Employment Law in Context

PEARSON

At Pearson, we take learning personally. Our courses and resources are available as books, online and via multi-lingual packages, helping people learn whatever, wherever and however they choose.

We work with leading authors to develop the strongest learning experiences, bringing cutting-edge thinking and best learning practice to a global market. We craft our print and digital resources to do more to help learners not only understand their content, but to see it in action and apply what they learn, whether studying or at work.

Pearson is the world's leading learning company. Our portfolio includes Penguin, Dorling Kindersley, the Financial Times and our educational business, Pearson International. We are also a leading provider of electronic learning programmes and of test development, processing and scoring services to educational institutions, corporations and professional bodies around the world.

Every day our work helps learning flourish, and wherever learning flourishes, so do people.

To learn more please visit us at: www.pearson.com/uk

Fourth Edition

Employment Law in Context
An Introduction for HR Professionals

Brian Willey

With contributions from:
Adrian Murton
Enda Hannon
Susan Mison
Sanjiv Sachdev

PEARSON

Harlow, England • London • New York • Boston • San Francisco • Toronto • Sydney
Auckland • Singapore • Hong Kong • Tokyo • Seoul • Taipei • New Delhi
Cape Town • São Paulo • Mexico City • Madrid • Amsterdam • Munich • Paris • Milan

Pearson Education Limited
Edinburgh Gate
Harlow
Essex CM20 2JE
England

and Associated Companies throughout the world

Visit us on the World Wide Web at:
www.pearson.com/uk

First published 2000 by Pitman Publishing, a division of Pearson Education Ltd
Second edition published 2003 by Pearson Education Limited
Third edition published 2009
Fourth edition published 2012

ISBN 978-1-4082-7047-9

British Library Cataloguing-in-Publication Data
A catalogue record for this book is available from the British Library

Library of Congress Cataloging-in-Publication Data
Willey, Brian.
    Employment law in context: an introduction for HR Professionals/Brian Willey; with contributions from Adrian Murton . . . [et al.].
        P. cm.
    ISBN 978-1-4082-7047-9 (pbk.)
1. Labor laws and legislation–Great Britain.   I. Murton, Adrian.   II. Title.
KD3009.W55 2012
344.4101–dc23
                                                          2011047409

10 9 8 7 6 5 4 3 2 1
16 15 14 13 12

Typeset in 9/12.5pt Stone Serif by 35
Printed and bound in Malaysia (CTP-VP)

Brief contents

Contents

6 Implementing equality in the workplace

253

12 Health, safety and welfare at work   **472**

Visit **www.mylawchamber.co.uk/willey** to access study support resources including realistic HR documentation to accompany the case studies in the book, an online chapter on collective labour law, interactive multiple choice questions, annotated weblinks, a glossary, glossary flashcards, key case flashcards, a legal newsfeed and legal updates.

unrivalled support for legal education

Your complete learning package

Visit **www.mylawchamber.co.uk/willey** to access a wealth of resources to support your studies and teaching.

Self study resources

- HR documentation supporting the case studies in the book to highlight the documents you are likely to encounter in practice
- An online chapter covering collective labour law
- Interactive multiple choice questions to test your understanding of each topic
- Annotated weblinks to help you read more widely around the subject and really impress your lecturers
- A glossary to use as a quick reference for legal terms and definitions
- Glossary flashcards to test yourself on legal terms and definitions
- Key case flashcards to test yourself on legal principles and major cases
- Legal newsfeed to help you read more widely, stay right up to date with the law and impress examiners
- Legal updates to help you stay up to date with the law and impress examiners

Teaching support materials

- PowerPoint slides with visual support in explaining key legal concepts

Also: The regularly maintained mylawchamber site provides the following features:

- Search tool to help locate specific items of content.
- Online help and support to assist with website usage and troubleshooting.

Particularly over the past 40 years, individual employment law has had a growing significance for managers – whether as general managers or human resource practitioners. It influences and may constrain action that they want to take. One principal aim of this textbook is to help those with day-to-day responsibilities for employment relations and human resource management to manage within the law. Its purpose is to promote understanding of four aspects:

- the essential provisions of European law and statute and case law in the United Kingdom;
- the application of the law to employment relations in respect of policy making and problem solving;
- the social purposes behind the legislation (i.e. what the UK Parliament and the European Union are trying to achieve);
- the contextual issues that affect the implementation of the law (e.g. particular social trends and economic considerations).

The development of corporate policies is more likely to be effective and well-informed if they are not seen, narrowly, as a series of conditions of employment to be applied mechanistically. For example, when family leave and 'work–life balance' policies are formulated, an understanding of the social trends against which they are developed is important (i.e. greater labour market participation by women; longer working hours; greater interest by fathers to be involved in childcare; the practical difficulties of reconciling work and non-work life). The social purposes underpinning the legislation should be appreciated to help ensure that the organisation's policies are compliant with the law. A manager who understands these purposes is better able to defend and argue for policy developments with colleagues.

One particular aspect of law that has grown hugely in significance since the previous editions of this textbook is the wide sweep of equality law across the range of 'protected characteristics'. The employment relationship, the application process for jobs and post-employment practices are all governed by legislative provisions. From time to time, some of these provisions are being clarified and creatively interpreted by the higher courts in Britain and by the European Court of Justice. It is a commonplace to say that no HR practitioner can afford to ignore the ramifications of such bodies of law. So, an attempt has been made in the book to structure the examination of discrimination law in a way that is hopefully both illuminating and also helpful in informing problem solving and policy formulation. There are three related chapters: Chapter 4 examines the historic, social and economic context in which discrimination law is located; Chapter 5 outlines the essential framework of equality law; and Chapter 6 raises a number of considerations for practitioners on how their employment policies should be legally compliant.

This textbook, then, aims to be integrative. It will aim principally to examine relevant law and provide a firm base knowledge for HR practitioners and other managers. It is also informed by relevant research and source material from economics and sociological studies. It is hoped that managers as students using this book will then have a full appreciation of the context of the law and will gain familiarity with and an enthusiasm for the subject of employment law; and also a confidence to analyse and handle a greater range of workplace problems.

Market for the book

This textbook is designed, principally, for those engaged in academic study. It is written for non-lawyers who wish to gain a basic understanding of the key areas of employment and equality law. Primarily, it is for students on postgraduate and post-experience courses. This would obviously cover those on programmes leading to graduate membership of the Chartered Institute of Personnel and Development; those on a Diploma of Management Studies course; and those studying employment law modules on, for example, Masters in Business Administration courses. It will also be useful for undergraduate students on, for example, BA Business Studies courses who are undertaking an employment law option.

Furthermore, an additional, related and important market is tutors on these courses who may be non-lawyers but wish to develop a wider understanding of the subject area.

Authorship

The first two editions of this textbook were, largely, written by myself as main author. The third, and this fourth edition are collaborative, drawing on the expertise of a number of colleagues who teach and undertake research and consultancy in the area of human resource management. The authorship is as follows:

Chapter 1: An introduction to employment law
Brian Willey

Chapter 2: Regulating the employment relationship
Brian Willey

Chapter 3: Managing change in the employment relationship
Brian Willey; and *Sanjiv Sachdev* on transfers of undertakings

Chapter 4: The context of discrimination at work
Brian Willey; contributions on equal pay and age discrimination from *Adrian Murton*

Chapter 5: Equality law and the workplace
Adrian Murton: age discrimination
Susan Mison: disability discrimination
Brian Willey: discrimination because of gender reassignment, marriage and civil partnership, pregnancy and maternity, race, religion or belief, sex and sexual orientation

Chapter 6: Implementing equality in the workplace
Brian Willey

Chapter 7: Harassment and bullying at work
Brian Willey

Chapter 8: Discipline and dismissal
Enda Hannon

Chapter 9: Wages and equal pay
Adrian Murton

Chapter 10: Regulation of working time
Adrian Murton

Chapter 11: Family leave and work–life balance
Enda Hannon

Chapter 12: Health, safety and welfare at work
Brian Willey

Chapter 13: Conclusion
Brian Willey

Website chapter: Collective representation and the law
Brian Willey

Approach to learning

In attempting to bridge, on the one hand, knowledge of legal provisions and, on the other, consideration of employment relations and HR issues, the textbook provides a number of opportunities for the reader to undertake exercises and activities. **Appendix 1** provides some feedback on the issues that should have been considered in discussions on the exercises.

There is also a case study – based around a fictional supermarket, Frishco – which forms the basis of scenarios in most chapters. The case study itself is on the accompanying website, **www.mylawchamber.co.uk/willey**. Additionally, some of the HR documentation necessary for completion of the scenarios is there, together with some feedback on the key issues to look out for.

Structure of each chapter

Most chapters are structured around the following sections:

- *Learning objectives*: the reader is given a list of objectives that should be attained once the chapter and the associated exercises have been completed.

- *Introduction*: this sets out the broad issues to be considered.

- *The context*: this identifies and discusses, as appropriate, social, political, economic and technological issues that form the background against which particular law is developing.

- *The legal framework*: the essential framework is outlined and discussed. As appropriate, material is drawn from European law, statute law, case law and statutory codes of practice.

- *Employment policies and practice*: this will consider the application of the law to the workplace. Drawing on research evidence, it will consider the experience of organisations and difficulties that have been encountered. It will provide some assistance for policy formulation and ways in which employment relations might be tackled.

- *Exercises*: most chapters have exercises which invite the reader to apply the concepts and legal provisions to the circumstances that are set out. The exercises are suitable for both individual study and syndicate work in the classroom. Feedback on the exercises is provided in Appendix 1.
- *References* of publications and research material used in each specific chapter.
- *Glossary*: this provides definitions of terms which may not be in everyday usage, that are used on several occasions within the book. The first or any significant occurrence of a glossary term in any given chapter is **highlighted** in the text.

Website

The website is designed to assist both students and tutors in several ways:

- **Law on collective representation**: an additional chapter, covering the essentials of this subject, is included. This meets a demand from some tutors who, whilst satisfied with the focus of the textbook on individual employment matters, indicated that this extra material would be helpful.
- **Legal updates**: these are provided periodically each year.
- **Frishco case study**: material associated with this case study is available together with appropriate weblinks relevant to some of the key material in the chapters.
- **Weblinks**.
- **Multiple choice questions**.
- **Flashcards and online glossary**.
- **Suggested further reading**.

Acknowledgements

The initial idea for this book arose from a previous collaborative text, *The Corporate Environment: a guide for human resource managers* (Pearson Education), written with my colleague, Huw Morris. The discussions we held about that textbook stimulated ideas about this present one as a complementary piece of work. Also, my involvement over a number of years in teaching the Employment Law module on the CIPD-accredited human resource management Masters/Diploma course at Kingston University Business School further reinforced my view that such a textbook could be useful. Furthermore, my teaching on the University's MA/LLM course in Employment Relations and Law helped me recognise more fully the complexity of issues that non-lawyer HR practitioners often have to manage. My thanks to them for helping to germinate and sustain the idea and my admiration to many of those who wrestle with the application of the law on a day-to-day basis.

The responsibility for this text is mine as editor and principal author. However, it could not have been written without the contributions, comments, advice and support of various people. In particular, I would mention Adrian Murton who 'nudged' me into the third and fourth editions after Pearson had approached me. Thanks also to Susan Mison who agreed to contribute on the seemingly ever-changing area of disability discrimination law. Also, my two colleagues at Kingston University with whom I teach the Employment Law module on the HRM courses, Enda Hannon and Sanjiv Sachdev, have shown considerable support for this project. All co-authors have demonstrated commitment to the concept of the book as a means of helping HR practitioners evaluate the contribution they may make to the application of the law to employment relations.

I would, furthermore, like to mention two people who have helped in different but important ways. Elaine Heslop, from the University of Kent at Canterbury and a colleague on a CIPD Employment Law programme, kindly agreed to review my draft of the gargantuan chapter on the Equality Act 2010. As an expert in this area, she provided many helpful comments and suggestions. They were all very much appreciated. But, as indicated above, the final text is my responsibility.

The second person is Karen Baldwin. Through her complex and successful constructive dismissal claim, she helped me appreciate, at first-hand, the impact of the employment tribunal process on claimants – in particular, how incredibly time-consuming and stressful it can be. Trying to balance case preparation and 'mitigating loss' by finding another job is not, in a difficult labour market, the easiest of tasks. The support of friends and family are essential – and she had these. So, thanks for letting me be involved in the experience and confirming that the enforcement of employment rights is not as straightforward as sometimes suggested.

Finally, such textbooks are rarely written without the support of families. In particular, I would like to thank my wife, Ann. She has, yet again, coped with me being welded to the computer during the early summer months.

I hope that readers will find the textbook useful and, above all, that it will give them the confidence to deal with the issues that employment law will present.

Brian Willey
Visiting Fellow
Faculty of Business and Law
Kingston University

January 2012

Publisher's acknowledgements

We are grateful to the following for permission to reproduce copyright material:

Tables

Table 2.1 from Labour Market Statistics (November 2009 – January 2011) Office for National Statistics (ONS), **www.statistics.gov.uk**, Crown Copyright material is reproduced with permission under the terms of the Click-Use Licence; Table 3.1 from Labour Force Survey, **www.statistics.gov.uk**, Office for National Statistics, Source: Office for National Statistics licensed under the Open Government Licence v.1.0.; Table 3.2 from Statistical Bulletin (7 June 2011), **www.statistics.gov.uk**, Office for National Statistics, Source: Office for National Statistics licensed under the Open Government Licence v.1.0.; Table 4.1 adapted from Office for National Statistics (2004), Source: Office for National Statistics licensed under the Open Government Licence v.1.0.; Table 4.2 from *The First Fair Treatment at Work Survey: Executive Summary – Updated.* Employment Relations Research Series No. 63, DTI, **www.berr.gov.uk** (Grainger, H. and Fitzner, G. 2007); Tables 4.4, 4.9 from *Labour Force Survey*, Spring Office of National Statistics (2005), Source: Office for National Statistics licensed under the Open Government Licence v.1.0.; Tables 4.5, 4.10 from *Labour Force Survey*, Spring, Office of National Statistics (2005), Source: Office for National Statistics licensed under the Open Government Licence v.1.0.; Table 4.6 from *The State of the Modern Family, the Millennium Cohort Survey*, Equality and Human Rights Commission (Equal Opportunities Commission 2007). The copyright and all other intellectual property rights in the material to be reproduced are owned by, or licensed to, the Commission for Equality and Human Rights, known as the Equality and Human Rights Commission ("the EHRC") . . ."; Table 4.7 from *Labour Force Survey*, Spring, Office for National Statistics (2005), Source: Office for National Statistics licensed under the Open Government Licence v.1.0.; Table 4.8 from *Labour Force Survey*, Spring, Office of National Statistics (2001), Source: Office for National Statistics licensed under the Open Government Licence v.1.0.; Table 4.11 from *Labour Force Survey*, Office of National Statistics, Source: Office for National Statistics licensed under the Open Government Licence v.1.0.; Table 4.13 from Census 2001 Statistics, **www.statistics.gov.uk** Office for National Statistics, Source: Office for National Statistics licensed under the Open Government Licence v.1.0.; Table 9.2 from Low Pay Commission Historical rates **www.lowpay.gov.uk**; Table 10.2 from **www.justice.gov.uk**, Crown Copyright material is reproduced with permission under the terms of the Click-Use License; Table 11.4 adapted from The Third Work-Life Balance Employee Survey: Main Findings, *Employee Relations Research Series*, No. 58 (Hooker, H., Neathey, F., Casebourne, J. and Munro, M. 2007), BERR, Crown Copyright material is reproduced with permission under the terms of the Click-Use License; Table 11.5 from Caring and Flexible Working, *Research Summary* (Elsmore, K. 2009), Department for Work and Pensions, Crown Copyright material is reproduced with permission under the terms of the Click-Use License.

Text

Exhibit 3.7 from Shropshire Council issues notices to all 6,500 staff (6 July 2011), **http://www.personneltoday.com/**; Exhibit 7.1 from £790,000 payout for bullied News of the World reporter, 24 November 2009 **http://www.personneltoday.com**; Exhibit 8.1 adapted from *Introduction to the (draft) ACAS Code of Practice on Discipline and Grievance*, ACAS (2009); Exhibit 9.9 from *NMW Annual Report, 2003/04*, BERR. Department for Business Innovation & Skills (BIS), Contains public sector information licensed under the Open Government License v1.0; Exhibit 10.7 from *Your Guide to the Working Time Regulations: Section 1–4*, Example 2, Section 2, Department for Business Innovation & Skills (BIS) (2008); Exhibit 13.2 from *Resolving workplace disputes: public consultation* (2011), Department for Business Innovation & Skills (BIS).

In some instances we have been unable to trace the owners of copyright material, and we would appreciate any information that would enable us to do so.

About the authors

Brian Willey is a Visiting Fellow, lecturing in employment law and human resource management in the Faculty of Business and Law, Kingston University, London. He undertakes consultancy in various aspects of individual dispute resolution. He was a member of the arbitration panel of the Advisory, Conciliation and Arbitration Service.

Adrian Murton is Subject Group Leader for Human Resource Management and Organisation Studies at the London Metropolitan Business School, London Metropolitan University.

Enda Hannon is Senior Lecturer in Employment Relations and Employment Law in the Department of Leadership, Human Resource Management and Organisation, at the Faculty of Business and Law, Kingston University, London.

Susan Mison is Senior Employment Law Editor for a major business media publishing company.

Sanjiv Sachdev is Senior Lecturer in Employment Law in the Department of Leadership, Human Resource Management and Organisation, at the Faculty of Business and Law, Kingston University, London.

Guided tour

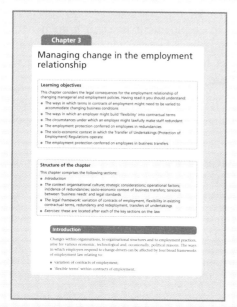

Use the **learning objectives** and **chapter structure outlines** at the start of every chapter to identify the key points within each chapter supporting your study and forming a useful checklist for revision.

Read the **exhibits** throughout the chapters to identify the most important points, concepts and facts of key illustrative cases and statutes you should know about.

Complete a range of interesting practical **activities** to consolidate your knowledge of the legal principles by putting the law into practice in a human resources context.

Use the **exercises** located throughout the book to test your understanding of what you have read by applying your knowledge to problem scenarios. Feedback to the exercises can be found at the end of the book.

See how law and policy interact in the real world using the **tables** which display informative figures and statistics.

Refer to the **end of chapter references** to access relevant further reading that can help with assignments or provide additional information

Look up any unfamiliar terms in the **glossary** at the end of the book.

Put your knowledge into practice by carrying out the activities contained in the **Frischo supermarket case studies** which run throughout the book.
A wide range of supporting documentation, such as Frishco's staff handbook and other HR documents, are available at www.mylawchamber.co.uk/Willey and highlight the sorts of documents you'll be dealing with as a HR professional in practice.

mylawchamber
unrivalled support for legal education

Your complete learning package

Visit **www.mylawchamber.co.uk/willey** to access a wealth of resources to support your studies:

- HR documentation supporting the case studies in the book to highlight the documents you are likely to encounter in practice
- An online chapter covering collective labour law
- Interactive multiple choice questions to test your understanding of each topic
- Annotated weblinks to help you read more widely around the subject and really impress your lecturers
- A glossary to use as a quick reference for legal terms and definitions
- Glossary flashcards to test yourself on legal terms and definitions
- Key case flashcards to test yourself on legal principles and major cases
- Legal newsfeed to help you read more widely, stay right up to date with the law and impress examiners
- Legal updates to help you stay up to date with the law and impress examiners

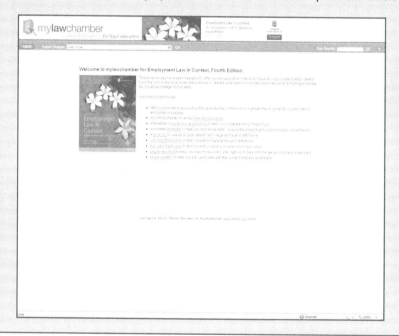

List of abbreviations

ACAS	Advisory, Conciliation and Arbitration Service
AML	Additional maternity leave
BIS	Department for Business, Innovation and Skills
BPR	Business process re-engineering
CA	Court of Appeal
CAC	Central Arbitration Committee
CBI	Confederation of British Industry
CEEP	European Centre for Enterprises with Public Participation
CIPD	Chartered Institute of Personnel and Development
CMCHA 2007	Corporate Manslaughter and Corporate Homicide Act 2007
CRB	Criminal Records Bureau
CRE	Commission for Racial Equality
DDA 1995	Disability Discrimination Act 1995
DPA 1998	Data Protection Act 1998
DRC	Disability Rights Commission
DSE	Display screen equipment
DTI	Department of Trade and Industry
DWP	Department for Work and Pensions
EA 2002	Employment Act 2002
EA 2010	Equality Act 2010
EAP	Employee assistance programme
EAT	Employment Appeal Tribunal
EC	European Community
ECHR/ECtHR	European Court of Human Rights
ECJ	European Court of Justice
EEC	European Economic Community
EHRC	Equality and Human Rights Commission
EOC	Equal Opportunities Commission
EqPA 1970	Equal Pay Act 1970
ERA 1996	Employment Rights Act 1996
ERA 1999	Employment Relations Act 1999
ET	Employment Tribunal
ETO	Economic, technical and organisational
ETUC	European Trade Union Confederation
EU	European Union
EWC	European Works Council
FIFO	First in first out
GEO	Government Equalities Office
HASAWA 1974	Health and Safety at Work etc. Act 1974
HC	High Court
HL	House of Lords
HMRC	Her Majesty's Revenue and Customs

HRA 1998	Human Rights Act 1998
HRM	Human resource management
HSC	Health and Safety Commission
HSE	Health and Safety Executive
HSI	Health and Safety Inspectorate
ICT	Information and communications technology
ILO	International Labour Organisation
IRA 1971	Industrial Relations Act 1971
ISA	Independent Safeguarding Authority
IT	Industrial Tribunal
LGB	Lesbian, gay and bisexual
LIFO	Last in first out
LPC	Low Pay Commission
MHSW	Management of Health and Safety at Work [Regulations 1999]
NICA	Northern Ireland Court of Appeal
NIRC	National Industrial Relations Court
NMW	National minimum wage
NMWA 1998	National Minimum Wage Act 1998
OHS	Occupational health service
OML	Ordinary maternity leave
OR	Occupational requirement
PPP	Public–private partnership
QMV	Qualified majority vote
RDP	Registered disabled person
RIDDOR	Reporting of Injuries, Diseases and Dangerous Occurrences Regulations 1995 SI 1995/3163
RORR	Range of reasonable responses
RRA 1976	Race Relations Act 1976
SAP	Statutory adoption pay
SC	Supreme Court
SDA 1975	Sex Discrimination Act 1975
SI	Statutory instrument
SMEs	Small and medium sized enterprises
SMP	Statutory Maternity Pay
SOSR	Some other substantial reason
SPP	Statutory Paternity Pay
TQM	Total quality management
TUC	Trades Union Congress
TULRCA 1992	Trade Union and Labour Relations (Consolidation) Act 1992
TUPE 2006	Transfer of Undertakings (Protection of Employment) Regulations 2006
WERS	Workplace Employee Relations Survey
WLB	Work–life balance
WTR 1998	Working Time Regulations 1998

Table of cases

Table of statutes

Table of statutory instruments

Table of statutory codes of practice

Table of European Community law

Council of Europe: conventions

List of useful websites

Advisory, Conciliation and Arbitration Service	www.acas.org.uk
Cabinet Office	www.cabinetoffice.gov.uk
Central Arbitration Committee	www.cac.gov.uk
Chartered Institute of Personnel and Development	www.cipd.co.uk
Citizens Advice Bureaux	www.citizensadvice.org.uk
Confederation of British Industry	www.cbi.org.uk
Criminal Records Bureau	www.crb.gov.uk
Department for Business, Innovation and Skills	www.bis.gov.uk
Department for Education	www.education.gov.uk
Department for Work and Pensions	www.dwp.gov.uk
Employment Tribunals and Employment Appeal Tribunal	www.justice.gov.uk
Equality and Human Rights Commission	www.equalityhumanrights.com
European Commission	www.europea.eu.int/comm
European Court of Human Rights	www.echr.coe.int
European Court of Justice	www.curia.eu.int
European Parliament	www.europarl.eu
European Union	www.europa.eu
Government Equalities Office	www.equalities.gov.uk
Health and Safety Executive	www.hse.gov.uk
HM Revenue and Customs	www.hmrc.gov.uk
Home Office (Human Rights Act issues)	www.homeoffice.gov.uk/hract
Information Commissioner's Office	www.ico.gov.uk
Institute of Employment Studies	www.employment-studies.co.uk
International Labour Organisation	www.ilo.org/global
Joseph Rowntree Foundation	www.jrf.org.uk
Low Pay Commission	www.lowpay.gov.uk
Ministry of Justice	www.justice.gov.uk
Public Concern at Work	www.pcaw.demon.co.uk
Stationery Office	www.thestationeryoffice.com
Stonewall	www.stonewall.org.uk
Supreme Court	www.supremecourt.gov.uk
Trades Union Congress	www.tuc.org.uk
UK Statistics Authority	www.statistics.gov.uk
United Kingdom Parliament	www.parliament.uk
Work Foundation	www.theworkfoundation.com

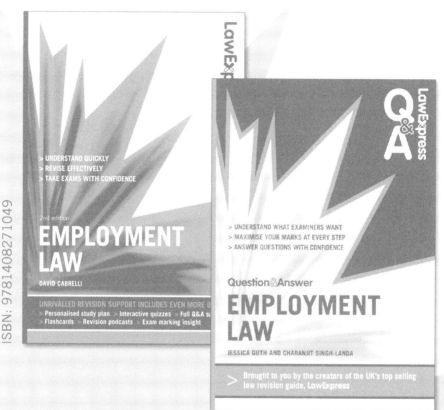

Chapter 1

An introduction to employment law

Learning objectives

This chapter considers the ways in which the employment relationship is regulated by both voluntary and legal measures. Having read it, you should understand:

- The nature and purpose of both voluntary and legal regulation in general
- The principles that underpin employment and discrimination law
- The relationship that can exist between voluntary and legal regulation
- The various roles of courts, tribunals and statutory agencies

Structure of the chapter

- *Introduction*: the role of legal and voluntary regulation; economic and political perspectives
- *The nature of legal regulation and enforcement*: common law; statute law; secondary legislation; European law; the European Convention on Human Rights; tribunals and courts; the role of statutory agencies; statutory codes of practice; redress
- *Some underpinning principles*: ethics; human rights; fairness; reasonableness; equal treatment; harmonisation; natural justice; consent and freedom

Introduction

Broadly speaking, the employment relationship is regulated by both voluntary and legal measures. Voluntary measures comprise agreements and other decisions that derive from collective bargaining, arbitration, conciliation, mediation, and grievance and discipline handling. They also include voluntarily accepted standards of good employment practice (for example, those advocated by the Chartered Institute of Personnel and Development). Legal measures are European Union (EU) treaties and directives, the European Convention on Human Rights and Fundamental Freedoms 1950, British statute law, the common law of contract and of tort, case law, statutory codes of practice and some international standards. In practice, these are not isolated sets of measures. As we shall see, voluntary and legal measures invariably interlink and influence each other.

▶ What are the purposes of voluntary and legal measures?

There are two broad purposes. First, at various points, they influence the function of management – i.e. the ways in which managers exercise power, control and organise workforces and manage conflicts of interest. This influence can be illustrated in the following way. It is widely accepted that the employment relationship is characterised by an imbalance of power in favour of the employer. Both voluntary and legal regulation can restrain the unfettered exercise of this employer power. So, for example, collective bargaining with a trade union can minimise the exploitation of individuals at work by agreements on pay and conditions, and also by helping to process grievances. Furthermore, legislation can establish minimum conditions of employment (e.g. national minimum wage), and set limits on the action that an employer might take against employees (e.g. in relation to discipline and dismissal).

The second purpose of this regulation is to assert certain principles. On the one hand, there are those principles that influence the nature and quality of decisions (e.g. fairness, equal treatment, reasonableness, etc.). In addition, there are those principles which mould the regulatory process itself. Examples of this include the fundamental importance of consent in agreeing and changing contracts of employment, and of fairness and reasonableness in disciplinary procedures.

▶ How does the law influence substantive issues?

Traditionally, it was accepted in British employment relations that, as far as terms and conditions of employment (the substantive issues) are concerned, the law may set a general framework but the details would be determined either by employers alone or after negotiation with trade unions. Indeed, in 1954, one academic lawyer was able to make the following comment: 'There is, perhaps, no major country in the world in which the law has played a less significant role in the shaping of (industrial) relations than in Great Britain and in which the law and legal profession have less to do with labour relations' (Kahn-Freund 1954).

This characterisation, however, soon began to change. Increasingly, over the following decades, statute law was enacted to establish both certain principles to guide employer behaviour and also the terms and conditions of employment offered to staff. So, for example, 'fairness' is now a basic criterion used to judge the reason for sacking an employee. 'Reasonableness' is widespread as a reference point for assessing health and safety standards. The prohibition of 'less favourable treatment' is fundamental to equality law.

There has also been a growing tendency towards more detailed prescription of certain terms and conditions of employment. This has arisen from some statute law and, in part, from case law. These more detailed requirements have an impact on all employers. For example, the outlawing of indirect sex discrimination – unless it can be justified – has created a body of case law which steers employers to scrutinise their employment practices. This law requires consideration about the legality and justification for such practices as, for example, seniority-based promotion, requirements that work should be full time, age barriers in employment, etc.

Academic commentators have pointed to growing evidence in Britain (as in other European countries) of 'juridification'. This is defined as the tendency to which the behaviour of employers and unions is determined by reference to legal standards.

Indeed, it is suggested that, in Britain, we have moved to a 'minimum standards' contract of employment that has been created through the continued intervention of statute law (see Chapter 2).

▶ How does law affect procedural issues?

The procedural aspects can be subdivided into those that concern the individual employee and those which concern collective relationships.

Individual employees work under a contract of employment agreed with the employer. Consent is at the heart of contract formation and also contract variation. The courts have asserted, in numerous cases, that when an employer wishes to change terms and conditions of employment, then, procedurally, the employee must be consulted and agreement sought (see Chapter 3).

In disciplinary matters involving individuals, procedural fairness is essential. This is specified in the ACAS *Code of Practice on Disciplinary and Grievance Procedures* (2009). This has been confirmed in case law (see Chapter 8). As far as grievances are concerned, it has been established that individuals have the right, through an implied term of their contract of employment, to raise grievances through an appropriate procedure (*WA Goold (Pearmak) Ltd* v *McConnell and Another* [1995] IRLR 516). Also, new statutory requirements on grievance handling are explained in the ACAS code of practice. Furthermore, a worker has a statutory right to be accompanied in a grievance and a disciplinary hearing (ERA 1999, s 10).

As far as collective relations are concerned, Britain, historically, had a strong tradition of voluntarism for determining employment relations procedures. So, employers could freely decide whether or not to negotiate with trade unions and about which terms and conditions of employment. They could also determine any consultation arrangements. There is still considerable employer freedom in this area. However, European and British law have circumscribed it to some extent. The principal examples are:

- *Collective redundancies*: consultation with unions or employee representatives over specified redundancies (Trade Union and Labour Relations (Consolidation) Act 1992).

- *Transfers of undertakings*: consultation with unions or employee representatives about the transfer (Transfer of Undertakings (Protection of Employment) Regulations 2006).

- *Health and safety*: consultation with unions or employee representatives about safety standards and safety organisation in the workplace (Safety Representatives and Safety Committees Regulations 1977; Health and Safety (Consultation with Employees) Regulations 1996).

- *General workplace information disclosure and consultation*: relating to the economic circumstances of the organisation, likely changes in the labour force, and contractual changes (Information and Consultation of Employees Regulations 2004).

- *Information disclosure and consultation*: in specified multinational companies operating in the European Union (Transnational Information and Consultation of Employees Regulations 1999; and the 2010 Regulations).

- *Recognition for collective bargaining purposes*: statutory obligations to negotiate with trade unions on certain employers who meet various statutory hurdles (Trade Union and Labour Relations (Consolidation) Act 1992).

Economic perspectives

A labour market is, arguably, defined by the limits set by law. As mentioned above, a key economic function of labour law is to determine how and when managerial authority is limited (e.g. limits to working time, minimum wages, protection against unfair dismissal). According to a leading labour law theorist, the 'main object of labour law has always been, and we venture to say will always be, to be a countervailing force to counteract the inequality of bargaining power which is inherent and must be inherent in the employment relationship' (Otto Kahn-Freund in Davies and Freedland 1983). So, labour law is seen as a potential force to counteract inequality.

Labour law can provide incentives or disincentives for improving skills and productivity. The nature of labour legislation affects the efficiency of a firm in a competitive market. For some, this role of promoting economic efficiency is central. So, for example, it is argued that minimum wage laws can encourage investment in skills and technology rather than reliance on cheap labour. Labour law can also affect the movement of labour both nationally and internationally. Furthermore, such law can have, as outlined above, an important moral dimension covering such issues as slavery, child labour, unfair discrimination, privacy and bullying.

As far as disincentives of labour law are concerned, these can be found largely in the human resource management experience of employers. For example, information obligations (e.g. about the contract of employment and changes) were found to be significant (Lambourne *et al.* 2008). The Better Regulation Executive (2010: 16) reported, from a survey of 500 micro businesses (i.e. employing fewer than 10 people), that respondents stated that 'employment law does have a negative effect on business growth, and the concern about employment law is less about paperwork but probably more about cost, complexity and the perceived cost of "getting it wrong"'. In particular, as far as dismissal is concerned, 'it is believed that it is becoming increasingly hard to dismiss people and that employers have to go through an onerous process' (2010: 17).

Furthermore, globalisation, as an economic phenomenon, has led to a lively debate about the declining power of national labour laws and the need for labour regulation across national boundaries.

▶ Globalisation and the changing role of labour law

One major labour law study notes that the 'study of comparative employment law has increased in importance in recent years largely because of the growing tendency towards international economic integration and the development of transnational labour standards' (Deakin and Morris 2005: 3). Globalisation has made a significant impact on the nature and profile of labour rights arguably diminishing the efficacy of national level employment law and labour market regulation with issues of labour abuses and the degradation of workers' rights being a common theme. According to Hepple (2005: 9), the 'features of the new economy mean that labour law is now inevitably global law and not just the concern of a particular nation state'. The role of international labour regulation has acquired renewed attention and pertinence. Issues of child labour, slave labour, forced labour and a variety of other forms of economic exploitation have been prominent in debates. To these debates have also been added the issue of 'social dumping' (whereby companies seek to relocate in countries with fewer or weaker employment law regimes), and the responsibilities of transnational companies in implementing and maintaining labour standards. The regulation of these transnational corporations poses many difficulties. Attempts have been made to introduce 'privatised' forms of regulation such as codes of conduct and social labelling systems. Transnational collective bargaining with international trade union confederations is barely formed. There are, however, examples of policy agreements. In 2010, PPR, the Paris-based multinational retail and luxury goods company (which includes Gucci and La Fnac) agreed a European charter setting out commitments on 'quality of life and work-related stress' (Carley 2010). In the developed world, collective bargaining often 'takes place under the shadow of threats to relocate or to merge with foreign corporations: domestic labour laws rarely offer rights to bargain about strategic corporate-level decisions such as these' (Hepple 2005: 10).

▶ Is there a crisis of labour law?

The consequences of 'footloose' multinational companies, of expanding globalised markets, and of migrant workers all raise serious questions about the feasibility of providing effective employment protection for working people against the exercise of employer economic power. In the United Kingdom, the cornerstone of employment protection is the contract of employment. But this is an imperfect instrument (see Chapter 2). Its defects in failing to recognise fairness and non-discriminatory treatment are gradually being rectified by statute law. However, whilst the contract of employment is effective to some degree, there are many 'atypical' (as well as some 'standard') workers who remain outside its limited protection. Some of the political wrestling involved in creating the current framework of employment law and regulation is considered in the next section.

Political perspectives

It is important to remember that legislation arises within political arenas – both in Britain and also in the European Union. Shifts in approach to employment regulation reflect various political views which change over time. Politicians have views about the nature and extent of employment law, the range of voluntary measures and the degree to which protection should be accorded to working people. It is possible to identify three different broad models of political approach which help consider the underpinning politics of employment law (Morris, Willey and Sachdev 2002: 229):

- the free collective bargaining model;
- the free labour market model;
- the employee protection or social justice model.

Each of these models, in different ways and with different emphases, considers a range of economic, social, political and human rights issues: the management of the economy, the economic consequences of collective bargaining and employment law, the concept of social justice, entitlement to job security, anti-discrimination policies, the human rights of freedom of association and freedom of expression. The models are designed to review and analyse broad trends in the development and natures of employment law. 'None of these models exists in its pure form. Contemporary employment relations in Britain are, in fact, governed by the interpenetration of the three' (Morris *et al.* 2002: 232).

▶ The free collective bargaining model

This reflects the traditional pattern of British industrial relations which developed, particularly, from World War One onwards. Collective bargaining was seen as the central process of employee relations, usually resulting in voluntary agreements between an employer and particular trade unions. The role of consultation was comparatively marginal. This model reflected, in part, international standards on freedom of association set in the 1940s and 1950s by the International Labour Organisation (ILO) and which British governments signed.

Philosophically, this model emphasised **voluntarism** which was broadly subscribed to by employers, unions and governments. It was characterised by the general, though not complete, 'abstention of the law' (Kahn-Freund 1954). The limited law enacted had two principal functions. First, it created a permissive framework in which trade unions could lawfully exist, engage in collective bargaining and call for and organise industrial action. Public policy promoted collective bargaining as an acceptable method of regulating terms and conditions of employment and of 'institutionalising' conflicts of interest endemic in employment relations.

Secondly, the law provided some very limited explicit protection for working people. One example was through Wages Councils (originally set up in 1909 and abolished in 1993). These councils set minimum pay for vulnerable groups of workers for whom collective bargaining was difficult to achieve. Another key example was health and safety legislation. A partial framework of such legislation owed its origins to social pioneers in the nineteenth century. It was only in 1974 that more comprehensive legislation was enacted.

Voluntarism was subject to numerous strains in the postwar years. Governments increasingly tried to balance the sectional interests and claims of unions and their members, on the one hand, and the public interest, on the other. So when, for example, the level of pay settlements achieved through free collective bargaining was perceived to be inflationary and economically damaging, governments, both Conservative and Labour, enacted voluntary and statutory incomes policies and also legislative attempts to limit trade union power. After 1979, under the Thatcher government, this free collective bargaining model became subject to a major political onslaught.

▶ The free labour market model

This was gradually introduced from 1979 to support the wider economic policies of Thatcherism. It decisively broke the prevailing consensus on industrial relations policy – which, admittedly, had been subject to considerable strains since the 1960s. The principles underlying this model were reflected in several broad policy approaches:

- Of principal importance was deregulation of the labour market. This involved the removal of certain protective measures for employees which were characterised as 'burdens on business'. Furthermore, EU employee protection polices were challenged because they were seen as obstructing overriding free market objectives.

- The promotion of economic objectives encouraging cost-effectiveness, competitiveness and flexibility in the use of labour.

- The primary importance of individualism in the employment relationship and the marginalising of collective interests and collective representation.

- The curbing of trade union power by abolishing, rather than reforming, statutory recognition rights and by constraining unions' ability to organise industrial action.

The policies pursued were principally driven by the economic interests of employers. Arguably, the countervailing interests of working people received much less consideration. The exceptions were in relation to discrimination law and health and safety. Here, the initiatives to improve protections largely derived from EU policies and from ruling of the European Court of Justice (ECJ).

❱ The employee protection or social justice model

This reflects the broad interventionist approach adopted by the EU – at least until the late 1990s. As articulated in EU law, the principles underpinning this model are:

- protection of employees throughout the employment relationship;
- a recognition that employees have both individual and collective interests and that these have to be accommodated in a framework of employment law;
- harmonisation of conditions of employment across member states – complementing economic convergence;
- consideration of economic issues (cost effectiveness, competitiveness and labour flexibility) in the formulation of employee protection measures;
- the promotion of consensus about employment protection measures to be adopted between the social partners (i.e. employers and their organisations and employees and their trade unions);
- an acceptance of the principle of '**subsidiarity**' – that is to say that some issues are more appropriately regulated at the level of the member state rather than at the level of the EU.

Consequently, the European Union has led to the enactment of the following law which has moulded terms and conditions of employment: equal treatment on the grounds of sex, race, sexuality, age, religion or belief, disability; equal pay; protections for pregnant workers; leave entitlements for parents; the establishment of wide-ranging health and safety standards; restrictions on excessive working time; protection of part-time workers, fixed-term employees and agency workers. As far as employment procedures, it has been much less interventionist. However, as mentioned above it has developed, in a number of aspects of employment relations, the duty of employers to consult and disclose information to its employees to provide better understanding of corporate polices and, to some extent, influence their direction.

❱ The current situation

Contemporary British employment relations continue to be characterised by the interpenetration of all three models. The Labour government (1997–2010) sought to maintain the Thatcherite commitment to the free market. However, it also aimed to ameliorate the worst aspects of this for working people by enacting various social justice measures – some deriving from European law (e.g. the Working Time Regulations 1998), and some from home-grown initiatives (e.g. the National Minimum Wage Act 1998). The Conservative-Liberal Democrat coalition government formed in May 2010 committed itself to a clear set of economic and social objectives, many of which have affected the regulation of terms and conditions of working people. Its employment relations policies are an (often uneasy) amalgam of Thatcherite objectives tinged with some commitment to social policy standards of good practice (see Exhibit 1.1).

Two key questions, as always, can be asked in judging political policies and legislation:

- in whose interests does this legislation exist and whose interests are adversely affected?
- can there be a balance of interests between those of working people and those of employers?

EXHIBIT 1.1

Conservative–Liberal Democrat coalition: employment relations policies

The context in which this government's employment relations policies have been formulated is one where a significant economic structural change has been initiated: substantial cutbacks in public expenditure and consequential redundancies, a two-year pay freeze for public sector workers and measures to change public sector pensions. The strands of its employment relations policies are:

- Broad commitment to the Equality Act 2010 – subject to some key changes (see Chapter 5).
- A commitment to promote the right to request flexible working for all employees – not just for employees with specified dependants (see Chapter 11).
- Abolition of the default retirement age (see Chapter 5).
- A review of and some amendments to health and safety legislation (see Chapter 12).
- Amendments to dispute resolution procedures and enforcement of statutory rights (see Chapter 8).
- Proposed restriction of the statutory right to claim unfair dismissal (see Chapter 8) (BIS, 2011).

Ideologically, these changes reflect a 'business friendly' approach and, in particular, a sympathy with the interests of small businesses. Data on the experience of micro businesses, for example, was provided by the Better Regulation Executive (2010).

Underpinning the government's policies are two specific political positions (see **www.bis.gov.uk**):

- A concern about what is characterised as the 'gold plating' of EU directives – i.e. where provisions of legislation, when a directive is transposed into UK law, are better than in the original directive.
- The promotion of deregulation by cutting 'red tape'; and by having a 'one in one out' policy in respect of new regulations (see Chapter 13).

The legal regulation of employment

This will be examined by looking at the following:

- *How are legal standards set?*
  - common law;
  - primary legislation: Acts of Parliament;
  - secondary legislation: regulations;
  - European law;
  - European Convention on Human Rights 1950;
  - statutory codes of practice.

- *How do working people enforce their rights?*
  - Employment tribunals;
  - Employment Appeal Tribunal;
  - Court of Appeal;
  - Supreme Court and the former House of Lords;
  - European Court of Justice;
  - European Court of Human Rights;
  - International Labour Organisation.
- *What is the role of statutory agencies?*
  - Advisory Conciliation and Arbitration Service;
  - Equality and Human Rights Commission;
  - Health and Safety Executive;
  - Low Pay Commission;
  - Information Commissioner;
  - Criminal Records Bureau;
  - Independent Safeguarding Authority;
  - Central Arbitration Committee.
- *What redress is available for infringements of rights?*
  - the effectiveness of redress and remedies.
- *What are the key underpinning principles?*
  - *substantive issues*:
    - fairness;
    - reasonableness;
    - equal treatment;
    - harmonisation;
  - *procedures*:
    - natural justice;
    - consultation;
    - consent;
    - freedom.

▶ How are legal standards set?

As indicated above, there are several sources of law affecting the employment relationship. We will look at each in turn.

Common law

This is formulated by judges through **case law**. It has set and developed various principles (e.g. the concept of reasonableness). Various legal tests (e.g. to define an employee) have been created. **Common law** is used in interpreting statute law. Under the doctrine of **precedent** rulings of judges in the higher courts are binding on the lower courts – unless overturned by Parliament in new legislation. There are two aspects of common law:

- *Law of contract.* A **contract** is an agreement between two or more parties which is intended to be legally enforceable. It may be oral or in writing. These parties create their own rights and duties. So, they voluntarily decide the content of the contract. Courts may be involved in discovering the intention of the parties (i.e. what they meant by a particular provision), and whether the contract was breached. Contracts may be ruled by the courts to be void if certain provisions are unlawful (e.g. contrary to equality law). Within employment, this branch of law has considerable significance through the contract of employment (see Chapter 2).

● *Law of tort.* A **tort** is a civil wrong other than a breach of contract. Obligations here are imposed by law. This branch of law concerns the interests of a 'person' (it can be an individual or an organisation) which may be injured by another. So, a person may be injured by another's **negligence** as a result of poor health and safety organisation, or an employer's interests may be damaged by unlawful **industrial action** organised by a trade union. (This second example can be referred to as an 'economic tort'.) A central concern for the courts in this branch of law is the issue of liability (i.e. who is liable for causing the injury). In some instances the issue of **vicarious liability** arises. This is where one person assumes liability for the actions of another. An example is where an employer is liable for all breaches of health and safety rules – even where the breach is committed by a manager or another employee. The complainant will be seeking **damages** (compensation) for the injury sustained.

Primary legislation

This is **statute law – Acts of Parliament**. These may set new legal requirements and can also overturn case-law decisions of the judges; and repeal or amend existing legislation. It is the most common way through which new general rights and duties are established. Among the most notable examples in employment and discrimination law are the Employment Rights Act 1996 and the Equality Act 2010. In considering complaints that may arise under statute law, courts and tribunals will consider the following:

● Does the individual have a right, under the Act, to make a complaint (e.g. is the person an 'employee' in law with the necessary qualifying service to claim unfair dismissal)?

● Has a provision of the legislation been infringed (e.g. the right to paid annual leave)?

● Does the complainant have a remedy (e.g. compensation and possible reinstatement)?

● Has the specific legislative provision been interpreted in any previous judgments (particularly by the Court of Appeal, the Supreme Court or, if European law is involved, the European Court of Justice)?

● Does the legislation have to be interpreted in conformity with European law?

● Are there any implications arising from the Human Rights Act 1998? Is the legislation compatible? (See later section on the European Convention on Human Rights.)

Secondary legislation

This subordinate legislation, made by way of **statutory instruments**, is often referred to as 'regulations'. They are laid before Parliament for approval in a simpler process than passing an Act. They are made under particular statute law (e.g. the European Communities Act 1972 or the Health and Safety at Work Act 1974). As with Acts of Parliament, regulations must be compatible with the European Convention on Human Rights (see below). Increasingly, employment law is enacted this way. The regulations include rights and entitlements which are enforceable in the courts in the same way as those under Acts of Parliament. Examples of some common secondary legislation in employment are:

● Employment Relations Act 1999 (Blacklists) Regulations 2010;

● Transfer of Undertakings (Protection of Employment) Regulations 2006;

- Part-time Workers (Prevention of Less Favourable Treatment) Regulations 2000;
- Management of Health and Safety at Work Regulations 1999;
- Working Time Regulations 1998.

European Union law

In employment regulation, there are three principal and relevant aspects of European law: Treaties of the European Union; **directives**; and rulings of the European Court of Justice.

- *Treaties*

  The original Treaty of Rome 1957, founding the then European Economic Community, has been amended on several occasions since – by the Single European Act 1986, the Treaty on European Union 1992 (the Maastricht Treaty), the Treaty of Amsterdam 1997, the Treaty of Nice 2000 and the Treaty of Lisbon 2008. As a consequence of the Lisbon Treaty which came into force in December 2009, two treaties govern the European Union:

  - **The Treaty on European Union (TEU):** This outlines the aims of the Union and its institutions.
  - **The Treaty on the Functioning of the European Union (TFEU):** This replaced the original Treaty of Rome and came into force in December 2009. It includes articles of relevance to employment law (e.g. Article 157 on equal pay).

  A treaty article can be enforced as a direct right in the courts of member states where it is 'sufficiently clear, precise and unconditional as to require no further interpretation'. Such a treaty article can have 'direct effect' both 'vertically' and 'horizontally'. This means that, in the first situation, the article confers rights for the citizen against the state. In the second situation, it confers rights for the citizen to exercise against another (e.g. an employer). A clear example of such **'direct effect'** is the principle of equal pay for equal work between men and women. This was in the original Treaty of Rome and has subsequently been enacted as Article 157 in the current treaty (the TFEU).

  In addition to the Treaties, there are three sets of EU secondary legislation: regulations, directives and decisions. Directives are the principal means for establishing employment rights within the European Union (see Table 1.1).

- *Directives*

  These are adopted through a legislative process known previously as 'co-decision' and, under the TFEU (art. 251), as the 'ordinary legislative procedure'. This involves the European Council (which comprises the heads of government of all member states) and the European Parliament (comprising elected MEPs from each member state). After many ministerial meetings and discussions in the European Parliament, ultimately they can be agreed and adopted. Originally, agreement had to be unanimous. However, in 1987 amendments were made to permit the adoption by **'qualified majority vote'** (QMV) of certain directives (those defined as health and safety measures).

It is also possible, under procedures adopted in the Maastricht Treaty, for the **'social partners'** to negotiate a **'framework agreement'** on a particular policy proposed by the Commission. These 'social partners' are BUSINESSEUROPE (formerly UNICE), the European private-sector employers' confederation; CEEP, the public-sector equivalent; UEAPME (representing small and medium-sized enterprises); and the ETUC, the

Table 1.1 **Some key European directives on employment policy**

1989	Safety and health of workers	1999	Fixed-term work
1990	Display screen equipment	2000	Racial discrimination
1991	Contract of employment information	2000	Equal treatment in employment
1992	Pregnant workers	2001	Transfers of undertakings
1994	European Works Councils	2002	Information and consultation
1994	Protection of young people at work	2003	Working time
1995	Data protection	2006	Equal treatment: men and women
1996	Posted workers	2008	Temporary agency work
1997	Part-time workers	2008	Insolvency
1998	Collective redundancies	2010	Parental leave

European Confederation of Trade Unions. Framework agreements may then be adopted by the Council of the European Union as the basis of a new directive. Three significant examples are the 2010 Directive on Parental Leave, the 1997 Directive on Part-time Workers and the 1999 Directive on Fixed-term Work.

The main advantage of such framework agreements is the ability to take into account, at the drafting stage, the practical implications (reflecting the experiences of employers and unions) of such policies proposed by the Commission. It may be that rather than provide detailed provisions, general principles are agreed which can guide employment practice in individual workplaces. This is particularly so with the 1997 Part-time Workers Framework Agreement and Directive (see Chapter 2).

Generally, directives are enforceable against member states. Each country is obliged to transpose a directive into national law within a specified number of years. In Britain, this is achieved by passing an Act of Parliament or laying regulations before Parliament (under the European Communities Act 1972) for approval. So, for example, the original Working Time Directive 1993 was enacted through the Working Time Regulations 1998.

The enforcement of directives has a particular significance for those employed in the public sector (and in certain private-sector companies which carry out public functions under law). These employees may use a directive in a national court without it having been transposed into national law. This arises because they work for the state (the civil service) or 'an emanation of the state' (e.g. a local authority, an NHS trust or an agency created as a result of the reorganisation of central government). The directive is said to have 'direct effect'. However, a directive must be 'sufficiently precise and unconditional' to be enforced without the need for domestic legislation. In practical terms, this means that a person employed in any public-sector body can complain that a specific right has been infringed from the date of adoption of the directive by the Council of the European Union – even if there is no British legislation. Unlike a treaty article, a directive can only have '***vertical* direct effect**' – i.e. enforceability against the state or an emanation of the state.

Some employees who work in certain parts of the private sector may be able to use this route to enforce rights. The concept of '**emanation of the state**' has been interpreted by the courts to embrace certain privatised corporations (notably British Gas and water companies). Three tests have been developed to help establish whether an organisation can be so defined:

- Is there a public service provision?
- Is there control by the state?
- Does the organisation have special powers?

It was ruled in a judgment of the European Court of Justice that 'A state body is a body, whatever its legal form, which has been made responsible, pursuant to a measure adopted by the state, for providing a public service under the control of the state, and which has, for that purpose, special powers beyond those which result from the normal rules applicable in relations between individuals' (*Foster v British Gas plc* [1990] IRLR 353).

- ### *Rulings of the European Court of Justice*
  The Court is responsible for determining the application and interpretation of European law (see Table 1.2). Together with Treaty articles and directives, its rulings have been the other most significant European influence on the development of employment regulation within Britain. These rulings are binding on all member states, irrespective of the country of origin of a particular case. The Lisbon Treaty 2008 provided for the EU's accession to the European Convention on Human Rights 1950 (see below) so that ECJ rulings must be compatible with the Convention.
  Among the key rulings to affect British employment relations are the following:

- *Deciding whether an EU member state has failed to fulfil a treaty obligation*. For example, the ECJ decided that because of the failure of the Italian government to implement the 1980 Insolvency Directive by the due date in 1983, citizens could sue their government for the loss they had sustained, provided that there was a clear link between a government failure and the damage suffered by an individual (*Francovich and Bonifaci v the Republic of Italy* [1992] IRLR 84). The consequence of this case is that '*Francovich* claims' can now be made in the British courts, subject to certain conditions.

- *Dealing with infraction proceedings*. For example, the United Kingdom's failure to provide for full consultation rights in respect of redundancies and business transfers was referred by the Commission to the Court for a ruling (*EC Commission v United Kingdom* (C-383/92) [1994] IRLR 412). Ultimately, this case resulted in the adoption of new consultation regulations in Britain that were compliant with EU law.

- *Reviewing the legality of decisions of the Council of the European Union and the Commission*. For example, the court determined, following a complaint by the British Conservative government, that the Working Time Directive 1993 was properly made as a health and safety measure under the treaty procedures (*United Kingdom v European Council* (C-84/94) [1997] IRLR 30).

- *Reviewing the failure to act of the European Council and the Commission where the treaty obliges them to act*.

Table 1.2 **The impact of European law: some key cases**

Non-discriminatory retirement ages between men and women	House of Lords judgment resulted in amendments to British law in the Sex Discrimination Act 1986 (*Marshall* v *Southampton & SW Hampshire Area Health Authority* [1986] IRLR 140)
Discrimination on the grounds of pregnancy a 'direct discrimination'	This arose from an ECJ ruling which elaborated equal treatment law (*Dekker* v *Stichting Vormingscentrum* [1991] IRLR 27). The concept was also incorporated in the Pregnant Workers' Directive
Pensions being defined a 'pay'	The Court of Appeal ruled that superannuation payments were subject to European equal pay provisions (*Barber* v *Guardian Royal Exchange* [1990] IRLR 240)
Part-time workers' access to statutory rights	The House of Lords ruled that, in interpreting European equal treatment law, it was indirect discrimination against women to have an hours qualification for access to redundancy pay and unfair dismissal compensation (*R* v *Secretary of State for Employment ex parte Equal Opportunities Commission* [1994] IRLR 176). New regulations were introduced which provided a one-year qualification period for all employees (full time or part time)
Removal of ceiling on compensation in sex discrimination cases	A ceiling on compensation payments was ruled as limiting the effective implementation of the principle of equal treatment (*Marshall* v *Southampton & SW Hampshire Area Health Authority (No. 2)* [1993] IRLR 455). As a consequence, the ceilings on compensation were removed in successful sex and race discrimination cases (SI 1993/2798; SI 1994/1748). In the long term, no ceilings were imposed in other strands of discrimination law
Discrimination on the grounds of trans-sexual status ruled contrary to equal treatment law	This was determined by the ECJ in *P* v *S and Cornwall County Council* [1996] IRLR 347. In 1999 the Sex Discrimination (Gender Reassignment) Regulations amended the Sex Discrimination Act 1975
Defining 'working time' when 'on call'	The Working Time Directive 1993 was interpreted in *SIMAP* v *Conselleria de Sanidad y Consumo de la Generalidad Valenciana* [2000] IRLR 845; and *Landeshauptstadt Kiel* v *Jaeger* [2003] IRLR 804
Dismissal of woman undergoing IVF treatment can be discriminatory	*Mayr* v *Backerei und Konditorei Gerhard Flockner OHG* [2008]
Calculating length of service and age discrimination	Excluding service before age 25 in calculating length of service was contrary to the Employment Directive 2000 (*Kücükdeveci* v *Swedex GmbH & Co* [2010] IRLR 346)

● *Giving preliminary rulings on points of European law at the request of a national court.*

● *To hear complaints on the application and interpretation of European law.*

● *To determine the wider application of European law.* For example, in 1990, the court ruled that national courts are obliged to interpret that country's domestic legislation in the light of European directives regardless of whether the domestic legislation pre-dates or post-dates the directives. This wide view of interpretation also concerns law enacted in the member states prior to that country's entry into the EU (*Marleasing SA* v *La Comercial Internacional de Alimentacion* (C-106/89)).

In interpreting the law, the ECJ adopts a '**purposive**' (as opposed to 'literal') approach to interpretation. So, it will consider the intention of the legislators and the 'spirit' of the legislation rather than the strict 'letter'. This is compatible with the character of much law in the original EU member states which is in the form of broad statements of over-riding aims and principles. The House of Lords has accepted that such an approach might be accepted in the British courts for complying with European law (Lord Justice Templeman in *Pickstone* v *Freemans plc* [1988] IRLR 357).

❱ European Convention on Human Rights 1950

From 2 October 2000, this Convention was incorporated into law in the United Kingdom through the Human Rights Act 1998. The Convention was drafted under the auspices of the Council of Europe – an intergovernmental body, founded in 1949, primarily to promote democracy, human rights and the rule of law throughout Europe. It is separate from the European Union, although member states of the EU are also members of the Council and the EU accepts and expects compliance with the Convention.

The Convention was ratified by the UK in 1951. Until 2000, those alleging that their human rights had been infringed needed to embark on a lengthy process to the European Court of Human Rights in Strasbourg. Following the implementation of the Human Rights Act 1998, the Convention is gradually woven into the fabric of law in the UK and complainants have easier access to possible redress in the domestic courts.

Exhibit 1.2 sets out the key Convention rights. The Human Rights Act 1998 has three fundamental effects which in varying ways can have an effect on law relating to employment:

- *Common law*. This must be developed compatibly with Convention rights. This means that previous judgments can be questioned. In relation to employment, this is likely, over time, to affect the common law of contract.
- *Legislation*. All legislation (Acts of Parliament, regulations and orders) must be inter-preted and implemented in compliance with the Convention 'so far as it is possible to do so' (HRA 1998, s 3(1)). Where there are two possible interpretations of a statutory provision (i.e. one compatible with the Convention and one not), that which is com-patible must be adopted. Previous interpretations, under case law from courts in the United Kingdom, may no longer be relied upon. Where it is not possible to interpret particular legislation compatibly, a court (in England and Wales, the High Court and above; and in Scotland, the Court of Session and the High Court of Justiciary) may:
  - Quash or disapply secondary legislation (regulations and orders).
  - Issue a 'declaration of incompatibility' (HRA 1998, s 4) for primary legislation (an Act of Parliament). This will not rescind the legislation. It will remain in force. However, the declaration will draw the issue to the government's attention and enable the appropriate minister to invoke the 'fast track' procedure to amend the legislation in Parliament by a remedial order.
  - Require UK courts and tribunals to take account of case law from the European Court of Human Rights in Strasbourg but not necessarily be bound by it.
- *Activities of public authorities*. It is unlawful for a public authority to act incompatibly with Convention rights. The Human Rights Act covers all activities of a public authority, for example: policy-making, rules and regulations, personnel issues, administrative procedures, decision-making. There are three broad categories of public authorities:
  - *'Obvious' or 'pure' public authorities*. This describes, for example, a government department or statutory agency, a Minister of the Crown, local authorities, NHS

EXHIBIT 1.2

Key rights, European Convention on Human Rights 1950

The detailed provisions of these rights are in Schedule 1 to the Human Rights Act 1998.

Absolute rights

These have no restrictions or limitations:

Article 7: protection from retrospective criminal penalties

Article 3: protection from torture, inhuman and degrading treatment and punishment

Article 4: prohibition of slavery and enforced labour

Limited rights

These can be limited in specific circumstances defined in the Convention:

Article 5: The right to liberty and security

A person may be detained if the detention is lawful. It covers, for example, arrest by the police and imprisonment following conviction by a court.

Qualified rights

Many rights with a bearing on employment relations are in this category:

Article 8: right to respect for private and family life

Article 9: freedom of thought, conscience and religion

Article 10: freedom of expression

Article 11: freedom of assembly and association

It is permissible to interfere with these qualified rights in the following circumstances:

- If the interference is provided for in law.
- If the interference is necessary in a democratic society. It must fulfil a pressing social need; pursue a legitimate aim; be proportionate to the aims being pursued; and be related to a permissible aim set out in the relevant Article (e.g. the prevention of crime or the protection of public order).

Other rights

Article 6: right to a fair trial

Article 14: prohibition of discrimination (in the exercising of Convention rights)

trusts, education authorities, fire and civil defence authorities, the armed forces, the police and the immigration service, and the prison service. Everything done by these is covered by the Human Rights Act – whether in their public functions or in their private functions (e.g. offering an employment contract).

- *Courts and tribunals.* Their responsibility for interpreting and implementing the law is outlined above. In the employment context, neither employment tribunals nor the Employment Appeal Tribunal have power to quash or disapply secondary legislation not to issue declarations of incompatibility. If this were done in an employment case, it would be at the appeal stages in the Court of Appeal or the Supreme Court. Nevertheless, employment tribunals and the EAT must interpret the law compatibly with the Convention.

○ *'Hybrid' or quasi-public bodies*. These are bodies which carry out some public functions. They are not a public authority for all their activities. Examples include the privatised utilities (gas, electricity and water companies).

● *Remedial action*. The Human Rights Act 1998 creates two effects:

1 *A direct effect*. This is where a person (i.e. a victim) can enforce Convention rights directly in court through starting legal proceedings (s 7). Such action can only be taken against a 'public authority'. A victim may be a company or other organisation as well as a private individual. The complaint has, normally, to be made within one year of the act complained of. If a court finds that a public authority has breached a person's Convention rights, it can award whatever remedy is available to it within its existing powers and is just and equitable (s 8(1)). This may include the award of damages; quashing an unlawful decision; ordering the public authority not to take the proposed action.

2 *An indirect effect*. There is no means of enforcing Convention rights directly against private individuals (including private companies or quasi-public bodies when they are carrying out their private functions). In these cases, where a private individual or organisation is involved, there is an indirect effect. This means that the law (statute and common law and secondary legislation) in cases involving such private 'individuals' must be applied and interpreted compatibly with the Convention.

Complaints under the Human Rights Act may be initiated in a number of courts or tribunals, depending on which is appropriate. If the claim is based on a contract or in tort (e.g. a claim for personal injury), action should start in the High Court or the county court (or, in Scotland, in the Sheriff Court or Court of Session). Where the case relates to the decision of a public body, the appropriate action will usually be judicial review in the High Court. It is still possible for a complaint to be made, ultimately, to the ECHR (see Exhibit 1.3).

▶ Human rights and employment law

The *explicit* significance for employment law cases of the Human Rights Act 1998 and the European Convention has been slow and gradual. In two areas Convention rights have been explicitly referred to by the Courts in their judgments:

● legal representation in internal disciplinary procedures where a person's prospect of future employment is jeopardised (see *R (on the application of G) v Governors of X School and Y City Council* [2011] IRLR 222 in Chapter 8); and

● the determination of whether a particular 'belief' is protected under equality law (see *Grainger plc v Nicolson* [2011] IRLR 4, EAT in Chapter 5, Exhibit 5.19).

▶ Statutory codes of practice

In hearing complaints, tribunals and courts may be required to take account of statutory codes of practice. These have to be approved by Parliament. The main ones currently in force which are relevant for individual employment rights are:

EXHIBIT 1.3

Union expulsion of a British National Party member

Associated Society of Locomotive Engineers and Firemen (ASLEF) v United Kingdom [2007] **IRLR 361**

Facts. Lee was a train driver and a member of ASLEF, the train drivers' union. In 2002, it was reported to the union's general secretary that Lee was a well-known British National Party activist who had stood as a candidate in elections. He was said to have written and distributed racist material and harassed Anti-Nazi League protestors and been reported to the police.

The union's executive committee took the view that Lee's activities with the BNP were likely to bring the union into disrepute. A resolution to expel him was passed unanimously. Under its rules, ASLEF states that it aims to promote and enact equal treatment policies and is committed to campaigning vigorously to expose 'the obnoxious policies of political parties such as the National Front'.

Lee complained, in the first instance, that he had been unlawfully excluded from ASLEF membership (contrary to TULRCA 1992, s 174(3)). The employment tribunal upheld Lee's complaint. ASLEF appealed to the Employment Appeal Tribunal which upheld the union's claim about the law. The matter was referred back to a further ET hearing; and again Lee was successful in his application. ASLEF then made an application to the European Court of Human Rights in Strasbourg. Its complaint was that it was prevented from expelling a member because of his membership of a political party that advocated views contrary to its own policies, and that this was an infringement of its right to freedom on association (under Article 11 of the ECHR).

Law. Article 11 of the Convention: freedom of assembly and association:

1 Everyone has the right to freedom of peaceful assembly and to freedom of association with others, including the right to form and join trade unions for the protection of his interests.

2 No restrictions shall be placed on the exercise of these rights other than such as are prescribed by law and are necessary in a democratic society in the interests of national security or public safety, for the prevention of disorder or crime, for the protection of health or morals or for the protection of the rights and freedoms of others. This article shall not prevent the imposition of lawful restrictions on the exercise of these rights by members of the armed forces, of the police or of the administration of the state.

The UK law which was considered as, arguably, incompatible with this Convention article was the Trade Union and Labour Relations (Consolidation) Act 1992, s 174.

ECHR judgment. The court's view was that Lee's expulsion did not impinge on his freedom of expression (Article 10). It noted that he had suffered no particular detriment apart from loss of union membership. Even in workplace employment relations, ASLEF was the bargaining agent for the terms and conditions of all train drivers, irrespective of whether they were members or not.

The court gave more weight to ASLEF's right to choose its members. It acknowledged that the union had its own clear political views. It noted that there was no suggestion that in the internal union procedures that ASLEF had erred in its finding that Lee's views and those of the union's clashed. In the absence of any identifiable hardship suffered by Lee or any abusive or unreasonable conduct by ASLEF, the court concluded that the balance between the competing Convention rights had not been properly struck.

Consequences:

● TULRCA 1992, s 174 was amended in 2004 to allow a union to exclude an individual from membership on the grounds of his or her activities as member of a political party.

● Membership of a specified political party, in itself, remained as an unlawful ground for expulsion. However, the Employment Act 2008 amends the law in this respect.

- *Advisory Conciliation and Arbitration Service:*
  - Disciplinary and Grievance Procedures (2009).
  - Disclosure of Information to Trade Unions for Collective Bargaining Purposes (1998).
  - Time Off for Trade Union Duties and Activities (2010).
- *Health and Safety Executive:*
  - Code of Practice on Safety Representatives and Safety Committees (1978).
  - Code of Practice on Time Off for the Training of Safety Representatives (1978).
- *Equality and Human Rights Commission:*
  - Code of Practice on Employment (2011).
  - Code of Practice on Equal Pay (2011).
  - Guidance on matters to be taken into account in determining questions relating to the definition of disability.
- *Border and Immigration Agency:*
  - Avoidance of Unlawful Discrimination in Employment Practice While Seeking to Prevent Illegal Working (2008).
- *Information Commissioner:*
  - Employment Practices Data Protection Code (2005). (N.B. this code is not required to be laid before Parliament.)

The status of statutory codes (as, for example, those published by ACAS) is as follows:

- Failure of a person to observe any provision of a code 'shall not of itself render him liable to any proceedings';
- However, in any proceedings before an employment tribunal, any appropriate code of practice 'shall be admissible in evidence', and 'if any provision of such a code appears to the tribunal to be relevant to any question arising in the proceedings it shall be taken into account in determining that question' (TULRCA 1992, s 207).

▶ How do working people enforce their rights?

Normally, complaints about individual employment rights are made to an employment tribunal. It is possible for a complainant (the employee or worker) or a respondent employer to appeal, on a point of law, to the Employment Appeal Tribunal (EAT); and, then, usually with permission, to the Court of Appeal (or Court of Session in Scotland); and, then, to the Supreme Court (until October 2009, the House of Lords). If the complaint involves European law (for example, on equality, working time or transfers of undertakings), an ultimate appeal, with the permission of either the Court of Appeal or Supreme Court, would be to the European Court of Justice in Luxembourg. Alternatively, the British courts might refer a particular matter to the ECJ for a ruling on its interpretation. In 2011, for example, the Court of Appeal asked the ECJ to rule on when an employer's duty to consult workers' representatives over collective redundancies is triggered – when a strategic decision has been made or at an earlier stage when the employer is contemplating redundancies (*United States of America v Nolan* [2011] IRLR 40, CA see Chapter 3) (for more detail on these bodies see below).

In addition, various statutory agencies have responsibility for assisting in the enforcement of employment law. They provide advice and information and most have some enforcement powers. The most notable are the Advisory Conciliation and Arbitration Service, the Health and Safety Executive, the Equality and Human Rights Commission, the Low Pay Commission (for more detail on these bodies see below).

Employment tribunals

Originally set up in 1964 as industrial tribunals to deal with training levy complaints, their jurisdiction was extended to unfair dismissal in 1972. They now cover a very wide range of employment rights (e.g. all strands of equality law, equal pay, maternity and parental rights, rights of trade union membership, unlawful pay deductions) (**www.justice.gov.uk**). In 1998, they were renamed 'employment tribunals'. They now operate under the Employment Tribunals Act 1996 and the Employment Tribunals (Constitution and Rules of Procedure) Regulations 2004 (as amended). A full tribunal comprises three people. It is chaired by an employment judge, a legally qualified person. He or she may sit alone or may be assisted by two lay people who have experience of employment relations and are drawn from an employer list (including managers and HR practitioners); and from an employee list (including people with trade union experience). The President of the Employment Tribunals has powers to issue practice directions to promote consistency of case management. For example, in 2010, he issued guidance on the reading out loud of some witness statements in tribunal hearings which he described as achieving 'nothing of value' and 'wast[ing] the time of the tribunal and the parties'.

The use of tribunals to deal with employment rights complaints was supposed to be beneficial in offering informality and speed. This, however, has not proved to be so (see later section on redress). Exhibit 1.4 outlines, as an illustration, the employment tribunal process for an unfair dismissal complaint. The role and operation of employment tribunals was considered in a consultation paper, *Resolving workplace disputes: a consultation*, published by the Conservative-Liberal Democrat Government in January 2011 (**www.bis.gov.uk**).

EXHIBIT 1.4

Employment tribunals: dealing with unfair dismissal complaint

Scenario

Hannah has been employed for just over two years as an administrator in a facilities management company, World Class Facilites plc (WCF). Her performance has been reasonably satisfactory – although she was taken through the company's capability procedure six months ago when she was performing some new tasks unsatisfactorily. In the past couple of months she has been late for work on three or four occasions and has, generally, not been working to an acceptable standard. Her manager, in consultation with the human resources department, has decided to start disciplinary action. (She is given the statutory right to be accompanied which she declines.) The hearing results in her dismissal with one month's pay in lieu of notice. During the disciplinary appeal hearing she informed the company that she was pregnant. She says that she is going to complain to an employment tribunal of unfair dismissal. She discusses the situation with Sunita, a friend who works in human resource management in another company.

Time limits

Hannah has three months from the date of her dismissal to submit a claim to an employment tribunal. Late applications can be accepted only where the tribunal thinks it is 'just and equitable' to do so.

Hannah needs to consider whether she qualifies to make a claim. She may, also, within this three-month period, use the ACAS pre-claim conciliation service (**www.acas.org.uk**).

Assistance

Hannah will not receive any financial assistance towards her tribunal claim. If she was a member of a trade union she could receive some help making and presenting her claim. In her case, however, she has to bear any costs herself and rely on the voluntary support of a friend, Sunita. She might obtain some advice on her complaint from Citizens Advice (**www.citizensadvice.org.uk**). (After the employment tribunal hearing, she can claim some specified expenses – travel and accommodation.)

Does the complainant qualify?

- *'Employee' status*: The tribunal must be satisfied that the complainant is an 'employee' and not a 'worker on some other contract'. In some cases, an employer will state that the claimant is not an 'employee' and it is then a matter for the tribunal to determine his or her employment status (see Chapter 2). In Hannah's case she has a contract of employment – the essentials of which are set out in a written *Statement of Initial Employment Particulars* (Employment Rights Act 1996, s 1).

- *Length of continuous service with the employer*: The complainant must have the appropriate continuous service with the employer. If, however, the dismissal relates to a 'protected characteristic' under the Equality Act 2010, then, he or she does not require a qualifying period. In Hannah's case, she is claiming that her dismissal is because of her pregnancy. She is also eligible to claim 'ordinary' unfair dismissal (see Chapters 5, 8 and 11).

- *Dismissal*: An employment tribunal needs to be satisfied that the complainant was dismissed. Hannah was given a letter terminating her employment.

ACAS pre-claim conciliation

ACAS (**www.acas.org.uk**) has a statutory duty (Employment Tribunal Act 1996, s 18) to try, through its conciliation officers, to promote a settlement in employment tribunal complaints – but *not* to advise the parties. In 2009, it expanded this free service. This involves conciliation officers assisting the parties to discuss the complaint. The aim is to find a solution acceptable to both parties and which avoids the costs, stress and time associated with a tribunal hearing. The ex-employer may offer a sum of money to settle the claim. In Hannah's case either she or the company could ask for pre-claim conciliation. It is, of course, for the parties to see if an agreement is possible. The conciliation officer cannot impose one. If none is reached, a complaint may be submitted to the tribunal.

More information

Hannah may use the statutory questionnaire available under the Equality Act. This asks the ex-employer to respond to a number of specific questions to help her support her claim of discriminatory treatment (**www.equalities.gov.uk/news/equality_act_2010_forms_for_ob_aspx**) (see also Chapter 5).

Filling in the forms

ET1: An ex-employee making a complaint must complete the necessary form (see the Ministry of Justice website: **www.justice.gov.uk**).* It should be completed electronically within three months from the

---

* Some different arrangements for dealing with the forms apply in Scotland.

date of the dismissal. Among the information required is the nature of the complaint. In Hannah's case, she would say she was unfairly dismissed because the reason for her dismissal was her pregnancy and not her overall performance. She might also say that, if there were performance issues, these were related to pregnancy. So, she would include two grounds for complaint. If it is claimed that there is more than one reason for a dismissal, it is for the tribunal to determine the *principal* reason. A complainant is asked to indicate on the ET1 the remedy that he or she is seeking. In dismissal cases, this will be compensation and, possibly, re-engagement or reinstatement. Hannah could claim these.

ET3: The employer receives a copy of the ET1 form from the tribunal office and should complete an ET3 form, responding to the claims made by the ex-employee (**www.justice.gov.uk**). In Hannah's case, the employer might deny that the reason for dismissal was pregnancy. It would refer to her poor performance record and state that the decision to dismiss was as result of a fair disciplinary procedure. It might point out that it only became aware of her pregnancy when the decision to dismiss for capability had already been taken. The forms provide an outline of the issues in dispute. If the tribunal accepts the complaint, then these issues will be dealt with in more detail at a full hearing.

The government are proposing fees to be introduced from April 2013 for complainants to pay 'up front'.

Pre-hearing review

This can be ordered by the tribunal or at the request of either the respondent employer or the complainant. It is held, in advance of a full hearing, by an employment judge (usually sitting alone) to decide preliminary matters – e.g. deciding whether, on the face of it, a complaint looks weak; has no reasonable prospect of success; or is vexatious. If a tribunal decides there is no reasonable prospect of success, the complainant is allowed to continue only if he or she deposits a sum of money ordered by the tribunal. Such decisions can, sometimes, be successfully challenged (*A v B* [2010] EWCA Civ 1378).

Who are the 'representatives'?

Both the complainant and the respondent employer will need to decide who is to represent them at the tribunal hearing. Complainants may represent themselves or, alternatively, may use a trade union official, a solicitor or a 'friend' (someone who may not be legally qualified who will assist in preparing and discussing the case). An employer usually uses a solicitor or a senior manager supported by staff from the HR department (see later section in this chapter). In Hannah's case, she is being assisted by a friend. WCF plc is represented by its HR Manager.

Claim 'activated'

If the claim is not settled in the ACAS pre-claim conciliation process, and the employment tribunal has formally accepted it for a full hearing, then various steps take place. The hearing may not be scheduled for several months from the ET1 being submitted.

Further opportunity for ACAS conciliation right up to the date of the hearing. An agreement would be legally binding and made through ACAS on form COT3. Tribunal proceedings would be withdrawn.

Case management. Various steps are ordered by the tribunal office to ensure that documentation is available and, as appropriate, exchanged between the parties. This includes papers that each party is relying on to support their case. Hannah's ex-employer is likely to provide all the paperwork relating to her performance and the relevant minutes of disciplinary hearings. Hannah herself may produce documentary evidence to show when she told her employer of her pregnancy; and also any evidence she has about how her pregnancy may have affected her performance.

Witnesses. Each party will have to indicate who they will bring as witnesses. (It is possible for a tribunal to order a witness to attend to give evidence or produce documents or information.) Witness statements should be prepared and exchanged in advance of the tribunal hearing. These may be read or, in some cases, 'taken as read'. Hannah may be the only witness for her complaint. WCF plc, on the other hand, may have various witnesses: her supervisor, her line manager, the senior manger who heard the appeal and, possibly, relevant HR staff.

Preparation. Hannah should meet her 'friend', Sunita, well in advance to prepare the presentation of her case; to try and anticipate the issues likely to raised by WCF plc; and to prepare questions that she might ask the company's witnesses.

The full tribunal hearing

The tribunal comprises a legally-qualified employment judge who chairs and two lay members. Proceedings are, normally, public. In unfair dismissal cases, the complainant presents his or her case first. Hannah will read her witness statement and Sunita may then ask her to elaborate, orally, on some aspects. Then, Hannah can be cross-examined by the representative of WCF plc, the HR Manager. Sunita may re-examine particular points, if necessary, and the tribunal may also ask questions to clarify or elaborate particular issues. This process is repeated with all witnesses. So, Sunita may cross-examine WCF plc witnesses on Hannah's behalf. She may consult with Hannah, during the proceedings, on particular issues and questions that need to be asked.

Tribunal decision

This will involve consideration of both fact and law. In Hannah's case the tribunal will, having heard all the evidence, decide on the principal reason for her dismissal. Was it the 'fair' reason of 'capability' (under the Employment Rights Act 1996, s 98); or was it the automatically unfair reason of 'pregnancy and maternity' (under the Equality Act 2010, s 39)? If it is for 'capability', then the issue would be whether it was 'reasonable in the circumstances' for the employer to dismiss Hannah for that reason; and whether WCF plc used a fair procedure (in accordance with the ACAS *Code of Practice on Disciplinary Procedures* 2009) (**www.acas.org.uk**). If it is found to be a dismissal because of the 'protected characteristic' of 'pregnancy and maternity', the tribunal would rule it to be an unfair dismissal. The Court of Appeal has reaffirmed an established view that, in unfair dismissal claims, the role of the tribunal is to review the fairness of the employer's decision and ***not*** to substitute its own view (*London Ambulance Service NHS Trust* v *Small* [2009] IRLR 563).

Remedy hearing

A complainant indicates on the ET1 form the remedies he or she is seeking. A tribunal will hold a remedy hearing to hear evidence of the loss sustained by the complainant. The respondent employer is able to challenge this evidence. A dismissed complainant must show evidence of attempting to 'mitigate their loss' (e.g. by applying for or obtaining other employment). If Hannah is successful in her discrimination claim, she is likely to seek compensation and an award for injury to feelings (see Chapters 5 and 8).

Compensation

The compensation awarded by tribunals is, invariably, well below the maximum sums available. The maximum compensatory award for unfair dismissal complaints is £68,400 (February 2011). Compensation is unlimited in discrimination claims. The ***median*** compensation for unfair dismissal is £4,591; and for sex discrimination (which at the time covered pregnancy complaints), £6,078 (Employment Tribunal and EAT statistics 2010–2011, **www.justice.gov.uk**).

Appeal

It is possible for either party to appeal against an employment tribunal decision to the Employment Appeal Tribunal. However, the appeal must relate to a 'point of law', e.g. alleging that the employment tribunal misconstrued the law. Rarely are such appeals made.

▶ Employment Appeal Tribunal

This was established in 1976 as a superior court of record to hear appeals on points of law from the (then) industrial tribunals. Each bench comprises a judge (drawn from the High Court and Court of Appeal) and two lay members from people who have experience of employment relations. In various areas of employment law, it has provided guidance for tribunals on particular issues (website: **www.justice.gov.uk**). In 2010–11, the EAT received 2048 appeals from employment tribunals (Employment Tribunal and EAT statistics, **www.justice.gov.uk**).

Court of Appeal

The jurisdiction of the Court of Appeal covers England and Wales. (In Scotland the equivalent appeal court is the Court of Session). Created in the late nineteenth century, it comprises two divisions: the Civil Division (presided over by the Master of Rolls) and the Criminal Division (presided over by the Lord Chief Justice). Under employment law, appeals against rulings of the EAT are heard in the Civil Division. Further appeals can be made to the Supreme Court – with the 'leave' (permission) of either the Court of Appeal or of the Supreme Court itself (**www.justice.gov.uk**).

Supreme Court (formerly the House of Lords)

The Supreme Court was established in October 2009, under the Constitutional Reform Act 2005, replacing the judicial committee of the House of Lords. It 'hears appeals on arguable points of law of the greatest public importance' (see website). It is the final court of appeal for civil and criminal cases from the Court of Appeal in England and Wales, for civil cases from the Court of Session in Scotland, and for civil and criminal cases from the Court of Appeal in Northern Ireland. Decisions of the Supreme Court bind all lower courts.

If the law derives from the European Union, there can be a further appeal stage to the European Court of Justice. If there is some uncertainty about the application or meaning of a provision of European law, the Supreme Court may refer this to the ECJ for authoritative guidance.

There are 12 Justices of the Supreme Court, who are appointed by the monarch on the advice of the Prime Minister, from senior appeal court judges from each part of the UK. The first female Law Lord – now a Justice – Lady Justice Hale was appointed in 2004. The Justices of the Supreme Court are debarred from sitting in the House of Lords (as a legislative chamber in Parliament) whilst holding that office. Usually, these Justices sit as a panel of five. The number of appeals dealt with each year varies – tending to be between 80 and 100. A few concern employment-related issues. For example, in 2011, it heard appeals from Court of Appeal rulings in relation to *Parkwood Leisure Ltd* v *Alemo-Herron and Others* [2010] IRLR 298 (see Chapter 3 on Transfers of Undertakings); and *R (on application of G)* v *Governors of X School* (see Chapter 8 on disciplinary action) (**www.supremecourt.gov.uk**).

European Court of Justice

Based in Luxembourg, this is the principal judicial body of the European Union. It is officially known as the Court of Justice of the European Communities. It has jurisdiction in Britain under the European Communities Act 1972 in relation to European competition and company law; and also employment and equality law (see earlier section in this chapter on European Union law).

The ECJ comprises 27 judges and eight Advocates-General who assist the court. Judges are nominated by member states for a six-year term. The ECJ makes final rulings on the application of European law (see Table 1.2). The role of Advocates-General has no equivalent in the English and Scottish legal systems. They provide a reasoned submission (an Opinion) in open court. This is a preliminary opinion on points of law in a specific case. An Advocate-General will refer to other relevant rulings and recommend a judgment. Some months later, the court will pronounce its ruling. It is usual for the Court to accept an Advocate-General's view. In its Annual Report 2009, the Court noted that there is an increase (from 41 per cent in 2008 to 52 per cent in 2009) in the determination of cases *without* an Advocate-General's Opinion where a case raised no new point of law (**www.europa.eu**).

European Court of Human Rights

Based in Strasbourg, this court operates under the Council of Europe and is separate from the European Union. Its responsibility is to adjudicate on alleged violations of the 1950 European Convention for the Protection of Human Rights and Fundamental Freedoms to which Britain is a signatory. This Convention is now incorporated into UK law through the Human Rights Act 1998. Although it is still possible for a complainant to appeal to the ECHR, initially, he or she should apply through the domestic courts (**www.echr.coe.int**).

International Labour Organisation

The ILO was established in 1919. Now an agency of the United Nations, it is charged with setting universal labour standards. It is a tripartite body comprising representatives of government, employers and workers. De-colonisation has meant that its membership has grown from 52 states in 1946 to 177 in 2003. The 1944 Declaration of Philadelphia redefined the ILO's objectives and reaffirmed the key principles on which the ILO is based:

- Labour is not a commodity.
- Freedom of expression and association are essential to sustained progress.
- Poverty anywhere constitutes a danger to prosperity everywhere.

ILO standards are set by the International Labour Conference in the form of Conventions and Recommendations. If a state ratifies a convention, it undertakes to ensure that its domestic law conforms to the convention's standards. Recommendations do not create legal obligations. Any dispute relating to ratified conventions can be referred to the International Court of Justice in the Hague.

The effectiveness of the ILO and of labour standards has been widely criticised (Hepple 2005: 66). In particular, it lacks effective sanctions against states which argue that down-scaling labour standards is necessary to remain competitive and attract investment. The implementation of ratified standards is also decidedly uneven. In response to this, the ILO has, since 1997, focused on 'core' standards: those relating to freedom of association and collective bargaining; forced labour; non-discrimination; child labour and minimum age in employment. However, difficulties remain in translating these principles into practice.

In 2011, for example, it published a proposed Convention concerning decent work for domestic workers. It noted that these are mostly female and continue to be 'under-valued and invisible'. They tend to be 'vulnerable to discrimination in respect of conditions of employment and of work and to other abuses of human rights'. Certainly, in the United Kingdom, they frequently fall 'below the radar' of employment protection because they work in private residences. However, the Department for Business, Innovation and Skills was reported as saying that 'it would not be ratifying the convention to bind the UK by its rules "for the foreseeable future", so felt it would be wrong to vote for it at all' and so would abstain (*Guardian*, 16 June 2011) (**www.ilo.org/global**).

What is the role of statutory agencies?

▶ Advisory Conciliation and Arbitration Service

Established initially in 1974, ACAS became a statutory body in 1975. It is an independent service, charged with the general duty 'to promote the improvement of industrial relations, in particular, by exercising its functions in relation to the settlement of **trade disputes**' (TULRCA 1992, ss 209–14). It is governed by a Council, comprising a full-time chairperson; and 11 members appointed after consultation with the Confederation of British Industry (CBI) and other specified employers' organisation; and the Trades Union Congress and other specified employees' organisations. Three members are appointed by the Secretary of State for Business. It is required to publish an annual report (TULRCA, ss 247–53).

Among its functions are the following:

- *Individual conciliation*: to offer conciliation in disputes over individual statutory employment rights (e.g. in unfair dismissal, discrimination claims, etc.) between individual employees and their employers or ex-employers. (See Exhibit 1.4 and Chapter 8 for a detailed outline of the role of ACAS in unfair dismissal cases.)
- *Collective conciliation*: to offer and provide this in industrial disputes.
- *Arbitration*: to provide facilities for **arbitration** in industrial disputes; and to provide a scheme for arbitration in relation to individual unfair dismissal claims (as an alternative to an employment tribunal hearing).
- *Statutory codes of practice*: to draft **codes of practice** to be approved by Parliament (see earlier). (See Chapter 8 for discussion about the *Code of Practice on Disciplinary and Grievance Procedures*) (**www.acas.org.uk**).

▶ Health and Safety Executive

This was established in 2008 arising from a merger of the former Health and Safety Commission and former Health and Safety Executive. It is responsible for taking appropriate steps to secure the health, safety and welfare of people at work and to protect the public generally against dangers to health and safety arising from work activities. It is headed by a governing board of up to 11 members and a chairperson. In formulating its policy it consults on all aspects of health and safety. It publishes an annual report. Its health and safety inspectors advise on health and safety legislation and have powers of enforcement (see Chapter 12) (**www.hse.gov.uk**).

▶ Equality and Human Rights Commission

Established in 2007, the Commission took over the work of the Equal Opportunities Commission, the Commission for Racial Equality, and the Disability Rights Commission. Its principal functions are:

- to take legal action: this can be taken on behalf of individuals where legal requirements need to be clarified;

- to initiate formal inquiries into employing organisations;

- to make representations to government on the implementation of discrimination and human rights law;

- to provide advice and information on discrimination and human rights law; and to provide some financial support to external organisations;

- to promote good practice in relation to equal opportunities (**www.equalityhuman rights.com**).

▶ Low Pay Commission

Established initially in 1997 as a non-statutory body to report on the introduction of a national minimum wage, the following year it was made a statutory body under the National Minimum Wage Act 1998. It comprises a chairperson and eight other members. These generally consist of nominees from employer bodies, trade unions and academics with low pay expertise. Its role is to carry out tasks specified by the Secretary of State for Business. Before making recommendations it is required to consult employers' and workers' organisations. It is also obliged to have regard to 'the effect of this Act on the economy of the United Kingdom as a whole and on competitiveness' (NMWA 1998, s 7) (**www.lowpay.gov.uk**).

▶ Information Commissioner

Initially known as the Data Protection Commissioner, the name was changed in 2000. The Commissioner has several principal functions:

- He or she is empowered to take enforcement action against 'data controllers' (i.e. companies and other organisations) which are in breach of the 'data protection principles' (Data Protection Act 1998, Sch 1).

- A 'data subject' (in the employment context, usually a 'worker') may complain to the Commissioner that the 'principles' are not being complied with in a particular case. The Commissioner may investigate by initiating an assessment (DPA 1998, s 42).

- He or she is under a statutory duty (DPA 1998, s 51) to promote and disseminate good practice – which includes the preparation of codes of practice.

- He or she must maintain a register of 'data controllers' who are required to notify their data processing.

- He or she may serve an *Enforcement Notice* on a 'data controller' (e.g. an employer). This requires the data controller to stop processing any personal data or any specified personal data, or processing it in a specified manner.

- He or she may serve an *Information Notice* on a 'data controller' specifying information required in a given time period to respond to a request for an assessment, or to decide whether the data protection principles have been complied with. Appeal can be made to the Information Tribunal on both Information and Enforcement Notices (DPA 1998, s 48). Further appeal is possible to the High Court in England and Wales, the Court of Session in Scotland, and the High Court in Northern Ireland (**www.ico.gov.uk**).

◗ Criminal Records Bureau

This is an executive agency of the Home Office established in 2002 (under the Police Act 1997). It provides a disclosure service for organisations in the private, public and voluntary service to inquire about the criminal records of specific applicants for employment; and those in employment. There are two checks available in England and Wales:

- *Standard disclosure*: This shows current and spent convictions, cautions, reprimands and warnings held on the Police National Computer. It also shows whether a person is on a government department list as unsuitable to work with children or vulnerable adults.

- *Enhanced disclosure*: This is the highest level of check and contains the same information as standard disclosures; but also includes other relevant information held by local police forces. This level of disclosure is primarily for positions involving regular caring for, training, supervising or being in sole charge of children or vulnerable adults.

In Scotland, there is also a *basic disclosure*. This is issued to individual applicants and provides details of convictions at national level that are not spent under the Rehabilitation of Offenders Act 1974.

Both the standard and enhanced disclosures are issued to the individual and to a registered employer. Organisations wishing to use the CRB checks must comply with its code of practice. The aim of the code is to ensure that the disclosed information is used fairly and that sensitive personal information is handled and stored appropriately and is kept for only as long as necessary. To assist employers, the CRB has also developed a sample policy statement on the recruitment of ex-offenders (**www.crb.gov.uk**).

◗ Independent Safeguarding Authority

This authority began work in 2009. It vets those who apply to work with children or vulnerable adults. It does this by:

- working with the CRB, which will gather information on those who want to work with vulnerable groups;

- using that information to decide on a case-by-case basis who poses a risk of harm to vulnerable groups;

- storing information about an individual's ISA status for employers and voluntary organisations.

In 2010, the Conservative-Liberal Democrat Government began a review of the criminal records and vetting and barring regime. In February 2011 it was announced that, among other measures, the Criminal Records Bureau and the ISA would be merged. (This is a provision in the Protection of Freedoms Bill.)

Central Arbitration Committee

Set up in the 1970s, it is an independent tribunal with statutory powers to adjudicate in various employment disputes. Its key functions are:

- to receive applications from trade unions for recognition rights with an employer;
- as appropriate, make a declaration granting recognition;
- receiving employers' applications for derecognition of a trade union;
- receiving complaints about the disclosure of information for collective bargaining;
- to help resolve disputes under the Information and Consultation Regulations 2004;
- dealing with claims and complaints regarding the establishment and operation of European Works Councils (**www.cac.gov.uk**).

What redress is available for infringements of rights?

It is, of course, pointless enacting employment rights without ensuring adequate redress. In this section we will look at the effectiveness of existing processes.

The effectiveness of redress and remedies

The effectiveness of redress for individuals depends upon the effectiveness of complaints procedures and on ease of access for complainants. There are two relevant sets of procedure:

- in-house dispute resolution: i.e. internal grievance, harassment, whistleblowing, capability and disciplinary procedures;
- external complaints procedures: especially through employment tribunals.

Considerable attention by governments has focused on these procedures as a way of promoting better, speedier dispute resolution; improving the quality of workplace relations; and reducing public expenditure on tribunals.

In-house procedures

Detailed consideration of these is provided later in the textbook (see Chapter 8). Guidance is provided in the ACAS *Code of Practice on Disciplinary and Grievance Procedures* (2009). ACAS also advises on mediation as a contribution to workplace dispute resolution (**www.acas.org.uk**).

Employment tribunals

An illustration of the steps in an employment tribunal claim are outlined in Exhibit 1.4.

Originally, tribunals as institutions were commended in comparison with the ordinary courts because they were said to offer 'cheapness, accessibility, freedom from technicality, expert knowledge of a particular subject' (Franks 1957). Employment tribunals, when allocated jurisdiction for individual employment rights complaints in 1972, were expected to have these characteristics. However, over the past 40 years, these characteristics have been increasingly questioned in various academic studies (Dickens *et al.* 1985; Leonard 1987; Lewis and Clark 1993; Hepple *et al.* 2000). A contemporary evaluation of the tribunal process in providing adequate redress can be considered under the following headings:

- *Access of complainants*. This may be limited formally in legislation depending on employment status (i.e. whether the person is, in law, an 'employee'), on length of service with the employer; and on the implementation of 'up front' fees.

- *Duration of procedure*. This may be slow; 75 per cent of hearings of single cases before an employment tribunal should be held in 26 weeks. This target was achieved in 2007–08 and 2008–09. However, the figure for 2009–10 was 65 per cent (Tribunals Service Annual Statistics 2009–10, **www.justice.gov.uk**). The median number of days spent on a case that involved a tribunal decision was one (Peters *et al.* 2010).

- *Resources*. There are several categories of resources necessary for complainants and respondents: professional advice, financial resources and time.

  Professional advice: Case law under the Convention on Human Rights saw the development of the concept of 'equality of arms' (*Neumeister* v *Austria* [1968] 1 EHRR 91). Essentially, this refers to the balance of resources between each side in a dispute or court case. In a subsequent case before the European Court of Human Rights, the concept was described as follows: '. . . as regards [civil] litigation involving opposing private interests, "equality of arms" implies that each party must be afforded a reasonable opportunity to present his case – including his evidence – under conditions that do not place him at a substantial disadvantage vis-à-vis his opponent' (*Dombo Beheer BV* v *Netherlands* [1993] 18 EHRR 213).

  Resources available to complainants and to respondent employers in employment tribunal cases differ widely. Data on this is available in the 2003 and 2008 surveys of employment tribunal applications (Hayward *et al.* 2004; and Peters *et al.* 2010). For example, 32 per cent of claimants nominated a professional representative on the ET1 form, compared with 54 per cent of employers on the ET3. Particularly for claimants, this represents 'a large decrease' from 2003 when the respective figures were 40 per cent and 55 per cent (Peters *et al.* 2010). 'The proportion of claimants who received no representation or advice [40 per cent] has risen compared with 2003' when it was 34 per cent (*ibid.*). At the full tribunal hearing, as in the 2003 survey, 'employers were much more likely than claimants to be represented (73 per cent versus 34 per cent)' (*ibid.* 48).

  Financial resources: 55 per cent of claimants incurred personal financial costs as a result of the case (*ibid.*: 91). The median amounts for legal and professional fees were £2,000 for claimants and £2,500 for employers. As in 2003, discrimination claims were the most expensive for both parties. The most expensive cases for complainants were those concerning wage deductions (£5,502); and for employers, redundancy payments (£7,050) (*ibid.* 55).

  Time: The median number of days a complainant spent on a case was seven (compared with four in 2003). Cases where a discrimination claim was the primary jurisdiction involved more time – the median was 14 days (*ibid.*: 92–3). As far as respondent employers were concerned, the mean number of days spent on a case was 13 and the median was 5. For discrimination cases the figure was 9 days (*ibid.*: 95).

- *Technicality*. Increasingly, this has become the hallmark of the tribunal process. The presence of lawyers has encouraged tribunals to appear more like courts. Indeed, by the mid-1980s, they were described as 'quasi-courts' (Dickens *et al.* 1985). Also, some bodies of employment law together with associated **case law** (e.g., equal pay and transfers of undertakings legislation) are particularly complex for lay complainants. Reliance on the expertise of lawyers is almost inevitable in these complaints.

- *Stamina*. Complainants need stamina and resources to enter and remain in the tribunal process: 36 per cent said that they had experienced stress and depression as a result of their complaint. As in the 1998 and 2003 surveys, 'these were the most common non-financial negative effects mentioned by claimants' (Peters *et al.* 2010: 96). Complainants bringing unfair **dismissal** or discrimination cases were most likely to report stress and greater incidence of loss of confidence/self-esteem (Peters *et al.* 2010: 96; Hayward *et al.* 2004: 162–3).

- *Remedies*. Where complainants are successful, the **remedies** can frequently be small. In successful unfair dismissal the remedies are limited compensation (capped at £68,400 in February 2011); and possible reinstatement or re-engagement. The *median* award in unfair dismissal cases was £4,591. Under equality law the remedies are unlimited compensation; an award for injury to feelings; a declaration; and a recommendation. An 'appropriate recommendation' (Equality Act 2010, s 124) to deal with discrimination in relation to the complainant or other staff can be made by the tribunal. In most discrimination cases *median* compensation was around £6000 (Employment Tribunal and EAT statistics 2010–11, **www.justice.gov.uk**).

❱ Employment consequences

By the time of the survey interview, 73 per cent of claimants were in new work and 8 per cent were still working for the employer against whom they had made the complaint. 'Where claimants had moved into new work, the average time it had taken to find this work was 15 weeks, whilst the median was 8 weeks' (*ibid.*); 41 per cent said that their pay was less than that in their previous job; and the same proportion said that it paid better (Peters *et al.* 2010: 99). Forty-one per cent said that their new job was at a higher level or about the same when compared to their previous job; 32 per cent saw their new employment as 'something to do until something better comes along' (*ibid.*).

What are the key principles underpinning employment law?

In the previous sections, we have referred to various principles which infuse employment law. Here, we consider them more fully and indicate their relationship to human resource management and employment relations. These underpinning principles can be divided into those that concern the substantive issues of employment relations (i.e. the outcomes – the terms and conditions of employment and other decisions); and those that affect the processes by which decisions on terms and conditions and other employment relations matters are made.

- *Substantive issues*:
  - Fairness
  - Reasonableness
  - Equal treatment
  - Harmonisation.

- **Procedural issues:**
  - **Natural justice**
  - **Consultation**
  - Consent
  - Freedom.

Substantive issues

In recent years, two overarching and interconnected policy perspectives have become increasingly influential: *ethical standards* and *human rights*. These encompass, in varying ways, the concepts of fairness, reasonableness, equal treatment and harmonisation. They are used as benchmarks to assess the treatment of employees and behaviour in society at large. So, for example, equality law (relating to both employment and the provision of goods, services and facilities) provides a clear standard of acceptable treatment. The promotion of ethical standards and the commitment to human rights also concerns business employment practices beyond Britain. They are a means of evaluating corporate behaviour in international supply chains which may be founded, in part, on child labour and exploitative conditions. Third World charities have expressed strong concern about this; and, indeed, Oxfam has published a code of practice to encourage employers to address the issue and take steps to establish a more ethical supply chain.

❱ Fairness

In defining fairness, people are invariably subjective (considering the concept in relation to their own personal values). They tend to define it relatively or comparatively (e.g. this is fair and that is not). When asked why they say something is fair or unfair, the tendency is quickly to move away from the abstract and explore details and practical elements of what constitutes fairness.

For example, at the heart of the debate on a statutory minimum wage is the notion of a fair wage. The idea of such a wage is long-standing. The Catholic Church has, historically, referred to a 'just' wage; and the Council of Europe defines and quantifies a 'decency threshold' – an acceptable level of pay. It is the latter that provides a clue to the practical ways in which the concept of fairness is defined. There are social expectations that pay should be sufficient, as a minimum, to enable a person to buy food and provide adequate shelter and appropriate care for both himself or herself and any dependants. Indeed, there are campaigns in Britain for a 'living wage'. It is claimed that the statutory national minimum wage is insufficient (see Chapter 9). Fair treatment, then, is determined against reference points. These are likely to change over time – particularly as social expectations and values shift.

❱ Reasonableness

Reasonableness is, likewise, an undefined term. It is a long-established concept in law generally. For example, in criminal law there are the concepts of 'reasonable force' in relation to self-defence; and the 'reasonable chastisement' of children. In civil proceedings, the 'reasonable man' test can be used to make value judgements about a person's conduct. The fundamental difficulty with such a test and with the concept of reasonableness is that it is invariably measured against shifting criteria. As social attitudes change, even within 20 or 30 years, the socially accepted notion of reasonable behaviour changes. Also, at any one time, there will probably be differences in attitude between men and women, between older and younger people, and between people from different social and ethnic backgrounds on the standards that they have in mind when assessing reasonableness.

In the employment arena, reasonableness is of particular significance in cases involving unfair dismissal, disability discrimination, and health and safety. In the former, tribunals have to satisfy themselves of the reasonableness of an employer's conduct in dismissing an employee for a particular fair reason. (See *Iceland Frozen Foods Ltd* v *Jones* [1982] IRLR 439 in Chapter 8 for more detailed discussion.) In legislation on disability discrimination, employers are required to make reasonable adjustments. Under health and safety legislation, the general duties imposed on an employer must be complied with 'so far as is reasonably practicable' (see, respectively, Chapters 5 and 12 for more details). Implied in the legislative provision of 'reasonableness' is the idea of a balance being struck between various factors: for example, cost, time and trouble involved in aiming to comply with the law.

❱ Equal treatment

Equal treatment as a concept has developed in British employment relations as a result of a number of parallel influences: social movements originating in the United States of America and policy initiatives from the European Union. In the 1960s, in the USA, the women's movement critically questioned the role and status of women in society and the opportunities available. Simultaneously, also in the USA, the civil rights movement challenged endemic racism and asserted social, voting and employment rights. The significance of these movements was felt in Britain and energised groups who sought changes here.

Within the European Community (as the Union was then called), commitment to equal treatment has had an uneven history. The founding Treaty of Rome 1957 refers only to equal pay between men and women – and that as a result of a political compromise. No specific social provisions were included because, initially, the community was conceived primarily as a free-trade area or 'common market'. Pragmatically, a Social Action Programme in the 1970s promoted equal treatment on the grounds of sex and equal pay. By 1989, under the Community Charter of Fundamental Social Rights of Workers, a clear shift had taken place in the importance of social policy. The preamble states that 'the same importance must be attached to the social aspects as to the economic aspects and . . . therefore, they must be developed in a balanced manner'. The social policy objectives of the European Union have, as a consequence, moulded much UK legislation on equal treatment.

There are two aspects to equal treatment law. First, 'like must be treated alike'. A basis of comparison is, then, established. The objective legal test has been defined in a House of Lords judgment on direct sex discrimination in this way: 'would the complainant have received the same treatment but for his/her sex?' (*James v Eastleigh Borough Council* [1990] IRLR 288). This is known in shorthand as the 'but for' test (see Chapter 5). The second aspect concerns policies and practices which appear neutral in effect but should be scrutinised to see if they create some institutionalised disadvantage for a person with particular characteristics (e.g. sex, race, disability, age) – i.e. indirect discrimination.

▶ Harmonisation

As an issue in British employment relations, this has developed from the early 1970s in a pragmatic and voluntary way primarily as a result of management–union negotiations. It is an aspect of equal treatment and concerns the establishment of 'single-status' terms and conditions of employment and the removal of the differential status and treatment of manual and non-manual workers (i.e. blue-collar and white-collar) workers. In particular, it resulted in common holidays and working hours and common access to sick pay and pensions. Traditionally, status distinctions had been the norm – with manual workers granted shorter holidays, working longer hours and, invariably, having no access to sick pay or pension schemes.

Under employment law, there has been no explicit differentiation between blue- and white-collar workers. The principal limitations on access have related to the number of hours worked each week and continuity of service with an employer. Although length of service remains for entitlement to some employment rights, the 'hours' threshold has been ruled to be unlawful (*R v Secretary of State for Employment* **ex parte** *Equal Opportunities Commission* [1994] IRLR 176). So, part-time workers have entitlements and, under the Part-time Workers Directive 1997, are eligible for *pro rata* treatment with full-time workers.

Procedural issues

There are four key underpinning principles evident within employment relations processes:

▶ Natural justice

This is a long-standing legal concept. There are two key rules:

- that no person may be a judge in their own cause;
- that a person must be given a fair opportunity to know the allegation against them, to state their case and to answer the person making the allegation.

In employment relations, these rules have particular importance in disciplinary and dismissal cases. Procedural fairness is as important a consideration for employment tribunals as the other tests (viz. whether the dismissal is for a fair reason and whether the employer behaved reasonably in all the circumstances). The ACAS *Code on Practice on Disciplinary and Grievance Procedures* embodies the principles of natural justice (see Chapter 8).

▶ Consultation

Within employment relations, conflicts of interest are endemic. Employers and their workforces will have different views and expectations about pay levels, job security arrangements, other terms and conditions of employment. Two processes can contribute to resolving workplace differences: collective bargaining and consultation. The former involves negotiations with recognised trade unions and results in 'joint regulation' (i.e. terms and conditions agreed between the employer and the recognised union).

Consultation is a weaker form of employee participation in management decision-making. Nevertheless, it is significant because it can arise in any workplace – unionised or not. Also, legislation (for example, the Information and Consultation with Employees Regulations 2004) and case law (for example, *R v British Coal Corporation and the Secretary of State for Trade and Industry* ex parte *Price* [1994] IRLR 72) have to some degree, over the past 30 years, enhanced its role. Its growth is, in part, a result of the promotion by the European Union of 'social partnership' and the way this concept has been woven into the fabric of employment relations.

In academic literature, distinctions are drawn between 'pseudo consultation' (Pateman 1970) and 'genuine consultation'. The former is essentially information giving by management. There is little, if any, expectation that a management decision or proposal will change as a result of discussion. This form of consultation maintains the 'right to manage'. 'Genuine consultation' can be assessed by various benchmarks. Examples of these can be seen in European law on, for example, collective redundancies and transfers of undertakings. In particular, the indicators of such consultation include:

- the extent to which appropriate information for discussion is disclosed by management;
- the extent to which management representatives listen actively to the views of the workforce and its representatives;
- the depth to which managers genuinely engage in discussion;
- the extent to which managers respond to the comments, views and ideas of the workforce; and
- the willingness of management to amend a policy proposal or change a decision.

It is possible for this form of consultation to develop into what is sometimes characterised as 'integrative consultation'. This can focus on problem-solving or the implementation of substantial changes to the organisation of work and the deployment of staff. Necessarily, it involves detailed discussions about interrelated issues.

❯ Consent

Following from the principle of 'consultation', 'consent' or agreement is an important element in employment procedures. It is central to the law on contract formulation, contract variation and to terms and conditions negotiated with trade unions or other worker representatives (see Chapter 2). It is also important to note that 'managing by consent' is good employment practice because of its contribution to minimising workplace conflict.

❯ Freedom

Traditionally, within employment relations, employers have asserted their commitment to managerial freedom. This has often been encapsulated in the term 'the right to manage'. As such, this 'right' has no legal standing. It is, arguably, a moral right deriving from economic ownership. It is an assertion that management should have unfettered freedom and discretion to take whatever decisions are appropriate for the prosperity of the business. Frequently, it is strongly associated with operational issues – particularly the deployment and organisation of resources (including employees). It embraces, for example, a 'right to hire and fire', rights to determine promotion, staffing levels, disciplinary matters, production control, technological change and quality issues.

There are, however, circumstances in which managements have been, and continue to be, willing to limit their freedom to act. In determining pay and conditions, some employers have felt that their interests could be met by agreeing to negotiate with unions. Although such a concession would reduce management's freedom of action, it would be compensated for by the creation of a more orderly system of employment relations based on workforce consent.

The traditional management 'ideology' described here has been substantially challenged and changed in the past 50 years or more. The right to manage has been constrained by various frameworks of legal regulations (particularly those on discrimination and dismissal). Where **collective bargaining** continues to exist, its complete 'freedom' is open to question. Provisions of collective agreements are not isolated from the specifications of employment law. So, no collective agreement can infringe discrimination law. The terms of collective agreements (as well as the terms of contracts of employment) must not provide for terms that are inferior to those prescribed in law.

The extent to which employers have freedom and discretion is variable. It is dependent upon the combined extent to which employment law intervenes and the employer has conceded collective bargaining rights to unions. Storey (1980: 45) describes the right to manage as 'the residue of discretionary powers of decision left to management when the regulative impacts of law and collective agreements have been subtracted'.

Conclusion

The interlocking of legal and voluntary measures remains an important feature of employment regulation. The balance has decisively swung towards significant juridification over the past 30 years or more. Managers are much less likely to determine policies, employment practices and terms and conditions of employment without reference to legal standards. Nevertheless, there are still areas for management to exercise discretion and to determine some of their own standards above the statutory minima. It is unlikely that there will be a return to the high level of 'voluntarism' that existed in Britain until the 1960s. Indeed, evidence of future legislative developments suggests that voluntarism within a legal framework will continue to be the norm.

Further reading

Access relevant websites for recent annual reports of:

- Advisory Conciliation and Arbitration Service
- Equality and Human Rights Commission
- Health and Safety Executive
- Employment Tribunals and Employment Appeal Tribunal
- Low Pay Commission.

Key websites for developments in employment and discrimination law:

- Department for Business, Innovation and Skills: **www.bis.gov.uk**
- Department for Work and Pensions: **www.dwp.gov.uk**
- Employment Tribunals and Employment Appeal Tribunal: **www.justice.gov.uk**
- Equality and Human Rights Commission: **www.equalityhumanrights.com**
- European Union: **www.europa.eu**
- Advisory Conciliation and Arbitration Service: **www.acas.org.uk**
- Chartered Institute of Personnel and Development: **www.cipd.co.uk**
- Confederation of British Industry: **www.cbi.org.uk**
- Trades Union Congress: **www.tuc.org.uk**

References

ACAS (2009) *Code of Practice on Disciplinary and Grievance Procedures.*

Better Regulation Executive (2010) *Lightening the Load: the Regulatory Impact on UK's Smallest Businesses* (www.bis.gov.uk).

Carley, M. (2010) *International: PPR Signs Charter on Stress Prevention with EWC*, European Employment Review, IRS.

Davies, P. and Freedland, M. (1983) *Labour and the Law.* London: Stevens.

Deakin, S. and Morris, G. (2005) *Labour Law.* Oxford: Hart.

Department for Business, Innovation and Skills (2011) *Resolving Workplace Disputes: a Consultation* (see www.bis.gov.uk/publications).

Department of Trade and Industry (2002) *Findings from the Survey of Employment Tribunal Applications 1998*, Employment Relations Research Series, No. 13. London: Department of Trade and Industry (see www.bis.gov.uk/publications).

Dickens, L. *et al.* (1985) *Dismissed.* Oxford: Blackwell.

Franks, Lord (1957) *Committee on Administrative Tribunals and Enquiries: Report*, Cmnd 218. London: HMSO.

Hayward, B. *et al.* (2004) *Findings from the Survey of Employment Tribunal Applications 2003*, Employment Relations Research Series, No. 33. London: Department of Trade and Industry (see www.bis.gov.uk/publications).

Hepple, B. (2005) *Labour Laws and Global Trade.* Oxford: Hart.

Hepple, B. *et al.* (2000) *Equality: a New Framework: Report of the Independent Review of the Enforcement of UK Anti-discrimination Legislation.* Oxford: Hart.

Kahn-Freund, O. (1954) 'Legal Framework', in Flanders, A. and Clegg, H. (eds) *The System of Industrial Relations in Great Britain.* Oxford: Blackwell.

Lambourne, E. *et al.* (2008) *Employment Law Admin Burdens Survey 2008* (for the Department for Business, Innovation and Skills) ORC International (www.orc.co.uk).

Leonard, A. (1987) *Judging Equality.* London: The Cobden Trust.

Lewis, R. and Clark, J. (1993) *Employment Rights, Industrial Tribunals and Arbitration: the Case for Alternative Dispute Resolution.* London: Institute of Employment Rights.

Ministry of Justice (2010) *Employment Tribunal and EAT Statistics 2009–2010*, www.justice.gov.uk.

Morris, H., Willey, B. and Sachdev, S. (2002) *Managing in a Business Context: an HR Approach*. London: Prentice Hall.

Pateman, C. (1970) *Participation and Democratic Theory*. Cambridge: Cambridge University Press.

Peters, M. *et al.* (2010) *Findings from the Survey of Employment Tribunal Applications 2008*, Employment Relations Research Series, No. 107. London: Department of Business, Innovation and Skills (www.bis.gov.uk).

Storey, J. (1980) *The Challenge to Management Control*. London: Business Books.

Visit **www.mylawchamber.co.uk/willey** to access study support resources including realistic HR documentation to accompany the case studies in the book, an online chapter on collective labour law, interactive multiple choice questions, annotated weblinks, a glossary, glossary flashcards, key case flashcards, a legal newsfeed and legal updates.

Chapter 2

Regulating the employment relationship

Introduction

▶ The employment relationship

This is an exchange relationship: the exchange of work for payment. It is often known as the 'work–wage' bargain. The parties are an individual worker and an employing organisation. Because it is voluntarily entered into, it is different from other relationships under which work is performed – e.g. slavery, serfdom, conscription.

It is also characterised as a power relationship. The two parties – the employer and the employee – are often spoken of as if they are of equal status. However, the economic reality of employment shows that, in practice, there is, usually, no equality. In discussing the employment contract, Wedderburn (1986) described the situation this way: 'The individual employer is from the outset an aggregate of resources, already a collective power in social terms . . . In reality, save in exceptional circumstances, the individual worker brings no equality of bargaining power to the labour market and to this transaction central to his life whereby the employer buys his labour.'

▶ Means of regulating the employment relationship

The employment relationship is not a 'free for all'. It is regulated. Four formal instruments may be used:

- the **contract** of employment between an employer and an employee;
- other contracts under which work is undertaken personally;
- **statute law** and **statutory instruments** together with **case law**;
- collective agreements with trade unions (or other workforce representatives).

All these 'instruments' produce sets of 'rules' which govern the employment relationship. The first three clearly have force of law and breaches can, as appropriate, be taken to employment tribunals and courts. The fourth set, in origin, is the result of a voluntary decision by an employer to negotiate directly with a trade union or, alternatively, to accept the provisions of a collective agreement negotiated elsewhere. Whilst collective agreements are, invariably, voluntary agreements and are presumed to be so (Trade Union and Labour Relations Consolidation Act 1992, s 179), they can and do have legal force in respect of terms and conditions of employment. The provisions of collective agreements, relating to pay, hours, holidays, etc. are, as appropriate, '**incorporated**' in law into an individual's contract of employment. So, in practice, all four formal instruments have legal force. (See also website chapter.)

In this chapter we will examine, in particular, the contract of employment with an individual; and other contracts under which work is undertaken personally. Throughout the textbook the various pieces of legislation will be considered; and, as appropriate, reference will be made to the ways in which collective agreements assist in the regulation of the employment relationship.

Context

In recent years, several developments have had an impact on the employment relationship and consequently on contractual issues. These are of fundamental significance because they force a reappraisal of various traditional models and practices. We will consider:

- concepts of work and employment;
- the psychological contract;
- the growing diversity of employment status.

▶ Concepts of work and employment

In the period since 1945, 'employment' has been the predominant model through which work has been carried out. Essentially, it involves a long-term arrangement between an individual and an organisation with work provided on a continuing basis – day in day out, week in week out, even year in and year out. Traditionally, in employment, a 'job for life' was presumed. Contractual benefits and entitlements were often service-related – based on seniority and continuous service. For individuals, a job, in these terms, was and remains a very valuable asset.

This model is essentially based on male employment patterns. This gender-based perspective is important in considering the issues raised in this chapter and elsewhere in the textbook. Linda Dickens (1992: 5) has commented:

> A key to women's disadvantage in the labour market . . . is that structures of employ-ment, although apparently neutral, are in fact moulded around the life patterns and domestic obligations of men. Our systems of labour law and social security have similarly taken the male as the neutral standard of the worker to the disadvantage of women who, in not conforming to the male life and work pattern, fall outside various protections. The adoption of the male as the normal standard is revealed immediately we consider the label 'atypical' employee . . . the 'typical' employee is the male; the 'atypical' employee female.

This traditional model has been subject to considerable buffeting in the past 40 years as a result, principally, of three related factors: employers' need for both greater flexibility in resource utilisation; their drive for greater efficiency and cost-effectiveness; and the challenges, in particular, of the law on sex discrimination. The changes initiated by employers from the early 1980s have been explored by academic writers in such theoretical models as 'the flexible firm' (Atkinson 1984), and the 'shamrock organisation' (Handy 1991).

Handy argues that we should reconsider our attitude to work as a wider activity and 'stop talking and thinking about employees and employment'. His reason is that 'if work were defined as activity, some of which is paid for, then everyone is a worker, for nearly all their natural life'. He proposes a portfolio of five categories of work – the balance of which will constantly alter as people grow older:

1 *Wage or salaried work*: Individuals are paid for the time given. This is the traditional employment model – whether a person's contract is full time, part time or temporary.

2 *Fee work*: Money is paid for results delivered. Its incidence increases as jobs move outside organisations.

3 *Home-work* (or '*domestic work*' to prevent confusion with the concept of 'homeworking'): This includes all tasks taking place in the home – cooking, cleaning, caring for children and other relatives; and maintaining and improving the home. This area of work is particularly susceptible to the use of other providers – depending on a person's economic circumstances.

4 *Gift work*: This is done for free outside the home for relatives, friends, neighbours, charities, local groups and as a public service. This unpaid work is particularly significant for the charitable organisations providing personal services for ill or disabled people.

5 *Study work*: This is education/training designed to improve skills and increase know-ledge. In an employment culture emphasising training, development, continuous improvement and life-long learning, this work is of great value to individuals and organisations.

This 'portfolio' concept of work clearly challenges the social convention that paid employment is the only appropriate definition both of people's contribution to society and of their status. So, if we were to adopt a different perspective, the domestic work, primarily undertaken by women would be recognised. The concept of 'unemployment' would be redefined. The notion of 'retirement', traditionally seen as disengagement from paid employment, would be reappraised. Furthermore, we might also acknowledge the financial contribution to society as a whole of uncosted and unpaid 'domestic' and 'gift' work.

The psychological contract

This concept, initially outlined by Schein (1988), has since been elaborated. Essentially, it is about the expectations and assumptions that parties bring to an employment relationship. These are likely to be moulded by previous employment experiences; by the process of socialisation in the family and the education system; by a person's values; and by economic imperatives involving the need, for example, for income and an appropriate living standard.

One author (Mant 1995: 48), summarising the nature of this contract states that:

within that implicit contract are embedded three kinds of individual expectations and needs:

- The need for equity and justice – that employees will be treated fairly and honestly and that information and explanation about changes will always be provided.

- The desire for security and relative certainty – that employees can expect, in return for their loyalty, that they need not be fearful, uncertain or helpless (as they contemplate who might be the next to go).

- The need for fulfilment, satisfaction and progression – that employees can trust the value that the organisation places on their current contributions and prior successes and relationships.

The achievement of 'deals' under the psychological contract is highly problematic. For the employee, it depends on several factors. First, the extent to which the employer is serious about what is on offer; and through employment practices and the employment contract, aims to deliver on these 'offers'. Secondly, the psychological contract can shift over time – possibly rapidly. Whether or not this is so, there is the question of feasibly reconciling the expectations of employee and employer. Mismatches can be sources of conflict, demotivation and disaffection. Thirdly, in terms of successful delivery of the psychological contract, much will probably depend on organisational size and the grades of staff concerned. So, larger organisations with developed human resource management policies may be more successful.

The growing diversity of employment status

The labour market has been characterised, historically, as comprising two broad categories of working people: 'standard' and 'non-standard' (or 'atypical' or 'marginal') workers. The first category comprises those who are, usually, employed on full-time, open-ended contracts and who may expect long, continuous service. This remains the largest group in the labour market (see Table 2.1). The second group consists of a wide diversity of employment status. As a group it has been growing in the past 20 years or so. These working people can be characterised as, for example, part-time, temporary,

Table 2.1 **Labour market structure**

Total in employment		Number of employees		Number of self-employed		Other groups (unpaid family work and training programmes)	
29.1 million		24.9 million		3.9 million		227,000	
Full time	Part time	FT	PT	FT	PT	n/a	n/a
21.2 m	7.9 m	18.2 m	6.7 m	2.9 m	1.1 m	–	–
Male	Female	M	F	M	F	M	F
15.6 m	13.5 m	12.7 m	12.2 m	2.8 m	1.2 m	115,000	111,000

Source: Labour Market Statistics (November 2009–January 2011) (**www.statistics.gov.uk**) © ICLR

freelance, agency, casual and zero hours workers and homeworkers (see Exhibit 2.1). The overwhelming majority of working people (nowadays estimated at around 85 per cent) are either 'employees' or 'dependent workers' and 13 per cent are clearly 'independently self-employed'. However, as we shall see in the later discussion of case law, these labels may not always be used accurately.

EXHIBIT 2.1

'Standard' and 'atypical' forms of employment

Full-time workers. This has long been regarded as the typical or 'standard' form of employment. Most work on open-ended contracts; although some may be on fixed-term contracts. This group represents around 75 per cent of the labour force (**www.statistics.gov.uk**).

Part-time workers. These are usually defined as those who work less than the scheduled full-time hours in a specific organisation: 27 per cent of those in employment work part time; 60 per cent of part-timers did *not* want full-time work (*Labour Market Statistics*, March 2011). In survey data, average working hours is 15 per week. Around 85 per cent of part-timers are female. By sector, two-thirds of part-time jobs are in 'public administration, education and health' and 'distribution, hotels and restaurants'. Some part-time employment is structured on a job-share basis. Also, the incidence of 'double jobbing' is continuing to grow with 1.1 million workers having a second job (for, on average, nine hours per week) – about 60 per cent of these are women. Traditionally, many of the terms and conditions of employment under which part-time workers have worked have been inferior in comparison with full-time workers; although, in some organisations the *pro rata* principle was established (see Part-time Workers Regulations 2000 below).

Temporary workers. Temporary jobs can take a variety of forms. They can be for a defined time period (days, weeks or years); or for the completion of a specific task. They include many other forms of 'atypical' employment: seasonal work, casual work, zero-hours contracts, non-permanent jobs through a temporary employment agency ('agency temps'). Temporary workers comprise 6 per cent of all employees. Just over half of temporary workers are female. By sector, 10 per cent of employees in the public sector are temporary (particularly in public administration, education and health care), compared with 6 per cent in the private sector. By occupation, the greatest concentrations are in professional occupations. The reasons most commonly cited by employers for recruiting temporary workers are:

providing cover for absent permanent staff (e.g. on maternity leave); to cope with seasonal workload fluctuations; to staff short-term projects; and to acquire people with specialist skills which are only needed on a short-term basis or which are only available on a non-permanent basis. Thirty-seven per cent of temporary employees could not find a permanent job (*Labour Market Statistics*, March 2011). (See the Fixed-term employees Regulations 2002 below.)

Agency workers. There are two categories of 'agencies' (Employment Agencies Act 1973):

- *employment agencies* introduce working people to be employed by or to establish a business relationship with the client themselves; and

- *employment businesses* supply their staff to a client to work on a temporary basis under the control of the hirer. They are usually paid by the agency.

Overall, the total numbers of agency workers is small. However, in certain sectors and occupations, their incidence is significant (i.e. clerical and secretarial work, personal and protective services, and plant and machine operatives). There is also a growth in 'banks' of professional agency workers (e.g. nurses, further education lecturers and supply schoolteachers). (See the Agency Workers Regulations 2010 below.)

Zero-hours contract working. This has been defined as an arrangement 'where the worker was not guaranteed any work at all but in some way was required to be available as and when the employer needed that person' (Cave 1997). The worker has the right to refuse work. This is not a new form of working. It has, however, grown in importance as a result of variable customer demand, changing technology and managerial strategies to be more cost effective. In 1998, the government reported some 200,000 such workers (DTI 1998). In Cave's study, 22 per cent of employers used zero-hours contracts. It was also reported that women are more likely to be employed on such contracts, and that in 91 per cent of organisations, zero-hours contract workers did not have the same benefits as other employees.

Self-employed workers. There are 3.9 million self-employed persons – almost three-quarters of whom are male. This category has grown fitfully since the early 1980s – depending on economic circumstances. The term encompasses people in other 'atypical working' (e.g. temporary working, homeworking/teleworking).

Homeworking. Homeworking is a long-established feature of certain parts of manufacturing industry. It involves routine tasks carried out at home, invariably for low pay. National surveys of homeworking suggest that there are around 700,000 such workers (Social Trends 31). Over 70 per cent of homeworkers are women. They are more likely to have dependent children than women in the workforce generally. Overwhelmingly, these workers undertake clerical and secretarial work; and craft and related work. Teleworking is a 'high tech' variant of this traditional model.

Teleworking. This is a growing 'high tech' variant of homeworking – accounting for 8 per cent of the workforce. In 2010, around 3.7 million people worked mainly from home using both a telephone and a computer to carry out their work. An important difference from the traditional model of homeworking is that home is a base and homeworking as such may constitute only part of their working life – the other parts being on the employer's premises or 'on the road'. The majority of such workers are male (**www.statistics.gov.uk**).

The legal issues of employment status and the employment protection conferred upon these various categories of working people are outlined later in this chapter.

Source: unless otherwise stated, data drawn from *Labour Force Surveys* (**www.statistics.gov.uk**).

Interest in these more flexible forms of employment derives from employers' need for greater operational flexibility and reducing unit labour costs (Atkinson 1984). However, their use is not new. These forms have a long history in the labour market where they have, traditionally, been regarded as marginal or 'atypical' forms of working. Despite this growth of more flexible working, it is important to note that 'the shift away from permanent and full-time jobs to temporary, short-term or part-time work is exaggerated' (Taylor 2002).

The legal framework

In this section, we will consider three broad sets of legal issues:

- employment status: 'employees', 'workers' and 'independent contractors' and the common law tests, mutuality of obligation, personal service, continuity of work;
- the characteristics of the contract of employment;
- employment protection for 'atypical' workers.

Employment status

In law, three broad terms are used to describe working people: employee, worker and independent contractor (i.e. self-employed). It has become increasingly important to appreciate the distinctions between these categories. This is because access to statutory rights and also determining the contractual arrangements under which a person works. Statute law draws a distinction but to a very limited extent. Much of the guidance is set out in case law as will be seen below. Indeed it is admitted by government that 'the definitions of "employee" and "worker" in legislation are not sufficiently clear and "user-friendly"' (DTI 2002: 7).

The starting point for considering the distinctions between these categories must be the principal employment statute, the Employment Rights Act 1996. This states:

> In this Act 'worker' (except in the phrases 'shop worker' and 'betting worker') means an individual who has entered into or works under (or, where the employment has ceased, worked under) –
>
> (a) a contract of employment, or
> (b) any other contract whether express or implied and (if it is express) whether oral or in writing, whereby the individual undertakes to do or perform personally any work or services for another party to the contract whose status is not by virtue of the contract that of a client or customer of any profession or business undertaking carried on by the individual. (ERA 1996, s 230(3))

This definition is, however, insufficient to distinguish effectively between the facts and circumstances of individual working people. Consequently, case law is necessary to determine whether a person is either an employee on a contract of employment, a worker on some other contract, or an independent contractor. In Table 2.2 an attempt is made to distinguish the different aspects of the employment status of each category. The terminology used in the table is then discussed below.

Table 2.2 **Determining employment status**

Employee (i.e. a worker with a contract of employment)	Worker (who is not an employee)	Independent contractor (genuinely self-employed)
People in this category are sometimes described as having an 'employment relationship'	People in this category are sometimes described as having an 'employment relationship'	Usually described as 'in business on their own account'
Common law tests: Multiple, control, integration, economic reality Compliance with these is necessary	**Common law tests:** The issue is likely to be: how many of these tests does the person comply with when the employment relationship is analysed?	**Common law tests:** Usually, there is little or no evidence of compliance with these tests. However, there might be an issue about control. Economic independence.
Mutuality of obligation: Extent that this exists in relation to both current and the future performance of work Must be an 'irreducible minimum' of mutuality	**Mutuality of obligation:** To what extent (if any) does this exist? If no mutuality, person cannot be an 'employee' and could be a 'worker on a contract to work personally' (ERA 1996)	**Mutuality of obligation:** There will be no evidence of mutuality of obligation in respect of a particular employer. An independent contractor may 'pick and choose' the work undertaken
Personal service: Is there evidence of this? Is 'substitution' permitted – if so, on what terms? Is substitution 'unfettered'?	**Personal service:** Is there evidence of this? Is 'substitution' permitted – if so, on what terms? Is it 'unfettered'?	**Personal service:** Personal service is not necessary and work may be subcontracted
Duration of work: Is the work continuous or intermittent? If intermittent, is there a 'global contract' covering all work engagements?	**Duration of work:** Is the work continuous or intermittent? If intermittent, is there a 'global contract' covering all work engagements?	**Duration of work:** Generally, such work is for a fixed time period or until the completion of a task
Contract: A 'contract of employment' will exist if the person satisfies the common law tests and evidence of mutuality of obligation	**Contract:** A person thought to be a 'worker' (on some 'other contract' to work personally) may be an 'employee' if the common law tests and mutuality of obligation are satisfied. However, if they are only partially satisfied, then he or she may be such a worker	**Contract:** No employment contract will exist. It will be a contract for services – a commercial contract. However, the self-employed contract may be a 'sham' and the person may, in fact, be an employee or a worker
Remuneration: An employee will receive wages (of at least the national minimum wage) and is entitled to claim for non-payment and unauthorised deductions. Likely to be deduction of tax under PAYE and national insurance	**Remuneration:** A 'worker' (who is not an employee) is likely to receive wages (of at least the national minimum wage) and is entitled to claim for non-payment and unauthorised deductions. May be deductions of tax under PAYE and national insurance	**Remuneration:** Payment is likely to be a fee. Likely to make own arrangements for tax and National Insurance

In determining a person's employment status against these tests and criteria, courts and tribunals look at the facts and circumstances of the individual case. They do not just accept the label that is given to a particular individual's employment relationship by the employer. This may be inaccurate. Determining employment status involves a mixture of law and fact.

❱ Common law tests

These tests have been developed by the judges over many decades. In particular, they help distinguish whether a person is an employee or self-employed – i.e. in business on his or her own account. They are as follows:

- *The control test.* This concerns the degree of control exercised by the employer. This long-standing test was at one time considered conclusive of 'employee' status. However, it is now regarded by the courts as one of the factors to be taken into account. The nature of control has, in practice, changed for various reasons. For example, as a result of human resource policies of 'empowerment', and the need to recruit skilled and professional staff who can exercise discretion and can work with some degree of autonomy. Courts and tribunals recognise that control may nowadays be more a question of the employer retaining 'ultimate authority' over the employee in relation to the performance of work. The Court of Appeal has indicated that the test considers 'who lays down what is to be done, the way in which it is to be done, the means by which it is to be done and the time when it is done' (*Lane v Shire Roofing Co (Oxford) Ltd* [1995] IRLR 493). In respect of the self-employed, it has been argued that, applying this test, they have greater autonomy and discretion in the way work is carried out. However, one writer suggests that 'the right of control fails to distinguish employment from self-employment because its presence is entirely consistent with either type of contract' (Brodie 1998: 140).

- *The integration test.* This involves considering the ways in which a person contributes to an organisation and is part of its structure: is the person 'integrated' into the organisation or 'accessory' to it? To what extent does the person contribute to service delivery or the production of goods? It focuses on the organisation of work and less on control or subordination. If integration is established, then a person is likely to be an 'employee'.

- *The economic reality test.* This is closely associated with the integration test and covers the issue of who bears financial risks and, as appropriate, who provides the resources for work to be done (i.e. staff, tools and equipment). It should help provide a clearer answer to the question of whether the individual is 'in business on their own account' – i.e. self-employed. Buchell *et al.* (1999: 6), quoting Lord Justice Nolan in *Hall v Lorimer* [1994] IRLR 171, say that it 'implies a test of economic dependence, in the sense that employee status is the result of "the extent to which the individual is dependent or independent of a particular paymaster for the financial exploitation of his talent"'. Genuine self-employed persons are likely to provide their own tools and be responsible for their own training and not be integrated into the structure and operation of the employer's organisation. They may hire their own staff and/or make subcontracting arrangement to carry out work. However, in practice, it may not always be possible to identify the genuine self-employed. Some self-employed may have a relationship of economic dependence on an employer. Burchell *et al.* (1999: 12) comment that this category of 'dependent self-employed', 'potentially included freelance workers, sole traders, homeworkers and casual workers of various kinds'.

- *Mutuality of obligation.* This is an essential test. Its use by the courts has grown in significance. It was initially laid down in *O'Kelly* v *Trusthouse Forte* [1983] IRLR 369, CA. In determining whether or not a person is an employee and whether or not a contract of employment exists, courts and tribunals will examine the obligations that the person who is working owes to the employer and vice versa. The essential requirement is to establish whether, in an employment relationship, an employer has an obligation to offer work to an individual and whether he or she has an obligation to undertake the work offered. Normally, in a 'standard' employment relationship, an employer expects to offer work on a regular basis. The employer, also, expects the worker to undertake the work offered. If the worker refuses without good reason, then, disciplinary action may result. However, there are circumstances where this may not arise. For example, an NHS trust may phone a nurse (who is a member of a nurse 'bank') and offer a night shift at a hospital. He or she may refuse (for any reason – however trivial), but the employer will not take any disciplinary action and work may well be offered for the following night. So there are no obligations on either side to offer or perform work. However, there would, normally, be an obligation to undertake any work that has been accepted.

It has been suggested (Deakin and Morris 1998: 164–8) that there may be a second level of mutuality – mutual promises of future performance of the employment relationship. This provides the stability and continuity which is characteristic of the employment relationship of the 'standard' worker. If this second level is missing, then, there is probably no contract of employment.

One difficulty is that the contract may be silent on the issue of mutuality of obligation. The person working may have a long-established relationship with the employer; and the person may have made assumptions that he or she is an employee because of length of service, the degree of economic dependence on the employer for pay and the extent of integration into the organisation – albeit intermittently. The **landmark case**, *Carmichael and Leese* v *National Power plc* [2000] IRLR 43, HL, illustrates this (see Exhibit 2.2).

Genuine self-employed people are, in respect of mutuality of obligation, free to 'pick and choose' the work they do. Where they agree to do work, they need not provide it personally. They may delegate it to another person to undertake it. So, no mutuality exists which points to an employment contract.

- *The multiple test.* The Court of Appeal has stated that any decision on 'employee' status does not involve a mechanical checking off of factors. An overall view must be taken of the facts and circumstances (including whether or not the individual makes his or her own arrangements for tax and social security contributions). This overall view would involve weighing the significance of particular factors; and considering, if appropriate, the intentions of the parties and their behaviour. No factor is seen as sufficient in itself. However, control, the payment of wages and mutuality of obligation are seen as essential (in *Hall* (*Inspector of Taxes*) v *Lorimer* [1994] IRLR 171).

▶ Personal service and substitution

Most employers expect that both 'employees' and 'workers' will personally undertake the work offered. The implication is that if there is no personal service then the person may be self-employed. However, in case law, there have been specific rulings which suggest that the issue is not clear-cut. The Court of Appeal ruled in *Express & Echo Publications* v *Tanton* [1999] ICR 693, that an 'irreducible minimum' for there being a contract of employment is personal service; and that a provision in a contract allowing

EXHIBIT 2.2

No mutuality of obligation

Carmichael and Leese v *National Power plc* [2000] **IRLR 43, HL**

Ms Leese (together with Ms Carmichael) had been employed since 1989 as a guide at a power station. She was obliged to supervise parties of visitors, explain various activities and answer questions. She also gave talks to schools. She was given training for the post. In her offer letter she was described as working on a 'casual as required' basis. The company did not have to provide work and she could refuse work. She had been unavailable for work on eight occasions.

She worked as a guide for up to 25 hours a week. She was paid, after deduction of tax and national insurance contributions at an employed person's rate. But she was only employed when she worked. There was no sick pay and no pension provision. No notice to terminate the contract was indicated. She was provided with a uniform. She was accountable to the company for the quality of her work. The grievance and disciplinary procedures for regular staff did not apply. There was no written contract of employment nor any contractual information other than that in the offer letter.

The complaint to an employment tribunal was that the company had failed to provide a written statement of initial employment particulars (under ERA 1996, s 1). The company contended that the two women were not 'employees' in law.

The case went through various appeal stages and eventually reached the House of Lords. It ruled that the objective inference from the situation as described was that when work was available the applicants were free to undertake it or not as they chose. It saw the flexibility as suiting both parties. The arrangement was based on mutual convenience and good will and had worked well in practice over the years. But it took the view that, in the circumstances of the case, there was no 'irreducible minimum of mutual obligation necessary to create' a contract of employment.

the substitution of a 'suitable person' was 'fatal' to him acquiring status as an employee. This approach was also adopted by the EAT in *Staffordshire Sentinel Newspapers Ltd* v *Potter* [2004] IRLR 752. However, in *MacFarlane* v *Glasgow City Council* [2001] IRLR 7, EAT, it was held that a gym instructor whose contract provided that he could select a substitute from a list pre-approved by the gym, did not cease to be an employee because of that provision. A similar approach was adopted in *Byrne Brothers (Formwork) Ltd* v *Baird* [2002] IRLR 96, EAT, where the ability to provide a substitute was limited and had to be approved.

Commenting on this situation, Daniel Barnett (web bulletin, 5 May 2004, **www.danielbarnett.co.uk**) stated that 'the position therefore appears to depend on the extent of the substitution clause. If the worker has an unfettered discretion to appoint a substitute, he cannot be an employee. If he has a heavily fettered discretion or requires the employer's approval, the substitution clause will not prevent him accruing employee status.'

▶ Continuity of service

This is particularly significant in three related respects:

- considering a person's status as an employee;
- access to statutory rights which may be service-related;

- qualifying for employment benefits under a contract of employment (e.g. enhanced holiday entitlements, sick pay, access to 'flexible' benefits).

General statutory provisions

The statutory provisions on continuous employment are defined in the Employment Rights Act 1996 (ss 210–19). Generally, continuity is in relation to one employer (the exceptions are considered below). Also, continuous employment can encompass a number of contracts of employment with that one employer.

To calculate continuous employment, the legal starting point is set out as follows:

> Any week during the whole or part of which an employee's relations with his employer are governed by a contract of employment counts in computing the employee's period of employment.   (ERA 1996 s 212)

The importance of establishing the existence of a contract of employment is signalled by this provision. The number of hours a person works each week is not relevant. There is a statutory presumption in favour of continuous employment, unless the contrary is shown by the employer. Certain weeks count (under particular rules): where the employee is:

- 'incapable of work in consequence of sickness or injury' (ERA 1996, s 212(3)(a)); or
- 'absent from work wholly or partly because of pregnancy or childbirth' (ERA 1996, s 212(3)(d)).

In addition and significant for certain atypical workers, are weeks which may count:

- where the employee is 'absent from work on account of a temporary cessation of work' (s 212 (3)(b)); or
- 'absent from work in circumstances such that by arrangement or custom, he is regarded as continuing in the employment of his employer from any purpose' (s 212(3)(c)).

Temporary cessation of work

It has been ruled in various cases that 'temporary cessation of work' need not break continuity of employment. No time period is prescribed for the cessation. The cessation is a question of fact: did it or did it not take place? The cessation can be for any reason. The 'work' referred to is the paid work of the individual employee – not the general work of the employer's business.

In handling cases involving the temporary cessation of work, two approaches have been used by the courts: the broad-brush approach; and the mathematical approach. Both remain available. In the former, the focus is on the whole employment history of the individual employee. This would obviously be done in retrospect and could take account of the expectations and intentions of the parties. The second approach considers the proportions of time spent at work and the times absent because of the temporary cessation (see Exhibit 2.3).

Absent by arrangement or custom

This provision can cover secondments, special leave of absence, working-time scheduling such as job-share or limited hours. This arrangement must be in place when the absence begins and should not be an afterthought.

EXHIBIT 2.3

A 'temporary cessation of work'

Ford v *Warwickshire County Council* [1983] **IRLR 126, HL**

This case involved a succession of fixed-term contracts for a further education lecturer (long before the enactment of the Fixed-term Employees Regulations 2002). Ms Ford had a series of 11-month contracts (covering September–July inclusive) over a 9-year period. She was not required to work in August. The issue came before the courts because she wished to claim unfair dismissal and there was uncertainty about whether she had the necessary qualifying length of continuous service: was it 11 months or 9 years?

Using the mathematical approach to the advantage of the complainant, Diplock LJ ruled that the interval when there was no work should be 'characterised as short relative to the combined duration of the two fixed-term contracts. Whether it can be so characterised is a question of fact and degree.' Of course, it is possible that this approach might lead to pedantic arguments about what is meant by 'short duration'. So, the broad-brush approach may have much to commend it.

Note: The approach in this case was used by the EAT in *Hussain* v *Acorn Independent College Ltd* [2011] IRLR 463, EAT in determining that a teacher had one year's continuous service (covering a temporary contract, the summer holiday and a permanent contract) in order to make an unfair dismissal complaint.

Service with more than one employer?

As mentioned earlier, continuous employment is normally with one employer. However, there are circumstances in which the acquired service might be preserved if the employee's employer changes in the following circumstances:

- A transfer of an undertaking (as specified in the Transfer of Undertakings (Protection of Employment) Regulations 2006).
- One corporate body replaced another as employer under **Act of Parliament**.
- The employer dies and the employee is then re-employed by the personal representatives or trustees of the deceased.
- A change in the partners, personal representatives or trustees who employ the individual.
- The individual is taken into the employment of an 'associated employer'.

This final circumstance can create difficulties. Control is the central issue. For the purposes of the Employment Rights Act 1996,

> any two employers shall be treated as associated if – (a) one is a company of which the other (directly or indirectly) has control, or (b) both are companies of which a third person (directly or indirectly) has control. (s 213)

Finding 'control' can be difficult. There are technical ways of establishing it through majority shareholding. Some cases have explored the channels of influence exerted on corporate policy. The presence of these can be particularly important for employment relations issues. Although there is no authoritative guidance on this issue, there is statutory authority for courts and tribunals to inquire into organisational decision-making structures.

▶ Contracts

As indicated above, there are three broad types of contract that might exist to regulate a working relationship:

- a contract of employment (sometimes referred to as a contract *of* service);
- some other contract under which an individual agrees to work personally; and
- a contract *for* services with an independent contractor (i.e. a self-employed person).

An issue that has been considered by the courts is whether the contract that is in force accurately reflects the true position of the employment relationship and in particular the correct employment status of the person undertaking work. Complaints have been made to employment tribunals and courts about whether a contract is a 'sham' (see Exhibit 2.4).

Volunteers

The employment status of volunteers is an issue that has come before the courts more frequently. The key issues are the nature of the agreement under which a volunteer works, whether there are any mutual obligations and the issue of payments. The following cases outline some of these issues.

South East Sheffield Citizens Advice Bureau v *Grayson* [2004] IRLR 353, EAT: The EAT held that for a volunteer to be an 'employee' it was necessary to identify an arrangement under which, in exchange for 'valuable consideration' (this generally, means payment),

---

EXHIBIT 2.4

'Sham' contracts

Protectacoat Firthglow Ltd v *Szilagyi* [2009] IRLR 365: A firm of builders argued that a written 'partnership agreement' showed that Mr Szilagyi was a partner and not an employee so he could not claim unfair dismissal. The Court of Appeal said that rather than consider whether a written agreement was a sham, tribunals should simply look at what the true legal relationship was between the parties. A court or tribunal has to consider whether or not the words of the written contract represent the true intentions or expectations of the parties, not only at the start of the contract but, if appropriate, as time goes by.

Autoclenz v *Belcher and others* [2009] EWCA Civ 1046: The employer claimed that the car valets were self-employed sub-contractors and that this was stated in their contracts. The Court of Appeal ruled that the clauses in the contracts which expressly provided for 'substitution' and the ability to refuse work were a 'sham'. There was, in practice, an obligation to work. Furthermore, it found that the control test and the requirement for personal performance were satisfied. It ruled that the car valets were 'employees' and they were able to claim in relation to paid annual leave and the national minimum wage. (The Employment Appeal Tribunal had found them to be 'workers on some other contract to work personally'.) In July 2011, the Supreme Court upheld the Court of Appeal decision on the issue of 'sham' contracts, it stated that where a party asserts that a written term of contract does not reflect the reality of the agreement, then tribunals/courts may look beyond the contractual terms to find the true nature of the agreement. A court or tribunal may disregard contractual provisions that do not reflect the reality of the contracts. Autoclenz v Belcher and others [2009] UKSC 41 the volunteer was contractually obliged to provide services or work personally for the employer. In this case, the 'volunteer agreement' aimed to 'clarify the reasonable expectations of both the volunteer and the Bureau'. The implication was that there was no intention for the agreement to be legally binding. There was no obligation for the CAB to provide work, nor for the volunteer to undertake it. The only obligations on the CAB were to reimburse expenses and to indemnify the volunteer against negligence claims if the volunteer worked for the CAB.

X v Mid Sussex Citizens Advice Bureau [2011] EWCA Civ 28: This involved a claim under the former Disability Discrimination Act 1995. X argued that the CAB's decision asking her to stop attending as a volunteer was connected with her disability. The court ruled that she was a volunteer and did not have a paid 'occupation'. The volunteer agreement was 'binding in honour only' and was not a contract of employment. She was not under a legal obligation to attend work.

Breakell v *Shropshire Army Cadet Force* UKEAT/0372/10: This also concerned a claim for disability discrimination by a paid volunteer adult instructor with Shropshire Army Cadet Force. The EAT ruled that there was no obligation for the ACF to provide work, nor any for him to accept the work offered, and he was only paid for the work he undertook. There was no mutuality of obligation in this arrangement. It found that he was a volunteer, not an employee or a worker under the former Disability Discrimination Act 1995 (s 68(1)).

FRISHCO SUPERMARKET CASE STUDY

Scenario 2.1

What is Jason's employment status?

In January 2010 Frishco's Head Office introduced a casual work scheme for additional store staff. They recruited a 'bank' of general assistants who would be available to meet emergencies in stores and, in particular, help out during peak times of customer demand (e.g. prior to Christmas and Easter; and on Friday, Saturday and Sunday). 'Bank staff' would also be available to cover in holiday periods. **Jason**, who has been in the 'bank' since it started, has only been an average performer and, in fact, he has not been called into work very often. In April 2012, after he was found by his team leader not to be stacking shelves quickly enough or putting goods in the correct places, he was told by **Winona**, an assistant manager, that he was being removed from the 'bank' and that he need not expect any more work. He says that he will 'see them at the tribunal'. The 'terms of engagement' for 'bank staff' state: 'Frishco will offer you work from time to time depending on the company's operational requirements. Staff are expected to undertake the work offered unless they have a good reason not to. They will be paid at the National Minimum Wage.'

Question

Does Jason have grounds, in law, for claiming unfair dismissal at an employment tribunal? Give reasons for your view.

Visit www.mylawchamber.co.uk/willey *to access sample HR documents to support this case study.*

The characteristics of the contract of employment

▶ A flawed instrument

Our focus in this section is on the predominant form of contract – the contract of employment. It is the starting point for so many issues: workplace grievances; disciplinary action and dismissal; and complaints to employment tribunals. However, although it is so fundamentally important, it is still a flawed instrument.

First, as mentioned above, it regulates an asymmetrical employment relationship which is characterised by a power imbalance under which an employee can be vulnerable to employer action. Secondly, many aspects of the contract can reinforce employer power. It provides a means of direction and control of the employee and, consequently, has been described as 'a command under the guise of an agreement' (Kahn-Freund 1983: 18). Thirdly, when it is formulated and agreed, a legal fiction is adopted that the contract is 'freely arrived at'. Technically, this is so. No employee is forced to enter a contract of employment. However, in reality, few job applicants or employees have influence over the terms of their contract. Force of economic circumstances means that most people 'take it or leave it'.

Fourthly, there are still echoes of the old 'master and servant' relationship in the way that the contract of employment is perceived. This submissive relationship which governed employment law during the nineteenth century has gradually been replaced by the, theoretically, more egalitarian contractual relationship. However, occasionally, judges in their rulings reflect this old-fashioned perspective based on status. Finally, the contract of employment has limitations as far as the adoption of universal minimum standards is concerned. Statute law is often seen as necessary to ensure universal fair treatment. For example, the former Equal Pay Act 1970 (s 1) (now the Equality Act 2010, s 66) deemed that 'an equality clause' be included in contracts of employment if one is not provided for 'directly or by reference to a collective agreement or otherwise'. This means that no term of a contract of employment can be discriminatory on grounds of sex. It will be void if it is. The need for anti-discrimination law has been commented on by academic lawyers. 'The common law with its emphasis on freedom of contract, sees nothing inherently wrong with discrimination . . . as long as no pre-existing contract or property right is infringed' (Deakin and Morris 1998: 543). So, through statute law, Parliament is eroding 'contractual autonomy'.

▶ Defining the contract of employment

It is a promise or an agreement made by an employer and an individual employee following an employer's offer of work. It is freely arrived at by the parties that make it. No one compels them to agree. It is legally enforceable in the courts and is intended to be so. It is usually of indefinite duration. It involves 'consideration' – i.e. something of value – usually pay, with which the employer obtains the promise of the employee to be ready, willing and able to undertake the agreed work. It may be in writing, verbally agreed or part verbal and part in writing. It need not be signed.

Key elements in this definition are examined in more detail below:

- *Offer.* This is an offer to the individual employee of work to be provided by the employer. It may be conditional on, for example, the receipt of acceptable references; medical and/or Criminal Records Bureau checks; and work permits being provided. (See also the guidance from the Information Commissioner: Employment Practices Data Protection Code (2005) Part 1.) An employer can withdraw an offer before the prospective employee has accepted it. There can, however, be difficulties of timing. When does the job applicant know of the withdrawal? Has he or she given notice to terminate existing employment?

- *Agreement.* It is an agreement between an employer and an employee that the employee will be ready, willing and able to undertake work offered. If this offer was conditional, then the contract is binding once the conditions have been fulfilled. If the offer has been accepted (but the prospective employee has not yet started work) and the employer withdraws the offer, then there can be a breach of contract. Usually, this can be dealt with by a payment in lieu of notice. If the prospective employee changes his or her mind about the job, it is unlikely that an employer would sue for breach of contract because it would be difficult for the employer to quantify the loss (see 'Express terms' below).

- *'Consideration'.* This legal term describes something of value with which the contract is 'sealed'. Usually, it is the pay given by the employer for the employee to be 'ready, willing and able' to undertake the work required.

- *Parties to the contract.* The term *employer* is, generally, fairly clear – although there can be occasional difficulties defining who the employer is in large conglomerate organisations where there may be associated companies. Also, as far as certain agency workers are concerned, defining their employer can pose some problems. The term *employee* is even more problematic as we have discussed above.

- *Legally enforceable.* The agreement is legally enforceable in the courts and at tribunals and is intended by the parties to be so. As a consequence, claims in the tribunals and courts can be made concerning allegations of breach of contract.

- *Freely arrived at.* Importantly, the agreement is freely arrived at – i.e. no one compels an employee to agree to enter a contract of employment on particular terms. Only exceptionally is an employee able to influence the terms.

- *Verbal and/or in writing.* Such contracts may be verbal or in writing or part verbal or part in writing. The reality, for most employees, is that they will not receive a legally drafted contractual document. They are more likely to receive a statement of initial employment particulars (as required under s 1, Employment Rights Act 1996) (see Exhibit 2.5). This outlines the employer's statement of the essential terms and conditions of employment. In addition to this, there will be other terms of the contract (see 'Sources of contractual terms' below) – some of which may be in writing. This statement of employment particulars is important to employees in respect of the balance of information in the employment relationship. However, *Which?* Legal Service (2010), in a survey of 4,075 people, found that 26 per cent only skim-read their contracts; and 6 per cent did not read them at all. The survey also recorded that 12 per cent (2 million people) had no contractual information at all (**www.whichlegalservice.co.uk**).

- *Duration.* A contract of employment can be for any period of time. So, it may be for a fixed term; or may be open-ended (sometimes said to be 'permanent'). The latter is the most common. Effectively, the contract exists until such time as one of the parties brings it to an end – either by the employee's resignation or dismissal by the employer.

Contractual information (required under Employment Rights Act 1996, s 1)

Information to be given to an employee within eight weeks of starting employment. If there is no information under any headings this should be stated. Even if the person leaves before the eight weeks, they are entitled to receive the information.

- Names of the employer and the employee.*
- Date employment began.*
- Date when continuous employment began (may include previous employment with that employer, or the consequences of a business transfer, or of transfers between companies within a group).*
- Scale or rate of remuneration; or method of calculating remuneration.*
- Intervals at which remuneration is paid (weekly, monthly or some other interval).*
- Hours of work and normal working hours.*
- Holiday entitlement, public holidays and holiday pay. (The particulars given being sufficient to enable the employee's entitlement including any entitlement to accrued holiday pay on the termination of employment to be precisely calculated.)*
- Job title or brief job description.*
- Place or places of work where the employee is required or permitted to work.*
- Terms relating to sickness, injury and sick pay.†
- Pensions and pension schemes.†
- Notice periods to terminate the contract – by both the employer and the employee.
- If employment is temporary, how long it is to last; or termination date of the fixed-term contract.
- Any collective agreement affecting terms and conditions of employment (including, where the employer is not a party to the agreement, the names of the employers and the unions by whom they were made).
- Where the employee is required to work outside the United Kingdom for more than a month:
  - the period for which he or she is to work outside the UK;
  - the currency in which he or she will be paid;
  - any additional remuneration payable; and any benefits to be provided whilst outside the UK;
  - any terms and conditions relating to return to the UK.
- A note (which can refer to a reasonably accessible document) specifying:
  - any disciplinary rules applicable to the employee;
  - disciplinary procedure relating to the employee;
  - an indication of a person 'to whom the employee can apply if dissatisfied with any disciplinary decision relating to him' (s 3(1)(b)(i)) including dismissal;
  - an indication of a person 'to whom the employee can apply for the purpose of seeking redress for any grievance relating to his employment and the manner in which any such application should be made' (s 3(1)(b)(ii));
  - appeal steps should also be indicated.

* This information shall be 'included in a single document' (s 2(4)).
† For these particulars, the employee may be referred to some other reasonably accessible document (s 2(3)).

Contractual terms: express and implied

▶ Express terms

These usually originate from management decisions and collective agreements. They set out explicitly certain terms under which an employee is to work. For example, in addition to pay and working time arrangements, an employer may want an employee to accept a mobility clause; or a restrictive covenant; or some commitment to confidentiality. Other examples, concerned with the specific circumstances of the employer's business, can include the circumstances in which an employer can physically search an employee and his or her property; dress codes; and testing for substance abuse.

Garden leave in the absence of an express term was considered by the High Court (*SG&R Valuation Service Co LLC* v *Boudrais and Others* [2008] IRLR 770). In the circumstances of the case, it was ruled that the employer was entitled to place the complainants on garden leave because of their misconduct. The EAT (in *Christie* v *Johnson Carmichael* EAT/0064/09) ruled that the employer had the right to put a chartered accountant on garden leave in the absence of an express contractual term. In this case, he had resigned as a result of a dispute about his contract of employment. These cases demonstrate the clear advantage of having an appropriate express term in contracts.

A slightly unusual example of where an express term can be valuable to an employer is a 'no show' clause. Normally, if a job applicant changes his or her mind, having accepted an offer of employment, it is unusual for an employer to take any action. However, the High Court ruled in a case involving a City of London investment firm where there was a 'no show' clause in the contract. It found that the employer was entitled to recover £293,000 from the employee (*Tullett Prebon Group Ltd* v *El-Hajjali* [2008] EWHC 1924).

▶ Implied terms

These, generally, derive from common law (the historic decisions of judges) or from specific statute law. Terms might be implied by judges for one of several reasons:

- for 'business efficacy' (i.e. where a term is necessary to make a contract work);
- where, on the facts, such a term is so obvious (even though it is not provided as an express term);
- on the basis of custom and practice (see below);
- to give effect to a statutory requirement;
- to meet changing circumstances.

Both express and implied terms will be explored in more detail in the discussion below.

Activity 2.1

Your contract of employment

Find out all the detailed terms of your own contract of employment. What are the sources? Which terms are in writing and which are verbal? Answer these questions as you read the following section.

Sources of contractual terms

There are several sources of a contract of employment:

- management decisions on terms and conditions of employment;
- collective agreements between an employer and recognised trade unions;
- workplace rules;
- custom and practice;
- statute law;
- implied terms under common law.

▶ Management decisions on terms and conditions of employment

An employer's ability to determine the terms and conditions under which a person works has, traditionally, been quite wide. However, two constraints affect these decisions:

- the requirements of employment and discrimination law;
- any collective agreements with recognised trade unions.

So, for example, an employer may determine the pay to be offered to an individual. However, it is necessary to ensure that such a pay is compliant with law on equal pay and, also, set at or above the rates of the national minimum wage. Furthermore, if there is a collective agreement in place, then the pay should be appropriate in relation to an agreed grading structure. However, it is important to remember that the constraints on employers are, in some respects, not always as strict as they appear at first sight. Even under law, they have areas of discretion. So, for example, employers can ask staff to agree to opt-out from the 48-hour maximum working week; certain terms, which may be regarded as indirectly discriminatory under discrimination law, can be 'objectively justified'; and requests by parents and carers to work flexibly can be refused for specified 'business reasons'.

▶ Collective agreements between an employer and recognised trade unions

Collective agreements can be important in determining and influencing an individual employee's terms and conditions of employment. An employer who, for example, has agreed to negotiate the terms and conditions of employment for particular grades of staff will apply the relevant provisions of the collective agreement to staff in that grade – irrespective of whether they are union members or not.

In law, the terms of the collective agreement relevant to an individual employee will then be 'incorporated' into that person's contract of employment. So, their pay, working time, holidays, shift pay, overtime rates, sick pay, etc. will derive from the collective agreement.

There are four important aspects that need to be borne in mind in relation to collective agreements and contracts of employment:

- Which contractual terms are appropriate for 'incorporation'? Those that have been tested in the courts are not the essential issues relating to pay, but those that are procedural or 'aspirational' in terms of good employment practice. For example, the Court of Appeal ruled on the status of a 'no compulsory redundancy' agreement (*Kaur* v *MG Rover Group Ltd* [2005] IRLR 40). It stated that the job security provision of the agreement which included the words, 'There will be no compulsory redundancy', when construed in the context of the agreement as a whole was no more than 'a statement of collective aspiration' and was not appropriate for incorporation into individual contracts. The Court has also ruled on a collective agreement between British Airways plc and the trade union (*Malone and others* v *British Airways plc* [2011] IRLR 32, CA). BA had unilaterally reduced crew complements on its aircraft below the agreed levels. The Court stated that the provision in the agreement was 'apt for incorporation' in that it related to working conditions (i.e. cabin crew complements). However, it stated that there would be 'disastrous consequences' for the business if this provision was individually enforceable. It ruled that the provision was intended by the employer as an undertaking towards its cabin crew employees collectively and not to be incorporated into individual contracts of employment. It was 'binding in honour' only.

- The role of the union when contractual changes are made. (This is considered in Chapter 3 under the issue of contract variation.)

- What happens when a collective agreement is rescinded by the employer? In brief, the relevant terms of a collective agreement can 'live on' in the individual employee's contract of employment. In the 1980s, British Gas unilaterally terminated an incentive bonus scheme which had been voluntarily agreed with a union. The company was entitled to give notice to terminate this collective agreement – which it did. However, the terms of the agreement had been incorporated into individual contracts. Lord Justice Kerr, in the Court of Appeal, said: 'the terms (of a collective agreement) are in this case incorporated into the individual contracts of employment and it is only if and when those terms are varied collectively by agreement that the individual contract of employment will also be varied. If the collective agreement is not varied by agreement but by some unilateral abrogation or withdrawal or **unilateral variation** to which the other side does not agree, then, it seems to me that the individual contract of employment remains unaffected' (*Robertson and Jackson* v *British Gas Corporation* [1983] IRLR 202).

- The effect on a collective agreement of a business transfer. (This is considered in Chapter 3 in the discussion on the Transfer of Undertakings (Protection of Employment) Regulations 2006).

❱ Workplace rules

The law on these is so varied that it is impossible to provide anything but broad guidelines. The rules are likely to be in an employee's contract if the employee signs them or if they are posted on notices in the workplace. But, even if they are signed, the rules may not become contractual but merely be lawful and reasonable instructions on how a job is to be carried out. The differences between a contractual rule and a lawful instruction can be described as follows:

- *Rules* can only be changed with the employee's consent. By 'working to rule' an employee is merely carrying out the contract.

- *Instructions* can be changed by the employer without consultation or agreement. By disobeying instructions which are lawful and reasonable an employee is breaking the contract.

▶ Custom and practice

In any workplace there are ways of working and, in some cases, terms and conditions which are not written down and have evolved over a period of time. A critical issue can be whether or not these customary ways have become contractual. To be binding, the courts have determined that **custom and practice** must meet three conditions:

- It must be widely known and almost universally observed by the relevant employees.
- It must be reasonable.
- It must be so certain that the individual employee can know exactly the effect that the custom has on him or her.

The implication of 'customary' terms into contracts of employment can be difficult. In *Cook and Others* v *Diageo* [2005] EATS/007/04, the issue of whether an employer's policy on local holidays had achieved the status of a contractual term was considered. The EAT, drawing on the approach in previous case law (*Solectron Scotland Ltd* v *Roper* [2004] IRLR 4, EAT) ruled that a custom or established practice regularly applied may become the source of an implied contractual term only when 'the courts are able to infer . . . that the parties must be taken to have accepted that the practice has crystallised into contractual rights'.

▶ Statute law

This affects the terms of contracts of employment in a number of particular ways:

- *Statutory imposition.* The direct intervention by legislation into contracts of employment. The principal example was the former Equal Pay Act 1970 which deemed that an equality clause should exist in all such contracts. This is now in Equality Act 2010, s 66.
- *General obligations.* These are designed to influence the way employers behave in the employment relationship. They cover, for example, the provisions of equality and of health and safety legislation.
- *Minimum conditions.* These must be met by employers (e.g. in respect of notice to terminate employment; paid annual leave; and maternity and paternity leave). An employer may provide enhancements under the individual's contract – i.e. terms and conditions better than the statutory minimum.

▶ Implied terms under common law

The discussion above has focused to a large extent on terms and conditions that are either formally in writing or, if not, at least generally recognised by the parties concerned. These implied terms are one source which many employees may not fully appreciate. Yet their importance is considerable. They are drawn from case law over many decades where the courts have implied into contracts of employment terms which make them work effectively and clarify the rights and duties of the parties. In some instances, as we shall see below, these implied terms have been modified by provisions of statute law. Certain key implied terms are explored below as general duties on employers and general duties on employees.

General duties on employers

▶ To pay wages

Failure to pay wages that are agreed and due to the employee is regarded as a fundamental breach of the contract of employment. An employee may resign and claim constructive dismissal if a grievance does not resolve the issue. Also, under statute law (Employment Rights Act 1996, ss 13–27), the employee (irrespective of length of service) may complain to an employment tribunal about the non-payment.

▶ Not to make unauthorised deductions

An employer may only make deductions if there is legal authority to do so under:

- *Act of Parliament*: for example, the authorised deduction of income tax, National Insurance contributions and, as appropriate, deduction through Attachment of Earnings Orders ordered by the courts.
- *Contract of employment*: this might provide for deductions to be made in certain specific circumstances. Examples include fines for disciplinary offences; deductions for cash deficiencies and stock shortages permitted, under the Employment Rights Act 1996, in the special circumstances of retail employment (see Chapter 9).
- *Individual agreement*: an employee can give agreement for the deduction of, for example, union subscriptions; or to reimburse the employer for overpayment of wages.

▶ To take reasonable care of the employee

This wide-ranging duty encompasses not just physical care of the employee but also exposure to psychiatric harm in employment. The issues under this heading are explored in Chapter 12 on health, safety and welfare. It is also important to note that this implied duty on employers covers the provision of references for ex-employees (see Exhibit 2.6).

▶ Not to breach mutual trust and confidence

This duty concerns the co-operation between the employer and the employee. Arising, over the years, from unfair dismissal cases, it has frequently been stated that an employer should not destroy the 'mutual trust and confidence' on which co-operation is built. This duty has been stated in this way: an employer will not, without reasonable and proper cause, act in a manner calculated or likely to destroy or seriously damage the relationship of confidence and trust between employer and employee (*Courtaulds Northern Textiles Ltd* v *Andrew* [1979] IRLR 84, EAT). Examples of breaches of mutual trust and confidence include:

- where an application for transfer had not been dealt with fairly;
- where there was failure to investigate a genuine safety grievance;

EXHIBIT 2.6

References

There is no general duty on an employer to provide a reference for an employee applying for another job. However, it can be expressly stated in a person's contract that a reference will be provided. Where they are provided, they should comply with guidance under case law.

A duty of care is owed to the ex-employee to provide a reference that is true, accurate and fair (*Bartholomew v London Borough of Hackney* [1999] IRLR 246, CA). It must not give an unfair or misleading impression when considered in its totality. As a general rule, a reference does not have to provide a full and comprehensive report on all the facts relating to the person in question.

Difficulties may arise in one particular set of circumstances: when an employee resigns under threat of disciplinary action or before that action is complete. Again, case law has asserted that the principle of telling the truth is important. If the ex-employer omits any mention of the disciplinary proceedings, it could be a breach of duty owed to the recipient of the reference. It could make the referee liable for negligent mis-statement. On the other hand, a referee should not make comments about an employee on matters which have not been properly investigated. In terms of natural justice, a proper investigation involves giving the employee a chance to state his or her case. In *Cox v Sun Alliance* [2001] IRLR 448, the Court of Appeal found that the referee was negligent in relying on unexplored allegations of dishonest conduct attributed to the ex-employee and the communication of these views to Mr Cox's new employer. (However, see *Jackson v Liverpool City Council* [2011] EWCA Gvi 068)

The burden of proof is on the referee to show that the contents were true. The referee's defence might be that he or she 'honestly believed that the contents were true'.

It is also important to note that all strands of equality law extend to the 'post employment' situation (see Chapters 5 and 6). The Equality Act 2010 (s 108) covers 'relationships that have ended'. It prohibits as unlawful any discrimination or harassment which 'arises out of and is closely connected to a relationship which used to exist between them' (i.e. between an employer and an employee). Clearly, the provision of references is one of the possible issues which could be discriminatory.

Because references inevitably involve the disclosure of personal data, the Information Commissioner provides relevant guidance on the drafting of references. This covers not just requests by ex-employees but also references given in relation to legal proceedings and financial references. Furthermore, there is guidance on the detail which can be disclosed to the ex-employee requesting the reference (see Employment Practices Data Protection Code 2005, section 2.9) **www.ico.gov.uk**.

- where there was a false accusation of theft on the basis of flimsy evidence;
- where the right to suspend an employee was exercised unreasonably;
- where a mobility clause was not operated reasonably (see Exhibit 2.7).

The EAT has held (*Morrow v Safeway Stores plc* [2002] IRLR 9 EAT) that breach of mutual trust and confidence will 'inevitably' be a repudiatory breach of the contract of employment and can result in the employee's resignation and a claim for constructive dismissal (subject to the qualifying length of service). The Court of Appeal (in *Buckland v Bournemouth University* [2010] Higher Education Corp EWCA Civ 121) ruled that the test for a constructive dismissal claim in such circumstances is whether there has been a fundamental breach of contract and not whether the employer behaved 'unreasonably'. Furthermore, the employer cannot 'cure' or remedy the breach by attempting to correct its own wrongdoing.

EXHIBIT 2.7

Implementing a mobility clause

United Bank v *Akhtar* [1989] **IRLR 507, EAT**

Mr Akhtar worked at the Leeds branch of the bank as a junior clerk. In his contract of employment he had a mobility clause which stated: '*The bank may from time to time require an employee to be transferred temporarily or permanently to any place of business which the bank may have in the UK for which a relocation allowance or other allowance may be payable at the discretion of the bank.*'

On 5 June he was informed that as from 8 June he would be required to transfer to the Birmingham branch. He requested that the transfer be delayed for three months because of his wife's illness and the impending sale of his house. This request was refused. He then asked if he could take 24 days' leave which was due to him, to sort out his affairs. He offered to start work in Birmingham on 10 July. He received no reply to this request. His pay was stopped from 5 June. So he resigned and claimed that he had been constructively dismissed because the employer had fundamentally breached his contract of employment. His claim succeeded.

In the EAT's view, the employer, even if there is an express term in the contract, must behave reasonably in implementing it. Otherwise, the employer's behaviour may be such as to destroy or seriously damage the relationship of 'trust and confidence' between the employer and the employee.

General duties on employees

▶ To co-operate with their employer

Under case law, this has been construed to mean helping to promote the employer's business interests by working according to the terms of the contract. However, in working to contract, employees must not wilfully disrupt the employer's business.

▶ To obey lawful and reasonable instructions

Any instruction to an employee must be both lawful and reasonable. Lawfulness means that an instruction must not, for example, breach equality law; or require an employee to exceed working time restrictions which are applicable to that individual. Reasonableness will be judged in the circumstances. However, factors which might be taken into account would be whether the particular employer is able (in terms of knowledge and skill) to obey the instruction and whether the instruction is consistent with the 'status' of the work he or she is employed to do. (See the discussion on contract variation in Chapter 3 and in particular the case of *Cresswell and Others* v *Board of Inland Revenue* [1984] IRLR 190, HC.)

▶ To be trustworthy

This duty is complementary to the employer's duty of mutual trust and confidence. The implied duty of fidelity generally ends when the contract ends. Breaches of trust by an employee are invariably regarded as serious and are likely to lead to dismissal and, in certain circumstances, criminal proceedings. Depending on the employer's business interests, this implied term might be elaborated into express terms setting out clear specific duties on employees as seen in some of the five aspects following:

- *A general duty to be honest*. Acts of deception, theft, embezzlement, forgery, etc. are breaches of trust and can lead to instant dismissal. They may also result in criminal proceedings brought by the Crown Prosecution Service in the Crown Court or in magistrates' courts.

- *An obligation not to wilfully neglect a contractual duty*. The Court of Appeal found that the failure of two company directors to report evidence of serious fraud was a 'wilful neglect of duty' and so a fundamental breach of their contracts of employment. The employer was entitled to dismiss them (*Dunn and Another* v *AAH Ltd* [2010] IRLR 709).

- *Obligation not to compete with the employer*. This obligation can be included in a restrictive covenant (as an express term in a contract of employment). Such a term restricts the work undertaken by a former employee in three possible ways:
  - *non-competition*: limiting the ex-employee from taking work with a competitor organisation;
  - *non-solicitation*: prohibiting the making of contact with clients and customers of the ex-employer;
  - *non-dealing*: not engaging in business activities with such clients and customers.

  The employer must show that it has a legitimate business interest to protect. The 'reasonableness' of restrictive covenants is an issue that can be determined by the courts. For example, the High Court ruled that the prohibition by an estate agency on a former employee from working in a specified area for two years was unreasonable and unenforceable. No other firm of estate agents in the area imposed a non-competition covenant for longer than six months. There was no evidence to suggest that the employer's business was so different to justify a longer period (*Barry Allsuch and Co* v *Harris* [2001] Industrial Relations Law Bulletin 680, HC) (see also Exhibit 2.8).

- *Obligation not to disclose confidential information*. This can bind both current and, if it exists as an express term, ex-employees. Such express obligations are likely to co-exist with restrictive covenants. Breach of the duty of confidentiality is likely to be regarded as gross misconduct resulting in instant dismissal. However, there may be special circumstances in which an employee might believe that unauthorised disclosure is in the public interest (see Whistleblowing below).

- *Obligation not to benefit from work undertaken for the employer*. This relates to work covered by legislation on patents, intellectual property right and copyright. Subject to this limitation, an employer cannot prevent a former employee from using the general knowledge and skill that has been acquired in the course of employment.

▶ Duty to take reasonable care

This duty requires that employees should take care of themselves and their fellow-workers and co-operate with the employer and other agencies in complying with health and safety requirements. It is supplemented by the provisions of the Health and Safety at Work etc. Act 1974 (s 7) and its associated regulations (see also Chapter 12).

EXHIBIT 2.8

Enforcing a restrictive covenant

Standard Life Health Care Ltd v *Gorman* [2010] **IRLR 233, CA**

Mr Gorman resigned from Standard Life without notice to go and work for a competitor. This was a breach of the implied term of fidelity under his contract. The company sought to hold him to the full three month period of his notice. The High Court granted an injunction preventing him from working for any private health insurance business other than Standard Life. It also upheld the company's right to suspend him and not provide him with work. The Court of Appeal ruled that, where the employee had seriously breached his or her contract, the employer could require the employee to continue the contract. In the circumstances, the employer was not obliged to provide him with work. In this case, the consequences for Mr Gorman were significant because he was paid on a commission only basis.

Probationary periods and contracts

Employers, usually, have a probationary period for new employees (and sometimes for promoted employees). As far as new employees are concerned, there is no legal requirement covering the length of this. It may, depending on the nature of the post, be reasonable to have a period of any time up to 12 months.

The critical problem for employers is how they deal with the termination of employment of an individual who 'fails' his or her probationary period. The following are factors that need to be taken into account:

- Does the contract of employment offered at the start of employment indicate that it is conditional on satisfactory completion of the probationary period and may be terminated at the end of this period?

- A probationary period for a specific time period does not guarantee employment to that date. The contract might be terminated earlier with due notice from the employer (*Dalgleish* v *Kew House Farm Ltd* [1982] IRLR 251, CA; *Fosca Services (UK) Ltd* v *Birkett* [1996] IRLR 325, EAT).

- Is the employee given notice to terminate at the end of the probationary period? It is uncertain, in law, whether notice needs to be given. So, best practice suggests that it is given or, alternatively, that pay in lieu of notice is provided.

- Any termination of the contract of employment is, from the start of employment, potentially affected by equality law (Equality Act 2010, s 39(2)(c)). This can result in employment tribunal claims, irrespective of length of service, alleging unfair treatment. An employer, therefore, needs to be clear on the reasons for dismissal after a probationary period. Whether or not the employee qualifies for making an unfair dismissal claim, it is advisable that these reasons should relate to those for fair dismissal among which are 'capability' and 'conduct' (Employment Rights Act 1996, s 98).

- Is the employee entitled to use a contractual disciplinary and dismissal procedure? If so, failure to allow a probationer to do so could be a breach of contract and might lead to a wrongful dismissal claim, which can be made irrespective of length of service.

- Has the employee, during the course of the probationary period, been given appropriate support and advice relating to capability and conduct?

- An employee whose probationary period is longer than 12 months will accrue employment rights.

As far as promoted employees who are on a probationary period in a new post are concerned, equality law and unfair dismissal legislation would need to be considered. In addition, if unsuitability is demonstrated in the new post, then the employer would need to consider the steps to be taken under the contract. For example, would a return to a lower position be consistent with the original offer of promotion or would there be a breach of mutual trust and confidence?

Whistleblowing

There may be circumstances when an employee believes it is 'in the public interest' to disclose information and, potentially, breach the duty of confidentiality (see Exhibits 2.9 and 2.10).

Legislation was enacted in 1998 on public interest disclosures. This is now in Employment Rights Act 1996, Part IVA. It is designed to protect workers who make certain disclosures from both detrimental treatment and unfair dismissal by their employer. The legislation defines 'qualifying disclosures' and 'protected disclosures'.

▶ Qualifying disclosure

This is a disclosure of information which a worker reasonably believes tends to show some malpractice – whether this is currently happening, has happened or is likely to happen in the future. Specifically, the legislation refers to:

- a criminal offence;
- the breach of a legal obligation;
- a miscarriage of justice;
- a danger to the health and safety of any individual;
- damage to the environment;
- deliberate covering up of information tending to show any of the above matters.

It does not matter that after investigation the worker's belief is found to be mistaken. However, the worker must show that, at the time of the disclosure, it was reasonable to hold the particular belief; that the information and allegation was substantially true; and that the worker acted in good faith and did not act for personal gain. (Disclosures in breach of the Official Secrets Act 1989 are excluded.) The EAT has ruled, however, that the worker must produce 'facts'. An allegation alone (in this case in a solicitor's letter) was not sufficient (*Cavendish Munro Professional Risks Management Ltd v Geduld* [2010] IRLR 38, EAT). This is, arguably, a restrictive interpretation of the legislation.

EXHIBIT 2.9

A whistleblower: dismissal

ALM Medical Services Ltd v *Bladon* [2002] **IRLR 807, CA**

Complainant. Bryan Bladon had 20 years' experience as a nurse. In June 1999 he joined ALM at one of its private nursing homes. From mid-August to September 1999, when the matron was on sick leave, he temporarily 'acted up'.

His concerns. On 19 August he phoned Mr Sinclair, PA to the Managing Director, Dr Matta. He was concerned about some matters relating to the management of the home and the welfare and care of patients. These included poor drug records, staffing levels, patient neglect and a wound to a resident. He was asked to put his concerns in writing which he did by fax. (This was a 'protected disclosure'.) Sinclair said he would deal with the issue on his return from holiday. By 31 August, Bladon saw further deterioration in patient care. He decided to take further action and phoned the Social Services Inspectorate (SSI) (although this was not a 'prescribed person').

The inspection. On 1 September, an inspection was carried out by the SSI and an inspector from the health authority's nursing home inspectorate. On 8 September, the inspectors wrote to Dr Matta saying that four of the six concerns raised by Bladon were 'substantiated in whole or in part'. These should be investigated and addressed by the company.

Disciplinary action. On 9 September, Bladon was summoned to a disciplinary hearing without prior warning about what was to be discussed. He was given a written warning on 10 September by Matta. It was claimed in the letter that Bladon's own alleged lack of professional care was partly responsible for problems; and that they were motivated by poor relations he had with colleagues. He was denied any internal right of appeal.

Dismissal. On 16 September Bladon was summarily dismissed. It was said that in carrying out his professional duties, he fell below the standards expected of him.

ET complaint. Bladon complained that he had been subject to a detriment (the written disciplinary warning), and unfairly dismissed because he had made 'protected disclosures'.

Tribunal's consideration. It was appropriate for Bladon to raise his concerns with Sinclair. Bladon had a 'reasonable belief' that the information disclosed was covered by the 'qualifying disclosure' provisions. The disclosure was made in good faith because of his concern about his professional responsibilities and, in particular, about patient welfare. His disclosure to the inspectorate was reasonable since this was the appropriate body. It was reasonable for Bladon to raise the issue with the inspectors and not await Sinclair's return. Furthermore, in the absence of a whistleblowing policy and of any indication that the company would investigate his concerns, it was reasonable for him to go to the inspectorate. The tribunal accepted the employer (in particular, Dr Matta) had 'acted in a demeaning, insensitive, unprofessional, unreasonable and arrogant way' that left Bladon feeling 'belittled, professionally slurred, isolated and unable to respond in an effective way'. The employer had 'manufactured' or 'fabricated' a disciplinary situation; failed to follow its own procedures; and made no attempt to investigate Bladon's concerns. The ET only permitted evidence from the Managing Director and not from three other ALM witnesses.

Tribunal's decision. It ruled that Bladon was subject to a detriment (both the written warning and the refusal of a right of appeal); and that he was dismissed unfairly.

Financial award. Bladon was awarded £5,500 compensation for net losses to the date of the hearing; £7,500 for future losses; and £10,000 aggravated damages (taking account also of injury to feelings) for the detrimental treatment. Total compensation: £23,000.

Court of Appeal. This ruled that ALM was entitled to call evidence, particularly on the issue of 'protected disclosures'. This evidence was also relevant to the reasonable belief and good faith of Mr Bladon. It allowed the company's appeal and remitted the case for a tribunal rehearing.

EXHIBIT 2.10

Whilstleblowers: detrimental treatment

Fecitt and Others v *NHS Manchester* [2011] **IRLR 111, EAT**

Facts. Three registered nurses, Ms Fecitt (a clinical co-ordinator), Ms Woodcock and Ms Hughes (a 'bank' nurse) were employed by NHS Manchester at the Wythenshaw Walk-in Health Centre. In March 2008 they raised concerns about a general nurse, Mr Swift, who had exaggerated his qualifications. The employer accepted these concerns as a 'protected disclosure'. When Swift apologised, the employer decided that no further action would be taken. This did not satify the three women, who decided to pursue the matter. The result was a deterioration in staff relations. The three nurses raised grievances about their treatment by other staff; Swift complained of bullying and harassment; and Ms Fecitt made a formal complaint under the employer's whilstleblowing policy.

Detriments. Ms Fecitt was removed from her managerial responsibilities. She and Ms Woodcock were redeployed away from the Walk-in Centre. Ms Hughes, a 'bank' nurse, was not given further work.

EAT ruling. It overturned the employment tribunal's decision on the grounds that it had taken the wrong approach to 'causation'. The EAT found in favour of the claimants and remitted their cases back to an employment tribunal for further consideration.

'Causation' and liability. The EAT ruled that where a worker has made a 'protected disclosure' and has subsequently suffered detrimental treatment, it is for the employer to prove that its actions (or failure to act) was 'in no sense whatever' on the ground of the protected disclosure. The employer was vicariously liable for the treatment by their work colleagues of the three complainants. This ruling means that the approach adopted in whilstleblowing cases is consistent with that in discrimination cases. The approach to the burden of proof in *Igen Ltd* v *Wong* [2005] IRLR 258, CA is applicable (see Chapter 5). So, the employer has the burden of proving, on the balance of probabilities, that the relevant act or failure to act was *not* done on the ground that the worker made a protected disclosure.

▶ Protected disclosure

A qualifying disclosure will be a protected disclosure where it is made either directly to the employer or through internal procedures authorised by the employer; and also if it is made to a legal adviser in the course of obtaining legal advice. Furthermore, disclosure to a person prescribed by the Secretary of State may be 'protected'. 'Prescribed persons' include, as appropriate, the Health and Safety Executive, the Audit Commission for England and Wales, HM Revenue and Customs, the Serious Fraud Office, the Financial Services Agency.

The issue of the extent of a 'protected disclosure' was considered in *Hibbins* v *Hesters Way Neighbourhood Project* [2009] IRLR 198, EAT. In this case the issue was whether or not a disclosure that does not reveal any 'wrongdoing' or 'failure' by an employer (or a person for whom the employer is responsible) was 'protected' under the Employment Rights Act 1996. The EAT ruled that a teacher's disclosure to the police and also to her manager that a student (i.e. a third party) was a suspect in a rape case was a 'protected disclosure'.

❱ Detrimental treatment and dismissal

Protection from suffering detriments (in respect of a wide range of statutory rights) is covered by the Employment Rights Act 1996, Part V. Case law originally interpreted the law as covering detriments during employment. However, the Court of Appeal (*Woodward* v *Abbey National plc* [2006] EWCA Civ 822) has ruled, in a whistleblowing case, that an employer was liable for a detriment imposed after the termination of the employment contract. Following an earlier House of Lords ruling (*Rhys-Harper* v *Relaxion Group plc and other appeals* [2003] IRLR 484), Lord Justice Ward stated that 'limiting such protection against victimisation to acts committed during the existence of the employment contract and excluding acts connected with the wider "employment relationship" but committed after termination of the contract was absurd, irrational and arbitrary'. The decision in this case has much wider significance. The rights not to suffer a detriment (in ERA 1996, Part V) cover, among others, health and safety, maternity, paternity, parental and adoption leave, working time and flexible working and employee representatives. The principle established in the *Woodward* case affects all categories. An employer will be liable for post-employment retaliation – for example, refusal to provide a reference. (Similar protection is provided under equality law.)

If a worker resigns because of detrimental treatment by the employer and then claims constructive dismissal, the cut-off date for calculating compensation is the date of his or her dismissal and not the date at which the employer's conduct first amounted to a repudiation of the contract (*Melia* v *Magna Kansei Ltd* [2006] IRLR 117).

In *El-Megrisi* v *Azad University (IR) in Oxford* [2009] UKEAT 0448/08, the EAT ruled on the principal reason for dismissal relating to whistleblowing. The complainant raised concerns with her employer about the immigration status of staff and students and also other alleged irregularities. She was dismissed shortly afterwards. She claimed 'ordinary' unfair dismissal and also a detriment and dismissal for making a 'protected disclosure' contrary to Employment Rights Act.

On the question of the dismissal, the EAT ruled that the employment tribunal had wrongly focused only on her most recent disclosure when it held that, because of previous difficulties with her employer, this disclosure was not the principal reason for her dismissal. The EAT stated that the tribunal had failed to take into account that the history of difficulties had consisted of other protected disclosures. These were the principal reason for her dismissal.

❱ Employment tribunal applications

The public interest disclosure legislation covers a wide group of 'workers'. Complaints alleging unfair dismissal or detrimental treatment may be made to an employment tribunal irrespective of length of service. The tribunal will consider:

- the identity of the person to whom the disclosure was made (e.g. an appropriate professional body);
- the seriousness of the relevant failure;
- whether the relevant failure is continuing or is likely to occur again;

- whether the disclosure breaches the employer's duty of confidentiality to others (e.g. clients);

- what action has been taken (or might reasonably be expected to have been taken) if a disclosure was made previously to the employer or a prescribed person;

- whether the worker complied with any internal procedures approved by the employer if a disclosure was made previously to the employer.

The Department for Business, Innovation and Skills (**www.bis.gov.uk/employment**) has confirmed that, for claims received after 6 April 2010, employment tribunals can pass to a prescribed regulator allegations (made in a claim) that the claimant has suffered a detriment or has been dismissed. It will be effected by a complainant ticking the appropriate box on the ET1 claim form to indicate consent. The aim of the process is to encourage claimants who may not have considered passing information to the relevant regulator to consider doing so.

In *BP plc* v *Elstone and Another* [2010] IRLR 558, EAT the Employment Appeal Tribunal, adopting a purposive approach in its interpretation of the legislation, ruled that a worker was entitled to bring a complaint under the whistleblowing provisions of the Employment Rights Act 1996 in respect of a detriment that he allegedly suffered in his current employment because of a protected disclosure that he had made while in previous employment. Mr Elstone, while employed by Petrotechnics, had made protected disclosures to two senior BP employees because of concerns about health and safety issues. (Petrotechnics evaluated safety processes for BP.) Petrotechnics dismissed him for breach of confidentiality which was seen as gross misconduct. Subsequently, he was to be employed as a consultant by BP. However, after Petrotechnics infomed BP that he had disclosed confidential information, BP chose not to engage him. He claimed, at employment tribunal, that he had suffered a detriment from BP.

Breach of contract

A contract of employment can be breached either by the employer or by the employee.

- *By employee*. If the employee breaches his or her contract, the employer will usually initiate disciplinary action (see Chapter 8). Depending on whether the breach is regarded as either minor or persistent minor misconduct or as gross misconduct, the employer will either dismiss the employee or impose a disciplinary penalty short of dismissal (usually, some form of warning).

- *By employer*. Breach of contract by an employer may be relatively minor or fundamental. A minor breach is likely to result in some form of grievance which may be resolved through the relevant grievance procedure. A fundamental breach is much more serious and can have a number of important consequences for the both the employee and the employer (see the following section).

▶ What is a fundamental or repudiatory breach of contract?

It is behaviour by an employer which is so serious that effectively 'tears up' the contract. Lord Denning, in the Court of Appeal, said 'if the employer is guilty of conduct which is a significant breach going to the root of the contract of employment or which shows that the employer no longer intends to be bound by one or more of the essential terms of the contract, then the employee is entitled to treat himself as discharged from any further performance . . . [T]he conduct must . . . be sufficiently serious to entitle him to leave at once' (*Western Excavating (ECC) Ltd v Sharp* [1978] IRLR 27). Examples can include not paying wages that are due, providing hazardous working conditions, failing to tackle harassment or other discriminatory treatment. It is likely that such conduct would be a breach of the implied mutual trust and confidence and also, possibly, a breach of the contractual duty to take reasonable care of the employee.

Usually, it is expected that an employee will initially raise a grievance (see the ACAS *Code of Practice on Disciplinary and Grievance Procedures* 2009). However, the employee must not stay too long after the unacceptable conduct by the employer because he or she might be thought by the tribunal or court to have waived the right to terminate. Of course, in some cases the behaviour may be so unacceptable that the employee might resign immediately without using the grievance procedure.

When an employee terminates the contract of employment in these circumstances, this forced resignation is regarded, in law, as equivalent to a 'dismissal'. The Employment Rights Act (s 95(1)(c)) states that an employee is dismissed by his or her employer if 'the employee terminates the contract under which he is employed (with or without notice) in circumstances in which he is entitled to terminate it without notice by reason of the employer's conduct'. In everyday speech (but not in law) this is known as 'constructive dismissal'.

Termination of a contract of employment

This issue is considered in detail in Chapter 8. Here, it is sufficient to outline briefly those circumstances in which a contract might end.

- *Notice to terminate*. Notice can be given by either the employer or the employee in accordance with the terms of the contract. The notice given by the employer should comply with the statutory minimum periods of notice (ERA 1996, s 86). If the contract is silent about notice, then the employee should be guided by the statutory minima.

- *Summary dismissal*. This refers to the instant termination of the contract. It can arise where there is gross misconduct by an employee (e.g. violence or theft) and there has been appropriate investigation and a disciplinary hearing.

- *Wrongful dismissal*. This is where the contract is terminated in breach of the contractual terms (e.g. in breach of the implied term of mutual trust and confidence, or where insufficient notice is given to terminate the contract). The restrictions on making unfair dismissal claims do not apply.

- *Constructive dismissal*. This arises in circumstances where an employee resigns because of what is perceived to be a repudiatory breach of the contract of employment by the employer (see above).

- *End of a fixed-term contract*. This refers to those contracts that have either a specific termination date or which end on the completion of a particular task.

- *Frustration of contract.* This is a complex area. Much will depend on the specific circumstances. It involves termination of the contract as a result of some unforeseen event which makes it difficult for the contract to be carried out. Frustration would cover death, long-term ill-health or imprisonment (particularly if the sentence is lengthy).

Subsistence of a contract

It is important to remember that there are certain circumstances when a contract of employment can subsist (i.e. it remains in existence but no work is carried out under it). An example of such circumstances arises in respect of maternity and paternity leave (see Chapter 11). There may be other circumstances where a person is absent from work by agreement with the employer. In all these circumstances, the contract remains in existence and, even if there is no remuneration paid, certain specified terms – express and or implied – are enforceable (e.g. confidentiality, restrictive covenants, mutual trust and confidence).

Employment protection for 'atypical' workers

In Exhibit 2.1 above, various categories of 'atypical' workers were identified. In this section, we will consider the employment protection afforded to these categories. Some will have to establish 'employee' status before they can claim employment rights; whilst other rights are extended to the wide category of 'workers' (see Exhibit 2.11). A significant driver of employment protection for 'atypical' workers has been the European Union as can be seen from the outline and discussion below.

▶ Part-time workers

There have been three broad developments in law which have begun to improve protection and rights for part-time workers:

- *Access to statutory rights.* The European Court of Justice ruled in 1994, in respect of statutory employment rights, that it was indirect sex discrimination for Britain to have differential qualifying rights for access for full-timers and for part-timers to unfair dismissal compensation and redundancy pay.

- *Requirement to work full time.* The requirement to work full time may be indirect sex discrimination which has to be objectively justified. Claims have been made by women returning from maternity leave to vary the scheduling and the number of working hours.

- *Comparable treatment with full-time workers.* The European Union adopted a directive in 1997 implementing a social partners' Framework Agreement on Part-time Work. This deals with the contractual rights of part-timers. It concerns any part-timers who have a contract of employment or are in an employment relationship. Part-timers are workers whose normal hours of work, averaged over a period of up to a year, are less than the normal hours of comparable full-timers.

EXHIBIT 2.11

Access to certain key statutory rights

'Employee' status (i.e. workers who have contracts of employment)

- **Contractual information**: must be provided within eight weeks of employment starting (ERA 1996, s 1).
- **Minimum contractual notice**: (ERA 1996, s 86).
- **Protection against unfair dismissal:**
  - qualified by length of service (ERA 1996, ss 94, 108, 109);
  - restricted right when dismissal relates to industrial action (TULRCA 1992, ss 237–9).
- **Written reasons for dismissal:**
  - one year's continuous service (ERA 1996, s 92);
  - no qualifying service if employee pregnant or on maternity leave.
- **Maternity leave**: an unqualified right (ERA ss 71–8).
- **Shop and betting shop workers: protection in relation to Sunday working:**
  - irrespective of age or length of service (ERA ss 36–43, 45).
- **Right to parental leave**: qualified by length of service.
- **Right to request flexible working** (ERA 1996, ss 80F–80I):
  - qualified by length of service;
  - qualifying conditions re child or dependant.
- **Protection for fixed-term employees against discrimination** (Fixed-term Employees Regulations 2002):
  - irrespective of age or length of service.
- **Transfers of undertakings: dismissal/substantial detrimental change to contracts** (TUPE 2006, reg 4):
  - qualified by length of service.

'Workers' (i.e. those with contracts of employment *and* those on some 'other contract' to work personally)

- **Protection against discriminatory treatment because of a protected characteristic:**
  - protected characteristics (Equality Act 2010, s 4);
  - in relation to 'employment': employees and applicants (EA 2010, s 39);
  - contract workers (EA 2010, s 41);
  - post employment (EA 2010, s 108).
- **Right to equal pay**: this covers 'the ordinary basic minimum wage or salary and any other consideration whether in cash or in kind which the worker receives directly or indirectly in respect of his employment from his employer' (Article 141, Treaty of Rome). (EA 2010, Chapter 9)
- **Protection from deduction from wages**: available irrespective of length of service (ERA 1996).
- **Working Time Regulations 1998:**
  - maximum working week; paid annual leave; rest entitlements and health requirements;
  - irrespective of length of service and hours worked.
- **Statutory national minimum wage**: minima for workers of 16 years and above (NMWA 1998).
- **'Whistleblowing' rights**: protects from detrimental treatment/dismissal for making protected disclosure (ERA 1996).

- **Protection for part-time workers**: against discrimination (Part-time Workers Regulations 2000).

- **Protection for agency workers**: the right to equal treatment is available to agency workers after 12 weeks' employment (Agency Workers Regulations 2010).

- **Protection against 'blacklisting' for participation in trade union activities**: (Employment Relations Act 1999 (Blacklists) Regulations 2010).

- **Statutory right to be accompanied:**
  - applicable in grievances and disciplinary action (Employment Relations Act 1999, 10);
  - explicitly covers agency workers and homeworkers.

The directive outlines certain general principles to be transposed into national law:

- Part-timers may not be treated less favourably than full-timers.

- Member states should in consultation with the **social partners** work to remove obstacles to part-time work.

- Employers, as far as possible, should make opportunities for part-time work at all levels; and should give consideration to requests from workers for changes from part-time to full-time work and vice versa.

- Refusal to transfer from full-time to part-time work (or vice versa) is not in itself a valid reason for dismissal.

The directive has been partially transposed into UK law through the Part-time Workers (Prevention of Less Favourable Treatment) Regulations 2000 (which were amended in 2002) (see Exhibit 2.12).

▶ Fixed-term contract workers

There are three legal issues involving these workers:

- *Continuity of service*. This is a basic and, in many cases, a vitally important issue for those workers on successive fixed-term contracts. It may be possible to 'stitch together' such contracts to establish continuity of service. In this context, it is also important to consider the significance of temporary cessations of work and the significance of breaks between contracts (see earlier discussion and also *Ford* v *Warwickshire County Council* [1983] IRLR 126, HL).

- *Statutory employment rights*. These accrue to fixed-term contract workers depending on whether they can, under the legal tests discussed earlier, be defined as an 'employee' or as a 'worker' on some other contract to work personally.

- *Comparable treatment with permanent workers*. The European Union adopted the Fixed-term Workers Directive 1999 implementing a social partners' framework agreement. This is to be transposed into the law of member states. The purposes of the framework agreement were stated as follows:
  - to improve the quality of fixed-term work by ensuring the application of the principle of non-discrimination;

EXHIBIT 2.12

Part-time Workers (Prevention of Less Favourable Treatment) Regulations 2000

Who is a part-time worker? This is defined by exemption – as a person who is not a full-time worker in a particular workplace. Also, the regulations cover 'workers' and not just 'employees'.

Who is the comparator? The part-time worker and the full-time worker comparator are to be employed at the same time, by the same employer, at the same establishment, under the same type of contract, and be engaged in the same or broadly similar work (taking into account, as appropriate, whether they have a similar level of qualification, skills and experience) (reg 2(4)). A comparison can be made with either a full-time worker on a permanent contract; or one on a fixed-term contract.

If there is no comparator at the same establishment, a person who works at a different establishment of that employer can be chosen. It is *not* possible to have a hypothetical comparator.

The principle of equal treatment. In respect of the terms of the contract, a part-timer has the right not to be treated by the employer less favourably than a full-time worker is treated. This right applies only if the less favourable treatment 'is on the ground that the worker is a part-time worker' and that the discriminatory treatment is 'not justified on objective grounds'. To test whether there has been less favourable treatment, the *pro rata* principle shall apply unless it is 'inappropriate' (reg 5(3)). The EAT has ruled that the less favourable treatment need not be solely on the ground of part-time status. But this status should be the effective and predominant cause of the treatment (*Carl v University of Sheffield* [2009] IRLR 616).

The regulations also prohibit a part-timer being subject to any '**detriment** by any act, or deliberate failure to act, of the employer' (e.g. denial of promotion opportunities) (reg 5(1)).

Objective justification. Discriminatory treatment can only be justified if it can be shown that the less favourable treatment is necessary to achieve a legitimate objective (e.g. a genuine business objective) and is an appropriate way of achieving that objective.

Rate of pay. A part-time worker must not receive a lower basic rate of pay than a comparable full-time worker. This protection also covers special rates of pay (e.g. bonuses, shift allowances and unsocial hours and weekend payments).

Overtime. Under current case law, part-timers do not have an automatic right to overtime payments when they work beyond their normal hours. However, once a part-timer exceeds the normal hours of a full-timer, the part-timer has a legal right to the applicable overtime payments (*Stadt Lengerich v Helmig* [1995] IRLR 216, ECJ).

Contractual sick and maternity pay. There must be no less favourable treatment in calculating rates of pay; the qualifying length of service for the pay; and the length of time for which the payment is received. The benefits must be provided *pro rata* unless the differential treatment is objectively justified.

Other contractual benefits. A part-timer must not be treated less favourably in terms of benefits such as health insurance, company cars, subsidised mortgages and staff discounts.

Conditions of access. There should be no discrimination over access to an occupational health scheme, a profit-sharing scheme or a share option scheme unless it is objectively justified.

Leave entitlements. Part-timers are entitled to statutory leave entitlements. Where an employer provides enhanced arrangements under contractual terms, then, part-timers should have the same entitlements as full-timers – on a *pro rata* basis.

Access to training. Part-time workers should not be excluded from training. Training provision should be at convenient times for the majority of staff including part-timers.

Redundancy. Selection criteria and different treatment of part-timers must be justified objectively.

Conversion to part-time status. This is not a right. The employer must consider requests. A full-time worker who converts by reducing working hours is entitled to be treated no less favourably than he or she was treated in terms and conditions of employment; or being subject to a detriment (reg 3).

Statement of reasons for treatment. A worker who believes he or she has been discriminated against may ask the employer in writing for 'a written statement giving particulars of the reasons for the treatment' (reg 6). If there is a case for objective justification, this should be stated. This statement is admissible at employment tribunal. A tribunal may draw 'any inference that it considers just and equitable, including an inference that the employer has infringed the right in question' if the employer has 'deliberately and without written excuse' not provided such a statement; or considers the statement 'evasive or equivocal' (reg 6(3)).

Unfair dismissal and victimisation. Dismissal or selection for redundancy is automatically unfair if the reason or principal reason concerns the exercise of rights under the regulations. A worker may complain to an employment tribunal; and also in relation to victimisation.

Employment tribunal application. A worker may complain within three months of either the date of the alleged discriminatory action; or the last in a series of discriminatory actions. It is for the employer to identify the ground for the less favourable treatment or detriment (reg 8(6)).

Liability. Reflecting the provisions of other discrimination law, an employer is vicariously liable for the behaviour of managers, supervisors and other workers 'in the course of employment' whether or not the behaviour was with the employer's knowledge and approval (reg 11(1)). An employer's defence is that it 'took such steps as were reasonably practicable' to prevent the discrimination (reg 11(3)).

Remedies. If an employment tribunal finds a complaint to be well-founded, it is required, as it considers 'just and equitable' (reg 8):

- to make a declaration of the rights of the complainant and the employer;
- to order the employer to pay compensation to the worker. A two-year limitation on remedies in relation to an occupational pension was ruled by the House of Lords to be incompatible with European law and was removed in 2002 (*Preston v Wolverhampton Healthcare Trust (No. 2)* [2001] ICR 217);
- to recommend that, within a specified period, the employer takes action, which appears to the tribunal to be reasonable in the circumstances of the case, to deal with the discrimination. Failure to comply with the recommendation may result in increased compensation.

  - to establish a framework to prevent abuse arising from the use of successive fixed-term employment contracts or relationships.

    The directive has been partially transposed into UK law through the Fixed-term Employees (Prevention of Less Favourable Treatment) Regulations 2002 (see Exhibit 2.13).

EXHIBIT 2.13

Fixed-term Employees (Prevention of Less Favourable Treatment) Regulations 2002

Who is covered? The regulations apply to 'employees' (whose status will have to be determined under the common law tests). The directive, however, applies to 'workers'.

The principle of equal treatment. A fixed-term employee should not be treated less favourably, in respect of terms and conditions, than a 'permanent' employee on the grounds of being fixed-term (reg 3). Also, the regulations prohibit the fixed-term employee, because they are fixed-term, being subject to any 'detriment by any act or deliberate failure to act of the employer' (reg 3(1)(b)).

Objective justification. Less favourable treatment may be objectively justified. Justification depends on the circumstances of the case. The regulations provide that discrimination in relation to a particular contractual term will be justified where the fixed-term employee's overall package of terms and conditions is not less favourable than the comparable permanent employee's (reg 4) (see *Manchester College v Cocliff* UKEAT/0035/10 for guidance on the approach to be taken).

Which contracts are covered? A fixed-term contract means a contract of employment which is one of the following (reg 1(2)):

- one which is made for a specific term which is fixed in advance (e.g. three months, a year); or
- one which ends automatically on the completion of a particular task or upon the occurrence or non-occurrence of any specific event. Examples include those contracts covering maternity leave breaks; peak demands for a service or production; or tasks covering defined projects like setting up a database.

Who is the comparator? This is a 'permanent' employee – i.e. someone on an open-ended contract of employment (reg 2). He or she should be employed by the same employer at the same establishment doing the same or broadly similar work. Where relevant the comparator should have similar skills and qualifications to the fixed-term employee. Where there is no comparator in the same establishment, then a comparison can be made with a similar permanent employee working for the same employer in a different establishment.

Successive fixed-term contracts. The use of successive fixed-term contracts is limited to four years, unless further fixed-term contracts can be justified on objective grounds. It is possible for employers and employees to increase or decrease this period through a collective agreement or, in non-union organisations, through a workforce agreement (reg 8 and sch 1).

There is no limit on the duration of the *first* fixed-term contract. However, if this contract is of four years or more and is renewed, it will be treated from then as 'permanent' unless the use of a fixed-term contract is objectively justified.

Furthermore, if a fixed-term contract is renewed after the four-year period, it will be treated as a contract for an indefinite period unless the use of a fixed-term contract is objectively justified. A fixed-term employee has the right to ask the employer for a written statement confirming that their contract is permanent or setting out objective reasons for the use of a fixed-term contract beyond the four-year period. The employer must provide this statement within 21 days (reg 8).

Written statement of reasons. A fixed-term employee has a right to ask their employer for a written statement setting out the reasons for the discriminatory treatment that they believe has occurred. The employer must provide this within 21 days of the request (reg 5). The statement is admissible in employment tribunal proceedings. A tribunal may draw 'any inference that it considers just and equitable, including an inference that the employer has infringed the right in question' (reg 5(3)) if the employer has 'deliberately and without written excuse' not provided such a statement or considers that 'the written statement is evasive or equivocal'.

Redundancy waiver. If included in a fixed-term contract agreed, extended or renewed after 1 October 2002 it will be invalid.

Protection against unfair dismissal and victimisation. Dismissal or selection for redundancy is automatically unfair if the reason or principal reason concerns the exercise of rights under the regulations. An employee may complain to an employment tribunal irrespective of age or length of service. Similar protection is provided against victimisation (reg 6).

Termination of a fixed-term contract. From 1 October 2002, the end of a 'task' contract that expires when a specific task has been completed or a specific event does or does not happen will be a dismissal in law. Likewise, the non-renewal of a fixed-term contract concluded for a specific period of time will be a dismissal. Employees of one year or more have the right to a written statement of reasons for dismissal and the right not to be unfairly dismissed. If the contract lasts for two years or more and it is not renewed because of redundancy, the employee has the right to statutory redundancy pay.

Application to employment tribunal. A worker may complain to an employment tribunal about less favourable treatment or victimisation (reg 7). The complaint should be made within three months of either the date of the action or of the last in a series of discriminatory actions. Where an employee complains, it is for the employer to identify the ground for the less favourable treatment or detriment (reg 7(6)).

Liability. An employer is vicariously liable for the behaviour of managers, supervisors and other workers 'in the course of employment' whether or not the employer knew or approved the behaviour (reg 12(1)). The defence is that he or she 'took such steps as were reasonably practicable' to prevent discrimination (reg 12(3)).

Remedies. If an employment tribunal finds a complaint to be well-founded, it is required, as it considers 'just and equitable' (reg 7):

- to make a declaration of the rights of the complainant and the employer;
- to order the employer to pay compensation to the worker which the tribunal considers to be just and equitable;
- to recommend that, within a specified period, the employer takes action to deal with the discrimination against the complainant which appears to the tribunal to be reasonable in the circumstances of the case. Failure to comply with the recommendation may result in increased compensation.

Statutory sick pay. Employees on contract of less than three months are entitled to statutory sick pay from October 2008.

❱ Casual and zero-hours contract workers

The role of casual workers is of growing importance in particular sectors (e.g. as nurses, supply teachers or in hotels and catering). Clearly, they have an employment relationship. The question is, what kind of relationship? What is the employment status? Is it one that confers statutory rights?

There is no specific statutory framework governing the position of casual workers. However, as noted below, casual workers may be able to claim under the Working Time Regulations 1998 and the National Minimim Wage Act 1998. Furthermore, they are protected under the Equality Act 2010 (see Chapter 5) and under the Health and Safety at Work Act 1974 (see Chapter 12).

Case law and casual workers

Various legal issues have arisen in case law over the past 20 years or so:

- Whether there is explicit 'mutuality of obligation'?
- Whether the person can be defined, under common law tests as an 'employee' in law?
- Whether there is a 'global contract' covering all assignments of work?
- Whether they have sufficient continuous service as an 'employee' to claim unfair dismissal?
- What counts as 'working time'?
- Whether they are eligible for the national minimum wage?

'Regular casuals' in catering

The case of *O'Kelly* v *Trust House Forte plc* [1983] IRLR 369, CA concerned waiters whose names were on a list to be called first for banqueting functions. They worked only for THF and did so virtually every week for varying hours (from three to 57). They were paid weekly, deductions were made for tax and National Insurance and they also received holiday pay. They worked under the control of the head waiter and were provided with uniforms. However, they did not have to agree to work if they did not wish to. Likewise the company was not required to provide work. Refusal could, however, result in removal from the list. The Court of Appeal ruled that there was no mutuality of obligation and so they were not 'employees'.

'Bank' nurses

It was ruled by the Court of Appeal in *Clark* v *Oxfordshire Health Authority* [1998] IRLR 125, CA that no contract of employment existed, even if there was a 'global contract' in existence, if there was no mutuality of obligation 'subsisting over the entire duration of the relevant period'.

Long-serving tour guides

In the landmark ruling in *Carmichael and Leese* v *National Power plc* [2000] IRLR 43, HL the House of Lords determined that there needed to be an 'irreducible minimum' of mutuality of obligation for a person to be an employee (see Exhibit 2.2 above).

▶ Relevant legislation and casual workers

Working Time Regulations 1998

The paramount importance of 'mutuality of obligation' deprives many long-serving working people of statutory employment rights (viz. on unfair dismissal, redundancy pay, parental rights, the provision of contractual information). However, such workers may have some rights and entitlements in respect of the Working Time Regulations 1998. These provide an entitlement to a maximum working week and to paid annual leave (on, if appropriate, a *pro rata* basis). Furthermore, case law from the European Court of Justice has defined 'working time' for working people who are 'on call' (*SIMAP v Consellaria de Sanidad y Consumo de la Generalidad Valenciana* [2000] IRLR 845; *Landeshauptstadt Kiel* v *Jaegar* [2003] IRLR 804) (see Chapter 10).

National Minimum Wage Act 1998

This legislation can also provide entitlements for certain casual and zero hours contract workers. Such workers should not be paid less than the national minimum wage. Furthermore, an associated issue tested in the courts was what constituted the eligible 'working time' of a nightwatchman who was allowed, during his shift, to sleep on duty. The EAT ruled that where a worker was required to be on the employer's premises to carry out his duties over a specific number of hours, then, all the hours were eligible for the national minimum wage (*Wright* v *Scottbridge Construction* [2001] IRLR 589) (see Chapter 9). In addition to a claim relating to the national minimum wage, a casual worker is entitled to claim for non-payment of wages under the Employment Rights Act 1996.

▶ Homeworking

The status of homeworkers can be problematic. Each case has to be considered on its own facts and circumstances to determine whether or not there is compliance with the common law tests and, therefore, 'employee' status. The issues that can arise in cases are:

- the fact that the work is undertaken in premises not under the control of the employing organisation;
- the provision, probably by the employer, of equipment and materials to be used;
- whether there is mutuality of obligation;
- whether the work is continuous or intermittent;
- whether there is a global contract in existence governing the employment relationship.

Two notable cases have arisen in this area:

- *Airfix Footwear* v *Cope* [1978] IRLR 396, EAT. This concerned Mrs Cope who worked at home making shoe heels. The company provided her with tools and issued instructions and, over a seven-year period, she generally worked a five-day week. There was close supervision of her work. She was paid on a piecework basis without deductions for tax and national insurance. She was held by the EAT to be an employee.

- *Nethermere (St Neots) Ltd* v *Gardiner & Taverna* [1984] IRLR 240, CA. In this, homeworkers worked for a company for three years for between five and seven hours a day sewing children's clothes. In some weeks, there was no work, and Ms Taverna usually took off 12 weeks each year. Subject to a minimum set by the company, the workers could specify the amount of work they wanted to be supplied with. The Court of Appeal found that contracts of employment existed. It stated that well-founded expectations of continuing homework consisting of the regular giving and taking of work for periods of a year or more could crystallise into an enforceable contract of employment spanning weeks in which no work was done and preserving continuity. So, the length of the relationship and the regularity of dealings between the homeworker and the employer were sufficient to establish an 'irreducible minimum of obligation'.

▶ Agency workers

There are a number of uncertainties about the position of agency workers in employment law. Their degree of employment protection is not always clearly established. This situation is complicated by the existence of a triangular relationship between the agency, the worker and the 'end user' or client organisation. The legal issues that have arisen in the past ten years or so have concerned case law in Britain, the European Union Temporary Agency Work Directive 2008, the previous Labour government's policy initiatives for 'vulnerable' workers and in political concerns about the behaviour of gangmasters in their treatment of migrant agency workers. The key legal issues are:

- the employment relationship of an agency worker;
- determining the status of an agency worker;
- the employment obligations to the worker;
- the employment relationship with the 'end user';
- the EU principles of equal treatment for agency workers;
- the specific employment protection for migrant agency workers.

The employment relationship of an agency worker

Agencies must comply with the Employment Agencies Act 1973 and the Conduct of Employment Agencies and Employment Businesses Regulations 2003. There are two categories of organisation: the employment agency and the employment business. (Although, it is fair to say that the term agency is used to encompass all organisations which provide staff.) The 'agency' provides introductions to a hiring organisation for whom the worker will work on either an open-ended or fixed-term contract. In such a case the hirer will be the employer. The 'employment business', however, will place staff on a temporary basis with a client. The contractual relationship is with the employment business (or 'temp agency' as these are commonly known).

Determining the status of an agency worker

This issue is left to the courts to consider on the facts of each individual case using the common law tests. In *McMeechan v Secretary of State for Employment* [1997] IRLR 353, the Court of Appeal considered whether, following the insolvency of the agency, the worker was entitled to a payment from the National Insurance Fund as an 'employee'. The Court of Appeal weighed the various facts in the case which point to or away from an employment relationship. Among the evidence was a document signed by McMeechan which stated that he would provide his services as a 'self-employed worker and not under a contract of service'. However, there was also evidence that the agency had power of dismissal for misconduct and the right to end assignments. It had the right to make deductions from an hourly rate of pay for poor performance or bad time-keeping.

His pay was subject to deduction of tax and National Insurance contributions. Also, the agency provided a grievance procedure and he owed a duty of fidelity and confidentiality. The Court found that there was an employment relationship with the agency but only for the purposes of the specific engagement.

The employment obligations to the worker

Where a worker has an employment relationship with the agency, it must provide a written statement of employment particulars and an indication of whether the person is employed on a contract of employment or a contract for services (i.e. as an independent contractor). Subject to whatever qualifications exist in law, agency workers are eligible for the national minimum wage, entitlements under the Working Time Regulations and statutory sick pay. Apart from in the entertainment and modelling sectors, the agency worker should not be charged by the agency for finding work. Whilst the employment contract might be with the agency, the 'end user' has a number of legal obligations to the worker – particularly under equality law and health and safety legislation.

The employment relationship with the 'end user'

There have been instances of some agency workers being placed with a client organisation and, for various reasons, remaining with that 'end user' for a prolonged period of time. As a consequence, the courts have dealt with a number of cases to consider how the nature of the contractual relationship has evolved over time between the agency worker and the 'end user'.

Initially, in the triangular relationship, the contractual relationships are likely to be as follows:

● *Agency worker and agency* – a contract of employment (i.e. the worker is an 'employee'), or a contract for services (i.e. the worker is self-employed).

● *Agency and client organisation or 'end user'* – a commercial contract to provide staff as specified.

● *Agency worker and client organisation or 'end user'* – whilst there are legal obligations governing the conduct of both and the performance of the worker, there is no contract of employment between these two parties. The agency is the employer.

In recent years, several complaints to employment tribunals by agency workers who had worked for long periods of time with 'end users' resulted in rulings by the Court of Appeal to determine the issue of employment status and contractual obligation in these triangular relationships (*Dacas* v *Brook Street Bureau (UK) Ltd* [2004] IRLR 358, CA; *Cable & Wireless plc* v *Muscat* [2006] IRLR 354, CA; *James* v *London Borough of Greenwich* [2008] IRLR 302, CA). In the first of these cases, the possibility of an implied contract of employment evolving over time with the 'end user' was raised. Eventually, the Court of Appeal elaborated the issue of an 'implied contract of employment'. In *James* v *London Borough of Greenwich* [2008] IRLR 302 it was stated that the implication of a contract should only be done on the grounds of 'necessity'.

The key issues arising from the *James* case are:

● *'Necessity' and 'business reality'*. Where there is no express contract between an agency worker and the 'end user', the first question for the purposes of determining employment status is whether or not it is necessary, according to established common law principles, to imply a contract between these parties to give the situation business reality.

- *The implication of a contract with the 'end user'.* On the facts, the relationship between the agency worker and the end user was fully explained by express contracts between the agency and the worker and between the agency and the 'end user'; and the arrangements were not a sham. In these circumstances, it was not necessary to imply a third contract between the worker and the 'end user'. 'The mere passage of time did not justify the implication of a contract between the worker and the end user as a matter of necessity'.

- *The contractual situation.* As there was no express or implied contract between the worker and the 'end user', it followed she could not be an employee of the 'end user'.

The view of many commentators is that the emphasis on 'necessity' in the *James* case will now make it more difficult for agency workers on long-term placements to establish an employment relationship with the 'end user'. It is only likely to arise where the entire relationship with an agency is a sham (see Exhibit 2.14).

EXHIBIT 2.14

Necessity

Tilson v *Alstom Transport* [2011] **IRLR 169, CA**

Facts. Mr Tilson worked for Alstom from August 2004. He was eventually promoted to a management role. His employment arose from a complex network of three contracts for the supply of labour. He brought an unfair dismissal claim against Alstom following his dismissal on 7 November 2006. It had to be determined whether he was an 'employee' of Alstom. In his position as manager, the employment tribunal heard, he managed Alstom employees; could recruit permanent staff; was authorised to discipline and dismiss permanent employees; signed time sheets for permanent staff; had to apply to his line manager for annual leave; and had negotiated contracts on behalf of Alstom. It was reported that he had rejected, more than once, Alstom's offer of permanent employment because he was receiving significantly higher pay under the agency arrangements.

Judgments. The employment tribunal found that a contract of employment should be implied with Alstom. The EAT overturned this decision. The Court of Appeal upheld the EAT decision and elaborated on the issue of 'necessity'.

Necessity. The Court of Appeal referred to the principle that a contract of employment can only be implied if it is 'necessary' to do so. In an earlier case, the Court had stated that the correct question to ask is whether it is necessary or not to imply a contract 'to give business reality to a transaction and to create enforceable obligations between parties who are dealing with one another in circumstances in which one would expect that business reality and those enforceable obligations to exist' (*The Aramis* [1989] 1 Lloyd's Rep 213, 224). The Court in the *Tilson* case noted that where the parties would or might have acted exactly as they did in the absence of a contract, then this would be fatal to the implication of a contract. It stated further that the mere fact that there was a significant degree of integration of Mr Tilson into Alstom was not inconsistent with an agency relationship in which there was no contract between him and Alstom. Furthermore, there was no common intention that there should be a contract nor any decision of contractual terms. So, this reinforced the view that no contract could be implied.

EU principles of equal treatment for agency workers

The Temporary Agency Work Directive 2008 is a companion piece of legislation to the directives governing part-time workers and fixed-term contract workers (see above). Among the key provisions of the directive are the following:

- *The purpose of the directive* is:
  - 'to ensure the protection of temporary workers and to improve the quality of temporary work by ensuring that the principle of non-discrimination is applied to temporary workers and recognising temporary agencies as employers';
  - 'to establish a suitable framework for the use of temporary work to contribute to creating jobs and the smooth functioning of the labour market' (Article 2).

- *The principle of non-discrimination.* 'The basic working and employment conditions of temporary workers shall be, for the duration of their posting at a user undertaking, at least those that would apply if they had been recruited directly by that enterprise to occupy the same job' (Article 5).

- *Access to permanent quality employment.* 'Temporary workers shall be informed of any vacant posts in the user undertaking to give them the same opportunity as other workers in that undertaking to find employment' (Article 6).

The Agency Workers' Regulations 2010, implementing the directive, came into force on 1 October 2011. This legislation is on the basis of a 'social partners' agreement reached in May 2008 between the Confederation of British Industry and the Trades Union Congress (see **www.bis.gov.uk/employment**) (see Exhibit 2.15).

EXHIBIT 2.15

Agency Workers' Regulations 2010: some key provisions

Scope. Department for Business, Innovation and Skills *Guidance* (April 2011) states that an agency worker is someone with a contract with the temporary work agency (TWA). This is an employment contract or an agreement to provide services personally. But he or she 'works temporarily for and under the direction and supervision of a hirer'. The unique, tripartite relationship between agency worker, agency and hirer is a key feature of these regulations and those who are covered by them. The key elements required for an agency worker are:

- there is a contract (an employment contract or an agreement to provide services personally) between the worker and a TWA;
- that worker is temporarily supplied to a hirer by the TWA; and
- when working on assignment the worker is subject to the supervision and direction of that hirer; and
- the individual in question is not in a business on their own account.

The *Guidance* also states that those working for 'in-house temporary staffing banks' are 'likely to be outside the scope' of the regulations. Issues of scope are, of course, very likely to be tested at employment tribunal.

Qualifying period. Agency workers to be provided with a right to equal treatment after 12 calendar weeks in a given job (regardless of whether this is a full-time or part-time job). A new qualifying period will begin only if a new assignment with the same employer is 'substantially different' or if there is 'a break of more than six weeks' between assignments in the same role.

Anti-avoidance provisions. Agency workers will have grounds for an employment tribunal claim if a structure of assignments develops – the most likely explanation for which is an intention to deprive them of equal treatment rights. For example, rotation between a series of 11-week assignments in 'substantially different' roles with a hirer.

Information. A TWA cannot supply an agency worker to a hirer without certain information. Also, agency workers are entitled to information relating to their equal treatment entitlements (see *Guidance*).

Equal treatment. There are two sets of entitlements:

Day 1 rights for all agency workers: The regulations give agency workers:

- the same access to certain facilities provided by the hirer such as the staff canteen, transport facilities, car parking and child-care facilities; and
- the same information on job vacancies as comparable permanent workers and employees within the hirer's organisation.

After 12 weeks in the same job:

These additional new equal treatment entitlements relate to 'relevant terms and conditions', namely pay and other basic working conditions, and will only come into effect after an agency worker completes a 12-week qualifying period with the same hirer, in the same role.

Pay. This includes:

- *basic pay*, based on the annual salary an agency worker would have received if recruited directly (usually converted into hourly or daily rate, taking into account any pay increments);
- *overtime payments*, subject to requirements regarding the number of qualifying hours;
- *shift/unsocial hours allowances, risk payments for hazardous duties*;
- *payment for annual leave* (above the statutory minimum of 5.6 weeks, at a full-time equivalent rate), which can be added to the hourly or daily rate;
- *bonuses or commission payments*, directly attributable to the amount or quality of the work done by the individual, including where sales or production targets achieved and payments related to quality of personal performance;
- additional discretionary, non-contractual payments that are paid with such regularity that they have become *custom and practice* but which do not fit the excluded types of bonus described below;
- *vouchers or stamps*, which have monetary value and are not 'salary sacrifice schemes' – e.g. luncheon vouchers, child-care vouchers.

Pay **excludes**, among other matters, occupational sick pay and occupational pensions.

Liability. 'The agency will be responsible for any breach of a right in relation to equal treatment for which they are responsible but will have a defence if they have taken "reasonable steps" to obtain the necessary information from the hirer and acted "reasonably" in determining the agency worker's basic working and employment conditions. In such cases the hirer will be liable.'

Remedies. At employment tribunal, these will be compensation for the agency worker's loss – subject to a minimum award provision and the possibility of an additional award when the 'anti-avoidance provision' is breached.

FRISHCO SUPERMARKET CASE STUDY

Scenario 2.2

What rights does Tracey have under the Agency Workers' Regulations?

Tracey works as a part-time assistant to **Debbie**, the Administrative Assistant. She was placed through an employment agency, Instant-Resourcing, 15 weeks ago. There is another part-time assistant, **Indira**, who works different hours and, in fact, the two part-timers normally never meet. However, on one occasion, **Tracey** was asked to work extra hours to help out with a workload peak. She agreed to do this. Her hours overlapped with those of Indira who was also working some overtime. At a lunch break they chatted about working at the company. **Indira** commented that she welcomed the overtime because she needed the extra cash. **Tracey** learned that **Indira** was being paid time and a quarter for each hour of overtime (i.e. £8.00 ph) whereas she was being paid at flat rate (£6.00 ph). **Tracey** had heard about some regulations relating to the equal treatment of agency workers and was looking for some advice on whether or not she might have a claim and so raise a grievance with the agency and with Frischco.

Question

What advice would you, as an HR practitioner, give Tracey about her employment rights?

Visit mylawchamber.co.uk/willey **to access sample HR documents to/support this case study.**

The specific employment protection for migrant agency workers

Many, but certainly not all, legal migrant workers are likely to be covered by British employment legislation. However, at the margins of the labour market there are certain vulnerable groups. One such group are those who work for gangmasters in, for example, agriculture, horticulture, dairy farming, gathering shellfish and related fish processing and packaging. The Gangmasters (Licensing) Act 2004 was enacted to deal with what were described in Parliament as 'unscrupulous rogue gangmasters who are exploiting and intimidating workers, often breaching human rights and engaging in a range of criminal activities such as illegal deductions from wages, failure to pay the minimum wage or sickness pay, tax fraud, human trafficking, smuggling and the supply of drugs' (7 January 2004).

Labour providers in these sectors require a licence and details are available on a public register maintained by the Gangmasters Licensing Authority. The legislation creates two new criminal offences: supplying labour without a licence and using an unlicensed labour provider. Offenders can face up to 10 years in prison. Workers provided by the labour provider (agency) have various employment rights and also protection under discrimination and health and safety legislation (see **www.gla.gov.uk**).

Activity 2.2

'Atypical' workers in your organisation

Check whether or not your organisation employs people who may be defined as 'atypical' workers. Which of the categories outlined above are used? Undertake an audit of a particular small group. It may be helpful to select from the following questions:

- What is the gender and ethnic profile of the staff you have selected?
- What description (from the categories of 'atypical' workers discussed above) would you use for these people?
- Using the common law tests, is the description of their employment status by the employer accurate?
- Is there evidence of mutuality of obligation?
- Is there evidence of a global contract?
- Are any of them provided by an employment agency?
- If so, have any problems arisen from the triangular relationship with the agency? How have they been resolved?
- How do their terms and conditions compare with employees on open-ended contracts of employment?
- Is there any evidence of breaches of discrimination law?
- Would you be recommending any reforms to your employer? What would these be?

Complaints relating to employment contracts

Complaints relating to contracts are likely to fall into one of the following categories:

- *Grievances that certain contractual terms and/or statutory rights have not been complied with.* If the grievance is not satisfactorily dealt with through the internal grievance procedure, most of these issues can be raised as complaints at an employment tribunal (subject, of course, to the complainant's employment status and length of service with the employer). The remedies will be those outlined under the appropriate legislation (see the other chapters in this textbook). It is possible for certain contractual grievances to be raised in the High Court where they do not relate to specific employment rights or discrimination law but rather to specific terms of the contract. Examples can be found in respect of claims concerning restrictive covenants or allegations about unlawful contract variation (*Burdett-Coutts and Others v Hertfordshire County Council* [1984] IRLR 91, HC; *Cresswell and Others v Board of Inland Revenue* [1984] IRLR 190, HC).

- *Unfair dismissal claims* (including those relating to redundancy) which can be made at an employment tribunal – depending on qualifying service (see Chapter 8).

- *Wrongful dismissal claims* which concern the termination of the contract which breaches the terms of that contract including the providing of insufficient notice (see Chapter 8).

Conclusion

The regulation of the employment relationship continues to be subjected to two parallel developments in law. First, statute law is progressively determining a framework of minimum rights which mould the terms of the contract of employment. Other 'contracts to carry out work personally' are also being influenced by statutory requirements. Although these are more limited in scope, they do cover two of the essential bases of an employment relationship: pay (through the national minimum wage and equal pay legislation); and working time regulation. The general political thrust of British and European employment law acknowledges that those in the 'flexible labour market' are entitled to minimum rights and that the general restriction of access to statutory rights to full-time permanent employees has ceased to be defensible. Consequently, legislation is gradually recognising the circumstances of part-time workers, some of those on temporary contracts, in agency work and in homeworking arrangements. Where there are gaps in employment protection, case law is taking some tentative steps towards improvement. However, a principal obstacle is the combined effect of restricting so many employment rights to those with 'employee' status; and the impact of 'mutuality of obligation' in excluding so many 'atypical' workers – particularly, casual workers – from employment protection.

References

Advisory, Conciliation and Arbitration Service (2009) *Code of Practice on Disciplinary and Grievance Procedures*. London: ACAS.

Atkinson, J. (1984) 'Manpower Strategies for Flexible Organisations', *Personnel Management*, August 28–31.

Brodie, D. (1998) 'The Contract for Work', *Scottish Law and Practice Quarterly*, 2.

Burchell, B. *et al.* (1999) *The Employment Status of Individuals in Non-standard Employment*, Employment Relations Research Series 6. London: Department of Trade and Industry.

Cave, K. (1997) *Zero Hours Contracts*. Huddersfield: University of Huddersfield.

Deakin, S. and Morris, G. (1998) *Labour Law*. London: Butterworth.

Department of Trade and Industry (1998) *Fairness at Work*, Cm 3968. London: Stationery Office.

Department of Trade and Industry (2002) *Discussion Document on Employment Status in Relation to Statutory Employment Rights*. London: Department of Trade and Industry.

Dickens, L. (1992) *Whose Flexibility? – Discrimination and Equality Issues in Atypical Work*. London: Institute of Employment Rights.

Handy, C. (1991) *The Age of Unreason*. London: Arrow Business Books.

Information Commissioner (2005) Employment Practices Data Protection Code. (www.ico.gov.uk)

Kahn-Freund, Sir Otto (1983) *Kahn-Freund's Labour and the Law* (P. Davies and M. Freedland, eds). London: Stevens.

Mant, A. (1995) 'Changing Work Roles' in Tyson, S. (ed.). *Strategic Prospects for HRM*. London: Chartered Institute of Personnel and Development.

Schein, G. (1988) *Organisational Psychology*, London: Prentice Hall.

Social Trends 31, *Homeworking by Occupation and Gender, 1996 and 2000*. (www.statistics.gov.uk)

Taylor, R. (2002) *Britain's World of Work – Myths and Realities*. London: Economic and Social Research Council.

Wedderburn, Lord (1986) *The Worker and the Law*. Harmondsworth: Penguin Books.

Useful websites

Gangmasters Licensing Authority **www.gla.gov.uk**

Information Commissioner's Office **www.ico.gov.uk**

UK Statistics Authority **www.statistics.gov.uk**

Visit **www.mylawchamber.co.uk/willey** to access study support resources including realistic HR documentation to accompany the case studies in the book, an online chapter on collective labour law, interactive multiple choice questions, annotated weblinks, a glossary, glossary flashcards, key case flashcards, a legal newsfeed and legal updates.

Chapter 3

Managing change in the employment relationship

Learning objectives

This chapter considers the legal consequences for the employment relationship of changing managerial and employment policies. Having read it you should understand:

- The ways in which terms in contracts of employment might need to be varied to accommodate changing business conditions
- The ways in which an employer might build 'flexibility' into contractual terms
- The circumstances under which an employer might lawfully make staff redundant
- The employment protection conferred on employees in redundancies
- The socio-economic context in which the Transfer of Undertakings (Protection of Employment) Regulations operate
- The employment protection conferred on employees in business transfers

Structure of the chapter

This chapter comprises the following sections:

- *Introduction*
- *The context*: organisational culture; strategic considerations; operational factors; incidence of redundancies; socio-economic context of business transfers; tensions between 'business needs' and legal standards
- *The legal framework*: variation of contracts of employment, flexibility in existing contractual terms, redundancy and redeployment, transfers of undertakings
- *Exercises*: these are located after each of the key sections on the law

Introduction

Changes within organisations, to organisational structures and to employment practices, arise for various economic, technological and, occasionally, political reasons. The ways in which employers respond to change-drivers can be affected by four broad frameworks of employment law relating to:

- variation of contracts of employment;
- 'flexible terms' within contracts of employment;

- redundancy and redeployment of **employees**;

- the transfers of undertakings (i.e. business transfers).

It is important to note that, in some circumstances, all four aspects of law can and do interweave in the day-to-day operation of employment relations.

Having briefly considered the nature of the changing business context, we will look at each of these areas of law in turn.

Context

It is a commonplace to say that management is increasingly the management of change, and that business is always in a state of flux. The principal drivers of change are pressures to compete more effectively in product markets; trends in the global economy; the consequences of government economic policy; the need to respond to technological changes in product manufacture, service delivery, information storage and communication; and the need to achieve satisfactory standards of quality. Additionally, changes may be a consequence of political decisions. Examples include the operation of public–private partnerships; the shifting of government funding and subsidies; the reorganisation and privatisation of public organisations.

Whatever the source of the change, there are several aspects that should be taken into account when considering the impact of change on employment relations. These, to a greater or lesser extent, have implications in law. They are: the organisation's culture; strategic considerations; operational factors; aspects of the economic context; and the tensions between business needs and legal requirements. We will look at each of these in turn.

▶ Organisational culture

The culture of a particular organisation may be difficult to define. Indeed it might be argued that, in some organisations, no *single* culture exists. Culture has been described as 'the characteristic spirit and belief of an organisation, demonstrated, for example, in the norms and values that are generally held about how people should behave and treat each other, the nature of the working relationships that should be developed and attitudes to change. These norms are deep, taken-for-granted, assumptions, which are not always expressed, and are often known without being understood' (Torrington and Hall 1998: 100). Clearly, there is a strong connection with the 'psychological contract' (see Chapter 2).

Cultural norms develop over a long period of time. They can and do, for example, mould recruitment and selection policies, day-to-day working practices and attitudes to reward systems. They can pose significant barriers to change – particularly in rooting out discriminatory treatment and patterns of harassment; and also where there are business transfers. Many large organisations have reputations for promoting 'cultural change'. This is seen by chief executives and senior management as a means of eradicating what are perceived to be inefficient practices and failures to achieve corporate business objectives. Given the entrenched nature of cultures, change programmes can encounter consider-able difficulties. Indeed, there is likely to be a cultural clash between what is believed by senior managers to be the new formal culture and the traditional cultural norms that staff aim to preserve. It may be that a 'counter-culture' emerges.

The extent to which an organisation's culture can facilitate change is particularly dependent upon the effectiveness of the techniques of communication, persuasion and consultation within that organisation.

▶ Strategic considerations

'Strategy' is a term frequently used in management texts in an approving way. It is an *integrative* process that involves *planning*. Strategic decisions have a medium to long-term perspective and are likely to have major resource implications. They bring together data and assessments from a wide range of organisational activities (production or service delivery, marketing, finance, employment relations, etc.). As a result of the fluidity of the business context, strategies are implemented in a context of ongoing uncertainty and risk. Finally, the outcome of strategic decision-making tends to involve significant change in the size, equipment, staffing arrangements or other aspects of the organisa-tion's physical and human resources. So, to have any prospect of success, a change in management strategy has to take account of various relevant factors: organisational culture; internal 'politics' (i.e. power structures – both formal and informal); the nature and degree of actual or potential resistance to change; ways of achieving economic and operational outcomes; and whether changes are legally compliant.

▶ Operational factors

In dealing with the management of change, the repercussions of particular changes need to be anticipated and considered. This is particularly so when operational changes are initiated. One example will illustrate the wide range of possible consequences. If an organisation is considering the installation of new, more technologically advanced, equipment there are various implications:

- *Economic factors*: e.g. the cost of purchase; the effect on unit costs and unit labour costs; the impact on product market competitiveness.

- *Operational*: e.g. the organisation of work, the working practices to be adopted; the redefinition of jobs; staffing levels; the scheduling of working time.

- *Health and safety*: compliance with the employer's general duties in law and with any appropriate specific regulations.

- *Employment relations*: i.e. requirements to consult about changes; whether redundancy or redeployment is proposed; consequences for terms in contracts of employment; impact on payment systems; consequences for working practices and for the schedul-ing of working time.

So, a coherent implementation plan should enable likely difficulties to be anticipated and appropriate action to be taken.

Finally, one particular aspect of operational factors, relevant to contractual change, is the nature and extent of 'flexibility' in the way work is undertaken. The flexibilities that are likely to arise are mobility and working from and at home (*geographic flexibility*); the schedule of working time or *temporal flexibility* (e.g. annualised hours contracts, overtime working, shift working, part-time working, **job share**, weekend working and flexitime); payments by results and performance-related pay (*reward flexibility*); and *functional flexibility* (i.e. requirements to undertake a variety of tasks) (Atkinson 1984) (see Chapter 2).

The economic context

For the purposes of this chapter, there are two broad aspects: the extent to which staff are made redundant; and the socio-economic and political context of business transfers.

▶ Incidence of redundancies

During the period 1997–2007, a period of labour market growth, the quarterly statistics recorded between 111,000 and 196,000 redundancies. In the first quarter of 2009, the figure peaked at 299,000. The most recent figures for the equivalent quarter were 176,000 (2010) and 123,000 (2011) (**www.statistics.gov.uk**). The spread of redundancies varied across industrial sectors. Using Standard Industrial Classification the percentage of redundancies was highest in 'wholesale, retail and vehicle repair' at 16.5 per cent; in 'professional scientific and technical services' at 13.8 per cent; and in 'construction' at 13.6 per cent. It was lowest in 'manufacturing' at 9.6 per cent. There were none recorded for 'finance and insurance and real estate'. Obviously, this is a snapshot at a particular time and future statistics will reflect prevailing economic conditions.

In terms of gender, the Office for National Statistics (ONS) *Labour Force Survey* reported that, of the 123,000 people (2011 Q1) 79,000 were men and 44,000 were women. In respect of age, the figures recorded the following (see Table 3.1).

An important consideration when reviewing redundancy statistics is the issue of re-employment. The ONS *Labour Force Survey* recorded the following situation for 2011 (Q1): the re-employment rate for men was 25.2 per cent; and for women was 30.9 per cent. In terms of age, the only re-engagement was in the 35–49 age bracket – at 31.8 per cent. In 2010, the 25–34 age group found re-employment. But, in 2010 and 2011, there was a nil return for both the 16–24 year group and the 50-plus group. (This rate is the percentage of those made redundant in the previous three months who were in employment during the survey reference week. It is not seasonally adjusted.) Again, these statistics provide a snapshot which can change.

As far as redundancy pay is concerned Wedlake Bell, the City law firm reported, following a Freedom of Information Act request to HMRC, that for 2011 the expected redundancy settlement would £9,362. Its Head of Employment, David Israel commented that 'on average businesses have been paying far more than the minimum redundancy

Table 3.1 **Percentage of those redundant by age**

	16–24 years	*25–34 years*	*35–49 years*	*50 years and above*
2011	20.1	24.1	30.7	25.1
2010	17.5	29.1	29.4	24.0
2009	22.9	25.2	32.7	19.2

First quarter figures – *not* seasonally adjusted.
Source: Office for National Statistics, *Labour Force Survey* (**www.statistics.gov.uk**)

payments that they are required to pay by law' (**www.wedlakebell.com**). Three reasons were suggested for this:

● helping to maintain morale of existing staff and preserve the employer's reputation for looking after staff;

● the scale of redundancies suggests that employers are having to shed staff they would prefer to keep;

● to help prevent employees from making unfair dismissal claims. Higher redundancy payments are often offered on the basis that the employee agrees not to pursue any legal claims against the employer. [No doubt, in a compromise agreement – Chapter 8.]

▶ Socio-economic and political context of business transfers

There are several aspects to this:

Mergers and acquisitions

These now play a significant part in the UK economy. The ONS has recorded the following (see Table 3.2):

Table 3.2 **Number of mergers and acquisitions involving UK companies**

	Acquisitions abroad by UK companies	*Acquisitions in the UK by foreign companies*	*Acquisitions in the UK by UK companies*
2011 Q1 provisional	48	38	60
2010	199	212	325
2009	118	112	286

Source: Office for National Statistics: *Statistical Bulletin*, 7 June 2011 (**www.statistics.gov.uk**)

Clearly, substantial numbers of employees are potentially affected by such transactions in respect of possible rationalisation of workforces and redundancies, harmonisation and variation of terms and conditions of employment, and obligations under business transfers legislation.

Outsourcing

Outsourcing has been defined as circumstances 'where an organisation passes the provision of a service or execution of a task, previously undertaken in-house, to a third party to perform on its behalf' (Reilly *et al.* 1996). It is far from being a new economic activity. In the sixteenth century Machiavelli, the Italian political philosopher, in *The Prince* criticised a form of military outsourcing – the employment of mercenaries – on the ground that 'there is no loyalty or inducement to keep them on the field apart from the little they are paid and this is not enough to make them die for you'.

Since the late 1970s, the scale of outsourcing, subcontracting or contracting has grown significantly. These practices now play an important part in the organisation of most firms. Within public services, some commentators argue that we are witnessing the emergence of a 'contract state'. This is where public services are organised around market relations and commercial contracts between purchasers and providers. So, the state has a lesser role in providing services but a greater role in co-ordinating and monitoring service delivery through contracts (Collings 1999; Timmins 2005). Areas such as health care, criminal justice and the military now see the private sector playing an increasingly prominent role in the delivery of public services (Sachdev 2006). The Conservative–Liberal Democrat government has shown a strong commitment to expand such policies further as part of its deficit reduction strategy and its ideological objective to reduce the nature and scope of state activity and, consequently, cut public expenditure.

Disquiet at some of the implications of outsourcing – especially loss of knowledge and control – has led one commentator to argue that 'there are signs everywhere that the outsourcing fashion has gone too far' (Shapinker 2003, 2005). Controversy has dogged certain forms of outsourcing including the school meals service, gangmaster labour, hospital cleaning and the organisation of the railways.

As far as the Transfer of Undertakings (Protection of Employment) Regulations 2006 (TUPE) are concerned, these may have prevented (or at least played a key role in preventing) a more extensive or even wholesale privatisation of the Prison Service. Private sector involvement was eventually more modest and piecemeal (see Exhibit 3.1). TUPE acted as an effective countervailing force to the deregulatory labour market ideology of the Conservative government and (in significantly modified form) the New Labour government.

Incidence of outsourcing

Evidence is reported in the Workplace Employment Relations Survey (WERS) 2004 (Kersley *et al.* 2006). Managers in organisations employing 10 or more staff were asked whether independent contracts provided any of 11 services. In 86 per cent of private-sector

---

EXHIBIT 3.1

TUPE and the prison service

According to Derek Lewis, the former Director General of the Prison Service, Sir Peter Levene (the efficiency adviser of Prime Minister John Major) 'believed that the *whole* service could be contracted out to the private sector'. It was only the re-interpretation of TUPE by the European Court of Justice that prevented the (then) Home Secretary, Kenneth Clarke, from 'privatising up to twenty prisons at a stroke. It is, also, obviously, another reason why only the private sector is being allowed to bid for newly built prisons' (Ryan 1994).

When it was discovered that TUPE applied to the prison service, Lewis says that 'disaster struck'. In a leaked letter the Home Secretary said: 'In relation to prison education services, my view is that the consequences of the [TUPE] case are very damaging because we stand to lose almost all the efficiency and cost savings achieved if all existing staff have to be taken on by new contractors on their present terms and conditions' (cited in Foley 1994).

Sir Richard Tilt, Director General (1995–2000) highlighted the impact of TUPE in limiting the scope of privatisation: 'At the time I was involved in it we on the whole were not enthusiastic about [private sector providers running existing prisons] mainly because, well I think TUPE was one problem, we couldn't really see how the private sector people were necessarily going to make huge inroads into the way in which the prison was run if they had to take on existing staff and their existing conditions.'

workplaces and 87 per cent of those in the public sector 'at least one' of these services was contracted out. The key findings were:

- *The incidence of contracting out*: building maintenance (in 59 per cent of workplaces); cleaning (52 per cent); training (34 per cent); transport of documents or goods (29 per cent); security (29 per cent); payroll (28 per cent).

- *Reasons for contracting out*: cost savings (47 per cent); improved service (43 per cent); focus on core activities (30 per cent).

- Within human resource activities, the scale of outsourcing is significant although the extent of it appears to have levelled out (1998 figures in brackets):
  - 34 per cent of workplace outsourced training (34 per cent);
  - 28 per cent outsourced payroll (19 per cent);
  - 16 per cent outsourced temporary filling of vacant posts (22 per cent);
  - 12 per cent outsourced recruitment (12 per cent).

▶ Tensions between 'business need' and legal standards

The legal framework which is discussed in this chapter is, then, set in the context of often rapid and substantial organisational and operational change. Given the speed of response demanded by employers, it is not surprising that attempts may be made to short-circuit or, perhaps, deliberately ignore legal obligations. Also, in some instances, with the growing complexity of legal requirements, employers may not fully understand the 'juridification' of employment relations that has been taking place since the 1970s. So, at the heart of the management of change, there is likely to be a tension between, on the one hand, the economic imperatives of business and, on the other hand, employees' interests (for example, in respect of job and income security and fair treatment).

Activity 3.1

The employment consequences of organisational change

Draw up a list of the changes that your organisation has experienced in the past 12 months (and may be still experiencing). Are these a consequence of technological, economic or political factors? What impact have they had on the organisation's structure and way of working?

Using the sections below on the legal framework as your guide, as appropriate, think about:

- the impact of changes on employees' terms and conditions of employment and whether they were changed;
- whether any employment changes could be accommodated under existing terms of contracts of employment;
- whether any redundancies occurred and how they were handled;
- whether the changes experienced occurred within a 'transfer situation' and how this was managed.

How would you assess the effectiveness of your organisation's employee relations/human resources functions in dealing with the changes? What lessons could be learned?

The legal framework

Four aspects of the law relating to business and organisational change are examined:

- **Flexibility available with existing contracts of employment.** This covers situations where the existing terms of a contract of employment have sufficient flexibility to help an employer achieve operational objectives (e.g. relating to the mobility of staff; or the range of tasks an employee carries out).

- **Variation of contractual terms.** This concerns those circumstances where an employer wishes to change an existing term or terms of a contract of employment (e.g. pay or hours of work).

- **Redundancy and redeployment.** This concerns employers' policies to reduce and reorganise workforces because of changing business circumstances.

- **Transfers of undertakings.** This relates to the protection of an employee's existing terms and conditions of employment when the undertaking they work for is transferred to another organisation.

▶ Flexibility within the contract of employment

Changes to contracts of employment are extremely common because a contract is agreed at a particular point in time. However, an organisation is likely to experience, sometimes considerable, changes over time: in the technology used; in its product market; in terms of the skills and competences needed; to respond to competition and so on. Consequently, a contract of employment cannot remain static. It will need to be adapted to new circumstances. Some changes are beneficial to the employee (e.g. pay increases, increased holidays and shorter working hours). Other changes, of course, can be adverse (e.g. relocation and redeployment, pay cuts, increased working time).

However, rather than changing contractual terms, some employers may be able to respond to operational changes by using terms of existing contracts of employment to implement changes to working practices. There is evidence from case law of the use of both *implied* terms (e.g. the **duty** to obey lawful and reasonable instructions) and *express* terms (e.g. a mobility clause, a flexible working hours clause, or a general variation clause).

Implied terms

An important illustration is seen in a case from the early 1980s which, in terms of law, is still applicable today (*Cresswell and Others* v *Board of Inland Revenue* [1984] IRLR 190). It involved the computerisation of certain clerical and administrative tasks which hitherto had been performed manually. In this case, the trade union concerned claimed that the employer had breached the employees' contracts of employment by requiring them to use the new computerised technology. However, it was ruled in the High Court that the employer's instruction was lawful and reasonable and so was consistent with the contracts of employment.

Mr Justice Walton stated that employees could not conceivably have the right to preserve their working obligations completely unchanged during their employment. They could reasonably be expected, after proper training, to adapt to new techniques. All that would happen with the computerisation was that jobs would remain 'recognisably the same but done in a different way'. However, this ruling does not give the employer free rein. Each case would be considered by the tribunal or court on its merits to decide whether or not the employer was 'reasonable'. It is also likely that the implied duty to obey lawful and reasonable instructions would apply only to work practices and related *operational* issues.

It is also accepted that each contract of employment has an implied duty on the employee to co-operate with the employer. This irreducible minimum of co-operation includes an obligation not to obstruct technological change or changes to work organisation. However, with contractual terms relating to pay, employee benefits and hours cannot be overridden by invoking the duty to co-operate. Essentially, these can only be changed by engaging in the process of variation.

Express terms

There are several examples of these.

Mobility clauses and place of work

At the heart of mobility clauses in contracts of employment is the implied term of mutual trust and confidence. Effectively, courts and tribunals consider the nature of the provisions of a mobility clause; its application to the circumstances of an employee's employment; and the consequences for the employee. In implementing the mobility clause the employer should be reasonable. If the employer's conduct is not reasonable, then mutual trust and confidence may be breached and there can be a consequential repudiation of the contract of employment. The employee may, then, resign and claim **constructive dismissal** (see Exhibit 3.2 and also Exhibit 2.7 dealing with *United Bank* v *Akhtar* [1989] IRLR 507, EAT).

Transfers between posts

The Court of Appeal has held that when an employer acts within the contract, the fact that loss is thereby caused to the employee does not render that action a breach of contract (*Spafax Ltd* v *Harrison* [1980] IRLR 442). However, a malicious or grossly unfair transfer could amount to a breach of mutual trust and confidence. Various other cases, relating to express terms, illustrate the potential for flexibility. For example, in *Bex* v *Securicor Transport Ltd* [1972] IRLR 68, the nature of the employee's work was changed. Although he regarded this as a demotion, it was found that the company was expressly entitled to require him to carry out these duties. There was no repudiation of contract. In other cases, the transfer might be subject to a proviso. So, in *White* v *Reflecting Roadstones* [1991] ICR 733, EAT, redeployment to a less well-paid job was permissible provided operational efficiency made it necessary. In *Risk Management Services (Chiltern) Ltd* v *Shrimpton* [1977] EAT 803/77, short notices of changes in shift and duties had to be 'in an emergency'.

▶ Variation of contract

The critical question for an employer is: *how is a contract of employment varied lawfully?* In answering this question, it is important to remember that a contract of employment is an agreement and, therefore, it cannot be changed arbitrarily by the employer. Broadly, there are three alternative courses of action available to employers who wish to make contractual changes:

EXHIBIT 3.2

Mobility clauses

An express mobility clause

Home Office v Evans and another [2008] IRLR 59, CA

Facts. Mr Evans and Mr Laidlaw were employed as immigration officers at Waterloo International Terminal. It was announced that this was to close on 13 May 2004. The employer proposed to transfer staff who had an express mobility clause in their contracts of employment (to work anywhere in the UK or abroad) to positions that met its operational needs. Evans and Laidlaw refused to engage in consultation and in August 2004 they were told that they would be transferred to Heathrow airport. They resigned claiming constructive dismissal.

Court of Appeal ruling. It agreed that the Home Office had a choice about whether to invoke the contractual mobility clause to avoid redundancy dismissals or to implement the agreed redundancy procedure. The employer did not propose dismissals; was able to transfer staff under the terms of their contracts; and, in fact, chose this course of action. The instruction to the staff to relocate was not a breach of the contract of employment.

An implied mobility clause

Courtaulds Northern Spinning Ltd v Sibson and the Transport and General Workers' Union [1988] IRLR 305, CA

A heavy goods vehicle driver was transferred from one depot to another a mile away. There was no express term within his contract of employment. The Court of Appeal ruled that this transfer did not breach his contract because there was an *implied* term that the employee could be transferred anywhere within reasonable commuting distance of his home. His constructive dismissal claim failed. Having ruled on the facts and circumstances of this particular case, the Court emphasised that each case will depend on its own facts.

Moving departments

BPCC Purnell Ltd v Webb EAT 129/1990

The employee was transferred from one pre-press department of a printing company to another. Because of the different nature of shift working in the new department, he was likely to lose £80 per week in earnings. His employment contract contained a clause requiring 'total flexibility between all pre-press departments'. The EAT, finding unfair constructive dismissal, stated that this term must not be used in such a way to destroy mutual trust and confidence. The £80 reduction in weekly wages out of a total of £305 was unacceptable and was a clear breach of the term.

- **Consensual variation**: The employer attempt to make the changes by discussion and agreement with the employees concerned, either individually or through trade union or other employee representatives.
- **Contractual authority**: They may have the authority as the employer to make contractual changes as explicitly stated within the contracts of employment.
- **Termination of contract**: The employer may terminate the existing contract, after consultation and with due notice (i.e. whatever a particular individual is entitled to)

and offer a new contract embodying the changed terms and conditions of employment (see also Chapter 8).

It is important to remember that there are particular provisions in law where the variation takes place in a 'transfer situation' (Transfer of Undertakings (Protection of Employment) Regulations 2006, regs 4 and 9) (see later section in this chapter).

Consensual variation

This refers to agreed changes to contractual terms (see Exhibit 3.3). This agreement can be by the individual employee or through a collective agreement with a trade union. This may be express agreement – clear and unequivocal in writing; or it may be implied by the behaviour of the employee. The courts, on occasion, have been reluctant to find implied consent particularly where the effect of the contractual change has no immediate effect.

EXHIBIT 3.3

Consensual variation: guidance

In order to achieve **consensual variation**, good practice suggests that a number of steps should be considered by the employer:

- Consider whether the changes relate to specific contractual terms or may concern lawful and reasonable instructions.
- Provide information about the proposed contractual changes to each affected employee.
- Be prepared to discuss, consult and/or – if unionised – negotiate.
- Try to obtain the employee's consent. This might involve making some concessions or offering 'consideration'.
- Be prepared to justify contractual changes against the organisation's operational requirements and business needs.
- Anticipate the arguments that might be put at a court or tribunal – for example, in terms of the scale of the change and the issue of reasonableness.
- Check to ensure that none of the proposed changes infringe statutory employment rights or discrimination and equality law (see Chapters 5 and 6).
- Check whether the affected employees are not protected by the Transfer of Undertaking (Protection of Employment) Regulations 2006 (see later section in this chapter).

So, for example, if an employer imposes a pay cut and the employee continues working without objection, then, because the change has 'immediate practical application', the employee could be taken to have impliedly agreed (*Jones* v *Associated Tunnelling Co Ltd* [1981] IRLR 477, EAT). In contrast, in a case involving the implementation of a mobility clause some five years after it had been introduced (*Anglia Regional Cooperative Society* v *O'Donnell* EAT 655/1991), the EAT ruled that the fact that the employee had continued to work after 1987 did not necessarily mean that she had agreed to the mobility clause which was not applied to her until 1992.

Variations can be agreed through a recognised trade union which has authority to negotiate collective agreements covering particular groups of staff. Usually, appropriate terms of collective agreements are expressly incorporated into contracts of employment (see Chapter 2 in relation to '**incorporation**'). An employer may include a phrase in contractual information saying that an individual's terms and conditions are 'as negotiated from time to time by XYZ Union'. The employee (whether or not he or she is a union member) is bound by an agreement reached with the union, regardless of whether he or she agrees to it. If there is no express incorporation, then it might be implied by **custom and practice**. If a collective agreement is rescinded by the employer, then any relevant terms of a collective agreement can 'live on' in the individual employee's contract of employment. (See the Court of Appeal's ruling in *Robertson and Jackson v British Gas Corporation* [1983] IRLR 202 outlined in Chapter 2.)

It is important to remember that the contractual terms that may be incorporated are most likely to be those relating to an individual's terms and conditions of employment. Other provisions of collective agreements may be more problematic. The Court of Appeal has ruled on the status of a 'no compulsory redundancy' agreement (*Kaur v MG Rover Group Ltd* [2005] IRLR 40). It stated that the job security provision of a collective agreement which included the words, 'There will be no compulsory redundancy', when construed in the context of the agreement as a whole was no more than 'a statement of collective aspiration' and was not appropriate to be incorporated into individual contracts of employment. The Court of Appeal took an interesting view on this issue in a subsequent case (see Exhibit 3.4).

Contractual authority

An employer might attempt to implement changes using a term in the existing contract. There must, then, be contractual authority and some residue of consultation otherwise the consequential changes could constitute a breach of contract. Three issues have arisen in cases involving this kind of employer action:

- Whether a **general variation clause** exists in the contract.
- Whether there is some other specific **contractual authority** for the employer-imposed changes.
- Whether the changes can be characterised as a **unilateral variation** of contract and, possibly, a breach of mutal trust and confidence.

EXHIBIT 3.4

'Apt for incorporation' but . . .

Malone and Others v British Airways plc [2011] **IRLR 32, CA**

The Court of Appeal ruled on a collective agreement between British Airways plc and UNITE, the trade union. BA had unilaterally reduced crew complements on its aircraft below the agreed levels. The Court stated that the provision in the agreement was 'apt for incorporation' in that it related to working conditions (i.e. relating to cabin crew complements). However, the Court took the view that there would be 'disastrous consequences' for the business if this provision were to be *individually* enforceable. It ruled that the provision was intended by the employer as an undertaking towards its cabin crew employees collectively and not to be incorporated into individual contracts of employment. It was 'binding in honour' only.

General variation clause

A wide-ranging clause in contracts of employment enabling the employer to change all contractual terms is unlikely to be enforceable. It is doubtful whether an agreement including such a term could be a contract at all. There would be, in effect, no agreement on the terms of the contract. In one case where there was a general express term, the EAT ruled that it would not permit substantial changes but only those of a minor and non-fundamental nature (*United Association for the Protection of Trade Ltd* v *Kilburn* EAT787/84). To use such a clause, the employer must give notice of the proposed change and be prepared to consult.

Some other contractual authority: a staff handbook

There are few examples of this, but one recent case illustrates a possible way in which such an approach may be lawful (see Exhibit 3.5).

Unilateral variation

Consent to proposed contractual changes is, of course, not always forthcoming. Unilateral variation arises where an employer imposes a contractual change (either because agreement cannot be reached on the variation or because there has been no attempt at discussion to try and reach agreement). In most cases, this is unlawful. So, where an employer imposes a pay cut without consultation and agreement, he or she is in breach of contract. Even if the employer has good economic reasons for reducing labour costs, the courts will hold the employer to the existing contracts; and (as in *Burdett-Coutts and Others* v *Hertfordshire County Council* [1984] IRLR 91, HC) award **damages** in the form of back-pay to the employees concerned.

Employees faced with unlawful unilateral variation have four possible courses of action:

- to work under protest;
- to accept the new contractual terms;

EXHIBIT 3.5

The staff handbook and contractual authority

Bateman and Others v *ASDA Stores* [2010] **UKEAT/0221/09**

Facts. ASDA attempted to harmonise the terms and conditions of employment of a group of staff who refused to agree to a new pay structure.

Employment Appeal Tribunal ruling. That a broad contractual right to alter terms and conditions of employment in line with business needs (which was set out in the Company's Staff Handbook) permitted the employer to make unilateral changes to contractual terms (including pay rates and hours of work) without the need for the express consent of employees.

This handbook was incorporated into the contracts of employment of staff. It stated that *'the company reserves the right to review, revise, amend or replace the content of this handbook and introduce new policies from time to time to reflect the changing needs of the business and to comply with new legislation.'* The power of the employer to amend, in these circumstances, can extend beyond the right to alter non-contractual policies to cover changes to terms of the contract – without gaining further consent.

The proviso is that the changes are properly implemented and the employer acts in compliance with the implied duty to maintain trust and confidence. In this case there had been considerable consultation and no evidence of a breach of mutual trust and confidence.

- make a claim for unlawful deduction of wages if appropriate (Employment Rights Act 1996, Part II) (see also Chapter 9);
- to resign, alleging a repudiatory breach of contract, and claim constructive dismissal (if they qualify in terms of employment status and length of service).

Working under protest

For an employee, this is one response to unilateral variation. The employee continues to work – but 'under protest'; and he or she holds the employer to the original contract. In *Rigby* v *Ferodo* [1988] IRLR 517 (a case involving the imposition of a pay cut), the House of Lords outlined the essential elements of 'working under protest':

- The employer's action amounted to a repudiatory breach of contract but not to termination of the contract.
- The employees had not accepted the employer's proposed changes in terms and conditions of employment.
- The employees were entitled to sue for the difference between the amount of wages they should have received and that which they had in fact received.
- As long as there is a continuing contract, not terminated by either side, the employer will remain liable for any shortfall in contractual wages.
- If the employer wants to limit liability, he must bring the contract to an end, although in doing so, he will run the risk of unfair dismissal claims.

Acceptance of the new terms by the employee

An employer might impose a unilateral variation and the employee(s) might impliedly consent – in that they do not protest and continue to work under the new terms and conditions. As indicated earlier, there can be uncertainty about how reliable an employee's agreement is in these circumstances.

A constructive dismissal claim

This might arise if the employee takes the view that the employer's conduct (e.g. imposing a pay cut) is such that it fundamentally breaches the contract of employment. In these circumstances, the employee may resign and, subject to having the appropriate length of continuous service, may claim unfair constructive dismissal at an employment tribunal. In the leading case, Lord Denning described the circumstances in which repudiation of a contract can arise in the following terms: 'If the employer is guilty of conduct which is a significant breach going to the root of the contract of employment, or which shows that the employer no longer intends to be bound by one or more of the essential terms of the contract, then the employee is entitled to treat himself as discharged from any further performance . . . The conduct must . . . be sufficiently serious to entitle him to leave at once . . .' (*Western Excavating (ECC) Ltd* v *Sharp* [1978] IRLR 27, CA). Clearly, pay is an essential term of the contract. The imposition of a pay cut without consent would go 'to the root of the contract'.

Terminating existing contracts and fair dismissal

If an employer wishes to change existing contracts and, in particular, encounters difficulties in reaching an agreed variation, it is possible to terminate the existing contract and offer a new one including the changed terms. Such a termination will be a dismissal in law.

So, to avoid the possibility of an allegation of unfair dismissal and an employment tribunal complaint, the employer must ensure that various steps are complied with:

- *Reason for the dismissal.* This is likely to be 'business need' and would be 'some other substantial reason for dismissal' (Employment Rights Act 1996 s 98) (see Exhibits 3.6 and 3.7); and the reasonableness of the employer's decision to dismiss (*Garnside and Laycock Ltd v Booth*, EAT/0003/11).

EXHIBIT 3.6

Hollister and the National Farmers' Union

Hollister v *National Farmers' Union* [1979] **IRLR 238, CA**

Facts. Mr Hollister was employed by the National Farmers' Union as a group secretary in Cornwall. To rectify anomalies between group secretaries throughout the country, the employer terminated the contracts of employment of the Cornish group secretaries and offered them new contracts on the same terms as those employed elsewhere. In most respects, Mr Hollister would have been better off. However, his pension rights would have been reduced. He refused the new contract and complained of unfair dismissal.

Judgment. The case, on appeal, eventually reached the Court of Appeal and became a 'leading' case in this area of law. The Court rejected his claim of unfair dismissal. It accepted that the reorganisation of the business was 'some other substantial reason' for dismissal. Since this case, employment tribunals have usually accepted 'business need' as some other substantial reason for dismissal – provided the employer adduced evidence to show why the changes were required. 'Reasonableness' in handling the whole process is also expected with the employer showing that the employee's interests have been considered and that reasonable procedures have been followed before the employer insisted on the adoption of the changes.

EXHIBIT 3.7

6,500 redundancy notices

'Shropshire Council has handed redundancy notices to its 6,500-strong workforce, informing them that they will be re-hired the next day if they agree to a 5.4% pay cut.

'The council said that the move would eventually reduced its staffing bill by £7 million per year and help it to cope with a total buget reduction of £76 million over the next three years. The alternative was "large scale redundancies which would involve the loss of at least 400 jobs and have a detrimental effect on frontline services for local people" it added.

'Jackie Kelly, head of organisational development at the council, said that the decision to terminate employment contracts from 30 September 2011 was reached after failure to reach a collective agreement with the unions. "The council is following a legal process in order to introduce changes to terms and conditions which is known as dismissal and re-engagement", she said. "We are continuing to meet with the unions to see if there is still a possibility of getting a collective agreement, before 30 September, to implement the necessary changes."

'The new terms and conditions of employment offered to council workers also include reductions in the rate of sick pay and an increase in annual leave.'

© *Personnel Today*, 6 July 2011.

- *Consultation.* The House of Lords ruled (in *Polkey* v *AE Dayton Services* [1987] IRLR 503) that there should be consultation before dismissal unless it was pointless. The ACAS *Code of Practice on Disciplinary and Grievance Procedures* (2009) recommends consultation; and it is expected as good employment practice. If the termination involves 20 or more people then the collective redundancy requirement to consult is invoked (TULRCA 1992, s 195).

- *Due notice.* The employer must give the amount of notice to terminate the contract that the individual employee is entitled to under the contract of employment and bearing in mind the statutory minima (Employment Rights Act 1996, s 86). Failure to do this could lead to a wrongful dismissal claim.

Exercise 3.1 Contract variation

Read these scenarios and decide:

- *Which legal issues do you think might be involved?*

- *What would you recommend to the employer as ways of dealing with the issues – taking account of both law and good human resource practice?*

3.1.1 Samantha is employed as an assistant in the Gateshead branch of Listeria Foods. On Friday, her manager tells her that from the following Monday she is to work at the Newcastle branch, some four miles away.

3.1.2 Locksmith Engineering in Birmingham has been in severe financial difficulties over the past six months. As part of its response for dealing with the problems, the owner has decided not to award a pay increase from 1 April this coming year.

3.1.3 Administrators in the admission department of Polygon University in the north-west of England have been instructed to implement a new and complex computerised system of student records. This replaces a system that has been in place for the past six years. Beryl, an experienced administrator who is two years away from retirement, is unhappy about the change. She has refused to attend the required training course.

3.1.4 Jamila works as a retail assistant in a large department store in Swansea. As a result of a change in company policy, she is required to ask all customers who did not have a company store card whether they would like information on the scheme. Increasingly, she comes to dislike this aspect of her work. She does not see it as a task that she is employed to do. She also resents the disparaging comments of the customers about the high rates of interest charged. She tells her manager that she is thinking of resigning and that a friend has told her that she could claim constructive dismissal.

Feedback on these exercises is provided in the Appendix to this textbook.

FRISHCO SUPERMARKET CASE STUDY

Scenario 3.1

Contract changes

As part of its business strategy to improve cost-effectiveness and promote flexibility, Frishco are proposing to change the scheduling of working hours of the Team Leaders, **Winston**, **Ashley**, **Sandra** and **Naomi** and the work that they undertake. Usually, they work from 7am–4pm (Monday–Friday) with a lunch break of an hour – a total of 40 hours per week. This enables them to be available to supervise at the peak time when deliveries arrive and the produce is brought to the shop floor and the shelves are replenished. During the times when the Team Leaders are not available, the Deputy Manager on duty will oversee their responsibilities. It is rare for there to be deliveries late in the day or at weekends – but there may be issues with the replenishing of stock. Deputy Managers have no contracted hours.

It is known by the company that **Winona**, a Deputy Manager, is likely to be moving to another store (see Scenario 5.2) and Frishco are considering not replacing her. If they are to make an appointment it might be of another Team Leader rather than a Deputy Manager. However, prior to that decision, it has been decided by **Caroline**, the HR Manager, that there need to be changes in the way in which Team Leaders work.

The four Team Leaders have been given a document outlining the following plans:

- Each product area is to be 'partnered' with another: 'fresh fruit and vegetables' with 'meat and fish products'; and 'dairy, yoghurts and desserts' with 'general groceries'. The relevant Team Leaders are to familiarise themselves with the jobs of their 'partners' and be able to cover for their 'partner' on an 'as and when basis'.

- Working hours are to be changed. To ensure that the store is properly ready for customers when it opens, there will be an early shift (between 6.30am and 2.30pm); and a late shift (between 12 noon and 8pm). The one hour lunch break would be retained. The total working hours would, however, be reduced to 35 per week and pay would be reduced accordingly. (Team Leaders receive an hourly rate of £15.) It is planned that a shift rota will be drawn up so that normally, each week, three Team Leaders would cover the early shift, and one would undertake the late shift.

The Team Leaders met after work in the local pub to discuss the plan. They all agreed that the company cannot do what is planned and that they should do something about it. They arrange a meeting with Caroline to discuss their concerns. She has asked them to itemise those issues where they think the company is breaking their contracts of employment and not behaving lawfully.

Question

What could be the issues that the Team Leaders might raise with Caroline which could have some legal implications?

What advice would you give Caroline both about how she might respond and, also, to support her view that the company has the legal authority to make the changes?

If the Team Leaders cannot satisfactorily resolve their complaints, what action at employment tribunal might they take?

Visit mylawchamber.co.uk/willey **to access sample HR documents to support this case study.**

▶ Redundancy and redeployment

Redundancy is a potentially 'fair' reason for dismissal (Employment Rights Act 1996, s 98(2)(c). The law influencing the conduct of redundancy programmes, however, also comes from other sources as described below. There are several key aspects to the law on redundancy that we will consider in this chapter:

- the definition of redundancy;
- tests of redundancies;
- 'establishment';
- selection 'pools';
- the criteria for selection;
- the use of alternative employment strategies;
- the right to time off work;
- consultation and information disclosure about redundancies
  - collective consultation
  - individual consultation;
- notice of dismissal;
- the availability of redundancy pay.

Definition

A person is dismissed for reason of redundancy:

- If the dismissal is 'wholly or mainly attributable' to 'the fact that his employer has ceased or intends to cease (i) to carry on business for the purposes of which the employee was employed by him, or (ii) to carry on that business in the place where the employee was employed' (ERA 1996, s 139(1)(a)).
- Alternatively, if the reason for the dismissal is 'wholly or mainly attributable' to 'the fact that the requirements of that business (i) for employees to carry out work of a particular kind or (ii) for employees to carry out work of a particular kind in the place where the employee was employed by the employer, have ceased or diminished or are expected to cease or diminish' (ERA 1996, s 139(1)(b)).

Tests of redundancies

Two important sets of tests have been before the courts to determine the question of whether a person is actually redundant: the geographical *v* contract test; and the function *v* contract test.

Geographical v contract test

The 'geographical' test obviously relates to the 'place of work' where the employee is employed. It is possible that a contractual mobility clause might be an important factor in deciding that a person is *not* redundant. In *High Table Ltd v Horst and others* [1997] IRLR 513, the Court of Appeal ruled that neither test can be determinative of a 'redundancy'. The question of where an employee is employed must be considered on the facts and circumstances of the employment relationship up to the dismissal. If a mobility clause is implemented, then it is important to ensure that this is done 'reasonably' otherwise there may be a breach of mutual trust and confidence (see Exhibit 2.7).

Function v contract test

The issue here is whether, under a person's contract, he or she may be required to undertake a range of functions. The EAT, in *Safeway Stores plc v Burrell* [1997] IRLR 200, ruled that neither test was determinative. It stated that the correct approach involved a three-stage process which reflected the wording of the statute:

- Was the employee dismissed?

- Have the requirements of the employer's business for employees to carry out work of a particular kind ceased or diminished; or were they expected to cease or diminish? This is a factual issue relating to the resourcing of the business and the contract of employment is not relevant.

- Was the dismissal 'wholly or mainly attributable' to these business circumstances?

'Establishment'

The term 'establishment' is not defined in the legislation. There have been some early cases where the matter has been considered. The judgment of the European Court of Justice was given in *Athinaiki Chartopoiia AE v Panagiotidis* [2007] IRLR 284 which concerned the interpretation of the Collective Redundancies Directive 1998. The Court ruled that an 'establishment', in the context of an undertaking, 'may consist of a distinct entity, having a certain degree of permanence and stability, which is assigned to perform one or more given tasks; and which has a workforce, technical means and a certain organisational structure allowing for the accomplishment of those tasks'. In Britain, tribunals have adopted an approach consistent with this definition. It has allowed them to rule that, for example, national networks of sales staff are a relevant 'establishment' (*Mills & Allen Ltd v Bulwich* EAT/154/99; *Tierney-Rymer v Sainsbury's Supermarkets Ltd* ET/1803829/09).

Selection 'pools'

In a redundancy exercise the employer will identify the 'pool' of employees who are liable to be considered. In *Lomond Motors Ltd v Clark* EATS/0019/09 the Employment Appeal Tribunal ruled that the employer's choice of who to include in a redundancy selection pool was within the range of reasonable responses because it was based on genuine, sound business reasons. Lady Smith stated that 'employers are to be afforded a good measure of flexibility in the determination of the pool and a finding that their judgement was unreasonable must be based on a sound rationale.' It was emphasised that it is not for an employment tribunal to substitute its own view for that of the employer in determining the scope of the redundancy selection pool. In this case, Mr Clarke claimed that his dismissal was unfair because the 'pool' should have been drawn differently. The EAT found that the dismissal was fair in view of its decision about the 'reasonableness' of the pool.

Criteria for selection

In selecting employees for redundancy, an employer must have fair and objective criteria against which an individual's selection can be defended. Traditionally, **LIFO** ('last in first out') has been a customary way of selecting staff for compulsory redundancies. Millward *et al.* (1992) reported its incidence in 47 per cent of workplaces as against other criteria:

Table 3.3 **Selection criteria for compulsory redundancy (%)***

Main selection criteria	Manufacturing industry	Services	Public services	All
Role within the organisation	64.4	70.2	80.6	68.1
Job performance/efficiency	61.1	63.9	36.1	61.7
Employee ability/flexibility	51.8	52.9	41.7	51.6
Length of service	30.8	23.9	13.9	26.5
Absence/disciplinary record	29.6	19.3	8.3	23.4

* Survey of 536 organisations: respondents asked to indicate the three most important criteria used (CIPD 2002)
Source: Based on CIPD (2002) *Survey of Redundancies*, **www.cipd.co.uk**

employee's level of skills or qualifications at 29 per cent; employee's performance record at 23 per cent; and disciplinary record or attendance at 19 per cent. The CIPD (2002) survey of HR professionals records the nature of the shift in criteria that has been taking place (see Table 3.3).

The selection criteria must be disclosed in writing to employee representatives for the purpose of consultation (TULRCA 1992, s 188(4)(d)). The EAT has ruled that reasonable employers should use criteria 'which as far as possible do not depend solely upon the opinion of the person making the selection but can be objectively checked against such things as attendance record, efficiency at the job, experience or length of service' (*Williams* v *Compair Maxam Ltd* [1982] IRLR 83). There is no statutory obligation to follow customary arrangements such as LIFO.

There are several factors an employer should be aware of when using particular selection criteria – especially where LIFO is used to some extent:

- the likelihood of detrimental treatment against a specific employee;
- subjective and objective criteria;
- direct discrimination;
- the possibility of indirect discrimination;
- points-based criteria;
- consistency of application.

Detrimental treatment

This can arise on various grounds: e.g. where an individual is being victimised for involvement in an employment tribunal complaint; asserting trade union membership rights; participating in elections as a workplace representative; carrying out functions as a workplace representative; or asserting certain statutory employment rights (ERA 1996, s 104).

Subjective and objective criteria

As we will see below, most redundancy selection schemes involve objective criteria. Examples of these, although not used in every case, are length of service or attendance record. Subjective criteria can also used and are particularly susceptible to bias. An example could be assessment of standards of performance. How these matters have been viewed by the courts is discussed in the subsequent sections.

The Employment Appeal Tribunal has ruled on subjectve criteria in a disability discrimination case (*Lancaster* v *TBWA Manchester* EAT/0460/10). The claimant, a senior art director, was in a pool of three such directors who were at risk of redundancy. He contended that a 'reasonable adjustment' under disability law would be the removal of subjective criteria, leaving only the objective criteria.

The subjective criteria were the ability to perform as a team player; the extent of influence on performance and attitude to others; and active participation in company activities and improving the organisation's creative output. These subjective criteria accounted for 75 points out of a possible total of 425. Mr Lancaster was disabled within the meaning of the Disability Discrimination Act 1995 (the relevant law at the time). He had a social anxiety disorder. He argued that because of this, he should have been assessed solely against objective criteria. Both the employment tribunal and the EAT disagreed because, from the scores achieved, it was clear that the removal of the subjective criteria would have had no effect on the outcome. However, the EAT affirmed that if there was a real prospect of the requested 'adjustment' having the desired effect, then 'it might be reasonable to expect the employer' to remove the subjective criteria.

Direct discrimination

This is a relatively clear-cut issue. It is unlawful to select employees for redundancy on grounds prohibited under equality law (Equality Act 2010 s 4). The employees in question would need to show that they had received 'less favourable treatment' because of a 'protected characteristic' (see Chapter 5).

Indirect discrimination

This relates to a 'provision, criterion or practice' which, although apparently neutral, can be discriminatory in effect. It must be justified as a 'proportionate means of achieving a legitimate aim' (i.e. some clear business objective) (Equality Act 2010, s 19) (see Chapter 5). There have been some notable examples from case law (under previous discrimination law). In each case it would be a matter for each tribunal to determine, on the facts, whether or not the use of a provision, criterion or practice (including LIFO where that was adopted) is justifiable and non-discriminatory under discrimination law (see Exhibit 3.8).

Points-based criteria

Following the *Rolls Royce* case, it is clear that courts will consider, on the facts of each case, the inter-weaving of points-based systems and LIFO (see Exhibit 3.9) Nevertheless, caution needs to be adopted in two respects: the implications of equality law; and the opportunity for employees to make representations about criteria. The Employment Appeal Tribunal ruled on this second issue in *Pinewood Repro Ltd t/a County Print* v *Page* [2010] UKEAT/0028/10. It stated that fair consultation in a redundancy exercise does involve giving the employee an explanation for his or her scoring and, also, a meaningful chance to comment on the scores. This was particularly important where there were subjective criteria. (See also *Dabson* v *David Cover + Sons* [2011] UKEAT/0374/10.)

In *Eversheds Legal Services Ltd* v *de Belin* [2011] IRLR 448, the issue of point-based criteria was considered in an allegation of direct sex discrimination (under the former Sex Discrimination Act 1975, s 2(2)). This statutory provision stated that in considering sex discrimination against men, 'no account shall be taken of special treatment afforded to women in connection with pregnancy or childbirth'. (This provision is now in the Equality Act 2010, s 13(6)(b).)

EXHIBIT 3.8

Redundancy selection: indirect discrimination

Part-time workers first in a redundancy programme. All part-timers in the company were female. The EAT stated that this criterion had a disproportionate and adverse impact on women in the workforce and could not be justified objectively (*Clarke* v *Eley (IMI) Kynoch Ltd* [1982] IRLR 482).

Fixed-term employees first in a redundancy situation. The Court of Appeal ruled that this was indirect sex discrimination (*Whiffen* v *Milham Ford Girls School and Another* [2001] IRLR 468). In this case it was also said that LIFO might be discriminatory because 'by reason of childbearing and other domestic commitments, fewer women than men might have long service'.

Length of service as a criterion for redundancy selection. The Court of Appeal ruled (*Rolls Royce plc* v *Unite* [2009] EWCA Civ 387) on the application of the Employment Equality (Age) Regulations 2006. It stated that this long service award (i.e. length of service as a criterion in redundancy selection) came within the long service exception under the Regulations. It would be lawful if it reasonably appeared to the company that it met a business need. The Court considered whether it was indirectly discriminatory and concluded that, if it were, it could be justified. The legitimate aim was to reward loyalty; and that proportionality was demonstrated by the fact that the length of service criterion was only one of a number of criteria measuring employees' suitability for employment. The other criteria included achievement of objectives; self-motivation; expertise/knowledge; versatility/application of knowledge; and wider personal contribution to the team. Against these criteria an employee could score points. As far as length of continuous service was concerned, an employee would receive one point for each completed year. Employees with the least points in total would be selected for redundancy.

In this case, the firm proposed to make one of two solicitors redundant. The pool comprised one male and one female, who was on maternity leave. The selection criteria involved consideration of 'lock up' (i.e. the period of time between a piece of work being undertaken and the receipt of the client's payment). The reference period was the 12 months preceding 31 July 2008. Mr de Belin scored 0.5 points. Ms Reinholz, who was on maternity leave in July 2008, was awarded the maximum of 2.0 points as a *notional* score. The aggregate scores of each, using the points-based criteria, were: de Belin 27 points; Reinholz 27.5 points.

De Belin's grievance was that the artifical inflation of Reinholz's score resulted in the firm treating him unfairly and in a discriminatory way; and that, had she not been on maternity leave, she would have scored lower than him and would have been selected for redundancy. He brought a claim for sex discrimination to an employment tribunal.

There is an obvious tension in law between, on the one hand, the 'principle of equal treatment between men and women' and, on the other hand, the 'special treatment' afforded to women in relation to pregnancy and childbirth. The Employment Appeal Tribunal ruled that it was not unlawful sex discrimination to give more favourable treatment to an employee on maternity leave to compensate her for the disadvantage of being absent. However, the special treatment needed to be 'no more favourable than was reasonably necessary for that purpose'. This clearly raises the issue of proportionality in such cases.

EXHIBIT 3.9

Redundancy selection: points-based scheme

(A hypothetical scheme relating to redundancies of HR practitioner posts in a large organisation – for illustration only.)

Criteria	Method	Description	Points
Skills, knowledge and experience	Written evidence and three interviews	Competency-based assessment requiring evidence of contribution	**Up to 120 points against each assessment of a competency**
Relevant professional qualification	Relevant evidence	Chartered Member of the CIPD or equivalent membership	20
		Log of continuous professional development and preparation for Chartered Member assessment	15
		Graduate CIPD membership or equivalent	10
		Graduate CIPD membership or equivalent qualification in progress	5
Attendance	Employee record over the past three years	Annual average of 10 or fewer working days lost – excluding those associated with disability, pregnancy, industrial injury or hospitalisation	0
		Annual average of 11–20 working days lost (with the same exclusions)	–5
		Annual average of 21 or more working days lost (with the same exclusions)	–10
Disciplinary and/ or capability warnings	Employee record	No live formal warnings	0
		Current recorded warnings	–5
		Current written warning	–10
		Current final warning	–15
Length of service	Employment record	One point for each year of service	
		TOTAL SCORE	

Consistency of application

The EAT has ruled on the application of selection criteria (*McCormack v Sanmina SCI (UK) Ltd* [2006] All ER (D) 138). In this case, it accepted that the selection criteria were reasonable and sufficiently precise. However, there were defects in the way that they were applied. There was an inconsistent approach by the employer in the assessment of an employee's willingness to work overtime and in the assessment of employees' skills.

Alternatives to redundancy

There are various alternatives:

- Restrictions on recruitment of permanent staff.
- Leaving vacancies unfilled and so allowing for a gradual decrease in numbers through 'natural wastage'.
- Where practical (and taking account of equality law), terminating the employment of temporary or contract staff.
- Using short-time working to cover temporary fluctuations in labour requirements.
- Retraining and redeployment, where appropriate, of existing staff into internal vacancies which arise or are expected to arise.
- Seeking applicants for early retirement or voluntary redundancy amongst existing staff before declaring compulsory redundancy.

Suitable alternative employment

Where an employee is offered and accepts re-engagement on the same terms as previous employment, that person is *not* regarded as dismissed and there is no entitlement to redundancy pay. If the terms offered by the employer (or an associated employer) are different from those in the previous contract, then, when the old contract has ended, a trial period of four consecutive weeks can be invoked (ERA 1996, s 138(3)). It is possible to extend a trial period for the purposes of retraining. This must be in the form of a written agreement between the employer and the employee (or their representative) (s 138(6)). This offer must be made before the previous employment ends and the take-up of the new offer must be within four weeks of the end of the previous employment. During the trial period, the employee may resign and be treated as dismissed (by the employer under the old contract by reason of redundancy).

If an employee unreasonably refuses an offer of suitable alternative employment or unreasonably terminates the contract during the trial period, the entitlement to statutory redundancy pay is lost. Employment that could be considered as unsuitable would be that involving adverse changes in pay, changes in skill requirements, loss of status and requirements for travelling time (see Exhibit 3.10).

There are special factors relating to women on ordinary maternity leave (OML) and additional maternity leave (AML). Such employees, if they are to be made redundant, are entitled to be offered a 'suitable alternative vacancy' where one exists. This may be at an associated employer (Maternity and Parental Leave Regulations 1999, reg 10). The new job must be such that the work is suitable and appropriate for her to do in the circumstances and, in addition, with provisions as to capacity, place and other terms and conditions that are 'not substantially less favourable' than if she had continued to be employed under the previous contract (see Exhibit 3.11).

If an employer fails to offer suitable alternative employment in these circumstances, any subsequent dismissal on grounds of redundancy will be automatically unfair (Employment Rights Act 1996, s 99). The implication is that employers are essentially required to discriminate in favour of women on maternity leave.

There are similar sets of provisions and consequences for the following employees:

- Employees on ordinary and additional adoption leave (Paternity and Adoption Leave Regulations 2000, reg 23).

EXHIBIT 3.10

Unsuitable alternative employment

Commission for Healthcare Audit and Inspection v *Ward* **EAT/0579/07**

Facts. Ms Ward's job was identified as redundant in a restructuring exercise. She was offered an alternative post that the employer considered suitable. Ms Ward felt that the job was unsuitable on the grounds of the reduced status of the job; differences in job content; inferior job prospects; and weaker job security. She also alleged that the employer had not properly discussed the alternative job with her.

Tribunal ruling. The EAT, agreeing with the employment tribunal, stated that whether or not an employee's refusal of alternative work is unreasonable must be judged on the basis of *the facts as they appear to him or her at the time*. The *degree of suitability* of the post can also be relevant. Where the new job offered is overwhelmingly 'suitable' it may be a little easier for the employer to show that an employee's refusal was unreasonable. In this case, Ms Ward was successful. Her refusal was reasonable and she was awarded a statutory redundancy payment of £2,175.

EXHIBIT 3.11

Maternity and suitable vacancies

Simpson v *Endsleigh Insurance Services Ltd and others* [2010], **UKEAT 0544/09**

It is for the employer to determine whether a position is suitable and appropriate, although it is advised that they consult closely with the affected employee in this regard.

In *Simpson* the Employment Appeal Tribunal held that a tribunal had not been mistaken in finding that the employer did not have a suitable vacancy to offer a London-based employee on maternity leave, because the available positions that might have suited her were based in Cheltenham and there was no evidence that she was willing to relocate.

The EAT in this case was also not willing to accept that an employer might be permitted to test a woman's suitability for a position by means of assessment or interview, as this would negate the special protection provided by this regulation, that women in this situation *must* be offered any position that satisfies the above criteria.

- Men on additional paternity leave (APL) (Additional Paternity Leave Regulations 2010, reg 28).
- Men on additional paternity leave (adoption) (Additional Paternity Leave Regulations 2010, reg 28).

Time off work

An employee who is under notice of dismissal because of redundancy and who has two years' continuous service on the date on which the notice is due to expire, 'is entitled to be permitted by his employer to take reasonable time off during the employee's working hours before the end of his notice in order to (a) look for new employment or (b) make arrangement for training for future employment' (ERA 1996, s 52(1)). The employee is entitled to remuneration for the time off (s 53). If an employer unreasonably refuses and the employee is successful at employment tribunal, the maximum award payable is two-fifths of a week's pay for that employee.

Consultation and information disclosure

Much of the legislation in this area is founded on European Union law (the Collective Redundancies **Directive** 1998). There are three aspects to this topic:

- *Information disclosure*: information which is essential to effective consultation.
- *Collective consultation*: the duty on an employer to consult with either a recognised independent trade union or, in non-union workplaces, with employee representatives.
- *Individual consultation*: the obligation on an employer to discuss the employee's **dismissal** in accordance with ACAS guidance and ACAS *Code of Practice on Disciplinary and Grievance Procedures* (2009) does not apply to redundancy dismissals.

Information disclosure

For the purposes of consultation the employer should disclose in writing the following information to the 'appropriate representatives' (TULRCA 1992, s 188(4)):

- the reasons for the redundancy proposals;
- the numbers and descriptions of the employees whom it is proposed to dismiss;
- the total number of employees of any such description employed by the employer at the establishment in question;
- the proposed method of selecting the employees who may be dismissed;
- the proposed method of carrying out the dismissals 'with due regard to any agreed procedure including the period over which the dismissals are to take effect' (s 188(4)(e));
- the proposed method of calculating any redundancy pay which is in excess of statutory redundancy pay.

Collective consultation

Under statute law it is stated that 'where an employer is proposing to dismiss as redundant twenty or more employees at one establishment within a period of ninety days or less, the employer shall consult about the dismissals all the persons who are appropriate representatives of any of the employees who may be affected by the proposed dismissals or may be affected by measures taken in connection with those dismissals' (TULRCA 1992, s 188(1)). Where the employer is proposing to dismiss 100 or more, there should be 'at least' 90 days' **consultation**; and where between 20 and 99 employees are involved, the period should be 'at least' 30 days.

'Trigger point' for collective consultation

This is an important issue that has come before the courts. In *United States of America* v *Nolan* [2011] IRLR 40, a case concerning the closure of an army base in Hampshire, the Court of Appeal has referred a question to the European Court of Justice (see Exhibit 3.12). The directive (article 2) requires consultation when an employer is 'contemplating' redundancies. The Trade Union and Labour Relations Act 1992 (as set out above) uses the word 'proposing'.

The European Court of Justice addressed an aspect of this issue – particularly in relation to conglomerate organisations (*Akavan Erityisalojen Keskusliitto AEK Ry and others* v *Fujitsu Siemens Computers Oy* [2009] IRLR 944, ECJ). The Court ruled that the duty to consult, under the Collective Redundancies Directive 1998, was triggered when

EXHIBIT 3.12

The Court of Appeal's question

Does the duty to consult arise when the employer has made a strategic business or operational decision that will foreseeably or inevitably lead to collective redundancies; or only when that decision has actually been made and the employer is then proposing consequential redundancies?

strategic decisions or changes in activities compel the employer to contemplate or plan collective redundancies. This can arise in a corporate group when the decision on redundancies is taken by the parent company without the relevant subsidiary employer being informed. The duty to consult falls on the subsidiary when that has been identified. The subsidiary employer must conclude consultation *before* it dismisses employees for redundancy. (This last point confirmed the ECJ ruling in *Junk v Kuhnel* [2005] IRLR 310, ECJ.)

The nature of consultation

This is not explicitly detailed in legislation. However, from case law and the principles set out in the Directive, it is possible to discern standards that might be adopted. The Collective Redundancies Directive 1998 (Article 2) envisages consultation 'in good time with a view to reaching an agreement' with workers' representatives.

In one Court of Appeal case involving redundancies in the coal-mining industry, Lord Justice Glidewell stated that 'fair consultation involves giving the body consulted a fair and proper opportunity to understand fully the matters about which it is being consulted and to express its view on those subjects, with the consuler thereafter considering those views properly and genuinely' (*R v British Coal Corporation and Secretary of State for Trade and Industry* ex parte *Price* [1994] IRLR 72, CA). This guidance is relevant for consultation on both collective redundancies and individual cases.

The legislation on collective consultation, reflecting the Directive, states that it shall begin 'in good time' (TULRCA 1992, s 188(1A)). It 'shall be undertaken by the employer with a view to reaching agreement with the appropriate representatives' (s 188(2)). The purpose of the consultation should be to include discussion on avoiding the dismissals, reducing the numbers of employees to be dismissed and mitigating the consequences of the dismissals.

The European Court of Justice (*Junk v Kuhnel* [2005] IRLR 310) elaborated the last point by ruling that, under the originating 1998 Directive, consultation 'shall, at least, cover ways and means of . . . mitigating the consequences by recourse to accompanying social measures aimed, *inter alia*, at aid for redeploying or retraining workers made redundant'.

The Employment Appeal Tribunal (in *UK Coal Mining Ltd v NUM (Northumberland Area) and Another* [2008] IRLR 4) has clarified, in an authoritative judgment, the extent of consultation under TULRCA 1992 (s 188) following legislative amendments arising from the 1998 Directive. In this case consultation should have included the 'reasons for the redundancies'. Employers are required to consult, among other things about ways of 'avoiding dismissals'. The EAT agreed with the union's claim that if there was no obligation to discuss the decision to close a workplace, then this made a mockery of the obligation to consult about avoiding dismissals. It noted that, given the broad duties to consult about economic decisions under the Information and Consultation of Employees Regulations 2004 (see below), it would be strange if this obligation to consult applied up to the point of redundancies being proposed and then ceased as the 1992 Act took effect.

Failure to consult

If the employer fails to consult according to the statutory requirements, the employees are entitled to a protective award. This will be an award of pay for the protected period which the employment tribunal considers just and equitable having regard to the seriousness of the employer's default (TULRCA 1992, s 189). Pay is not subject to the statutory cap – it is the actual remuneration for the protected period of those (to be) dismissed.

The Court of Appeal has provided detailed guidance to employment tribunals on this matter (*Susie Radin Ltd* v *GMB and Others* [2004] IRLR 400) in the following terms:

- The purpose of the award is to provide a sanction for the employer's breach of their statutory obligations (TULRCA s 188) and *not* to compensate the employees for their loss as a result of that breach.

- Tribunals have a wide discretion to determine what is 'just and equitable' but they should focus on the degree of seriousness of the employer's default – whether this is a technical breach or a complete failure to comply with the obligations on information and consultation.

- The deliberateness of the failure may be relevant.

- It is a matter for the tribunal to determine the length of the protected period. But a proper approach where there has been no consultation is to start with the maximum period and reduce it only if there are mitigating circumstances justifying a reduction to an extent which the tribunal considers appropriate.

'Special circumstances' for not consulting are permitted. This term is not defined. Nevertheless, the employer must 'take all such steps towards compliance . . . as are reasonably practicable in those circumstances' (s 188(7)). In *Shanahan Engineering Ltd* v *Unite the Union* UKEAT/0411/09, the Employment Appeal Tribunal stated that even in 'special circumstances' there can still be some obligation to consult (see Exhibit 3.13).

EXHIBIT 3.13

'Special circumstances' and consultation

Shanahan Engineering Ltd v *Unite the Union* UKEAT/0411/09

Facts. Shanahan was a construction contractor engaged in work for Alstom, a transport infrastructure company. The contractor was told by Alstom to stop work on a project within three days. This would result in redundancies. In fact, 50 employees were dismissed.

EAT ruling. 'It remained for Shanahan to decide whether employees should be dismissed for redundancy, how many employees should be dismissed, when they should be dismissed and what if anything ought to be done to mitigate the consequences of dismissal.' The contractor was not wholly relieved of the obligation to consult even if the normal period of consultation in the statute is not feasible.

As indicated above, it is important to remember that consultation with 'appropriate representatives' (under TULRCA 1998, s 188) might well be affected by duties under the Information and Consultation of Employees Regulations 2004. These impose a duty on an employer to inform and consult on matters that have a considerable bearing on the economic context in which redundancy is taking place; and in relation to the measures affecting individual employees. The following provisions are key (reg 20):

- *Disclosure of information* on 'the recent and probable development of the undertaking's activities and economic situation'.

- *Information and consultation* on 'the situation, structure and probable development of employment within the undertaking and on any anticipatory measures envisaged, in particular, where there is a threat to employment within the undertaking'.

- *Information and consultation* on 'decisions likely to lead to substantial changes in work organisation or in contractual relations'. The duty on this last point will cease once the employer is consulting about redundancies under TULRCA 1992 (s 188).

Individual consultation

This arises under the law on unfair dismissal (see Chapter 8). A person who has been made redundant might complain to an employment tribunal of unfair dismissal. Redundancy is a fair reason (ERA 1996, s 98(2)). However, the tribunal would need to consider whether there was a genuine redundancy; whether the complainant had been fairly selected; and whether it was reasonable to dismiss the person for that reason. Evidence of individual consultation would go a long way to establishing procedural fairness. Such consultation is particularly important where there is no statutory duty to consult (i.e. where there are fewer than 20 people being made redundant). Even in the context of collective redundancies (i.e. involving 20 or more staff) individual consultation is good practice. The EAT affirmed the importance of individual consultation in *Dabson* v *David Cover + Sons* [2011] UKEAT 0374/10.

Case law has a bearing on this issue:

- The House of Lords ruled (in *Polkey* v *AE Dayton Services* [1987] IRLR 503) that there should be consultation before dismissal unless it was pointless.

- The Employment Appeal Tribunal ruled in *Pinewood Repro Ltd t/a County Print* v *Page* [2010] UKEAT/0028/10 that fair consultation in a redundancy exercise involves giving the employee, where 'points-based' selection criteria are used, an explanation for his or her scoring in points-based selection; and, also, a meaningful chance to comment on the scores.

Notice of dismissal

An employee being made redundant is entitled to due notice (bearing in mind the statutory minima and any enhanced notice under the contract of employment). The trigger date for this notice has been clarified by the European Court of Justice (*Junk* v *Kuhnel* [2005] IRLR 310). It ruled that giving notice of redundancy is not the same as notice of dismissal. So, an employer must consult and notify employees of the redundancies *before* issuing notice of dismissal.

Redundancy pay

Potentially, there are two kinds of redundancy pay: that provided under statute (ERA 1996, ss 135 and 162) which is a minimum entitlement; and enhancements to the statutory minimum provided at the discretion of the employer under the individual's contract of employment.

Statutory redundancy pay

The right to statutory redundancy pay is set out as follows: 'An employer shall pay a redundancy payment to any employee of his if the employee (a) is dismissed by the employer by reason of redundancy or (b) is eligible for a redundancy payment by reason of being laid off or kept on short-time' (ERA 1996, s 135(1)).

Under European equal treatment law, it has been ruled by the European Court of Justice that 'pay' includes redundancy pay (now under Article 157 of the Treaty on the Functioning of the European Union 2009). Consequently, redundancy benefits must be provided to men and women on the same terms.

Exclusions to the right to statutory redundancy payment arise in various circumstances:

- where the employee is dismissed for gross misconduct during the obligatory notice period;
- where an employee unreasonably refuses an offer of suitable alternative employment;
- when the employee is taking part in a strike (but not other forms of industrial action) before the employee is under the redundancy notice to terminate employment.

Statutory redundancy pay is calculated as follows (ERA 1996, s 162):

- one and a half weeks' pay: for a year of employment in which the employee was not below the age of 41;
- one week's pay: for a year of employment between 40 and 22 years;
- half a week's pay: for each year of employment between the ages of 18 and 21 years.

This structure was amended in 2006 to take account of age discrimination law. Nevertheless, employment before the age of 18 is not included. The maximum number of years that can be taken into account is 20. A 'week's pay' is revised annually and in February 2011 was set at £400 maximum (see **www.bis.gov.uk/employment** for updates). Redundancy pay (both statutory and contractual) is tax free up to a specified limit which varies from time to time (see **www.hmrc.gov.uk**).

Enhanced redundancy pay

- The Equality Act 2010 (Schedule 9, para 13) specifically requires enhanced redundancy pay not to be discriminatory. It should mirror the structure of the statutory scheme.

Case law, to date, largely comes under the previous Employment Equality (Age) Regulations 2006. The employer can be required to justify the enhancement objectively as a proportionate means of achieving a legitimate aim (see Exhibit 3.14).

EXHIBIT 3.14

Enhanced redundancy pay and a 'cap'

Kraft Foods UK Ltd v *Hastie* [2011] **3 All ER 956**

The Employment Appeal Tribunal considered the cap the employer placed on payments under its redundancy scheme – enhanced above the statutory scheme.

Mr Hastie took voluntary redundancy two and a quarter years prior to his 65th birthday. The company scheme imposed a cap that the maximum amount payable should not exceed the amount that employee would have earned at the current rate of pay had he or she worked to the normal retirement age. Mr Hastie received a 'capped' payment of £76,560. Without the cap the payment would have been about £90,100. The legal issue was whether the employer could objectively justify the cap as a proportionate means of achieving a legitimate aim. It was found to be so – in preventing employees from receiving a 'windfall' and it was not age discriminatory.

FRISHCO SUPERMARKET CASE STUDY

Scenario 3.2

Redundancy Selection

As part of its business strategy to improve cost-effectiveness and promote flexibility, Frishco is installing, as a 'pilot' scheme, some customer-operated checkouts in its four south-west London stores. These stores are all within a six mile radius. As a consequence, it is proposing to have a freeze on the recruitment of check-out staff and to make some of the existing check-out assistants redundant. The principal features of the redundancy exercise are these:

- The 'pool' is to include all four stores. There would be 80 staff in total in the pool: 50 are full-time staff and the remaining 30 are part-timers; 75 per cent are female and 25 per cent male. In fact 28 part-timers are female – and two are male.

- The company intends to reduce the number of check-out staff by 10 in total.

- It is has been decided by **Caroline**, the Human Resources Manager, that the fairest way would be to select staff on the following basis:
  - To rank order all 80 staff according to their length of service – giving 50 points for each year's service – irrespective of whether they were full-time or part-time staff.
  - Then, to award points to each individual in relation to attendance and whether he or she had any disciplinary warnings. Full attendance in the past 12 months would be awarded 200 points. There would be a deduction of one point for each day's absence in past 12 months. There would be a deduction – providing the penalties were 'live' – of 5 points for a verbal warning, 10 points for a written warning, and 20 points for a final written warning.
  - Then, a good annual appraisal in the past 12 months would accrue 50 points.

This scheme was discussed with store managers and implemented without any communication

with the staff. The staff with the 10 lowest scores were to be dismissed.

Caroline arranged for a member of staff in the HR Department to liaise with the store managers to prepare the ranking of the staff. The arrangement, then, was for the staff selected for redundancy to be notified in writing on a specific day. They were told that if they had any queries about being selected for redundancy, they should contact **Caroline** in writing. Staff not selected were not given any information.

When the calculations had been done, there were various consequences for **Tony's** staff:

- Two were to be made redundant. They were among those who scored the lowest points because of short service. Each had just under 12 months' service.
  - One, **Wanda**, was female and part time who had dependent pre-school children.
  - The other, **Sally**, also female and part time, was concerned that her for sickness absence had resulted in a lower score. In fact, she had had a considerable number of days' absence recently for pregnancy-related illness.

- Because a neighbouring store was to lose five members of staff, a further member of **Tony's** checkout staff, **Christine**, was to be redeployed there (some three miles away). She was told that she was expected to be mobile.

Question

What advice would you give Caroline about how the scheme had been structured and implemented; and how the company might prevent claims at employment tribunal?

Visit mylawchamber.co.uk/willey **to access sample HR documents to support this case study.**

Exercise 3.2 Managing redundancies

Read the scenarios and decide on the following:

- *What legal issues do you think might be involved?*
- *Taking account of law and good employment practice, what would you recommend to the employer?*

3.2.1 The owner of a small print shop, because of technological change, has decided to make two print operators redundant. He is planning to give them a written notice of dismissal with their pay cheque.

3.2.2 Because of a fall in sales, a medium-sized regional grocery chain is proposing redundancies. The managing director suggests that staff employed on temporary contracts should be dismissed. The HR manager asks to discuss the proposal with him.

3.2.3 Because of technological change and a reorganisation to 'promote greater administrative efficiency', Trisha has been told that her post as a course administrator in a further education college's administration department will no longer exist. She is one of two such staff to be made redundant. To date, Trisha has worked for a course leader and has had a reasonable amount of autonomy in the day-to-day organisation of her work. Now, she has been offered a new position as a member of the 'course support team'. This will involve carrying out a wider range of administrative and secretarial functions together with two other members of staff. It means greater functional flexibility. She, along with the other administrators, will have contact with course leaders – but it will be a pool of five rather than one. Her monthly pay and hours will remain the same, but she will be expected to schedule her working hours differently to provide greater cover. This will involve occasional work until 7pm.

Feedback on these exercises is provided in the Appendix to this textbook.

▶ Transfers of undertakings

Evolution of the regulations

The Transfer of Undertaking (Protection of Employment) Regulations 2006 have had a convoluted evolution. They are an aspect of law that is sometimes seen as lacking clarity, stability, and has been viewed by most practitioners as being unduly complex. Case law has been particularly prominent in the law's development – and, arguably, its confusion. The original 1981 Regulations supposedly transposed the EU Acquired Rights Directive 1977 into British law. One particularly significant flaw was the 'unjustified restriction' (Cavalier 1997: 6) of these regulations to 'commercial ventures' – so excluding public sector bodies. This was rectified in 1993, ahead of a ruling in the European Court of Justice (*European Commission* v *UK* (C-383/92) [1994] IRLR 392). A consequence of this early partial implementation of the Directive was that, in the 1980s, competitive tendering exercises in local government and the National Health Service, which resulted in changed and adverse terms and conditions for staff, were not challenged.

In 2001, the European Directive was amended and eventually transposed into British law as the Transfer of Undertaking (Protection of Employment) Regulations 2006 – rescinding the 1981 Regulations. Crucially, the new Regulations go beyond the Directive's requirements bringing within the scope of TUPE's employment protection the vast majority of service provision changes (i.e. those arising from outsourcing, insourcing and re-tendering exercises).

Purpose of the regulations

Initially, arising from concerns about the effects on employees of increased competition and, in particular, greater worker insecurity, arising from mergers and from the EU's 'single market', this European legislation sought to protect employees when the business they work for changes hands through a takeover, a merger or a form of subcontracting. The main effect of the regulations is to enable the contract of employment of an employee to be transferred over to the buyer of a business in the event of a business sale. They also apply where work is contracted out from a central organisation to subcontractors; or where one subcontractor succeeds another.

The pre-existing contractual terms and conditions of the relevant employees are to be preserved (with separate and specific provisions for occupational pensions). A transfer should not affect their security of employment. Their continuity of employment is not broken. Also, both the seller and the purchaser (i.e. the '**transferor**' and the '**transferee**', respectively) are under an obligation to inform and consult representatives of those employees who may be affected by the transfer. This consultation should be with a view to seeking agreement on any proposed measures affecting these employees. Whilst TUPE potentially benefits employees, it can also be advantageous to employers: it 'may have indirect benefit for management by reducing the probability that experienced staff will seek to leave once a potential transfer is mooted' (Rubery and Earnshaw 2005: 169).

Conceptually, TUPE constitutes a significant legal innovation. The regulations are '. . . a major limitation on both the principle of freedom of contract and the power of employers to arrange their commercial and corporate affairs in such a way as to minimise or fragment their employment law liabilities' (Deakin and Morris 2005: 216).

Coverage

The regulations apply:

- when a business or undertaking, or part of one, is transferred to another organisation;
- when a 'service provision change' takes place.

So, the regulations apply to 'public and private undertakings engaged in economic activities whether or not they are operating for gain' (reg 3(4)). They clearly cover the public and voluntary sectors. These provisions would determine whether there was a 'relevant transfer' or not (see below).

Effectively, there are two employing organisations described in the regulations as the:

- *transferor*: the employer who is transferring the staff;
- *transferee*: the new employer who is taking on the staff.

The working people to be protected under the 2006 regulations are 'employees'. They define (reg 2) an 'employee' as 'any individual who works for another person whether under a contract of service or apprenticeship or otherwise but does not include anyone who provides services under a contract for services'. Clearly, workers who have a contract of employment are covered; and the self-employed who are under contracts for services are excluded. It is not explicit, however, what 'otherwise' means and whether workers 'on some other contract to work personally' might be protected (see Chapter 2).

Although the regulations are silent on this matter, the Business Transfers Directive 2001 (Article 2(2)) states that member states shall not exclude from the scope of this directive contracts of employment or employment relationships solely because:

- of the number of hours performed;
- there is a fixed-duration contact of employment;
- there is a temporary employment relationship.

What is a 'relevant transfer'?

To determine this, three other questions must be answered:

- Was there a transfer to another 'person'? (In this context, an organisation would be regarded, in law, as a 'person'.)
- Did an 'economic entity' transfer?
- Did the 'economic entity' retain its 'identity' after the transfer?

Was there a transfer to another person?

This is relatively straightforward. The regulations cover transfers as a result of a legal transfer or merger – generally a sale of a business between a vendor and a purchaser. Generally, share sales are not covered. The regulations also cover service provision changes:

- outsourcing and contracting out: i.e. where a service previously undertaken by an organisation is contracted out;
- where a contract is assigned to a new contractor on subsequent re-tendering;
- insourcing: i.e. where a contract ends with the service being performed 'in house'.

Did an 'economic entity' transfer?

An 'economic entity' is defined as 'an organised grouping of resources which has the objective of pursuing an economic activity, whether or not this activity is central or ancillary' (reg 3(2)). This is a question of fact for a tribunal or court to determine. The Employment Appeals Tribunal outlined guidance to determine whether an economic entity exists (*Cheeseman and Others* v *R. Brewer Contracts Ltd* [2001] IRLR 144):

- It must be a stable economic entity.
- It must be sufficiently structured and autonomous.
- It need not have significant tangible or intangible assets. (So, for example, in cleaning or surveillance, the assets are often reduced to their most basic and the activity is essentially based on manpower.)

- A group of wage earners who are specifically and permanently assigned to a common task may (in the absence of other factors of production) amount to an economic entity.
- An activity is not an entity – other elements are needed.

Did the 'economic entity' retain its 'identity' after the transfer?

Identity must be retained for the regulations to apply. This is the decisive criterion. The EAT (in *Cheeseman and Others* v *R. Brewer Contracts Ltd* [2001] IRLR 144), drawing on the ECJ in the *Spijkers* case (1986), indicated a multifactoral test identifying the factors which were important. As the ECJ commented in a later case: 'It should be noted, however, that all those circumstances are merely single factors in the overall assessment which must be made and cannot therefore be considered in isolation' (*Sophie Redmond Stichtung* v *Bartol* [1992] IRLR 366, ECJ). The factors to be considered are:

- Did the operation of the activity resume or continue?
- Are most of the employees taken over by the new employer?
- Are tangible assets transferred?
- What is the degree of similarity of the activities carried on before and after the transfer?
- Are the customers transferred?
- A transfer may exist without the existence of a formal contract.

The first case involving a service provision change involving the transfer of staff to two new service providers, resulted in some guidance from the Employment Appeals Tribunal (*Kimberley Group Housing Ltd* v *Hambley and Others; Angel Services (UK) Ltd* v *Hambley and Others* [2008] IRLR 682). The EAT stated that the apportionment of liabilities in a service provision change should be treated in the same way as a traditional transfer (i.e. the transfer of an economic entity which retains its identity). It ruled that Kimberley Group had taken the vast majority of the activities to which the employees were assigned. Therefore, it was responsible for all liabilities under their contracts of employment. 'The EAT has confirmed that the approach in the case of a service provision change should be no different to the approach already established for traditional transfers. This means that tribunals must determine as a matter of fact whether the employee is assigned to activities involved in the service provision change. If so, the employee will transfer to the new service provider taking on those particular activities' (Helen Hall, Partner, DLA Piper, *Personnel Today*, 8 July 2008).

Temporary cessation of business

It is possible for the regulations to apply to circumstances were there is a temporary cessation in the operation of a business. The Employment Appeal Tribunal ruled (in *Wood* v *Caledon Social Club Ltd* EAT/0528/09) that the temporary cessation of a bar on the loss of its premises licence to sell alcohol did not prevent TUPE applying. The economic entity did not cease. The transferee intended to re-open the bar when it obtained a new alcohol licence and to run the bar as the transferor had done.

Cross-border transfers

As long as the economic entity being transferred retains its identity, the regulations are theoretically capable of applying to cross-border transfers. McMullan (2008) comments that 'case law . . . is thin on the ground, perhaps, because the issue does not often arise as a matter of contention: if there is a transfer of a business across borders, the employees rarely wish to move, especially when the transfer is to a geographically distant jurisdiction. The employees and trade unions tend to focus on negotiating the best redundancy package from the UK-based transferor.'

The European Union has published a case for cross-border applications within the European Union (CMS Employment Practice Area Group study at **ec.europa.eu**). Neither the 2001 directive (nor the 2006 regulations which transpose this into British law) applies itself to this issue. Theoretically, the directive could do so. It could potentially extend its scope across the EU and so significantly increase its significance.

The Employment Appeal Tribunal, under the 2006 regulations, has considered the issue in a case that involved the transfer to Israel of an undertaking which made curtain poles and tracks in *Tamworth (Holis Metal Industries Ltd* v *GMB and Another* [2008] EAT/0171/07). McMullan (2008) comments that, 'from the starting point that TUPE expressly applies to transfers of undertakings situated immediately before the transfer in the UK (as was the case here), the EAT held that set against the purpose of protecting the rights of workers in the event of a change in employer, a purposive approach to workers' rights requires that they should be protected even if the transfer is transnational. Enforcement might present a problem, but not an insuperable one.'

Contractual issues

There are several contractual issues arising in respect of business transfers:

- Rights and duties arising under the contract.
- Variation of contract.
- Liabilities for employment claims.
- Collective agreements and the impact of a business transfer.
- Right to refuse transfer by individual employees.
- Occupational pensions.
- Dismissals.

Rights and duties arising under the contract

The transferee takes over all the transferor's rights, powers and duties in respect of contracts of employment in force immediately before the transfer (reg 4). Apart from the usual contractual terms such express terms as mobility clauses and restrictive covenants will also be transferred. The only exception, as far as terms and conditions are concerned, relates to occupational pensions (see below).

An employee's service under their contact of employment will continue and not be regarded as broken by the transfer. So accrued service with a previous employer or employers will count towards entitlements to statutory and contractual rights.

In Britain, as far as terms and conditions of employment in the public sector were concerned, a voluntary *Code of Practice in Workforce Matters in Public Contract* (2005) was adopted by the Labour government. This was withdrawn by the Conservative–Liberal Democrat government with immediate effect in December 2010. It was replaced with *A statement of principles that reflect good employing practice for Government, contracting authorities and suppliers* (**www.cabinetoffice.gov.uk**). A *Code of Practice in Workforce Matters in Local Authority Service Contracts* (2003), at the time of writing, remains but it likely to be reconsidered by the Department for Communities and Local Government (**www.communities.gov.uk**).

These two *Codes*, as supplementary documents, were drafted to set out guiding principles and guidance on transfers resulting from public–private partnerships; second and subsequent transfers; transfers back into the public sector; and transfers and reorganisations in the civil service. They addressed the concern of trade unions about the possible evolution of a two-tier workforce in contracted-out public services. The *Codes* were to protect pay and conditions of new staff hired by companies who take over public sector contracts so that their terms and conditions were broadly comparable with those received by former public sector workers transferred under TUPE.

Variation of contract

● *General law on contract variation.* The basic principle applies that an employer can only change a contract of employment with the agreement of the employee (see earlier section in this chapter). However, there are some important qualifications to be made under the Transfer of Undertakings Regulations which are considered here.

● *No inferior terms and conditions.* Other than in the special circumstances of insolvency, it is unlawful to make 'a substantial change in working conditions to the detriment' of an employee who is transferred. In these circumstances, the employee can regard the contract as terminated and he or she as being dismissed (reg 4(9)). The employee may then claim at an employment tribunal. This statutory right to complain does not prevent the employee resigning and claiming constructive dismissal for a repudiatory breach of contract (reg 4(11)) (see Exhibit 3.15).

● *No variation in transfer period.* As indicated above, the purpose of the regulations is to protect employees during business transfers; and so, to ensure that the terms of their contracts of employment remain unchanged in the transfer period. A question that often arises from human resource managers is whether it is possible to change contracts after

---

EXHIBIT 3.15

'A substantial change'?

Tapere v South London and Maudsley NHS Trust UKEAT/0410/08

Ms Tapere had a term in her contract of employment with her original employer (the transferor), permitting it to change her place of work to another location 'within the Trust', providing it was reasonable to do so. After a transfer (under the TUPE Regulations 2006), the transferee required her to move to another location. She contended this was a 'substantial change' that would cause 'material detriment'.

The EAT determined important issues relating to the interpretation of the regulations.

● *Substantial change.* The employment tribunal had taken the view that the phrase 'within the Trust' added nothing to the mobility clause. The EAT stated that this was an error. The words were 'vital' in defining 'the scope' of the mobility clause. Ms Tapere objected to the extension, after the transfer, of the geographic boundary of the clause. The EAT held that she could not be required to move to a work location outside the area set in her original contract. It would fundamentally breach her contract.

● *Material detriment.* The EAT held that this does not have to be 'objectively determined' (in the sense of balancing the competing contentions of the employee and the employer) and, then, 'weighed and arbitrated upon by the employment tribunal'. The 'correct approach' is that suggested by Lord Scott (in a discrimination case) (*Shamoon v Royal Ulster Constabulary* [2003] IRLR 285) – namely to consider the employee's view about the detriment experienced and ask whether it is reasonable in the circumstances for him or her to adopt that view about the detriment.

the transfer has taken place. Until 2006, the short answer was 'no' if the proposed variation related to the transfer. Indeed, the situation is still that 'any' variation of a contract related to the transfer is 'void' (reg 4(4)). The restrictions on changing terms and conditions of employment also apply to anticipatory changes – i.e. where the transferor is contemplating changed terms and conditions for those employees who are likely to transfer. However, under the latest iteration of the regulations, there are specific circumstances when variation might take place. These are where the change is for an 'economic, technical or organisational reason entailing changes in the workforce', and in insolvency situations.

- **ETO** *reasons*. Changes to contracts of employment are permitted if the sole or principal reason for the variation is either:
  - a reason connected with the transfer that is an 'economic, technical or organisational reason entailing changes in the workforce';
  - a reason entirely unconnected with the transfer (for example a sudden loss of an order or an upturn in demand for a service).

  There is no statutory definition of these ETO reasons. However, the following have been suggested in guidance from the former Department of Trade and Industry:
  - *Economic*: a reason relating to the profitability or market performance of the transferee's business.
  - *Technical*: a reason relating to the nature of the equipment or production processes which the transferee operates.
  - *Organisational*: a reason relating to the management or organisation structure of the transferee's business.

  The phrase 'entailing changes in the workforce' also has no statutory definition. The DTI described it this way: 'interpretation by the courts has restricted it to changes in the numbers employed or to changes in the functions performed by employees'. If any changes of terms and conditions are proposed by the employer, they should be agreed with the recognised trade union or with the individual employees.

- *Beneficial contractual changes*. A case, under the 1981 regulations, involving a beneficial contractual change (concerning contractual retirement age and prior to the enactment of age discrimination legislation) which a transferee had initially proposed and then reneged on, was ruled on by the Court of Appeal (*Regent Security Services Ltd* v *Power* [2008] IRLR 66). The Court of Appeal took the view that nothing in public policy, reflected in European or British legislation nor in case law, prevents an employee from obtaining an additional right (i.e. an improved contractual term). The employee is able to agree with the transferee to obtain an additional right by reason of the transfer. The employee would be treated as obtaining an additional right, not as waiving a transferred acquired right. So, Mr Power's reliance on the retirement age of 65 agreed with the transferee, even for a reason connected with the transfer of the undertaking, was *not* contrary to the prohibition on employees contracting out of the protection and safeguards of the TUPE.

  This case was brought under the 1981 regulations. The 2006 regulations, as indicated above, preclude 'any' variation (unless it is for an ETO reason) and rule that it would be 'void' (reg 4(4)). This obviously raises some uncertainty in the application of the law. John McMullen (2008) comments that 'it is perhaps more likely that the tribunals and courts will interpret reg 4(4) in line with the Court of Appeal decision in *Power* given the strong message that the purpose of the Acquired Rights Directive is to protect employees' and not employers' rights.'

- *Insolvency situations.* In these circumstances, where an insolvent business is being transferred, the restrictions on the variation of contracts would be waived subject to certain conditions (reg 9):
  - *Permitted variation.* These must be agreed with appropriate representatives of the affected workforce. The purpose of such variations must be 'to safeguard employment opportunities by ensuring the survival of the undertaking' (reg 9(7)(b)). Such variations may include, in the exceptional circumstances of insolvency, pay reductions and other inferior terms and conditions. No variations should breach any statutory entitlements.
  - *Agreements.* These may be with representatives of recognised **independent trade unions** and will be in the form of a collective agreement. Non-union representatives are empowered to agree permitted variations subject to the following requirements: the agreement must be in writing and signed by the representatives; and before signature, the employer must provide all affected employees with a copy of the agreement and any necessary guidance.

Liabilities for employment claims

These are also transferred. The transferee inherits the transferor's liability in, for example, employment tribunal claims and other civil proceedings. The following are some examples of the transfer of claims:

- *Sex discrimination*: ***DJM International v Nicolas*** [1986] IRLR 76.

- *Accident at work*: ***Bernadone v Pall Mall Services Group and Another*** [1999] IRLR 617.

- *Transferor's right of indemnity* under an employer's liability insurance policy is a right which transfers: ***Martin v Lancashire County Council*** [2000] Court of Appeal.

The regulations impose a requirement on the transferor to disclose this information to the transferee (reg 11) (see Exhibit 3.16). It must be in writing or made available in reasonably accessible form or provided by a third party at least two weeks before the

---

EXHIBIT 3.16

Employee liability information

The information to be provided by the transferor to the transferee:

- Identity of employees who will transfer.
- The ages of those employees.
- Information in the 'statements of employment particulars' of each employee (ERA 1996, s 1).
- Information relating to any collective agreements which apply to those employees.
- Instances of any disciplinary action within the preceding two years taken by the transferor in respect of those employees.
- Instances of any grievances raised by those employees within the preceding two years.
- Instances of any legal actions taken by transferring employees against the transferor in the previous two years. (This would cover employment tribunal complaints and other civil proceedings in the courts.)
- Circumstances where transferor reasonably believes legal action may be brought.

completion of the transfer. The transferee may complain to an employment tribunal, within three months of the date of the relevant transfer, that the transferor has failed to provide specific information (reg 12). If the complaint is well-founded, the tribunal shall make a declaration and may award compensation to the transferee that it considers 'just and equitable'.

Collective agreements and the impact of a business transfer

Collective agreements and union recognition agreements are transferred to the new owner (regs 5 and 6) until they are terminated or are replaced. Two particular issues should be noted in respect of the application of collective agreements. First, their terms will be incorporated into individual contracts and can 'live on' after a collective agreement has been rescinded (see Chapter 2). Secondly, the normal principles of contract variation are applicable; but are in the case of relevant transfers supplemented by special provisions (see below).

A particular issue of concern relating to collective agreements has come before the courts and, at the time of writing, is not resolved. This concerns circumstances where the transferee is *not* a party to a collective agreement but the transferring employees have been because their previous employer was a party to those negotiations with a recognised union (see Exhibit 3.17).

Right to object to the transfer

The enforced transfer of an employee to a new employer is not permissible (reg 4 (7 and 8)). The employee's objection terminates the contract of employment and he or she shall not be regarded as being dismissed by the employer. He or she is not obliged to give notice of resignation, other than to make an objection (which does not have to be done in writing). This provision arises from an earlier case in the European Court of Justice (*Katsikas v Konstantinidis* [1993] IRLR 179). The employee in these circumstances is not entitled to any statutory or contractual rights (for example, relating to dismissal or redundancy pay).

Occupational pensions

These remain excluded from the terms and conditions of employment transferred; and were specifically excluded in the original Acquired Rights Directive 1977. There are certain caveats that can be made about the current situation.

- *The general private sector position.* Occupational pension rights earned up to the time of the transfer are protected by social security legislation and pension trust arrangements. The transferee is not required to continue identical occupational pension arrangements for the transferred employees. Where these employees were entitled to participate in the transferor's occupational pension scheme, the new employer must establish a minimum level of pension provision for the transferred employees. Under the Pensions Act 2004 and the Transfer of Employment (Pension Protection) Regulations 2005, the minimum 'safety net' requires the transferee to match employee contributions up to 6 per cent of salary into a stakeholder pension or offer an equivalent alternative.
- *Public sector employees.* The Conservative–Liberal Democrat government continues to follow the policy set out in HM Treasury note, *A Fair Deal for Staff Pensions* (2004). A private sector transferee, receiving public sector workers, must offer 'a good quality pension scheme' that is 'broadly comparable' to that previously enjoyed by these employees. However, HM Treasury is consulting about this issue.

EXHIBIT 3.17

TUPE and collective bargaining

Parkwood Leisure Ltd v *Alemo-Herron and others* [2010] **IRLR 298, CA**
Parkwood Leisure Ltd v *Alemo-Herron and others* [2011] **IRLR 696, SC**

Facts. The employees were transferred from the London Borough of Lewisham to CCL Ltd and then to Parkwood Leisure Ltd. When employed by Lewisham council, they were paid according to collective agreements negotiated at the National Joint Council for Local Government Services (NJC). From 2002–2004, CCL Ltd increased their pay in line with relevant NJC settlements. However, Parkwood Leisure, which did not take part in the national negotiations, did not make pay awards reflecting NJC increases.

The legal arguments. The employees complained to an employment tribunal of unauthorised deduction of wages. Parkwood Leisure argued that it was not obliged to increase the transferred employees' pay in accordance with collective agreements negotiated 'from time to time' at the NJC. The issue was heard at an employment tribunal and, on appeal, at the Employment Appeal Tribunal.

(The timing of this complaint means that it related to the 1981 TUPE Regulations and the 1977 Acquired Rights Directive. However, the issues are relevant to the implementation of the 2006 Regulations and the 2001 Directive.)

Court of Appeal. This overturned the EAT ruling. It determined that the transferee (Parkwood Leisure Ltd) was *not* bound by the terms of a pay increase that was made under a collective agreement that was incorporated into contracts of employment prior to the transfer in circumstances where the increase was made under a collective agreement reached *after* the transfer in which the transferee (Parkwood) played no part.

The Court held that the TUPE regulations did not expand employees' rights as set out in the directive to include future increases. The Court stated that decisions such as the earlier EAT ruling in the case of *Whent* v *T. Cartledge* [1997] IRLR 153 were a wrong interpretation of TUPE and that the interpretation outlined by the European Court of Justice in *Werhof* v *Freeway Traffic Systems GmbH & Co KG* [2006] IRLR 400, ECJ should be followed.

The ECJ had ruled that where a contract with a worker who has been transferred refers to a collective agreement negotiated by a body that the old employer was a member of – but which the new employer is not – the new employer is not bound by any subsequent changes to the agreement made by that negotiating body.

Supreme Court. In June 2011, the Court referred the issue to the European Court of Justice for a ruling, on this specific point, about the interpretation of the TUPE Regulations in the context of the EU directive.

The transfer period

Determining this period of time is important – particularly in relation to complaints of changes to contract of employment. It is often difficult – understandably so – for HR practitioners and other managers to determine this 'period'. There is no certainty about its duration. Guidance (from the former Department of Trade and Industry, **www.bis.gov.uk**) states the following: 'There is likely to come a time when the link with the transfer can be treated as no longer effective. However, this must be assessed in the light of all the circumstances of the individual case and will vary from case to case. There is no "rule of thumb" used by the courts or specified in the regulations to define

EXHIBIT 3.18

TUPE and harmonisation

Taylor v *Connex South Eastern Ltd* EAT/1243/99

Facts. Mr Taylor, in 1995, started work as a company administrator with British Rail. With privatisation, his contract of employment was transferred in 1996, under TUPE 1981, to Connex South Eastern Ltd. In 1997, he was offered a new contract by Connex but the terms and conditions were never agreed between the parties. He continued employment on his transferred British Rail terms. In 1998, Connex began a rationalisation involving SE Ltd and another part of the group, South Central Ltd. As a result, Taylor was presented with another new contract which was to his detriment in relation to contractual redundancy and holiday entitlements. All but a couple of the 250 staff agreed the new terms. As a result of his refusal to agree the new contract, Taylor was dismissed. He complained of unfair dismissal to an employment tribunal; and then went on appeal to the EAT.

EAT judgment. The crucial issue for the EAT to consider was whether his dismissal was *connected with the transfer*. When there was an elapse of time since the date of the transfer there was an issue of whether there was a weakening of 'the chain of causation' which maintained the connection. However, the EAT ruled, that the mere passage of time without anything happening does not *in itself* constitute a weakening to the point of dissolution of the chain of causation. It also ruled that the fact that the overwhelming majority had accepted the changes was not relevant. The rights under the Regulations were individual not collective rights; and were capable of being asserted by the individual.

Comment. '. . . once the Regulations are found to apply to a transfer (which is a matter of law that cannot be excluded by the agreement of the parties) its effects are far-reaching and can continue for a considerable time after the point of transfer. This can cause severe practical problems for transferees seeking to harmonise terms and conditions. This case emphasises that if an employee is dismissed for refusing to accept a variation of terms and conditions, something more than the mere passing of time is needed to sever the connection between the reason for dismissal and the transfer' (Industrial Relations Services, *Industrial Relations Law Bulletin*, 662).

TUPE Regulations 2006. These now permit contract variation for ETO reasons (see above). If that is not achievable by an employer, then, the principles established in the *Taylor* case still apply.

a period of time after which it is safe to assume that the transfer did not impact directly or indirectly on the employer's actions' (see Exhibit 3.18).

Dismissal

A dismissal is automatically unfair if the reason or principal reason for the dismissal is the transfer or a reason connected with it. The only exception to this is where the dismissal is for an 'economic, technical or organisational reason entailing changes in the workforce' of either the transferor or the transferee before of after the relevant transfer (reg 7). The responsibility rests with the employer who is dismissing the employee to show that the dismissal is for an ETO reason. The phrase 'entailing changes in the workforce' can mean changes in the numbers of people employed or a change in employees' functions. The test of reasonableness will apply to dismissals (see Chapter 8).

A transferred employee who experiences a 'substantial adverse change' in his or her contract of employment as a result of the transfer has the right to end the contract and claim unfair dismissal. The grounds would be that the action, or proposed action, of the employer constitutes a *de facto* termination of the contract of employment (reg 4(9)). This statutory right exists independently of the right, under the common law of contract, to claim constructive dismissal (see Chapter 8).

If the reason for the dismissal is redundancy, then the usual arrangements for handling redundancies apply and the dismissed employee may be entitled to statutory redundancy pay (see above in this chapter). The reason for redundancy must be for an 'economic, technical or organisational reason entailing changes in the workforce'.

The European Court of Justice has ruled that if an employee is dismissed in breach of the, then, 1977 Acquired Rights Directive (Article 4(1)), he or she must be considered still to be employed by the undertaking at the date of the transfer (*Bork (P) International A/S v Foreningen af Arbejdsledere i Danmark* [1989] IRLR 41). This was implied into the 1981 regulations by the House of Lords.

Consultation and information disclosure

The requirement for the employers (the transferor and the transferee) to share information and to consult with 'affected employees' collectively both before and after a transfer has taken place is a key feature of the regulations (reg 13). Obligations are placed on both employers. The workforces which may be affected include:

- those employees who are to be transferred;
- staff of the transferor who will not transfer but whose jobs might be affected;
- existing employees of the transferee whose jobs might be affected.

The Employment Appeal Tribunal (in *Unison v Somerset County Council* [2010] IRLR 207) ruled on the term 'affected employees'. It stated that these were 'those who will be or may be transferred or whose jobs are in jeopardy by reason of the proposed transfer or who have job applications within the organisation pending at the time of the transfer'. It did not accept that the regulations covered employees of the transferor whose future career opportunities might be diminished by changes in recruitment arrangements.

Since 1999, where there is a recognised independent trade union, it must be consulted. In non-union workplaces, appropriate employee representatives must be consulted (reg 13). Sargeant (2002) found that 'where trade unions were present then effective consultation seemed to take place at an early stage and at quite a detailed level. It is in other situations that there must be a real concern.'

Duty to inform

This requires the disclosure of the following information:

- the date or proposed date of the transfer;
- why the transfer is taking place;
- the legal, economic, organisational and social implications of the transfer;
- measures envisaged arising from the transfer.

Duty to consult

This duty is to consult with employee representatives but not with individual employees (although good practice suggests that, on occasion, that might be sensible). The consultation must be with a view to seeking their agreement to the measures to be taken. It must take place long enough before the transfer. The employer must respond to any representations made by workforce representatives; and if the representations are rejected, reasons must be given.

The Employment Appeal Tribunal has ruled (in *Amicus v City Building (Glasgow) LLP and Others* [2009] IRLR 253) that consultation is 'forward looking'. The Business Transfers Directive did not require any specified information to be given *after* the transfer. Consequently, if this is the case, then an obligation to consult after the transfer would be meaningless. So, the cut-off date for consultation is the date of the transfer.

Rights of representatives

They are entitled to facilities to enable them to carry out their function; and to protection against dismissal or any detrimental treatment (ERA 1996, s 103).

Failure to consult

A complaint may be made to an employment tribunal. This may award compensation which it considers 'just and equitable' up to a maximum of 13 weeks' pay for each employee in question (regs 15 and 16).

Conclusion

The consequences of business change can be fraught with complexities – not just for operational reasons but also, as indicated above, as far as the law is concerned. This is particularly so where the various bodies of law interpenetrate. Clear business objectives, careful planning, understanding of the employer's duties and their liabilities in law, genuine consultation and appropriate information disclosure, and attention to the good employment practice will help contribute to a satisfactory outcome.

FRISHCO SUPERMARKET CASE STUDY

Scenario 3.3

'In house' cleaners?

Frishco has been unhappy about the quality of cleaning being delivered by FastKleeners. They have complained to the contract cleaning company and believe the problems are that:

- there are insufficient staff allocated to the contract with Frishco;
- occasionally, no cover is provided when individual cleaners are absent;
- the cleaning staff that attend do not have sufficient time to do a thorough job.

Because of concerns, in particular, about hygiene, senior management of Frishco have decided that the best option is to bring the cleaning service 'in house' to be under the direct management responsibility of **Tony**, the store manager.

Caroline, the HR Manager, has been asked to produce a discussion draft of the employment relations issues that are likely to arise and to provide proposals as to how these may be managed by Frishco which, in the circumstances, would be the 'transferee'. The issues are:

➡

- **Yasmin** and **Magda** are likely to be transferred to Frishco. They live locally and, despite the problems with FastKleeners, are viewed as helpful and conscientious workers who, if their performance was managed, would be able to do a better job. **Hamida** is seen as rather lazy and Frishco do not want to employ her.

- What employee liability information should FastKleeners give to Frishco?

- What consultation and information disclosure should there be and who should be consulted?

- What would **Hamida's** situation be, in law, if she is not transferred? Would she have any complaint? If so, against whom?

- What terms and conditions issues might arise if the staff are transferred? Currently, **Yasmin**, **Hamida** and **Magda** are paid the national minimum wage; they are required to work fixed hours; they have 28 days' annual leave which, by agreement, can be taken at any time; there is no pension scheme and no sick pay arrangements.

Frishco would want to make some changes to harmonise with its own staff's terms and conditions. So, there would a slight increase in the hourly rate; a requirement to work flexible hours; a restriction on the timing of annual leave; a pension scheme but no sick pay scheme.

Question

What advice would you give to Caroline about how to deal with these specific issues and about the relevant law?

Visit mylawchamber.co.uk/willey *to access sample HR documents to support this case study.*

Exercise 3.3 Managing transfers

Read the scenarios and decide on the following:

- *What legal issues do you think might be involved?*
- *Taking account of both law and good employment practice, what would you recommend to the employer?*

3.3.1 A facilities management company has acquired a contract cleaning company. The managing director tells the HR manager that he wants there to be a common pay structure for existing and recently acquired cleaning staff. In addition, work rotas and holiday arrangements must be harmonised.

3.3.2 A non-union catering company has successfully bid for the contract to provide facilities at Somerset University. The existing terms and conditions of the staff to be transferred have been negotiated with the recognised union, UNISON. Relevant provisions of collective agreements have been incorporated into the individual contracts of employment. The managing director of the transferee tells the HR manager that he wants to preserve a union-free company.

3.3.3 Some weeks after the transfer of a security company the transferee receives correspondence from an employment tribunal citing it as respondent employer in a race discrimination complaint involving harassment. The single incident of harassment is said to have occurred several weeks before the transfer date when the complainant and the perpetrator were employed by the transferor.

3.3.4 A company which manages parks and gardens is to acquire staff who work at a large, privately-owned country house. Some of the staff to be transferred are permanent employees, some are on seasonal contracts (working between March and October) and some are called self-employed (although they work most of the year in the park). The HR manager of the transferee questions whether these 'self-employed' staff should be transferred; and also how the contract staff should be dealt with.

Feedback on these exercises is provided in the Appendix to this textbook.

References

Advisory, Conciliation and Arbitration Service (2009) *Code of Practice on Disciplinary and Grievance Procedures*. London: ACAS.

Atkinson, J. (1984) 'Manpower strategies for flexible organisations', *Personnel Management*, August.

Cavalier, S. (1997) *Transfer Rights: TUPE in Perspective*. London: Institute of Employment Rights.

Chartered Institute of Personnel and Development (2002) *Survey of Redundancies* (www.cipd.co.uk).

Collings, H. (1999) *Employment Law*. Oxford: Oxford University Press.

Deakin, S. and Morris, G. (2005) *Labour Law in Britain*. Oxford: Hart.

Foley, K. (1994) 'The lessons of market testing: the experience of prison education', in *Privatisation and Market Testing in the Prison Service*. London: Prison Reform Trust.

Kersley, B. *et al.* (2006) *Inside the Workplace: Findings from the 2004 Workplace Employment Relations Survey*. London: Routledge.

McMullen, J. (2008) 'TUPE Case Law Update', Industrial Relations Services, *Employment Review* 892, February.

Millward, N. *et al.* (1992) *Workplace Industrial Relations in Transition*. Aldershot: Dartmouth.

Reilly, P. *et al.* (1996) *Outsourcing: a Flexible Option for the Future?* London: Gower.

Rubery, J. and Earnshaw, J. (2005) 'Employment policy and practice: crossing borders and disordering hierarchies', in Marchington, M., Grimshaw, D., Rubery, J. and Wilmott, H. *Fragmenting World*. Oxford: Oxford University Press.

Ryan, M. (1994) 'Privatisation and corporate interest and the future shape and ethos of the prison service', in *Privatisation and Market Testing in the Prison Service*. London: Prison Reform Trust.

Sachdev, S. (2006) *The Impact of Contracting Out on Employment Relations in Public Services*. London: Institute of Employment Rights.

Sargeant, M. (2002) 'New transfer regulations', *Industrial Law Journal*, Vol. 31, March.

Shapinker, M. (2003) 'A cost-effective way to lose control of your business', *Financial Times*, 15 October.

Shapinker, M. (2005) 'Outsourcing the essentials is bad for your health', *Financial Times*, 26 January.

Timmins, N. (2005) 'Revolution in the way public services are delivered heads towards fruition', *Financial Times*, 26 October.

Torrington, D. and Hall, L. (1998) *Human Resource Management* (4th edn). Hemel Hempstead: Prentice Hall Europe.

Useful websites

Department for Business, Innovation and Skills **www.bis.gov.uk**

Chartered Institute of Personnel and Development **www.cipd.co.uk**

European Commission **ec.europa.eu**

HM Revenue and Customs **www.hmrc.gov.uk**

UK Statistics Authority **www.statistics.gov.uk**

Visit **www.mylawchamber.co.uk/willey** to access study support resources including realistic HR documentation to accompany the case studies in the book, an online chapter on collective labour law, interactive multiple choice questions, annotated weblinks, a glossary, glossary flashcards, key case flashcards, a legal newsfeed and legal updates.

Chapter 4

The context of discrimination at work

Introduction

The extensive framework of discrimination law covering employment and the wider society was enacted from the early 1970s to deal with a wide range of employment and other policies and practices founded on stereotyping, prejudice and in some instances, hatred. The genesis of such discriminatory behaviour, for many different reasons, is, generally, in the past. This historical origin means that many of the attitudes are deeply embedded in our culture, have often formed part of socialisation and so can be difficult to challenge and eradicate. This chapter is designed to consider the key concepts that arise in discrimination law; and set out the social and economic context of discrimination. The law relating to the various strands of discrimination, now covered by the Equality Act 2010, is examined in Chapter 5, and employment policies and practices are outlined in Chapter 6.

General concepts in equal opportunities

These concepts are central to any examination of discrimination across all 'protected characteristics' as defined in the Equality Act.

❱ Discrimination

Discrimination occurs widely both within employment and within society at large. It is about the exercise of choice – for example, in recruitment or in promotions. Implicit in this exercise of choice is the fact that action can be taken *in favour* of one person and *against* another. The critical issue is the grounds on which that discrimination or choice is made. So, for example, when a manager appoints a person to a post, the key question is: 'What were the grounds for making that choice and rejecting other applicants?' Were the applicants considered against *objective criteria* for the position – e.g. experience, skills and qualifications? Was there evidence that *unlawful criteria* were used – e.g. avoiding the recruitment of a pregnant woman or a disabled person?

The concept of discrimination, of course, encompasses wider patterns of social, economic and political behaviour whereby particular groups of people are stereotyped, victimised and discriminated against on the presumption that they possess certain characteristics. Various social and employment barriers can reinforce unfair discrimination and prevent a person achieving equal treatment. For example, the social role of caring for children which is, traditionally, ascribed to women has been found to be a considerable obstacle in the attainment of promotion, career progression and equal pay.

❱ Equal opportunities and equal treatment

Anti-discrimination measures are invariably discussed in the context of equal opportunities and equal treatment policies. 'Equal opportunities', as a concept, derives from the United States of America and was imported into British law in the 1970s. Less common in usage is the term 'equal treatment' originating from European Union discrimination law. Differentiating between these two terms is difficult and, probably, pointless. In practice – in the thinking of managers, in the experience of working people and, usually, in the interpretation of the law – they have become synonymous. Superficially, 'equal opportunities' is an attractive term because it is aspirational. It seems to go beyond the present situation to consider access to improved conditions and circumstances, the provision of better standards and the encouragement of those who are disadvantaged. Nevertheless, it is important to note that it is EU equal treatment law that has facilitated an expansion of opportunities for women. In terms of outcomes, there may be little that is preferable in either term.

❱ Managing diversity

In some literature in the early 1990s (Kandola *et al.* 1994), 'managing diversity' was seen as a concept *opposed* to 'equal opportunities'. The latter was seen as restrictive and relying on piecemeal compliance with separate pieces of legislation. Managing diversity was seen as more inclusive, business-related and strategic. However, 'managing diversity' has been a controversial concept. As originally conceived, it individualises equal opportunities, so distracting attention from the group basis of discrimination. However, when promoting the concept in Britain, from the mid-1990s, the Chartered Institute of Personnel and Development saw it as an evolutionary step in the development of equal opportunities. It saw equal opportunities and managing diversity as 'complementary', 'interdependent' and 'not alternatives'. In the CIPD's view, managing diversity was related to management strategy and it encompassed the entire employment relationship. It was seen as helpful in making 'the business case' for equal opportunities.

Diversity management can now be characterised as follows:

- It provides *a coherent approach* integrating both business and personal needs with ethical standards and equal treatment law. It is 'based on the concept that people should be valued as individuals for reasons related to business interests, as well as for moral and social reasons' (CIPD, 1996).

- It provides *a strategic approach* to equal opportunities. So, it is associated with such strategic business and human resource issues as quality management, productivity and cost effectiveness, empowerment, performance management and continuous development. It has an explicit economic focus in respect of labour cost-effectiveness.

- It is *inclusive*. It embraces all corporate policies and working practices and expects that they are tested against the criteria of diversity management. Such policies and practices should be assessed when formulated, implemented, audited and revised.

- The essential focus is on *the individual employee*. It is concerned with his or her characteristics, needs, aspirations and differences. The success of the policy is, then, determined by the extent to which the interests of individuals are accommodated by corporate policies. (Having said that, there must be acknowledgement that discriminatory treatment also has a group base. Stereotyping of individuals arises because they are presumed to have the same characteristics as similar people. Unlawful discrimination can only be tackled effectively by addressing both the individual and the group dimensions.)

- It is *management driven*. Line managers, team leaders and human resource managers are responsible for establishing the ways in which both legislative requirements and individual needs result in corporate action. The human resource department or individual equality officers should not be left as the isolated 'guardians' of equal opportunities. There must be a clearer and wider management responsibility.

▶ Institutional discrimination

In the report of the Stephen Lawrence Inquiry (1999), institutional racism was reported as a characteristic of the Metropolitan Police Service. It was defined as: 'the collective failure of an organisation to provide an appropriate and professional service to people because of their colour, culture or ethnic origin. It can be seen or detected in processes, attitudes and behaviour which amount to discrimination through unwitting prejudice, ignorance, thoughtlessness and racist stereotyping which disadvantage minority ethnic people.'

This useful definition of one type of discrimination can be generalised. It is possible for organisations to be institutionally discriminatory across many, if not all, 'protected characteristics', in their employment practices, service delivery and how they deal with suppliers and contractors. Recognition that this may be a characteristic of organisations has resulted in two related initiatives: the 'mainstreaming' of equal treatment; and the enactment of a statutory public sector duty to promote equal opportunities (see Chapter 5).

▶ Positive action and positive discrimination

These two concepts are, theoretically, defined separately. However, in practice, they can be blurred. *Positive action* is provided for in relation to all 'protected characteristics' (Equality Act 2010, s 158–9). Largely, it is conceived as encouragement for under-represented groups to apply for posts and promotion and to participate in training opportunities. However, the decisions to appoint or promote must be made against objective criteria. *Positive discrimination*, by contrast, is sometimes referred to as 'reverse discrimination'. Essentially, it is preferential treatment on the grounds of a particular characteristic, for example, sex or race. Apart from a House of Lords ruling on the duty to make reasonable adjustments under disability discrimination law (see Exhibit 5.14), it is unlawful under British equality law. However, in practice, there may be no clear-cut theoretical distinction. For example, preferential access to training and development opportunities may be both positive action and positive discrimination – particularly if the course is 'rigidly confined' to the disadvantaged group (Pitt 1992: 283).

As a general comment, Deakin and Morris (1998: 592) state that 'as part of an equal opportunities policy it is arguable that an employer may legitimately decide to employ or promote, for example, a woman, who is found to be *equally well-qualified* with a male applicant or colleague with the aim of improving the balance of women and men in particular parts of its workforce'. This practice reflects the 'tie-break' situation which has been ruled upon by the European Court of Justice (see Exhibit 5.4). A measure similar to the 'tie-break' has been enacted under the Equality Act 2010 (s 159) (see Chapter 5).

The arguments for and against positive action are various. Two in favour are particularly compelling:

● *Eradication of historic patterns of disadvantage*. This argument is based on the view that historic patterns are still influential today in framing social attitudes and expectations towards women, members of various ethnic groups and religions, disabled people, and homosexual and transgender people. Various historic obstacles to equal opportunities have included male social dominance; the legacy of colonialism, slavery and racism; the social marginalisation and low expectations held of disabled people; and the legacy of criminality and 'perversion' influencing opinions about sexual orientation. So, 'the point of positive discrimination is to give them [disadvantaged people] the capacity and the confidence to decide their goals for themselves, to empower them, to remove their existential marginality and to assure them that no area of life is necessarily and inherently inaccessible to them' (Parekh 1992: 270).

● *Compensatory action*. 'Social justice' implies compensatory action for past systematic breaches of fair treatment. Such action can take various forms (public training courses for women or different ethnic groups; assistance with childcare; appointing people from disadvantaged groups to public office as both representatives of particular inter-ests and as role models; and, in employment, setting quotas for the recruitment or promotion of particular under-represented groups). This action helps avoid social exclusion, promote social cohesion and the moral obligations and rights of a liberal democracy.

Arguments against positive discrimination are that it is inappropriate to compensate for the past wrongs experienced by previous generations; and that it is, potentially, socially divisive. Also, any compensatory action may only benefit some members of the disadvantaged group. Furthermore, in employment in particular, it is argued that it may result in a 'backlash' because the discrimination cannot be defended on objective grounds; and it may result in further discrimination if better qualified applicants for jobs and for promotion are rejected.

▶ Language and 'political correctness'

One of the more controversial aspects of tackling discrimination and promoting of equal opportunities is the acceptability of language (or what is called 'political correctness' by certain commentators, journalists and some politicians who appear hostile to any attempts to examine the connotations of particular language). Words are powerful instruments for identifying, categorising, stereotyping and demeaning people. They carry with them connotations and coded messages.

Over time there can be shifts in the use of acceptable language. For example, the word 'negro' has ceased to be used because it was associated with racism and slavery in the southern states of the USA and in particular with its corrupted form 'nigger'. It was replaced in the late 1960s by the term 'black' – reflecting the growth of 'black consciousness' and 'black power' political movements. In recent years, the term African-Caribbean (or, if appropriate, African-American) has become more acceptable, and has closer associations with ethnicity in the way that colour does not.

This process of challenging and modifying language reflects attempts to arrive at descriptions that are acceptable and without pejorative connotations; and which, above all, demonstrate respect. Whether the recipients of the language are women, young people, older people, people from various ethnic groups, people of various sexual orientations, disabled persons or those with specific religious beliefs, the connotations of the words used should be considered. If not, they may be found to be discriminatory or even evidence of harassment (see Chapter 7). It is particularly important when advertising jobs that employers are careful about the language used because this may infringe equality law (see Chapter 5).

The social and economic context of discrimination

▶ An overall view

The incidence of discrimination at work is considered and then the historic and contemporary context of each strand of discrimination law is examined.

The population profile

The total population of Britain is just over 58 million people (Census 2001) comprising:

- *disabled people*: 10 million;
- *ethnic minority people*: 4.6 million;
- *gay, lesbian and bisexual people*: estimated between 2.3 million and 3.2 million;
- *belonging to non-Christian religions*: 3.2 million;
- *gender and age profile*: see Table 4.1.

Table 4.1 **Population profile on basis of gender and age**

Age bands	Women	%	Men	%
Under 16 years	5,489,000	18	5,773,000	20
16–64 years	18,847,000	63	18,668,000	66
65 and above	5,353,000	18	3,994,000	14
Total	29,690,000	100	28,435,000	100

Source: Adapted from Office for National Statistics (2004) licensed under the Open Government Licence v.60.

◗ The incidence of discrimination at work

It is difficult to be precise about the scale of employees' experience of discrimination at work. This is for various reasons: for example, determining whether a victim views particular conduct as discriminatory; the possibility a victim may deny they are being discriminated against; whether objectively others would regard the behaviour as discrimination.

In the 2003 British Social Attitudes Survey (Kaur 2004: 8), 'very few employees said that they were aware of their employer discriminating unfairly against an employee on the grounds of sex, age, disability, race or ethnicity, sexual orientation or religion or belief when getting a job. Employees were mostly aware of their employer treating an employee unfairly in the last five years when getting promotion. This was across sex, age and race discrimination.' More detailed data is in *The First Fair Treatment at Work Survey* (Grainger and Fitzner 2007) (Table 4.2).

Table 4.2 **Personal experience of discrimination at work in the last two years by equality strands (%)**

	Male	Female	White	Non-white	Total
Disability discrimination (including long-term illness)	1.4	0.9	1.3	0.4	1.2
Sex discrimination (including marital status and pregnancy)	0.5	1.4	1.0	0.7	0.9
Race discrimination	1.0	0.6	0.4	4.0	0.8
Age discrimination	0.9	0.8	0.9	0.7	0.8
Religious discrimination	0.3	0.2	0.2	1.1	0.2
Sexual orientation discrimination	*	*	*	*	*
All types of discrimination at work	3.6	3.5	3.3	5.6	3.5

Survey population: 3,936 employees. Interviewed between November 2005 and January 2006.
* Fewer than 10 cases

Source: Heidi Grainger and Grant Fitzner (2007) *The First Fair Treatment at Work Survey: Executive Summary – Updated*, Department of Trade and Industry (**www.bis.gov.uk**)

In this survey (Grainger and Fitzner 2007: 10), employees who said that they had been treated unfairly at work in the last two years were asked if they would consider it discrimination: 70 per cent said they did; and significantly more respondents said that they had witnessed others being treated unfairly than had experienced unfair treatment personally. Employment tribunal complaints and their outcomes also provide some indication of the extent of discrimination and harassment. However, these data and official statistics need to be considered with some caution. Nevertheless, they provide a reasonable snapshot of the situation at a particular point in time (Table 4.2).

Other research for ACAS (Denvir *et al.* 2007) suggests from an analysis of employment tribunal claims (made between January 2004 and September 2006) that there is clear evidence of discrimination and particularly harassment (sometimes over a number of years) on the grounds of sexual orientation in the private sector. As far as discrimination on the grounds of religion or belief, bullying and harassment was significant. Some applicants also cited problems around working hours, time off or leave (in relation to religious observance).

The statistics relating to the number of employment tribunal complaints also provide a further, if imperfect, snapshot of the extent of discriminatory treatment (Table 4.3). The outcomes of these complaints suggest that there is substance behind many allegations of discriminatory treatment. The overall incidence is, of course, far from clear cut. For example, in 2010–11, a sizeable minority of claims were settled through ACAS concili-ation, ranging from 28 per cent of sex discrimination cases to 46 per cent of disability discrimination cases. However, in terms of success at employment tribunal, 3 per cent or fewer of discrimination claims were successful. Median compensation for a successful complainant was below £10,000 (Employment Tribunal and EAT Statistics 2010–11, **www.justice.gov.uk**).

Taken overall, the Equality and Human Rights Commission (2010: 4) in its triennial review of equality, *How Fair is Britain?*, takes the view that 'some forms of discrimination have diminished and some of the disparities in achievements between different groups have narrowed . . . In simple terms, Britain has become a fairer place'. This is not a com-placent conclusion. There is a clear acknowledgement in the review that much still

Table 4.3 Employment tribunal discrimination complaints

Claims	2004/05	2005/06	2006/07	2007/08	2008/09	2009/10	2010/11
Sex discrimination	11,726	14,250	28,153	26,900	18,600	18,200	18,300
Pregnancy	1,345	1,504	1,465	1,600	1,800	1,900	1,900
Equal pay	8,229	17,268	44,013	62,700	45,700	37,400	34,600
Race discrimination	3,317	4,103	3,780	4,100	5,000	5,700	5,000
Disability discrimination	4,942	4,585	5,533	5,800	6,600	7,500	7,200
Age discrimination	n/a	n/a	972	2,900	3,800	5,200	6,800
Religion or belief discrimination	307	486	648	710	830	1,000	880
Sexual orientation discrimination	349	395	470	580	600	710	640

Source: Selected statistics (**www.justice.gov.uk**). © Crown Copyright needs to be done and that the snapshot is a marker of some gradual progress on a long journey. The discussion below in this chapter draws attention to the continuing issues relating to specific 'protected characteristics'.

Sex discrimination: the context

There are several important contextual issues in this section: the historic situation of women; changing perspectives; women's participation in the labour market; and women's pay.

▶ The historic situation of women

Historically, predominant social attitudes have seen women's contribution to society outside the home as largely peripheral. Women were generally regarded as inferior and dependent upon men, having no separate legal identity. Blackstone, the eighteenth-century jurist, put the situation as follows: 'by marriage, the very being or legal existence of woman is suspended, or at least incorporated and consolidated into that of the husband, under whose wing, protection and cover she performs everything.' In the middle of the nineteenth century, a fictional lawyer in George Eliot's novel, *The Mill on the Floss*, commented, 'We don't ask what a woman does, we ask to whom she belongs'.

The overwhelming emphasis was on the importance of male roles in society. It was not until the late nineteenth century that slow legislative progress started which began piecemeal improvements in both status and rights. This gradual process of legislative change continues to the present day. Some of these key changes are outlined below.

First of all, on marriage, *a woman's property and income* became her husband's by law. In 1882, the Married Woman's Property Act enacted the principle, revolutionary at the time, that married women should have the same rights over their property as unmarried women and that husbands and wives should have separate interests in their property. Wives were also enabled to carry on trade and business using their property.

Secondly, *government and political activity* were regarded as male preserves (in fact, largely the preserve of property-owning males). It was not until 1918 (following campaigning by the Women's Suffrage Movement) that certain women (those over the age of 30 years) were granted the vote in Parliamentary elections; and 1928 before they acquired it on equal terms with men in respect of age. The first woman to be elected to Parliament, who took up her seat, did so in 1919. Women have, however, continued to remain a small minority of elected MPs. Following the 2010 election, of the 650 MPs there were 144 women – the largest number being Labour (**www.parliament.uk**).

Thirdly, *education* was seen as essential for boys but not for girls. Various views – often eccentric by present-day standards – were used to justify this discriminatory attitude. In the mid-nineteenth century 'educating girls was thought to damage their health as adolescence was the time their reproductive organs were growing and so . . . rest was essential. Schooling might damage this process by being too taxing. Experts predicted infertility or, at the very least, an inability to breastfeed' (Holdsworth 1988: 41). Biologically, 'Women were thought to have smaller brains and, it followed, less intellectual potential. It was also a common belief that women were behind men in evolution as their prime function, motherhood, kept them closer to nature. In short they were inferior' (*ibid.*: 42).

In 1870, compulsory education, up to the age of 14 years in elementary schools, was introduced. 'Such official thought as went into the education of working-class girls (and that does not appear to have been a great deal) concentrated on preparing them to be wives and mothers or taking work as domestic servants' (*ibid.*: 47). Cookery, hygiene, laundry work and housewifery were all on the curriculum of elementary school girls, sometimes supplemented by infant-care lessons. At university level, access was gradually available from the latter part of the nineteenth century. For example, in 1878, the University of London admitted women for the first time. Oxford permitted women to take degrees from 1920; Cambridge not until 1947. Although Girton College had opened there in 1870 it was not recognised by the university.

Finally, ***full-time work and the 'breadwinner role'*** were ascribed to men. Women, on marriage, were generally expected to give up work and ultimately care full time for their husband and children. 'Men lost face if they could not support their wives' (Holdsworth 1988: 62). The two World Wars (1914–18 and 1939–45) did disturb the conventional views about men's and women's roles – both in society and in employment. Women took up employment in jobs which were previously thought unsuitable for them such as ambulance drivers, stokers, tool setters, welders, carpenters and bus conductors. However, they did not establish any rights to equal pay. It is generally agreed that any changes in the world of work were short-lived and the general expectation by employers, politicians, men and many women was that, after both wars, women would return to their 'proper' roles of being wives and mothers. After World War Two, however, one factor was different from the situation after World War One: immediately the economy began to grow and there were labour shortages. This was a primary influence in the subsequent growing labour market participation of women.

▶ Changing perspectives

It would be a mistake to see the emergence of changing perspectives of women's role in society, politics, the economy and employment as a recent phenomenon. Questioning and challenging the inferior and dependent status ascribed to women has been evident in Britain for the past two centuries. One early writer who articulated the problems of women's status and advocated alternative views was Mary Wollstonecraft in *A Vindication of the Rights of Women* (1792). Her ideas influenced other women in the nineteenth century and the gradual action taken through legislation.

It was not, however, until the 1960s that a feminist critique of gender roles in society received more serious consideration among a wider audience. One of the fundamental objectives of the feminist movement was 'consciousness raising'. Essentially, this involved women appraising and understanding their social, economic and political roles and status together with the expectations that usually underpinned these. Invariably this diagnostic approach was restricted to women only. This deliberately fostered segregation and the focus on 'women's issues' was controversial. On the one hand, it was argued that this approach gave women confidence and facilitated more in-depth discussion of women's concerns. On the other hand, it was contended that it would perpetuate the segregation and marginalisation of 'women's issues'. Added to this was the view that, given that the power structures necessary for effecting change (e.g. the political system, the judicial system, employing organisations, and the trade union movement) were male-dominated, attention should be focused on changing these and creating alliances with sympathetic men. The feminist movement was not a single entity. It was charac-terised by diversity. It was cross-cut by class differences, ethnic differences, different political perspectives, different employment experiences and different attitudes about tactical alliances.

From the experience of the past 40 years, it is possible to draw the following tentative conclusions. Structurally, male dominance persists in many aspects of society: for example, in the political system, the judicial system, corporate and public service management, health care and education. Nevertheless, there is some evidence of slow, piecemeal change and there have existed since the mid-1970s legal mechanisms to challenge discriminatory practice. Despite the proof of poor compliance, there is also evidence of some achievements. The reality is that the progress made constitutes small steps on a very long road to full equal treatment.

In summary, since World War Two the following key expectations have changed:

- initially, that married women should be able to return to work;
- increasingly, that women with childcare responsibilities should be encouraged to return to work;
- increasingly that women returners should be able to fulfil career aspirations;
- that employers should facilitate parenting as a joint female and male responsibility;
- increasingly that employers should accommodate to some extent the dependency responsibilities of their staff.

▶ Participation in the labour market

There are five important aspects to female participation:

- the prevailing economic conditions;
- greater tendency for women to have peripheral or flexible employment (see Tables 4.4 and 4.5);
- increasing economic activity in child-bearing/rearing years (see Tables 4.4 and 4.5);
- women with dependency responsibilities (Table 4.7);
- a tendency for women to be segregated often into lower skilled, lower paid and lower status employment – and in particular sectors.

▶ Prevailing economic conditions

The impact of prevailing conditions in the economy can have profound and disparate effects on women and on men – whether in periods of growth or in recession. At the time of writing, it is difficult to be certain about the direction of what is a fluid and uncertain economic situation. However, various commentators have identified one important theme in the current economy which is likely to remain significant for some time to come: the differential and adverse gender impact of economic policy initiatives.

Irrespective of current political arguments about the scale and speed of the Conservative-Liberal Democrat government 'deficit reduction strategy', there have been important comments and observations about the *process* under which public expenditure cutbacks are made – in particular whether an informed and credible 'equality impact assessment' has been undertaken; and, also, about the differential *consequences* on women and on men of government spending decisions.

Table 4.4 **Employment by age and gender**

	In employment full-time (%)	In employment part-time (%)	Employment rate (%)	Unemployment rate (%)
Women				
16–24 years	56	44	57	10.0
25–44 years	60	40	74	3.6
45–64 years	55	45	63	2.3
65 and above	18	82	4	–
All aged 16–64 years	58	42	67	4.1
Men				
16–24 years	72	28	60	13.4
25–44 years	96	4	88	3.9
45–64 years	91	9	77	3.3
65 and above	37	63	9	est 2.1
All aged 16–64 years	91	9	79	5.1

Source: ONS (2005) *Labour Force Survey*, Spring, Office of National Statistics 2005, licensed under the Open Government Licence v.1.0

Table 4.5 **Part-time and flexible working: employees 16–64 years**

	Women		Men	
	(000s)	%	*(000s)*	%
Part-time	4,845	42	1,093	9
Flexitime	1,387	12	1,055	9
Annualised hours	514	4	524	4
Term-time working	888	8	162	1
Job share	150	1	16	–
Homeworking	195	2	124	1
Any flexible arrangement	**6,538**	**57**	**2,766**	**23**

Source: ONS (2005) *Labour Force Survey*, Spring, Office of National Statistics 2005, licensed under the Open Government Licence v.1.0

● ***Process***: An initial legal challenge was made in 2010 by the Fawcett Society (**www. fawcett-society.org.uk**), a women's pressure group. Its argument was that the emergency budget, presented to Parliament in June 2010 shortly after the general election, would unfairly impact on women. It sought a judicial review in the High Court because HM Treasury had not provided an 'equality impact assessment' which should have been undertaken to comply with the public sector gender equality duty in force at that time under the Sex Discrimination Act 1975. The Fawcett Society assessed that 72 per cent of the public expenditure cuts outlined in the budget would be met from women's income; and the remaining 28 per cent from men's. Furthermore, the changes to the tax system would discriminate against women. Following the High Court hearing in late 2010, Mr Justice Ouseley said that the Equality and Human Rights Commission would be best placed to conduct the analysis needed.

The government was reported as saying, at the High Court, that it was 'regrettable' that there had been no equality impact assessment. It did undertake one on spending decisions announced in the autumn 2010 Comprehensive Spending Review (CSR). Furthermore the ECHR also began a formal, independent assessment of the extent to which the Treasury has met its legal obligations to consider the impact of these CSR decisions.

- *Consequences*: Government economic policy decisions will, inevitably, have consequences not only for those reliant on various social security benefits and public services but on such important employment relations issues as earnings, job security, levels of employment and unemployment. If economic policies are geared to have a differential impact on the public sector as against the private sector and those sectors have clear gender differences in the composition of their workforces then, potentially, women are more likely to be adversely affected than men. For example, nationally, around 40 per cent of women's jobs are in the public sector compared to around 15 per cent of men's jobs. Women comprise 65 per cent of the public sector workforce. Much of this can be explained by 'occupational segregation' where women predominate in, for example, health, social care and education (see later section in this chapter).

  Analysis of measures and policies by the government led the Trade Union Congress (2010) to identify the 'gender impact of the cuts'. It drew on official data and research material to show the differential impact of benefit cuts on women – in particular, on lone parents who are overwhelmingly female; and on female pensioners. As far as pay is concerned, more women than men will be affected by the two-year public sector pay freeze. This freeze is imposed on those earning £21,000 and above. It will result in a substantial erosion of real earnings (and so purchasing power) particularly at a time of rising inflation. The £250 flat-rate payment to those earning under £20,000 is calculated by the TUC to be a 0.125 per cent pay increase.

  Drawing on the *Annual Survey of Hours and Earnings 2009*, the TUC reports that the 'gender pay gap', which is better in the public than in the private sector, is likely to be adversely affected by public sector contraction. Median hourly earnings (excluding overtime) by gender, hours and sector are:

Sector	Male	Female
Full-time public sector	£15.26	£13.39
Full-time private sector	£12.20	£9.66
Part-time public sector	£11.43	£9.43
Part-time private sector	£6.81	£6.78

These changes to pay and benefits are occurring against the backdrop of a reduction of 500,000 public sector jobs over the four years to 2014. The government's intention is to promote a structural shift of employment from the public to the private sector. Given the earnings figures outlined above, there will be a likely shift to lower paid employment.

In respect of employment and unemployment, the picture is more complex. Whilst in early 2011 there was some increase in employment, the issue is whether it can be sustained in the context of reduced real earnings, higher inflation and public sector contraction. Despite the overall recorded growth in employment, official unemployment statistics show an increase in female unemployment even if there is a marginal decrease in unemployment overall. Predicting the medium term, the Chartered Institute of Personnel and Development (2010) has calculated that there would be 1.6 million jobs lost by 2016 – across both public and private sectors. Taken overall, the gender impact of employment levels and structural changes cannot be precisely predicted. However, analysing the 500,000 public sector job losses announced by the government, the TUC comments that 'it is likely that at least 325,000 of those losing their jobs will be women' (2010: 8).

◗ Dependency

The provision of care is a complex issue. However, it is still largely a female role and can inhibit a women's participation in the labour market or, if she is in employment, can limit career opportunities and affect the number of hours worked. There is some evidence of changing attitudes but, also, still some structural barriers in both law and employment practice. In an Equality and Human Rights Commission research report, Campbell-Barr and Granham (2010: iv), commenting on earlier research, stated that 'today's parents defy stereotypes and want to share work and family care more equally. Their choices are constrained by inflexible and low paid family leave provisions based on a traditional division of paid work and care. Britain stands out internationally for its relatively long leave reserved for mothers, mostly at a low rate of pay and its relatively weak parental leave. It also has short paternity leave . . . There is evidence of unmet demand from fathers for more leave with their children.'

In this regard, the Conservative–Liberal Democrat government issued a consultation document, *Modern Workplaces* (2011), which focused to two related issues: flexible parental leave and flexible working. In the *Foreword* the government's intention is stated: 'we want to create a society where work and family complement one another. One where employers have the flexibility and certainty to recruit and retain the skilled labour they need to develop their businesses. And one where employees no longer have to choose between a rewarding career and a fulfilling home life.' The aim, after consultation, is to legislate on these issues 'as soon as possible in this Parliament' (**www.bis.gov.uk**).

In general terms there are two particular phases of care: for children, and for adult dependants. Reporting on the Millennium Cohort Survey (of some 30,000 parents), the former Equal Opportunities Commission (2007) stated that the 'breadwinner dad, homemaker mum' family model represented fewer than three in ten millennium families. From a sample of mothers interviewed, the following profile was recorded of family arrangements when their child is three years old (Table 4.6):

Table 4.6 **Millennium families when their child is three, partnership and economic status**

Status	Percentage
Lone parent not employed	11
Lone parent employed	6
Father employed, mother not employed	29
Both parents employed full time	11
Father employed full time/mother part time	35
Mother employed/father part time or not employed	4
Both not employed	4

Source: Equal Opportunities Commission (2007) *The State of the Modern Family*, the Millennium Cohort Survey, Equality and Human Rights Commission

Having dependent children has a substantial impact on a women's participation in the labour market. The former Equal Opportunities Commission (2006), reviewing Labour Force Survey data, showed that as far as fathers with children up to the age of 18 years were concerned, there was no shift to part-time employment. Over 90 per cent worked full time whatever the age of their youngest child. The response rates for women were significantly different (see Table 4.7).

Underlying these data is evidence of divisions of social class in respect of childcare and family support. The Millennium Cohort Survey (EOC 2007) showed that there is a substantial difference in the experience of semi-skilled/unskilled mothers in comparison to managerial/professional mothers. For example, 7 per cent of the former used formal childcare when the child was 9–10 months in contrast to 65 per cent of the managerial/professional group. Access to family-friendly provisions for mothers when a child was three years was mentioned by 59 per cent of semi-skilled/unskilled mothers as opposed to 79 per cent of managerial/professional ones.

Table 4.7 **Women's employment and dependent children**

	In employment full time (%)	In employment part time (%)	Employment rate	Unemployment rate
All women parents	42	58	67	4.4
Youngest child				
0–4 years	36	64	55	5.5
5–10 years	39	61	71	4.8
11–15 years	50	50	77	3.1
16–18 years	56	44	79	3.2
No dependent children	67	33	67	4.0

Source: ONS (2005) *Labour Force Survey*, Spring, Office for National Statistics 2005, licensed under the Open Government Licence v.1.0

As far as caring for adults is concerned, there is a gender divide here. The Department for Work and Pensions (2005) found that for women adult carers, 54 per cent were in full-time employment (in contrast to 89 per cent of male adult carers); and 46 per cent of women were in part-time employment (as opposed to 11 per cent of men). The ageing of the population will produce more demands on adult carers. The 2001 Census recorded that of employees in full-time work, some 1.6 million are providing at least some unpaid care.

◗ Occupational segregation

The Equality and Human Rights Commission (2010: 25) in its Triennial Review comments that 'the British labour market continues to be characterised by a high level of occupational segregation . . . [This] continues to feed pay differences, especially in the private and voluntary sectors where at age 40 men are earning on average 27 per cent more than women.'

There are two forms of segregation: horizontal and vertical. *Horizontal segregation* describes the situation where, for example, men and women in an organisation may work in different types of jobs – men's work and women's work. Workforce surveys indicate heavy concentrations of women workers in relatively few occupations. These are frequently those with a large demand for part-time labour (e.g. clerical and related work, catering, cleaning, hairdressing, personal services, professional and related in education, welfare and health, retail selling; and, in manufacturing, repetitive assembly and product packaging). This occupational segregation reflects, in large part, stereotypical female responsibilities: caring, cleaning and cooking. Such occupational segregation is a factor in the difficulties of achieving equal pay (see Chapter 9).

Vertical segregation describes the situation where men predominate in the higher graded posts in an organisation and women in the lower grades. Its existence has been described as evidence for many women of 'a glass ceiling blocking their aspirations, allowing them to see where they might go, but stopping them from arriving there' (Hansard Society 1990). The Labour Force Survey (Spring 2001) highlighted a 'glass ceiling' that was more or less penetrable depending on the sector concerned (see Table 4.8).

According to research published by the Equality and Human Rights Commission (2008), women's progress into top positions of power and influence across public and private sectors has stalled or reversed.

Table 4.8 **Proportion of female managers in selected managerial occupations**

Occupation	Female managers as a proportion of all managers (%)
Production managers	6
Financial institution managers	37
Advertising and PR managers	45
Personnel, training and IR managers	57
Office managers	66
Health and social services managers	73
All managers and senior officials	**30**

Source: ONS (2001) *Labour Force Survey*, Spring, Office of National Statistics, 2001, licensed under the Open Government Licence v.1.0

In 2010, the Conservative–Liberal Democrat government commissioned Lord Davies of Abersoch to investigate and report on women on the boards of listed companies. In the report (Davies 2011) he recommended, among other measures, that UK listed companies in the FTSE 100 should be aiming for a minimum of 25 per cent female board member representation by 2015; and that FTSE 350 companies should set their own 'challenging' targets. The Business Secretary, Vince Cable, said that the government would 'seriously consider' the recommendations (**www.bis.gov.uk**).

▶ Segregation and education

The discrimination, attitudes and behaviour underpinning this segregation can be difficult to eradicate because most is a result of socialisation. This is the process through which attitudes, values and standards of behaviour are inculcated and developed particularly within the family, within education, within religious organisations, within the workplace and within society at large. Examples of this can be seen in a number of the early life-time choices made by girls and young women which often determine ultimate employment and careers.

For example, the EOC (2006) (data for England from the Learning and Skills Council, 2005) reported on the educational choices of young women and men. These show marked gender segregation which will be reflected in employment and careers. Overwhelming numbers of young women (at least 85 per cent of those enrolled in courses) chose apprenticeships in 'early years care and education'; hairdressing; health and social care. The overwhelming male choices (at least 97 per cent) were engineering; automotive industry; construction; plumbing; and electro-technical.

Subject segregation in further education and higher education is almost as extreme. The choice of 'hairdressing and beauty therapy' courses was overwhelmingly female (93 per cent of those enrolled); with 'health and social care' at 66 per cent. By contrast 'engineering, technology and manufacturing' and 'construction' courses had predominantly male students (at 87 per cent and 95 per cent respectively). In other subject areas there was a closer balance between the sexes: 'science and mathematics' and ICT.

First degree segregation in higher education was also evident (data for Britain from the Higher Education Statistics Agency, 2005). 'Education' was predominantly female (at 82 per cent). There were smaller majorities of women in 'law' and 'medicine and dentistry'. 'Computer science' and 'engineering and technology' were predominantly male (at 81 per cent and 86 per cent respectively). There were smaller majorities of men in 'physical sciences' and 'mathematical sciences'.

▶ Women's pay and the gender pay gap

Pay discrimination against women was outlawed by the Equal Pay Act 1970. Progress in addressing the underlying causes of unequal pay has been slow and uneven. Some professions (e.g. teaching and the civil service) established the principle and practice of equal pay – at least for 'like work' – in the 1950s. However, research evidence shows flawed progress overall. Most of the decline in the full-time 'pay gap' took place in the 1970s. It remains a third higher than the average for the European Union as whole. It has been noted, pointing to the inadequacy of the legislation, that 'in the twenty-two years from 1974 to 1996, the gap narrowed by a mere 5.9 per cent' (Fredman 1997: 225) (see Chapter 9 and Exhibit 9.1).

The aggregate figures disguise important variations in the pay gap. The gap increases with age. At present it is largest for those women in their forties: 22.8 per cent for full-time workers; and 41.2 per cent for part-timers. It also varies by region – being the highest in London and the South-east. In the City of London it is estimated to be as high as 40 per cent (TUC 2008a: 17).

Recent reductions in the gap for both full- and part-time employees are largely attributable to the impact of the national minimum wage. The former Equal Opportunities Commission stated to the Low Pay Commission that 'the NMW's contribution to the narrowing of the pay gap at the bottom end of the pay distribution represented a substantial achievement both for the LPC and for the government'. One discrimination lawyer has argued further that the NMW also has had an important indirect impact on pay above the rates it sets by incentivising employers to up-skill low paid jobs – jobs that are again undertaken disproportionately by women (Ashtiany 2007: 6).

It is estimated that around 36 per cent of the gender pay gap could be explained by gender differences in lifetime working patterns – including periods of part-time work and interruptions to careers. A further 18 per cent is the result of labour market rigidities including gender segregation; the fact that women are more likely to work in small firms; and are less likely to be unionised; 38 per cent is explained by direct discrimination and women's and men's career preferences and motives; and 8 per cent the result of educational attainments (Olsen and Walby 2004). In earlier work, these authors estimated that these factors contributed to a major productivity gap because skills and deficits and labour market failures are particularly pronounced for women (Walby and Olsen 2002).

▶ Social and economic factors

Three factors have been identified as underlying the gender pay gap (Grimshaw and Rubery 2007):

Undervaluing of women's work

Two factors are critical: women tend to be paid less than men for the same performance in the same job; and the jobs women are likely to perform tend to attract lower wages than do men's jobs. The authors identify five 'V's that they claim work to create lower pay:

- *Visibility*. Women's skills are often not recognised by 'large undifferentiated' pay and grading bands.
- *Valuation*. Even where skills are recognised there is a long tradition of not giving a high value to such skills (for example, caring, nurturing skills).
- *Vocation*. It is assumed that women's skills are natural, which underlines their low valuation.
- *Valued added*. Men's jobs are more likely to involve high 'value-added' processes or service delivery. This can lead them to be more highly rated even where there is little difference in the skills involved.
- *Variance*. The existence of women's caring responsibilities underscores the view that women's work is in a separate sphere; and, indeed, less central or necessary for women. Part-time work, in particular, is frequently seen as synonymous with unskilled work both by employers and by women themselves.

Gender segregation and pay

The characteristics of labour markets is important in analysing the 'pay gap'. Research data points to a number of complexities and entrenched problems. Sixty per cent of women work in 10 occupations (out of a total of 77); and 60 per cent of women part-timers work in industries where 70 per cent or more of the employees are women (*Kingsmill Report* 2001). A related aspect of this is that women are 'vastly over-represented in low paid, part-time unskilled work' (Ashtiany 2007: 6). The Women and Work Commission (2006) linked gender segregation to broad features in our society: gender-stereotyped early environments; limited choices for girls in education; attitudes of teachers, parents and carers; and the images of women in the media and in popular culture.

Employment penalty for mothers

The Equalities Review (**www.equalities.gov.uk**) confirmed this penalty – identifying that 'becoming mothers' is the biggest cause of women's labour market inequality. Specific evidence relied on by the Review indicated that women with children under 11 years, irrespective of whether they were on their own or with a partner, face significant problems in getting jobs; and are over 40 per cent more disadvantaged than men with partners (Berthoud and Blekesaune 2007) (see Chapter 11).

Race discrimination: the context

❱ Britain's ethnic diversity

Britain is a diverse society in terms of the ethnic and national origins of its citizens. It has become particularly so since the middle of the nineteenth century. This ethnic diversity derives from a number of principal causes of migration:

- Britain's position adjacent to continental Europe which has been characterised by religious and political persecution, ethnic cleansing and genocide. Examples are the migration of Jews fleeing pogroms in Russia and eastern Europe in the late nineteenth century; and from the Nazi genocide after 1933.

- Britain's former role as an imperial power with colonies in all other continents and the perception of Britain as 'the mother country'.

- Occasional severe labour shortages, particularly after World War Two, which encouraged recruitment campaigns by employers (for example, in the Caribbean in the 1950s and 1960s for employment in public transport and the National Health Service).

- A loose, imperfectly implemented, moral commitment to protect people whose human rights have been abused in other countries. Examples are East African Asians who were expelled from Kenya (1968) and Uganda (1972) as a result of 'Africanisation' policies.

Additionally Britain, like most industrialised societies, has experienced other *ad hoc* migration. For example, internal migration between England, Scotland, Wales and Northern Ireland (and from the Republic of Ireland); migration as a consequence of the EU 'free movement of labour' policy; and migration by people seeking asylum from other countries undergoing political, religious and racial turbulence (e.g. Iraq, Afghanistan and the Congo).

◗ Concepts

To explore the issue of racial discrimination we need to consider the meaning of two key concepts: race and ethnicity; and in addition, the issue of 'colour'. All are used in everyday language and also indicated in race relations legislation as characteristics of 'racial groups'.

Race

This, as a concept, originally emerged in the late eighteenth century and led to the development of a 'race science' based on *biological* differences. It established a hierarchy of inferiority and superiority between races and was used to reinforce existing power structures (primarily, the domination of white people over other races). This 'science' enabled certain races to be defined as 'non human' and, therefore, they could be enslaved, treated as a commodity and denied any basic human rights. These 'non human' 'out groups' were often equated with animals. Dilip Hiro (1973: xii) records the historic comment that Africans were regarded as 'an equivocal race between man and monkey'. 'Race science' underpins Nazi ideology. Under this, the Aryan people are seen as supreme. The north-European Aryans and the Jews were 'as far apart as humans and animals' (Boonstras *et al.* 1993: 76). By the end of World War Two this 'science' had become generally discredited.

'Race' has also been defined as a *sociological* concept. But as a form of categorisation it is imperfect. Among the categories identified are: European, African, Semitic, Chinese. The implication is that people organise themselves and behave in certain ways according to racial origin. Given that these are extremely broad categories, which themselves cover a wide degree of diversity, the sociological definition of 'race' is comparatively unhelpful.

Ethnicity

This, on the other hand, is a more useful term for helping to structure discussions on discrimination. Most academic commentators would 'stress some sort of cultural distinction as the mark of an ethnic grouping' (Mason 1995: 12). Evidence of this distinctiveness can be seen in common descent (e.g. Jews originating in what is today the state of Israel); common cultural heritage or traditions; common traditions relating to marriage and family life (e.g. the arrangement of marriages); possibly, a common religion (which may be linked to the two previous characteristics); probably, a common language; and such factors as dress (for example, the hijab worn by some Islamic women). At the heart of ethnicity is a sense of belongingness to a group and to certain 'roots' – with distinctions drawn, especially by first generation immigrants, between 'natural' and 'adopted' home countries. The significance of these indicators of ethnicity will vary, often substantially, between different ethnic groups. In part, this depends on the extent to which such groups are integrated into the 'host' society.

In Britain, ethnicity has also been defined, conventionally, by skin colour. As a consequence, various European groups, for example, are not generally perceived as ethnic groups (e.g. Italians, Poles, Ukrainians) – but as white people. Indeed, 'white British people are apt to see ethnicity as an attribute only of others – something that distinguishes "them" from "us"' (Mason 1995: 14). This is a distortion of the concept and, in this text, ethnicity will be used to reflect any cultural distinctiveness.

In part, then, ethnicity is rooted in 'the self-definitions of members' (Mason 1995: 12). Rather than being an entirely ascribed category, like race, ethnicity enables individuals to determine their belonging to an ethnic group. So a person can have a range of different ethnic identities depending on the situation. A person might be a Hindu *and* an Indian *and* a Kenyan *and* British – depending upon the circumstances they are in and the treatment they receive at the hands of other people. As subsequent generations become established in the host society, more individuals will probably manifest these multi-ethnic characteristics.

Colour

This term features in the Equality Act 2010 (s 9). Historically, it has been used to differentiate between people. Indeed, in most ethnic monitoring schemes there can be, even today, an unsatisfactory confusion of racial, ethnic and colour categories. Mason (1995: 6) comments that characterising people by colour is 'of considerable importance because of the way in which the colours black and white were emotionally loaded concepts in the English language'. These colours are 'polar opposites'. 'White' represents 'good, purity and virginity' whilst 'black' is 'the colour of death, evil and debasement'. Such contrasts are long-standing features of our language, literature and philosophy as well as being elements in racist political rhetoric. Colour can be useful as *one* characteristic of an ethnic group (or 'racial group' under the legislation) but that is all. Otherwise, it is a crude and unhelpful categorisation.

▶ Historic labour market experience

Within the labour market after World War Two, there is considerable evidence of racist practices, reflecting attitudes in the wider society. In one substantial research project, union officials and employers' representatives were interviewed (Daniel 1968: 89). Three general conclusions were drawn about attitudes to the, then, new African-Caribbean migrants:

> The first is that there was a high degree of generalisation and stereotyping and little attempt to distinguish between different types of coloured people in terms of level of ability, personality or character, although some distinctions were drawn in terms of race or country of origin. The second is that . . . whether or not they themselves saw coloured immigrants in all the ways described, informants said or assumed that other people (their clients in the case of employment exchanges and bureaux; their members in the case of trade unions; their other employees, customers or clients in the case of employers) objected to coloured people for these reasons.

Indeed, in this context, the retail and distributive trade sector were 'the most resistant to the employment of coloured people . . . [and] most of them displaced responsibility on to customers or the public'. The third and most important point, and this is partly a consequence of the first two, is that 'coloured immigrants had been and were being considered by employers, if at all, only where no suitable white English personnel were available'.

In terms of promotion, there were even more difficulties. Non-white ethnic workers 'become less acceptable or unacceptable in jobs that imply authority over white subordinates, reciprocal relationships with white colleagues in other departments and other functions and contact with clients and the general public' (*ibid.*: 107). Daniel (1968: 83) commented that it was not surprising that 'many of the coloured immigrants who were interviewed had been very disappointed and even bitter about their experience of life in Britain and of the white British people with whom they had come into contact'.

▶ Taking legislative action

In the 1960s, two legislative steps were taken by the Labour government. In 1965 it enacted legislation to prohibit racism in 'certain places of public resort' (e.g. hotels, restaurants, public houses, theatres, dance halls, swimming pools, public transport, etc.). In 1968, further legislation extended protection by outlawing direct (but not indirect) discrimination in employment. In 1976, the Race Relations Act was passed and implemented. Most provisions of this Act were subsequently included in the Equality Act 2010.

Comparing Britain with other EU member states, Justice, the human rights group commented some years later that it was 'unique' in having had legislation against discrimination on racial grounds on the statute book for some 30 years. Although all EU states 'have written Constitutions that prohibit race discrimination in some way, detailed implementing legislation is often lacking. Where it does exist, it may be limited to acts committed by organs of the State' (1996: 28). The situation within the EU gradually moved on with the enactment in 2000 of the directive requiring equal treatment on the grounds of racial and ethnic origin.

▶ Labour market participation today

Although there continues to be evidence of racism in employment, there has been some incremental change for the better over the past 30 years. Whilst, on the one hand, there is evidence of some segregation in employment (which may be exacerbated by both gender issues and social class), there is also evidence of a more positive approach being taken to equal opportunities, particularly in the public sector. Of particular importance is the commitment of public policy (through equality duties) and legislation to the eradication of racism and the promotion of equal opportunities.

An overview of employment by ethnic group is given in Table 4.9, and some more detailed outline of concentrations of ethnic minority employment is set out in the following data (Annual Population Survey 2004, **www.statistics.gov.uk**):

Self-employment: this status was more evident among Pakistanis (21 per cent); Chinese (16 per cent) and white Irish (15 per cent) than among the white British population (12 per cent). *Industry concentrations*: certain ethnic groups are concentrated in particular industries:

- *distribution, hotel and restaurant industry*: three-fifths of Bangladeshi men and just under half of Chinese men in employment worked in this sector compared with one-sixth of white British counterparts. Forty per cent of Chinese women and one-third of Bangladeshi women worked here compared with 20 per cent of all women in employment;

- *transport and communications*: Pakistani men were the group most likely to work in this industry – 23 per cent of them compared with 10 per cent of all men employed;

- *construction*: white Irish men were more likely than other men to work in this industry – 20 per cent compared with 13 per cent overall;

- *public administration, education or health sector*: 54 per cent of Black Caribbean and 52 per cent of Black African women worked in this sector.

Table 4.9 **Employment by ethnic group (Great Britain: people aged 16–64 years)**

	In full-time employment (%)	In part-time employment (%)	Employment rate	Unemployment rate
Women				
White	57	43	69	3.7
Mixed	66	34	64	10.3
Indian	68	32	61	5.8
Pakistani	55	45	23	21.7
Bangladeshi	52*	48*	18	–
Black Caribbean	73	27	64	7.6
Black African	73	27	48	9.4
Chinese	74	26	55	–
All ethnic groups[†]	**68**	**32**	**50**	**9.1**
All aged 16–64 years	**58**	**42**	**67**	**4.1**
Men				
White	91	9	80	4.6
Mixed	85	15	63	9.9*
Indian	91	9	75	6.4
Pakistani	80	20	63	10.1
Bangladeshi	61	39	54	19.1
Black Caribbean	87	13	71	14.6
Black African	78	22	63	15.4
Chinese	82	18*	49	14.4*
All ethnic groups[†]	**84**	**16**	**66**	**10.7**
All aged 16–64 years	**91**	**9**	**79**	**5.1**

* Estimate may be unreliable
[†] All non-white groups including those not listed separately

Source: ONS (2005) *Labour Force Survey,* Spring, Office of National Statistics 2005, licensed under the Open Government Licence v.1.0

Occupations:

● *managerial or professional occupations*: those most likely to be employed in managerial or professional occupations were Chinese, Indian, white Irish and other non-British white groups (between 32 and 38 per cent). White British people were at 27 per cent. The lowest proportions in this occupational group (between 19 and 22 per cent) were Black Caribbean, Black African and Bangladeshi;

- *driving*: one in seven Pakistani men in employment was a taxi driver, cab driver or chauffeur compared with one per cent of white British men;

- *catering*: over a quarter of Bangladeshi men were chefs, cooks or waiters;

- *healthcare*: 4 per cent of Indian men worked as medical practitioners – 10 times higher than the rate for white British men. Around one in 10 Black African women and one in seven women from the Other Asian group were working as nurses compared with one in 30 white British women;

- *packers, bottlers, canners and fillers*: Indian, Pakistani and Black African women were around four times more likely than white British women to be working at these jobs;

- *sewing machinists*: Pakistani and Indian women were, respectively, six times and four times more likely than white British women to be working at this job.

Disability discrimination: the context

▶ Defining disability

The most common problems affecting people with a disability (Twomey 2001) are:

- musculoskeletal (relating to arms, legs, back, hands and feet): 36 per cent;

- chest or breathing problems: 13 per cent;

- heart, blood pressure and circulatory conditions: 11 per cent;

- mental illness: 8 per cent.

▶ Models of disability

There are two distinct approaches to defining disability: The 'medical model' and the 'social model'. The traditional definition (the 'medical model') is that used by the World Health Organisation (Wood 1991). This categorised the following:

- *Impairment*: any loss or abnormality of psychological, physiological or anatomical structure or function.

- *Disability*: any restriction or lack of ability (resulting from an impairment) to perform an activity in the manner or within the range considered normal for a human being.

- *Handicap*: a disadvantage for a given individual, resulting from an impairment or a disability that limits or prevents the fulfilment of a role (depending on age, sex and social and cultural factors) for that individual.

This 'medical model' concentrates on dysfunction and on how to make the person well or on the aids necessary for the person to function 'normally'. So, the amputee is fitted with an artificial limb. The implication is that people with functional limitations need to adapt to fit into society. The TUC (2008b), in a critique, has commented that 'the medical model underlying the DDA has a long history. For a long period, disability was thought by almost everyone to signify an inability to live a "normal life". Disabled people were seen as either the pathetic and helpless objects of charity or else, if they managed despite everything to succeed in their careers and lives, as heroic figures overcoming their "defects" (not, note, the barriers) by superhuman effort.'

The 'social model' sees disability as 'resting in society rather than in any factor inherent in disabled people' (Massie 1994). This is not to deny the medical aspects of disability which may be considerable. It acknowledges that the impact of disability frequently depends on the 'context in which someone lives' (*ibid.*). Against this background, Disabled Peoples' International has adopted the following definitions:

- *Impairment*: the functional limitation within the individual caused by physical, mental or sensory impairment.
- *Disability*: the loss or limitation of opportunities to take part in the normal life of the community on an equal level with others due to physical or social barriers.

This 'social model' enables people to have an impairment without having a disability. It is social factors that translate the 'impairment' into a 'disability'. So, if the physical and attitudinal barriers that exist within society are reduced, then so is the disability. Individuals will still have the physical or mental impairment and the consequent pain and emotions but their ability to participate in society will be enhanced. The importance of this second model is that it focuses attention on the individual's interface with the environment and not on the individual's impairment. Thus, people are seen as individuals – and not as 'the disabled' – with effort being put into addressing any social and physical barriers that exist. It helps move away from the notion that 'disability' equates with 'inability'.

The original statutory disability duty on public authorities (Disability Discrimination Act 1995, s 49A) was based on the social model of disability and is now part of the Equality Act 2010 (s 1). Godwin (2008a: 10), in a survey of 132 employers, found that 44 per cent of organisations said that they used the 'social model'; 21 per cent said that they had not; and 35 per cent did not know. She commented that this suggests that 'a substantial number of organisations have adopted policies without first establishing the fundamental principles underlying such a policy'.

▶ Social context

There are two relevant dimensions which affect the day-to-day living and employment opportunities of disabled people: prevailing social attitudes; and social infrastructure.

Attitudes

Disabled people are frequently subject to stereotyping and preconceptions about the nature and consequences of their disability. First, there is the ever-present tendency to regard 'the disabled' as an undifferentiated group. In reality, the spectrum of impairment is extremely wide. Consequently, the impact of an impairment on a person's ability to carry out day-to-day activities, to live independently, to travel and so on varies very significantly from person to person. This may seem an obvious statement but it is surprising how it is still forgotten in the whole range of social activities and in the employment arena.

Secondly, disabled people can be treated with suspicion, apprehension, ridicule and pity. They may also experience well-meaning patronising attitudes from people who think that they 'know best' about any assistance required. Thirdly, social attitudes frequently fail to consider the situation of a disabled person from that person's perspective. For example, expressions are used such as 'confined to a wheelchair' when, in fact, the wheelchair may liberate the user by providing mobility. Someone may be described as suffering from a particular condition when that person does not regard the condition as a disability but as a normal part of life. There can be a failure to allow the disabled person to take the initiative in deciding the adjustments and assistance that they want or do not want. One survey (Honey *et al.* 1993) found that employers tended to hold inaccurate or exaggerated beliefs about the restrictions that impairments place on employment. Many of the prevailing social attitudes reflect the traditional medical model of disability where the focus is on the individual's condition and care and welfare.

A final comment on attitudes (and evident in all areas of discrimination) is the pernicious and deterrent effect that stereotyping, prejudice and insulting behaviour has on the self-esteem of disabled people. This creates a further psychological obstacle that needs to be overcome so they may become active participants in society and employment. This has been described as the 'discouraged worker' syndrome – whereby people withdraw from the labour market after repeated rejection and lack of opportunities. They tend to devalue their own potential. Recent research confirms the persistence of many negative attitudes (Fevre *et al.* 2008).

Social infrastructure

People with impairments face difficulties associated with public transport and building design. These, inevitably, can cause access problems in relation to training, employment, the purchase of goods and services, entertainment. Access problems in one area can exacerbate access in others. For example, difficulties in acquiring education and training, which may be caused in part by transport problems, can obstruct entry into the labour market and employment. The ability to lead a constructive and rewarding life is inhibited.

Attitudes and social infrastructure issues are linked in providing five obstacles to the entry of disabled people into employment (Weiss 1974: 457):

- physical and vocational problems during rehabilitation and training;
- barriers created by architectural design and transport systems;
- resistance by employers to hiring disabled persons;
- self-doubt as a result of previous prejudice;
- overcoming ill-focused and often unnecessary medical tests.

◗ Historical perspective

Until the enactment of the Disability Discrimination Act 1995, there had been little progress in protecting disabled people from discrimination and facilitating full social and economic participation. Aside from legislation relating to the provision of information to disabled people and a requirement (in 1980) on companies employing 250 or more staff to include a general statement in their annual report about their treatment of disabled people, the principal legislation was the Disabled Persons (Employment) Act 1944. This was seen as a major piece of legislation when enacted towards the end of World War Two. It was expected to go some way to assisting demobilised and injured members of the armed forces. It introduced a registration scheme for disabled people; a quota scheme in employment; and reserve occupations. The quota scheme required employers with 20 or more employees to have at least 3 per cent of their workforce as registered disabled persons (RDPs). It was unlawful to engage an able-bodied person or to dismiss an RDP without reasonable cause if the quota was, or would fall below, 3 per cent. In fact, the number of people registering gradually fell to approximately one per cent of the working population. Employers universally were unlikely to achieve the quota and many applied for exemption certificates. Prosecutions for non-compliance were few and the last was in 1975. The maximum fine was £100. As far as reserve occupations, only the positions of passenger electric lift attendant and car park attendant were ever designated as occupations to be carried out by RDPs.

A political shift was necessary to provide a more coherent and effective framework of law for all disabled people in employment and in the provision of goods and services. Initiatives were being developed within the EU. In 1986 there was a non-binding Recommendation of the European Council on the Employment of Disabled Persons in the European Community. From the early 1980s, campaigning took place in Britain by pressure groups, trade unions and the solicitors' organisation, the Law Society. There were 15 unsuccessful attempts by backbench Members of Parliament to gain consent for private member's Bills. The Conservative government remained opposed until 1994 when, eventually, it proposed legislation and Parliament enacted the Disability Discrimination Act 1995 (with an exemption for small employers). This Act was subsequently improved as a result of both the European Employment Equality Directive 2000 and, in 2005, domestic legislation. Its provisions are now largely included in the Equality Act 2010 (see Chapter 5).

▌ Employment context of the 1995 Act

Surveys (Honey *et al.* 1993; Pidduck 1995) undertaken in the mid-1990s show that the employment context in which the new legislation was enacted was not generally propitious.

Honey *et al.* (1993) found that overall, it was the larger employers who were more likely to employ people with disabilities; to have a written policy which included disabled people; to have realistic perceptions of the costs and problems involved; to use the disability '*Two Ticks*' symbol; to seek to recruit and accommodate disabled persons; and to look for external help and advice. Employers who adopted one of these initiatives were more likely to have adopted others. On the whole, smaller organisations did not appear to have taken on board the legal, moral and good practice reasons for employing people with disabilities. Those employers who did not employ anyone with a disability were more likely to perceive physical and safety problems and to anticipate costly accommodations. They tended to hold stereotyped and exaggerated views of 'wheelchair bound' applicants bringing a range of difficulties relating to the type or level of work and to safety and to the premises.

Pidduck (1995), surveying mostly 'good practice' employers just prior to the implementation of the Disability Discrimination Act, suggested that employers' perceptions and their associated behaviours could be categorised into one of five groups. The incidence of the first three was reported to be generally found among small to medium-sized employers. The other two categories tended to be medium to large organisations.

- Those who were ignorant of the legislation and deliberately disregard it.
- Those who adopt an approach of minimal compliance. They generally have sufficient knowledge of the law to avoid being seen as directly discriminatory but they have little understanding of indirect discrimination.

- Those whose position is one of neutral reactivity. They have the potential to comply with not just the letter but also the spirit of the law. However, they need direction and encouragement.

- Those who, in both the public and private sector, have started to review their policies and to implement changes. They have seen the wider business reasons for accommodating those with disabilities.

- Those (many in the public sector) who constitute a positive and proactive group. Often they are members of the Employers' Forum on Disability. They are well-informed and have and continue to take a wide range of initiatives to facilitate the recruitment and retention of people with disabilities. The impetus for their initiatives has both a moral and business foundation dating back prior to the 1995 Act. The Act provided an added stimulus to their activities. They have developed a clear strategy.

Data (Disability Rights Commission 2004) in a survey of 1,000 small organisations employing up to 50 staff (some of whom came under the requirements of the Act for the first time that year) found a variety of responses – some optimistic and some stereotypical:

- 64 per cent of small business owners do not think that disabled people will take more sick leave than other people;

- 80 per cent do not think that disabled people will be 'less productive' than other workers;

- 45 per cent believe it would be 'very/quite difficult' to employ a disabled person;

- 87 per cent think that disabled people 'would fit into their team';

- 41 per cent said that when they hear the word 'disability' they immediately think of people in a wheelchair or someone with a physical impairment. (In fact, only around 7.5 per cent of disabled people are wheelchair users.)

Since the enactment of the 1995 Act and its subsequent amendments there has been progress – some fitful – in employment policies. Dewson *et al.* (2010: 1), in a survey of 1,000 respondent organisations, reflected this in their findings. For example, *'awareness'* of the Disability Discrimination Act 1995 (in force at the time) was partial: 20 per cent of employers could name the DDA 'spontaneously'; 49 per cent were 'aware of some legislation related to employment but were unable to name it'; and 30 per cent did not know of any such legislation.

As far as *'employment-related adjustments'* were concerned, the researchers found the following: 61 per cent of employers had made such an adjustment in the past or planned to do so. 'There had been a statistically significant fall since the last survey (the figure was 70 per cent in 2006).' Flexible working time or working arrangements were the most commonly reported adjustments (53 per cent and 50 per cent respectively). The proportion of employers making adjustments in response to a request from an employee increased from 22 per cent (2006) to 30 per cent (2009). The in-depth qualitative interviews with 97 respondents 'revealed that, in a few cases, employment-related adjustments had been made for new employees, but in most cases they had been made for existing employees, in response to specific needs' (*ibid.*).

▶ Labour market participation

Despite an increase of 8 per cent since 1999, the participation of disabled people in the labour market is markedly lower than for the non-disabled (see Table 4.10).

Table 4.10 **Employment by disability (Great Britain: people of working age)**

	In full-time employment (%)	*In part-time employment (%)*	*Employment rate*	*Unemployment rate*
Women				
Disabled*	54	46	49	6.2
Not disabled	59	41	75	3.9
All of working age (16–59 years)	**58**	**42**	**70**	**4.3**
Men				
Disabled*	87	13	52	8.8
Not disabled	91	9	85	4.5
All working age (16–64 years)	**91**	**9**	**79**	**5.1**

* People with a current disability, including DDA disabled and work-limiting disabled

Source: ONS (2005) *Labour Force Survey,* Spring, Office for National Statistics 2005, licensed under the Open Government Licence v.1.0

Employment rates vary greatly according to a person's type of impairment. Those with mental health issues have the lowest employment rate (at 21 per cent). People with diabetes have the highest at 68 per cent. The rate for people with learning difficulties was 23.2 per cent (down marginally from 1999).

Age discrimination: the context

▶ The concept of 'ageism'

According to Age Concern, the term 'ageism' was first coined in the 1960s by Robert Butler to denote a process of stereotyping and discrimination against people just because of their age. It is concerned with prejudice and discrimination based on age and more formally as 'a set of attitudes that generate fear and denigration of the ageing process and stereotyping presumptions regarding competence' (Bytheway 1995). More recently, MacNicol (2006: 11) has defined ageism in terms of attitudes and social relations as age-based group characteristics applied to individuals which are seen as embedded in patterns of thinking and which are 'rampant' in modern western societies. These in turn give rise to discrimination based on age – 'the most complex and difficult of discriminations that affect modern societies in that it is very difficult to identify, detect and prove' (*ibid.*: 6).

Other writers have also noted that age discrimination is unusual in that unlike other discrimination grounds where we can usually identify a distinct category of persons, we all have an age and could potentially be affected at some point in our lives. The life cycle also involves members of an 'in group' (prime age workers) eventually becoming members of an 'out group' (older workers). So, young people experience ageism as do older people. The definition of 'older people' can also be problematic. For some commentators it is an undifferentiated group over 50 years (the so-called 'Saga' generation); whilst others distinguish between 'young' old age (60–75 years) and 'old' old age (75 years and above).

▶ The incidence of ageism

There is overwhelming evidence that ageist attitudes and prejudice are widespread in Britain and that age discrimination is strongly embedded in many parts of social and economic life (Bytheway 1995; MacNicol 2006; Abrams *et al.* 2009). The Discrimination Law Review estimated that around 28 per cent of people have suffered discrimination on the grounds of age. A further survey reported that one in five employers indicated that they felt some jobs were more suitable for some age groups than others (Metcalf and Meadows 2006).

In evidence to the House of Lords Select Committee on the Economics of an Ageing Population (2003), the Trades Union Congress and a number of individual representations suggested that many line managers were simply unaware that the processes and procedures they used might be age discriminatory. The Report stated: 'we conclude from the evidence that there is significant age discrimination in employment and that this discrimination . . . is frequently the unconscious outcome of an employer's more general human resource management policy and procedure.'

Indeed, it is reasonable to comment that 'almost any HR policy or practice, term or condition is likely to have a disproportionate impact on some age group or another' (Rubenstein 2006) and as a result could be 'potentially indirectly discriminatory' (Fredman 2003: 58). So, as O'Cinneide (2005) comments, 'experience, "know-how", educational qualifications, decisionmaking capabilities, emotional maturity and almost any other neutral criterion that might be applicable in the employment context could put persons of a particular age at a disadvantage'. The experience of the past 25 years, then, suggests that the issue of age discrimination in the labour market is complex, with particular groups disproportionately affected.

▶ The 'drivers' of legislation

Despite evidence of ageism and age discrimination, proposals to legislate against it have, until recently, been rare. In Britain, some age-related discrimination was tackled through sex discrimination law (see Chapter 5). In some countries (Canada, the Netherlands and, to some extent, Ireland) measures to tackle age discrimination have emerged from a 'human rights' perspective. In the United States and the European Union the approach has been more pragmatic, reflecting a more utilitarian orientation (O'Cinneide 2005) aimed at addressing public policy issues. These policy concerns have centred on older workers and have sought to deal with their **economic activity rates** (see Tables 4.11 and 4.12). The underlying issues are possible social exclusion; the wider concerns surrounding an impending pensions crisis in many European economies; and concerns about a 'rising dependency ratio' (Exhibit 4.1). So, European policy initiatives have emphasised a 'supply side' agenda – removing barriers to the greater participation of older workers in the labour market. By the 1990s in Europe there was a greater willingness to consider age discrimination legislation. In 2000, the EU Employment Equality Directive included provisions for equal treatment on the grounds of age.

Table 4.11 **Economic activity rates by age (%)**

	1975	*1981*	*1985*	*1990*	*1995*	*2000*	*2006*
Men aged							
55–59	93.0	89.4	82.5	81.4	73.7	74.8	76.1
60–64	82.3	69.3	55.4	54.6	50.1	50.3	53.9
Women aged							
55–59	52.4	53.4	52.0	54.8	55.7	57.6	62.0
60–64	28.6	23.3	18.8	22.7	25.0	25.9	31.9

Sources: Labour Force Survey 2006; OECD (2001) 1985–2000 data; Taylor and Walter (1994) (1975–81 data)

Table 4.12 **Economic activity rates: above state pension age (%)**

	1992	*1994*	*1998*	*2002*	*2006*
Men (65+)	7.5	8.1	7.1	8.1	9.8
Women (60+)	7.6	7.7	8.1	8.9	11.7

The fourth quarters in the years indicated

Source: Labour Force Survey (various), Office for National Statistics. Licensed under the Open Government Licence v.1.0

EXHIBIT 4.1

Drivers of age discrimination legislation

Population, life expectancy and dependency ratios. In Europe, the median age of people is projected to rise from 29.2 years (1950) to 49.5 years (2050). At this date the average man in Britain will live to 83 years and the average woman to 90 years. Projections from the Department of Work and Pensions (2010) on the number of future centenarians suggest that, given 'underlying assumptions about future fertility, mortality and migration', there will be 21,900 in 2020 and 58,800 in 2030. This contrasts with 6,800 in 2000 (**www.dwp.gov.uk**).

To ensure that rising numbers drawing state pension do not impose a huge financial burden on those in work requires two possible policies for both government and employers:

- that people save more through pensions whilst in work; and
- the rate at which people retire is raised to maintain the level of the pensions.

The old-age dependency ratio (the number of people of pensionable age as a proportion of the working age population) was around 24 per cent in the OECD states in 2005 – approximately a fifth higher than in 1980. In Germany, Greece, Italy and Japan it was between 30 and 35 per cent; in the UK around 30 per cent; whilst in Turkey it was only 10 per cent. By 2050, it is estimated that with no change in retirement ages, this ratio will rise to 52 per cent in the OECD area; with rises to over 70 per cent in Italy, Spain and Japan (OECD 2006). The UK estimate is of a rise to 49 per cent (ONS 2008).

Raising economic activity rates of those over 50 years. This rate fell off sharply in the 1980s and 1990s. Official statistics show it has started to recover. Most of the reduction in older people's employment rates was involuntary. Evidence of activities undertaken by this cohort suggests that capability is not an issue.

Promoting the 'knowledge economy'. A key element of the EU Lisbon summit was a commitment to develop Europe as 'the most dynamic, knowledge based economy in the world'. The shift to this kind of service economy places far less premium on physical attributes. Knowledge may continue to be gained throughout working life and decays slower than physical ability. This underlines the continuing utility of older workers.

Social inclusion and exclusion. A major EU concern is that those leaving the labour market risk being isolated, unable to participate economically, socially and politically and may experience serious problems. 'Far from retirement being a time of passive dependency, most of those interviewed were making a real contribution to society. They were taking part in a huge range of activities, including various forms of unpaid work, learning activities, domestic work and caring for family, helping out friends and neighbours, and leisure and educational pursuits' (Barnes *et al.* 2002).

Equality principles. The principles of social justice, fairness and dignity have informed legislation in a number of jurisdictions.

❱ Older workers in the labour market

The labour market position of older workers has become a major policy concern throughout industrial and post-industrial economies. This has been prompted by a steady flow of these workers leaving the labour market in the 1980s and 1990s (see Tables 4.11 and 4.12). Those exiting were principally men: in manual occupations where there was a lack of demand for their skills; and those in financially secure higher occupations who chose economic inactivity. In contrast, the growing service economy created significant employment opportunities that benefited women generally and older and younger women in particular.

The Discrimination Law Review (**www.equalities.gov.uk**) (Rubenstein, 2007a) helpfully refocused attention on the labour market disadvantages faced by certain groups. It remains the case that some are significantly more disadvantaged with respect to age than others. Furthermore, as with other forms of discrimination, age combines with other factors to reinforce disadvantage. The labour market vulnerability of some groups of older men is evidenced by the fact that a fifth have no formal qualifications. They have a greater chance of becoming unemployed than their younger counterparts; and once unemployed are more likely to remain so for longer. Such data potentially self-reinforce and shape stereotypes of older workers as 'slow', 'resistant to change' and 'unwilling to embrace new ideas'. These are particular concerns when employers are increasingly looking for flexibility, dynamism and new ideas.

This situation will change because of greater access to tertiary education. It is estimated that the share of older workers with University or equivalent qualifications will rise from 22 per cent (2000) to 31 per cent (2025) in OECD countries. The proportion with less than an upper-secondary level of education will fall over the same period from 40 per cent to 21 per cent (OECD 2006).

There is also evidence that over the past ten years an increasing number of people over the age of 65 years have remained in work. The Office for National Statistics (**www.statistics.gov.uk**) reported that in 2001, 412,000 people over 65 were in work. In the last quarter of 2010 this had risen to 870,000. Disaggregating the figures, it recorded that 270,000 worked full time and 600,000 worked part time. There was also some evidence of continuity of employment for these older workers: 41 per cent had worked for the same employer for 20 years or more; and 24 per cent for between 10 and 20 years. The 2010 statistics were collated at a time when the default retirement age (DRA) was still in force and employees could request continued employment after the age of 65 years.

From October 2011, the DRA was abolished (see Chapter 5, Exhibit 5.10). It might therefore be reasonable to expect more workers above the age of 65 years to be active in the labour market. It is important to note that in another survey, 'the main reason for [economic] inactivity for people aged 50 to SPA [i.e. state pension age of 60 years for women and 65 years for men] was being long-term sick or disabled. Looking at unemployment, a smaller percentage of people aged 50 years to SPA were unemployed, 3.8 per cent compared to 5.2 per cent for people aged 25 to 49' (Barrett 2010: 22).

Sexual orientation discrimination: the context

Law on discrimination in employment was first enacted in 2003 on the grounds of *all* sexual orientation. However, the social wrongs committed historically have largely been on the grounds of homosexuality and, in particular, male homosexuality.

▶ Historic legal prohibitions

Negative social attitudes and punitive legislation in relation to homosexuality have a very long history. Stonewall (**www.stonewall.org.uk**) records evidence of the first mention in English common law of a punishment for homosexuality as 1290, with sodomites being burned alive in 1300. Under the first statute law, the Buggery Act 1533, hanging was the penalty. Whilst capital punishment for buggery was abolished in 1861, the nineteenth century saw the continued possibility of criminal liability. Legislation was passed in 1885 which created the offence of 'gross indecency' for a homosexual act. This criminal activity could result in blackmail. It was for an allegation of 'indecency' that the writer Oscar Wilde unsuccessfully sued the Marquis of Queensbury for criminal libel and was himself subsequently arrested and sentenced, in 1895, to two years' imprisonment with hard labour. The criminal law was slowly dismantled in the United Kingdom between 1967 and 2001.

▶ Social attitudes

Homosexuals, both historically and in the present day, have been the subject of abuse, harassment, assault and murder on the grounds of sexual orientation. Furthermore, views about the cause of their sexual orientation have often fuelled unacceptable conduct. Some historic attitudes, drawing on false science, have characterised homosexuality as a disease that can be 'cured'. Grotesque 'medical treatments' were perpetrated in Britain until the 1960s. This view continued to be propagated despite arguments from the late nineteenth century onwards that it was neither a disease nor a crime. It was asserted that homosexuality was innate. In recent years, ongoing scientific research has established satisfactorily that this is so.

Acceptance of differences in sexual orientation and more positive social attitudes have been more in evidence in recent years. Stonewall, the campaigning gay rights group, commissioned a *YouGov* survey of some 2,000 adults (2006) which reported the following among its findings:

- Only a quarter of people surveyed said they have a low opinion of lesbians and gay men.

- However, 55 per cent think that there is general public prejudice against gay people in Britain today. 'Women, people from ethnic minorities and younger people are most likely to acknowledge that anti-gay prejudice exists and to want it addressed' (para 2.3).

- 'In general, older white British men are least likely to support legal equality for lesbian and gay people. They are more likely to believe that anti-gay prejudice is not an important issue and should not be tackled' (para 2.3).

- Fifty-nine per cent of those surveyed 'think that public prejudice is caused by religious attitudes, despite the fact that this research demonstrates that "people of faith" are no more likely to be prejudiced than anyone else' (para 2.4). In fact, 84 per cent of religious people *disagreed* with the statement that 'homosexuality is morally unacceptable in all circumstances'. Also, 64 per cent of religious people would be 'comfortable if their local religious representative was gay' (para 3.6).

- 'Anti-gay bullying at work is also widespread. Thirteen per cent have witnessed verbal anti-gay bullying at work . . . Physical bullying also occurs at work and has been seen by 4 per cent of workers' (para 2.5) (see Chapter 7).

▮ Developments in legislation

Over the past 50 years, there have been a number of important incremental steps to achieve civil and employment rights for homosexuals.

Criminal law

After considerable campaigning, the report of the Wolfenden Committee (1957), and press publicity relating to homosexual acts by high profile individuals (including journalists, actors and politicians), in 1967 Parliament started the process of decriminalisation and moves towards positive human rights. The legislative action was as follows:

- *Decriminalisation*. The Sexual Offences Act 1967 decriminalised, in England and Wales, homosexual acts 'in private' between two consenting men over 21 years of age. Eventually, homosexuality was decriminalised in Scotland in 1980. Age of consent reduced to 18 in 1994; and to 16 (the same as for heterosexuals) in 2001. In 1981, the British government was ruled to be breaching Article 8 of the ECHR by refusing to legalise consenting homosexual behaviour in Northern Ireland. It was eventually decriminalised there in 1982. It was not decriminalised in the Isle of Man, under its special constitutional circumstances, until 1992.

- *Civil Partnerships Act 2004*. This legislation enabled a couple of the same sex to register their partnership. It confers on them the same rights as a married couple in respect of tax, social security, inheritance and workplace benefits. The first registrations took place in December 2005. The Equality Act 2010 provides protection against direct and indirect discrimination because of civil partnership (see Chapter 5). Since 2007, discrimination in the provision of goods and services has been unlawful.

- *Criminal Justice and Immigration Act 2008*. This provides protection against incitement to homophobic hatred and violence. There is a controversial 'religious defence' in the legislation.

Employment

Conferring employment rights and protection against discrimination has been a long, tortuous process. The Conservative government (1979–97) did not provide a facilitating political environment, with legislative opposition to 'the promotion of homosexuality'. The European Union took its first significant step to legislation in the Employment Directive 2000. It was transposed into British law as the Employment Equality (Sexual Orientation) Regulations 2003. In employment, it is also important to note that the Civil Partnership Act 2004 has a bearing on an employee's entitlements under their contract; and eligibility for non-contractual benefits (for example, the travel concessions in dispute in (*Grant v South West Trains Ltd* [1998] IRLR 188, ECJ case). Such claims are likely to be brought under the Equality Act 2010 (see Chapter 5).

Views on legislation

The Stonewall survey (2007) reported the following findings:

- 93 per cent supported the Employment Equality (Sexual Orientation) Regulations 2003 the original legislation concerning discrimination and harassment at work;
- 68 per cent supported the Civil Partnership Act 2004 concerning the legal status and rights of homosexual partners;
- 85 per cent supported the Equality Act (Sexual Orientation) Regulations 2007 concerning the provision of goods and services.

▌ The quality of employment relations

Stonewall has constructed a Workplace Equality Index to measure progress in the achievement of equal treatment on the grounds of sexual orientation. It undertook its 7th Index in 2011 (**www.stonewall.org.uk**). Employers are ranked according to various criteria using 25 questions covering 8 areas of good practice. In 2011, 387 organisations entered the Index to have their work recognised. The top five organisations were: the Home Office, Lloyds Banking Group, Ernst and Young, the Hampshire Constabulary and IBM.

Discrimination because of religion and belief: the context

▌ Incidence of religion/belief

Historically and formally, Britain is a Christian country. The Census 2001 for England and Wales reported that 37.3 million people stated that their religion was Christian (see Table 4.13). Much of this stated religious adherence may be nominal because it contrasts with the small percentage who attend Sunday worship. Indeed, it is argued that Britain is a more secular society than its formal commitment to Christianity suggests. Christianity reflects a wide spectrum of belief and religious practice, ranging from the puritanical Plymouth Brethren through various non-conformist religions to the 'established' Church of England (of which the monarch is the 'Defender of the Faith') and to the Catholic Church. A similar spectrum of orthodoxy and belief is also reflected in the two other major and historically important religions in European societies: Judaism and Islam. Neither has a high degree of uniformity of either belief or practice.

Table 4.13 **Recorded membership of religions**

	England	*Wales*	*Scotland*
Christian	35.3 m	2.1 m	3.3 m
Muslim	1.5 m	21,700	43,000
Jewish	257,600	2,200	6,400
Hindu	546,900	5,400	5,600
Sikh	327,343	2,000	6,600
Buddhist	139,000	5,400	6,800
No religion	7.17 m	538,000	1.4 m
Religion not stated	3.77 m	234,000	278,000

The question was voluntary

Source: Census 2001 statistics. National Statistics website: **www.statistics.gov.uk** Office for National Statistics, licensed under the Open Government Licence v.1.0

▶ Social tensions and religion

Religious belief can, of course, be the source of good works. However, there are circumstances in which tensions, sometimes serious, with religious organisations can arise:

● *Fundamentalism*: debates about the extent to which a relevant holy text (the Bible, the Torah or the Qur'an) is to be interpreted literally have been and remain consistent aspects of religions. This can give rise to 'fundamentalist' views and, as a consequence, a religion may become embedded in a political ideology. 'Fundamentalist' forms of such religious ideology can lead to the justification of intolerance, violence and murder. There is evidence of this 'fundamentalist' form of all three major religions.

● *Conflicting values*: this can arise from the relationship between an individual's personal religious belief and prevailing social values and legislation (see Exhibit 5.18).

● *Political activity*: the involvement of religion in politics by campaigning for specific objectives and trying to influence public policy and legislation, whilst legitimate, may not reflect the prevailing social views (on for example, abortion or gay rights).

● *Religious observance*: efforts to influence employers and society at large to facilitate particular religious observance. For employers this can arise in respect of observance of days of worship, religious festivals, religious dress and not being required to undertake work that conflicts with religious belief (see Chapters 5 and 6).

▶ Other beliefs

Alongside religious belief, it is important to remember that there are also the values and views of secularism. Within British society there is a long-standing strand of opinion that supports and promotes atheism, agnostic views, rationalism and humanism. Many adherents of these opinions and values seek to minimise the social and political role of religion and restrict it to a person's private life. Under the Equality Act 2010, political beliefs can also potentially be protected (see Chapter 5).

Table 4.14 **What clothes or accessories should people not be allowed to wear for work?**

Clothes/accessories	Percentage
Burkha/niqab/covering the whole body and face	65
Veil/hijab/covering the face	56
Religious knife or kirpan	19
Turban/kiffayeh/similar male headwear	8
Crucifix	5
Jewish skull cap/yamulke	3
Silver ring of abstinence	2
Orthodox Jewish hair and hat	2
Bindi/red Hindu dot on the face	2
Sari	2
Dreadlocks	2
Beard	1
Star of David/Mogon Davod	1

1,000 face-to-face interviews (December 2007). Based on statistically representative sample of religious and non-religious populations in Great Britain

Source: Employers Forum on Belief (**www.efbelief.org.uk**)

▶ Incidence of discrimination/attitudes to religion or belief

A survey commissioned by the Employers' Forum on Belief (2008, **www.efbelief.org.uk**) indicated a fairly consistent general view (across religions and non-religious people) that people should not be allowed to wear whatever they wanted according to their religious views. Almost half (48 per cent) agreed with this statement. Attitudes to specific religious clothes or accessories were tested (see Table 4.14). Views about the acceptability of wearing clothes that express their religion varied: 64 per cent thought teachers should not be allowed to wear such clothes; 51 per cent for police officers; and 44 per cent for doctors and nurses.

The state of the law

▶ What progress and what problems?

Since the enactment of the first legislation in the 1970s, various commentators have drawn attention to problems with discrimination law – particularly as it has developed across six strands. Aside from technical-legal issues, the key areas of concern are:

▶ Grounds of discrimination

These have expanded considerably but an inevitable question is whether or not they are sufficiently comprehensive. Some commentators point to the absence of discrimination on the grounds of **social origin** (which is included explicitly in the European Convention on Human Rights (Article 14)). The Chair of the Equality and Human Rights Commission commented in a speech (21 July 2008): 'While we are used to talking about inequality between different groups based on race, gender, disability and age, we need to think much bigger than that. We need to regain the habit of talking about vertical inequality – or, in other words, that taboo subject, economic class . . . The divide between rich and poor has widened to its highest level for 40 years according to recent research by the Joseph Rowntree Foundation.' In the British Social Attitudes Survey, 76 per cent of people considered the gap between rich and poor to be too large.

The Equality Act 2010 (s 1) imposes a duty on public authorities 'regarding socio-economic inequalities'. It is not to be implemented by the Conservative–Liberal Democrat government. In an 'equality strategy' speech (17 November 2010) the Home Secretary and Minister for Women and Equalities, Theresa May, characterised the duty this way: 'It was meant to force public authorities to take into account inequality of outcome when making decisions about their policies. In reality, it would have been just another bureaucratic box to be ticked . . . But at its worst, it could have meant public spending permanently skewed towards certain parts of the country' (**www.homeoffice. gov.uk/media-centre/speeches/equality-vision**).

Other commentators draw attention to discrimination in respect of **genetic information**. 'As biotechnology progresses, it is becoming increasingly feasible to test for genetic traits that indicate a susceptibility to developing specific illnesses or disorders' (Rubenstein 2007b: 31). Federal legislation was enacted on this issue in the United States in 2008 (to be implemented in 2009) covering employers and health insurers (*Equal Opportunities Review*, 177, June 2008). The Labour government stated it had decided 'not to extend protection against discrimination on the ground of genetic predisposition. We have recently agreed to the insurance industry's proposal to extend until 2014 the existing arrangements for a voluntary moratorium on insurers' use of predictive genetic test results and consider that this, along with continued monitoring [by the Human Genetics Commission] of the use of genetic testing in the UK should provide sufficient reassurance' (*The Equality Bill – Government Response to the Consultation*, 2008, para 15.1). The UK is behind many other EU member states who have legislated. Action in the UK to extend protection against discriminatory treatment will only arise from both social and political pressure.

Other writers and lobby groups point to the failure to cover effectively those with **criminal convictions**. Given it is recorded that a third of men have a criminal record, the potential for discrimination is considerable. The legislation, the Rehabilitation of Offenders Act 1974, was described in a Home Office report (2002) as being 'confusing' and 'not achieving the right balance between resettlement and protection'. No immediate action looks likely to clarify this area. Nevertheless, the circumstances should be propitious for greater clarification of the law and a public policy commitment in favour of rehabilitation – particularly given the excessively high (mostly male) prison population. The CIPD research (2007) has found that three-quarters of employers would consider recruiting ex-offenders if they had relevant skills but only if government improves support for employers (in respect of rehabilitation and training; and guidance on risk assessments). But relatively few employers offer work to people just released from prison.

Finally, the issue of protection against **caste discrimination** could easily be implemented. It is provided for in the Equality Act 2010 (s 9(5)). The Labour government commissioned a research report from the National Institute of Economic and Social Research on the issue. It was published in December 2010 and awaits a decision on implementation by the Conservative–Liberal Democrat Government.

The researchers reported that 'caste awareness in Britain is concentrated amongst people with roots in the Indian sub-continent (who comprise five per cent of the population). It is not religion specific and is subscribed to by and affects members of any or no religion' (Metcalfe and Rolfe 2010: i). The study identified evidence of work-related discrimination and harassment (bullying, recruitment, promotion, task allocation) which could be covered by the Equality Act 2010; and in the provision of services. 'The caste discrimination and harassment identified in this study was by higher castes against the lowest castes.' The researchers added that 'relying on the Indian community to take action to reduce caste discrimination and harassment is problematic' (*ibid.*).

❯ Implementing public-sector equality duties

Criticism has arisen in part as a result of the ways in which the initial statutory duties on public authorities (particularly in relation to race) have been implemented. Surveys in *Equal Opportunities Review* show that 'organisations can become too focused on process rather than outcomes'. They 'can view the publishing of their equality scheme as the completion of the legal requirement rather than the starting point' (Godwin 2007). The Commission for Racial Equality (2007) (in a final report before it was wound up) listed its main areas of concern: a failure to collect data for all required areas; a failure to collect data using appropriate ethnic monitoring categories; the very high numbers of staff whose ethnicity was not known; a failure to analyse data; a failure to publish employment data; no action plan in the organisation's race equality schemes; and schemes that just reiterated the wording of the race equality duty.

Other research suggests a slightly more positive aspect. Research among 113 public-sector organisations (mostly in the health service and local government) reported that 44 per cent of the respondents had chosen to produce a single equality scheme or adopt a combined approach across all strands of discrimination law. The reasons being: to avoid duplication, reduce costs in communication and in staff training. However, two-thirds of organisations had separate equality schemes as well as an overall single scheme (Schneider-Ross 2007).

The complexity and 'bureaucratisation' of equal opportunities inherent in having parallel duties may start to be tackled with the single duty in the Equality Act 2010.

❯ Covert discrimination

Secrecy bedevils the identification of discriminatory treatment; and in particular the achievement of equal pay. The limitations on obtaining reliable evidence and data make it difficult to formulate a persuasive and convincing complaint. The explicit use of contract law to compound the secrecy is a serious problem because of the likely consequence of breach of contract by the employee that might arise. Equal Opportunities Commission research (2004, **www.equalityhumanrights.com**) recorded that 22 per cent of employers did not permit employees to share pay information with colleagues. A provision to outlaw secrecy clauses is in the Equality Act 2010. It should be one step towards diagnosing more accurately the nature of a gender pay gap.

▶ Positive action

As indicated earlier in this chapter, this action can be particularly contentious and confusing. A survey by the Confederation of British Industry (2007) reported that just over a quarter of companies said that they had not adopted it because they were unsure of what was allowable positive action and unlawful positive discrimination. The extension of positive action through the use of the 'tie break' has been evident in some other European countries and is compatible with European law (see Exhibit 5.4). It has obvious merits in dealing with under-representation. However, clarity on its objectives and operation are particularly important (see Chapter 5).

▶ Compound discrimination

Currently, people can only bring a claim that someone has treated them unfairly because of *one* particular characteristic. But there are situations where people are discriminated against because of a particular combination of characteristics. This means that 'there is little information about the number of people that are prevented from bringing claims as a result of this limitation' (Moon 2008). Drawing on evidence from Ontario which includes Toronto, one of the most diverse cities in Canada, it has been noted that 'the Ontario Human Rights Commission, which can support claims of multiple discrimination, found that 48 per cent of its cases between 1997 and 2000 involved multiple discrimination . . . it seems likely that a similar pattern could be found in some parts of Britain too'. Other evidence points to potential multiple discrimination, such as:

- Bangladeshi and Pakistani women experiencing racism, sexism and anti-Muslim prejudice;
- African people with HIV experiencing racism and homophobia (and sexism if they are female).

This is a complex issue and the specific provision 'combined discrimination: dual characteristics' was included in the Equality Act 2010 (s 14). However, it is not being implemented by the Conservative–Liberal Democrat Government.

▶ Monitoring

This remains a perennial problem for the achievement of effective equal opportunities. The Discrimination Law Review (**www.equalities.gov.uk**) stated that 'a reporting regime which could guarantee the necessary degree of accuracy would be bureaucratic, burdensome on employers and costly to run and enforce'. Behind these, perhaps dispiriting, words are the essential problems of monitoring: time, trouble and cost. Evidence on the limited compliance with statutory equality duties (see above) shows the difficulties. Although a statutory duty on employers (with more than ten employees) to monitor and report does exist under religious discrimination law in Northern Ireland, it is not part of discrimination law in the rest of the UK. The Equality Act 2010 made no provision along similar lines. Monitoring is only recommended in the statutory *Code of Practice on Employment* (2011) published by the Equality and Human Rights Commission (**www.equalityhumanrights.com**).

❱ Weak enforcement

There are several issues that have been commented upon:

- *Recommendations by employment tribunals*. As around 70 per cent of employees involved in discrimination complaints leave the organisation, this 'ties the hands of tribunals' who may only make recommendations for that complainant (Rubenstein 2007a). However, the Equality Act 2010 (s 124) does allow an employment tribunal to make a wider recommendation on employment/human resource policy and practice.

- *Individual complaints*. Current legislation is founded upon individual complaints. One proposal for overcoming this limitation to the enforcement process would be to permit 'representative actions' (where a common problem affected a group of employees). The Discrimination Law Review was 'not persuaded' there should be a move to these.

- *Workplace enforcement*. There are two aspects of this: collective bargaining and workplace trade union representation. Both have limitations because of the relatively low density of trade union membership and recognition. Twenty years ago, in one survey of research studies, Dickens and Colling (1990) pointed to the weakness of collective bargaining as an instrument for promoting and reinforcing equal opportunities policies. Largely the negotiating focus was on a traditional pay and conditions agenda. Recent steps to help overcome these problems include unions appointing equality workplace representatives. A report to the Wales TUC (May 2008) concluded that unions had made considerable progress mainstreaming equal pay and incorporating flexible working into their bargaining priorities. Large unions like UNITE have adopted a Model Agreement for such representatives; and the government-funded Union Modernisation Fund is promoting training (Godwin 2008b).

Conclusion

This chapter aimed to provide a flavour of the diversity and Britain's labour market and society and of the basis on which discriminatory treatment might arise. No apology is made for indicating the historical context of such treatment. Long-standing views, stereotypes and prejudices have embedded discriminatory attitudes in society and, as a consequence, in the workplace. Eradication of these remains a long haul. The achievement of equal opportunities is probably something that, to use the old advertising strapline, we 'are working towards' and are unlikely to achieve. There will always be challenges to policies, practices and conduct in employment and in society at large. Nevertheless, the issue is to improve these and, where appropriate, to modify corporate cultures through the adoption and effective implementation of proactive equal opportunities policies (see Chapter 6). Success will be measured, in part, by occupational profiles that better represent opportunities for all individual employees. Success will also be measured by reductions in grievances and employment tribunal complaints rather than in a utopian dream of their total elimination.

References

Abrams, D. *et al.* (2009) *Attitudes to Age in Britain 2004–8*, London: Department of Work and Pensions (www.dwp.gov.uk).

Ashtiany, S. (2007) 'Discrimination law – where did it come from and where is it going?', Industrial Law Society Conference, May.

Barrett, R. (2010) 'Disadvantaged Groups in the Labour Market', *Economic and Labour Market Review*, Vol. 4 No. 6, London: Office for National Statistics.

Berthoud, R. and Blekesaune, M. (2007) *Persistent Employment Disadvantage*, Research Report No. 416. London: Department of Work and Pensions.

Boonstras, J. *et al.* (eds) (1993) *Antisemitism: a History Portrayed*. Amsterdam: Anne Frank Foundation.

Bytheway, B. (1995) *Ageism*. Buckingham: Open University Press.

Campbell-Barr, V. and Granham, A. (2010) *Childcare – a Review of What Parents Want*, Equality and Human Rights Commission Research Report 66 (www.equalityhuman-rights.com).

Chartered Institute of Personnel and Development (1996) *Managing Diversity: a Position Paper*. London: CIPD (www.cipd.co.uk).

Chartered Institute of Personnel and Development (2007) *Employing Ex-Offenders to Capture Talent*. London: CIPD (www.cipd.co.uk).

Commission for Racial Equality (2007) *CRE Monitoring and Enforcement Report 2005–07*. London: Commission for Racial Equality.

Confederation of British Industry (2007) *CBI/Pertemps Survey of 507 Employers* (www.cbi.org.uk).

Daniel, W.W. (1968) *Racial Discrimination in England*. Harmondsworth: Penguin Books.

Lord Davies of Abersoch (2011) *Women on Boards*, London: Department for Business, Innovation and Skills, www.bis.gov.uk.

Deakin, S. and Morris, G. (1998) *Labour Law*. Oxford: Hart.

Denvir, A. *et al.* (2007) *The Experiences of Sexual Orientation and Religion or Belief Discrimination Employment Tribunal Claimants*. London: Advisory, Conciliation and Arbitration Service (www.acas.org.uk).

Dewson, S. *et al.* (2010) *Organisations' reponses to the Disability Discrimination Act: 2009 Study*, Research Report 685, London: Department for Work and Pensions (www.dwp.gov.uk).

Dickens, L. and Colling, T. (1990) 'Why Equality Won't Appear on the Bargaining Agenda', *Personnel Management*, April.

Disability Rights Commission (2004) *Small Employers' Attitudes to Disability*. DRC archive at www.equalityhumanrights.com.

Equal Opportunities Commission (2006) *Facts about Women and Men in Great Britain*. Manchester: Equal Opportunities Commission (www.equalityhumanrights.com).

Equal Opportunities Commission (2007) *The State of the Modern Family*, Millennium Cohort Survey. Manchester: Equal Opportunities Commission (www.equalityhumanrights.com).

Equality and Human Rights Commission (2008) *Sex and Power 2008*. London: Equality and Human Rights Commission (www.equalityhumanrights.com).

Equality and Human Rights Commission (2010) *How Fair is Britain?*: triennial review of equality (www.equalityhumanrights.com).

Fevre, R. *et al.* (2008) Work Fit for All: Disability, Health and the Experience of Negative Treatment in the British Workplace. London: Equality and Human Rights Commission.

Fredman, S. (1997) *Women and the Law*. Oxford: Oxford University Press.

Fredman, S. (2003) 'The age of equality', in Fredman, S. and Spencer, S. (eds) *Age as an Equality Issue*. Oxford: Hart.

Godwin, K. (2007) 'Positive Action: Possibilities and Limits', *Equal Opportunities Review*, 170, November.

Godwin, K. (2008a) 'Disability Policies: EOR Survey 2008', *Equal Opportunities Review*, 177, June.

Godwin, K. (2008b) 'The Missing Link: Union Equality Representatives at Work', *Equal Opportunities Review*, 173, February.

Grainger, H. and Fitzner, G. (2007) *The First Fair Treatment at Work Survey: Executive Summary – Updated*, Employment Relations Research Series, No. 63. London: Department of Trade and Industry (www.bis.gov.uk).

Grimshaw, D. and Rubery, J. (2007) *Understanding Women's Work*. Manchester: Equal Opportunities Commission.

Hansard Society (1990) *Women at the Top: the Report of the Commission on Women at the Top*. London: The Hansard Society.

Hiro, D. (1973) *Black British, White British*. Harmondworth: Penguin Books.

HM Government (2011) *Consultation on Modern Workplaces*, London: Department for Business, Innovation and Skills (www.bis.gov.uk).

Holdsworth, A. (1988) *Out of the Doll's House*. London: BBC Books.

Home Office (2002) *Breaking the Circle: a Report of the Review of the Rehabilitation of Offenders Act*. London: The Home Office.

Honey, S. *et al.* (1993) *Employers' Attitudes Towards People with Disabilities*. Brighton: Institute of Manpower Studies.

Justice (1996) *The Union Divided: Race Discrimination and Third Country Nationals in the European Union*. London: Justice.

Kandola *et al.* (1994) *Diversity in Action: Managing the Mosaic*. London: Chartered Institute of Personnel and Development.

Kaur, H. (2004) *Employment Attitudes: Main Finding from British Social Attitudes Survey 2003*, Employment Relations Research Series, No. 36. London: Department of Trade and Industry (www.bis.gov.uk).

MacNicol, J. (2006) *Age Discrimination: an Historical and Contemporary Analysis*. Cambridge: Cambridge University Press.

Mason, D. (1995) *Race and Ethnicity in Modern Britain*. Oxford: Oxford University Press.

Massie, B. (1994) *Disabled People and Social Justice*. London: Institute for Public Policy Research.

Metcalf, H. and Meadows, P. (2006) *Survey of Employers' Policies, Practices and Preferences Relating to Age*, Employment Relations Research Series, No. 49. London: Department of Trade and Industry (www.bis.gov.uk).

Metcalfe, H. and Rolfe, H. (2010) *Caste Discrimination and Harassment in Great Britain*, London: National Institute of Economic and Social Research (www.equalities.gov.uk).

Moon, G. (2008) 'Multi-dimensional Discrimination: Justice for the Whole Person', *Equal Opportunities Review*, 173, February.

O'Cinneide, C. (2005) *Age Discrimination and European Law*. Brussels: European Commission.

Olsen, L. and Walby, S. (2004) *Modelling Gender Pay Gaps*. Manchester: Equal Opportunities Commission.

Parekh, B. (1992) 'A Case of Positive Discrimination', in Hepple, B. and Szyszczak, E.M. (eds) *Discrimination: the Limits of the Law*. London: Mansell.

Pidduck, J. (1995) (unpublished) 'The Implications of the Disability Discrimination Act for People with Disabilities'. Kingston-upon-Thames: Kingston University Business School.

Pitt, G. (1992) 'Can Reverse Discrimination be Justified?', in Hepple, B. and Szyszczak, E.M. (eds) *Discrimination: the Limits of the Law*. London: Mansell.

Rubenstein, M. (2006) 'Age regulations 2006 – part 1: key general principles', *Equal Opportunities Review*, May, No. 152.

Rubenstein, M. (2007a) 'Discrimination Law Review: EOR Guide', *Equal Opportunities Review*, No. 167: 30.

Rubenstein, M. (2007b) What is the Next Frontier for Discrimination Law? *Equal Opportunities Review*, July, No. 166.

Schneider-Ross, diversity consultants (2007) *The Public Sector Equality Duties – Making an Impact* (www.schneider-ross.com).

Stephen Lawrence Inquiry Report (1999) Cm 4262-1. London: Stationery Office.

Stonewall (2007) *Living Together: British Attitudes to Lesbian and Gay People* (www.stonewall.org.uk).

Taylor, P. and Walter, A. (1994) 'The ageing workforce: employers' attitudes towards employing older people', *Employment and Society*, Vol. 8, No. 4.

Trades Union Congress (2008a) *Closing the Gender Pay Gap: an Update Report for TUC Women's Conference 2008*. London: Trades Union Congress (www.tuc.org.uk).

Trades Union Congress (2008b) *Trade Unions, Disabled Members and the Social Model*. London: Trades Union Congress (www.tuc.org.uk).

Trades Union Congress (2010) The Gender Impact of the Cuts. London (www.tuc.org.uk).

Walby, S. and Olson, L. (2002) *The Impact of Women's Position in the Labour Market on Pay and Implications for UK Productivity*. London: Women and Equality Unit.

Weiss, S. (1974) 'Equal Treatment and the Disabled: a Proposal', *Columbia Journal of Social Problems*, 10.

Wood, P. (1991) *International Classification of Impairments, Disabilities and Handicaps*. Geneva: World Health Organisation.

Useful websites

Advisory, Conciliation and Arbitration Service **www.acas.org.uk**

Chartered Institute of Personnel and Development **www.cipd.co.uk**

Confederation of British Industry **www.cbi.org.uk**

Department for Business Enterprise and Regulatory Reform **www.bis.gov.uk**

Employment Tribunals and EAT **www.justice.gov.uk**

Equality and Human Rights Commission **www.equalityhumanrights.com**

Government Equalities Office **www.equalities.gov.uk**

Joseph Rowntree Foundation **www.jrf.org.uk**

Schneider-Ross **www.schneider-ross.com**

Stonewall **www.stonewall.org.uk**

Trades Union Congress **www.tuc.org.uk**

UK Statistics Authority **www.statistics.gov.uk**

Visit **www.mylawchamber.co.uk/willey** to access study support resources including realistic HR documentation to accompany the case studies in the book, an online chapter on collective labour law, interactive multiple choice questions, annotated weblinks, a glossary, glossary flashcards, key case flashcards, a legal newsfeed and legal updates.

Chapter 5

Equality law and the workplace

Learning objectives

To understand:

- The 'protected characteristics' for which discrimination is prohibited
- The underpinning by European Union directives of equality law
- The terminology and provisions in the legislation
- The enforcement process for individuals to obtain remedies

Structure of the chapter

This chapter is organised as follows:

- *Introduction*: European directives; transposition into UK law; status of previous discrimination case law; the language of equality law; statutory Codes of Practice; other related legislation; Equality and Human Rights Commission.

- *Equality Act 2010*: protected characteristics; public sector equality duty; who is covered? Prohibited conduct – direct discrimination, comparators, indirect discrimination, objective justification, occupational requirements, positive action, instructing, discriminatory advertsisements, aiding unlawful acts. Enforcement – employer's liability and defence; personal liability; burden of proof; statutory questionnaire; complaints to employment tribunal; time limits; victimisation. Remedies – declaration, compensation, award for injury to feelings.

- *'Protected characteristics', legal issues and case law*: age, disability, gender reassignment, marriage and civil partnership, pregnancy and maternity, race, religion or belief, sex and sexual orientation.

- *Exercises*

Introduction

This chapter provides an outline of equality law. The social, economic and political context in which this law was formulated and enacted was discussed in Chapter 4. The key employment policy implications for human resource practitioners are outlined in Chapter 6. The related issues of harassment at work, equal pay and pregnancy and maternity are examined in detail later (in Chapters 7, 9 and 11 respectively).

▶ EU directives

The bulk of UK equality legislation is underpinned by European law. In most cases it is compliant with the principles and provisions of EU **directives**. However, there are aspects of some UK legislation, as outlined below, which are 'home grown'; and there are some cases where compliance is challenged. The relevant EU directives are:

● *Equal treatment of men and women (2006)*: This consolidates and updates four major directives: equal pay (1975); equal treatment (1976); occupational social security schemes (1986); and the **burden of proof** (1997). These earlier directives are repealed.

● *Directive for establishing a general framework for equal treatment in employment (2000)*: This Employment Equality Framework Directive provides anti-discrimination measures relating to age, disability, sexual orientation and religion or belief.

● *Equal treatment irrespective of racial or ethnic origin (2000)*: This is often referred to as the Race Directive.

▶ Transposition into UK law

As appropriate, the principal implementation of these directives in the UK was through the following legislation:

● Sex Discrimination Act 1975;

● Equal Pay Act 1970;

● Race Relations Act 1976;

● Disability Discrimination Act 1995;

● Employment Equality (Sexual Orientation) **Regulations** 2003;

● Employment Equality (Religion or Belief) Regulations 2003;

● Employment Equality (Age) Regulations 2006.

From October 2010, most of the Equality Act 2010 came into force. This new statute re-enacts most previous statutory provisions and repeals that legislation. Also, as noted below, it overturns certain case law.

One significant consequence of the European base of equality law is that the interpretation of **statutory** provisions and claims of non-compliance have been taken to the European Court of Justice. In the chapter there are references to important ECJ rulings.

▶ Previous case law and the Equality Act 2010

A considerable body of case law has developed under the previous discrimination law. What is its relevance now? This case law is likely to be applicable to the interpretation of the Equality Act 2010 where it clearly relates to common provisions in the new legislation. Examples of this are likely to be the 'but for' test applicable to defining direct discrimination (*James* v *Eastleigh Borough Council* [1990] IRLR 288, HL); and the definition of employer vicarious liability as set out in *Jones* v *Tower Boot* [1997] IRLR 68, CA. Where the Equality Act 2010 contains provisions which are substantially different to those in previous legislation, new case law may arise in the future. In some areas, previous case law has been explicitly overturned by the Equality Act. An example of this is the ruling (in *London Borough of Lewisham* v *Malcolm* [2008] IRLR 700) on 'disability-related discrimination' (a concept that no longer exists in the new Act). So, obviously, great care needs to be taken in relation to previous case law. Practitioners should be alert to new cases and rulings as they come through the courts.

❱ The language of equality law

Before discussing the detailed provisions of the legislation, it is useful to give a *broad* overview of the concepts used in equality law:

- *Direct discrimination* refers to 'less favourable treatment' than a particular comparator.

- *Indirect discrimination* is where an apparently neutral employment practice (for example, the requirement that a particular job is 'full time') may be discriminatory in effect. It is important to note that claims of direct and indirect discrimination can arise from the same facts.

- *The issue of 'justification'* is where, in specific circumstances, an employer might defend discriminatory treatment – usually for reasons of business necessity.

- *Occupational requirements*: this is where a person specification requires an individual with a particular characteristic that appears to infringe equality law. An employer has to show that such a requirement is an 'exception' under the relevant provisions of the law.

- *Positive action* is the encouragement of applications in recruitment, promotion and training of people from under-represented groups.

- *Liability* for discriminatory treatment. There are three possible aspects: the strict liability of the employer; the employer's vicarious liability (for the conduct of its employees); and the personal liability of perpetrators of discrimination and harassment.

- *Defence against vicarious liability* is where an employer argues that it took all reasonable steps to deal with discrimination.

- *Burden of proof* in discrimination claims to an employment tribunal involves two broad aspects: the employee needs to make a *prima facie* case outlining the facts. The burden, then, shifts to the respondent employer to show that there was no discrimination. The complainant may use the statutory questionnaire procedure to obtain information from the employer to support his or her claim.

- *Victimisation* is where those involved in employment tribunal complaints; those who have information or evidence for tribunal proceedings; and those who make an allegation of contravention of the Equality Act are treated detrimentally and have protection from detrimental treatment.

- *Remedies* include compensation, award for injury to feelings, and recommendations.

- *Public sector equality duty* concerns the equality obligations on public authorities in the way they carry out all their functions.

❱ Statutory codes of practice

The Equality Act 2010 is supported by statutory Codes of Practice which replace earlier codes. Two new Codes of Practice have been drafted by the Equality and Human Rights

Commission: the *Code of Practice on Employment*; and the *Code of Practice on Equal Pay*. These relate to Part 5 of the Equality Act, '*Work*', and came into force on 26 January 2011. A further Code of Practice, whilst not **directly** concerning employment, will have importance for many employers: the *Code of Practice on services, public functions and associations*. This relates to Parts 3 and 7 of the Equality Act 2010. All Codes can be downloaded from the ECHR website (**www.equalityhumanrights.com**). The ECHR has also published guidance on the single public sector duty and on the positive action provisions (see also Chapter 6 and Exhibit 6.1).

▶ Other related legislation

It is important to note that equality law (apart from that relating to age) also encompasses provisions relating to the treatment of individuals in a wider range of social relationships (i.e. in the provision of goods, facilities and services). In this chapter, however, the focus is, obviously, on the employment relationship. Nevertheless, interpretations of the law in non-employment cases may be relevant.

Finally, it should be remembered that five other bodies of law (largely deriving from European directives) are linked with the equality law discussed in this chapter:

- law on equal pay (included in the Equality Act 2010 (see Chapter 9);
- law on *harassment* (which is prohibited under the Equality Act 2010) (see Chapter 7);
- legislation relating to *family leave and flexible working* (see Chapter 11);
- law concerning discrimination on the grounds of *'atypical' employment status* of agency, part-time and fixed-term working (see Chapter 2);
- legislation concerning the rights of trade union members and employee representatives not to be subject to a detriment or dismissal; and also protection against 'blacklisting' (see **web chapter** on *Collective employment law*).

Furthermore, two other Acts have a bearing on sexual orientation and gender re-assignment: the Civil Partnership Act 2004 and the Gender Recognition Act 2004. These cover wider social rights but may, occasionally, be relevant to specific employment relations issues.

▶ The Equality and Human Rights Commission

Established in 2007, it took over the responsibilities of the former equality commissions. It has responsibilities for advice to government on and enforcement of all strands of discrimination law (see Chapter 1) (**www.equalityhumanrights.com**).

Equality Act 2010

This Act covers a wide range of social and economic behaviour. It deals with the provision of goods, services and facilities and with employment. For the purposes of this textbook, the focus will be on employment – with some passing reference to the other provisions. It refers to 'protected characteristics' and 'prohibited conduct'. These are summarised in Exhibit 5.1 (Y indicates that there are some provisions). All the issues identified in this table are discussed subsequently in some detail.

EXHIBIT 5.1

Protected characteristics and prohibited conduct at work

	Age	Disability	Gender reassignment	Marriage/ civil partnership	Pregnancy/ maternity	Race	Religion or belief	Sex	Sexual orientation
Direct discrimination	Y-may be justified	Y-no justification	Y-no justification	Y-no justification	Y-no justification	Y-no justification	Y-no justification	Y-no justification	Y-no justification
Associative discrimination	Y	Y	Y	Y	N?	Y	Y	Y	Y
Discrimination by perception	Y	Y	Y	N	N	Y	Y	Y	Y
Indirect discrimination	Y-may be justified	Y-may be justified	Y-may be justified	Y-may be justified	N	Y-may be justified	Y-may be justified	Y-may be justified	Y-may be justified
Occupational requirement	Y-may be lawful	Y-may be lawful	Y-may be lawful	Y-may be lawful	N	Y-may be lawful	Y-may be lawful	Y-may be lawful	Y-may be lawful
Harassment	Y	Y	Y	N	N	Y	Y	Y	Y
Harassment by third party	Y	Y	Y	N	N	Y	Y	Y	Y
Victimisation	Y	Y	Y	Y	Y	Y	Y	Y	Y

❭ 'Protected characteristics'

The Act identifies nine 'protected characteristics' (EA 2010, s 4):

- *Age*: This refers to an 'age group' – whether by reference to a particular age or a range of ages (s 5).

- *Disability*: This refers to a person who has a physical or mental impairment which has a substantial and long-term adverse effect on his or her ability to carry out normal day-to-day activities (s 6).

- *Gender reassignment*: This is where a person intends to undergo, is undergoing or has undergone a process (or part of a process) for 'the purpose of reassigning a person's sex by changing physiological or other attributes of sex' (s 7). Medical supervision is no longer required for the person to be protected.

- *Marital status or civil partnership*: Where a person is married or is a civil partner (s 8).

- *Pregnancy and maternity*: This relates to pregnancy, pregnancy-related illness, access to maternity leave (s 18). This covers the 'protected period' between the start of the pregnancy and the end of maternity leave (or a woman's return from leave if earlier). (For more information on pregnancy rights see also Chapter 11.)

- *Race*: This includes colour, nationality, ethnic or national origin (s 9(1)). A reference to 'race' is a reference to a person of a particular 'racial group'. A 'racial group' is a group of persons defined by reference to race. 'The fact that racial group comprises two or more distinct racial groups does not prevent it from constituting a particular racial group' (s 9(2)–(4)).

- *Religion or belief*: 'Religion' refers to any religion or lack of religion. 'Belief' refers to any religious or philosophical belief; or a lack of belief (s 10).

- *Sex*: This is a reference to either a women or a man (s 11).

- *Sexual orientation*: Refers to orientation to the opposite sex, the same sex or either sex (s 12).

These 'protected characteristics' are examined later in this chapter in relation to relevant legal issues and case law.

❭ Public sector equality duty

The Equality Act 2010 (s 149) provides for an encompassing equality duty covering all protected characteristics apart from 'marriage and civil partnership':

> A public authority must, in the exercise of its functions, have due regard to the need to:
>
> (a) eliminate discrimination, harassment, victimisation and any other conduct that is prohibited by or under this Act;
>
> (b) advance equality of opportunity between persons who share a relevant protected characteristic and persons who do not share it;
>
> (c) foster good relations between persons who share a relevant protected characteristic and persons who do not share it (s 149(1)).

The relevant public authorities are listed in Schedule 19.

The single equality duty, originally to come into force in April 2011, has been put back until April 2012 (see **www.equalities.gov.uk**). The Equality and Human Rights Commission has published guidance on this duty (see **www.equalityhumanrights.com**).

The Equality Act also sets out a public sector duty relating to 'socio-economic equalities' (ss 1–3). The Conservative–Liberal Democrat government decided against the implementation of this socio-economic duty (see **www.equalities.gov.uk**).

Under previous discrimination legislation, there were three such statutory duties:

- *Race discrimination* (in force from 2002 with specific CRE Code of Practice).

- *Sex discrimination* (in force from April 2007 with specific EOC Code of Practice).

- *Disability* (in force from 2006 together with accompanying specific DRC Code).

These are replaced by the over-arching duty in the Equality Act 2010.

▶ Who is covered?

The employment provisions of the Equality Act 2010 cover a range of people (s 39) including the following:

Applicants for employment

An employer must not discriminate against a person nor victimise them:

- in the arrangements he makes for deciding to whom to offer employment

- in the terms on which employment is offered

- by not offering employment (s 39(1) and (3)).

So, for example, a job specification should not contain discriminatory criteria unless there is a lawful occupational requirement. Pay should not be discriminatory between men and women. A decision to refuse employment should be for an objective, non-discriminatory reason.

Employees

An employer must not discriminate against an employee nor victimise them:

- in the terms on which that person is employed

- in ways in which there is access (or no access) to the following: opportunities for promotion, transfer or training; or for receiving any other benefit, facility or service

- by dismissing the employee

- by subjecting the employee to any other **detriment** (i.e. any disadvantage in his/her employment) (s 39(2) and (4)).

Those personally performing work

The Act (s 83(2)), in defining 'employment' and related expressions, states that it means: 'employment under a contract of employment, a contract of apprenticeship or a contract personally to do work'. This gives the legislation a wide coverage. The intricate employment status issues discussed earlier in the textbook (see Chapter 2) are unlikely to be scrutinised as part of any employment tribunal complaint except, perhaps, in respect of self-employed workers. Under the previous Sex Discrimination Act 1975, this issue was tested in one case (*Quinnen v Hovels* [1984] IRLR 227, EAT). A self-employed salesman of 'fancy goods' who had 'pitches' in various department stores recruited some temporary assistants to work for him on a commission basis. Although they were self-employed, the EAT ruled that they were protected by the Act because they were employed under contract 'personally to execute any work or labour'.

Contract workers

Contract **workers** are also covered (s 41). The 'principal' (the person for whom the work is undertaken) must not discriminate against or victimise a contract worker (s 42(1) and (3)):

- in the terms on which he allows the worker to do that work;

- by not allowing the worker to do or continue to do the work;

- in the way he affords the worker access to opportunities for receiving any benefits, facility or service;

- by subjecting the worker to any other detriment.

A 'principal' is defined as 'a person who makes work available for an individual who is: (a) employed by another person; and (b) supplied by that other person in furtherance of a contract to which the principal is a party' (s 41(5)).

Ex-employees

It is unlawful to discriminate against a person after an employment relationship has ended and where 'the discrimination arises out of and is closely connected to a relationship which used to exist between them'. The Act states that the nature of the conduct would be discriminatory, had it occurred during the employment relationship (EA 2010 s 108). This protection covers all 'prohibited characteristics' and reflects the development of the law since 1997.

The European Court of Justice ruled on protection for ex-employees (*Coote v Granada Hospitality Ltd* (C-185/97) [1998] ECR I-5199; [1998] IRLR 656, ECJ). The case involved a refusal to provide a reference to an employment agency for a woman who had alleged that she had been dismissed because of pregnancy. Retaliatory measures by an employer (whether in cases of dismissal or not) were unlawful. They could deter workers from pursuing claims and might seriously jeopardise the Equal Treatment Directive's aim.

A change in UK discrimination law, then, arose from the House of Lords decision in *Rhys-Harper* v *Relaxion Group plc*; *DeSouza* v *London Borough of Lambeth*; and *Jones v 3M Healthcare Ltd* [2003] IRLR 848. It ruled in these joint appeals that employees should be protected against certain post-termination discrimination by their employer. It was stated that it is the employment relationship that triggers the employer's obligation not to discriminate; and it makes no sense to draw an arbitrary line at the point when the contract ends. This case was decided on the wider definition of 'the employment relationship' under European equality law.

Offshore work

Part 5 of the Equality Act, 'Work', applies to offshore workers (Equality Act 2010 (Offshore Work) Order 2010).

▶ Prohibited conduct

The 'prohibited conduct' outlined in the Act includes the following: direct discrimination; combined discrimination – dual characteristics; indirect discrimination; and victimisation. The Equality Act also covers harassment at work. This is discussed in Chapter 7.

▶ Direct discrimination

The Equality Act states that 'A person (A) discriminates against another (B) if, because of a protected characteristic, A treats B less favourably than A treats or would treat others' (s 13). This concept of 'less favourable treatment' arises in relation to the following aspects of the employment relationship (s 39(1) and (2)):

- Arrangements made for determining who should be offered employment.
- Terms on which employment is to be offered.
- Refusals to offer employment.
- Opportunities for promotion, training and transfer or for receiving any other benefit, facility or service.
- Dismissal.
- Subjecting a person to any other detriment.

Several issues arise in respect of this issue.

- *'Because of'*: This means, for example, that the less favourable treatment could be because of age or sexuality rather than because of B's *actual* age or sexuality.
- *Associative discrimination*: The 'less favourable treatment' could be because of a 'protected characteristic' of another person. (See later in this chapter the disability discrimination case of *Coleman* v *Attridge Law and Another* [2008] C-303/06, ECJ which interpreted the meaning and extent of the European Employment Framework Directive 2000). Associative discrimination does not apply to the protected characteristic of marriage and civil partnership; and, arguably, not to pregnancy and maternity.
- *Perceived discrimination*: This arises where someone is believed or regarded as having a particular protected characteristic even if this is untrue. It does not apply to the protected characteristic of marriage and civil partnership.
- *Possible (anticipatory) discrimination*: This arises from the phrase 'or would treat others'. An example of a racially discriminatory advertisement providing evidence of this is considered later in this chapter (*Centrum voor gelijkheid van kansen en voor racismebestrijding* v *Firma Feryn NV* [2008] IRLR 732, ECJ).

There is *no* objective justification for direct discrimination – except in the case of age (s 13(2)). Other specific exceptions relate to lawful *occupational requirements* (Sch 9).

Comparators

There are several important aspects to this issue. There are four steps that should be undertaken in considering the relevance of a comparator:

- An identification of the person who is believed to be the (actual or hypothetical) comparator (see Exhibit 5.2).

- Ensuring that there is 'no material difference' between the circumstances of the comparator's case and that of the complainant (EA 2010, s 23(1)).

- In direct discrimination complaints, the application of the 'but for' test (see Exhibit 5.3).

- Giving the reason for the treatment.

EXHIBIT 5.2

Comparators

Comparators apply to direct discrimination (s 13), to indirect discrimination (s 19) and to the duty to make adjustments (s 20). The comparator can be an actual or hypothetical person who does not share the complainant's 'protected characteristic'. But, otherwise, there must be no material difference between the circumstances of the complainant and the comparator. **Particular comparators are discussed later in the chapter in relation to each of the 'protected characteristics'. The following provides a summary:**

- *Age*: No comparator.
- *Disability*: Other people for a reason related to disability; or association with disability. (NB: More favourable treatment of a disabled person is permitted.)
- *Gender reassignment*: Other people throughout the reassignment process.
- *Married person/civil partner*: Another person.
- *Pregnancy and maternity*: No comparator.
- *Sex*: A man (for a woman); a woman (for a man).
- *Race*: Other people on racial grounds.
- *Religion or belief*: Other people because of a person's religion or belief, perceived religion or belief, or association with religion or belief, lack of religion or belief.
- *Sexual orientation*: Other people because of sexual orientation, perceived sexual orientation, or association with sexual orientation.

In direct discrimination claims, comparison must be between treatment received by the complainant and actual or hypothetical treatment of another, who had all the characteristics of the complainant apart from the specific 'protected characteristic' in the complaint. The Court of Appeal has ruled that if there is no actual comparator, then an employment tribunal must construct a hypothetical one. Failure to do so is an error in law (*Balamoody v UK Central Council for Nursing, Midwifery and Health Visiting* [2002] IRLR 288). The House of Lords has strongly emphasised that if there is no actual comparator whose circumstances are the same, then the statutory comparison should be with how a hypothetical comparator in those same circumstances would be treated (*Shamoon v Chief Constable of the Royal Ulster Constabulary* [2003] IRLR 258).

> EXHIBIT 5.3

The 'but for' test

This has been and is likely to remain the key test for determining direct discrimination (*James* v *Eastleigh Borough Council* [1990] IRLR 288). Lord Goff in the House of Lords judgment (in a case brought under the previous Sex Discrimination Act 1975) stated that 'cases of direct discrimination ... can be considered by asking the simple question: would the complainant have received the same treatment from the defendant but for his or her sex?'. It is important, in this context, that the court or tribunal has to arrive at a view, *on the facts*, that the less favourable treatment was on the grounds of sex (even in part) and on no other grounds. Motive and intention are not relevant in cases of direct discrimination. No justification or defence is allowable (apart from direct age discrimination).

❱ Combined discrimination: dual characteristics

Under this provision, 'a person (A) discriminates against another (B) if, because of a combination of **two** relevant protected characteristics, A treats B less favourably than A treats or would treat a person who does not share either of those characteristics' (s 14). Here the 'relevant protected characteristics' which may be considered are age, disability, gender reassignment, race, religion or belief, sex and sexual orientation. Pregnancy or maternity and marriage or civil partnership are not included. This provision applies only to direct discrimination and ***not*** to indirect discrimination, harassment or victimisation. A dual claim need not preclude separate claims on other matters.

The Conservative–Liberal Democrat government delayed implementation of this provision and then announced on 23 March 2011 that it would not be implemented. This was announced under the *Plan for Growth,* published at the time of the 2011 Budget. This was described as setting out 'plans for reducing burdens on business in order to achieve sustainable economic growth' (**www.equalities.gov.uk**).

The rationale for the combined discrimination protection was to ensure more effective enforcement of the law where the interaction of protected characteristics might be causing more serious instances of discrimination – for example for a black woman; or for an elderly woman. Whilst complaints relating to combined discrimination may not be available, it is still possible to submit, simultaneously, parallel claims relating to each of the allegations of discriminatory treatment.

❱ Indirect discrimination

Whilst the direct discrimination provisions cover clear and blatant unfair discrimination, those relating to indirect discrimination in employment are designed to tackle the less obvious and unintentional discriminatory treatment that might arise in the course of employment. Welcoming the original incorporation of the concept into the earlier legal framework, Mary Redmond (1986: 476) said that 'the proscription of indirect discrimination represents a landmark in British anti-discrimination legislation. The continuing absence of women and of minority groups from important areas of employment is due, in large measure, to indirect discrimination.' However, she adds an important word of warning that 'the road to be travelled by a person alleging indirect discrimination is strewn with complexities'. So, indirect discrimination provisions are designed to deal with employment policies and practices which are apparently non-discriminatory but which, in practice, may have a discriminatory effect (e.g. on people of a certain age or ethnic origin).

Under the Equality Act 2010 (s 19), the indirect discrimination provision states:

s 19(1) A person (A) discriminates against another (B) if A applies to B a provision, criterion or practice which is discriminatory in relation to a relevant protected characteristic of B's.

s 19(2) For the purposes of subsection (1) a provision, criterion or practice is discriminatory in relation to a relevant protected characteristic of B's if –

(a) A applies, or would apply, it to persons with whom B does not share the characteristic,
(b) it puts, or would put, persons with whom B shares the characteristic at a particular disadvantage when compared with persons with whom B does not share it,
(c) it puts, or would put, B at that disadvantage and,
(d) A cannot show it to be a proportionate means of achieving a legitimate aim.

This section of the Act does not apply to pregnancy or maternity discrimination (though such discrimination may be challenged as discrimination 'because of' sex).

Several issues arise in respect of this definition:

'Provision, criterion or practice': Examples could include access to benefits, requests for part-time working, working time flexibility, opportunities for religious observance. Under earlier anti-discrimination law, a number of employment arrangements were challenged as discriminatory on the grounds of sex (and would still be relevant under current law). These illustrate the issues:

- *Age barriers in recruitment.* These may be discriminatory against women who have taken time out of employment to care for children (*Price v Civil Service Commission* [1978] IRLR 3, EAT).

- *Requirements on length of service.* These can disadvantage women who have had breaks in employment to bring up children.

- *Mobility conditions.* These may cause disadvantage to women in contrast to a man because of childcare responsibilities.

- *Unsocial hours requirements.* These can disproportionately affect women because of family responsibilities.

- *Requirement to work full time.* This may be indirectly discriminatory against women returners from maternity leave if the work can be undertaken on a part-time or more formal job share basis (see Chapter 11).

- *Redundancy selection.* A decision to select part-time workers first for redundancy could be indirectly discriminatory because of the predominance of women in part-time employment (*Clarke v Eley (IMI) Kynoch Ltd* [1982] IRLR 482).

'Disadvantage': The individual alleging discrimination needs to show that he or she experienced a disadvantage (e.g. the inability to work on a full-time basis; and/or the inability to undertake a particular job for which he or she was qualified). The discrimination by the employer would have to be justified objectively. The complainant requires a comparator.

▶ The 'justification' of indirect discrimination

Unlike direct discrimination (apart from age), indirect discrimination can potentially be justified. The employer needs to show the discrimination to be 'a proportionate means of achieving a legitimate aim'. The 'legitimate aim' would be a relevant business objective which can include business operational needs and efficiency; health safety and welfare requirements; particular training requirements. The means of achieving that aim should be 'proportionate'. The Equal Treatment Directive 2006 (Article 2) refers to 'means' as being 'appropriate and necessary'. The reference to 'necessity' reflects earlier **case law**. The European Court of Justice ruled that the objective standards of 'justification' require that the employer has a real need and that the discriminatory action is necessary and appropriate to achieve that end (*Bilka-Kaufhaus Gmbh* v *Weber von Hartz* [1986] IRLR 317, ECJ).

▶ Occupational requirements

These provisions (Schedule 9) permit an employer to select for employment people on particular grounds which on the face of it are discriminatory. The employer must be able to give credible reasons for such decisions and why the 'exception' applies. The provisions in the Act require that the employer shows that:

- the protected characteristic' is 'an occupational requirement';
- 'the application of the requirement is a proportionate means of achieving a legitimate aim';
- 'the person to whom [the employer] applies the requirement does not meet it (or [the employer] has reasonable grounds for not being satisfied that the person meets it)'.

The occupational requirement provisions apply to both direct and indirect discrimination. The EHRC *Employment Code of Practice* (2010) states that 'the requirement must not be a sham or pretext and there must be a link between the requirement and the job' (para 13.7).

Under previous discrimination law, there were specific provisions for what were called 'genuine occupational requirements and qualifications'. Examples, deriving from the previous legislation and case law, are considered in Chapter 6. They are likely to provide the basis for employers wishing to implement this part of the Equality Act.

▶ Positive action

The concept of positive action has two principal objectives (see also Chapter 4):

- It concerns the encouragement to apply for jobs or for promotion; or have access to training.
- It is to prevent or compensate for (historic) disadvantage (Employment Directive 2000).

The Equality Act 2010 (ss 158–9) provides for positive action in various circumstances. Employers may take 'proportionate' steps (s 158):

- to enable or encourage persons *who share the protected characteristic* to overcome or minimise the relevant disadvantage;
- to meet the relevant needs;
- to enable or encourage persons who share the protected characteristics to participate in the relevant activity;
- these 'steps' must be objectively justified as *a proportionate means of achieving a legitimate aim.*

Examples of positive action can include: work shadowing; mentoring; courses on filling in application forms, interviewing skills, selection tests; courses to develop confidence; courses in skills such as computer programming; short-term work placements in a relevant department. Positive action in recruitment and promotion is specifically provided for under the Equality Act 2010 (s 159). It allows employers to treat more favourably individuals with a 'protected characteristic' when there are two or more candidates of equal merit. This treatment is designed to address under-representation or a disadvantage that is connected to the protected characteristic. This provision came into force in April 2011.

These positive action steps in respect of recruitment and promotion are ***not*** *positive discrimination* or affirmative action which, apart from the specific circumstances of disability discrimination law (see ***Archibald*** v ***Fife Council*** [2004] UKHL 32) (Exhibit 5.14), is generally unlawful under British law. However, similar German law has been tested in the European Court of Justice to judge compliance with European equal treatment law. It was found to be compatible (see Exhibit 5.4).

▶ Instructing

It is unlawful to instruct, cause or induce a person to discriminate against another (EA 2010 s 111). Proceedings may be brought by (a) the person to whom the instruction was given if he or she suffered a detriment; (b) the person against whom the instruction or inducement was directed if he or she suffered a detriment; and (c) the Equality and Human Rights Commission. The discriminatory 'grounds' on which an instruction was based were heard by the Employment Appeal Tribunal in the early 1980s. In ***Showboat Entertainment Centre Ltd*** v ***Owens*** [1984] IRLR 7, the issue was considered of a white receptionist who was told not to hire out vehicles to 'coloureds and Asians'. She resigned and complained of unlawful race discrimination. Mr Justice Browne-Wilkinson stated that 'certainly the main thrust of the legislation [the Race Relations Act 1976] is to give protection to those discriminated against on the grounds of their own racial characteristics. But the words "on racial grounds" are perfectly capable in their ordinary sense of covering any reason for an action based on race, whether it be the race of the person affected by the action or of others.' This approach was subsequently endorsed by the Court of Appeal in ***Weathersfield Ltd t/a Van & Truck Rentals*** v ***Sargent*** [1999] IRLR 94, CA. Although the terminology under the Equality Act is different – in that the discrimination is 'because of' a protected characteristic rather than 'on the grounds of' – this established approach is likely to continue to be taken by the courts to provide the wide protection expected by the legislators.

EXHIBIT 5.4

Equal treatment, positive discrimination and the 'tie-break'

Marschall v Land Nordrhein-Westfalen [1998] IRLR 39

Facts. A German secondary school teacher, Helmutt Marschall, applied for promotion to a higher-grade teaching post. The civil service law of the Federal State of North Rhine-Westphalia provides that where 'there are fewer women than men in the particular higher-grade post in the career bracket, women are to be given priority for promotion in the event of equal suitability, competence and professional performance unless reasons specific to an individual (male) candidate tilt the balance in his favour'. He was informed that an equally qualified woman was to be appointed. He initiated legal proceedings in Germany.

ECJ ruling. This practice was not incompatible with the Equal Treatment Directive. The provision in civil service law was compatible provided that:

- in each individual case there is a guarantee that the candidates will be subject to an objective assessment which takes account of all criteria;
- where one or more of those criteria tilts the balance in favour of a male candidate, the priority accorded to female candidates will be overridden; and
- such criteria are not discriminatory against female candidates.

Although approving the possible legality of the 'tie-break' in the *Marschall* case, the ECJ has asserted that 'positive discrimination is incompatible with equal treatment law'. In an earlier German case it stated that rules which guarantee women absolute and unconditional priority for public sector appointments (where women are under-represented) go beyond promoting equal opportunities and overstep the limits of the Equal Treatment Directive (*Kalenke v Freie Hansestadt Bremen* [1995] IRLR 660). Disapproval of positive discrimination was confirmed in a later case (*Abrahamsson and Anderson v Fogelqvist* (2000) C-407/98).

Positive action in the form of targets, for recruitment, selection and promotion, has been considered and ruled to be compatible with equal treatment law. The proviso was that women should not be offered automatically and unconditionally preferential treatment over men (*Badeck v Land Hessen* (2000) C-158/97, IRLR 432).

▶ Discriminatory advertisements

The European Court of Justice has ruled that, under the Race Directive 2000, it is not necessary to have an identifiable victim of discriminatory job advertisements (*Centrum voor gelijkheid van kansen en voor racismebestrijding v Firma Feryn NV* [2008] IRLR 732, ECJ). The company's stated general refusal to employ immigrants because of customer attitudes was ruled to be direct race discrimination. The Equality Act 2010 prohibits discrimination in 'the arrangements [an employer] makes for deciding to whom to offer employment' (s 39(1)(a)). This encompasses advertisements for a job. Proceedings may be brought by the EHRC.

The Employment Appeal Tribunal has, in *Berry v Recruitment Revolution* EAT/0190/10, indicated some caution in dealing with complaints about advertisements. It stated, in this age discrimination case, that an employer is only liable for the discriminatory act if it affected the complainant in some way. Berry was not deterred from applying for the post of 'junior administrator/administrative assistant'. When the wording of the advert was rectified he declined to apply. The EAT commented that the law on age discrimination was not to provide 'a source of income for those who complain about job advertisements which they have no intention to fill'. It was recorded that Berry had, previously, made 50 similar employment tribunal applications.

▶ Aiding unlawful acts

It is unlawful (s 112) for a person to knowingly aid another person to discriminate in contravention of s 111 or s 39 (see preceding sections); or in relation to relationships that have ended (s 108). For example, under previous discrimination law, a manager was jointly and severally liable to pay compensation for acts of sex discrimination against the claimant even though some of the acts were carried out by other managers in circumstances in which the manager could be regarded as having unlawfully aided and consciously encouraged the discrimination (*Gilbank v Miles* [2006] IRLR 538, CA).

▶ Enforcement

▶ Liability and vicarious liability

An employer is strictly liable for discrimination and also vicariously liable for such acts carried out by its employees and managers (s 109). Vicarious liability is stated in these terms:

● Anything done by a person *in the course of his employment* shall be treated as done by his employer as well as by him whether or not it was done with the employer's knowledge or approval.

● An employer is liable for discriminatory behaviour of third parties who discriminate against/harass their staff (see also Chapter 7).

● An employee may be personally liable for discrimination/harassment (s 110). However, this personal liability would only arise in the context of a claim against the employer (s 109).

Two specific issues arise from the provisions on liability:

In the course of employment: The Court of Appeal ruled on the meaning of this phrase (*Jones v Tower Boot Co Ltd* [1997] IRLR 68). It stated that these words should be interpreted broadly, in line with 'the natural meaning of those everyday words'. It added that:

> [T]his is not to say that when it comes to applying them to the infinite variety of circumstances which is liable to occur in particular instances – within or without the workplace, in or out of uniform, in or out of rest breaks – all laymen would necessarily agree as to the result . . . The application of the phrase will be a question of fact for each [employment tribunal] to resolve in the light of the circumstances presented to it, with a mind unclouded by any parallels sought to be drawn from the law of vicarious liability in tort.

This wide construction of the phrase 'in the course of employment' would cover not just presence on the employer's premises, but probably travelling to work, travelling during working hours, work-related training events and conferences. The EAT has also ruled that an employer can be liable for discrimination in a social gathering where people are having drinks after work (*Chief Constable of Lincolnshire Police* v *Stubbs and Others* [1999] IRLR 81). This would, of course, cover Christmas parties.

On the related issue of motivation to discriminate, Lord Goff (in *R* v *Birmingham City Council* ex parte *EOC* [1989] IRLR 173) stated that 'the intention or motive of the defendant to discriminate . . . is not a necessary condition to liability; it is perfectly possible to envisage cases where the defendant had no such motive and yet did in fact discriminate on the grounds of sex'.

Personal liability: Under previous discrimination law, this issue was considered by the courts (Race Relations Act 1976 (s 32(2)). In *Yeboah* v *Crofton* [2002] IRLR 634, CA, the Court of Appeal, in a case where a senior council employee 'knowingly' aided unlawful discrimination, confirmed that employees can be personally liable for acts of unlawful discrimination against colleagues and can be so liable even where the employer itself is not found to have acted unlawfully.

Employer's defence

An employer's defence against liability for discrimination involves proving that it took *all reasonable steps* (s 109) to prevent the employee from doing that act or from doing, in the course of his or her employment, 'that thing' or 'anything of that description'. 'Reasonable steps' would include the following:

- The existence of an operational equal opportunities policy (see relevant statutory Codes of Practice).
- Training of managers and relevant staff on equality issues.
- The use of relevant workplace procedures:
  - Grievances: a procedure that complies with the ACAS *Code of Practice on Grievance and Discipline* (2009).
  - Harassment and bullying: a special procedure that might involve advice, counselling and mediation (see Chapter 7).
  - Disciplinary and dismissal: A procedure that complies with the ACAS *Code of Practice on Grievance and Discipline* (2009).
  - Compliance with the statutory right to be accompanied.
- Monitoring of equal opportunities practice.

▶ Statutory questionnaire

A statutory questionnaire may be used by a complainant to enable a person to obtain information about his or her claim of discrimination, victimisation or harassment (EA s 138) (**www.equalities.gov.uk/news/equality_act_2010_forms_for_ob_aspx**). Subject to guidance from the EAT (see below), inferences may be drawn by employment tribunals if this questionnaire is not completed adequately or at all.

▶ Burden of proof

The burden of proof has shifted in discrimination cases in the past ten years or so by tilting the balance more in favour of the complainant. The Equality Act (s 136) enacts this approach. Essentially, the complainant must make a *prima facie* case of discriminatory treatment. This is an outline of the key facts known to him or her which in the view of the complainant point to discrimination. Under previous case law, it has been stated that there does not have to be *positive evidence* that the difference in treatment is on grounds of race or sex in order to establish a *prima facie* case (*Network Rail Infrastructure Ltd* v *Griffiths-Henry* [2006] IRLR 865, EAT). It is then for the respondent employer to demonstrate that there was no unlawful discriminatory treatment whatsoever. The Court of Appeal has approved 13-point guidance on how the burden of proof rules in discrimination cases should be applied (*Igen Ltd* v *Wong* [2005] ICR 931) (see Exhibit 5.5).

The question of inferences has been ruled on by the EAT (*D'Silva* v *NATFHE* [2008] IRLR 412, EAT). Mr Justice Underhill stated that it was not a 'correct approach' for complainants to 'rely' on a respondent employer's failure to either answer a statutory questionnaire or otherwise provide documents. In a later case (*Deer* v *Walford and Another* UKEAT/0283/10), he stated that 'there are no special rules of law about what inferences should be drawn from unsatisfactory answers to the statutory questionnaire. The process involved in deciding what, if any, inference should be drawn in the case of an evasive or equivocal answer is no different in principle from that to be applied in any other case where an inference of discriminatory behaviour is sought to be drawn. The question is always whether, in the circumstances of the particular case, the act or omission in question tends to show that the respondent acted in the way complained of – typically that he acted with a discriminatory motivation.'

EXHIBIT 5.5

Guidance on the burden of proof

Igen Ltd v *Wong* [2005] ICR 931 (paraphrased)

1 *The complainant*. He or she must prove, on the balance of probabilities, facts from which the tribunal could conclude (in the absence of an adequate explanation) that the respondent employer has committed an act of unlawful discrimination against the claimant.

2 If the claimant does not prove such facts he or she will fail.

3 *Direct evidence*. It is important to bear in mind, in deciding whether the claimant has proved such facts, that it is unusual to find direct evidence of sex discrimination. Few employers would be prepared to admit such discrimination even to themselves.

4 *Inferences*. In deciding whether the complainant has proved such facts, it is important to remember that the outcome, at this stage of the analysis by the tribunal, will usually depend on what inferences it is proper to draw from the primary facts it finds.

5 *Could there be discrimination*? At this stage, the tribunal is not reaching a definitive determination that such facts **would** lead to a conclusion that there was an act of unlawful discrimination. It is looking at the primary facts before it in order to see what inferences of secondary fact could be drawn from them.

6 In considering what inferences or conclusions can be drawn from the primary facts, the tribunal must assume that there is no adequate explanation for those facts.

7 *Evasive and equivocal replies*. These inferences can include (in appropriate cases) those that it is just and equitable to draw from an evasive or equivocal reply to a questionnaire or any other questions that fall within discrimination legislation.

8 *Relevant code of practice*. The tribunal must decide whether any provision of an applicable code is relevant and has been taken into account in determining such facts. Inferences may be drawn from failure to comply with any relevant code.

9 *The burden of proof*. This moves to the respondent employer where the claimant has provided facts from which conclusions could be drawn that he or she has been treated less favourably on the ground of sex (or other unlawful grounds of discrimination).

10 It is, then, for the respondent to prove that he or she did not commit, or as the case may be, is not treated as having committed that act.

11 *Discharging the burden of proof*. It is necessary for the respondent to prove, on the balance of probabilities, that the treatment was in no sense whatsoever on the grounds of sex (or, as appropriate, other unlawful grounds).

12 *Tribunal assessment*. That requires the tribunal to assess whether the respondent has proved an explanation for the facts from which such inferences can be drawn; but further that it is adequate to discharge the burden of proof on the balance of probabilities that unlawful discrimination was not a ground for the treatment alleged.

13 *Cogent evidence from respondent*. Since the facts necessary to prove an explanation would normally be in the respondent's possession, the tribunal would normally expect cogent evidence to discharge the burden of proof. In particular, the tribunal will need to examine carefully explanations for failure to deal with the questionnaire procedure and/or code of practice.

▶ Complaints to an employment tribunal

Complaints to an employment tribunal under equality law (ss 120–3) may be made by a person with an employment relationship, an applicant for employment, or someone whose employment relationship has ended (see above). There is normally an initial attempt at conciliation under the auspices of ACAS (the Advisory, Conciliation and Arbitration Service). Various issues arise in relation to complaints: the nature of the complaint and whether it relates to a specific 'wrong' under the legislation; time limit for the complaint; whether there has been victimisation; remedies for a successful complaint; the right of appeal to the Employment Appeal Tribunal. A complaint to an employment tribunal should be made within three months of the discriminatory act complained of. However, an employment tribunal may nevertheless consider any such complaint which is out of time if it thinks it is 'just and equitable' to do so by extending the time (s 123(1)). Discrimination law has envisaged two types of situation: a single act of discrimination; and a pattern of discrimination that might extend over a period of time (s 67(6)(b)). Greater difficulties in establishing the appropriate time limit can arise with the latter. There is information and advice on the Tribunal Service website (**www.justice.gov.uk**) on the process: describing the making of the complaint (on an ET1 form) and the response from the employer (on the ET3 form).

▶ Victimisation

The Equality Act (s 27) prohibits victimisation of people who perform a 'protected act'. The victimisation would be detrimental treatment. Specific 'protected acts' mentioned in the legislation are:

- 'bringing proceedings under the Act';
- giving 'evidence or information in connection with proceedings' under the Act;
- doing 'any other thing for the purposes of or in connection with the Act;
- 'making an allegation' that a person has contravened the Act.

Case law under previous discrimination law pointed to a number of principles and issues that are likely to be relevant in the interpretation of the Equality Act 2010. Although under previous case law a comparator was needed for a victimisation claim, the Equality Act (s 27(1)) no longer requires this. However, on the nature of the alleged victimisation, two cases are important. In an equal pay case (*St Helens Borough Council* v *Derbyshire and Others* [2007] IRLR 540), the House of Lords drew a distinction between what might be an employer's attempt to 'settle or compromise a claim' and a letter which 'contained what was effectively a threat'. It was asserted by Lady Justice Hale that an employer must avoid doing anything that might 'make a reasonable employee feel she is being unduly pressurised to concede her claim'. It must be demonstrated that the less favourable treatment is a direct result of the involvement in the discrimination case (*Aziz* v *Trinity Street Taxis Ltd* [1988] ICR 534, CA).

▶ Remedies

Where an employment tribunal upholds a complaint, it may grant one or more of the following remedies (s 124). These primarily existed under previous discrimination law:

1 *A declaration*. This is a declaration of the rights of the complainant and the respondent in relation to the matters before the employment tribunal. In itself, it can have little deterrent effect, unless the employer is concerned about adverse publicity. In practice, a declaration is usually accompanied by compensation and/or a recommendation.

2 *Compensation*. In practice, this is the remedy that complainants most frequently seek and, if successful, are awarded. Since 1993, the upper limit (originally set in UK discrimination law) has been removed as a result of a ruling in the European Court of Justice (*Marshall* v *Southampton and South West Hampshire Area Health Authority (No. 2)* [1993] IRLR 445). The court reasoned that 'where financial compensation is the measure adopted in order to achieve the [1976 Equal Treatment Directive's] objective, it must be adequate, in that it must enable the loss and damage actually sustained as a result of the discriminatory dismissal (or other circumstances) to be made good in full in accordance with applicable national rules.' In this case it was also ruled that interest is 'an essential component of compensation'. Compensation is awarded for **financial loss**, if any, and for **injury to feelings**.

  - *Financial loss*. This can comprise loss of earnings, past and projected; loss of fringe benefits (e.g. pension rights, subsidised travel or company car; and expenses associated with the discrimination claim). The assessment of compensation is based on the principle that the complainant must be put into the position they would have been in had the unlawful discrimination not happened. In *Wardle* v *Credit Agricole Corporate and Investment Bank* [2011] IRLR 819, the Court of Appeal stated that when tribunals are calculating future loss, they should assess the loss suffered up to a particular point in time. This would be when a claimant would be *likely* to secure another job on equalivalent terms rather than the point when there was *certainty* about such an appointment. As an overall approach, the Court of Appeal (*Coleman v Skyrail Oceanic Ltd* [1981] IRLR 398) has indicated that the objective of restitution was subject to four qualifications:

- *Foreseeable damage*: compensation for damage arising directly from the unlawful discrimination.
- *Mitigation of loss*: the complainant is obliged to take all reasonable steps to minimise his or her loss (e.g. by seeking alternative employment).
- *Behaviour*: compensation may be reduced because of the conduct, character and circumstances of the complainant.
- *Non-financial loss*: this is difficult to establish and tribunals have fairly wide discretion.

- *Award for injury to feelings.* This refers to emotional harm; and it is almost inevitable that compensation under this heading will arise in discrimination cases. The issues which can influence this level of award are:
  - the complainant proving most or all of his or her claim;
  - evidence of a long-term campaign of discrimination;
  - the consequences of the discrimination (e.g. stress, depression);
  - a power relationship between the perpetrator and the victim;
  - management's approach in dealing with the matter through the organisation's grievance procedure.

  It has been stated that an award for injury to feelings should include an element of *aggravated damages* where the employer has 'behaved in a high-handed, malicious, insulting or oppressive manner' in discriminating against the complainant (*Alexander v Home Office* [1988] IRLR 190, CA). The Court of Appeal set out three bands for awards for injury to feelings (*Vento v Chief Constable of West Yorkshire Police* [2003] IRLR 102). These were increased by the Employment Appeal Tribunal in *Da'Bell v NSPCC* [2010] IRLR 19) (see Table 5.1). It has been commented that harbouring a legitimate and principled sense of grievance is not to be confused with suffering an injury to feelings (*Moyhing v Barts and London NHS Trust* [2006] IRLR 860, EAT).

- *Personal injury.* Claimants can also claim for personal injury (including psychiatric injury) arising out of discriminatory treatment without having to satisfy an additional test that the losses were reasonably foreseeable (*Essa v Laing* [2004] IRLR 313, CA).

3 *Recommendation:* The Act specifies that the tribunal may make 'an appropriate recommendation'. Defined in the legislation, it is 'a recommendation that within a specified period the respondent [employer] takes specified steps for the purpose of obviating or reducing the adverse effect of any matter to which the proceedings relate

Table 5.1 **Vento guidelines (amended in** *Da'Bell* v *NSPCC* **[2009] IRLR 19)**

Top band £18,000–£30,000	Designed to cover the most serious cases (e.g. lengthy campaign of discrimination). Awards over £30,000 should be exceptional
Middle band £6,000–£18,000	For serious cases that do not merit a top band award
Lowest band £500–£6,000	For less serious cases – e.g. where the discriminatory act is an isolated incident

(a) on the complainant; (b) on any other person'. This extends the provisions under previous discrimination law where recommendations were limited to recommendations for action that will only affect the individual complainant. Under the Equality Act it now possible to make general policy recommendations. If a respondent employer fails 'without reasonable cause' to comply with an appropriate recommendation 'in so far as it relates to the complainant', a tribunal may increase the amount of compensation to be paid or, if no order for compensation has been made, it may make one (s 124(7)).

Protected characteristics, legal issues and case law

▶ Age

Prior to the Equality Framework Directive (2000) and the Employment Equality (Age) Regulations 2006, no UK legislation protecting workers from age discrimination existed. Certain protection against elements of age discrimination was afforded by the indirect discrimination provisions of the former Sex Discrimination Act 1975 (see Exhibit 5.6). Unequal retirement and pension ages for men and women, seen as direct sex discrimination, were ultimately resolved through the harmonising of compulsory retirement and occupational pension ages (*Marshall* v *Southampton and SW Hampshire Area Health Authority* [1986] IRLR 140, ECJ; *Barber* v *Guardian Royal Exchange Assurance Group plc* [1990] IRLR 240, ECJ). Despite the significance of this area of law, it is protection afforded on the grounds of sex, not of age.

▶ Employment Equality Framework Directive 2000 and age discrimination

The importance of the directive can be seen not only on the way it is transposed into UK law but also in the significance of case law ruled upon by the European Court of Justice. These cases provide an important body of interpretation. The protection the directive affords those claiming age discrimination is limited to the areas of employment and occupations. However, these are defined broadly and include access to employment, recruitment, promotion, all types and levels of vocational training, working conditions, pay, dismissal and membership of or involvement in employer bodies, trade unions and professional organisations.

The directive provides for protection against direct discrimination, indirect discrimination, harassment and victimisation on the grounds of age (Article 2) although there are exceptions to this protection provided through Articles 4 and 6. Article 4 covers specific occupational requirements that may allow for discriminatory treatment and which are consistent with other areas of discrimination law, but Article 6 is more controversial. Reflecting both the complexity of this area of discrimination and the belief that it would be wrong to deny employers an age-based approach where this is appropriate it extends the defence of justification to both direct *and* indirect discrimination. The directive therefore marks out age discrimination as distinctive in permitting differences of treatment (both directly and indirectly discriminatory in respect of age) where these can be 'objectively and reasonably justified by a legitimate aim and where the means of achieving the aim must be 'appropriate and necessary' (Article 6(1)).

EXHIBIT 5.6

Age and the Sex Discrimination Act 1975

Price v Civil Service Commission [1978] IRLR 3

Facts. Price, a 35-year-old woman wanting to work for the Civil Service after maternity leave, challenged an age limit of 28 for a particular post. She argued that the age limit constituted indirect sex discrimination on the grounds that proportionately fewer women could apply for the post than men, because many women were engaged in child bearing and rearing in their late twenties.

Judgments. The original tribunal found in favour of the employer on the grounds that it was possible for any woman aged 17 and a half and 28 to apply and that in practice the proportion who were able to do so was not considerably smaller than the proportion of men who were able. However, the EAT found in favour of Price arguing that 'it is safe to say that the condition (of an age limit of 28) is one which it is in practice harder for women to comply with than it is for men'. Adding that there are clearly women who 'cannot comply with the condition, because they are women, that is to say, because of their involvement with their children' (Phillips J).

Jones v University of Manchester [1993] IRLR 218

Facts. This case was brought by a 44-year-old woman and concerned a situation where her employer had imposed a maximum age bar in order to achieve a better age balance in the relevant department (age band of 27–35). The employer argued further that a careers officer post should be occupied by a younger person, on the grounds that they would be able to relate more closely to the students that they would be giving advice to. Ms Jones had studied for a degree as a mature student and claimed that the age limit discriminated against women who obtained their degree as mature students.

Judgments. Although the tribunal found in her favour, both the EAT and the Court of Appeal found in favour of the employer on the grounds that the tribunal had erred in law in using a 'pool' which consisted of mature graduates with relevant experience only when it should have used the numbers of men and women who can comply with the requirement as a proportion of those in the whole of the relevant population, rather than using a subdivision of the larger pool (mature graduates with relevant experience).

Comment. It should be noted that today in light of the former Employment Equality (Age) Regulations (2006) and current Equality Act 2010, Jones would now be able to bring a claim for direct age discrimination. Although the employer could argue for 'justification' it is unlikely that a court would accept the argument that an age band would be justified in light of the target audience.

Article 6(1) of the directive provides some guidance as to what may constitute justifiable differences of treatment, although the list is not exhaustive. These include:

- setting special conditions on access to employment and vocational training;
- fixing minimum conditions of age, professional experience or seniority in service for access to employment;
- fixing maximum ages for recruitment, based on training requirements for the post, although the list is not exhaustive.

The Labour government implemented the requirements of the directive through the Employment Equality (Age) Regulations (2006), following the provisions of the directive closely. With the passing of the Equality Act and its implementation in October 2010, the Regulations were effectively repealed and the nature and scope of age discrimination law modified and extended. Before considering the recent changes introduced by the Act we review the impact of the Regulations in the four years of their existence.

▶ Evaluating the 2006 Age Regulations

The Regulations were subject to criticism from a number of sources. The fact that they were only to apply to employment disappointed many who felt that the legislation should also be extended to areas such as the provision of services (Fredman 2003). Moreover, in the employment field the inclusion of an objective justification defence for direct as well as indirect discrimination, whilst following the directive, was seen as substantially weakening the impact of the Regulations, and potentially increasing their complexity by handing over matters of interpretation to the courts. A further concern related to the decision by government to exempt a number of areas from the Regulations, notably the apprentice and young worker rates for the national minimum wage and the retention of the compulsory retirement age of 65.

▶ Equality Act (2010)

In October 2010 the Employment Equality (Age) Regulations were repealed by the Equality Act 2010 which modifies and extends the nature and scope of the law on age discrimination in important ways. In terms of its nature, age becomes one of the 'protected characteristics' covered by the legislation (s 5(1) and (2)). The protected characteristic relates to a person's age or his or her 'age group'.

As outlined above, the Act applies to all workers – employees, contract workers, job seekers and trainees. Age is now included as one of the protected characteristics within the public sector equality duty – promoting equality as part of the core business of public bodies (Government Equalities Office 2009). However, the age bands for the national minimum wage remain.

By expanding the scope of protection prohibiting discrimination, victimisation and harassment related to age beyond the area of employment to include the provision of services, considerably extends the reach of age discrimination law (see Hepple 2011: 29). Following consultation about this issue, it is intended to bring these provisions into force in April 2012 (**www.equalities.gov.uk**).

▶ Direct age discrimination

The distinctive characteristic of direct age discrimination, under the directive and in the Equality Act, is that is can be justified as a proportionate means to achieve a legitimate aim (s 13(2)) (see later discussion on this point). *Perceived discrimination* is retained in the Act ensuring that the definition of age includes 'B's apparent age'. It should also be remembered that it is not necessary for age to be the *sole reason* for a dismissal (see judgment in *Owen and Briggs* v *James* [1982] ICR 618, CA). An important new development in respect of age discrimination is that its scope is extended to include *associated discrimination* defined as: 'treating one employee or group of employees less favourably as a result of their association with a person against whom it would be unlawful to discriminate'. ACAS (2010) has helpfully synthesised these developments so that:

Direct discrimination occurs when someone is treated less favourably than another person because of a protected characteristic they have or are thought to have or because they associate with someone who has a protected characteristic.

There is no requirement that it is the employee who has the protected characteristic. However, the broadening of the scope of the protected characteristic in respect of age is tempered by the objective justification defence, which as well as weakening the ability to bring a successful claim for direct discrimination, considerably increases the complexity of this area of law and focuses attention on what might be permissible as both proportionate, and a legitimate aim.

▶ Objective justification and age discrimination

Because the 'objective justification' test applies to both direct and indirect age discrimination, it assumes particular importance under the Act. To qualify as a defence against age discrimination an employer must show that:

(a) in a claim for direct age discrimination, the less favourable treatment was 'a proportionate means of achieving a legitimate aim'; and that

(b) in a claim for indirect age discrimination, the provision, criterion or practice which placed persons of the claimant's age group at a disadvantage was a proportionate means of achieving a legitimate aim.

Under the 2006 Regulations, objective justification of direct discrimination attracted considerable attention and criticism, with arguments that it was too flexible to allow what is and what is not permitted to be predicted. Furthermore, because 'almost any criterion or practice can be potentially indirectly discriminatory' on the grounds of age (Fredman 2003: 58), it created potential uncertainty over the application of the Regulations and their interpretation by the courts and tribunals, further intensifying the pressure on employers to review their policies for evidence of potential age bias (Rubenstein 2006a; ACAS 2006). The government's position in *Coming of Age* (DTI 2005) was that 'the test of objective justification would not be an easy one to satisfy', a view that seems to have been confirmed by a series of ECJ decisions (see the ECJ decision in *Mangold* v *Helm* [2006] IRLR 143, but see *Wolf* [2010] (Exhibit 5.7). Before considering case law in this area we explore the concepts of *proportionality* and *legitimate aims* as they apply to age discrimination.

Proportionality

This requires that the legitimate aim be weighed against the discriminatory effect of the requirement. As the government put it (DTI 2006) at the time of the introduction of the 2006 Regulations:

> The discriminatory effect of any age-based practice should be significantly outweighed by the importance and benefits of its legitimate aim, and the employer should have no reasonable alternative.

In effect this is saying that 'one should not discriminate more than is necessary'. It suggests that because there is almost always going to be a less discriminatory way of achieving a legitimate aim than imposing a blanket age requirement that direct age discrimination will only be justified in extremely rare circumstances (Rubenstein 2006a: 13). The proportionality requirement was seen at the time as the key to how the regulations would operate in practice. It was acknowledged that because age frequently operates as a 'cheap screen' for employers, 'a key battleground for interpreting the age regulations, will be the extent to which tribunals find that an employer fails to satisfy the requirement of proportionality where it directly discriminates on grounds of age' (Rubenstein 2006a: 18). Some insight into the way in which the Courts have interpreted this can be seen below (see Exhibit 5.7).

Legitimate aims

In the consultation prior to the 2006 Regulations the government stated that to be considered legitimate an 'aim must correspond with a real need on the part of the employer', and therefore, was intended to correspond to the 'real need' test in EU sex equality law. As we noted above, Article 6 of the directive produced a non-exhaustive list of factors that might qualify under the objective justification defence and left open potentially difficult areas of employment practice. It remains unclear whether legitimate aims can themselves have an age-discriminatory aspect; and whether cost-saving might also be considered legitimate (but see discussion below). The general view appears to be that whilst these may in some circumstances constitute a legitimate aim, they are unlikely to be viewed by the courts as proportionate responses by employers. For example, where a high street clothes store is trying to target a particular age group as customers, it may also wish to target people of that age group as employees to support its business objectives. This may well constitute a legitimate business aim but the difficulty would be in arguing that the 'age discriminatory aspect' was a proportionate response. This is illustrated in the *O'Reilly* case (Exhibit 5.11).

▶ Objective justification and case law

Retirement ages: UK cases

Early cases under the 2006 Regulations concerned the objective justification of retirement ages. In *Seldon* v *Clarkson Wright and Jakes* [2010] IRLR 865, a law firm claimed that compulsory retirement provisions were introduced to meet legitimate business needs to facilitate long-term workforce planning. Dismissing Seldon once he reached the age of 65 was a proportionate means of achieving a legitimate aim. The Court of Appeal agreed and held that the firm had justifiably discriminated against him by retirement at 65. However, in *Hampton* v *Lord Chancellor and Another* [2008] IRLR 258, a south London recorder (part-time judicial officer) worked where a retirement age of 65 applied, rather than 70 for other judicial posts. The Ministry of Justice argued that this was necessary to ensure room for new appointments and therefore was a legitimate aim. However, the tribunal held that it had failed to show that the age requirement of 65 was a proportionate means of meeting that aim. Important questions about both occupational retirement ages and how specific an organisation can be about these is shown in *Martin & Others* v *Professional Game Match Officials Ltd* [2010] ET/28024 38/08, an employment tribunal case. Martin, a professional football referee, and a number of colleagues were forcibly retired by the Professional Game Match Officials, the organisation responsible for employing referees and assistant referees for the Premier League and Championship in England, on reaching 48 – the age stipulated by the PGMO in its retirement policy. Because it was not relying on the Default Retirement Age of 65 (in force at the time), it needed to objectively justify its retirement policy.

The case was brought by Martin and his colleagues alleging that the retirement age operated by the Professional Game Match Officials was age discriminatory and that in any event several other officials had been given exemptions to continue beyond the PGMO retirement age. The employment tribunal found the compulsory retirement age of 48 was discriminatory. Its reasoning was based on its view that although a retirement age could be justified, 48 constituted a rather arbitrary age and the PGMO had failed to provide a justification for its insistence on 48 rather than say, 46 or 49. It made reference to the fact that in other countries, retirement ages for referees varied between 45 and 50. Significantly this seems to be sending a message to employers that whilst a specific age for retirement may be very difficult to justify as *proportionate* in achieving a *legitimate aim*, an age range may well be. This raises the important question of how an employer might justify a retirement age, and points to greater analysis of performance data, in particular the point at which evidence suggests performance for a large proportion of staff appears to deteriorate.

Retirement ages: European cases

There have been a number of cases involving compulsory retirement ages in specific occupations that have been referred to the European Court of Justice. The decisions are of considerable significance. The objective justification defence for direct age discrimination has always had the potential to allow employers to defend policies (and the assumptions behind these) that suggest that individual performance and capability decline with age. What these recent ECJ decisions suggest is not only that such policies can potentially be used to justify age discriminatory rules but that the 'occupational requirement' defence may be more readily established in age discrimination cases than was previously thought.

Clearly establishing the extent to which such rules and policies are a proportionate means of achieving a legitimate aim remains complex and employers need to proceed with caution. However, the ECJ decisions in Exhibit 5.7 and the decision in *Martin* probably confirm what lawyers and many HR specialists already suspected: that where sufficient and rigorous evidence to support the association between declining performance and age can be established and on these grounds an employer seeks to apply an 'appropriate' age range for policies such as compulsory retirement, it may well be able to defend this successfully in the courts.

A Spanish case (*Palacios de la villa* v *Cortefiel Servicios SA* [2006] IRLR 989, ECJ) provided an early illustration of how objective justification might operate in practice. The case concerned the legitimacy of national laws relating to mandatory retirement ages and whether these were inconsistent with the directive. The European Court of Justice held that mandatory retirement ages were indeed discriminatory but that these could be justified in the context of employment policy and labour market objectives. More recently the UK government sought to justify its use of a mandatory retirement age on similar grounds in the *Heyday* case (*Age UK* v *Sec of State for Business Enterprise and Regulatory Reform and Others* (C-388/07) [2009] IRLR 373).

The ECJ handed down a similar ruling. Both cases held that mandatory retirement ages were a proportionate response to achieving the legitimate aims of promoting employment and labour market opportunities across different age groups. Similar ECJ rulings have been replicated in cases involving occupational rules and laws (Exhibit 5.7 below).

EXHIBIT 5.7

European Court of Justice rulings

Mangold v *Helm* [2006] **IRLR 143**

Facts. German laws set limits on the length of fixed-term contracts and the number of times they could be renewed. In an effort to combat unemployment, the laws were relaxed for those workers over a certain age giving them less job protection. In 2001 this age had been reduced from 60 to 52. The German government argued that the laws operated to assist with 'the vocational integration of unemployed older workers in so far as they encounter difficulties in finding work' and that this constituted a legitimate aim of policy, and therefore justified age discrimination. The case was referred to the European Court of Justice.

Judgment. The ECJ accepted the German government's argument that this constituted a *legitimate aim* **but** did not accept that the limits were 'appropriate and necessary' as required by the directive. The key issue for the ECJ was the argument that the limit applied to all workers over 52, 'whether or not they were unemployed before the contract was concluded and whatever the duration of any period of unemployment', which they argued infringed the principle of proportionality.

The ECJ therefore held that because the legislation being challenged took the age of the worker as the only criterion for the application of the legislation 'regardless of any other consideration linked to the structure of the labour market in question or the personal situation of the person concerned' it went 'beyond what is appropriate and necessary in order to attain the objective pursued'. As the judgment said: 'Observance of the principle of proportionality requires every derogation from an individual right to reconcile, so far as is possible, the requirements of the principle of equal treatment with those of the aim pursued.'

Wolf v *Stadt Frankfurt am Main* **(C-229/08) [2010] IRLR 244**

Facts. German legislation set a maximum recruitment age of 30 for specific and physically demanding fire service positions. This was challenged by Colin Wolf as age discrimination. The case was referred to the ECJ.

Judgment. The ECJ held that high physical capacities could be a 'genuine and determining occupational requirement related to age' (under Article 4(1) of the Directive) and that it could be considered necessary for employees to be under 50 in order to achieve this. It held that recruiting for fire-fighters over the age of 30 would be likely to result in an insufficient number of fire service employees being capable of performing the necessary physically demanding tasks. Wolf therefore represents a case here where the objective justification was deemed to be proportionate in achieving a legitimate aim.

Comment. 'This is a shocking decision . . . The claimant does not seem to have been represented at all . . . The ECJ's decision is based on scientific data put forward by the German Government showing that respiratory capacity, musculature and endurance diminish with age. On the basis of this very broad observation, the Court leaps to the conclusion that very few people over 45 and none over 50 have the capacity to be front-line fire-fighters. This is the first way in which the judgment does not comport with sound discrimination law principles. The very essence of equal opportunities is that each person has the right to be judged as an individual, rather than having a stereotype applied to them . . . Wolf was age 30 and presumably met all the fitness requirements for the job when he applied. To find that he was lawfully discriminated against on the basis of a presumption as to his fitness 15 or 20 years hence is quite extraordinary' (Rubenstein 2010a: 27).

Petersen v Berufungsuasschuss fuer Zahnaertze fuer den Bezirk Westfalen-Lippe (C-341/08)

Facts. The issue centred on the legitimacy of legislation that set a maximum employment age of 68 for doctors and dentists practising on German health system panels. Here the legitimate aim focused upon sharing employment opportunities – ensuring numbers retired to make way for new recruits into the profession. (German legislation did not impose an equivalent age limit for private sector dentists.)

Judgment. The Court held that on the assumption that there was a surplus of panel doctors and dentists, the use of a maximum age was an appropriate and necessary means of achieving the aim of sharing employment opportunities. The Court also noted that this would also help protect patients from declining performance, which would be a legitimate aim, but added that setting a maximum age in the health service when the same age was not used in the private sector would then raise questions as to whether it remained an appropriate and necessary means of achieving that aim.

The decisions in *Wolf* (arguably) and *Petersen* point to an emerging line of argument within the ECJ; that of the importance of 'inter-generational fairness', of sharing employment between the generations, one that suggests employers may find justifying the use of a mandatory retirement age relatively easy. Moreover, in the later case of *Rosenbladt v Oellerking Gebaudereinigungsges mBh* [2011] IRLR 51, it provided clear and specific guidance on when a compulsory retirement age of 65 in an employment contract could be justified. In its view this could be appropriate under the following conditions:

(a) That the term in the contract relating to retirement age, had been collectively negotiated with a union.

(b) That the employee will receive a pension, thus ensuring some replacement income.

(c) That compulsory retirement has been in widespread use in the relevant country for a considerable amount of time without having had an effect on employment levels.

▶ British government and the Default Retirement Age (DRA)

The government's decision to opt for a mandatory retirement age of 65 at the time of the 2006 Regulations was controversial and led almost immediately to a legal challenge (*Age UK v Sec of State for Business Enterprise and Regulatory Reform and Others* (C-388/07) [2009] see Exhibit 5.8 below). It seems to have been persuaded by employer arguments that a set retirement age made it easier to engage in workforce planning, and that any changes were likely to come from a gradual encouragement towards greater pro-ceduralisation and formalisation of 'good practice' in how employers dealt with age-related matters. This was to be achieved by the concept of 'fair retirement' (see Exhibit 5.9) and by 'signposting' that a review of the DRA would take place in 2011 – subsequently brought forward to 2010. If one accepts the extent of ageist attitudes and their embedded nature, a staged process of change could be seen as an attempt at a more fundamental culture change among employers, and in society generally. In acknowledging the symbolic nature of retirement and 'retirement age', the government could be seen as trying to move employers towards an acceptance of 'transitions out of work' and a more considered approach to retaining staff who are performing and wish to remain in work.

EXHIBIT 5.8

The *Heyday* case

Incorporated Trustees of the National Council on Ageing v Secretary of State for Business, Enterprise and Regulatory Reform [2009] **IRLR 373**

Heyday, a branch of Age Concern (now Age UK) mounted a legal challenge to the government's position that, despite the age discrimination regulations, a compulsory retirement age of 65 would remain, thus preserving an element of age discrimination in employment.

The case was referred to the European Court of Justice by the High Court and in September 2008 the Advocate General advised that the UK government position was lawful, a decision endorsed by the ECJ in March 2009. In general the ECJ held that discrimination can be justified if it satisfies a general test of being a proportionate means of achieving a legitimate aim. In the view of the ECJ, the default retirement age did meet a legitimate aim, that of wider economic and social policy, and the decision was remitted back to the High Court in London to determine whether the compulsory retirement age pursued legitimate aims in a way that was also proportionate.

Following a hearing the High Court, in September 2009, held that the default retirement age was indeed lawful. That the DRA was based on a social policy objective of 'maintaining confidence in the labour market' and that the DRA was a proportionate means of giving effect to this. However, the judgment was interesting in that the High Court made clear that its decision was influenced by the government's decision to bring forward a review of the DRA to 2010, and that had this not happened that it would not have found the DRA to be justified. Indeed in the High Court, Justice Blake argued that in light of 'substantial arguments' there was now a 'compelling case' for setting the age higher than 65.

EXHIBIT 5.9

The concept of fair retirement

The former Employment Equality (Age) Regulations 2006 introduced an element of proceduralisation through the concept of 'fair' retirement. Although this was re-enacted in the Equality Act 2010, it was rescinded in April 2011 when the DRA was abolished. However, it may remain significant in some residual claims that are made to employment tribunals.

Fair retirement requires employers to notify in writing their intention to retire an employee no more than a year but more than six months before the intended date of retirement. They must also have told employees of their right to request to continue working. The statutory right to request not to retire must be in writing; and the employer is under a duty to consider it. The employer is then required to hold a meeting with the employee but is under no obligation to agree to any request not to retire; nor to provide a reason although it would clearly be good practice to do so.

The abolition of the DRA from October 2011 (see Exhibit 5.10) has major implications for workforce management. In principle, it establishes that retirement will no longer be a fair reason for dismissal. Although it may still be possible to retire an employee lawfully at a specific age provided that this can be objectively justified (see *Rosenbladt* case above, ACAS 2011) the extent to which employers will try to or be able to rely on this defence is unclear. They will therefore need to examine carefully certain HR policies and how these are adhered to in practice.

Despite the emerging ECJ position, the general advice to employers has been to remove any references to compulsory retirement ages, emphasising the point that there are a number of alternatives to this including changes to hours, job sharing, changes in roles and responsibilities and deferring retirements (Short and Barnett 2011). However, as well as requiring changes to employment contracts to remove references to compulsory retirement age (or consider whether such an age can be objectively justified), retirement policies will need to be reviewed to clarify an employer's approach to retirement under new rules. Included within this will be judgements about dismissal concerning retirement, with employers needing to rely far more on formal performance management procedures (EOR 2011: 208, 210, 2011a, 210). This was always the hope of the fair retirement provisions under the 2006 Regulations but the DRA abolition has the potential to radically alter the role of appraisal, capability and performance management and, also, to further proceduralise decisions relating to retirement. The government has also emphasised the need for 'open dialogue' with older workers regarding retirement in order to avoid potential age discrimination or constructive dismissal claims, guidance reinforced by ACAS (2011).

EXHIBIT 5.10

Abolition of the DRA

Note: Although the DRA is now repealed, it is still possible for issues relating to it to be in the tribunal and court process for some time in the future.

Phasing out the Default Retirement Age
In January 2011, the government, following a consultation initiated in July 2010, announced that it would phase out the DRA (see *Phasing Out the Default Retirement Age: Government Response to Consultation* on **www.bis.gov.uk**). The transitional arrangements started on 6 April 2011. The government indicated the following measures which were implemented through the Employment Equality (Repeal of Retirement Age Provisions) Regulations 2011:

Transitional arrangements:

- From 6 April 2011 employers are prohibited from issuing notifications of retirement using the statutory retirement procedure.
- Notifications to employees issued on or before 5 April 2011 must only relate to retirements at the age of 65 years that occur on or before 30 September 2011.

Abolition. 1 October 2011: the DRA will be abolished completely.

Notification of retirement and right to request working. Both provisions are rescinded at the same time.

Compulsory retirement ages. Can be prescribed. However, they must be justified as a 'proportionate means of achieving a legitimate aim'. Complaints can be made to an employment tribunal.

No compulsory retirement age. Any dismissal must relate to the 'fair reasons' under the Employment Rights Act 1996, s 98. Retirement will no longer be a 'fair reason' for dismissal. In a number of cases, the 'real' reason for dismissing older workers is likely to be challenged (see Chapter 8).

Recruitment of older workers. An employer's right to refuse to employ an applicant who is 64 years and six months or more is rescinded. It is unlawful to discriminate because of age, irrespective of the age of the person, in selection arrangements and recruitment. Any age requirement must be justified.

▶ Age discrimination and redundancy selection and payments

One particular area that has led to some interesting legal cases is that of selection for redundancy. This has been a controversial area, in part because the age-banding of statutory redundancy pay has been deemed by governments to constitute justifiable age discrimination but also because redundancy schemes that relied on payments linked even in part to length of service were risky in terms of their age discriminatory component. Two cases have clarified matters somewhat in relation to the second of these issues. In *Rolls Royce* v *Unite the Union* [2009] EWCA Civ 387, CA, the company negotiated collective agreements with the union outlining the agreed approach to be taken in any redundancy situation. The approach outlined five criteria and assigned points to each of these, one of which was for length of service. Significantly the company was concerned that the length of service criteria could amount to unlawful age discrimination and wanted it removed, but the union wanted it retained, acknowledging that it did amount to indirect age discrimination but that this could be justified. The case originally went to the High Court which held the length of service criterion not to be discriminatory, but the company appealed the decision. The Court of Appeal found in favour of the union accepting that the criterion was indirectly discriminatory but that this could be objectively justified. The legitimate aim 'was the reward of loyalty and the overall desirability of achieving a stable workforce in the context of a fair process of redundancy selection. Proportionality was demonstrated by the fact that the length of service criterion was only one of a substantial number of criteria for measuring employee suitability for redundancy' (*Personnel Today* 2 June 2009; see also Chapter 3).

The second case, *Mayor and Burgesses of the London Borough of Tower Hamlets* v *Wooster* [2009] IRLR 980, concerned an employee of the council who had been seconded to a social landlord for a period which was due to come to an end shortly before his 50th birthday, he had over 30 years' service with the council. He was informed that unless alternative employment could be found he would be dismissed on the grounds of redundancy. None was found and he was duly dismissed. Significantly, had he continued in work until his 50th birthday he would have been entitled to an immediate retirement pension rather than having to wait until his 60th birthday. In 2007 Wooster claimed unfair dismissal and age discrimination. The employment tribunal upheld the claim but the council appealed and the case was heard at the EAT in 2009. This dismissed the appeal on the grounds that the council could have found alternative work but failed to do so because of their concerns over the more generous retirement package he would have been entitled to had he continued working beyond the age of 50. In effect the EAT judgment suggested the council had deliberately forced Wooster out of employment to avoid having to pay an enhanced pension and endorses the general position that cost on its own cannot be a basis for a justification of age discrimination.

The third illustration is a German case concerning redundancy payments that went to the ECJ. In *Kücükdeveci* v *Swedex GmbH & Co* [2009] the issue concerned the national law in Germany whereby the use of length of service for calculating redundancy payments discounted service before the age of 25. The claimant started work at the age of 18 and was dismissed at the age of 28. Instead of receiving benefits based on ten years' service she received them based on three and claimed age discrimination. The

ECJ held that this constituted unjustified age discrimination which could not be objectively justified. As *People Management* reported this:

> On the question of age discrimination, the ECJ decided the German law did give less favourable treatment to employees who entered an employer's service before the age of 25. The court held that although the historical aim behind the law – allowing German employers more flexibility over the dismissal of young workers – was legitimate, the law was not a proportionate means of achieving this aim because it applied to all employees joining an undertaking before the age of 25, irrespective of their age at dismissal. The ECJ confirmed the German law did not comply with the equal treatment directive.   (*People Management* 8 February 2010)

▶ Age discrimination and market considerations

There have been a number of allegations by women working in television media of age discrimination in the recent past. However, the *O'Reilly* case is the first to have been taken to tribunal and is significant for a number of reasons (Exhibit 5.11). The particular interest lies in the employer's defence that discrimination was legitimate, or objectively justified by a wish to appeal to a prime-time audience, including widening the appeal of the programme to encompass a younger audience profile. This can be interpreted in two ways which have important implications for employers and the effectiveness of the legislation. One is that the BBC is pursuing a diversity argument. To mirror more closely the target market it wished to appeal to, it needed to reflect the nature of that market in

---

EXHIBIT 5.11

O'Reilly v *BBC* [2010] ET/2200423/10

Miriam O'Reilly had been employed as a presenter on the BBC's *Countryfile* programme and was dismissed from this post in 2009 aged 52. She claimed age discrimination citing her replacement by significantly younger presenters. It was conceded that she had been dismissed 'almost entirely out of hand' with little documentation and a failure to use a formal procedure. However, it was held that this did not, of itself, evidence discrimination . . . although it made it more difficult for the BBC to account for its decisions and the grounds on which the decisions were taken.

A particular issue in the case was the fact that the BBC had argued its wish to appeal to a prime-time audience including younger viewers, which the tribunal acknowledged as a legitimate aim. It was accepted that the general age profile of the programme became considerably younger as a result of the dismissal of O'Reilly and her replacement by new presenters. Furthermore, this was particularly marked for what was deemed the second tier group for which O'Reilly might have been considered. However the tribunal held that:

> The new . . . presenters did not have the substantial network profile that might attract prime-time audiences that was supposed to be the [BBC's] principal criteria. We consider a significant factor in their choice [of presenters] was their comparative youth; and in the decision not to consider the claimant, her age.

The tribunal added that in its view the discrimination was not objectively justified, that is that the BBC's view that choosing younger presenters was required to appeal to such an audience, was not a proportionate response.

the profile of its presenters. In pursuing a diversity agenda the BBC might have to engage in discriminatory practices which could be objectively justified. A second interpretation is that an employer is choosing to discriminate, because its customers are discriminating. A simple extension of this is to argue that the market decides. If viewers say they want to watch programmes with younger presenters reflecting a more youthful outlook then the organisation should be able to change its presenters to reflect this. An issue that arises from the *O'Reilly* case is that age discrimination legislation could be vulnerable in the future to such claims (whether diversity or market based). However there remains the question (as in the *O'Reilly* case) as to whether responses of the kind seen in *O'Reilly* would be viewed as proportionate.

▶ Cost considerations

Extending the market or business case arguments for justifying age discrimination inevitably raises the question of whether employers can cite cost considerations as a legitimate aim particularly as 'economic factors such as business needs and considerations of efficiency may be legitimate aims' (Davies 2005: 11). As Rubenstein (2006a: 16) has argued: 'cost is an especially important consideration in the age discrimination context.' A consideration that has particular relevance for older workers' pay and benefits, and the sensitivity with which older workers are viewed in terms of their relative cost to organisations, particularly where length of service and seniority-based rewards are well established.

Case law suggests that costs should be considered but cannot be determinate, and it is unclear what weight should be placed on them. In *Cross v British Airways plc* [2005] IRLR 423 it was argued that costs alone cannot constitute a legitimate aim but that it is appropriate to take cost into account in deciding whether or not an employer's discriminatory treatment is a proportionate means of achieving the employer's aim. As the Employment Appeal Tribunal judgment concluded, economic justification may not often be highly valued, for example where discrimination is substantial, obvious and deliberate, (but) it must be considered.

In the more recent case, *Woodcock v North Cumbria Primary Care Trusts* EAT/0489/09, the Employment Appeal Tribunal came to a similar conclusion. Here a redundancy dismissal was timed so as to avoid 'enhanced' early retirement rights being triggered due to the appellant's age. At the EAT it was held that although dismissal was unfair it did not constitute age discrimination. This was because it was objectively justified on grounds *other than cost alone*. The fact that the Primary Care Trust had identified more than cost as a legitimate aim, that Woodcock was redundant, that no alternative job had been found for him and it was this need – to dismiss a redundant employee – that made the employer's aim legitimate. The EAT therefore followed its earlier decision in *Cross* that while cost alone may not justify a decision, cost plus other factors may do so.

▶ Seniority and length of service

A further area of controversy relates to age, seniority and length of service. Given the sensitivity of this area it is significant that both the former Regulations and the Equality Act have addressed it specifically. Direct discrimination by an employer using age-related pay or benefits has to be objectively justified. However, employers are permitted to award pay and benefits, such as enhanced holiday entitlement, to employees using the criterion of length of service. The argument is that employers may want to 'encourage loyalty', 'encourage motivation' and 'reward experience', benefits based on length of service of up to five years are permitted (Equality Act 2010, Schedule 9, Part 2, para 10).

Under the former Regulations and the Equality Act, benefits based on service beyond five years do **not** constitute unlawful service-based discrimination so long as it 'reasonably appears' to the employer that the way the criterion of length of service is used 'fulfils a business need of his undertaking (for example, either prospectively by encouraging loyalty or motivation, or retrospectively by rewarding experience, of some or all of his workers)' and that they have given consideration to whether or not they have that business need. This seems to be saying that an employer does not have to show objective justification for the use of length of service criteria. The use of service-related benefits is then a proportionate means of achieving the aim in question. The legitimate aim justifying the retention of service-related benefits is employment planning, in the sense of being able to attract, retain, and reward experienced staff. They help maintain workforce stability by rewarding loyalty, as distinct from performance, and by responding to employees' reasonable expectations that their salary should not remain static.

Although many employers clearly made significant changes to reward systems in the run up to and following the 2006 Regulations, seniority remains embedded in many organisations (MacNicol 2006). Separating out the wider influence of seniority from 'legitimate' rewards for loyalty, motivation and experience in many workplaces presents challenges. Furthermore, the issue of rewarding 'loyalty' could be interpreted as potentially giving rise to indirect sex discrimination claims if this is equated with long service and used as a justification for higher remuneration. The decision in *Cadman v HSE* [2006] IRLR 969, ECJ (an equal pay case), is relevant here. The Advocate General stated: 'I see no basis for a general and unconditional endorsement of a seniority criterion.' However, the European Court of Justice did not adopt this Opinion and held that since recourse to the criterion of length of service is generally appropriate to attain the legitimate objective of rewarding experience that enables a worker to perform his or her duties better, an employer need not specifically justify its use. This would apply unless serious doubts are raised about its appropriateness. This suggests that the use of a length of service justification should not be accepted unquestioningly by the courts, and that it needs to be subject to closer scrutiny in future.

Despite these important qualifications, the consensus among lawyers appears to be that length of service criteria would be relatively easy to satisfy. Employers would need to convince an employment tribunal why they believe that the service-related benefit is effective in fulfilling that need, and some evidence will be required to show that the belief was reasonable. 'Provided an employer complies with statutory requirements, the burden placed on them of justifying the length of service criterion appears to be extremely low' (Rubenstein 2006b: 26). Furthermore, length of service need not mean length of continuous service, it is about how long a person has been 'working for him in total', and pay and benefits can be based on service in a particular grade. Crucially, it is for the employer to decide which definition to use to calculate length of service – total time in employment or length of time working for him doing work he reasonably considers to be at or above a particular level.

▶ National minimum wage

The 2006 Regulations and the Equality Act (Schedule 9, Part 2, paras 11–12) expressly exempt the National Minimum Wage (NMW) in respect of its age bands. It remains lawful to operate an adult rate, apprentice rate and a separate rate for 18–20 and 16–17-year-olds. The Employers Forum on Age raised concerns about the continuation of age discriminatory pay bands in respect of the NMW. The government's view has remained that differential rates are needed to ensure continuing employment opportunities for younger workers (see Chapter 9).

Age discrimination: Conclusions

In a relatively short period of time age discrimination legislation is established as a key area of equality law. The provisions in the Equality Act 2010 reinforce and build on the foundation of the 2006 Regulations as one of the new 'protected characteristics'. It has been the issues surrounding the objective justification defence for both direct and indirect age discrimination that has attracted particular attention in the courts, resulting in a number of high profile cases, many of which have been referred to the ECJ. Although the legal position on objective justification has become clearer, particularly in respect of direct age discrimination, it remains a controversial area of the law and one where many employers are still 'feeling their way'.

FRISHCO SUPERMARKET CASE STUDY

Scenario 5.1

Is Marcus's failed promotion application evidence of age discrimination?

Marcus, a 48-year-old African-Caribbean man, had worked as a general assistant at the store for six years. He decided that he wanted to apply for promotion to the grade for checkout staff. This would involve him undergoing relevant training on the use of tills. He was interviewed for the post and rejected. **Trisha**, a 30-year-old African-Caribbean woman, was appointed.

  Marcus believed that he was not promoted because of his age and asked **Debbie**, the full-time administrator, why he didn't get the job. **Debbie**, incautiously, said that **Trisha** was 'young and enthusiastic and got on well with customers'. Marcus then spoke to **Tony** to complain that he had been discriminated against because he was one of the oldest general assistants and he wanted **Tony** to do something about

it. **Tony** said that the decision was made and that **Trisha** was the best person for the job and nothing could be done about the matter. **Marcus**, who is a union member, contacted **Des**, the Regional Official of the General Retail Workers' Union (GRWU) and asked what could be done.

Question

What advice would Des be likely to give Marcus about the action that he could take?

Visit www.mylawchamber.co.uk/willey to access sample HR documents to support this case study.

Disability

❱ The protected characteristic of 'disability'

Disability is a protected characteristic (Equality Act 2010, s 4). The concepts and principles established in the Disability Discrimination Act 1995 have been re-stated and harmonised to provide one approach under the Equality Act. So although the Disability Discrimination Act 1995 has been repealed much of it reappears in the Equality Act 2010. Furthermore, many of the disability discrimination cases decided under the Disability Discrimination Act 1995 remain good law.

❱ Defining disability

A disabled person is a person who has a disability within the meaning of the Act (EA, s 6(2)). A person has a disability if he or she has 'a physical or mental impairment' which has 'a substantial and long-term adverse effect on [the person's] ability to carry out normal day-to-day activities' (s 6(1)). Each aspect of this definition is considered below. The Act (s 6(5)) also provides for guidance to be issued about matters that should be taken into account in deciding any questions arising from this definition. The Equalities and Human Rights Commission (EHRC) has issued this. It replaces the previous guidance issued under the Disability Discrimination Act 1995. The EHRC's *Guidance on Matters to be Taken into Account in Determining Questions Relating to the Definition of Disability* considers each element of the definition in turn but emphasises the importance of reading the *Guidance* as a whole (**www.officefordisability.gov.uk/ docs/wor/new/ea-guide.pdf**). This is because each element has to be met by a person seeking protection under the Act.

It is important to note that the definition of disability is a legal definition and only adjudicating bodies such as a court or an employment tribunal can conclusively determine whether a person meets the definition. In everyday language the term 'disabled' is used widely to describe particular individuals. To claim protection under the legislation, however, the tests set out in the legislation must be complied with. It is also important to note that a tribunal might hear evidence from a medical practitioner about a complainant's impairment. However, it is not obliged to adopt this opinion in deciding whether a person is 'disabled' within the meaning of the legislation (*Abadeh* v *British Telecomms plc* [2001] IRLR 23). Furthermore, a tribunal may hear evidence from a complainant about what they cannot do.

The EHRC's *Guidance* is not, itself, an authoritative statement of the law but will be used by courts and tribunals to assist them in determining whether a person meets the definition. It is therefore important for any potential claimants to be aware of the *Guidance* and its illustrative examples and how it might influence judicial decision-making. In the case of *J* v *DLA Piper UK LLP* [2010] IRLR 936 the Employment Appeal Tribunal (EAT) considered the definition of disability in the context of a mental impairment. Although it determined that an employment tribunal should not proceed rigidly through the definition in consecutive stages it did suggest that a good starting point was to consider the claimant's ability to carry out day-to-day activities.

The EHRC's *Guidance* considers all elements of the definition but begins with what is meant by an impairment; the adverse effects which may be considered as substantial;

the meaning of long-term adverse effects; and, then, the meaning of day-to-day activities. These sections are to be considered together. The *Guidance* provides examples of a person with the particular protected characteristic of disability. The Appendix lists examples of activities that would or would not be considered as normal day-to-day activities.

The *Guidance* also considers the definition in relation to disabled children. Day-to-day activities in relation to a child under the age of six are considered as though for a child of six years or over. Considering whether a child meets the definition of disability would be important in the context of associative disability where an adult is claiming disability discrimination because of their association with a child. This might apply to the mother of a disabled child who alleges that she has been discriminated against because she has to care for her disabled child (see *Attridge Law* v *Coleman* [2008] IRLR 722 in Exhibit 5.12).

A physical or mental impairment

For the purposes of the legal definition the effects experienced by an individual must arise from a physical and/or mental impairment. The question is not how this impairment was caused. That is not important. The issue to be considered is its effect on the individual's ability to carry out normal day-to-day activities. However some conditions are specifically referred to in the *Guidance* so that an individual with the condition will either be deemed to be disabled or excluded from the definition. The Equality Act (Sch 1, para 6) provides that a person who has cancer, HIV infection or multiple sclerosis (MS) will be considered as a disabled person from the point of diagnosis. Similarly a person who is certified by an ophthalmic consultant as blind, severely sight impaired or partially sighted will be deemed to have a disability. However, certain other specific impairments such as addiction to alcohol or nicotine, or seasonal allergic rhinitis (hay fever) are specifically excluded. It is also important to note that a requirement in earlier disability discrimination legislation that mental impairments must be 'clinically well recognised' was repealed in 2005 and remains so.

Deciding whether an individual has a disability can be problematic where an individual has an impairment that is deemed to be a disability as well as another impairment that is excluded from the definition. An example of this might be an individual who is addicted to alcohol. This is an excluded condition but the alcoholism may have caused liver damage which is a physical impairment or depression which is a mental impairment. As the cause of the impairment is not relevant it is possible that such a person could meet the definition.

The Equality Act also covers past disabilities. This means that a person who no longer has a condition that they had in the past (which had met the definition of disability) will be able to claim protection under the Act. In the *Guidance* the example is given of a woman who has suffered from a mental impairment in the past and while not experiencing any further symptoms feels that she has been discriminated against because of her past mental illness. Furthermore, certain individuals registered as disabled under the Disabled Persons (Employment) Act 1944 were treated as disabled under the Disability Discrimination Act 1995 and continue to be so treated under the Equality Act 2010.

Substantial adverse effect

The physical or mental impairment must be shown to have a substantial adverse effect on the individual's ability to carry out normal day-to-day activities (s 6(1)(b)). 'Substantial' is defined as meaning 'more than minor or trivial' (s 212(1)). A cut on the

'Associative' discrimination

Coleman v *Attridge Law and Another* [2008] **IRLR 722**

Facts. Ms Coleman worked for a firm of solicitors as a legal secretary. Her son was born in 2002 with a severe breathing condition requiring specialised and particular care which she provided for him. She alleged that she was subjected to direct discrimination and harassment by her employer whom she claimed refused her requests for flexible working and subjected her and her child to abusive and insulting comments. In August 2005, she made a complaint at an employment tribunal alleging unfair constructive dismissal and that she had been treated less favourably because she had to care for her disabled son. The novel point in this case was that Ms Coleman was claiming that she had been treated less favourably on the grounds of her son's disability rather than her own.

Employment tribunal. The first question was whether Ms Coleman could plead discrimination against her former employer on the ground that she was subjected to less favourable treatment connected with her son's disability. This claim could not be raised under the Disability Discrimination Act 1995 (as amended). However, such 'associative' discrimination on the grounds of disability may have been unlawful under European law (the Employment Equality Directive 2000). The tribunal stayed (adjourned) the case whilst the matter was referred to the European Court of Justice for a ruling.

The reference. The employment tribunal asked the ECJ to consider whether the directive prohibited direct discrimination and/or harassment in a case of associative discrimination where the employee was not disabled but alleged less favourable treatment on the grounds of her son's disability. (The EAT dismissed an objection to this reference to the ECJ being made.)

ECJ ruling. It noted that the purpose of the Employment Equality Framework Directive was to lay down a general framework for combating discrimination on various grounds including disability. The principle of equal treatment meant that there was to be no direct or indirect discrimination 'whatsoever' on any of these grounds. The ECJ concluded that the directive which was designed to safeguard the principle of equal treatment could not be limited to people who were themselves disabled. Its purpose 'as regards employment and occupation, is to combat all forms of discrimination on grounds of disability.' In the present case, although Ms Coleman was not herself disabled, it was disability that caused the less favourable treatment that she complained of.

The directive was intended to combat all forms of discrimination on the grounds of disability in employment and occupation. The directive's application was not limited to a particular category of person but by reference, as appropriate, to religion or belief, disability, age or sexual orientation. This was the situation with regard to both direct discrimination and harassment.

Comment. By confirming that 'associative' discrimination on the grounds of disability is unlawful under European law, the ECJ has emphasised the importance of the directive and of national legislation implementing that directive in combating disability discrimination. In ruling that the protection applies to discrimination on grounds of disability and not to a particular category of person, the ECJ has reinforced the protection. 'This judgment has important implications for the rights of those who care for disabled people and elderly people' (*Equal Opportunities Review*, 179, August 2008).

Employment tribunal and EAT hearings. In December 2008, an employment tribunal accepted that it had jurisdiction to hear the case by interpreting the Disability Discrimination Act 1995 in conformity with the ECJ ruling. The employer appealed claiming that the employment tribunal had 'distorted and rewritten' the Act. The Employment Appeal Tribunal dismissed the appeal. It held that it was possible to construe the Act to prohibit associative discrimination (*EBR Attridge Law LLP* v *Coleman (No. 2)* [2010] IRLR 10, EAT). The case was further remitted to an employment tribunal to hear the discrimination complaint.

hand might therefore be considered as minor or trivial but the effect would be substantial if the hand had been amputated.

In considering whether the effect of impairment is substantial the *Guidance* compares factors such as the time taken by an individual with an impairment to carry out an activity compared with the time taken by a person without the impairment. The way in which an activity is carried out should also be considered. So for example, a person with obsessive compulsive disorder (OCD) might check many times to ensure that doors are locked on leaving home. The constant checking and re-checking would be a substantial adverse effect on a day-to-day activity.

The cumulative adverse effects of an impairment may become substantial, as for example with a person suffering from depression who is unable to plan and is forgetful. The effect of not buying food or doing household tasks would be cumulative. Furthermore a person with more than one impairment may experience a substantial adverse effect although in isolation the effect of the impairments individually may not be substantial. Many people with an impairment will modify their behaviour as a way of coping with the effects but the extent to which the individual should be required to modify their behaviour should be reasonable. So it would, for example, be reasonable to expect a person with chronic back pain to avoid skiing but not shopping. The fact that a person is able to use avoidance strategies to the extent that they do not appear to have an impairment does not mean that it is reasonable to conclude that they are not a disabled person. What must be considered are the things that the person cannot do or can only do with difficulty. Environmental effects are also relevant when assessing whether the adverse effects of an individual's impairment are substantial. An example of this would be rheumatoid arthritis, the effects of which may be less substantial in warmer, dryer weather. The overall substantial adverse effect of the condition should not be discounted because of seasonal variation.

'An impairment is to be treated as having a substantial adverse effect on the ability of the person concerned to carry out normal day-to-day activities' if, despite the effect of 'medical treatment and the use of a prosthesis or other aid', it would be 'likely' to have a substantial adverse effect (EA sch 1 para 5). The *Guidance* states that 'likely' is to be construed as meaning 'could well happen'. This reflects the decision of the House of Lords in *SCA Packaging Ltd* v *Boyle* [2009] IRLR 746 which resulted in a lower evidential test. The effect of treatment or correction is stripped out so that the impairment is to be treated as having a substantial adverse effect if it would do so without the treatment or correction. This means that for a person who wears a hearing aid the level of their hearing is to considered on the basis that were it not for the hearing aid the hearing impairment would be likely to have a substantial adverse effect. However, the use of spectacles or contact lenses to correct a sight impairment that is capable of correction is specifically excluded.

In cases where a person has a progressive condition this will be treated as having a substantial adverse effect from the point at which the condition begins to have such an effect and provided that in future the adverse effect is like to become substantial. We have already seen that certain progressive conditions such as cancer, HIV infection and MS will be considered as a disability from diagnosis.

'An impairment which consists of a severe disfigurement is to be treated as having a substantial adverse effect on the ability of the person concerned to carry out normal day-to-day activities.' However, this does not apply to deliberately acquired disfigurements.

Long-term effect

As well as being substantial the adverse effect on the individual's ability to carry out normal day-to-day activities has to be long term (s 6(1)(b)). This means that the condition must have lasted for 12 months, is likely to last for 12 months or is likely to last for the rest of the person's life (Sch 1, para 2(1)). The cumulative effect of related impairments will be relevant. This includes whether the impairment has developed from or is likely to develop from another impairment. So for example, anxiety disorder that has lasted for eight months then developed into depression that lasts for another five months would be considered as long term. However, separate and unconnected conditions lasting collectively for more than 12 months would not be considered as long term. The *Guidance* defines 'likely' in the context of likely to last for 12 months or likely to last for the rest of the person's life as meaning 'it could well happen'. Even if an impairment ceases to have a substantial adverse effect on a person's ability to carry out normal day-to-day activities it will be treated as having that effect if the effect is likely to recur (Sch 1, para 2(2)). In regard to progressive conditions a person will be taken to have an impairment that has a substantial adverse effect if the progressive condition is likely to have that effect (Sch 1, para 8). This is so even if the progressive condition is not yet having an adverse effect on day-to-day activities. Furthermore, an impairment will also be treated as having a substantial adverse effect if it would be likely to do so without treatment or other aids (Sch 1, para 5). This does not apply to a visual impairment that is correctable by using spectacles or contact lenses. In cases where stopping treatment would result in a recurrence of the condition then treatment is to be ignored and the substantial adverse effect is to be regarded as likely to recur.

It is important to note that it is the circumstances existing at the time of the alleged discrimination that are relevant rather than at the time of consideration at a judicial or other hearing. In *McDougall* v *Richmond Adult Community College* [2008] IRLR 227, the Court of Appeal confirmed that this was the correct approach. In relation to recurring effects the *Guidance* looks at the example of a person with rheumatoid arthritis which has a substantial adverse effect but then goes into a period of remission. Such a condition will be treated as long-term because the substantial adverse effect is likely to recur. The exception here is seasonal rhinitis (hay fever) which is a specific exclusion. In contrast to a condition such as rheumatoid arthritis which will be treated as likely to recur, two discrete episodes of depression – one caused by redundancy and another caused by bereavement over a period of 12 months – would not be treated as recurring because there is no evidence of an underlying condition.

Day-to-day activities

'Day-to-day activities' will mean very different things to different people. The previous Disability Discrimination Act 1995 included a prescribed list. These are no longer included in the Equality Act 2010. In general terms, the *Guidance* refers to day-to-day activities as 'things people do on a regular or daily basis'. This is considered to include activities such as 'shopping, reading and writing, having a conversation or using the telephone, watching television, getting washed and dressed, preparing and eating food, carrying out household tasks, walking and travelling by various forms of transport, and taking part in social activities'. Although specialist work activities such as reaching typing speeds standardised for secretarial work would not be considered as a normal day-to-day activity other more general activities that are part of everyday life in the workplace would be included. In this context the *Guidance* refers to activities such as 'interacting with colleagues, following instructions, using a computer, driving, carrying out interviews, preparing written documents, and keeping to a timetable or a shift pattern'.

'Normal' is given its ordinary everyday meaning to refer to an activity that is carried out daily or frequently. To be a normal day-to-day activity, however, the activity does not have to be carried out by the majority of the population. An example of this would be applying make-up which would not be a majority activity but would be a normal day-to-day activity. However, activities that involve highly specialised levels of attainment are not normal day-to-day activities. This would include for example the manual dexterity required of a watch repairer or concert pianist. It is not surprising therefore that the Equality Act does not provide one definition of day-to-day activities but the *Guidance* does give many examples in the Appendix. This lists the factors which, if experienced by a person, it would be reasonable or not reasonable to regard as having a substantial adverse effect on ability to carry out normal day-to-day activities. Examples are given in the *Guidance* of factors that it would be reasonable to regard as having a substantial adverse effect. They include, 'difficulty carrying out activities associated with toileting, or caused by frequent minor incontinence'. An example which would not be considered as having a substantial adverse effect would be 'inability to move heavy objects without assistance or a mechanical aid, such as moving a large suitcase or heavy piece of furniture without a trolley'. The examples given in the Appendix are indications rather than tests and all the circumstances of each individual case should be considered. This would include the cumulative effects of a condition, the interrelationship of physical and mental impairments as well as environmental factors such as noise which could be considerable for a person with a condition such as tinnitus. Possible indirect effects should also be considered as an impairment may not altogether prevent a person from carrying out a day-to-day activity but could still have a substantial adverse effect. This would include for example pain on writing or using a keyboard. In considering the effect of an impairment on day-to-day activities any treatment or corrective aid has to be ignored. This does not apply though when a person's sight is corrected by spectacles or contact lenses.

◗ The 'protected characteristic' summarised

To summarise (see Exhibit 5.13), it is explained in the Equality and Human Rights Commission *Code of Practice* (**www.equalityhumanrights.com**) that the protected characteristic of disability applies to individuals who meet the definition set out in the Equality Act 2010 (s 6(1)). This definition refers to a person who has a 'physical or mental impairment' which has 'a substantial and long-term adverse effect on [that person's] ability to carry out normal day-to-day activities'. Guidance from the Office for Disability Issues (**www.officefordisability.gov.uk/docs/wor/new/ea-guide**) explains what matters should be taken into account in determining questions relating to the definition of disability. Only an individual who can meet this definition will have the 'protected characteristic' of disability which does not simply apply to a person with a general medical condition. Section 6(3)(a) refers to 'a person who has a particular protected characteristic' as being a 'reference to a person who has a particular disability' rather than a particular medical condition. Accordingly people who have the same disability are considered to have a shared protected characteristic. Furthermore, an individual who has had a disability in the past will be considered to have the protected characteristic of disability.

Disability: summary of 'prohibited conduct'

NB: the employer must know or be reasonably expected to know of the disability (EA 2010, Sch 9, Part 3, para 20).

All these provisions are considered in detail below.

	Definition	Employer's possible defence
Direct discrimination	'Less favourable treatment' than others. No material difference between the cases (EA 2010, s 13)	None
Indirect discrimination	Where a 'provision, criterion or practice' causes particular disadvantage (EA 2010, s 19)	Objective justification: that the discrimination is a 'proportionate means of achieving a legitimate aim' (s 19)
Discrimination arising from disability	'Unfavourable treatment' because of something arising as a consequence of a person's disability (EA 2010, s 15)	Objective justification: that the discrimination is a 'proportionate means of achieving a legitimate aim' (s 15)
Duty to make adjustments	A duty on employer to change working practices and physical facilities and provide aids to assist a disabled person (EA 2010, ss 20–21; Sch 8)	Whether or not it is 'reasonable' to make the adjustments (EA 2010, ss 20–21; Sch 8; and relevant case law)

▶ Employer's knowledge of disability

An employer's knowledge of disability is particularly relevant to the issues of 'prohibited conduct', the duty to make reasonable adjustments and the pre-employment health questions. An employer can be exempted from the duty to make reasonable adjustments if it can show that it 'does not know' or 'could not reasonably be expected to know' of a person's disability (Equality Act, Sch 9, Part 3, para 20).

The former Disability Discrimination Act 1995 (s 4A(3)) exempted an employer from the duty to make reasonable adjustments if it does not know or could not reasonably be expected to know of a person's disability (within the meaning of the Act). The Employment Appeal Tribunal held that each of the following four limbs should *all* be satisfied by an employer (*Eastern & Coastal Kent Primary Care Trust* v *Grey* [2009] IRLR 429, EAT):

● that he or she does not know the disabled person has a disability;

● that he or she does not know that the disabled person is likely to be at a substantial disadvantage compared with persons who are not disabled;

● that he or she could not reasonably be expected to know that the disabled person has a disability; and

● that he or she could not reasonably be expected to know that the disabled person is likely to be placed at a substantial disadvantage compared with persons who are not disabled.

This approach is still good law.

Finding out if a disabled person has a disability requires a fine balance between legitimate questioning of an employee and respecting the employee's privacy. Knowledge acquired by a person providing services to an employer will be attributed or 'imputed' to the employer unless the service is provided to employees independently of the employer. An example of this would be counselling provided under an employer's Employee Assistance Programme (EAP) by an independent contractor whose contract specifically states that the counsellors are not acting on the employer's behalf. In such a case knowledge acquired by the counsellors would not be imputed to the employer. However, knowledge obtained by an occupational health advisor on the employer's behalf would be attributed to the employer.

▶ Direct discrimination

A person discriminates against another if 'because of a protected characteristic' that person is treated less favourably than others (EA s 13(1)). The EHRC *Code of Practice* provides that in the context of employment the comparison in treatment would be with other workers. It explains that it is not necessary for an individual to suffer financial loss in order to establish that they have been treated less favourably. A perception of less favourable treatment would be sufficient as in the example provided in the *Code of Practice* (albeit relating to sex discrimination) of a woman manager from whom appraisal duties are withdrawn while her male colleagues continue to perform appraisals. The woman is not demoted and suffers no loss of salary but feels that she has been demeaned in the eyes of those she managed and in the eyes of her colleagues. If this less favourable treatment is because of her sex this would be direct sex discrimination. A similar approach would be adopted if the protected characteristic was disability.

The phrase 'because of' replaces 'on grounds of' used in previous legislation on discrimination. The EHRC *Code of Practice* does not consider that this changes the legal meaning in any way. The protected characteristic does not need to be the main or only cause of the less favourable treatment but the circumstances would need to be investigated to establish that the less favourable treatment was due at least in part to the protected characteristic. The example is provided in the *Code of Practice* of a person with multiple sclerosis who is unsuccessful in applying for a job because the employer appoints a person who does not have a disability. It would be necessary to investigate the reason why the employer did not offer the job to the person with multiple sclerosis to establish whether the less favourable treatment was 'because of' the person's disability.

Comparators

The Equality Act refers to an individual being treated less favourably because of a protected characteristic than others would be treated (s 13(1)). In relation to disability the comparators are other employees who do not have a disability. The Act provides that 'there must be no material difference between the circumstances relating to each case' (s 23(1)). The *Code of Practice* explains that this does not mean that the circumstances have to be identical but they would have to be nearly the same. In the context of disability the circumstances would have to include a person's abilities (s 23(2)). To explain this, it provides the example of 'a disabled man with arthritis who can type at 30 words per minute'. The man applies for a clerical job that involves typing but he is rejected because his typing is too slow. The *Code of Practice* provides that the 'correct comparator in a claim for direct discrimination would be a person without arthritis who has the same typing speed with the same accuracy rate.' It would not be relevant for the man in this situation to compare himself with a comparator who was, for example, unable to lift heavy weights because this is not a requirement of the job and therefore not relevant to the circumstances.

▶ Associative and perceived discrimination

It is not necessary for an individual to have the particular protected characteristic in order to be protected against discrimination. The Equality Act has incorporated a developing trend in case law (*Coleman* v *Attridge Law* (C-303/06) [2008] IRLR 722, ECJ) (see Exhibit 5.12) to provide protection to an individual who is associated with someone who has a protected characteristic. For example, a father who is dismissed because he takes time off work to care for his disabled child could claim direct discrimination on the grounds of his association with his child's disability. It would also be direct discrimination if a person were to be treated less favourably because they were mistakenly perceived to have a particular protected characteristic.

▶ Duty to make adjustments

The duty to make reasonable adjustments for disabled people is a key difference between the way in which the protected characteristic of disability and other protected characteristics are dealt with under the legislation. This duty is one way of achieving, for a disabled person, a level playing field for individuals who might not otherwise be able to access and make progress in employment. The duty is undoubtedly important. It might be seen by employers as onerous but its impact is moderated by reference to the duty to make 'reasonable' adjustments. This introduces an objective assessment by which each case is to be considered. The EHRC *Code of Practice* summarises the duty to make adjustments as arising 'where a provision, criterion or practice, any physical feature or the absence of an auxiliary aid puts a disabled person at a substantial disadvantage compared with people who are not disabled'.

An employer has a duty to make reasonable adjustments for a person at all stages of employment (s 20 and Sch 8). This includes existing employees and a person who is an applicant for employment or simply a person who has notified the employer that they may be an applicant for employment. The duty also applies after employment has ended (s 108(4)).

The duty to make reasonable adjustments comprises three requirements:

● **Avoiding substantial disadvantage**. Where a 'provision, criterion or practice' of the employer puts a disabled person 'at a substantial disadvantage', the employer is required to 'take such steps as it is reasonable to have to take to avoid the disadvantage'. Although there is no definition of 'provision, criterion or practice' the *Code of Practice* suggests that the phrase should be widely construed to include any formal or informal rules, policies, practices or procedures in the workplace. For example access to the employer's car park on the basis of seniority could be adjusted so that a junior disabled employee is granted access. As far as the 'substantial ' nature of the disadvantage is concerned, the Equality Act (s 212(1)) defines 'substantial' as meaning 'more than minor or trivial'. The *Code of Practice* provides that it is a question of fact as to whether a disadvantage exists in a particular case and that this is to be assessed on an objective basis.

- **Physical features of work premises**. Where a physical feature puts a disabled person at a substantial disadvantage. Removing the substantial disadvantage caused by physical features such as access to a building would include removing the physical feature, altering it or providing a reasonable means of avoiding it. A common example of this would be a flight of steps to the entrance of a building, a substantial barrier to a disabled person using a wheelchair. Removal of the stairs might not be a reasonable adjustment but it could be reasonable to alter the entrance by building a ramp or avoiding the stairs altogether through another entrance. A physical feature could also include the furniture, fixtures or fittings or a building.

- **Auxiliary aid**. Where a disabled person would be put a substantial disadvantage without the provision of an auxiliary aid the employer is under a duty to take reasonable steps to provide such an aid (s 20(5)). An auxiliary aid would include, for example the provision of information such as training materials or correspondence in Braille or on audio tape or the provision of an auxiliary service such as the assistance of a support worker.

To be subject to the duty to make reasonable adjustments the employer must know or be reasonably expected to know that a disabled person may be an applicant for employment or an employee. The restrictions on asking applicants about their health prior to offering employment are described below but the restrictions do mean that employers may not be aware that a particular employee is disabled. There is no obligation on an employee to tell their employer about a disability but if the employer could not reasonably have known about the disability they will not be required to make adjustments. In practice it may be that the employee has to forgo some confidentiality in order that reasonable adjustments are made.

Defining 'reasonable'

The question to be addressed by an employment tribunal is whether, in all the circumstances, the employer has taken reasonable steps in order to make the adjustment. In assessing whether the cost of the adjustment is reasonable, the *Code of Practice* suggests that a comparison could be made between the cost of making the adjustment with the cost of recruiting and training a new employee. Other factors to consider would include the extent of the financial resources, the type and size of the employer, the practicality of the adjustment, including disruption to the employer's activities and how effective it would be in preventing the substantial disadvantage (see *Cordell v Foreign and Commonwealth Office* EAT/0016/11). It is possible for employers to obtain assistance under the Access to Work Scheme. Financial assistance available under this scheme can widen the scope of adjustments it would be reasonable to expect an employer to make. It is important to note that an employee cannot insist on a particular adjustment (*Secretary of State for Work and Pensions (Job Centre Plus) v Wilson* EAT/0289/09).

A failure to comply with the duty to make reasonable adjustments would constitute an act of unlawful discrimination. However, an employer is not required to make an adjustment if medical evidence suggests that it would be futile (*Hay v Surrey County Council* [2007] EWCA Civ 93). The Employment Appeal Tribunal has ruled (*Romec Ltd v Rudham* EAT/0069/07) that there should be 'a real prospect' that the adjustment would remove the substantial disadvantage. If not, it would not be reasonable to make the adjustment.

It is important to note that the Equality Act provides that it is not discrimination against a person who is **not** disabled if a disabled person is treated more favourably (s 13(3)). It is not therefore direct discrimination to treat a disabled person more favourably than a person who does not have a disability. This reflects the approach taken by the House of Lords in *Archibald v Fife Council* [2004] UKHL 32 (see Exhibits 5.14 and 5.15).

EXHIBIT 5.14

Positive discrimination and disability discrimination: the extent of the 'reasonable adjustment' duty

Archibald v *Fife Council* [2004] **UKHL 32, HL**

Facts. Ms Archibald was a road sweeper employed by Fife Council between May 1997 and March 2001. In April 1999, she underwent a minor surgical procedure that led to a rare complication resulting in severe pain over her heels, rendering her unable to walk. Initially, she had to use a wheelchair and later was able to walk only with the aid of sticks. The Council obtained medical advice in July 2000 that she remained unfit for work as a road sweeper but that she was fit for a sedentary job.

In the meantime, the employer had explored whether suitable alternative work could be offered to her. She applied, unsuccessfully, for over 100 posts in various departments. Some were office-based and on marginally more pay than she received as a road sweeper. Despite representations from her union, she had to undertake competitive interviews in line with the Council's redeployment policy.

In March 2001, the Council took the view that the deployment procedure had been exhausted and that she should be dismissed, given the length of her absence and the report that she would be unable to return to work as a road sweeper in the foreseeable future.

Her complaint.

- that she had been discriminated against on grounds of disability;
- that she should not have had to compete for alternative employment if she could show that she could perform the duties and responsibilities of the post applied for;
- that the council had failed to comply with the duty to make reasonable adjustment.

House of Lords ruling.

- The duty to make reasonable adjustments (Disability Discrimination Act 1995) *may* require an employer to treat a disabled person more favourably than a non-disabled person in order to remove the disadvantage caused by the disability. This may include transferring an employee to a suitable vacant position.

- Lady Justice Hale said that under the Sex Discrimination Act 1975 and the Race Relations Act 1976, everyone is treated equally. 'Men and women, black or white as the case may be, are opposite sides of the same coin . . . Treating men more favourably than women discriminates against women. Treating women more favourably than men discriminates against men.' The DDA does not expect disabled and non-disabled people to be treated in the same way. It makes provision for reasonable adjustments to be made to meet the special needs of disabled people. It is clear that the DDA 'entails *a measure of positive discrimination*, in the sense that employers are required to take steps to help disabled people which they are not required to take for others'. However, it is also the case that employers are required to take only those steps 'which in all the circumstances it is reasonable for them to take'. The steps that are reasonable include the extent to which it is practicable for the employer and the financial costs incurred.

EXHIBIT 5.15

Jelic v *Chief Constable of South Yorkshire Police* UKEAT/0491/09

In this case the Employment Appeal Tribunal considered a case where a police constable had been retired on medical grounds (with chronic anxiety syndrome) and whether the employer had failed to make reasonable adjustments – in particular whether the employer had considered the medical report recommending redeployment to a non-confrontational role involving limited public contact. The EAT ruled that it would be a reasonable adjustment to create a new job for a disabled employee. This extends the provision about access for a disabled person to a vacancy, as ruled by the House of Lords in *Archibald* v *Fife Council* [2004].

Consultation about adjustments

The Employment Appeal Tribunal ruled (*Tarbuck* v *Sainsbury's Supermarkets Ltd* [2006] IRLR 664, EAT) that the employer had no statutory duty to consult an employee on reasonable adjustments. However, it added that it would be wise for the employer to do so. It could help the employer defend itself against any complaint, if it had provided a full opportunity to explore the relevant issues raised by the employee and, also, that it had complied with the duty to make reasonable adjustments – even if, at the end of the consultation process, none could be made.

▶ 'Discrimination arising from disability'

The Equality Act (s 15) introduces discrimination 'arising from disability'. This new protection applies where a disabled person is treated 'unfavourably because of something arising in consequence' of their disability and it cannot be shown that 'the treatment is a proportionate means of achieving a legitimate aim'. However, discrimination will not be established if the alleged discriminator did not know and 'could not reasonably have been expected to know' that the individual had a disability.

The *Code of Practice* explains that discrimination arising from disability differs from direct discrimination because rather than arising because of the disability itself it arises in consequence of the disability. It provides the example of an employee who is dismissed for taking three months' sick leave. In the example the employer is aware that the employee has multiple sclerosis and that the sick leave was related to the employee's disability. The decision to dismiss was because of the length of absence but the absence arose because of the disability. This employee has therefore been treated unfavourably because of something arising in consequence of their disability. There is no need for the employee to cite a comparator because it is only necessary to show that the discrimination is because of something arising in consequence of the disability or that there is a connection between the unfavourable treatment and the disability.

Employers' defence

The employer will have a defence if it can show that the treatment was 'a proportionate means of achieving a legitimate aim' (s 15((1)(b)). This is the 'objective justification test'. The burden of proof rests with the employer to produce specific evidence in support of the contention that the unfavourable treatment is justified. However, the unfavourable treatment will not amount to discrimination if the employer can show it did not know that the disabled person had the disability in question and could not 'reasonably have been expected to know that the disabled person had the disability'.

▶ Enquiries about disability and health in recruitment

The Equality Act (s 60) prevents a prospective employer asking applicants for employment about their disability or health until an offer of employment has been made. The offer may have been made on a conditional or unconditional basis but it is only after this offer that health-related questions can be asked. Questions about an applicant's sickness absence record are also excluded as is the practice of requiring job applicants to complete a health questionnaire. These restrictions help to ensure that a disabled person is assessed on the basis of their ability to do the job rather than on the basis of their disability.

However, a complete ban on such questions could prevent employers asking legitimate questions designed to assist people with a disability gain employment. Accordingly, there are five specific situations when such questions will be allowed (s 60(6)(a)–(e)).

- The first is where the employer is asking questions to ascertain whether a job applicant will be able to undergo an assessment or whether any reasonable adjustment is required to enable them to participate in the recruitment process. This would only include questions about reasonable adjustments for the recruitment process leaving the issue of reasonable adjustments for the job itself until after recruitment. Replies obtained about the applicant's disability should be disregarded for the purposes of assessing suitability for the role in question.

- Secondly, questions are permitted to establish whether an applicant can carry out a function that is intrinsic to the work in question. Guidance from the Government Equalities Office provides the example of a person applying for a job as a care assistant in a residential care home. The job involves the lifting and physical support of residents so it would be permissible for the employer to ask questions about the applicant's ability to lift and physically support residents.

- The third situation relates to questions for the purpose of monitoring diversity among job applicants. It is important for employers to keep information collected for monitoring purposes separate from application forms so that there is no risk that the monitoring information will influence the decision-making process.

- Fourthly, employers may ask questions about health and disability in order to support initiatives for positive action. This is the sort of action that is taken to promote the recruitment of people with a disability where, for example, they may be under-represented in the workforce. Employers operating the guaranteed interview scheme will also need to ascertain whether a person has a disability. Under the guaranteed interview scheme employers guarantee to interview every applicant with a disability. The employer will therefore need to ascertain if the applicant has a disability.

- The fifth situation again relates to positive action where the work in question requires the job holder to have a particular disability. Again it would be necessary for the employer to establish whether the applicant has a disability.

Should the applicant volunteer information about his or her own disability the *Code of Practice* recommends that employers respond by only asking questions that relate to the intrinsic requirements of the job. If a conditional offer of employment is made the employer may proceed with health enquiries but should an applicant be rejected on the basis that they revealed a disability this would amount to direct discrimination. The *Code of Practice* recommends that in order to avoid such discrimination employers should only ask health questions that are relevant to the particular job and that reasonable adjustments are made for disabled applicants.

If an employer does ask a prohibited question about health or disability, and an applicant was unsuccessful for a job, this would not necessarily be discrimination. The burden of proof would be on the employer to show that no discrimination took place and give the reason why the applicant was unsuccessful. It could be that the reason involved 'discrimination arising from disability' (which could be objectively justified) rather than direct discrimination (which cannot be justified and triggers the duty to make reasonable adjustments).

❱ Indirect discrimination

Indirect discrimination occurs when an employer applies an apparently neutral 'provision, criterion or practice' which puts workers sharing a protected characteristic at a particular disadvantage (s 19).

Provision, criterion or practice

For establishing when a provision, criterion or practice will be discriminatory in relation to a protected characteristic four requirements must be met (EA 2010 s 19(2)).

- First, the employer applies the relevant provision, criterion or practice to everyone within the relevant group who does not share the particular characteristic. While not defined in the Act, the phrase 'provision, criterion or practice' is to be widely construed and as well as applying to current policies and procedures includes proposed policies and procedures and one-off decisions. The 'provision, criterion or practice' must be neutral in the sense that it applies to everyone in the relevant group.

- Secondly, the provision, criterion or practice puts or would put people who share the employee's protected characteristic at a particular disadvantage when compared with people who do not share the characteristic (s 19(2)(b)). The reference to 'would put' means that a provision, criterion or practice that has not yet been applied can be challenged. A particular 'disadvantage' is not defined in the Act but it is suggested in the *Code of Practice* that it could include 'denial of an opportunity or choice, deterrence, rejection or exclusion'. It is not necessary to establish financial loss but it must be something that a reasonable person would complain about rather than an unjustified sense of grievance.

- Thirdly, having established that the provision, criterion or practice puts people sharing the protected characteristic at particular disadvantage it is necessary to compare the situation of people in the relevant group who do not share the characteristic. There must be 'no material difference between the circumstances' relating to each group in order for a comparison to be made (s 23(1)). The *Code of Practice* also points out that it is important to be clear which protected characteristic is relevant. In the context of disability it would be people sharing, for example, an equivalent level of visual impairment rather than people generally with a disability. The pool used for comparison should consist of the group affected by the provision, criterion or practice with the comparison being made between its impact on people without the relevant protected characteristic and its impact on people with the relevant protected characteristic. It is required that the provision, criterion or practice puts the person concerned at that particular disadvantage rather than a group of people who share a protected characteristic. It must be established that the person has suffered (or could suffer) that particular disadvantage as an individual.

- Fourthly the provision, criterion or practice will be indirectly discriminatory if the employer cannot objectively justify it by showing it to be a 'proportionate means of achieving a legitimate aim'. There are two limbs to establishing this. The first question is whether the aim of the provision, criterion or practice is legal and non-discriminatory representing a real, objective consideration? Secondly, if the aim is legitimate, is the means of achieving it proportionate – in other words appropriate and necessary in all the circumstances? The *Code of Practice* points out that an employment tribunal is unlikely to accept reducing costs as a legitimate aim as this is tantamount to arguing that it is cheaper to discriminate than to avoid discrimination. In considering what is proportionate the *Code of Practice* looks to EU directives which use the term to mean an 'appropriate and necessary' means of achieving a legitimate aim although 'necessary' does not mean that the provision, criterion or practice is the only way of achieving a legitimate aim. The *Code of Practice* advises that it is sufficient that the same aim could not be achieved by less discriminatory means.

▶ Discriminatory adverts

An employer must not discriminate in the arrangements that are made for deciding to whom to offer employment (s 39(1)(a)). Arrangements in this context would include advertisements for jobs, the application process and the interview stage. The *Code of Practice* reiterates that an employer must not discriminate in its arrangements for advertising jobs or by not advertising a job. It is also important to ensure that the content of the job advertisement is not discriminatory. Advertising a job is a good way of encouraging applications from as diverse a section of the population as possible. For this reason recruitment on the basis of recommendation should be avoided as it will simply perpetuate any under-representation by employees with particular protected characteristics. If a job is only to be advertised internally the employer should ensure that it is as widely advertised as possible. Employees on long-term sick leave should also not be forgotten as failure to include them could amount to discrimination.

Job advertisements should be carefully worded to ensure that they accurately reflect the requirements of the job and do not directly discriminate by expressly excluding anyone with a protected characteristic. An example of this would be an advertisement for an 'able bodied' person for a clerical position that had no intrinsic requirement for any particular physical attributes. Similarly, the *Code of Practice* states that advertisements should not include wording that might indirectly discriminate by disadvantaging people with a particular characteristic unless that requirement could be objectively justified.

The *Code of Practice* provides that the question of whether an advertisement is discriminatory depends on whether a reasonable person would consider it to be so.

Job advertisements should not give any impression that reasonable adjustments will not be made for people with disabilities. The example is given in the *Code of Practice* of an advertisement for a job that is stated not to be suitable for wheelchair users because it is on the first floor. The employer should state instead that it is willing to make reasonable adjustments.

Discrimination on the grounds of disability is asymmetrical. This is because, unlike other protected characteristics, it is not discriminatory to treat a person with the protected characteristic of disability more favourably than someone who is not disabled (s 13(3)). Accordingly it would not be discriminatory to advertise for a job specifically requiring an applicant with a disability.

FRISHCO SUPERMARKET CASE STUDY

Scenario 5.2

What would be a reasonable adjustment for Winona?

Winona had worked for Frishco for ten years and had been promoted to be a deputy manager of the busy south-west London store. She had, however, developed a medical condition (fibromyalgia syndrome) which caused her pain and tiredness and muscle stiffness. She found the shift working and the pressurised working environment difficult to cope with some weeks. In fact, she had taken more sick leave during the past year than she had ever taken in her employment with the company.

Following a risk assessment, the company had made some adjustment – allowing her to take occasional breaks when she needed. However, these arrangements proved not to be satisfactory. **Winona** did not want to give up work; nor did she want to take a job that would be a demotion. She was a single parent with a teenage son and could not afford the loss of a regular income. There is a quieter store about five miles away in suburban Surrey. **Tony**, the store manager, following a discussion with **Caroline**, the HR manager, proposed to **Winona** that she move there on a permanent basis. A deputy manager there was about to go on maternity leave and cover was needed. **Tony** said that **Winona** could provide the cover and 'see how things worked out'. It was possible for her to travel there although the journey would have taken slightly longer on a less frequent train service. **Winona** responded that she was happy at the south-west London store, having worked there for five years. She had good work relations with the staff – some of whom she knew socially. She told him that she didn't want to move. **Winona** was uncertain about the action she could take and spoke to **Des**, a Regional Officer of the General Retail Workers' Union for advice.

Question

What advice would Des be likely to give Winona about the action that she could take?

Visit **mylawchamber.co.uk/willey** *to access sample HR documents to support this case study.*

Gender reassignment

The European Court of Justice ruled that discrimination on the grounds of gender reassignment was contrary to the principle of equal treatment in the 1976 Equal Treatment Directive (*P v S and Cornwall County Council* [1996] IRLR 347). In 1999, the Sex Discrimination Act 1975 was amended to incorporate protections. Under the Equality Act 2010 (s 16), a person is protected from direct and indirect discrimination and victimisation where that person is intending to undergo, undergoing or has undergone the process of gender reassignment. The Act has removed the original provision (in the Sex Discrimination Act) that the reassignment process has to be conducted under medical supervision. The proscribed 'less favourable treatment' can involve a comparison of arrangements for sick absence (for employees who are not reassigning their gender) and the absence necessary for gender reassignment medical treatment (EA 2010 s 16).

The need to clarify the application of the 'less favourable treatment' provisions to the gender reassignment *process* arose in one case involving the use of toilet facilities (*Croft v Royal Mail Group plc* [2003] IRLR 592). There are, effectively, three stages in the gender reassignment process: intention to reassign; undergoing the reassignment; and the completion of the reassignment (i.e. the post-operative stage). It is possible that a person at any of these three stages may experience different treatment. However, it is a matter for the courts to determine whether this is 'less favourable treatment' within the terms of the legislation.

In the case of Ms Croft, a *pre-operative* 'male to female' transsexual undergoing medical treatment, there were concerns from the existing workforce about her use of toilet facilities. The employer, as a pragmatic response, provided access to a gender-neutral disabled toilet rather than the women's toilet (the gender to which she was reassigning).

The Court of Appeal ruled that in considering what amounts to less favourable treatment on grounds of gender reassignment, it does not follow that all such persons are entitled *immediately* to be treated as members of the sex to which they aspire. It added that the moment at which a person at the 'real life test' stage is entitled to use female toilets depends on all the circumstances. The employer must take into account the stage reached in treatment, including the employee's own assessment and the way that they present themselves – although the employer is not bound by the employee's self-definition when making a judgement as to when the changes occurred. The employer is also entitled to take into account, though not to be governed by, the susceptibilities of other members of the workforce. In the circumstances of this case, the Court of Appeal ruled that the measures taken by the employers were appropriate in the circumstances. Therefore, they were entitled, for a period of time, to rely on the unisex disabled toilet as being a sufficient facility for Ms Croft to use. The time had not come when they were obliged to permit her to use the female toilets.

The House of Lords has held that for the purposes of employment law a *post-operative* transsexual should be treated as having their reassigned sex (*A v Chief Constable of West Yorkshire Police* [2004] IRLR 573). Following this stage, a person is entitled to formal recognition under the Gender Recognition Act 2004. This provides rights relevant to employment and in the wider society for people who have obtained a Gender Recognition Certificate. It arose from a ruling in 2002 by the European Court of Human Rights following an application from Christine Goodwin (*Goodwin v United Kingdom* [2002] IRLR 664, ECHR). The key provisions of the Act are:

- A person undergoing gender reassignment can apply for a Gender Recognition Certificate. Those born in the UK can obtain a new birth certificate.

- This new birth certificate is likely to have a bearing on any evidence provided to human resource departments for entry to, for example, occupational pension schemes.

- Any disclosure that a person has such a Gender Recognition Certificate is a criminal offence with a fine of up to £5,000. This obviously applies to employers, prospective employers and any of their employees.

As far as the issue of occupational requirement is concerned, the previous provisions under the Sex Discrimination Act excluding 'transgender' people from certain jobs have been repealed. There is now only the broad statutory provision (Sch 9) which permits the employer to specify and justify any occupational requirement (see also Chapter 6).

Marriage and civil partnership

The Equality Act prohibits direct and indirect discrimination and victimisation on the grounds of this protected characteristic. However, it does not encompass perceived discrimination. A civil partnership is formally specified as a relationship between two people of the same sex under the Civil Partnership Act 2004. It is not permissible to victimise or to discriminate directly or indirectly against a person because of their status as a married person or a civil partner. It is, however, permissible to discriminate against a single person of either sex – but not in their favour. This would constitute discrimination against a married person or a civil partner.

Pregnancy and maternity

'Pregnancy and maternity' is a 'protected characteristic' (s 4). There is no indirect discrimination provision relating to it. A particular provision relates to direct sex discrimination – 'less favourable treatment' – concerning breastfeeding *not* at work (s 13). Most relevant protection concerns 'unfavourable treatment' which does not require a comparator (s 18). Prohibited discrimination must be 'because of' this characteristic. The Act specifies the following protections against discriminatory treatment at work: (s 18(2)):

- 'A person (A) discriminates against a woman if, in the protected period in relation to a pregnancy of hers, A treats her unfavourably
  - because of the pregnancy, or
  - because of illness suffered by her as a result of it.'

- Unfavourable treatment (under s 18(2)) is regarded as occurring in the protected period even if 'the implementation is not until after the end of that period' (s 18(5)).

It is important to note that the prohibition in relation to 'pregnancy and maternity' is against 'unfavourable' treatment and not against 'less favourable' treatment. No comparison is required as it would be if the phrase 'less favourable treatment' was used. This reflects established case law.

The Act prohibits 'unfavourable' treatment in respect of compulsory maternity leave (s 18(3)). It also states that a person (e.g. an employer) discriminates against a woman if he treats her unfavourably because she is exercising or seeking to exercise (or has exercised or sought to exercise) the right to ordinary or additional maternity leave (s 18(4)). An employer must know that a woman is pregnant for her to be protected. The **protected period** (s 18(6)) 'begins when the pregnancy begins and ends' in one of two sets of circumstances:

- if the woman has the right to OML or AML, then at the end of AML or (if earlier) when she returns to work after the pregnancy;

- if the woman does not have the right to OML or AML, then the protected period finishes at 'the end of the period of 2 weeks beginning with the end of the pregnancy'.

Even if unfavourable treatment is activated after the protected period, it is possible that the woman *may* be protected if it can be shown that the decision to treat her unfavourably was taken by the employer prior to the end of the protected period (s 18(5)).

Direct discrimination (s 13): This section states that if the protected characteristic is sex, then if a man is claiming direct sex discrimination 'no account is to be taken of special treatment afforded to a woman in connection with pregnancy or childbirth'.

Breastfeeding (s 13(6)(a)): This section covers less favourable treatment of a woman because she is breastfeeding. However, it does not apply to the workplace (s 13(7)) (see Chapter 11).

Race

This 'protected characteristic' includes colour, nationality, ethnic or national origin (s 9(1)). A reference to 'race' is a reference to a person of a particular 'racial group'. A 'racial group' is a group of persons defined by reference to race. 'The fact that racial group comprises two or more distinct racial groups does not prevent it from constituting a particular racial group' (s 9(2)–(4)). There is provision in the Equality Act (s 9(5)) which allows it to be extended to cover 'caste' discrimination. This has not yet been implemented by the Conservative–Liberal Democrat government. As a preliminary to implementation, the previous Labour government commissioned a report on the matter (Metcalfe and Rolfe 2010).

The protections cover direct and indirect discrimination and victimisation. They also, importantly, encompass associative discrimination which has a number of recorded cases since the 1980s (e.g. *R v Commission for Racial Equality ex parte Westminster City Council* [1985] IRLR 426) (see also Exhibit 5.16).

◗ Racial group

This is defined by 'colour, race, nationality or ethnic or national origin' (s 3(1)). A person may be a member of several 'racial groups' simultaneously and these can be indicated in any complaint alleging discrimination.

In a **leading case** which tested whether Sikhs qualified as a racial group, the House of Lords (*Mandla v Dowell Lee* [1983] IRLR 209) ruled that 'ethnic origin' was a wider concept than 'race', to be construed in a 'broad, cultural historic sense'. To be an 'ethnic group' under the Act, a group must have certain essential characteristics:

The cable layers

Three young cable-layers from Bradford who were friends were sent to Warwick, a predominantly white town, to lay TV cables for a Manchester-based company. Ninja, Toffo and Parksy were white, Asian and African-Caribbean respectively. On arrival they were told they were 'too scruffy for our customers' by a senior manager. When they returned to their van to load up their gear, Ninja was taken aside by the manager. He was offered work and told that there was no problem with him – 'it's the other two'. He added, 'you know what I mean'. Ninja refused and returned to Bradford with his colleagues. Toffo commented that 'the guys who sacked me and Parksy were sly. They thought they'd not be found out because Ninja would have the same racist views as them.'

- a long shared history, of which the group is conscious as distinguishing it from other groups and the memory of which keeps it alive;
- a cultural tradition, including family and social customs and manners (which may be associated with religious observance).

Also, some of the following factors may be relevant in distinguishing the group:

- common geographical origin or descent from common ancestors;
- a common language (not necessarily restricted to the group);
- a common literature particular to that group;
- a common religion (different from that of neighbouring groups or from the general community);
- being a minority or being an oppressed or a dominant group within a large community.

In addition to these objective factors, self-designation is also a consideration: 'provided a person who joins the group feels himself or herself to be a member of it and is accepted by other members, then, he is for the purposes of the Act a member' (Lord Justice Fraser).

▶ More than one cause

The racial grounds underlying the less favourable treatment need not be the *sole* grounds for the less favourable treatment. There can be other non-racial grounds. Mr Justice Knox stated that where an employment tribunal 'finds that there are mixed motives for the doing of an act, one or some but not all of which constitute unlawful discrimination, it is highly desirable for there to be an assessment of the importance, from the causative point of view, of the unlawful motive or motives. If the tribunal finds that the unlawful motive or motives were of sufficient weight in the decision-making process to be treated as a cause, not the sole cause but as cause, of the act thus motivated, there will be unlawful discrimination' (*Nagarajan* v *Agnew* [1994] IRLR 61, EAT).

▶ Indirect discrimination

Under the former Race Relations Act 1976, various employment practices were challenged. Initially, in the original legislation, employees and applicants for employment could challenge a 'requirement or condition' imposed by the employer. The Court of Appeal ruled that a 'requirement or condition' should be a 'must' (*Perera v (1) The Civil Service Commission (2) The Department of Customs and Excise* [1983] IRLR 166). Under later European equality law, the new formulation of 'provision, criterion or practice' was enacted. This enables a wider range of employer decisions and employment arrangements to be scutinised and, as appropriate, challenged. The issue of objective justification is still relevant. This approach is adopted in the implementation of the Equality Act (s 19) where the legislation now defines indirect discrimination as a 'provision, criterion or practice' which causes disadvantage.

Cases under the earlier race discrimination legislation are outlined in Exhibit 5.17 to illustrate the employment issues that have arisen. It is important to note that some of these issues might, nowadays, come under the 'protected characteristic' of 'religion or belief' as well as 'race'. They were, nevertheless, regarded at the time as acceptable complaints relating to 'racial grounds'. Furthermore, it must be remembered that each case must be considered on its own facts and circumstances to determine whether there is disadvantage and whether the employer can justify the indirect discrimination as 'a proportionate means of achieving a legitimate aim'.

EXHIBIT 5.17

Race: examples of indirect discrimination

Hussein v *Saints Complete House Furnishers* [1979] **IRLR 337**

A job applicant was not considered because he lived in one of a group of Liverpool postal districts with a high proportion of non-white residents. It was found by the tribunal that 50 per cent of the population in the specified postal districts were non-white; compared with 2 per cent for the rest of Merseyside. The tribunal found the particular racial group was disproportionately affected.

Panesar v *Nestlé & Co Ltd* [1980] **IRLR 64, CA**

A rule in a chocolate factory that prohibited beards and long hair was challenged by a Sikh man. The Court of Appeal ruled that it was objectively justified in the interests of hygiene and safety.

Malik v *British Home Stores* [1980] **ET/2901/79**

A Muslim woman of Pakistani origin successfully claimed that she should be allowed to wear a uniform that included trousers rather than just a skirt to enable her to comply with her religious requirement to have her legs covered. The employer's uniform requirement was not justified.

Kingston & Richmond Area Health Authority v *Kaur* [1981] **IRLR 337, EAT**

In a case concerning the uniform to be worn by an enrolled nurse – which was, under statutory rules, to be a specified 'frock' and not to be subject to alteration 'of any kind' – the EAT ruled against the complainant. Ms Kaur claimed that she should be allowed to wear trousers as part of her uniform. In the circumstances of this case, it was unlawful for the Health Authority to permit a variation to the uniform. Consequently, the employer's approach was justified.

➡

Board of Governors of St Matthias Church of England School v *Crizzle* [1993] **IRLR 472, EAT**

A Church of England school was justified in specifying that a headteacher post should be held by a communicant of that religion. Ms Crizzle, who was Asian, was a Roman Catholic – albeit a non-practising one.

Kaur v *Butcher & Baker Foods Ltd* **ET/1304563/97**

Ms Kaur, who carried a Sikh dagger under her clothes as a religious obligation, worked on a food production line. When her supervisor became aware of the dagger she was eventually dismissed because it was an item of jewellery contrary to company policy. In response at the employment tribunal, the company said that it had to be removed for reasons of food hygiene. The tribunal 'could see no way in which the carrying of this dagger under at least some clothes could in any way interfere with or affect food hygiene' and found that Ms Kaur was indirectly discriminated against.

Hussain v *Midland Cosmetic Sales Ltd and Others* **ET/5204750/99**

Ms Hussain, a Pakistani Muslim, was required to remove a hajib (a headscarf covering her head and neck) which was required for religious observance and to wear protective headgear to conform to company health and safety policy. She was found not to have been indirectly discriminated against on grounds of race. The tribunal noted that other Muslim employees were able to comply with the health and safety rules.

Religion or belief

The former Race Relations Act 1976 did not expressly cover discrimination on the grounds of religion. However, in certain specific circumstances, some religious groups were ruled as 'racial groups' under that legislation following a House of Lords ruling (*Mandla* v *Dowell Lee* [1983] IRLR 209). Jews and Sikhs were protected as ethnic groups; but Muslims and Rastafarians (*Dawkins* v *Department of Environment* [1993] IRLR 284) were not protected.

The Employment Equality (Religion or Belief) Regulations 2003 transposed into British law the relevant provisions of the EU Employment Directive 2000. In 2007, supplementary regulations were implemented in respect of discrimination in the provision of goods, facilities and services. This legislation is now repealed and its provisions are in the Equality Act 2010.

There is a critical problem at the heart of this protected characteristic. Most other 'protected characteristics' relate to *innate* characteristics (age, gender reassignment, disability, race, sex and sexual orientation). 'Religion' or 'belief' are concerned with '*acquired*' characteristics – what a person chooses to believe; whether to accept the tenets of a particular religion; whether to adopt a literal translation of a holy book; whether to have a commitment to a political philosophy; or whether to reject theism as irrational. As a consequence, the issue of 'trumping' arises. There can be, and are, conflicts between one person's belief and another's right to be protected on other discriminatory grounds. So, courts and tribunals can be required to determine in particular cases whose rights are paramount (see Exhibit 5.18).

EXHIBIT 5.18

The registrar and civil partnerships

Facts. Ms Lillian Ladele was employed by the London Borough of Islington as a registrar. Until December 2007, registrars effectively worked on a freelance basis and could swap with each other to avoid civil partnership ceremonies. Since that date they came under the direct control of the local authority and there was said to be less flexibility in the arrangements. Ladele objected to officiating at civil partnership ceremonies because of her evangelical Christian beliefs. She claimed that she was picked on, shunned and accused of being homophobic for refusing to carry out civil partnership ceremonies, and that she was discriminated against on grounds of her religious beliefs.

Decisions. The **employment tribunal** found that she had been harassed and discriminated against directly and indirectly on the grounds of religious belief. The Council had assumed that protection against discrimination on the grounds of sexual orientation should be paramount. It had disregarded and displayed no respect for her genuinely held religious belief. The tribunal took the view that the starting point was that all rights are to be valued equally. The Council was able to provide facilities for civil partnership services without Ms Ladele by using staff who did not share her views. The **Employment Appeal Tribunal** ruled that the employment tribunal had erred in law. There was no unlawful religious discrimination by the Council (*London Borough of Islington* v *Ladele* UKEAT/0453/08). The **Court of Appeal** held that Ms Ladele was not discriminated against on the grounds of her religion; nor did she experience harassment. Furthermore, the policy of Islington Council was justified. So it had not indirectly discriminated against her on the grounds of religion.

The Court of Appeal also addressed the issue of the Equality Act (Sexual Orientation) Regulations 2007 which concerned the provision of public services. The Court ruled that it would have been unlawful discrimination under these regulations for Ms Ladele to refuse to perform civil partnership ceremonies. So, the Council was entitled to, and obliged to, require her to perform her designated duties as a Registrar (*Ladele* v *London Borough of Islington* [2009] EWCA Civ 1357, Court of Appeal). In March 2010, Ms Ladele was refused leave to appeal this case at the **Supreme Court**. The Court stated that the case did not raise legal points of 'general public importance'.

Reactions to ET ruling.

Public servants like Registrars have a duty to serve all members of the public without fear or favour. Once society lets some people opt out of upholding the law, where will it end?
(Peter Tatchell, campaigner for gay rights, BBC News website, 10 July 2008)

This important ruling confirms that gay rights should not be treated as trumping religious rights.
(Mike Judge, The Christian Institute, which financially supported the complainant)

[The decision] appears to place religious 'conscience of registrars' above their legal duty to carry out Parliament's legislation [. . .] Will registrars with similar religious convictions now be allowed to opt out of conducting civil marriages for divorcees, or for couples they believe have had sex before marriage or even couples from other faiths? [. . .] Would a racist council employee be allowed to excuse themselves in cases involving ethnic minorities on the basis of their 'deeply held beliefs' or 'religious consciences'?
(Terry Sanderson, President of the National Secular Society, press release, 10 July 2008 www.secularism.org.uk/registrarjudgementpotentiallycat.html)

◗ What is 'religion' and 'belief'?

'Religion'. There is probably a wide consensus in society about whether certain organisations constitute religions. If the tests are that there is belief in an external deity, collective worship, an authoritative holy book, some structure of leadership or priesthood, the use of prayer and the observance of certain holy days, then adherents of the three major religions in western society (Judaism, Christianity and Islam) would be covered. However, within these broad religious groups there are spectrums of opinion – some of a fundamentalist nature. Furthermore, there are also 'beliefs' which claim that they are 'religious' but may, arguably, be cults and are often regarded as anathema to the main religions. The extent to which non-orthodox views are protected must be tested on a case-by-case basis.

'Belief'. This is a potentially far-reaching category covering both 'religious' and 'philosophical' belief. The category encompasses humanism, various secular views and atheism; and political philosophies. An individual who is not part of a collective religious organisation might claim to have his or her own personal religious belief. Whether a person can successfully achieve protection for personal views is dependent on a number of considerations set by the courts (see Exhibit 5.19).

◗ Discrimination

The Equality Act 2010 prohibits direct and indirect discrimination and victimisation because of religion or belief. Direct discrimination is concerned with whether the less favourable treatment is because of a person's religion or belief. It is irrelevant whether the person discriminating has the same religion or belief. Indirect discrimination on the grounds of religion or belief is (as under the common provisions of the Act) where there is a provision, criterion or practice which creates a disadvantage to a person of a particular religion or belief (compared to other persons). It has to be objectively justified (see Exhibits 5.19–5.21).

◗ Occupational requirements

Although the employment implications of implementing occupational requirements under equality law are examined in more detail in Chapter 6, it is important to consider here the specific provisions about religion or belief in legislation (Equality Act, Sch 9, Part 1, paras 2–3). There are two sets of statutory provisions:

Employment for the purposes of an organised religion (Sch 9, para 2). The occupational requirement must be because of the work undertaken and it should either enable the person to comply with the doctrines of the religion (the 'compliance principle') or not be in conflict with the 'strongly held religious convictions of a significant number of the religion's followers' (the 'non-conflict' principle). In this context, the occupational requirement can be that the person is to be of a particular sex; not to be a transsexual; or relating to a person's sexual orientation. In addition, there are possible requirements relating to marriage and civil partnership. The requirements can be that the person:

- is not married or a civil partner;
- is not married to (or a civil partner of) a person who has a living former spouse (or civil partner);
- is subject to provisions about the circumstances in which a marriage or civil partnership came to an end.

EXHIBIT 5.19

Opinion and 'belief'?

McClintock v *Department for Constitutional Affairs* [2007] **IRLR 29**

The EAT considered a discrimination claim from a Justice of the Peace who, as a practising Christian, objected to hearing family court cases where a child was to be placed with a same-sex couple. He claimed that such placements had not been sufficiently researched and were 'an experiment in social science'. The EAT ruled that 'to constitute a belief there must be a religious or philosophical viewpoint in which one actually believes. It is not enough "to have an opinion based on some real or perceived logic or based on information or lack of information available".' The test for considering whether views can properly be considered to fall into the category of a philosophical belief is 'whether they have sufficient cogency, seriousness, cohesion and importance and are worthy of respect in a democratic society'. Mr McClintock was found to have an opinion and not a religious or philosophical belief.

Comment. This test for a philosophical belief is drawn from the European Court of Human Rights case, *Campbell & Cosans* v *United Kingdom* [1982] 4 EHRR 293. The concept of the belief being 'worthy of respect in a democratic society' is particularly interesting. This might form the basis for rejecting a claim for protection under the religion or belief regulations from someone such as a British National Party member who is claiming that 'fascism' or 'British nationalism' amounts to a 'philosophical belief' (*Equal Opportunities Review*, 175, April 2008).

Grainger plc v *Nicholson* [2010] **IRLR 4, EAT**

Mr Nicholson was made redundant from his position as head of sustainability in Grainger plc. He claimed that one reason for his dismissal was his belief in climate change and environmental policy. The EAT ruled on whether his 'belief' was covered by the former Employment Equality (Religion or Belief) Regulations 2003. In evidence, Nicholson stated that his belief about climate change and the environment was genuine. It comprised a belief in the urgent need to cut carbon emissions; and affected his whole way of life. Reflecting the employment tribunal consideration of case law from the European Court of Human Rights (*Campbell & Cosans* v *UK* [1982] 4EHRR 293), the EAT held that for a 'belief' to qualify for protection it must:

- Be genuinely held. (But it did not have to be shared with others; nor, to come within the statutory definition, did it have to be a fully developed system of thought that governs a person's life.)
- Be not merely an opinion.
- Be related to a weighty and substantial aspect of human life and behaviour.
- Be persuasive, serious, cohesive and important.
- Be worthy of respect in a democratic society and not incompatible with human dignity or in conflict with the fundamental rights of others.

In the EAT's view this approach could encompass 'belief' based on political philosophies but it would exclude homophobic and racist views because these would not be 'worthy of respect' in a democratic society. Nicholson was successful in his claim that he was discriminated against on the grounds of religion or belief.

EXHIBIT 5.20

Dress codes and 'objective justification'

Azmi v Kirklees Metropolitan Borough Council [2007] IRLR 484, EAT

Facts. Mrs Azmi was a schoolteacher who was suspended for refusing an instruction not to wear when in class with pupils, a niqab (a veil covering her face with only her eyes visible). She was employed as a bilingual support worker which required her to work as part of a team to support the learning and welfare of pupils, particularly ethnic minority pupils who were at risk of underachieving. Consequently, the employer stated that 'making verbal and non verbal-communication/facial expression/eye contact [is] vital'.

The headteacher had not previously received a request from someone to wear a veil at all times in the presence of male colleagues. Other Muslim women wore the headscarf and not the veil. The advice of the education service was that 'the desire to express religious identity does not overcome the primary requirement for optimal communications between adults and children'.

Prior to receiving this advice the headteacher had allowed Mrs Azmi to wear the niqab and her work was observed. It was concluded that she did not carry out her role as effectively when wearing the veil as when she was unveiled.

She was then instructed by the headteacher that she should not wear the veil when teaching children.

EAT ruling. This upheld the employment tribunal view that there had been *no direct discrimination* because a non-Muslim person (the correct comparator) would have been treated in the same way. It found that there was *indirect discrimination* but it could be *justified*. The employer's requirement not to wear clothing that covers a considerable part of the face and/or mouth was a 'proportionate means of achieving a legitimate aim'. This measure was to ensure effective teaching.

It was noted at the employment tribunal that, on the employer's part, the instruction was not given immediately; time was taken to consider the position; the instruction not to wear the veil was confined to times when she was teaching the children; and there had been observations on the effectiveness of her teaching.

Eweida v British Airways plc [2010] IRLR 322

The Court of Appeal ruled that Mrs Eweida, a Christian employee, did not suffer indirect discrimination on the grounds of her religion because she was sent home when she insisted on wearing a cross visibly, so breaching the company's uniform policy. The only religious exception was where jewellery or a religious item was a scriptural requirement.

Ethos based on religion or belief (Sch 9, para 3). It is possible for an organisation to require a person to be of a particular religion or belief if, having regard to the ethos and 'the nature or content of the work':

- it is an occupational requirement;
- the application of the requirement is a proportionate means of achieving a legitimate aim; and
- the person to whom the organisation applies the requirement does not meet the requirement.

The obvious example of the way in which this requirement could operate would be in the appointment of people required to promote a particular religious doctrine (see *Glasgow City Council* v *McNab* [2007] IRLR 476).

EXHIBIT 5.21

Proselytising religion and promoting belief

Under the previous 2003 Regulations, the EAT has established a distinction between protection for a person's religion or belief and the conduct of a person in promoting it.

Chondol v *Liverpool City Council* **UKEAT/0298/08**

In this case a distinction was drawn between less favourable treatment on the grounds of religious belief and treatment for improperly promoting those beliefs. Mr Chondol was a social worker who was dismissed for proselytising his Christian beliefs with clients with whom he was dealing. Overt promotion of religious beliefs was prohibited by the employer. The EAT, agreeing with the employment tribunal, took the view that the employer would have reached the same outcome and would have in acted the same way regardless of the religion or any other belief being promoted. It found that the dismissal did not contravene the Employment Equality (Religion or Belief) Regulations 2003 (reg 6).

Power v *Greater Manchester Police Authority* **EAT/0087/10**

The dismissal of a committed spiritualist, who was a police trainer, for inappropriate promotion and expression of his beliefs was ruled to be lawful.

EXHIBIT 5.22

Direct and indirect discrimination

Facts. Mr McFarlane, a trained psychosexual therapist, was summarily dismissed after a disciplinary hearing. The employer's reasons were that he had 'stated to Relate that [he] would comply with its equal opportunities policy and professional ethics policy in relation to work with same-sex couples and same-sex sexual activities when [he] had no and [has] no intention of complying with Relate's policies on those issues'. Mr McFarlane's evangelical Christian religious beliefs were that same-sex sexual activity is sinful and that he would not endorse such activity.

Decisions. The **Employment Appeal Tribunal** upheld the employment tribunal ruling that he was not directly discriminated against. Relate would not have treated differently another counsellor who (for reasons unrelated to Christianity) was believed to be unwilling to provide this counselling and was unwilling to comply with the equal opportunities policy. He was not indirectly discriminated against because his dismissal was a proportionate means of achieving the legitimate aim of providing non-discriminatory services (*McFarlane* v *Relate Avon Ltd* [2009] UKEAT/0106/09). The **Court of Appeal** refused permission to appeal. It found that the EAT had been correct that the 'provision, criterion or practice' (compliance with its policy on counselling same-sex couples) was a 'proportionate means to achieve a legitimate aim' (*McFarlane* v *Relate Avon Ltd* [2010] EWCA Civ B1).

In a combined application (*Ladele, McFarlane, Eweida and Chaplin* v *Royal Devon and Exeter NHS Foundation Trust* the European Court of Human Rights has been asked (July 2011) to rule on the qualified right under Article 9 (Freedom of thought, conscience and religion). The first two cases concern provision of services; and the others are about wearing Christian Crosses. This multiple application is supported by the Equality and Human Rights Commission (see Chapter 1).

Scenario 5.3

Does Hussain have a claim for direct indirect religious discrimination?

Hussain has just been recruited as a member of the warehouse staff. He began work on Monday and worked satisfactorily during the week. On Friday at about 11.30am he told one of his colleagues, **Terry**, that he was 'off to prayers'. Just before midday, **Phil**, the warehouse supervisor, asked where **Hussain** was. **Terry** told him. **Phil** swore about the explanation. **Hussain's** lunch break was at 1pm for half and hour. When **Hussain** returned to the warehouse at 1.30pm he was immediately called into **Phil's** office and asked for an explanation. **Hussain** said, 'I went to the mosque. I am entitled to observe my religion, the law says so. My previous employer let me go.' **Phil** told him that he couldn't go to prayers and would have to have a half hour

lunch break as scheduled on the rota like the other staff. **Hussain** accused him of discrimination and said he was going to see **Tony**, the store manager.

Question

What action might Tony take to deal with Hussain's complaint and what do you think might be the outcome?

Visit mylawchamber.co.uk/willey *to access sample HR documents to support this case study.*

Sex

The European Court of Justice has ruled that the elimination of discrimination based on sex is a 'fundamental right' and is 'one of the general principles of Community law (*Defrenne* v *Sabena* (1981) C-43/75). In Britain the original EU directives on equal pay and equal treatment were implemented through two companion pieces of legislation: the Sex Discrimination Act 1975 and the Equal Pay Act 1970. The latter dealt with discriminatory practice in relation to contractual terms, 'pay' in its widest sense; the former dealt with the treatment of individuals both in employment and in other social relations. Both statutes have been repealed and the relevant law is in the Equality Act 2010. In this chapter the issue of discrimination 'because of' sex is considered. The companion legislative provisions on equal pay are outlined and discussed in Chapter 9.

The former Sex Discrimination Act 1975 (as amended) covered a number of aspects of discriminatory treatment that are now enacted separately as 'protected characteristics' in the Equality Act:

- Sex.
- Pregnancy and maternity.
- Marriage and civil partnership.
- Gender reassignment.

The final three have been considered earlier in this chapter. Here we look at some key elements of case law on sex discrimination that are likely to be relevant under the new law.

▶ Indirect discrimination

Pool of comparators

In a case involving the refusal of a request for flexible working by a woman returning from maternity leave, the EAT reaffirmed (*Hacking & Paterson and Another* v *Wilson* UKEATS/0054/09) the House of Lords ruling (*Rutherford* v *Secretary of State for Trade and Industry* [2006] IRLR 151) in which it stated that the pool of comparison should be restricted to those who want a benefit and should not include those who have no interest in the advantage or disadvantage.

Work arrangements and working time

There have been various cases under the former Sex Discrimination Act where what appeared to be neutral requirements of employers were challenged because they were claimed to be indirectly discriminatory against women. The arguments in most of the cases – but not all – concerned the impact of the employer's requirements (for work to be carried out in a particular way or at particular times) on the role of a woman as a carer – usually of dependent children but, also, possibly, of dependent ill or elderly adults. Earlier in this chapter in the discussion on age discrimination, there are references to specific age barriers and the way they were successfully challenged (prior to the enactment of age discrimination law in 2006) under sex discrimination law.

Exhibit 5.23 gives examples of cases that raised issues that will no doubt continue to arise under the Equality Act.

EXHIBIT 5.23

Sex: examples of indirect discrimination

London Underground Ltd v *Edwards (No. 2)* [1998] **IRLR 364, CA**

Facts. A female train operator, who was a single parent, was required to work a new roster or face dismissal. Prior to this, for five years, she had been able to organise a shift pattern which enabled her to work and care for her child. The roster would have required her to work longer hours than previously. She complained of unfair dismissal.

EAT ruling. The tribunal ruled that London Underground had not established justification. It stated that it could have easily accommodated Ms Edwards without losing the objective of its business plan and reorganisation. It had been well aware of her misgivings and difficulties and had not addressed itself to them. She had been working for this employer for nearly ten years and there had been no complaints about her work performance. Her family demands were of a temporary nature. London Underground could have accommodated her reasonable demands.

Court of Appeal ruling. The court upheld the EAT ruling that the rostering system requiring an early morning start had an adverse impact on women even though only one out of 21 women drivers positively complained about the arrangement.

➡

British Airways v *Starmer* [2005] **IRLR 862, EAT**

Facts. The employer refused a request from a female pilot to go to a 50 per cent fractional contract in order to be able to look after her new baby, and instead only permitted her to move to a 75 per cent contract.

Judgments. A tribunal and subsequently the Employment Appeals Tribunal held that the decision to only permit part-time working at 75 per cent of a full-time contract was a 'provision, criterion or practice' for the purposes of the Sex Discrimination Act. The EAT held that the tribunal had been correct in finding that British Airways had not provided sufficient justification for this decision and that there had therefore been indirect discrimination against Mrs Starmer. Resource constraints including the burden of additional costs and inability to reorganise work had been put forward by the employer, with the tribunal finding that the reasons outlined were not sufficient to justify the discriminatory effect of the decision made. In addition, a general policy of BA that inexperienced pilots should not be permitted to work below 75 per cent of a full-time contract was rejected. The EAT ruled that the circumstances of individual workers needed to be considered.

Sexual orientation

The achievement of statutory protection took some time and various cases tested the scope of both the EU Equal Treatment Directive 1976 and also the European Convention on Human Rights 1950. In respect of the first challenge, the European Court of Justice ruled that sexual orientation was not covered by the Equal Treatment Directive 1976. It stated, in a case involving the eligibility of the partner of a lesbian member of staff for travel concessions, that 'an employer is not required by Community law to treat the situation of a person who has a stable relationship with a partner of the same sex as equivalent to that of a person who is married to or has a stable relationship outside marriage with a partner of the opposite sex' (*Grant* v *South West Trains Ltd* [1998] IRLR 188).

The judgment by the European Court of Human Rights (ECtHR) (*Smith and Grady* v *United Kingdom (No. 1)* [1999] IRLR 734) exposed gaps in protection on the grounds of sexual orientation. The complainants contended that investigations by the armed forces into their homosexuality constituted violations of the Convention Articles 8 (the right of privacy) and 14 (non-discrimination). The ECtHR found that the investigations, interviews and discharges of Ms Smith and Mr Grady were an 'exceptional intrusion'. It also found that there was not an effective remedy available to the complainants (as required under Article 13).

In 2000, the EU Employment Framework Directive (covering sexual orientation in addition to age, disability and religion or belief) was enacted. It was transposed into British law through the former Employment Equality (Sexual Orientation) Regulations 2003. In 2007, this was supplemented by further legislation to tackle discrimination in the provision of goods, facilities and services. The provisions of these regulations are now enacted in the Equality Act 2010.

The Equality Act covers direct and indirect discrimination because of a person's sexual orientation as a heterosexual, a homosexual or a bisexual. It also prohibits victimisation. To date, there have been three significant cases implementing the Employment Directive (see Exhibits 5.24, 5.25, 5.26).

EXHIBIT 5.24

Civil partner's rights

Maruko v *Versorgungsanstalt der deutschen Buhnen* [2008] **IRLR 450, ECJ**

Facts. Tadao Maruko entered into the German equivalent of a civil partnership. His partner was a member of a pension scheme, and when he died, the scheme refused to recognise Maruko's entitlement to a widower's pension. He claimed discrimination on the grounds of sexual orientation contrary to the Employment Equality Framework Directive 2000.

ECJ ruling. It asserted that member states must comply with EU law and with the principle of non-discrimination. It is direct discrimination on grounds of sexual orientation not to provide a surviving partner with a survivor's benefit equivalent to that granted to a surviving spouse.

EXHIBIT 5.25

The *English* case

English v *Thomas Sanderson Blinds Ltd* [2008] **EWCA Civ 1421, CA**

Facts. Mr English complained to an employment tribunal that he had suffered unlawful harassment on the grounds of sexual orientation. He alleged that he had been subjected to homophobic taunts from colleagues because he had been educated at a boarding school and lived in Brighton. These facts were perceived by colleagues as characteristics associated with a homosexual person. Mr English is hetero-sexual and, despite their alleged behaviour, he accepted that his workmates did not genuinely believe him to be gay.

Employment tribunal. This dismissed the complaint because someone who was not gay, and was not mistakenly or genuinely thought to be gay, and was not harassed because of any gay associations or friendships, could not fall within the provisions of harassment on the grounds of sexual orientation.

EAT. This dismissed the appeal. It said that the problem was that Mr English's alleged harassers did not perceive him to be gay, and he fully accepted that they did not. The homophobic behaviour was a vehicle for teasing him, but it could not be said to be 'on grounds of sexual orientation' as required under reg 5.

Court of Appeal. This held by a majority that the (now repealed) Sexual Orientation Regulations 2003 did cover homophobic abuse even where the victim is not gay and not perceived to be gay.

Comment. The importance of this case is about the scope of the legislation. It was argued that, irrespective of the sexuality of the victim, his treatment was, in the language of the former Regulations, 'on the grounds of' sexual orientation. Under the Equality Act 2010 such treatment would be 'because of' sexual orientation and would also be unlawful.

Note. The courts, having determined that this complaint was covered by the discrimination law in force at that time, returned it to an employment tribunal. Eventually the substantive issues were ruled on by the Employment Appeal Tribunal (*Thomas Sanderson Blinds Ltd* v *English* UKEAT/0316/10) (see Chapter 7 for a consideration of the harassment claim).

EXHIBIT 5.26

Re-positioning in the market

Lisboa v *Realpubs Ltd and Others* **UKEAT/0224/10**

Facts*.* Mr Lisboa was employed, for six weeks until 11 January 2009, by Realpubs as assistant manager at the Pembroke Arms pub in Earls Court, London. Until 2008 the pub had been a well-known gay pub, the Coleherne. The company's strategy was to 're-position' the pub under a new name as a gastropub and to widen its market appeal. Lisboa, who was gay, did not object to the strategy but to the way it was implemented. He was told by his manager to put up a board outside saying 'this is not a gay pub' and to seat customers who appeared to be heterosexual in prominent positions in the pub. He resigned and complained of direct discrimination. Essentially, the complaint concerned his manager's comments about his sexuality; and the pressure he was under to make the pub less welcoming to gay customers.

Employment Appeal Tribunal ruling*.* Lisboa was directly discriminated against on the grounds of his sexuality by his manager by the comments made to him. On the point of the 're-positioning' strategy, gay customers, on the facts given to the employment tribunal, were treated less favourably than customers who were not gay. As a consequence, Lisboa (who was required to implement the policy) was treated less favourably on the grounds of sexual orientation. The Tribunal referred to the Court of Appeal ruling in *Weathersfield Ltd t/a Van & Truck Rentals* v *Sargent* **[1999]** IRLR 94 concerning unlawful instructions.

Comment*.* It is important to note that had Mr Lisboa not been gay a complaint would have been possible because the implementation of the company's policy would have been discriminatory on grounds of sexual orientation. Although this case arose under the former Sexual Orientation Regulations 2003 (and also drew on the former 2007 Regulations concerning the provision of goods and services), the legal principles would be relevant to future cases under the Equality Act.

Conclusion

The years since 2010 have seen significant changes to the law on discrimination. There was a political will, as indicated in the Labour government's 'declaration of intent' – the **White Paper** *Framework for a Fairer Future – the Equality Bill (2008)* – to 'de-clutter and strengthen the law' on equality. This was achieved to a large extent in the Equality Act 2010 which was just granted the Royal Assent before the 2010 General Election.

Since 2010, most of the provisions of the Act have been implemented by the Conservative–Liberal Democrat government. However, there have been a number of key provisions that either remain on the statute book and not 'commenced'; or threatened with repeal. Most notable of these measures are:

- Non-implemenation of the socio-economic duty on public authorities (EA 2010 s 1).

- Non-implementation of the 'combined discrimination: dual characteristics' provision (EA 2010 s 14).

- Non-implementation of the requirement in the Act to enable the government to require all employers with more than 250 employee to report their gender pay gap from 2013. An alternative voluntary scheme was adopted (see Chapter 9).

- The consulting on the removing of the third-party harassment provisions which have already been implemented (EA 2010 s 40) (see Chapter 7).

Whilst some previous case law remains relevant, as indicated in the introduction to this chapter, there will be new case law which HR professionals will need to be alert to in the coming years. It will also be important for them to use the resources of the EHRC statutory *Code of Practice* (2011) (see also Chapter 6).

Exercises

5.1 **Whose rights are paramount?** Bearing in mind the issues raised in the *Ladele* case (Exhibit 5.18) and the reactions of various groups to the employment tribunals' decision, think of a situation in your own organisation where there may be a clash of rights.

What approach would you advise your employer to adopt, in the light of the Court of Appeal's decision, to ensure that you are compliant with the law and also able to deal with the relevant management and employment relations issues?

5.2 Mrs Hill was an accounts assistant/secretary for an agricultural contractor. All employees at the depot – apart from her and the female cleaner – were invited to a 'gentlemen's evening'. When a customer asked the depot manager, Mr Parker, why they were not taking Mrs Hill out, he said that the event was 'gentlemen only' to thank the lads for their hard work. He suggested that the customer took Mrs Hill out if he wanted to.

Mrs Hill felt dispirited and no longer part of the team. She told her line manager that she was thinking of resigning. When Mr Parker heard of this, he told her she was overreacting. He falsely told her that Mr Webster (who had started work the day before the event) had not been invited. Mr Parker said that had she been his wife he would not have wanted her to go. He told her that she ought to go home as it was time to make her husband's tea. Mrs Hill resigned shortly afterwards.

What are the relevant legal issues? What do you think the outcome of an employment tribunal complaint would be? What are your reasons?

5.3 You are an HR officer and your organisation is expanding and is advertising supervisory posts. The section manager says that the person specification must include 'commitment' to the organisation. He says that this means having worked for the company on a full-time basis for a number of years; and being prepared to work long hours as required and sometimes at short notice.

You have been asked to advise on this specification. Do you anticipate that there will be any implications under discrimination law?

5.4 Sarah, a young woman, was verbally offered employment at a small packaging company. When she mentioned, in passing, that she occasionally experienced panic attacks, the company did not formally write to her confirming the offer of employment. When she queried the situation on the phone she was told that she was 'not suitable' and was not being offered the job.

Does she have any rights under discrimination law to complain? What would be her remedies?

5.5   Lou, one of the marketing executives of a pharmaceutical company, was recently diagnosed as having multiple sclerosis. There are no obvious symptoms at the present time. He is working full time and is able to drive and carry out his normal day-to-day work responsibilities. He told his manager in confidence about his medical situation and said that he would notify him if any problems arise as regard his fitness to carry out particular duties. An opportunity for promotion has just arisen. Lou decided that he would like to apply for the post. It would involve more opportunities to work in the office and possibly, on an occasional basis at home. He was not shortlisted for interview. He was told by his manager 'we didn't think it was worth interviewing you in the circumstances. We are looking for a long-term appointment.'

Does he have any rights under discrimination law to complain? What would be his remedies?

5.6   A budget airline, in a highly pressured and competitive market, was advertising for a senior manager to be in charge of airline regulation. The rather buccaneering chief executive said that he wanted someone that was young and dynamic and to be available to undertake considerable travel to ensure that the best interests of the company were attended to. 'I know the sort of person I don't want!' he told his HR manager. 'For a start, I don't want someone who will be wanting flexible working hours and time off. They must show considerable commitment.'

What pitfalls in terms of discrimination law might arise? What advice should the HR manager give as far as the advertisement, the person specification and the selection process is concerned?

5.7   Fatima, who has permission to work in Britain, spent the first 18 years of her life in Iraq. She is now 30 years old. She has applied for a position as a receptionist in a large medical practice in a multi-ethnic city. The advertisement stated that applicants must have GCSE in English and Maths as a minimum qualification. You are the practice manager and, in the sifting process, a doctor who is the senior partner tells you that she should not be considered for an interview because she has no GCSE qualifications.

What advice would you give him or her?

5.8   You work as the HR adviser to a small charity that promotes cultural and artistic activities among the Chinese community in a large northern city. You are to appoint a fund-raiser and administrator who is to liaise with community groups and individual artists and promote its objectives. You have been told by the chair of the management board that you must appoint someone of Chinese ethnic origin and preferably who was born in Britain.

What advice would you give about the law?

5.9   Afzal is qualified as an electrician and has reasonable skills as a general handyman. Responding to an advertisement in a local paper, he calls into the offices of a Christian local charity which is looking for such a person to work in their various social welfare centres (for single parents, for drug users and for elderly people). The office manager says that they were specific in the advertisement that the postholder must be a Christian to fit in with the ethos of the various centres. Afzal replies that he is Muslim.

What advice would you give him about his rights under discrimination law?

Feedback on these exercises is provided in the Appendix to this textbook.

References

ACAS (2006) *Age and the Workplace: Putting the Employment Equality (Age) Regulations 2006 into Practice*. London: ACAS.

ACAS (2011) *Age and the Workplace: A Guide for Employers and Employees* (www.acas.org.uk).

Advisory Conciliation and Arbitration Service (2009) *Code of Practice on Disciplinary and Grievance Procedures* (www.acas.org.uk).

Davies, J. (2005) 'The Employment Equality (Age) Regulations: Sweeping Reform or Stop-Gap Measure'. Paper presented at Industrial Law Society Conference, Oxford, 9–11 September.

Deakin, S. and Morris, G. (2009) *Labour Law*. Oxford: Hart.

Department of Trade and Industry (2006) *Coming of Age: a Consultation Paper*. London: DTI (www.berr.gov.uk).

Equality and Human Rights Commission (2011) *Code of Practice on Employment* (www.equalityhumanrights.com).

Equality and Human Rights Commission (2011) *Code of Practice on Equal Pay* (www.equalityhumanrights.com).

Ewing, K., Collins, H. and McColgan, A. (2006) *Labour Law: Texts and Materials*. Oxford: Hart.

Fredman, S. (1997) *Women and the Law*. Oxford: Oxford University Press.

Fredman, S. (2003) 'The Age of Equality', in Fredman, S. and Spencer, S. (eds) *Age as an Equality Issue*. Oxford, Hart.

Fredman, S. (2004) 'European Developments – Marginalising Equal Pay Laws', *Industrial Law Journal*, Vol. 33: 3.

Hepple, R. (2011) *Equality: The Legal Framework*. Oxford: Hart.

MacNicol, J. (2006) *Age Discrimination: An Historical and Contemporary Analysis*. Cambridge: Cambridge University Press.

McColgan, A. (2005) *Discrimination Law*. Oxford: Hart.

Metcalfe, H. and Rolfe, H. (2010) *Caste Discrimination and Harassment in Great Britain*, London: National Institute of Economic and Social Research.

Redmond, M. (1986) 'Women and Minorities', in Lewis, R. (ed.) *Labour Law in Britain*. Oxford: Blackwell.

Rubenstein, M. (2006a) 'Age Regulations 2006, Part 1: Key General Principles', *Equal Opportunities Review*, No. 152, May: 15–21.

Rubenstein, M. (2006b) 'Age Regulations 2006, Part 2: Discrimination in Employment', *Equal Opportunities Review*, No. 153, June: 20–27.

Rubenstein, M. (2010a) 'In the Courts: Highlights of Key Cases', *Equal Opportunities Review*, No. 198.

Short, A. and Barnett, D. (2011) *Justifying retirement without a compulsory retirement age*, Outer Temple Chambers Seminar, 1 March 2011.

Useful websites

Advisory, Conciliation and Arbitration Service **www.acas.org.uk**

Department for Business Innovation and Skills **www.bis.gov.uk**

Government Equalities Office **www.equalities.gov.uk**

Equality and Human Rights Commission **www.equalityhumanrights.com**

Office for Disability **http://odi.dwp.gov.uk**

Employment Tribunals and Employment Appeal Tribunal **www.justice.gov.uk**

Visit **www.mylawchamber.co.uk/willey** to access study support resources including realistic HR documentation to accompany the case studies in the book, an online chapter on collective labour law, interactive multiple choice questions, annotated weblinks, a glossary, glossary flashcards, key case flashcards, a legal newsfeed and legal updates.

Chapter 6

Implementing equality in the workplace

Learning objectives

- To understand the strategic business perspective necessary for implementing equal opportunities
- To consider the implications of specific *key* provisions of legislation and of case law for human resource management policy and practice
- Have sufficient understanding of the relevant issues to provide initial advice on steps to be taken

Structure of the chapter

- *Introduction*: employer liability; the business case; social justice; statutory codes of practice
- *Human resource strategy*: establishing a strategic approach; evidence of strategy; and the incidence of equal opportunities policies
- *Specific aspects of the employment relationship*: recruitment and selection; contract of employment; pay and other terms and conditions; working time issues; training and development; promotion; dress and appearance; dismissal; post-employment issues

Introduction

There are three fundamental reasons for employers to consider effective implementation of equal opportunities policies: legal standards and duties; the 'business case'; and social justice (i.e. a moral commitment to fair treatment).

▶ Legal standards

- *Employer liability*. This issue has been outlined previously (Chapter 5). Equality law makes clear the employer's strict and vicarious liability for discrimination 'in the course of employment'. This phrase is widely construed within its everyday meaning. Liability covers applications for employment, employment and certain post-employment circumstances.

EXHIBIT 6.1

Statutory codes of practice and official guidance

Codes of practice

- Equality and Human Rights Commission *Code of Practice on Employment* (2010).
- Equality and Human Rights Commission *Code of Practice on Equal Pay* (2010).
- Equality and Human Rights Commission *Code on Services, Public Functions and Associations* (2010) (although this is not directly an employment code, it forms part of the overall business context for employers).

Status in law. These codes are laid before Parliament. They do not impose any legal obligations in themselves. However, they can be used in legal proceedings (e.g. an employment tribunal complaint) where a court or tribunal must take account of any part of the appropriate code that might be relevant to a question arising in those proceedings. They are available on **www.equalityhumanrights.com**.

Guidance approved by Parliament

- Secretary of State for Work and Pensions: *Guidance on matters to be taken into account in determining questions relating to the definition of disability* (2011) (**www.dwp.gov.uk**).

Other guidance

- Government Equalities Office: *Equality Act 2010 – what do I need to know? Quick start guide to the ban on questions about health and disability during recruitment* (2011) (**www.equalities.gov.uk**).
- Government Equalities Office: *Equality Act 2010 – what do I need to know? Quick start guide to using positive action in recruitment and promotion* (2011) (**www.equalities.gov.uk**).
- Government Equalities Office: *Equality Act 2010 – what do I need to know? Quick start guide to the public sector equality duty* (2011) (**www.equalities.gov.uk**).

- *Defence against liability*. The employer's potential defence is that he took 'all reasonable steps' (EA 2010 s 109) to deal with discrimination. These 'steps' are essentially policies, procedures and practices that can be adopted by the employer. The implementation of these is the main focus of this chapter. Guidance on employment policies and practice is provided by statutory codes of practice and other official guidance (see Exhibit 6.1).

▶ Business case

In human resource management, 'managing diversity' is about effective resourcing – accessing staff with the best skills and competences whatever their personal characteristics. It also concerns using the skills and capabilities of *all* staff; and so ensuring effective and, as appropriate, profitable links with other parts of a business. In product design and provision, knowledge of the diverse spectrum of customer needs can help businesses meet demands. In marketing, a diverse workforce can help establish effective sales relationships with customers. In public relations, a diverse organisation can achieve a positive reputation and credibility within the wider society. So, it is argued, diversity management and equal opportunities make 'business sense'.

▶ Social justice

The CIPD (2008) comments that 'arguably, the social justice and business case arguments for diversity are complementary because unless people are treated fairly at work they will feel less than fully committed and will therefore under-perform'. The Institute defines the social justice argument in these terms: it is 'based on the belief that everyone should have a right to equal access to employment and when employed should have equal pay and equal access to training and development, as well as being free of any direct or indirect discrimination and harassment or bullying'. This view of the social purpose of equality law is clearly reflected in the social policies of the European Union; and in the provisions of the European Convention on Human Rights and Fundamental Freedoms 1950.

Human resource strategy

The view that employers should have a more strategic approach to managing diversity has gained hold in management circles, particularly since the mid-1990s. Unfortunately, as research evidence suggests (see below), 'strategy' still tends to be more part of management rhetoric rather than reality. In fact, effective diversity management should be integral to both an organisation's human resource strategy and its corporate strategy. There are two principal 'drivers' of this 'joined up' approach: the 'business case' mentioned above which is applicable for private, public and voluntary organisations; and the statutory duty on public sector organisations to promote equal opportunities in all their functions.

▶ Establishing a strategic approach

To be effective in promoting equal opportunities all organisations need to undertake a circular process involving:

- diagnosis of the existing situation;
- the setting of objectives, planning of action to be taken, and the implementation of policies;
- monitoring and review, and so returning to further diagnosis.

Diagnosis

This requires, for example, collection of data of the existing workforce profile; the identification of any barriers to equal opportunities (e.g. in promotion to higher grades); evidence of complaints of unfair treatment and lessons that may be learned from them. Fundamental to diagnosis is critical examination of organisational culture and whether there is evidence of institutional discrimination in any functions.

Objective, planning and implementation

The debate about the concepts 'equal opportunities' and 'managing diversity' (see Chapter 4) drew attention to a view that equal opportunities policies are frequently marginal to wider organisational objectives and that diversity management, at least theoretically, has a more integrative approach. Consequently, objective setting and planning requires answers to several questions:

- Is the scope of the equal opportunities policy to be restricted to areas of unfair discrimination prohibited by law or is it to be extended?
- Which barriers to equal opportunities, both internal and external, are to be given priority for eradication?
- Are targets for 'positive action' to be set? Would these be compliant with legislation? (See Chapters 4 and 5.)
- How can the commitment of managers be ensured? (Research evidence indicates potential and real tension between the 'hard' day-to-day operational business needs of managers and what is perceived to be the 'soft' HRM issue of equal opportunities.)
- How can the workforce be engaged in policy formulation, implementation and review? This may require **consultation** arrangements and, as appropriate, engagement with union equality representatives.
- What resource allocation is necessary to make the policy effective?

Monitoring and review

This is an essential step in this circular process. Data acquired can inform further diagnosis about the degree to which equal opportunities objectives have been achieved. Evidence of systematic monitoring shows that it is patchy. When asked, in the Workplace Employment Relations Survey 2004, about the monitoring of gender, ethnicity, disability and age issues, less than a quarter of respondents said that they undertook it. 'Larger workplaces, public sector workplaces and workplaces with a recognised union were more likely to carry out monitoring and reviewing activities' (Kersley *et al.* 2006). The Industrial Relations Services study also found that only a quarter of their sample had conducted audits into employment (IRS 2006).

Looking at specific HR practices, it has been reported that a fifth of workplaces monitored and reviewed procedures relating to recruitment and selection in respect of gender and ethnicity but only 10 per cent did so in relation to promotions, and even fewer did so in respect of relative pay (5 per cent for ethnicity and 7 per cent for gender). Findings that cast 'some doubt on the effectiveness of organisational equality policies given that promotion and pay-setting processes can be infused with discriminatory bias' (Walsh 2007: 307).

It appears that effective monitoring will remain a matter for employers rather than for further statutory intervention given the views of the *Discrimination Law Review* (**www.equalities.gov.uk**) and the failure to include it in the Equality Act 2010 (see also Exhibit 6.2).

▌Equal opportunities policies

One important formal way of co-ordinating these practical steps is to formulate an equal opportunities policy. The 2004 Workplace Employment Relations Survey (WERS) (Kersley *et al.* 2006) recorded that 73 per cent of workplaces (having 10 or more **employees**) had such a formal policy – in contrast to 64 per cent in the 1998 survey. They were much more common in larger workplaces (with over 100 employees) where the incidence was

EXHIBIT 6.2

Ethnic monitoring

The identification of categories for *most* 'protected characteristics' under equality law are fairly straightforward. However, one of the more complex areas is ethnic monitoring. The Equality and Human Rights Commission, in the Employment Code 2011, recommends the use of the categorisation used for the 2001 Census. This would provide some standardisation and facilitates cross-employer comparisons.

- **White**: British; Irish; any other white background.
- **Mixed**: white and black Caribbean; white and black African; white and Asian; any other mixed background.
- **Asian or Asian British**: Indian; Pakistani; Bangladeshi; any other Asian background.
- **Black or Black British**: Caribbean; African; any other black background.
- **Chinese or other ethnic group**: Chinese; any other.

96 per cent. The question inevitably asked is whether such policies remain 'on the shelf' or are practical documents guiding and informing practice in the organisation. Research does suggest that many equality initiatives can be superficial gestures containing little of any substance, little more than 'an empty shell' (Hoque and Noon 2004).

A related issue is the scope of equal opportunities policies. They should be revised to cover all grounds of discrimination. However, there can sometimes be quite significant gaps – even where the 'grounds' for discriminatory treatment are set out in **statute law**. For example, the CIPD (2008) has recorded that 'although the vast majority of employers surveyed have a formal diversity policy, only one in three employers has an explicit policy on managing religious beliefs in the workplace. The proportion of employers surveyed with an explicit policy is far higher in the public sector (55 per cent) than in the voluntary sector (31 per cent), private sector services (30 per cent) and, especially, manufacturing and production, where fewer than one in five employers (17 per cent) have a policy'. Given that there may be contentious employment relations issues about religious observance, time off and dress codes, this incidence is surprisingly low.

▶ Evidence of a strategic approach

Research evidence suggests that a strategic approach to managing diversity is still ill-formed. A survey, commissioned by the Chartered Institute for Personnel and Development (2007a: 19), of staff responsible for diversity issues in private, public and voluntary sector organisations found that 'the state of the nation in managing diversity reflects a more cosmetic than deep-rooted success'. Two principal factors contributed to this situation: the limitations of corporate strategy, and the focus on legal compliance.

Limitations of corporate strategy

The researchers identified the concept of 'sophistication' of management approaches to diversity management. 'To be sophisticated in managing diversity, organisations need to meet their legal duties in addition to integrating diversity into all their operational activities' (*ibid*.: 19). They reported on variations between sectors: only 7 per cent of private sector organisations achieve the highest levels of sophistication compared to 34 per cent of public sector organisations and 18 per cent of voluntary organisations. Larger organisations are more likely to be 'sophisticated' (*ibid.*: 5).

Other findings indicated the weakness of a strategic and integrative approach and only limited achievement of diversity objectives at operational level:

- *Strategic objectives.* Seventy per cent of the diversity professionals admitted they do not set objectives to progress diversity. This 'suggests that it's not a strategic issue in their organisations . . . diversity management activities in the majority of UK organisations remain at a very superficial level' (*ibid.*: 10).

- *Senior management.* Only 16 per cent 'strongly agreed' that senior management encouraged diversity. As far as 'ownership of diversity', this decreased by job level from senior to middle management to junior management (*ibid.*: 13–14).

- *Operational management.* Whilst 54 per cent had undertaken manager diversity training, only 16 per cent of respondents included diversity objectives as part of managers' performance assessment (*ibid.*: 11).

- *Centrality of diversity.* Eighty-two per cent of respondents said that diversity is 'central to HR'. This contrasted with, among other findings, its stated centrality to customers and consumers (at 51 per cent); to marketing and sales (35 per cent); to manufacturing and production (18 per cent); and suppliers (23 per cent). On this last point, the researchers comment that this is 'despite the duty in the public sector to promote the importance of equality regarding race' (*ibid.*: 18).

Legal compliance

Law is the major influence on organisations in progressing diversity – indicated by 32 per cent of respondents as being the most important of the top five 'drivers of equality'. Only 16 per cent indicated the 'business case', and 13 per cent said 'because it is morally right' (*ibid.*: 7). When asked which skills were needed most in diversity management jobs, 'understanding the law' was the highest – cited by 79 per cent of respondents. It was closely followed, at 71 per cent, by 'understanding HR procedures', and 'understanding the business environment' was reported by 54 per cent. The researchers comment that 'this is because most activities focus on compliance with legislation and people management and development issues rather than operational activities and the production of goods and services' (*ibid.*: 16).

▶ A long way to go?

The research evidence presented above indicates that steps are being taken towards more strategic approaches – particularly in large organisations. But these are quite fitful requiring stronger business links and greater management commitment.

In the context of organisational strategy, the public sector equality duty is particularly important (EA 2010, s 149). The purpose of the equality duty is to 'integrate consideration of equality and good relations into the day-to-day business of public authorities' (Equality and Human Rights Commission, 2011: 6).

The duty covers all 'protected characteristics' apart from 'marriage and civil partnership'. Consequently, it is more extensive in its coverage than the earlier separate duties for race, sex and disability. The EHRC (2011: 4) in its guide stated that 'compliance with the general duty is a legal obligation but it also makes good business sense'. It added that the duty 'should also result in better informed decision-making and policy development and better policy outcomes. Overall, compliance can lead to services that are more appropriate to the user, and services that are more effective and cost-effective. This can lead to increased satisfaction with public services.' There is a clear interpenetration of the quality of service delivery and employment relations issues.

Recruitment and selection

There are likely to be particular concerns about employers' actions in this area. As seen in Chapter 5, the Equality Act prohibits discrimination 'because of' any of the nine 'protected characteristics'. Discrimination – in the meaning of making choices – is at the heart of this HR process. These choices must be made against objective criteria and not reflecting stereotyping and assumptions about particular categories of people. In considering recruitment policy, employers should, first of all, identify the existing profile of their workforce. This can reveal historic patterns of discrimination and evidence of occupational segregation. An employer may need to decide whether any positive action is necessary. Part of this process could involve establishing targets for the recruitment of particular groups under-represented in the workforce. Furthermore, consideration may need to be given to the appropriateness of 'occupational requirements'.

The Equality Act (s 39(1) and (3)) makes clear that an employer must not discriminate against or victimise a person in the arrangements for deciding to offer employment or not offering employment. These 'arrangements' encompass the normal practices and policies in recruitment and selection: advertising, recruitment targets, criteria for person specifications, job descriptions, and the interview process and the questions to be asked.

▶ Advertising and recruitment targets

- *The language of advertisements*. This must be non-discriminatory. This involves careful phrasing of language to avoid discriminatory connotations. For example, job descriptions with 'a sexual connotation' (e.g. stewardess, salesgirl, postman or fireman) are likely to be taken to indicate an intention to discriminate, unless there is evidence to the contrary. The *Employment Code of Practice* states that 'job titles should not show a predetermined bias for the recruitment of those with a particular characteristic' (para 16.6).

- *Occupational requirements*. If a requirement is relevant to the post then this should be stated on the advertisement indicating the specific legislation. The employer should be prepared to defend this requirement as an 'exception'.

- *Location of advertising*. This may be important as part of a positive action policy to encourage under-represented groups, or to assist with recruiting on the basis of an occupational requirement. Particular publications (e.g. those whose readership is predominantly female or of a particular age or ethnic group) and geographic locations may be chosen. Location and media used may be potentially discriminatory. Some media may lead to certain age groups being under-represented (e.g. e-recruitment). The issue of graduate recruitment has also attracted particular attention, in that a focus on recent *young* graduates may well discourage recent *older* graduates.

- *Information on jobs*. For disabled applicants, it is likely to be a reasonable adjustment for an employer to provide, on request, information in a format that is accessible to them – taking account of the use of IT and their requirements.

- *'Word of mouth' recruitment*. Given the cost of the recruitment process, this can, for certain jobs, be an attractive informal and cost-effective option for employers. Furthermore, managers may feel more certain of the reliability and acceptability of potential employees recommended through this process. However, it could be indirect discrimination which covers 'practices' – whether formal or informal. It can reinforce the existing profile of a work group – particularly on the grounds of gender or ethnicity and possibly age. For example, it is suggested that, probably because of the nature of informal social networks, men are more likely to mention job vacancies to other men; women to other women; members of ethnic groups to people of their group.

- *Targets*. If these are indicated, they should be part of a clearly articulated positive action policy. It is important that the distinction between 'targets' and 'quotas' is understood. Use of the latter would be evidence of unlawful positive discrimination.

▶ Criteria of person specifications and job descriptions

- *Relevant criteria for the post*. There are a number of criteria that traditionally have arisen in person specifications: qualifications; skills and competences; experience in relevant work; health; age; suitability; and occupational requirements. Equality law requires scrutiny of the relevance of these specifications to determine whether they can be defended under the appropriate legislation.

- *Relevant or marginal?* In relation to disabled people the inclusion of unnecessary or marginal requirements in a job description or person specification can be discriminatory. Also, stating that a certain personal, medical or health-related characteristic is essential or desirable can lead to discrimination if the characteristic is not necessary for the performance of the job.

- *Suitability*. This can be a complicating factor. It concerns the extent to which 'acceptability criteria' are used as opposed to 'suitability criteria'. The latter should more readily be objectively defensible (e.g. by reference to relevant experience, skills, and appropriate qualifications). 'Acceptability criteria' may be more difficult to defend as non-discriminatory. They are associated with 'fit' – and this involves, among other factors, an applicant's compatibility with the organisation's culture (which itself, of course, may be discriminatory).

- *Qualifications*. In terms of race discrimination, criteria like English language qualifications or degrees of proficiency in English should be justified by the nature of the job. Recognition of overseas qualifications should be accepted after appropriate investigations to establish equivalence.

- *Skills and competences*. Research evidence shows that two particular groups experience discrimination in relation to this criterion: older **workers** and disabled workers. Part of the discriminatory practice is the unwillingness to invest in training and development of these workers. Also, there can be stereotyping in regard to perceived capability – as opposed to actual capability. Given the abolition of the default retirement age (see Exhibit 5.10) and the greater participation of older workers in the labour market, greater sensitivity to skills, competences and training will be necessary.

- *Experience*. This is linked with skills and competences and the issue is the extent to which it is relevant and can be justified; and where the experience was gained: was it, for example, overseas; or in the voluntary sector; or in caring for dependent children or adults? An imaginative approach to examining experience gained – both in a formal workplace environment or otherwise – might avoid unfair discrimination.

- *Age*. Under the law on age discrimination, employers are encouraged to move away from an emphasis on the more potentially litigious factors such as length of service and an individual's chronological age. In research it has been found that almost half of establishments surveyed had a maximum recruitment age; and 60 per cent used some form of selection criteria that were likely to be problematic in light of the age regulations (which were in force at that time) but could be acceptable if they were objectively justified (Metcalf and Meadows 2006). The CIPD (2001) found that 10 per cent of those between the ages of 45 and 54 years claimed they had been rejected from a job in the previous 12 months because they had been too old (despite *little hard evidence* of discrimination). However, recent work has shown employers have responded to the former age regulations with considerable evidence of changed recruitment practices particularly with respect to job/person specifications (McNair and Flynn 2007).

- *Occupational requirements*. This concerns circumstances where an employer is saying that a person needs to have a particular 'protected characteristic' for a job. An example would be the requirement that a post-holder should be female. The EHRC *Employment Code of Practice* (para 13.7) emphasises that 'the requirement must not be a sham or pre-text and there must be a link between the requirement and the job'. For most 'protected characteristics' the Equality Act does not specify situations whereby an employer might say such a requirement exists. The exception to this is 'religion or belief' where there are detailed specifications relating to 'ethos' and potential conflicts with religious belief (see *Code* paras 13.12–13.18 and Chapter 5). It has been noted, particularly in faith-based schools and also in some religious charities, that virtually all posts can be reserved for those of a particular religion – even if the post does not require promoting a particular religious view (Stinson 2008). The issue of occupational requirement for religion in particular has been and remains contentious (see Exhibit 6.5). (Separate from the Equality Act in the specific circumstances of school education in England, the Education Bill currently before Parliament extends the right of religious schools to be more restrictive in appointments on the grounds of religious faith.) The bases for many occupational requirements under previous discrimination law were specified in the relevant statutes. These are noted in Exhibit 6.3 for illustration. ***Applying an occupational requirement lawfully***: The EHRC *Employment Code* (paras 13.19–13.20) recommends some of the issues an employer might consider:
  - Do any or all of the duties of the job need to be performed by a person with a particular characteristic?
  - Could the employer use the skills of an existing worker with the required protected characteristic to do that aspect of the job?

    'Employers should not have a blanket policy of applying an occupational require-ment exception . . . They should also re-assess the job whenever it becomes vacant to ensure that the statutory conditions for applying the occupational requirement exception still apply.'

> **EXHIBIT 6.3**

Previous genuine occupational qualifications

These examples are for illustration. The issues *may* arise in cases under the Equality Act 2010.

Sex as a genuine qualification for a job

- The essential nature of the job requires either a man or woman for reasons of *physiology* (excluding physical strength or stamina); or for *authenticity* in drama and other entertainment.

- The job needs to be held 'by a man or a woman' to preserve *decency or privacy*. This is because the job requires 'physical contact' or because the holder of the job might work in circumstances where members of the opposite sex 'are in a state of undress or are using sanitary facilities'.

- The job is likely to involve the job holder doing work, or living, in *a private home* and needs to be held by, for example, a man because objection might reasonably be taken to allowing a woman the degree of physical or social contact with the person living in the home; or the knowledge of intimate details of such a person's life.

- *Single-sex accommodation* where it is 'impractical' for the job holder to live elsewhere than in the employer's premises; 'the only such premises which are available' are for one sex and these 'are not equipped with separate sleeping accommodation . . . and sanitary facilities'; and 'it is not reasonable to expect the employer either to equip those premises with such accommodation and facilities or to provide other premises'.

- *Single-sex establishments* which are 'a hospital, prison or other establishment for persons requiring special care, supervision and attention'; and that 'it is reasonable, having regard to the essential character of the establishment or that part' that the job should be held by a person of a specified sex.

- The job holder provides individuals with *personal services* promoting their welfare or education, or similar personal services, and those services can most effectively be provided by a person of a specified sex.

Race as a genuine occupational qualification for a post

Two broad reasons:

- *Authenticity*. Examples are acting and entertainment; modelling for clothes and in the production of works of art; the provision of food and drink in a particular setting like a Chinese restaurant.

- *Personal services promoting welfare*. Examples cover counselling and other social welfare posts where specific knowledge of an ethnic group and its cultural practices is required; and these can be most effectively provided by a person of that racial group (see Exhibit 6.4).

❱ Application forms

Two principal issues arise: the format of the application form, and the information requested.

Format

The standard formats usually require completion in writing or on-line. Standard on-line forms may be discriminatory by excluding people with no access to or facility to use

EXHIBIT 6.4

Personal services promoting welfare

Tottenham Green Under Fives' Centre v *Marshall* [1989] **IRLR 147**

In a notable case, under the previous Race Relations Act 1976, the EAT set out guidance on the application of the genuine occupational requirement on personal services. This case law *may* guide future courts and tribunals if such issues arise under the Equality Act 2010.

- The particular racial group must be clearly, even narrowly, defined because it must be the same for the postholder and the recipient of the personal services.
- The postholder must be directly involved in the provision of the services. It is insufficient if they are merely directing others.
- If the postholder provides several personal services to the recipient, then provided one of these genuinely falls within the subsection, the defence is established.
- 'Promoting the welfare' is a very wide expression and the meaning should be interpreted widely in the light of the facts of each case.
- The [Race Relations] Act assumes that the personal services could be provided by others, but the question is whether they can be 'most effectively provided' by a person of that racial group.

EXHIBIT 6.5

An atheist teacher in a Catholic school

Glasgow City Council v *McNab* [2007] **IRLR 476, EAT**

Facts. Mr McNab worked as a teacher of mathematics and computing in a Catholic school maintained by Glasgow City Council. He was an atheist. He applied for the post of acting principal teacher of pastoral care. He was not shortlisted. The school argued that there was a non-statutory agreement between the Church and the local authority that certain posts would be reserved for Catholics only.

Employment tribunal. This found no statutory basis for the agreement, and stated that just because the agreement specified that a teacher had to be a Catholic for certain posts did not mean that the require-ment had to be regarded as a genuine occupational requirement. The respondent had not established the GOR, Genuine Occupational Requirement, (Employment Equality (Religion or Belief) Regulations 2003, reg 7(2)). Furthermore, the respondent could not rely on the claim that it had an 'ethos' (reg 7(3)). 'An education authority does not, in any event, have a religious ethos.'

EAT ruling. It upheld the employment tribunal's ruling that Mr McNab had been discriminated against because none of the exceptions under reg 7(2) and (3) applied.

computers. The EHRC *Code of Practice on Employment* (para 16.33) states that 'an employer must make reasonable adjustments for disabled applicants during the application process and must provide and accept information in accessible formats, where this would be a reasonable adjustment.'

Information

There are likely to be three categories of information that an organisation will request:

1 Information providing an indication of an applicant's competence and likely suitability for a particular job. Primarily, this will cover experience, skills and qualification (if appropriate). This information will be used in selection for interview and as an aid in the interview process. The EHRC *Code of Practice on Employment* (para 16.39) recommends that 'where an applicant's protected characteristics [such as age or sex] are suggested by information in an application form or CV (for example, qualifications or work history) those who are short-listing or interviewing must not use it to discriminate against the applicant'.

2 Information for monitoring purposes: to identify applicants and prospective employees in terms of age, gender, ethnicity, etc. to help assess the effectiveness of an equal opportunities policy.

3 Information about successful applicants in relation to, for example, health, criminal convictions, etc.

Good practice and legal compliance suggests that the first two categories of information can be requested of applicants – but separated before sifting – and the monitoring information not available to interviewers. The third category would be requested with a conditional offer of employment.

▶ Selection process

This process involves several stages: the short-listing of job applications; the interview process; possible administration of tests; and decisions to offer employment or to reject applicants. It is a process where various assumptions and stereotyping might arise on, for example, the abilities of a disabled person; the capabilities of an older worker; the experience of a younger worker; the likelihood of a young woman becoming pregnant. Decisions to accept or reject in this process need to be capable of being defended by the employer as not being discriminatory.

▶ Interview process

The CIPD commented (in a voluntary code on equal opportunities) that the interview 'as a predictive device is an extremely fallible instrument, highly susceptible to interviewer bias and stereotyped perceptions'. So, care must be taken to avoid questions which could be construed as discriminatory; to make offers of employment that can have been determined by structured decision-making; and to record the interview process. This implies proper training for managers who interview.

For particular groups of applicants there can be special issues which may arise in the interview process. For example, it has been commented by disability campaigners that there are four main barriers to the employment of ***disabled people***:

- *Lack of credibility*. Potential employees have to convince recruiters of their skills and abilities to complete the tasks required. This can be difficult for a disabled person if he or she is rejected prior to interview, or if the focus of the selection process is on what they cannot do rather than on identifying potential.

- *Anxiety over taking risks*. The risk perceived by employers often relates to the cost of adaptations; belief that the disabled person will have greater sick absence; the likelihood that he or she is accident prone; perceived attitudes, including possible hostility, of existing staff.

- *Lack of imagination*. Many employers may not know how technology can be used to enable full and active participation in work. Furthermore, there may be a lack of creative thinking about the way work can be organised, its location and its working hours.

- *Lack of appropriate access*. The majority of disabled people have no additional access requirements and need no additional equipment. Generally, the individual's impairment will have little or no bearing upon the capacity to realise their employment potential.

Another example concerns certain ***ethnic minority applicants***. Two interpersonal factors can enter the selection process, particularly at the interview stage: body language and cross-cultural communication. Clearly, there can be difficulties in both verbal and non-verbal communication between people of different ethnic origin. First, an applicant might have limited proficiency in the English language and may not fully understand the subtleties of expression, technical language, jargon and idioms. Secondly, 'ethnocentrism' on the part of the interviewer can involve the interpretation of another person's behaviour/communications in terms of the interviewer's own cultural framework. Frequently, this is done unconsciously. Thirdly, an applicant may have pronunciation difficulties.

The interview may be fallible as a predictive device, but it is well-known to HR practitioners that it is a critically important part of recruitment and selection. An ill-prepared, unsystematic process can result in careless and prejudiced decision-making – and, consequently, possible employment tribunal claims. So, it is strongly advised that records are kept. The EHRC *Employment Code of Practice* (para 16.44) states that 'if the employer does not keep records of their decisions, in some circumstances, it could result in an employment tribunal drawing an adverse inference of discrimination' (see Exhibit 6.6).

▶ Testing

Discrimination law does not prohibit the use of tests. However, the primary consideration is that they should be relevant to the requirements of the specific job. Recruiters need to be alert to the facts that selection tests could be discriminatory on racial grounds if they contain irrelevant questions or exercises which may be less familiar to ethnic minority applicants than to indigenous applicants. They may also be discriminatory on the grounds of disability if reasonable adjustments are not made to assist an applicant to complete the test.

▶ Training of recruiters

Staff responsible for short-listing, interviewing and selecting candidates should be:

- clearly informed of the selection criteria and the need for their consistent application;

- given guidance or training on the effects which generalised assumptions and prejudices about all grounds for discrimination can have on selection decisions;

- made aware of the possible misunderstandings that can occur in interviews between persons of different cultural backgrounds.

> **EXHIBIT 6.6**

Keeping records: recruitment and selection

The records that employers should keep include:

- Any job advertisements, job description or person specification used in the recruitment process.
- Application forms or CVs and supporting documentation from every candidate applying for the job.
- Records of discussions and decisions by an interviewer or members of the selection panel – for example, on marking standards or interview questions.
- Notes taken by the interviewer, or by each member of the panel, during the interviews.
- Each interview panel members' marks at each stage of the process – e.g. on the application form, any selection tests and each interview question (where a formal marking system is used).
- All correspondence with the candidates.

(Equality and Human Rights Commission, 2011 *Employment Code of Practice*, para 16.46.)

Comment. The Equality Act 2010 has enacted two new provisions which may result in complaints and for which the data mentioned above would, also, be very helpful for an employer to defend itself. These are complaints about enquiries relating to disability and health (s 60); and complaints arising under the 'positive action: recruitment and selection' provisions where there is a 'tie-break 'situation (s 159). Further guidance on these two issues is found in the *Employment Code of Practice*, paras 10.25–10.43; and paras 12.1–12.36 respectively.

Contract of employment

Statute law moulds the **terms** of **contracts** in various ways (see Chapter 2): by setting minimum standards; by imposing certain entitlements; and by requiring compliance with discrimination law. *Both* contracts and the terms of collective agreements (which are incorporated into contracts of employment) are subject to discrimination law. The detailed terms of contracts are considered below. As a preliminary, it is important to remember three important legal issues:

- The Equality Act 2010 (s 66) expressly imposes an 'equality clause' – relating to all contractual terms – into all contracts of employment in relation to discrimination between men and women.
- Discriminatory terms are unlawful and, in contracts and collective agreements, they are 'void' (EA 2010 ss 142–146).
- Contractual terms which are indirectly discriminatory need to be objectively justified by an employer as a 'proportionate means of achieving a legitimate aim' (s 19).

Pay and benefits

Discrimination law affects pay and contractual terms in two principal ways: in respect of indirect discrimination in relation to various 'protected characteristics'; and by explicit prohibitions against discriminatory pay and benefits. If there is indirect discrimination, then the employer must objectively justify the relevant terms. However, the *Employment*

Code of Practice states that 'cost alone is not sufficient to objectively justify the discriminatory rule or practice. Financial cost may be taken into account only if there are other good reasons for denying or restricting access to the benefit' (para 14.6).

❯ Gender

The Equality Act 2010 (s 66) statutorily imposes an equality clause affecting all terms of a contract of employment. Compliance with this is required in comparing the terms of women and men – unless a genuine material factor or difference is relevant (see Chapter 9).

Furthermore, employers need to be alert to other gender issues. First is the possibility of structural discrimination if the workforce is segregated on the basis of gender. Secondly, the possibility of indirect sex discrimination in respect of, for example, full-time employment requirement, working time requirements, work location and mobility requirements (see Chapter 5).

❯ Age and length of service

A key issue is the use of this as a basis in systems of remuneration. Research (in a national sample of over 2,000 establishments) shows that around a third of establishments had incremental pay scales; a third had some form of merit based pay; and over 40 per cent used length of service as a basis for reward; with a further 41 per cent using years of relevant experience (Metcalf and Meadows 2006: 9).

Although this criterion is generally ruled to be unlawful after its use for five years, it is possible in certain specified circumstances in the legislation to use it, with justification, for rewarding experience, loyalty and motivation. Work on reward systems undertaken six months after the introduction of the former Age Regulations 2006 suggests that significant changes have been made to pay and holiday entitlements in many larger employers, notably the Civil Service and some larger private sector firms.

❯ Disability

Particular issues arise in respect of pay and disability discrimination. The EHRC *Employment Code* makes clear that employers 'must avoid discrimination arising from disability and, in certain circumstances, may need to consider the duty to make reasonable adjustments to pay or to certain benefits that they provide' (para 14.1). It draws attention, in particular, to output-related pay. 'If a worker has a disability which adversely affects their rate of output, the effect may be that they receive less under a performance-related pay scheme than other workers. The employer must consider whether there are reasonable adjustments which would overcome this substantial disadvantage' (para 14.8).

Working time issues

The issue of working time features significantly under equality law for various specific reasons. Whatever the impact of discrimination law, the provisions of the Working Time Regulations 1998 also apply.

▶ Sex discrimination

The law relating to indirect sex discrimination enables a worker to claim that a 'provision, criterion or practice' causes them a disadvantage. The employer can justify objectively the particular employment practice. Applications to work some form of **'non-standard' employment** is one of the issues that has been considered in case law and is likely to be a continuing issue for employers. Dependency is the principal reason for such requests – whether it is to care for dependant children of whatever age or dependant adults. It is clear from the evidence that this issue will have a growing impact on employment relations in the foreseeable future (see Chapters 4 and 11).

The ability to make a request under equality law is additional to the right to request flexible working (Flexible Working (Eligibility, Complaints and Remedies) Regulations 2002). Under equality law, for example, a woman returning from maternity leave, having previously worked on a full-time **'standard'** contract, may request any of various forms of flexible working (e.g. part-time work; compressed working week; term-time working; job share). The employer will need to consider carefully the operational and employment relations implications of an application. Objective justification would involve showing that rejection of the application and the need to maintain the requirement to work standard hours was 'a proportionate means of achieving a legitimate aim' (see Chapter 5).

This sex discrimination route, under the Equality Act, has advantages for employees:

- *Qualification.* None is required under equality law in respect of employment status or length of service. The Flexible Working Regulations require that the complainant is an 'employee' and must have a minimum of 26 weeks' continuous service. There are various other relevant conditions relating to the application process (see Chapter 11).

- *Reason for refusal.* Under equality law, this needs to be set out in some detail as an objective justification. Under the Flexible Working Regulations refusal can be from a specified list of 'business reasons'.

- *Repeated requests.* Sex discrimination law does not limit the possibility of a repeated application. There is a restriction under the Flexible Working Regulations.

- *Remedies.* Under the Flexible Working Regulations, there is no penalty for refusal for rejection of the application, merely compensation for the employer's failing in his or her duty to consider the application. Under equality law, a complainant subject to unjustified indirect sex discrimination can receive compensation which is uncapped; an award for injury to feelings; a declaration of his or her rights; and a recommendation to the employer.

▶ Disability discrimination

An employer is under a duty to make a reasonable adjustment requested by a disabled person. **Flexibility** of working time might be an appropriate arrangement. The issue as to its 'reasonableness' is likely to depend on operational factors. The employer needs to be confident that any refusal is based on a sound business case.

▶ Religion or belief discrimination

This area of equality law raises a number of potentially contentious issues for the management of staff with religious beliefs. Essentially, there are two sets of issues: the

EXHIBIT 6.7

Religious belief and working time

	Manufacturing (%)	Voluntary sector (%)	Private services (%)	Public services sector (%)	All (%)
All special time off	69	82	74	81	76
Time off in addition to annual leave	21	20	20	13	14
Provide time/facilities in workplace for religious observance	38	69	56	78	61

Source: Based on CIPD (2007b) *Labour Market Outlook*, Winter. Survey of 1,369 employers (**www.cipd.co.uk**)

accommodation of religious observance during the working week; and arrangements for special leave of absence (see also Chapter 5) (see Exhibit 6.7).

● *Religious observance*. There are two aspects to this: observance during the working day; and time off for a religion's Sabbath or holy days. There is no obligation for employers to provide time for religious observance. The critical issue under equality law is whether or not there is direct or indirect discrimination against people of a particular religious view; and, in respect of indirect discrimination, whether or not the employer can justify their policy objectively. ACAS (2008) (**www.acas.org.uk**) provides detailed advice as to how employers might deal with requests. In essence, there is a need to balance the operational needs of the organisation, the interests of the religious adherents and the interests of other employees. Consultation and planning of the steps to be taken are particularly important. It may be that the use of rest breaks and the adoption of flexible working arrangements during the working week could accommodate some of the religious observance (for example, prayers for Muslims; observance of the Jewish Sabbath). The EHRC *Employment Code of Practice* draws attention to the possibility of an employer providing a 'quiet room' (paras 17.57–17.59).

● *Special leave of absence*. If this is requested for religious reasons, it might be accommodated under the annual holiday scheme or under standard policies for special unpaid leave of absence.

There is, clearly, a need to balance the operational needs of the organisation, the interests of the religious adherents and the interests of other employees who may have some other religious belief or none at all. It is essential for good employment relations that there is perceived consistency and fair treatment in respect of rest breaks, time off and special leave of absence. This can be achieved by the adoption of a policy which would cover all these issues for all staff whether or not they are adherents of particular religions or have no religious belief. Workplace tensions can arise if it is perceived that religious groups are privileged. CIPD research (2007b) found that although the vast majority of employers surveyed had a formal diversity policy, only one in three had an explicit policy on managing religious beliefs. This varied between sectors: public sector (55 per cent); voluntary sector (31 per cent); private sector services (30 per cent); and manufacturing (17 per cent).

▸ Age discrimination

Equality legislation is, in part, designed to encourage older workers to be economically active after retirement. However, there are very weak tools in the legislation to promote such participation in the labour market. Originally, under the former Employment Equality (Age) Regulations 2006, a retiree at 65 years could make a request to continue work; and procedural arrangements had to be complied with by the employer. (However, no reason for refusal needed to be provided by the employer.) Since October 2011, the default retirement age has been rescinded (see Exhibit 5.10). Now, there is no specific point in a person's employment at which there could be a discussion about the interests, aspirations and needs of older workers. Theoretically, an appraisal interview might provide such an opportunity but the incidence of these is limited (see following section on Training and development).

In managing older workers, an employer may need to consider several issues relating to working time. Full-time working might be regarded as indirect discrimination against old workers who might prefer some other contract to contribute to the business of the company. The whole gamut of flexible working should be open to consideration: e.g. part-time work; compressed working week; job share; short fixed-term contracts. In a survey undertaken by the Chartered Institute of Personnel and Development (2011), a small minority of workers over 65 years reported adjustments in their working time as the employer's reponse to a decline in their physical ability: 7 per cent reported the offer of reduced hours, and 6 per cent flexible working.

Training and development

▸ Employees

Training and development is a significant issue in terms of entry into employment; the achievement of performance standards in work; equipping people to gain promotion and enhance career progression; and being transferred to new responsibilities. Restricted access to training opportunities can be evidence of either direct or indirect discrimination (EA 2010 s 39 (1) and (3)). For example, women may have limited access where they are either in part-time employment or some other form of flexible working; or where they have been on maternity leave. In the latter situation, access to training during 'KIT days' ('Keeping in touch' days) is a possibility. Workers from certain ethnic groups may have limited opportunities to develop proficiency in the English language and in communication skills.

In respect of age discrimination, employers might argue that restriction of training opportunities could be justified. This would probably apply to training of older workers where the employer might argue that the costs of so doing will be unable to be recouped over the remainder of an individual's working life. However, as already pointed out earlier, cost can only be *part* of an 'objective justification' defence. Otherwise, in general, a refusal to train workers of a certain age is unlikely to be justified.

It is significant that in their study of employers, McNair and Flynn (2007) found that most claimed they did not discriminate on age grounds when selecting for training but did not actively encourage it among older workers. The Chartered Institute of Personnel and Development (2011) in a survey of 2,000 employees reported the following:

Formal appraisals

- Forty-six per cent of workers over 65 years reported having a formal appraisal either once a year or more frequently. This compared with 65 per cent of all employees.

- Forty-four per cent of workers over 65 years have not had a formal appraisal in the past two years or have never had an appraisal – compared to the survey average of 27 per cent.

Provision of training

- Fifty-one per cent of workers over 65 years reported that they had received no training in the last three years or had never received training – compared to 32 per cent across all age groups.

These results led to the comment by Dianah Worman, the CIPD diversity adviser, that older workers are often 'neglected when it comes to training and performance management'. She added that 'the removal of the DRA [default retirement age] will rightfully put a stop to lazy management of older workers with employers forced to maximise the talents of an ageing workforce. Failure to address poor performance of older workers may also pave the way for discrimination claims . . . if there is a dispute over capability.'

◗ Management development

To support the promotion of equal opportunities and to avoid potentially expensive litigation, managers and supervisors may benefit from various types of training:

- Familiarisation with the purposes of equal opportunities and with associated organisational policies.

- Appropriate training in interview skills, human resource management and grievance and disciplinary procedures handling – ensuring compliance with the ACAS *Code of Practice on Disciplinary and Grievance Procedures* (2009).

- Awareness training (e.g. relating to women, ethnic and religious groups, disabled workers).

◗ Possible policy measures

- As part of positive action, it is permissible to encourage under-represented groups into training schemes to develop particular skills for development and promotional opportunities.

- Provide mentoring schemes (particularly for women, ethnic groups and disabled workers). These schemes can assist in acclimatisation to work; the provision of advice and a 'sounding board' on career progression; and suitable training underpinning promotional opportunities. Recent evidence (Silcox 2007) of women in the medical profession shows that a lack of role models and mentoring is, among other factors, one of the barriers to promotion – particularly to surgery where participation rates are low.

- 'Keeping in touch days': these became available in 2007 under maternity leave provisions. They enable return-to-work training and support to be undertaken (see Chapter 11).

- As far as disabled workers are concerned, there may need to be reasonable adjustments to ensure access to and participation in appropriate training is facilitated (EHRC *Employment Code of Practice*, para 17.67).

Promotion

The issue of promotion raises similar issues to those discussed above in relation to selection. Employers need to identify competencies and promotion criteria need to be transparent and defensible. Training and development is integral to this issue. Testing whether or not there is indirect discrimination in any of the promotion criteria or availability of training opportunities is a critical part of any defence.

Harassment

This important dimension of discrimination law is considered in detail in Chapter 7.

Dress and appearance

This potentially contentious issue can arise under various aspects of equality law. Issues of human rights may also be invoked by complainants in relation to freedom of expression. Employers in most organisations have views and policies about standards of dress, uniforms and safety protection measures. Sometimes there is a clear rationale for these policies; sometimes they are introduced on a whim to enhance corporate image. Dress and appearance requirements are governed generally by the implied contractual term of mutual trust and confidence. So, a requirement to wear clothing that was demeaning to an employee may be argued to be a **repudiatory breach of contract**. As a consequence, the employee might resign and claim constructive dismissal.

A more likely legal **remedy** would be under equality law. The test in any particular instance will be whether the proposed dress code is directly or indirectly discriminatory in relation to a 'protected characteristic'; and whether, if it is indirectly discriminatory, it may be objectively justifiable. The *Employment Code of Practice* recommends that 'it is good practice for employers to consult with workers as to how a dress code may impact on different religious or belief groups and whether any exceptions should be allowed – for example, for religious jewellery' (para 17.40).

Particular issues (some of which are still not decisively resolved) are:

- *Gender*. An early case in this area involved a complaint that a woman shopworker was, unlike a male shopworker, not allowed to wear trousers (*Schmidt v Austicks Bookshops Ltd* [1977] IRLR 360, EAT). In a later case about hair length (*Smith v Safeway plc* [1996] IRLR 457) the Court of Appeal approved the earlier approach. It found no sex discrimination. Dress codes, it stated, were not discriminatory provided they merely imposed general rules that enforced a conventional or smart appearance (with relevant changes to account for the difference in sex). The question to be asked, taken overall, was whether there was 'less favourable treatment' in a particular case.

- *Gender reassignment*. This involves a process and different arrangements are likely to be adopted at different stages in that process. Guidance suggests that when the person is undergoing gender reassignment, dress code is one of the issues that the employer should consult about with the individual. At some point he or she will wish to attend work in the clothes appropriate for the gender to which he or she is reassigning. When the process of reassignment is completed, then, the appropriate clothes for employees of that gender will be worn.

- *Disability*. This can be a problematic issue in some cases. Certain appearances (like tattoos) are explicitly excluded from the Equality Act 2010. However, facial disfigurements caused by a medical condition are expressly protected from discrimination.

- *Race*. Issues of dress code *may* also relate to those on religious grounds. It could be an issue of direct discrimination. Although, essentially, it is likely to be indirect discrimination because of race. The employer would need to justify the provision, criterion or practice as a proportionate means of achieving a legitimate aim.

- *Religious grounds*. Two issues arise under equality law: religious dress requirements; and the wearing of religious accessories (Exhibit 6.8). Direct and indirect discrimination might be alleged. The intricacy of the problems that may face employers is seen in the cases of *Azmi* and *Eweida* (Exhibit 5.20 in Chapter 5). The issues that need to be considered will vary in importance from workplace to workplace. However, those issues that may be considered in drafting a dress code are: communication standards in the course of employment; potential health and safety hazards. In respect to the latter issue it is important to note that, under the Employment Act 1989 (s 11), Sikhs are exempt from any statutory requirement to wear safety helmets on construction sites.

Although not an employment case, the High Court, in ruling on whether a school could prohibit a Sikh female pupil from wearing a Kara, set out a view which *may* be adopted elsewhere (*R (on The application of Watkins-Singh) v Governing Body of Aberdare Girls High School* [2008], HC). The underlying principle set out by Mr Justice Silber is that: 'The need for equality of respect for those with different ethnic or religious beliefs . . . may mean taking reasonable steps to alter the "usual" rules so as to enable different situations to be dealt with differently.' Rubenstein (2008: 24) comments that 'this is akin to setting a standard of "reasonable accommodation" for manifestations of religious belief'.

As far as religious accessories are concerned, health and safety is a possible concern. The views of other staff, if the accessories are prominent, are a consideration. The symbolism of an accessory is also a factor. Employers need also to remember that accessories do not have to be about religious belief but about political and non-religious belief. So, badges and other insignia would be covered (including those of campaigning groups, mainstream political parties and extremist groups). Any policy would need to set standards of acceptability so as not to potentially inflame workplace relations.

EXHIBIT 6.8

Religious belief and dress

	Manufacturing (%)	Voluntary sector (%)	Private services (%)	Public services sector (%)	All (%)
Allow staff to meet religious dress code	51	64	61	74	65
Impose restrictions on religious dress	26	9	14	13	13

Source: Based on CIPD (2007b) *Labour Market Outlook*, Winter. Survey of 1,369 employers (**www.cipd.co.uk**)

Dismissal

There are standard issues of fair treatment in relation to dismissal (see Chapter 8). The ACAS *Code of Practice on Disciplinary and Grievance Procedures* (2009) is an essential starting point for establishing the framework of natural justice and reasonable conduct by the employer. It is important to note that the Equality Act 2010 is explicit in its protection against discriminatory dismissal. An employer must not discriminate against or victimise an employee by dismissing him or her (s 39(2)(c) and (4)(c)).

Post employment

Equality law extends protection to issues arising after the employment relationship has ended. The complaint about discriminatory treatment must arise out of the former employment relationship and be closely connected with it (EA 2010 s 108). One principal issue is likely to be the provision of references which may show evidence of discriminatory behaviour (see Chapter 2). It is, of course, possible that there could be discriminatory treatment in respect of contractual terms at the end of the relationship and, for example, in the enforcement of a restrictive covenant.

Conclusion

The range and complexities in equality legislation mean that an organisation should think systematically about employment relations/human resource management and formulate and implement a comprehensive range of policies and procedures. This is not 'bureaucratisation' but an attempt to ensure a number of important objectives for the benefit of the organisation: consistency in the treatment of staff; possible reasonable defences against employment tribunal complaints; and processes for managing disputes and workplace conflict.

References

Advisory, Conciliation and Arbitration Service (2008) *Religion or Belief in the Workplace: a Guide for Employers and Employees*. London: ACAS (www.acas.org.uk).

Advisory, Conciliation and Arbitration Service (2009) *Code of Practice on Disciplinary and Grievance Procedures*. London: ACAS (www.acas.org.uk).

Chartered Institute for Personnel and Development (2001) *Age Discrimination at Work*. London: Chartered Institute for Personnel and Development (www.cipd.co.uk).

Chartered Institute for Personnel and Development (2007a) *Diversity in Business: a Focus for Progress*. London: Chartered Institute for Personnel and Development (www.cipd.co.uk).

Chartered Institute for Personnel and Development (2007b) *Labour Market Outlook*, Winter 2007. London: Chartered Institute for Personnel and Development (www.cipd.co.uk).

Chartered Institute for Personnel and Development (2008) *Diversity: an Overview*. London: Chartered Institute for Personnel and Development (**www.cipd.co.uk**).

Chartered Institute for Personnel and Development (2011) *Economic Outlook: Focus on an ageing workforce*. London: Chartered Institute for Personnel and Development (**www.cipd.co.uk**).

Equality and Human Rights Commission (2011) *The Essential Guide to the Public Sector Equality Duty* (**www.equalityhumanrights.com**).

Hoque, K. and Noon, M., (2004) 'Equal opportunities policy and practice in Britain: evaluating the "empty shell" hypothesis', *Work, Employment & Society*, Vol. 18(3): 481–506.

Industrial Relations Services (2006) 'From recruitment to retirement', *IRS Employment Review*, 857: 49–56.

Kersley, B. *et al.* (2006) *Inside the Workplace: Findings from the 2004 Workplace Employment Relations Survey*. London: Routledge.

McNair, S. and Flynn, M. (2005) *The Age Dimension of Employment Practices: Employer Case Studies*, Employment Relations Research Series, No. 42. London: Department of Trade and Industry (**www.bis.gov.uk**).

McNair, S. and Flynn, M. (2007) *Employer Responses to an Ageing Workforce: a Qualitative Study*, Research Report, No. 455. London: Department of Work and Pensions (**www.dwp.gov.uk**).

Metcalf, H. and Meadows, P. (2006) *Survey of Employers' Policies, Practices and Preferences Relating to Age*, Employment Relations Research Series, No. 49. London: Department of Trade and Industry (**www.bis.gov.uk**).

Rubenstein, M. (2008) 'In the courts: highlights of key cases', *Equal Opportunities Review*, No. 181.

Silcox, S. (2007) 'Women in medicine: barriers to progression is professional roles', *Equal Opportunities Review*, December.

Stinson, H. (2008) 'Discrimination against the non-religious', *Equal Opportunities Review*, April.

Walsh, J., (2007) 'Equality and diversity in British workplaces: the 2004 Workplace Employment Relations Survey', *Industrial Relations Journal*, Vol. 38(4), 303–19.

Useful websites

Department for Work and Pensions **www.dwp.gov.uk**

Equality and Human Rights Commission **www.equalityhumanrights.com**

Equalities Office **www.equalities.gov.uk**

Visit **www.mylawchamber.co.uk/willey** to access study support resources including realistic HR documentation to accompany the case studies in the book, an online chapter on collective labour law, interactive multiple choice questions, annotated weblinks, a glossary, glossary flashcards, key case flashcards, a legal newsfeed and legal updates.

Chapter 7

Harassment and bullying at work

Structure of the chapter

- *Introduction*: Growing concern about harassment; how 'harassment' and 'bullying' are defined; contextual issues; the incidence of harassment and bullying; the characteristics of workplaces; the recipient's response
- *Legal framework*: contract of employment – employer's duties; employee's duties; discrimination and equality law – background, harassment provisions under equality law, reasonableness, direct discrimination, particular terminology, combined claims, post employment, employer vicarious liability and defence, burden of proof, victimisation; redress and remedies; Protection from Harassment Act 1997
- *Conclusion*
- *Exercises*

Introduction

Workplace bullying and harassment have, historically, featured in working life. Examples can be seen in, for example, initiation ceremonies for young new workers, in insulting nicknames, in the 'casting couch' in the film industry, and in the intimidation of 'out groups'. Only since the mid-1980s have harassment and bullying in the workplace gradually become high-profile issues of public concern. Generally, they are considered in the context of equal opportunities strategies like the management of diversity. The range of behaviour that constitutes harassment covers a very wide spectrum and, in extreme forms, can be a crime.

❯ Why the growing concern about harassment?

This has arisen for several reasons:

- The standards of acceptable behaviour in society at large are changing and being articulated more clearly.

- Some employers recognise the disruptive and economically damaging consequences of tensions and victimisation in the workplace. Also, corporate image can be adversely affected; and management costs of dealing with complaints can be considerable.

- Coherent workplace responses to harassment (through the adoption of policies and procedures) have been encouraged by the original equality commissions and their successor, the Equality and Human Rights Commission.

- More effective legal standards and remedies have become available since the original harassment case in 1986 which proscribed sexual harassment as 'direct sex discrimination' (*Porcelli* v *Strathclyde Regional Council* [1986] IRLR 134).

- Unlimited compensation in discrimination cases has influenced many employers.

- Finally, there are wider social concerns, expressed through criminal law, about the manifestations of sexual, homophobic, racial and religious harassment and violence – what are described as 'hate crimes'.

- Evidence of the wider public policy concern can be seen in the document, *Preventing Workplace Harassment and Violence* (2009), a joint guidance for implementing a European social partner agreement. Among the supporting organisations are ACAS, the Department for Business, Innovation and Skills, the Health and Safety Executive, the CBI and the TUC (**www.bis.gov.uk**).

❯ How 'harassment' and 'bullying' are defined

These terms are interrelated and, in practice, it can be difficult to distinguish between them. However, some distinction can be attempted. Harassment *may* be initiated for purely interpersonal reasons. However, it is *normally* for 'social' reasons – relating to the victim's membership or association with a particular social group. So, it concerns gender, sexuality, ethnic origin, disability, age, etc. The intention of the perpetrator is to demean and/or intimidate the victim because of a particular characteristic. It is in this context that 'harassment' arises as a provision in equality law.

Bullying, on the other hand, is more likely to be interpersonal and can often be related to the exercise of power. It may not necessarily relate to, for example, any 'protected characteristic' under the Equality Act 2010. Where it exists it is likely, but not exclusively, to be part of a management style that is aggressive, overbearing, heavily critical, demeaning and intimidatory. In these cases, it is invariably an abuse of power. Having said that, there can be circumstances where workgroups behave in a bullying way towards fellow workers or, in some instances, even towards supervisors and team leaders.

The characteristics of harassment and bullying, as defined in law, are outlined below. Essentially, it is behaviour which is unwanted by the recipient because it is unreasonable or offensive. Unacceptable conduct may be a single act or a pattern of behaviour.

▶ Contextual issues

There are two principal issues which are interrelated:

- *Power relations*. 'Power' is a key element in social relationships. Historically, in many organisations, it has been exercised by men and, in Britain, by white men. Consequently, there is likely to be both a sex and race bias in organisations and the way that they function (see Chapter 4). In a society that is increasingly redefining the role and contribution of women and also acknowledging its multi-ethnic character, tensions will inevitably exist. It is said by many commentators that all harassment is about power. Collier (1995: 27) argues from her experience as a counsellor and from a study of the literature that the common assumption that sexual harassment is about flirtation or about sex is incorrect. It too is about power.

- *Cultural factors*. Culture refers to the values, norms or standards and the traditions that exist in society at large or within particular groups in society. There are two issues that arise under this heading: tensions between groups; and the discriminatory character of an organisation's culture (see Exercise 7.1).
  - *Tensions*. These will exist when one group in society has different expectations and values from another. One example is the conflict of views about homosexuality. Some Christian and Muslim religious organisations are strongly critical about statutory rights relating to sexuality. The issue that inevitably arises in debate is whether one view can 'trump' another (see Chapter 5). Current debate suggests that a distinction can be drawn between those characteristics which are 'innate' (i.e. which an individual is unable to alter like sex, sexuality, race, age or disability) and those which are 'acquired' like religious belief or other philosophical belief. So, one argument is that discrimination/harassment against individuals on the grounds of sexuality 'trumps' religious views about whether or not homosexuality is socially acceptable.
  - *Discriminatory culture*. The pervasiveness of the cultural values of a particular group within an organisation can be illustrated best by the following comment from a police officer: 'Sexual harassment has always been an acceptable part of the police environment and any worthwhile female officer can deal with it herself and give as good as she gets' (Home Office 1993). This statement reflects a number of things:
    - that the standards of 'acceptable' behaviour are determined by male police officers;
    - that this behaviour is in-built – it has 'always' been so;
    - that the appropriate response is not to challenge the norms (the standards of behaviour) but to accept and 'give as good as you get';
    - there is no acknowledgement that the recipient might be upset and need support.

This use of harassment is 'political'. It is designed to preserve male 'power' and 'male reality'. Collier (1995: 36) goes further by characterising it is as heterosexual male reality, adding that this 'compulsory heterosexuality' is the foundation for much homophobia and hostility to transsexuals.

The police service is not alone in having these characteristics. There is evidence in many, if not most, organisations. The issue is how to tackle them. If the cultural fabric of an organisation is discriminatory, then attempts to deal with individual allegations of harassment will be very difficult.

To tackle these two contextual issues, there are two sets of suggested measures. First, there needs to be a diagnosis of the organisation's institutional discrimination – whether on the grounds of sex, race or otherwise. This should result in effective equal opportunities and managing diversity policies. It should, in theory, create a more conducive context within which harassment and bullying can be minimised. Secondly, for public authorities, there is a statutory duty to promote equal opportunities (Equality Act 2010, s 149) (see Chapter 5).

▶ The incidence of harassment and bullying

This is difficult to quantify with any accuracy because of several factors: an individual's perceptions, his or her interpretation of behaviour, the issue of subjectivity, and the occasional denial by the recipient that they are being treated in such a way.

A systematic analysis of fair treatment at work was undertaken, among 3,936 **employees**, by researchers for the former Department of Trade and Industry (Grainger and Fitzner 2007) (see **www.bis.gov.uk**). Bullying and harassment was defined to respondents as 'any unwelcome behaviour that creates a hostile working environment'. These employees were then asked whether in the past two years they had experienced such treatment. The incidence of bullying in British workplaces 'appears to be quite high – almost one million employees (3.8 per cent of all employees)' (*ibid.*: 13). Having said that, the authors acknowledge that their results show 'a lower incidence of unfair treatment at work than most other British or UK employee surveys have found' (*ibid.*: 16).

Disaggregating the overall statistic, the following results were reported:

- *Women* were 'significantly more likely to have been bullied than men' (4.9 per cent compared with 2.8 per cent).

- *Foreign-born employees* were more 'at risk of being bullied' than UK-born (5 per cent compared with 3.6 per cent).

- For *disabled employees or those with long-term illness*, the incidence was 10.6 per cent. For disabled women, it was 14.4 per cent ('almost four times the national average').

- *Sectors*: the incidence was twice as high in the public sector as in the private sector (5.8 per cent compared with 2.7 per cent). 'This is in part a compositional effect. The public sector hires a higher proportion of women and disabled employees than the private sector.'

The following results were also reported:

- *Perpetrators*: 'An employee's supervisor or manager was involved in two-thirds of bullying cases; and a work colleague in one-third.'

- *Duration*: 54 per cent of those who had been bullied said that it was still ongoing. Ongoing bullying was 'much more common for men' (74 per cent) than for women (45 per cent).

- *Advice*: 64 per cent of employees who had been bullied sought advice. In contrast, only 'one-quarter of black employees who had been bullied or harassed at work said that they had sought advice.'

- *Witnessing bullying*: 10.6 per cent of employees who worked with others said that they were aware of another person at work being bullied or harassed in the last two years.

- *Reporting bullying of others*: those most likely to do this were employees with a disability or long-term illness; public sector employees; those employed in larger organisations; and trade union members.

Sexual harassment

The researchers specifically inquired about this issue (*ibid.*: 15). They defined sexual harassment to the respondents as 'any unwelcome sex or gender-related behaviour that creates a hostile working environment'; and asked whether in the last two years with your current employer the respondent had 'experienced sexual harassment at work'.

The results showed that 'relatively few' employees (0.9 per cent) had experienced it. Women (at 1.1 per cent) had a higher incidence than men (at 0.7 per cent). 'Nonetheless, 41 per cent of British employees who said that they had been sexually harassed were men.' Of employees who worked with others, 3.7 per cent said that they were aware of another person at their place of work who had experienced sexual harassment in the last two years (*ibid.*: 15).

▶ The characteristics of perpetrators

The social factors outlined earlier are reflected in any workplace. There will be a range of power relations. The culture of the organisation will reveal particular values, attitudes, norms and traditional practices. Groups and individuals can be marginalised and regarded as (part of) an 'out group' – i.e. those who do not 'fit' into the existing situation.

There are three likely categories of perpetrators of harassment: managers/supervisors, individual fellow workers, and workgroups. These perpetrators, in various ways, wish to preserve the existing situation. So, harassment may be used as a tool – as a means of preventing disruption to the status quo; or to discourage applications for promotion and breaking through 'the glass ceiling', and so, to make working life sufficiently uncomfortable for individuals to leave.

Evidence from employment tribunal cases and from research shows that harassment can be particularly fierce where a 'different' person breaks through into a workgroup. Some of the worst examples of sexual and racial harassment have occurred in traditionally white male-dominated employment: City of London financial institutions, the construction industry, the railways, the police service and the armed forces. The few 'pioneering' women or members of minority ethnic groups have frequently been targeted. The nature of the harassment can and does cover the entire spectrum of unacceptable conduct (see Exercise 7.1 and Exhibit 7.1).

▶ The recipient's response

For recipients, there are four possible consequences deriving from incidents of harassment and bullying:

1 *Action to tackle it.* The employee may obtain advice, under a dignity at work procedure, from a harassment adviser, from a union representative, or from the human resources department; and then possibly raise the issue formally with the employer as grievance.

2 *Deliberate submission by the individual.* This may occur when the individual decides not to face the difficulties of making a complaint. The victim may isolate himself/ herself from the harassment and bullying as far as practicable; or behave in ways that the perpetrator(s) wants. So, a person might be sufficiently discouraged from applying for training courses or promotion or may keep out of the way of the work group at lunch breaks or tolerate or even engage in sexist, racist or homophobic banter.

3 *Denial of its occurrence.* This is where, particularly in the early stages of a pattern of unacceptable conduct, the recipient does not explicitly accept that it is occurring and tries to ignore it.

4 *Escape.* This is the most likely outcome. The recipient is moved by the employer away from the perpetrator; or resigns. As an outcome this does not tackle the fundamental source of the problem.

Any of these consequences may be accompanied, variously, by symptoms of physical or mental illness and behaviour changes. Examples can include migraine, raised blood pressure, loss of appetite, inability to sleep, panic attacks, becoming withdrawn, depression and increased consumption of tobacco or alcohol.

Exercise 7.1 Harassment in the City

- **The workplace**
  Money brokers act as independent intermediaries between two financial institutions, usually banks, assisting them in buying or selling money products on the wholesale money market. This market is not located in any one place as participants communicate through a global network of telecommunications and computer links. A money broker acts like an auctioneer between the client and other market participants, communicating bid and offer prices at high speeds. Millions of pounds can be transacted in a matter of seconds.

- **The money brokers**
  The brokers in broking houses and banks, as in the money market generally, are predominantly white men. There are few female brokers (mostly in junior grades), and about one per cent is of non-white ethnic origin. (Overall, women are concentrated in non-management grades.) Brokers work in teams in extremely pressurised and cramped conditions with up to 50 people in one small area. When the market is busy, it is a frenzied, noisy environment with brokers shouting prices at each other and at clients. They work long hours (nine per day plus evening entertainment). They rarely sustain their career beyond 45 years of age. Where they do, they usually move into management but retire at 55 years.

- **The issue**
  This close team environment breeds familiarity, friendships and, because there are few women, a 'laddish' culture. Brokers both talk openly and joke about their latest sexual conquests and physical attributes. Cartoons and pornographic pictures are adapted to depict fellow staff and are circulated. Everyone has a nickname which can usually be related to their physique, religion, race or personality. Pin-ups of women, some nude, are displayed in the dealing rooms. Women, who work in the back-office area, commonly hear sexual remarks and innuendoes. The motivation for this behaviour is varied. It can be to have 'fun'. So, 'bad' language, playing pranks and jokes on colleagues are seen as part of everyday life.

  Sometimes the pressure of the job leads to loss of tempers, to the use of foul and abusive language and to what could be perceived as crude behaviour among brokers

– particularly when a deal goes wrong. (This is not intentionally offensive. If it is so, it is only meant to be short-lived and is soon forgiven.) On other occasions, the purpose is to vent anger at a subordinate or to teach them not to repeat mistakes and to 'toughen' junior staff to make them better brokers. Sometimes unruly behaviour can be triggered by a broker after a 'boozy' client lunch.

The situation is compounded by the fact that departmental managers are brokers promoted because of their broking expertise. They have had no management or discrimination awareness training. The overwhelming majority have not read the company's equal opportunities policy. So, if someone reacts badly, the usual view is that they cannot handle the pressure. Indeed, over 80 per cent of managers do not consider foul language, verbal abuse when tempers fray or exclusion from the group on the grounds of sex or race as forms of harassment. They are seen as typical of the working environment. Nevertheless, just over 40 per cent of managers have received complaints about harassment. The HR department has recorded seven complaints in the past five years. In only one case did the dismissal of a broker result. The company is concerned that someone may claim racial or sexual discrimination at an employment tribunal.

What steps would you recommend for working towards effective culture change?

Feedback on these exercises is provided in the Appendix to this textbook.

The legal framework

The framework of law governing harassment and bullying encompasses both the law of contract and also equality law. In addition, the hybrid criminal and civil legislation, the Protection from Harassment Act 1997 can also be involved in tackling such issues.

The contract of employment

▶ Employer's duties

Two implied contractual terms are important in respect of harassment and bullying: the **duty** of the employer to take reasonable care of the employee; and the mutual trust and confidence that the employer should ensure underpins the employment relationship (see Chapter 2). A breach of mutual trust and confidence will invariably be regarded as a **repudiatory breach of contract** and may result in the employee's resignation and possible claim of **constructive dismissal**. Breach of the duty of care may, depending on the circumstances, be regarded as such a breach. So, an employer receiving a grievance complaint relating to harassment or bullying must deal with the issue promptly and properly in accordance with the organisation's grievance and/or harassment procedures. In respect of the duty of care it is, also, important to note that stress caused by bullying and harassment may trigger either physical or mental ill health which might result in a

EXHIBIT 7.1

Large payout for bullying and stress-related depression

'Sports reporter Matt Driscoll was sacked in April 2007 while on long-term sick leave for stress-related depression, having suffered, the East London employment tribunal found, from "a consistent pattern of bullying behaviour". The bullying was led by the then *News of the World* editor, Andy Coulson [who later became Prime Minister David Cameron's Director of Communications] . . . although the tribunal noted that senior managers were also involved. Driscoll was awarded almost £792,736 for unfair dismissal and disability discrimination. The *News of the World* had said that he was fired because of poor punctuality and inaccuracies in his reporting, according to the *Guardian*.'

Source: © *Personnel Today*, 24 November 2009

personal injury claim by an employee if the harm to health could be foreseeable (see Chapter 12 and Exhibit 7.1).

▶ Employee's duties

Employees are under an implied contractual duty to obey lawful and reasonable instructions; and to comply with the disciplinary rules set by their employer. In most organisations, it is likely that any form of bullying or harassment would be regarded as gross misconduct and could make the employee liable to instant dismissal. That dismissal must, of course comply with the requirements of the organisation's disciplinary and dismissal procedure and the guidance set out in the ACAS *Code of Practice on Disciplinary and Grievance Procedures* (2009).

▶ Harassment and bullying outside of discrimination law

Under equality law, as outlined below, there is an explicit free-standing right protecting working people from harassment 'related to a relevant protected characteristic' (Equality Act 2010 s 26). However, some harassment and bullying, as suggested earlier, may *not* be linked to grounds under equality law. It may be purely interpersonal and concerned with the exercise of power. In these circumstances, if the employer fails to deal effectively with the complaint about the unacceptable behaviour, the redress and remedies available to such a victim would only be those for a repudiatory breach of contract and not for breach of equality law.

If the victim of the unacceptable behaviour was to resign because of the employer's repudiation of the contract, then, he or she could only claim constructive dismissal if he or she had 12 months' continuous service with the employer and was also able to prove that he or she was an 'employee' in law (see Chapter 2). Clearly, outside of the provisions of equality law, working people are vulnerable with limited redress. The remedies available to them would be those for unfair dismissal: a capped award of compensation. (The maximum set in February 2011 is £68,400. This amount is updated annually – see **www.bis.gov.uk**.) An order for re-instatement or re-engagement may be made if requested. These remedies contrast poorly with those available under equality law (see below).

Discrimination law

▶ Background

Discrimination and equality law tackled harassment in a piecemeal way. It is only since 2005 that there has been a wide framework of free-standing prohibitions against harassment. A long campaign to have the issue treated seriously and effectively began, in the courts, with the case of *Porcelli* v *Strathclyde Regional Council* [1986] IRLR 134. Then, the original Sex Discrimination Act 1975 contained no express prohibition against harassment. Ms Porcelli invoked the direct sex discrimination provisions arguing that the harassment she experienced from her two male lab technician colleagues would not have been used against another man. She said that she, as a woman, was suffering 'less favourable treatment'. The Scottish Court of Session (equivalent to the Court of Appeal in England and Wales) accepted this argument and, consequently, sexual harassment as an issue was encompassed by the direct sex discrimination provisions. Because of the way the courts implemented the common legal provisions of the Race Relations Act 1976, it was also accepted that racial harassment was also 'less favourable treatment' and covered by its direct race discrimination provisions.

It was European Union policy and legislation which helped accelerate greater protections in the area. In 1991, a European Recommendation and a Code of Practice was published on the 'protection of the dignity of men and women at work'. Although this was not law it was to be taken into account by courts and tribunals in member states. National courts 'are bound to take Recommendations into consideration in order to decide disputes submitted to them, in particular where they clarify the interpretation of national provisions adopted in order to implement them or where they are designed to supplement community measures' (*Grimaldi* v *Fonds des Maladies Professionelles* [1990] IRLR 400 ECJ). From 2000, new EU **directives** were enacted and gradually transposed into various pieces of legislation in Britain. When the previous discrimination statutes and **regulations** were consolidated into the Equality Act 2010, then, a single free-standing protection against harassment was enacted (s 26).

▶ Equality Act 2010

This Act contains the following provisions:

▶ 'Protected characteristics' (s 4 and s 26)

Apart from 'pregnancy and maternity' and 'marriage and civil partnership', all others (i.e. age, disability, gender reassignment, race, religion or belief, sex, sexual orientation) are covered for the purposes of harassment protection.

▶ Who is covered?

The prohibition covers people with an employment relationship (s 39) and applicants for employment (s 40). Equality law also provides an important additional protection. Under the heading of 'relationships that have ended' (s 108 (2) and (3)) it prohibits post-employment harassment. The Act states:

A person (A) must not harass another (B) if –

(a) the harassment arises out of and is closely connected to a relationship which used to exist between them, and

(b) conduct of a description constituting the harassment would, if it occurred during the relationship, contravene this Act.

It does not matter whether the relationship ends before or after the commencement of this section (s 108(2) and (3)).

▶ The general prohibition

Three types of harassment (s 26) are specified. The first covers all relevant protected characteristics (see above). The other two relate to sexual harassment or harassment of a sexual nature.

The general prohibition will be examined first. It is expressed in these terms:

A person (A) harasses another (B) if

(a) A engages in unwanted conduct related to a relevant protected characteristic and

(b) the conduct has the purpose or effect of

    (i) violating B's dignity or

    (ii) creating an intimidating, hostile, degrading, humiliating or offensive environment for B.

Several legal and human resource management issues arise from this definition:

- **'Related to'**. To be offended, the individual does not have to possess the particular characteristic. The complaint may be 'perceived' to have the characteristic or be 'associated' with someone who has the characteristic. So, for example, a heterosexual male member of staff who socialised with colleagues after work – some of whom were gay – might be harassed because of his association with them or because he was wrongly perceived to be homosexual.

- **Reason for the harassment**. No proof of this is required.

- **Unwanted conduct**. This phrase introduces an element of subjectivity into the area. Harassing behaviour covers a very wide spectrum of conduct – ranging from an arm around a woman's shoulder to physical assault. So, for example, at the lower end of the spectrum, such behaviour might be judged acceptable by one woman but not by another. The issue of seriousness, then, arises. Clearly, at the extreme end of the spectrum, there are forms of conduct which are socially unacceptable and most are likely to be crimes. Some other forms of conduct may be 'shrugged off' with a riposte.

  In this context, then, the Equality Act refers to the issue of 'reasonableness' (see the following section). Clearly, the facts and circumstances of each incident or pattern of incidents need to be examined and decisions made by the employer as to 'reasonableness'.

- **Judging 'effect'**. In determining this, a tribunal will take into account:
  - the perception of the victim;
  - the other circumstances of the case;
  - whether it is reasonable for the conduct to have that effect (s 26(4)).

These factors embrace the subjective and the objective. Essentially, there is a two-step test for determining whether or not an act or acts amount to harassment:

- An employment tribunal will consider the facts and make an *objective assessment* about whether the conduct experienced by the complainant is unreasonable and disadvantageous to him or her.
- The *subjective test* considers how the recipient felt about the conduct.

This approach continues to be adopted under the Equality Act 2010. An illustration of its use under previous laws is provided in Exhibit 7.2.

Violating dignity and creating a harassing environment

These two provisions in the law are likely to be intimately linked. The 'violation of dignity' is, effectively, the 'personal' aspect of harassment law – in the sense that the

---

EXHIBIT 7.2

Employee's perceptions about harassment

Thomas Sanderson Blinds Ltd v *English* UKEAT/0316/10

Note. This case is referred to in Chapter 5, Exhibit 5.25. The original case concerned the issue of whether English had a right to claim under the former Sexual Orientation Regulations 2003. The Court of Appeal ruled that he did and the substance of his allegation about harassment was returned to an employment tribunal and, subsequently, to the Employment Appeal Tribunal.

Facts. English was an area sales manager. He was subject to homophobic banter and an article in an internal magazine. For some time he did not complain about this behaviour and, in fact, he was good friends with the two perpetrators. Following a further offensive magazine article in August 2005 he did complain of homophobic behaviour. Although the company arranged a meeting to discuss his complaint, he resigned.

Judgments. The **employment tribunal** found that, apart from one magazine article, the conduct did not constitute harassment. In coming to this view, the tribunal referred to the following evidence:

- English had participated in 'extremely offensive' behaviour himself. He had written a number of articles that were 'riddled with sexist and ageist innuendo'.
- He had been required to apologise to a woman for an offensive comment about her breasts.
- He was very friendly with his alleged tormenters.
- He had not complained about the conduct until August 2005.

The tribunal found that only the article of August 2005 had a degrading effect in English's eyes and so constituted harassment. However, he did not submit a claim until over three months after its publication and the harassment claim was 'out of time'.

Employment Appeal Tribunal. This held that the employment tribunal was right to ask about English's own perceptions and feelings. It was also right to consider the behaviour of English and his colleagues and, as a consequence, was entitled to reach the conclusion it did. It upheld the point about the time limit. The EAT dismissed English's appeal.

conduct demeans the victim. It could be a single incident that is demeaning or it could be a pattern of behaviour that is directed at a particular individual. The 'environment' refers to patterns of behaviour that may well reflect an organisation's culture. If this is the case, then more fundamental action needs to taken by the employer. It is also important to note that bystanders can make complaints. The provision of the Act (s 26) can be interpreted to provide protection for those offended by conduct even though it is not directed specifically at them – in that they do not have the 'protected characteristic'.

Sexual harassment and harassment related to sex

The Equality Act explicitly prohibits these two other forms of harassment.

- Under the first, 'A also harasses B if A engages in unwanted conduct of a sexual nature' and the conduct has the purpose or effect of violating A's dignity or of creating the type of environment described above (s 26(2)). This would include, for example, unwelcome sexual advances, touching, forms of sexual assault, sexual jokes, pornographic material.

- The second form is set out as follows (s 26(3)):
  A also harasses B if:
  - A or another person engages in ***unwanted conduct of a sexual nature that is related to gender reassignment or sex***;
  - the conduct has the purpose or effect of violating A's dignity or of creating the type of environment described above; and
  - because of B's rejection of or submission to the conduct, A treats B less favourably than A would treat B if B had not rejected or submitted to the conduct.

❱ Patterns of behaviour

Harassment may involve a single act of unacceptable behaviour. However, it is more likely that a person will be subjected to a sequence of incidents. A critical issue is the point at which he or she takes action against this behaviour both through the internal grievance procedure and in an employment tribunal complaint. This is particularly important when a constructive dismissal claim is made: at what point is the claimant saying that particular conduct is the 'last straw' and that there has been a breach of mutual trust and confidence (see Chapter 8 on constructive dismissal)? (See Exhibit 7.3 to illustrate the approach adopted by the EAT.)

❱ 'Third party harassment'

In the course of employment, employees may have dealings with contractors, suppliers and customers. An employer is liable for the treatment of employees during these contacts. Management are responsible for raising the issue with the 'third party'. 'Third party' means a person other than the employer or a person employed by the employer (for whom, of course, vicarious liability remains).

The Equality Act (s 40) states that an employer (A) is regarded as harassing an employee (B) if a third party harasses B in the course of B's employment; and the employer failed to take such steps as would have been reasonably practicable to prevent the harassment by the third party.

EXHIBIT 7.3

Enough is enough

Munchkins Restaurant Ltd v *Karmzyn* **UKEAT/0359/09**

This case involved four migrant workers who were waitresses and who had been subject to a pattern of sexual harassment for a number of years. They claimed against their employer and also against Mr Moss who was responsible for the harassment. The women complained that he made them wear skirts that were too short. He showed sex books and sexually explicit photographs. He made sexually suggestive comments and tried to initiate discussions about sexual matters. Eventually, the women resigned – they had between one and five years' service. The EAT judge stated: 'We do not find it at all extraordinary that these waitresses should have soldiered on as they did for the years that they did, in the circumstances they found themselves in, and that the [employment] tribunal should have found this was the case.'

The fact that the conduct was put up with for a long time does not provide grounds for finding that the conduct was not unwelcome. The EAT awarded £15,000 compensation for each waitress – finding both the company and Moss liable.

The employer's liability only arises when he knew of the harassment of the employee in the course of his or her employment on at least two other occasions by *a* third party. It does not have to be the same third party on each occasion. A third party would not be another employee of A but is likely to be a client or customer of the employer.

This 'third party' harassment is also subject to the test of reasonableness. So, as indicated earlier, conduct shall be regarded as violating dignity or creating a harassing environment 'only if, having regard to all the circumstances', including in particular the perception of the victim, 'it should reasonably be considered as having that effect'.

In March 2011, as part of its *Plan for Growth* (**http://cdn.hm-treasury.gov.uk/budget_growth.pdf**), the Conservative–Liberal Democrat government announced that it would consult to remove what it described as the 'unworkable' third party harassment provision that employers should take reasonable steps to prevent persistent harassment of their staff by third parties. The reason given was that employers had 'no direct control' over the circumstances. However, employment lawyers question whether the removal of this provision would 'result in any significant lightening of the regulatory burden on employers' (Newman 2011: 21). Newman (*ibid.*) makes two points. First, that 'the Equality Act does indeed widen the definition of harassment to cover conduct which is "related to" a protected characteristic (s 26(1)(a)) and there would no doubt be attempts to test the extent to which this widening has opened the way to claims based on an employer's failure to address the offensive conduct of third parties.' Secondly, 'potential claims would, of course, not be limited to claims under the Equality Act. It would certainly be argued that a failure to deal with harassment from third parties would amount to a breach of the implied term of mutual trust and confidence, with the result that the employer would be exposed to potential constructive dismissal claims.'

❱ Liability for harassment

An employer is vicariously liable for harassment in the course of employment as under the general law on discrimination and equality (s 109) (see Chapter 5). Effectively, an employer is liable for its behaviour towards staff in the course of employment. It is also liable for the conduct of all staff, supervisors and managers if their behaviour is harassing. This is known as employers' 'vicarious liability'. The Court of Appeal has ruled in *Jones* v *Tower Boot Co Ltd* [1997] IRLR 68 (see Exhibit 7.4) that the phrase 'in the course of employment' should be interpreted broadly in line with 'the natural meaning of these everyday words'. In another case, involving sexual harassment, the concept of 'employment' was extended to cover conduct that took place off the employer's premises after work (*Chief Constable of Lincolnshire Police* v *Stubbs* [1999] IRLR 81, EAT). So, employers need to note that liability extends to cover a wide range of work-related situations both formal and informal: training courses, conferences, travel to work, travelling in the course of work, parties, etc.

A problem relating to employer liability arose in a case concerning employment tribunal jurisdiction to hear a complaint. Sexual harassment (under the previous Sex

---

EXHIBIT 7.4

Harassment 'in the course of employment'

Jones v *Tower Boot Co Ltd* [1997] **IRLR 68, CA**

Facts*.* Raymondo Jones, whose mother was white and father was African-Caribbean, worked as a machine operative for one month until he resigned. During that time he was subjected to a number of incidents of racial harassment from work colleagues. One employee burnt his arm with a hot screwdriver; metal bolts were thrown at his head; his legs were whipped with a piece of welt; someone stuck a notice on his back bearing the words 'Chipmunks are go'. He was called names such as 'chimp', 'monkey' and 'baboon'.

EAT ruling*.* By a majority, the EAT determined that the company was not liable for the racial harassment because the conduct was not 'in the course of' the harassers' employment – i.e. the duties they were employed to do. The acts experienced by Raymondo Jones could not 'by any stretch of the imagination' be described as an improper way of performing unauthorised tasks.

Course of Appeal decision*.* Lord Justice Waite said that in the interpretion of discrimination law it was appropriate to use a '**purposive approach**' – to consider the intention of the legislators. This legislation had traditionally been given a wide interpretation. This should be so in respect to the phrase 'in the course of employment'. (This would be unlike the interpretation of the same phrase under the common law of tort.) He stated that, under discrimination law, the words 'in the course of employment' should be interpreted 'in the sense in which every layman would understand them. This is not to say that when it comes to applying them to the infinite variety of circumstance which is liable to occur in particular instances – within or without the workplace, in or out of uniform, in or out of rest breaks – all laymen would necessarily agree as to the result . . . The application of the phrase will be a question of fact for each industrial tribunal to resolve in the light of the circumstances presented to it, with a mind unclouded by any parallels sought to be drawn from the law of vicarious liability in tort.'

Discrimination Act 1975) was alleged to have taken place when the complainant was working in both London and in Paris. The EAT ruled that an employment tribunal had no jurisdiction to consider the complaints relating to Paris. However, evidence relating to alleged discrimination and harassment in Paris could be allowed by the tribunal as background material tending to support or weaken either party's case as to what occurred in London (*Tradition Securities and Futures SA v X and Another* [2008] EAT/0202/08).

It is important to note than an employee can be personally liable for discriminating against or harassing another employee (EA 2010, s 110). This liability is contingent on the employer also being liable (EA 2010, s 109). So, a complainant must sue the employer as well as the individual employee who was the perpetrator.

FRISHCO SUPERMARKET CASE STUDY

Scenario 7.1

A lack of customer care

Sean is 19 years old and has worked on the checkout for about a month. He has a slightly effeminate manner and way of speaking. A couple of weeks ago, an elderly male customer commented to **Ashley**, a Team Leader who was nearby, 'I don't want to be served by a "poof" next time I come in'. **Ashley** made some non-committal comment and tried to pass off the remark as a joke. **Sean** was upset by the comment and by the Team Leader's reaction to it. A week later, a young male customer he had seen at the local nightclub the previous evening commented about seeing him kissing a bloke. In fact, **Sean** had been at the club with his girlfriend and a group of friends who, at one point, had been 'messing about'. The remark was overheard by **Debbie**, the Admin. Assistant, who was buying some groceries as she finished her shift. She reprimanded the young customer for speaking to **Sean** that way and was, as a consequence, verbally abused herself. The following day, **Sean** again served the elderly male customer who commented to him, 'It's a queer old business being served by a poof'.

Sean was fed up with comments about what was perceived to be his sexuality. He wasn't sure what to do because he was on a probationary period and didn't want to 'make trouble'. He was keen to perform well at his job because, eventually, he wanted promotion to a Team Leader position. He mentioned his concerns to **Margaret**, another checkout operator, when they were having a coffee break. **Margaret**, who was about 45 years old and who had worked for the company for over 15 years, was very sympathetic to **Sean**. She said that he should not have to put up with this kind of treatment and that the management should do something about it. She knew **Mick**, a deputy store manager, quite well and would have a word with him.

Question

If Mick is told the full facts of Sean's complaint, what steps in law and in practice could and should the company take to avoid liability?

Visit mylawchamber.co.uk/willey
to access sample HR documents to
support this case study.

▶ Defence against liability

An employer can have a defence against liability if it can show that it took 'all reasonable steps to prevent' the harassment (Equality Act s 109). In individual cases, these reasonable steps are likely to comprise dealing with grievances seriously and promptly, and appropriate disciplinary action. In the more entrenched cases, the defence argument can cover a range of employment relations practices and policies and attempts to effect cultural change. So, the existence of an equal opportunities policy and a 'dignity at work' policy could be evidence that the employer views harassment as unacceptable. Training of managers and briefing staff about acceptable standards of conduct would be further supportive evidence.

▶ Combining contract and equality law

So far the discussion has outlined the two principal bodies of law involved in legal proceedings relating to harassment and bullying: contract law and equality law. It is important to remember that claims under the law of contract (for example, for repudiatory breach and constructive dismissal) and under both the direct discrimination and harassment provisions of equality law can and do co-exist in any single employment tribunal case. For an illustration of this see Exhibit 7.5.

▶ Burden of proof

As in equality law generally, the burden of proof, at employment tribunal, in harassment cases requires the complainant to make a *prima facie* case (EA 2010, s 136). The respondent employer then has to explain the behaviour and show whether or not there was discrimination/harassment. In *Igen Ltd* v *Wong* [2005] ICR 931, the Court of Appeal set out a 13-point guidance note on how the burden of proof rules in discrimination cases should be applied (see Chapter 5, Exhibit 5.5). In the Equality Act 2010 (s 138) provision is made for complainants to obtain information from the employer by means of a statutory questionnaire (**www.equalities.gov.uk/news/equality_act_2010_forms_for_ob_aspx**) (see Chapter 5).

▶ Victimisation

Under the Equality Act (s 27), there is protection against the **victimisation** of complainants. The protection extends to those alleging harassment under this law at an employment tribunal; or those providing evidence or information in relation to a harassment allegation (i.e. what is called a 'protected act'). A person is victimised by being subjected to a 'detriment' as an individual (s 27(4)). Each of the following is a 'protected act':

● The victim has brought proceedings under the Equality Act. In the case of work-related harassment this would, initially, be at an employment tribunal.

● The victim has given evidence or information in such a case. This could, for example, involve being a witness.

● The victim is making an allegation that discrimination/harassment has taken place.

The Act explicitly states that 'giving false evidence or information, or making a false allegation, is not a protected act if the evidence or information is given, or the allegation is made, in bad faith' (s 27(3)).

EXHIBIT 7.5

Offensive graffiti

Martin v *Parkham Foods Ltd* **ET case 1800241/06**

Chris Martin, an openly gay man, worked for Parkham Foods as a Quality Assurance Assistant. In May 2005, offensive graffiti appeared in the men's toilets with his name by it.

His verbal complaint was ignored. He wrote to the employer (11 May 2005) complaining about the graffiti and also about offensive homophobic remarks made to him the previous day in the presence of supervisors who had laughed. He indicated that he was reluctant to attend work because of this treatment.

At a meeting (24 May) he explained that he felt humiliated and undermined in his managerial role. Although his name had been painted over, the drawing remained (as it did for several months). The employer reacted by displaying the company's equal opportunities policy prominently and instructing managers to be vigilant about vandalism and graffiti.

In October 2005, Chris Martin wished to change his name because of his imminent civil partnership. His new name appeared by the graffiti. He sent the employer several letters setting out his grievances. His name – but not the graffiti – was removed. Notices were placed in the toilets warning against graffiti. At a meeting (7 November) the employer reported that it was not possible to identify the culprit.

On 11 November, Chris Martin wrote to request a copy of the employer's equal opportunities policy and also to ask what was happening to his grievance. According to the grievance policy this should have been investigated within five days.

Mrs Smith (who received the letter) regarded his conduct as aggressive and told him to stop harassing her. She recorded in a memo her belief that his complaints were not related to sexual orientation but were a 'transparent attempt to exploit his sexual orientation' as evidenced by his repeated (but factually incorrect) assertion that he was 'the only gay in the company'.

On 15 November, Chris Martin raised a further grievance about an incident with a colleague. That day the company suspended him on full pay in accordance with its stress policy. On 17 November he submitted a sick note for two weeks' absence. The next day he was removed from full pay and told he would receive only statutory sick pay.

He resigned in early December regarding his suspension as 'the last straw'. He complained to an employment tribunal in Leeds.

Tribunal findings

- That pornographic, offensive and homophobic graffiti remained on the toilet wall for months even after Chris Martin had complained about it.
- The employer failed to investigate his grievances properly.
- Action that the employer took did not address the underlying issue of homophobia but focused instead on the issue of graffiti.
- The employer could have taken firmer action to show how seriously they regarded homophobia and that perpetrators would be at risk of dismissal.
- There was evidence that the employer 'viewed the problem as being that of Mr Martin who needed personal counselling to cope with the "situation" he was in'.
- The employer wrongly treated his 'distress and despair' as aggressive behaviour and wrongly suspended him under the stress policy.

The tribunal upheld claims of direct discrimination and harassment on the grounds of sexual orientation. It also upheld the claim for unfair constructive dismissal.

A claim for victimisation on grounds of sexual orientation was dismissed.

❱ Redress and remedies

There are two possible sets of circumstances here: claims **not** covered by discrimination law; and those that are brought under the Equality Act 2010.

Claims for bullying and harassment *not* covered by discrimination law

- Grievance should be raised with the employer under the appropriate workplace grievance procedure and in accordance with the ACAS *Code on Disciplinary and Grievance Procedures* (2009).

- Prior to this, the complainant may have used the employer's confidential harassment or 'dignity at work' procedure or employee assistance programme. This would be optional and voluntary.

- Failure by the employer to resolve the grievance promptly and effectively could result in the employee resigning.

- He or she would need to show that there was a fundamental **breach of contract** of employment by the employer. This is likely to be a breach of 'mutual trust and confidence' or, possibly, a breach of the duty to take reasonable care of the employee.

- If a repudiatory breach was established and the employee resigned, he or she could claim constructive dismissal. The employment tribunal would only hear the claim if the person was an employee with the relevant period of continuous service with the employer.

- If the employment tribunal claim was successful, the claimant would receive compensation (as limited in unfair dismissal cases); and possibly reinstatement or re-engagement or, alternatively, further compensation where that was refused by the employer. There is no award for injury to feelings in unfair dismissal cases.

- Failure to use the internal grievance procedure and an 'unreasonable failure to comply' with the ACAS *Code* by either the employer or the employee *may* result, depending on the circumstances, in the amount of compensation being affected. If the non-compliance was the employer's fault any compensation may be increased by up to 25 per cent. If it was the employee's fault, then, reduced by up to the same percentage (see *Foreword* to ACAS *Code of Practice on Disciplinary and Grievance Procedures* (2009)).

Claims for bullying and harassment under equality law

- The first four of the steps outlined above would still apply.

- However, the employee need not resign to bring a claim under discrimination law. Although it may be unlikely, he or she can remain in employment and seek redress at employment tribunal. There is no qualifying length of service for a claim under discrimination law. Furthermore, there is no need to establish status as an 'employee'.

- If the employment tribunal claim was successful, the following remedies are available (Equality Act 2010, s 124):

- *Compensation* which is unlimited in discrimination cases.
- *Award for injury to feelings*: this refers to emotional harm and is almost inevitable in successful harassment claims. It may also be the only form of compensation if financial loss is not experienced. The EAT outlined two categories – higher and lower awards (*ICTS (UK) Ltd* v *Tchoula* [2000] IRLR 643). A higher level award is based on the following factors:
  - the complainant proving most of the complaint;
  - evidence of a long-term campaign of discrimination;
  - the consequences of the discrimination/harassment (e.g. stress, depression);
  - a power relationship between the perpetrator and the victim;
  - management's approach in dealing with a complaint through the grievance procedure.

In 2003, the Court of Appeal outlined guidance determining three broad bands (*Vento* v *West Yorkshire Police (No. 2)* [2003] IRLR 102, CA). These have been varied upwards by the Employment Appeal Tribunal (*da' Bell* v *National Society for Prevention of Cruelty to Children* [2010] IRLR 19):

  - *Top band*: between £18,000 and £30,000. This is for the most serious cases such as a lengthy campaign of harassment. Only exceptionally should the ceiling be exceeded.
  - *Middle band*: between £6,000 and £18,000. Used for serious cases that do not merit an award in the highest band.
  - *Lowest band*: between £500 and £6,000. Appropriate for less serious cases where, for example, the act of discrimination is an isolated or one-off occurrence. Awards of less than £500 should be avoided altogether.

An award for injury to feelings should include an element of **aggravated damages** where the employer has 'behaved in a high-handed, malicious, insulting or oppressive manner' in discriminating against the complainant (*Alexander* v *Home Office* [1988] IRLR 190, CA).

- A *declaration* of the rights of the complainant and of the respondent employer.
- An order for *re-instatement or re-engagement* (if dismissal is an element of the harassment).
- *An appropriate recommendation*: The Equality Act 2010 (s 124 (3)) states that such a recommendation involves the employer 'within a specified period' taking 'specified steps' to deal with the harassment or reduce the adverse effect of the harassment on the complainant and on 'any other person'. The implication of this last point is that any broader policy implications of unacceptable conduct should be addressed through, for example, workplace codes of conduct and harassment procedures.

   As indicated above, failure to use the internal grievance procedure may result, depending on the circumstances, in either an increase in compensation if the fault was the employer's, or a reduction if the fault was the employee's (see *Foreword* to ACAS *Code of Practice on Disciplinary and Grievance Procedures* (2009)).

Scenario 7.2

Banter or serious harassment?

Ken is a general assistant and the 'trolley wally'. He is 55 years old and has been employed by the company for three years. He has some learning disabilities. He has an inability to speak fluently and walks in a slightly 'jerky' way. He is also rather shy. Management regard him as a diligent worker who is, also, very willing to help customers take their purchases to their cars. Generally, he has good working relationships with the staff in the store.

However, **Winston**, a new Team Leader, has, out of hearing of other workers, made various unpleasant comments to **Ken** about his age and about his disability. He has also imitated some of his mannerisms. One day, **Winston** told **Ken** that he was a 'crippled old crock' and that he wouldn't have employed him. One of the other general assistants, **May-Ling**, overheard this and she saw **Ken** visibly distressed. She had been told by another general assistant about some of the previous comments.

Winston is her supervisor and she is afraid to raise the issue with him because she believes that he might victimise her. Nevertheless, she is upset by **Ken's** treatment and has, privately, told him that he should complain to **Tony**, the store manager. **Ken** tells her he doesn't want to do anything about it because it 'might cause trouble'.

Question

What, in law, could May-Ling do about the situation? If Tony is told about the harassment, how seriously should he regard it and what steps should he take to defend the company against liability?

Visit mylawchamber.co.uk/willey **to access sample HR documents to support this case study.**

The Protection from Harassment Act 1997

❱ Introduction

This legislation was enacted to deal with the issue of 'stalking'. It is not specifically an employment law measure. It relates to a 'course of conduct' causing harassment (s 2) and to a 'course of conduct causing fear of violence' (s 4). Magistrates' courts and the Crown Court have the power to impose a fine, a community penalty or custody where a criminal offence has been committed. The courts can also impose a restraining order on the offender. It is possible for the victim to bring a claim in the county court or High Court for damages for the conduct outlined in s 2 (see Exhibit 7.7 for some work-related cases).

Under the legislation, harassment is not defined in detail. It covers situations where a person causes another 'alarm' or 'distress' (s 7). Obviously, it can cover sending text messages or e-mail messages, phoning, sending messages through the post, making threats, loitering outside a person's home or workplace, sending unwanted gifts, and unsolicited contact at work, etc. It is not limited to incidents based on sex, race or the other areas covered by discrimination law. A 'course of conduct' involves conduct on at least two occasions. Such 'conduct' includes speech.

In enacting this legislation Parliament expected that the two principal parties would be the victim and another individual as perpetrator. There are no specific provisions in the Act making the employer vicariously liable for the acts of employees who may be engaging in a 'course of conduct' whilst in the course of their employment. However, the House of Lords ruled on this issue of employer vicarious liability (*Majrowski* v *Guy's and St Thomas' NHS Trust* [2006] IRLR 695) in the circumstances of this legislation (see Exhibit 7.6). The conduct complained of must be 'oppressive and unacceptable', not merely 'unreasonable'.

EXHIBIT 7.6

The *Majrowski* case

Majrowski v *Guy's and St Thomas' NHS Trust* [2006] UKHL 34, HL

The facts. Mr Majrowski was employed by the Guy's and St Thomas' Hospital NHS Trust as a clinical audit co-ordinator. He alleged (from April 1998) that during his employment he was bullied, intimidated and harassed by his departmental manager, Ms Freeman, who was acting in the course of her employment. He claimed that she was excessively critical of and strict about his time-keeping and his work; that she isolated him by refusing to talk to him and treated him differently and unfavourably compared to other staff; that she was rude and abusive to him in front of other staff; and that she imposed unrealistic targets for his performance, threatening him with disciplinary action if he did not achieve them. In June 1999, he was dismissed by the Trust for reasons unrelated to his complaint.

In February 2003, he brought proceedings, initially in the county court, claiming damages from his employer because of his manager's behaviour. In a preliminary hearing, the judge struck out his claim, ruling that the employer was not vicariously liable. The legislation was intended to protect individuals from harassment by other individuals and did not include the concept of employer's vicarious liability.

He appealed on the question of liability to the Court of Appeal (where broadly he was successful in his argument about liability). The case then went to the House of Lords because the NHS Trust appealed. The Law Lords dismissed the Trust's appeal.

The judgment

- Lord Nicholls observed that vicarious liability is a **common law** *principle* of strict, no-fault liability. A blameless employer is liable for a wrong committed by an employee while acting in the course of his or her employment.
- Their Lordships took the view that it is difficult to see a coherent basis for confining the common law principle of vicarious liability to common law wrongs.
- The Protection from Harassment Act 1997 does *not* expressly or impliedly *exclude* vicarious liability.
- An employer will be vicariously liable for breach of the statutory duty under this Act.
- For the principle to apply, the course of conduct must be *so closely connected* with the acts that the employee is authorised to do that his or her conduct may fairly and properly be regarded as being done in the course of employment.
- The conduct complained of must be 'oppressive and unacceptable', not merely unreasonable.

The case returned to the county court for a full hearing.

The implications

- Although the ruling was unanimous, four of the law Lords 'thought there was considerable force in the Trust's argument that Parliament's intention may have been that liability in damages should be personal to the perpetrator of the harassment'. However, their ruling arose from their construction of the language of the Act (*Industrial Relations Law Bulletin* 792, September 2006).

- 'Common law vicarious liability is strict: if the harassment took place in the course of employment, the employer will be liable' (*ibid.*).

- Unlike the vicarious liability provisions in discrimination law, the employer has no defence that he took such steps as were reasonably practicable to deal with the harassment.

- It was argued by the Trust that the ruling could lead to a greatly increased volume of employee claims based on stress, anxiety or other emotional problems at work.

- This ruling provides an alternative potential remedy for employees subjected to bullying without them having to resign and claim constructive dismissal.

- The time limit for bringing claims under this Act is six years.

- However, bringing claims in the county court is more expensive than an employment tribunal. There are cost implications for complainants where their claims fail.

It is important to remember that this legislation is ***unlikely*** to be a principal route under which harassment claims will be made for the reasons set out in Exhibit 7.6 – i.e. because the conduct complained about must be 'oppressive and unacceptable'. Claims are much more likely to continue to arise under equality law. Nevertheless, in those circumstances where discrimination law does not apply, and a person has either no redress or, if they qualify, their redress is to claim constructive dismissal, then, use of the Protection from Harassment Act 1997 may be a tempting – albeit financially risky – route. Even the remote possibility of such claims should prompt employers to make serious attempts to tackle that bullying behaviour which falls outside discrimination law (see Exhibit 7.7).

EXHIBIT 7.7

Protection from Harassment Act – employment cases

Green v Deutsche Bank Group Services (UK) Ltd [2006] IRLR 764

Helen Green, a company secretary, was subjected to a deliberate and concerted three-year campaign of bullying and harassment by fellow employees, including a group of four women who worked close to her. The bullying involved ignoring her, bursting out laughing when she walked past, making crude and lewd remarks, removing papers from her desk, hiding her post, removing or omitting her name from internal circulation lists and internal records and conducting loud conversations close to her desk making it difficult for her to make or receive phone calls. She complained and raised a formal grievance which was unsuccessful. She suffered two episodes of depression and absence. After her second relapse she was unable to return to work. The High Court ruled that her psychiatric injury resulted from the harassment and bullying, which was 'oppressive and unreasonable' for which the employer was vicariously liable. She was awarded over £800,000 damages.

Veakins v *Kier Islington Ltd* [2010] **IRLR 132, CA**

In this case, the Court held that the company was vicariously liable for a female supervisor's unusually serious campaign of harassment of a female employee which resulted in her prolonged sick leave absence for depression. In the Court's view, the supervisor's behaviour was 'oppressive and unacceptable'. Whilst the Court did not expect many workplace cases to give rise to liability under this criminal legislation, in the 'extraordinary' circumstances of this case, the employer was found to be liable.

Rayment v *Ministry of Defence* [2010] **IRLR 768, HC**

The High Court awarded damages for injury and distress under the Protection from Harassment Act. It found that there were incidents that satisfied the 'oppressive and unacceptable' test (as defined by the House of Lords in the *Majrowski* case). A total of £6,060 was awarded – of which £5,000 was for three incidents that exacerbated her depression.

Conclusion

The liability of employers for harassment and bullying in the workplace requires them to think strategically and develop policies, procedures and practices which will create a reasonably acceptable work environment and also enable an arguable defence to be made (see Chapter 6, *Implementing equality in the workplace*).

In brief, among the steps to be taken are the following:

- Ensuring that the issue of harassment and bullying is integral to an equal opportunities policy.
- If a public authority, ensuring that 'dignity at work' policies are compliant with the statutory duty to promote equal opportunities.
- Publicising and enforcing a code of conduct of acceptable behaviour for employees, customers and suppliers.
- Providing appropriate induction and 'awareness' training for managers and staff.
- Ensuring that managers understand the concept of the employer's vicarious liability.
- Ensuring that appropriate disciplinary rules are in force and, where disciplinary action is taken, that it is in accordance with the ACAS *Code of Practice*.
- Providing a dignity at work policy which encompasses access to confidential counselling for complainants.
- Ensuring that the formal grievance procedure is used and is compliant with the ACAS *Code of Practice*.
- Providing the facility, if necessary, for an independent external person to undertake a fact-finding investigation (particularly where a pattern of persistent harassing behaviour is alleged).
- Providing for mediation as an opportunity to resolve any interpersonal disputes.
- Ensuring that, alongside equal opportunities policies, the incidence and handling of harassment and bullying complaints is monitored.

Exercises 7.2–7.4

Exercise 7.1 is earlier in the chapter.

7.2   **Indira**. One morning, when Indira logged onto her computer at work in a large insurance brokers, she found an offensive e-mail message. It contained some sexist comments and a picture attachment. It appeared that it had been sent to everyone in the department by Jez who had a reputation for being a 'lad'. She was upset by the message and commented on it to her supervisor. He said that she should laugh it off and forget about it. When Indira mentioned the matter to other female staff, they told her to ignore it and said that Jez was 'just an idiot'. Tom, who worked with Indira, told her that he didn't like Jez's behaviour and that something should be done about it. The following day, Indira accidentally met Jez in the lift and he made an offensive personal comment to her and told her that she was 'soft' for moaning about his jokey e-mail. No one else was in the lift, so this conversation was not witnessed. She went to see Angela in the HR department and told her that she felt very uncomfortable working in the organisation and was thinking of leaving. The company had recently adopted a harassment policy as a result of a recent employment tribunal case which had attracted a great deal of adverse publicity.

What advice should Angela give Indira about the courses of action open to her? What reasonable steps would you expect the employer to take if Indira lodges a grievance?

7.3   **Ronke**. Ronke, a Nigerian woman, has worked for 12 years as a senior administrator for a company that runs a number of residential care homes. She had always been regarded by her managers as a good performer with good interpersonal skills who is interested in her own professional development. (In fact, she successfully undertook a management studies diploma course in the past three years.) Her new manager, Joan Philips, a white English woman, was very demanding. She was attempting to introduce new computerised administrative systems. She refused to listen to Ronke's advice which was based on her knowledge and experience of working within the company. The manager required long working hours and quick turnarounds for the tasks that she gave Ronke. When Ronke complained to her about her unreasonable behaviour, Joan said, 'That's the trouble with people like you, you don't know what hard work is.' Very upset by the slur, Ronke chatted to a friend who worked in a human resources department of another organisation.

What advice would you expect her friend to give Ronke about what the issues are and how she might tackle the situation?

7.4   **Issac and Harry**. Harry works in the warehouse of a department store. His eldest son is homosexual and had recently been seen on a television news broadcast about a Gay Pride march in London. Harry's supervisor, Issa, started making offensive comments to Harry about this. Issac belongs to an evangelical Christian church which believes that homosexuality is a sin. He has repeatedly told Harry that his son will 'go to hell' and that he should 'get him treated'. At first Harry thought that Issac was joking and told him to 'shut up'. The comments continued and, after a while, Harry became very irritated by what he found to be offensive behaviour. He mentioned the situation to the warehouse manager who had just overheard one of the comments. He told Harry to ignore the comments saying that 'you know that Issac's a bit of a religious maniac'. A few days later a fight broke out between Harry and Issac. Issac had repeated his comments about homosexuality being a sin and had wondered if Harry, himself, wasn't 'a bit queer'. At this point Harry had punched Issac in the face. The warehouse manager asked them to come to his office and explain themselves because he was thinking of disciplinary action. Harry has asked for his union representative to be present. He has advised Harry to lodge a grievance with the warehouse manager for not dealing with the harassment he had experienced from Issac.

What advice would you give to the various parties on the legal situation?

Feedback on these exercises is provided in the Appendix to this textbook.

References

ACAS (2009) *Code of Practice on Disciplinary and Grievance Procedures*. London: ACAS.

ACAS website: guidance on harassment and bullying (www.acas.org.uk).

Collier, R. (1995) *Combating Sexual Harassment in the Workplace*. Buckingham: Open University Press.

Department for Business, Innovation and Skills (2009) *Preventing Workplace Harassment and Violence*. This document is joint guidance for implementing a European social partner agreement. Among the supporting organisations are ACAS, the Department for Business, Innovation and Skills, the Health and Safety Executive, the CBI and the TUC (www.bis.gov.uk).

Grainger, H. and Fitzner, G. (2007) *The First Fair Treatment at Work Survey: Executive Summary (Updated)*, Employment Relations Research Series, No. 63. London: Department of Trade and Industry (see www.bis.gov.uk/employment).

Home Office (1993) *Aspects of Sex Discrimination within the Police Service*. London: Home Office.

Newman, D. (2011) *Impact of Removing Third-party Harassment Protection*, Equal Opportunities Review, No. 212, May (www.eordirect.co.uk).

Useful websites

Advisory, Conciliation and Arbitration Service **www.acas.org.uk**

Department for Business, Innovation and Skills **www.bis.gov.uk**

Visit **www.mylawchamber.co.uk/willey** to access study support resources including realistic HR documentation to accompany the case studies in the book, an online chapter on collective labour law, interactive multiple choice questions, annotated weblinks, a glossary, glossary flashcards, key case flashcards, a legal newsfeed and legal updates.

Chapter 8

Discipline and dismissal

Learning objectives

To be able to:

- Explain the importance of discipline and dismissal in the employment relationship
- Summarise the main provisions of UK legislation as well as accepted principles of best practice in relation to dismissal, disciplinary and grievance procedures
- Evaluate legal developments in the area of discipline and dismissal from the perspective of both employers and employees

Structure of the chapter

- *Introduction*: overview of current and historic issues relating to discipline and dismissal
- *ACAS Code of Practice on Disciplinary and Grievance Procedures*: its status and principles
- *Statutory protection from unfair dismissal*: Who qualifies? What is a 'dismissal' in law; fair and automatically unfair reasons for dismissal; reasonableness in the circumstances; fair procedures; written reasons for dismissal; statutory right to be accompanied
- *Obtaining redress for unfair dismissal at an employment tribunal*: Does the complainant qualify? When must a complaint be made? What is the role of ACAS in tribunal complaints? What is a compromise agreement? What issues concern an employment tribunal in making its decision? What remedies are available to successful complainants? Dismissal complaints and other grounds/causes of action; wrongful dismissal claims
- *Grievance procedures*
- *Exercises*

Introduction

For HR practitioners, rules and regulations in the area of discipline and dismissal are of central importance. The primary objective of most organisations, whether public or private, is to undertake particular activities in a profitable, efficient or cost-effective manner. The ability to set standards and control the performance of staff is therefore key, as is the possibility to deal with circumstances arising which impact on organisational perform-ance such as staff absence or sickness. Workers and employees, on the other hand, have an equally legitimate interest in the existence of limits on the exercise of managerial discretion, and in particular on management's ability to terminate the employment relationship.

Unfair dismissal has for many years been a very common reason for applications to employment tribunals. There were 47,900 unfair dismissal claims registered at tribunals in the year 2010–11 (Ministry of Justice/HM Courts and Tribunals Service 2011). This compared with 57,400 in 2009–10 and 52,700 in 2008–09. In total, unfair dismissal was raised in 22 per cent of claims registered with employment tribunals in 2010–11. The difficult economic conditions since 2008 are seen to have led to an increase in the number of claims between 2008–09 and 2009–10, with the subsequent decline in 2010–11 possibly partly due to the increasing success of organisations such as ACAS in promoting the settlement of disputes prior to formal tribunal claims being submitted (ACAS Annual Report 2010–11).

The fact that it is estimated that only around one in seven dismissals lead to a tribunal claim (Knight and Latreille 2000: 541) provides an indication of how significant a phenomenon dismissal is across the labour market more broadly. Indeed, the Department of Trade and Industry in 1999 estimated that over a million workers in the UK are dismissed each year, although this figure includes those made redundant or who retired or whose fixed term contracts expired.

Further information on the use of disciplinary and dismissal processes is provided by the results of the 2004 Workplace Employee Relations Survey (Kersley *et al.* 2006). This survey, which was sponsored by the Department of Trade and Industry (now the Department for Business, Innovation and Skills), ACAS and a number of other organisations, comprised a nationally representative survey of workplaces with five or more employees located in Great Britain, and is widely regarded as the most authoritative source of evidence on employment relations in Britain.

The survey included questions on the use of disciplinary sanctions. It found that 55 per cent of managers surveyed had used at least one of a range of disciplinary sanctions in the year prior to the survey, namely formal verbal or written warnings, suspension with or without pay, deduction from pay, internal transfer or dismissal. Forty-five per cent of workplaces had issued a verbal warning; 37 per cent a written warning; while one-fifth had suspended an employee without pay. Only 5 per cent of workplaces had made deductions from pay and 6 per cent internal transfers. Perhaps most notably for our purposes here, 28 per cent of workplaces had made at least one dismissal in the year preceding the survey (Kersley *et al.* 2006: 224–30). Common reasons for taking disciplinary action were poor performance, unauthorised absence, poor timekeeping and theft or dishonesty, with other reasons including negligence, abusive or violent behaviour, disobedience, health and safety breaches and alcohol or drug use.

The survey findings made it possible to calculate a disciplinary sanction rate for the workplaces surveyed, i.e. the average number of disciplinary sanctions applied per 100 employees. In this regard, the overall average was 5.7 sanctions per 100 employees. Average rates were somewhat higher in smaller firms (8.0 in workplaces of 10 to 24 employees), and in the private sector, 6.9, compared to the public sector at 1.9. The rate of disciplinary sanctions was highest in the 'other business services' sector, with hotels and restaurants and wholesale and retail also having relatively high rates. In contrast, sanction rates were comparatively low in the education, public administration and health and social work sectors (ibid.).

The WERS figures emphasise the importance of discipline and dismissal in the contemporary employment relationship and highlight the strong need for legislation in this area.

▶ Historic redress

Legislation outlining required procedures and standards in relation to discipline and dismissal of **employees** is comparatively recent. Historically, the nature and conduct of relationships at work was largely left to employers and employees to resolve among themselves, with a dismissed employee obliged to seek redress under the **common law** contract of employment either via a claim for wrongful dismissal or in the context of proceedings relating to frustration of contract. These grounds of action still apply today and are discussed in turn below. The primary focus of this chapter, however, is an examination of **statute law** and relevant codes of practice on dismissal and disciplinary procedures.

Wrongful dismissal

A claim for wrongful dismissal can only be successful if the employer has breached the contract of employment. Describing the situation under common law prior to 1971, Anderman (1986: 416) stated that 'as long as proper contractual notice of termination was given, an employer was legally entitled to dismiss an employee for whatever reason he wished. There was no obligation on the employer to reveal his reason for dismissal to the employee, much less to justify it.'

An employee dismissed in circumstances where his honesty was questioned and who, as a consequence, found it difficult to obtain other employment, might only have available an action for defamation – which would be costly, complex and uncertain. An employee dismissed on grounds that could be construed as **victimisation** or discriminatory would have had no special protection. Certainly, the common law, emphasising freedom of contract, did not proscribe discriminatory treatment.

If upheld, the **remedy** for a wrongful dismissal claim is **damages** equal to the amount of pay the employee would have received in their notice period (i.e. effectively pay in lieu of notice) or the amount of pay he or she would have received in both the period of notice and the period during which the procedural requirements in the contract would have been completed. However, as notice periods tend to be relatively short, a claim for wrongful dismissal is not particularly attractive for the majority of employees. It is arguably most attractive to very highly paid individuals for whom the potential loss of pay relating to the notice period is of greater significance.

Nowadays, actions alleging wrongful dismissal can still be made and sometimes are made, alongside unfair dismissal claims (see later section on obtaining redress, Table 8.2).

Common law doctrine of frustration

This doctrine is applicable where, because of an event outside the control of the employer or employee, it becomes impossible to perform the contract. Examples of the kinds of circumstances that can give rise to a finding of frustration of contract include death, imprisonment or long-term sickness or incapability on the part of an employee. Where there is frustration, the employment contract is terminated automatically and there is no dismissal in law.

In general terms, the doctrine of frustration has been superseded by the legislation on unfair dismissal and employers need to be very cautious in cases of incapability of an employee in claiming frustration of contract, as the tribunals and courts are reluctant to accept such a claim where to do so would allow the employer to get around their obligations under unfair dismissal law.

That said, in certain situations tribunals may still find that a contract has been frustrated and it is therefore important for employers and human resource management practitioners to be aware of the concept. It has emerged from a number of decisions that factors such as the length of service of the employee; the duration of the contract; the nature and likely duration of incapability; whether the contract makes provision for sick pay; and the nature and importance of the role undertaken, are important in establishing whether a contract has been frustrated or not (*Marshall v Harland and Wolff Ltd* [1972] 2 All ER 715, NIRC; *Egg Stores v Leibovici* [1976] IRLR 376, EAT). There is some historical precedent that the courts and tribunals may be more willing to establish a case of frustration where the employee in question is in a key post or where the contract is of relatively short duration, however more recent cases have challenged these positions and highlight the extent to which employers' claims for frustration will be examined very carefully, irrespective of such features or characteristics.

Legislation on unfair dismissal

During the 1960s, the UK government came under increasing pressure from a number of different sources to introduce greater protection for employees against dismissal. The adoption by the International Labour Organisation in 1963 of a Recommendation on Termination of Employment (No. 119), to which Britain as a member of the ILO subscribed, was important. In addition, a number of reports on industrial relations in the late 1960s highlighted the dissatisfaction of trade unions and employers with the lack of legal regulation in the area. Allied to wider support for change among politicians and the general public, these pressures culminated in the enactment of unfair dismissal provisions in the Industrial Relations Act 1971. This introduced mandatory standards and rules for employers to follow when dismissing employees which have been amended in subsequent legislation. Although there have been notable developments, the central components of the law on unfair dismissal have remained largely stable since then.

The current legislative provisions on unfair dismissal are contained in the Employment Rights Act 1996 (Parts X and XI). These are supplemented by the ACAS *Code of Practice on Disciplinary and Grievance Procedures* 2009. This statutory code sets out detailed guidance and recommendations for employers to follow in relation to discipline and dismissal. Failure to comply with the Code does not 'of itself render (a person) liable to any proceedings'. However it will be 'admissible in evidence' before an employment tribunal in deciding whether a dismissal is fair or unfair (TULRCA 1992, s 207).

The ACAS *Code of Practice* has recently been given greater force by the Employment Act 2008. This provides that where an employer or employee has unreasonably failed to comply with the code, an employment tribunal may, if it considers it just and equitable, increase or decrease any award it makes by up to 25 per cent.

The Employment Rights Act 1996 and the ACAS *Code* are further supplemented by the Employment Relations Act 1999 which outlines the statutory right for workers to be accompanied by a fellow worker or trade union official at disciplinary or dismissal meetings (ERA 1999, s 10).

The ACAS *Code of Practice*

The ACAS *Code of Practice* outlines a number of key principles and also numerous specific pieces of guidance and advice to employers in relation to discipline and dismissal and also grievance-handling in the workplace (see Exhibit 8.1). It is supplemented by a detailed handbook of good employment practice on discipline and grievances at work (ACAS 2011).

EXHIBIT 8.1

ACAS *Code of Practice on Disciplinary and Grievance Procedures* 2009

This code is designed to help employers, employees and their representatives deal with disciplinary and grievance situations in the workplace.

- *Informality*. Many potential disciplinary or grievance issues can be resolved informally. A quiet word is often all that is required to resolve a problem. However, where informality does not work the matter may be pursued formally.

- *Rules and procedures*. Fairness and transparency are promoted by developing and using rules and procedures for handling disciplinary and grievance situations. These should be set down in writing, be specific and clear and be agreed wherever applicable with trade unions or employee representatives. It is also important to ensure that employees and managers understand how they are to be used.

- *'Reasonable' formal action*. Where some form of formal action is needed, what action is reasonable or justified will depend on all the circumstances of the particular case. The size and resources of the employer should always be taken into account. In small organisations it may sometimes not be practicable to take all of the steps set out in this *Code*. However, the key elements of good practice that employers and employees should work to are set out below.

- *Workplace resolution*. Employers and employees should do all that they can to resolve disciplinary and grievance issues in the workplace. The use of an independent third party as a mediator should be considered. Recourse to an employment tribunal should only be a last resort.

- *The formal process*. Whenever a formal process is being followed, it is important to deal with issues fairly. There are a number of elements to this:
  - Issues should be dealt with *promptly*. Meetings and decisions should not be unduly delayed.
  - Employers and employees should act *consistently*.
  - Appropriate *investigations* should be made by employers to establish the facts of the case.
  - Any grievance or disciplinary meeting should, so far as possible, be conducted by a manager who was *not involved* in the matter giving rise to the dispute.
  - Where the employer is raising a *performance problem* the immediate manager should be involved.
  - An employee should be *informed* of the basis of the problem and have an opportunity to *put their case* in response before any decisions are made.
  - An employee has the right to be *accompanied* at any disciplinary or grievance meeting.
  - An employee should be allowed to *appeal* against any formal decision made.

- *Records*. It is good practice to keep written records during disciplinary and grievance cases. A written record should be kept of the outcome.

Summary of key provisions. For the full *Code of Practice* see: **www.acas.org.uk**.

Source: © ACAS

Several issues which arise in the extract contained in Exhibit 8.1 require some further elaboration:

- approach and aim of disciplinary action;
- disciplinary rules;
- acting reasonably;
- disciplinary penalties.

▶ Approach and aim of disciplinary action

The 2004 version of the ACAS *Code of Practice* set out explicitly that disciplinary procedures are seen primarily 'as a means of encouraging improved performance or conduct' from employees, as opposed to merely consisting of sanctions for wrongdoings. This objective is now implicit in the 2009 code. Nevertheless, the encouragement of improvement is an important principle for employers to have in mind.

▶ Disciplinary rules

Organisations' policies should clearly set out disciplinary rules and the likely consequence of breach of these, including examples of gross misconduct that may warrant **summary dismissal** (i.e. dismissal without notice). The statement of employment particulars which employers are obliged to provide their employees within two months of starting employment must contain a note specifying any rules and procedures relating to discipline and employee grievances, or alternatively refer employees to a document specifying such rules (ERA 1996, s 3).

Workplace rules will reflect the operational and business circumstances of each particular employer. Rules are likely to cover the following areas:

- attendance at work;
- compliance with safety standards;
- theft of company property;
- confidentiality when dealing with customers/clients;
- harassment and bullying of fellow workers, suppliers, clients and customers;
- alcohol and drug abuse;
- standards of behaviour outside work;
- misuse of company internet and e-mail facilities;
- behaviour which is likely to bring the organisation into disrepute.

▶ Acting reasonably

A key reference point in the code is that employers should act reasonably in dealing with employees. It is recommended that instances of minor misconduct or unsatisfactory performance be dealt with informally, for example by a manager having a quiet word with the employee in question. Where the issue is rather more serious, the code recommends that employers consider taking formal action. In this case the employee should be adequately informed of the issue or problem in question and invited to a meeting to discuss it, at which they should have the right to be accompanied by a fellow worker or a trade union representative.

At the meeting the employer should explain the complaint against the employee, going through relevant evidence, and the employee should be allowed to ask questions, set out their case and answer any allegations made. Following the meeting the employer should decide whether disciplinary action is necessary or not. The *Code* outlines that if disciplinary action is seen to be necessary this will usually take the form of a written warning which highlights the performance or conduct problem, the improvement or change in conduct required within a specified period, and information about any support the employer will provide to assist the employee. This warning should explain that failure to make the necessary changes could lead to a final written warning and subsequently dismissal, and also that the employee is entitled to appeal the decision.

Where the conduct or performance problem is sufficiently serious it may be appropriate to issue a final warning as the first stage of disciplinary action. Relatedly, where the conduct or performance problem involves a situation of 'gross misconduct', for example involving theft, fraud or violence, summary dismissal may be the appropriate disciplinary action to be taken. However even here, ACAS advise that reasonable behaviour from employers requires there to be an investigation and an opportunity for the employee to defend him- or herself and put their case across.

▶ Disciplinary penalties

The ACAS *Code of Practice* refers to several forms of disciplinary penalty. It is worth summarising them here and commenting briefly on some of the implications of imposing them (see Exhibit 8.2).

EXHIBIT 8.2

Disciplinary penalties

- **Informal verbal warning**. Recommended first step for minor poor performance and minor misconduct.
- **Formal written warning**. Normally, the penalty imposed after a disciplinary hearing for continuing poor performance and persistent minor misconduct.
- **Final written warning**. May be imposed as a result of the failure to comply with previous warnings, or may be a first penalty (short of dismissal) for an act of gross misconduct or serious unsatisfactory performance.
- **Dismissal with notice or pay in lieu of notice**. This would follow a disciplinary hearing. The notice here is that due to the employee based on the statutory minima (ERA 1996, s 86) and entitlements under the contract of employment.
- **Summary (or instant) dismissal**. This is likely to arise where there has been gross misconduct. The decision to dismiss must, however, have been reached after compliance with the workplace disciplinary procedure.
- **Suspension without pay; fines; demotion; and disciplinary transfer**. If an employer proposes to use these disciplinary penalties, then it is essential that the authority for doing so is provided through an express term of the contract of employment. The imposition of these penalties without contractual authority is likely to be regarded as a repudiatory breach of the contract and may result in resignation and a constructive dismissal claim by the employee.

Warnings should set out the nature of the improvement in performance or the change in conduct required, and should specify an appropriate time period for this improvement.

In some cases (those likely to lead to final written warnings or dismissal), the employee might be suspended on full pay pending the disciplinary hearing. Suspension without pay in these circumstances is likely to be a breach of contract.

It is recommended by ACAS that warnings should, after a period specified by the employer, be disregarded.

See the ACAS *Code of Practice* and guide for more detail: **www.acas.org.uk**.

Statutory protection from unfair dismissal

In order to deal with an application for unfair dismissal, an employment tribunal addresses a number of questions in turn (ERA 1996):

- *Who qualifies?* Is the individual complainant an 'employee' with the required continuous service?

- *A dismissal?* Has there been a dismissal in law?

- *Reasons for dismissal?* What was the reason or reasons for dismissal? Was the reason, or if there is more than one reason, the principal reason, potentially fair or automatically unfair?

- *Reasonableness?* Was the dismissal reasonable in the circumstances of the case?

- *Procedures?* Was a fair procedure used – reflecting the recommendations of the ACAS *Code of Practice* and/or was it compliant with the organisation's contractual disciplinary procedure?

If the answer to the first question is 'no', then a claim for unfair dismissal cannot be heard. If the answer to this question is 'yes', then the tribunal goes on to examine the second question. It will then consider, under the Employment Rights Act 1996, a number of categories of 'fair reasons' for dismissal as well as a list of 'automatically unfair' reasons. These are outlined in some detail below. If the reason for the dismissal was a fair one then the tribunal goes on to consider the fourth question, which is whether the decision to dismiss was reasonable in the circumstances. If, on the other hand, the reason for dismissal was not a fair one or was an automatically unfair reason then the process will stop at that stage, with the dismissal being found to be unfair. In addressing the issue of reasonableness, in addition to considerations such as whether the disciplinary punishment was proportionate to the act or situation in question, of central importance is an examination of procedural fairness, i.e. whether or not the employer has followed a fair procedure in dismissing the employee. It is important to remember that the Employment Appeal Tribunal and the Court of Appeal have reminded employment tribunals that they must not substitute their own view as to the action taken by the employer. Their role is to judge whether a dismissal was fair and within 'the range of reasonable responses' that an employer of the type in question could have been expected to adopt in the circumstances.

These elements of the law on unfair dismissal will now be discussed in turn.

❱ Who qualifies?

As a general rule, protection against unfair dismissal applies only to those with a contract of employment with one year's continuous service with an employer. This means that employees with less than one year's service are not covered. (Note that at the time of writing the government has proposed increasing the qualifying period from one to two years from April 2012 (Department for Business, Innovation and Skills, 2011)). In addition, casual or other 'atypical' workers who do not have employee status are also not able to claim unfair dismissal if dismissed by the organisation or person they are working for (see Chapter 2).

However, in certain specified circumstances the requirement for employees to have the required continuous service does not apply. There are a number of reasons for dismissal that are 'automatically unfair' (for example, dismissal on grounds of pregnancy; in contravention of equality law generally; or for claiming entitlement to the national minimum wage), and in these situations employees do not need the required service in order to claim unfair dismissal at an employment tribunal (see further below).

In relation to workers who do not have a contract of employment, although they are unable to claim unfair dismissal, this does not necessarily mean that they will have no employment law claim or remedy at all. For example, if an agency worker is dismissed by the client organisation (or 'principal') because she is pregnant, although she may not be able to claim unfair dismissal, she could have a claim for discrimination under the Equality Act 2010 (s 39(2)(c)). (It should be noted that employees, whether with or without the required service, may also be entitled to bring such claims in addition to or instead of a claim for unfair dismissal.)

Historically, employees aged 65 or over or who had reached the normal retiring age in their organisations were not eligible to claim unfair dismissal. These restrictions have now been removed (see further below).

Table 8.1 provides a summary of the position relating to complaints about dismissal depending on a worker's employment status.

❱ Is there a dismissal in law?

In unfair dismissal cases the onus is on the applicant (i.e. employee) to prove that a dismissal has taken place. The Employment Rights Act (s 95) defines the circumstances

Table 8.1 **Protection against unfair dismissal by employment status**

Employment status	*Protection*
Employee (i.e. with a contract of employment) with minimum of one year's* continuous service with an employer	Full/comprehensive protection against unfair dismissal and also claims in relation to wrongful dismissal
Employee with less than one year's* continuous service	Only able to claim unfair dismissal where dismissal for an 'automatically unfair' reason (but may, depending on the circumstances, be able to bring claim for 'wrongful dismissal')
Worker without 'employee' status (i.e. not having a contract of employment, but having some other contract to work personally)	Not entitled to claim unfair dismissal, but may have alternative claim (e.g. under equality law or for unlawful deduction of wages)

* Subject to Parliamentary approval, this will increase to two years from April 2012

that come within the meaning of a dismissal for the purpose of the unfair dismissal legislation. A 'dismissal' includes the following:

- termination of an employment contract by an employer either with or without notice;
- expiry of a fixed term contract;
- circumstances where an employee is entitled to terminate his or her contract without notice by reason of the employer's conduct (this is known as a 'constructive dismissal').

These various situations are now considered in turn.

Termination of contract by the employer

That this is classed as a 'dismissal' is arguably self-evident – the termination of an employee's contract by his or her employer is what immediately comes to mind when thinking of dismissal. However, it is important to note that the decision to dismiss should be clear and unambiguous. In determining whether or not there was a dismissal, an employment tribunal will consider how the language or expressions used might be interpreted in the circumstances of a particular industry (*Futty v D & D Brekkes Ltd* [1974] IRLR 130).

Fixed-term contracts

It is notable that a fixed term contract coming to an end comes within the definition of a dismissal: even though the contract merely comes to an end and there is no positive dismissal by the employer (for example relating to an employee's conduct or performance), this situation still constitutes a dismissal under the ERA 1996.

Constructive dismissal

At first glance the third category appears to be rather unusual. However, on closer inspection, it makes a lot of sense. This provision means that where an employer does not dismiss the employee but acts in such a way as to fundamentally breach the contract of employment, the employee is not obliged to stay in employment but can resign because of the employer's fundamental breach, and claim unfair dismissal. For this situation to arise there must be a breach which goes 'to the root of the contract' or which involves the employer demonstrating that they no longer intend to be bound by an essential term of the contract (*Western Excavating Ltd (ECC) v Sharp* [1978] IRLR 27, CA).

Possible examples of this would include an employer breaching an express term of the contract, for example by non-payment or late payment of wages or by cutting pay without an employee's consent. In addition, making changes to duties that are not provided for in the contract, changing working hours or the reallocation of job responsibilities could also be covered. Further, breach of the implied terms of the contract of employment will often provide grounds for a constructive dismissal, for example breach of the duty to take reasonable care of the employee (which may occur when an employer fails to adequately protect an employee from bullying or harassment), or the implied duty of trust and confidence between employer and employee.

The Employment Appeal Tribunal has ruled that an employer may commit a repudiatory breach of contract entitling an employee to resign and claim unfair constructive dismissal where its conduct is not directly targeted at the employee in question, but is nevertheless calculated or likely to destroy or seriously damage the relationship of mutual trust and confidence between them (*Hunter v Timber Components (UK) Ltd* UKEAT 0025/09). Bullying or intimidating behaviour directed at other employees may, for example, have this effect.

Notably, in addition to one-off, fundamental breaches of contract, an accumulation of minor infringements or unjustified actions has also been held to give rise to a situation of constructive dismissal (*Lewis v Motorworld Garages* [1985] IRLR 465, CA). Where a repudiatory breach has occurred this cannot subsequently be cured by remedial action on the part of the employer; it is up to the employee in question whether they accept the breach and treat it as dismissal or remain with the organisation (*Buckland v Bournemouth University Higher Education Corporation* [2010] EWCA Civ 121).

Importantly, as with other unfair dismissal claims, in order to claim constructive dismissal employees are required to have the required service.

The circumstances surrounding the ending of employment

Finally, in relation to the issue of establishing the existence of a dismissal, the tribunals and courts will carefully examine the circumstances surrounding the ending of employment in order to ascertain whether a dismissal has in fact taken place. It may be that an employee has not been dismissed but has instead voluntarily resigned his or her position, but tribunals will examine any supposed resignation very closely to determine whether or not the situation is more accurately interpreted as one of dismissal. There have been instances where an employee will resign instead of being dismissed, which the courts have held to constitute cases of dismissal (e.g. *Sheffield v Oxford Controls Co Ltd* [1979] IRLR 133, EAT).

▌ Reasons for dismissal

Having established the eligibility of the complainant and that there has been a dismissal in law, the next step an employment tribunal takes is to establish the reason for the dismissal. The Employment Rights Act 1996 outlines both a list of potentially fair and what are conventionally called 'automatically unfair' reasons for dismissal (the latter term does not actually feature in the legislation).

Fair reasons

The five categories of potentially fair reasons are:

1 capability and qualifications;
2 conduct;
3 redundancy;
4 contravening a statutory duty or restriction;
5 'some other substantial reason' (SOSR).

It is important to note that until April 2011, 'retirement' was a fair reason for dismissal (under the Employment Equality (Age) Regulations 2006). There are likely to be some cases in the tribunal and court system relating to these regulations for some time. This aspect of dismissal law is discussed below.

If an employer can show that the dismissal came within one of these reasons, the dismissal is potentially fair, and the tribunal will go on to consider the issue of reasonableness.

Just because an employer can demonstrate that the reason for dismissal came within those specified it does not mean that the dismissal will be found to have been fair.

Capability and qualifications

The ERA (s 98(3)(a)) outlines that capability refers to 'skill, aptitude, health or any other physical or mental quality'. Understandably, this includes a person's competence or ability to do the job they have been employed to do. Such a reason can be related to either a disciplinary or non-disciplinary matter. For example, poor performance or substandard work is likely, but not necessarily, to be a relevant disciplinary matter, while dismissal on the grounds of ill-health is not. If the former, the appropriate ground may be more appropriately classified as conduct instead of capability.

'Qualifications' means 'any degree, diploma or other academic, technical or professional qualification relevant to the position' (s 98(3)(b)). This encompasses the possession of educational and vocational qualifications (for example, A levels, university degree or apprenticeship). In addition, qualifications include the requirement to possess a valid driving licence and to pass an aptitude test (*Blackman v Post Office* [1974] ICR 151, NIRC). Misrepresentation of qualifications would probably be construed as gross misconduct.

Conduct

As with capability and qualifications, an employee's conduct at work may constitute grounds for a fair dismissal (ERA, s 98(2)(b)). The expectations in any workplace are likely to be set out in the disciplinary rules. As indicated above in the discussion of the ACAS *Code of Practice*, a common distinction made in this regard is between 'minor' or 'ordinary' misconduct and cases of 'gross' misconduct. The former would typically include issues such as lateness or excessive personal use of e-mail, and the latter violence or bullying, theft, fraud, a serious breach of health and safety or insubordination (i.e. a refusal to follow management instructions).

Redundancy

Where an employer's business has ceased or the specific work activity that an employee was undertaking has ceased or diminished, it is potentially fair for an employer to dismiss the employee or employees affected on grounds of redundancy (ERA, s 98(2)(c)) (see detailed discussion in Chapter 3).

Contravening a statutory duty or restriction

The Employment Rights Act provides for fair dismissal where 'the employee could not continue to work in the position which he held without contravention (either on his part or on that of his employer) of a duty or restriction imposed by or under an enactment' (s 98(2)(d)). This provision enables employers to dismiss an employee fairly where their employment or continued employment would be in breach of a statute. Examples here include dismissing an employee who has been disqualified from driving and, therefore, is unable to undertake a job where having a valid driving licence is a requirement; or dismissing an employee whose work permit has expired (see *Kurumuth v NHS Trust North Middlesex University Hospital* UKEAT/0524/10). Such dismissals will be fair, provided that they are carried out in a reasonable manner.

'Some other substantial reason' (SOSR)

This has been described as a 'residual' category which is used by employers to justify a dismissal which does not easily come within the other categories of potentially fair reason. The relevant provision of the ERA (s 98(2)(b)) defines this category of fair reason for dismissal as follows: 'some other substantial reason of a kind such as to justify the dismissal of an employee holding the position which the employee held'.

The Court of Appeal has emphasised that there is a burden on the employer to show that the reason in question is 'substantial' and not trivial (*Kent County Council v Gilham (No. 2)* [1985] IRLR 18).

Examples of potentially valid SOSRs from **case law** are outlined below:

- *Dismissing employees who do not agree to organisational restructuring or change in working patterns*. This may be a dismissal for a fair reason under the SOSR heading if the employer can demonstrate that the change in question was necessary. For example, in *Scott & Co v Richardson* [2005] All ER (D) 87, EAT, the dismissal of a debt collector who would not agree to work a new shift system when his other colleagues had agreed to do so, was found by the EAT to come within the definition of SOSR. It repeated an earlier **landmark case** on this subject (*Hollister v National Farmers' Union* [1979] IRLR 238, CA) which established that having a 'sound good business reason' for the change in question is sufficient to establish SOSR for dismissing an employee who refuses to accept the change to terms and conditions – provided that the employer adduced evidence to show why the change was necessary (see Exhibit 3.6). In *Scott v Richardson* an increased requirement for debt collection work to be undertaken in the evenings, which made the employer adjust working patterns such that evenings became part of the normal rota, was held by the EAT to constitute a sound business reason that potentially justified dismissal of Mr Richardson for 'SOSR'.

- *Transfers of undertakings*. Where an employer wishes to dismiss an employee for an 'ETO reason' (economic, technical or organisational reason) connected with a transfer of undertaking, this is also potentially fair under the SOSR category (Transfer of Undertakings (Protection of Employment) Regulations 2006, reg 7) (see also Chapter 3).

- *Pressure from customers or clients of the employer*. This may also provide valid grounds for a dismissal on the basis of SOSR. For example, in the case of *Edwards v Curtis t/a Arkive Computing* [1996] EAT 845/95, the EAT held that the dismissal of an employee following a complaint by the company's only customer regarding the quality of his work was fair, coming within the category of SOSR. Here the customer insisted that the employee in question be dismissed, but provided that there is clear evidence of customer pressure to dismiss, there does not need to be an express instruction to dismiss or an ultimatum from a customer. It is important to note, however, that customer pressure must not infringe discrimination law.

- *Employee charged or convicted of a criminal offence outside of work*. The ACAS *Code of Practice* 2009 states that the fact that an employee is charged with or convicted of a criminal offence is not normally in itself a reason for disciplinary action. Consideration needs to be given to the effect of the charge or conviction on the employee's ability to do their job and their relationship with their employer, work colleagues and customers. The employer should establish the facts and determine whether the matter is serious enough to warrant disciplinary action. It should be noted that the former ACAS *Code of Practice* 2004 notes that the primary determinant of an employer's response where a criminal offence comes to light should be whether it is one that makes the employee 'unsuitable' for the type of work they are undertaking. An employee should not be dismissed solely because they are absent from work as a result of being remanded in custody. This approach may continue to be adopted by employers as good employment practice.

- *Allegation of criminality*. In *A* v *B* UKEAT/0206/09, the Employment Appeal Tribunal held that a tribunal was entitled to find a dismissal fair in circumstances where a public authority had dismissed a senior employee who it was alleged was guilty of child sex abuse. The employer had been provided substantial evidence by the police suggesting guilt and it was held to have therefore been reasonable for it to dismiss due to the likely reputational damage the employer would suffer if the employee in question was subsequently found to have been guilty of the acts in question.

- *An employee's difficult personality*. This may be a possible 'substantial reason'. An example is the case of *Perkin* v *St George's Healthcare Trust* [2005] IRLR 934, CA. The employer, an NHS trust, instigated disciplinary proceedings against a finance director, Mr Perkin, on the basis that his aloof manner and intimidating management style were causing difficulties at work. At the disciplinary meeting Mr Perkin made a number of unfounded allegations against senior management at the Trust. He was subsequently dismissed on the basis of a breakdown of the relationship between him and the executive team and the fact that he was unable to establish good working relationships more generally. Mr Perkin brought a case for unfair dismissal which subsequently came to the Court of Appeal, which held that personality, of itself, could not be a ground for dismissal, but that an employee's personality must manifest itself in such a way as to bring the actions of the employee within one of the headings of fair reason for dismissal. In this regard it noted that an employee with a difficult personality could possibly be dismissed on grounds of conduct or SOSR. The Court of Appeal outlined that where there was a breakdown in confidence between an employer and a senior executive for which the executive was responsible and that was damaging to the operations of the organisation or meant that senior executives were unable to work as a team, such circumstances could amount to SOSR for a dismissal.

Dismissal on grounds of retirement

Historically employees aged 65 or over or who had reached the normal retiring age in their organisations were not eligible to claim unfair dismissal. These restrictions were removed as a consequence of the Equal Treatment in Employment **Directive** 2000 which outlawed age discrimination in the European Union (see Chapter 5). However, the possibility for older employees to bring successful unfair **dismissal** claims remained very limited up until April 2011, because the Employment Equality (Age) Regulations 2006 made it lawful for employers to dismiss employees on grounds of 'retirement' provided particular procedural requirements were complied with. The regulations introduced a statutory default retirement age of 65, with dismissals of employees on grounds of retirement at that age (or lower, if objectively justified) classified as fair provided certain procedures were followed. Retirement was therefore listed as a 'fair reason' for dismissal. These rules were consistent with the European directive, which permitted discrimination on grounds of age to be justified on certain grounds (for example relating to national governments' employment policies). The Labour government introduced the regulations in response to lobbying by employer organisations who supported rules enforcing a mandatory retirement age.

However, the Conservative–Liberal Democrat government elected in May 2010 decided to abolish the default retirement age. This was in recognition of the fact that with average life expectancy increasing, many people wish to continue working beyond 65 and are very able to do so. Official statistics show that there were 870,000 people over 65 in work in the UK in 2010, compared with 412,000 in 2001 (**www.statistics.gov.uk**). In addition, extending employees' working lives was seen as a way of potentially reducing the financial burden on the state and maximising tax income against the context of a difficult economic climate.

The statutory default retirement age was therefore abolished in April 2011 by the Employment Equality (Repeal of Retirement Age Provisions) Regulations 2011. However, it remains possible for employers to adopt a mandatory retirement age provided this direct age discrimination can be objectively justified as a proportionate means of achieving a legitimate aim, which is necessary in order to comply with the provisions on age discrimination in the Equality Act 2010 (s 13(2)) (see Chapter 5). A dismissal in line with an employer's mandatory retirement age will come under the 'some other substantial reason' heading of the unfair dismissal legislation. Both discrimination and dismissal law provisions therefore potentially apply.

Previous case law has provided examples of the types of situations or retirement policies which the courts may find legal. For example, it may be possible to justify a retirement age in order to create opportunities for promotion. The Court of Appeal held a law firm's policy of retiring partners at 65 was justified in part on grounds of giving senior solicitors the opportunity of partnership (*Seldon v Clarkson, Wright and Jakes* [2011] ICR 60, CA), although this case has since been appealed to the Supreme Court. Such a policy may be particularly justifiable where there are a small number of jobs at the top, for example as would apply in the case of university professors (EOR 2011b). A German case adjudicated on by the European Court of Justice (*Rosenbladt v Oellerking Gebaudereinigungsges mbH* [2011] IRLR 51, ECJ) is similarly authority for the position that fixed retirement ages may be a proportionate response to the need to share employment between the generations.

Overall, however, it is argued that the abolition of the mandatory retirement age allied to broader changes in demography and social norms means that employers will find it increasingly difficult to justify the application of general rules regarding retirement dates (*ibid.*). It is suggested that they will need to provide substantial supporting evidence in order to justify retirement dismissals (for example, of declining performance). It should also be noted that even though a retirement age may be objectively justified, a dismissal on such grounds may still be found to be unfair, for example on procedural grounds. Where no fixed retirement age is in place, to be fair a dismissal must come under one of the other headings of fair reasons for dismissal. Dismissing on grounds of capability is likely to be the most obvious approach employers will take in dealing with possible cases of declining performance due to increasing age.

Automatically unfair reasons for dismissal

In the same way that the Employment Rights Act 1996 outlines potentially fair reasons for dismissal, it also specifies a number of reasons for dismissal that are automatically unfair. Below is a non-exhaustive list of such automatically unfair reasons for dismissal (note that a number of these reasons are outlined in legislation other than the ERA):

- dismissal for family reasons (e.g. pregnancy, taking of maternity leave or applying for flexible working) (ERA 1996, ss 99 and 104C);
- dismissal for a health and safety reason (e.g. acting as a health and safety representative, or refusing to work for health and safety reasons) (ERA 1996, s 100) (see Exhibit 8.3);
- dismissal of an employee for exercising rights under the Working Time Regulations 1998 (reg 32) or the National Minimum Wage Act 1998 (reg 25);
- dismissal of an employee for asserting statutory rights (i.e. for bringing a grievance or tribunal claim in connection with a statutory right) (ERA 1996, s 104);
- dismissal of employees for pursuing or attempting to enforce their rights under the Part-time Workers Regulations 2000; the Fixed-Term Workers Regulations 2002; and the Agency Workers Regulations 2010;
- dismissal of shop workers and betting shop workers who refuse to work on Sunday (ERA 1996, s 101);
- dismissal for taking part in lawful, official **industrial action** within the statutory 12-week protected period (TULRCA 1992, ss 238A and 239) (see Exhibit 8.3);
- dismissal for trade union membership or participation in union activities (TULRCA 1992, ss 152 and 154);
- dismissal of an employee for acting as an employee representative in relation to redundancy and transfer of undertaking situations (ERA 1996, s 103) or as a trustee of an occupational pension scheme (ERA 1996, s 102);
- dismissal where the sole or main reason for the dismissal is a transfer of undertakings or a reason connected with a transfer that is not an 'economic, technical or organisational' reason (TUPE Regulations 2006, reg 7).

EXHIBIT 8.3

Dismissal for taking industrial action and refusal to work in hazardous conditions

Common law. Since the nineteenth century, employees who strike or, in most circumstances, take part in 'industrial action short of a strike', breach their contracts of employment. Such action is a fundamental breach for which the employer may decide to summarily dismiss the employee. Effectively, there has been no legal 'right to strike'. However, since 2000, statute law has provided some limitations on the employer's ability to dismiss where there is 'lawful' industrial action. Essentially, to be 'lawful' there must have been an individual secret ballot to approve the industrial action; and the issues in dispute must relate to the employees' own workplace. Any picketing in support of industrial action must be peaceful (Trade Union and Labour Relations Consolidation Act 1992, Part V).

There are three sets of circumstances to be considered:

1 *Dismissal for taking 'protected' industrial action.* It is unlawful for an employer to dismiss an employee for the reason that they are taking part in industrial action which has been approved by the trade union concerned following an individual secret ballot of its members (this is often known as 'official industrial action'). This protection lasts for 12 weeks. However, in circumstances where the employer fails to take 'reasonable procedural steps' to deal with the dispute (including seeking **conciliation,** mediation or **arbitration;** or restarting negotiations), the period of protection for employees can be

extended. A dismissed employee can complain to an employment tribunal irrespective of length of service. Note that this protection only applies to industrial action which is officially sanctioned by a trade union following an individual, secret ballot of its members. If this does not take place the industrial action is therefore unofficial/unlawful and employers may lawfully dismiss the employees engaging in such action (see below).

2 ***Unlawful selective dismissal or re-engagement***. In addition to being unfair for employers to dismiss employees for taking 'protected' industrial action, it is unlawful for employers to *selectively dismiss* employees taking official industrial action. Employers may validly dismiss all employees taking such action (provided that the principal reason for this was not the fact they were taking industrial action, or if this was the reason, that the protected period has expired; and, in addition, provided the reason for dismissal was not one of the automatically unfair reasons for dismissal outlined above). If an employer attempts to dismiss selectively, then these dismissals will be automatically unfair. It will also constitute automatically unfair dismissal if an employer dismissed all employees taking part in official industrial action but then *selectively re-engages* only some of them. However, the latter protection only applies for three months following the dismissal.

3 ***Dismissal for taking unofficial industrial action***. As discussed above, there is no legal protection for employees dismissed while taking unofficial industrial action. However, here again, there are exceptions – where the reason for dismissal is an automatically unfair reason then an employee taking unofficial action is entitled to claim unfair dismissal.

'***Taking part***' in industrial action is not defined in statute law. For the overwhelming majority of participants, the issue will be clear-cut. However, there have been cases where uncertainty exists and the employee contends that, for whatever reason, they were not involved. The tribunal will decide the issue on the facts. Generally, participation concerns behaviour and not the motives of the individual worker. The burden of proof is on the employer. Case law has provided some examples:

● *Sick absence from work*. This may not, depending on the facts and circumstances, preclude a ruling of 'participation' (*Williams v Western Mail & Echo* [1980] IRLR 222, EAT; *Bolton Roadways Ltd v Edwards and Others* [1987] IRLR 392, EAT).

● *Threatened industrial action*. If the threat was specific that industrial action would take place on a particular date when the employees were due to work, this would be regarded as an 'anticipatory' breach of contract and the employer can regard 'participation' as beginning from the moment the employer was told of the intention to take the industrial action (*Winnet v Seamarks Brothers Ltd* [1978] IRLR 387, EAT; *Midland Plastics v Till and Others* [1983] IRLR 9, EAT).

Health and safety: protection from dismissal. An employee or group of employees is protected from dismissal when they stop work in relation to workplace hazards. This is where an employee 'in circumstances of danger which he reasonably believed to be serious and imminent and which he could not reasonably have been expected to avert left or proposed to leave or (while the danger persisted) refused to return to his place of work or any dangerous part of his place of work' (ERA 1996, s 100(1)(d)); or where 'he took (or proposed to take) appropriate steps to protect himself or other persons from danger' (s 100(1)(e)) (see *Oudahar* v *Esporta Group Ltd* UKEAT/0566/10 where automatically unfair dismissal was found even though *the employer* genuinely believed there was no danger).

As noted earlier, where an employee has been dismissed for one of these 'automatically unfair' reasons there is no requirement that they have one year's service in order to be eligible to apply to an employment tribunal for unfair dismissal. However, dismissals relating to a transfer of undertakings are an exception in this regard – in this instance employees are still required to have one year's service (see Chapter 3).

It is rather curious that discriminatory dismissals (e.g. because of 'protected character-istics') are not included in the Employment Rights Act as automatically unfair reasons for dismissal. However, the Equality Act 2010 (s 39(2)(c)) expressly prohibits 'dismissal' as discriminatory treatment. It is made clear (s 39(7)) that reference to dismissal includes the termination of employment 'by the expiry of a period' (i.e. the non-renewal of a fixed term contract); or an act of the employee giving notice to terminate his or her employment in circumstances where he or she is entitled to because of the employer's conduct (i.e. a constructive dismissal situation). Schedule 9 (para 1) of the Act permits an exception to s 39(2)(c) if there is an 'occupational requirement'.

It is likely that dismissals contravening the Equality Act (for example those constitut-ing direct discrimination) will be unfair unless the occupational requirement applies. However, in respect of age discrimination it is possible for an employer to objectively justify such discriminatory treatment (and so, a dismissal) as a 'proportionate means of achieving a legitimate aim' (s 13(2)).

For an employee to claim discriminatory treatment under the Equality Act, he or she does not have any service qualification with the employer.

▶ 'Reasonableness' in the circumstances

If an employer has established a fair reason for dismissal, a tribunal will go on to con-sider the reasonableness of the decision to dismiss. The reasonableness of the employer's conduct is seen to be *the* central consideration in determining the fairness of a dismissal (Smith and Baker 2010). The Employment Rights Act (s 98(4)) states that where a fair reason has been established, whether a dismissal is fair or unfair:

(a) depends on whether in the circumstances (including the size and administrative resources of the employer's undertaking) the employer acted reasonably or unreason-ably in treating it as a sufficient reason for dismissing the employee, and

(b) shall be determined in accordance with equity and the substantial merits of the case.

The size and administrative resources at the disposal of the employer are specifically highlighted as factors to consider in determining fairness or unfairness. This means that what is expected of a small employer in terms of procedures and steps undertaken may be somewhat less than that expected of a larger, better resourced organisation.

Considered below are various other factors that should be taken into account by employers in addressing potential dismissal situations:

- the employee's length of service and previous record;
- his or her position within the organisation;
- the nature of the business;
- possible mitigating circumstances; and
- consistency of treatment.

Length of service and previous record of the employee in question

Employers have generally been expected to give long-serving employees more time to learn new skills or ways of working than new or recently recruited employees, while in cases of misconduct the past records of individual employees involved may justify differences in treatment between them, notwithstanding the requirement for consistency in decision-making which is discussed below. The EAT has ruled on the relevance of an employee's disciplinary record, noting that warnings for unconnected disciplinary offences (concerning conduct) could be taken into account by employers in deciding whether or not to dismiss (*Auguste Noel Ltd* v *Curtis* [1990] IRLR 326).

Employee's position

Employers may validly be more demanding and expect higher standards from employees in positions of authority or who hold senior posts involving substantial responsibility. For example, an employer would not be expected to give a chief executive or finance director who has been found to be incompetent, a lengthy period of time to improve their performance. These positions are of such responsibility that it is essential that the employees who hold them prove themselves to be competent soon after starting.

Nature of the business

Employers' assessments of reasonableness may validly differ based on differences in the nature of the businesses they operate. For example, lighting up a cigarette in a chemical plant would be substantially more serious then doing it in a university classroom. The courts have also held that an employer may treat the theft of a perishable item (e.g. fresh produce from a supermarket) more seriously than theft of a non-perishable item (e.g. office stationery) (see Exhibit 8.4). The former may lawfully be treated as gross misconduct warranting dismissal (providing this is clearly outlined in the workplace disciplinary rules), whereas with regard to the latter an employer may be required to issue a final written warning prior to dismissal.

Mitigating circumstances

In addition to having a good disciplinary record and long service, as discussed above, whether a breach of discipline was provoked in any way may be regarded by an employer as 'mitigating circumstances' in considering what disciplinary action to take or by a tribunal in deciding whether a dismissal was fair or unfair.

Consistency

For a dismissal to be fair it is important that the employee in question was dealt with in a manner consistent with how other employees had been treated in similar circumstances. If an employee is dismissed while other employees are not or were not in similar situations in the past, then an employer is likely to find it difficult to show that the dismissal was reasonable. Employers, however, are permitted some flexibility in this regard. As indicated above, they may validly apply a different disciplinary sanction to individual employees depending on their disciplinary records (*London Borough of Harrow* v *Cunningham* [1996] IRLR 256, EAT). The essential requirement is that employers act reasonably.

▶ The 'range of reasonableness responses' test

The application of the reasonableness standard in s 98(4) of the ERA has attracted considerable interest and attention from both employment practitioners and academics. Importantly, the courts have developed a test for determining whether dismissals for

EXHIBIT 8.4

Mr Howarth: a 'reasonable' decision?

British Bakeries Ltd v *Howarth* **EAT/322/92**

The facts and circumstances. Mr Howarth was employed by British Bakeries Ltd for 24 years. The bakery where he worked as a shift manager had introduced a system to reduce stock losses. Under this scheme staff who wished to buy the bakery's products had to make immediate payment and obtain a ticket recording the purchase. Mr Howarth was found leaving work with a loaf for which he had not paid. The company investigated the matter at a disciplinary inquiry carried out by the general manager, Mr Jenkins. Mr Howarth admitted that he had taken the bread but said that he had intended to pay for it the next day. Mr Jenkins' view was that there had been no such intention to pay. Mr Howarth was dismissed. There was an internal appeal to Mr Goodwin. He accepted that dismissal was the appropriate penalty.

Employment tribunal. Mr Howarth complained to an employment tribunal. This found that Mr Jenkins had carried out a reasonable investigation and had genuinely believed on reasonable grounds that Howarth was guilty of the alleged offence. It took the view that the company had acted reasonably in treating his conduct as a sufficient reason for dismissal.

However, the tribunal took the view that Mr Goodwin had acted unreasonably in not considering the particular circumstances of Mr Howarth's case and whether dismissal was the appropriate penalty. Mr Goodwin had told the tribunal that he 'could not conceive of any circumstances in which theft could result in any other penalty than dismissal'.

Employment Appeals Tribunal. The company appealed to the EAT, which declared the dismissal to be fair. It held that if a dismissal process was found to be intrinsically proper and that the employer's decision was proper, then, the fact that the penalty of dismissal was not considered at appeal did not necessarily mean that the dismissal was unfair overall. It stated that Mr Goodwin did not consider the penalty because he thought that dismissal was the only appropriate decision. He had satisfied himself that a fair disciplinary process had been undertaken.

potentially fair reasons were in fact fair. This test is known as the 'range of reasonable responses' (RORR) test, which was outlined by Lord Denning in the Court of Appeal in *British Leyland (UK) Ltd* v *Swift* [1981] IRLR 91, CA. Guidance for employment tribunals' determination of dismissal cases following this test was set out in *Iceland Frozen Foods Ltd* v *Jones* [1982] IRLR 439 (see Exhibit 8.5).

Essentially, this means that in judging fairness or unfairness, tribunals and courts are not to judge the reasonableness of an employer's actions according to one fixed, objective standard; and they also should not base a decision on their own personal views as to the reasonableness of the employer's conduct. Rather, they are required to ask themselves whether the decision to dismiss was within the range of actions that an employer could have been reasonably expected to take in the circumstances. The focus is on the reasonableness of the employer's conduct rather than the injustice suffered by the employee (see also *Garside and Laylock Ltd* v *Booth*, EAT/0003/11).

The 'range of reasonable responses' test is therefore designed to allow for the fact that individual employers may take a different view of a particular situation. It is arguably best described as a partly subjective and partly objective test, in that it allows for variation

EXHIBIT 8.5

The determination of 'reasonableness' by employment tribunals

EAT guidance for employment tribunals

Iceland Frozen Foods Ltd v *Jones* [1982] **IRLR 439**

- The starting point should be the legislation (see Employment Rights Act 1996, s 98(4), above).
- The determining issue is the reasonableness of the employer's conduct, not whether or not the tribunal considers the dismissal to be fair or unfair on its substantive merits.
- In judging the reasonableness of the employer's conduct, an employment tribunal must not substitute its own view or decision as to what was the right course to adopt for that of the employer.
- In many (though not all) cases there is a range of reasonable responses to the situation or employee's conduct, within which one employer might reasonably take one view and a second quite reasonably another.
- The function of a tribunal is to determine whether in the particular circumstances of each case the decision to dismiss fell within the range of responses which a reasonable employer might have adopted. If the dismissal falls within the range it is fair, if outside it is unfair.

according to the circumstances of individual cases, albeit within certain wider boundaries (Smith and Baker 2010).

For example, while in most cases it will not be reasonable for an employer to dismiss an employee for being a minute late for work on one occasion, one employer might decide to dismiss an employee for repeated absences following a written warning, while another might issue a final written warning. Both responses would arguably be valid and fall within the 'range of reasonable responses' which employers might bring to the situation.

Relatedly, an important feature of the RORR test is that an employer's actions are judged against the standards of other employers of their type in the circumstances in question, as opposed to those of a tribunal chairperson or judge. The case of Mr Howarth (Exhibit 8.4) is arguably a good example of the way in which the test is applied – the EAT ruled that the fact that the penalty of dismissal was not considered at the appeal did not make the dismissal unfair because the employer in question had followed a fair procedure and the decision made was in good faith. Other employers in the same sector may have been likely to make a similar decision.

▶ Fair procedure

It is a long established principle of unfair dismissal law that unless a fair procedure has been followed a dismissal will not be found to have been fair. The importance of procedural fairness is reflected in the fact that shortcomings or failures in procedure constitute a very common cause of unfair dismissal findings (Earnshaw *et al.* 1998). The guidelines as to disciplinary procedures contained in the ACAS *Code of Practice* 2009 are of central importance in this regard. This section will discuss accepted standards and procedures with regard to:

- general procedural rules and principles;
- work performance and capability;
- medical capability;
- conduct;
- failure to follow a fair procedure and the '*Polkey* principle'.

General procedural rules and principles

The ACAS *Code of Practice* outlines that it is important for employers to follow certain principles of 'natural justice' in drawing up and implementing disciplinary procedures. Essentially, this means that:

- employees should be informed of the nature of the case against them;
- there should be a reasonable investigation; and
- employees should have an opportunity to defend themselves against an allegation and also to appeal any disciplinary sanction that is imposed.

One aspect confirmed in case law is that employees should be given the opportunity of a meeting with someone who has not been involved in the matter. In the case of *Byrne v BOC Ltd* [1992] IRLR 505, EAT, a dismissal was found to be unfair in circumstances where a manager who had instigated a disciplinary hearing also conducted the investigation and decided on the appropriate punishment. The manager in question had been too involved with the case to deal with it fairly. The principles of 'natural justice' had been breached. Hence there is a need to ensure that different people are involved in and responsible for the various stages. In addition, the *Code of Practice* states that wherever possible appeals should be dealt with by a manager who is more senior than the manager who conducted the first hearing. The ACAS guide on discipline and grievance at work notes that such steps may not be possible in small firms. Where this is the case it is important for the employer or manager to communicate that they will act as fairly as possible (ACAS 2011).

While the tribunals and courts are very strict in requiring that the principles of natural justice are adhered to, this does not mean that any procedural irregularity will automatically make a dismissal unfair (see later discussion). Rather what is fair or unfair is very much dependent on the facts of each case. For example in *Bashir and Another v Sheffield Teaching Hospital NHS Foundation Trust* UKEAT 0448/09, a married couple were dismissed following grievance and disciplinary hearings held in their absence. The EAT held that while the circumstances in which relevant decisions were made were both unusual and very unsatisfactory, the fact that the claimants had behaved unreasonably and in an obstructive manner throughout and refused to attend any hearings, meant that the decision to dismiss in the circumstances was not unfair.

Organisations should ensure they provide employees with as much information as possible. For example in the context of redundancy dismissals, the Employment Appeal Tribunal has ruled that fair consultation involves the provision of adequate information or explanation, particularly in relation to subjective criteria scoring, which enables an employee to understand their scoring and puts them in a position to challenge it (*Pinewood Repro Ltd t/a County Print v Page*, UKEAT, 0028/10) (see Chapter 3).

The case of *Sarkar* v *West London Mental Health NHS Trust* [2010] IRLR 508, Court of Appeal EWCA Civ 289, highlights how, where it has been decided to adopt an informal procedure in dealing with what are perceived to be less serious matters, organisations need to take care, then, not to instigate formal procedures that could result in dismissal. In this case, a consultant psychologist accused of bullying and harassing colleagues was expressly dealt with under a policy aimed at resolving relatively minor issues by negotiation and agreement, which resulted in a decision to issue a formal written warning and relocate the employee to a different directorate. However at the end of the relevant meeting the Trust's medical director announced that she would report Mr Sarkar to the General Medical Council. Mr Sarkar consequently withdrew from the informal procedure and decided to subject himself to a formal disciplinary hearing instead. He was subsequently summarily dismissed for gross misconduct. He made a claim to an employment tribunal and his case subsequently came to the Court of Appeal. The Court of Appeal found that the tribunal had been correct in finding his dismissal unfair on the basis that it was inconsistent of the Trust to first agree to use the informal procedure, indicating it regarded his misconduct as relatively minor, and then dismiss him for gross misconduct based on the same evidence.

The case of *Secretary of State for Justice* v *Mansfield* UKEAT/0539/09 dealt with the issue of delay in holding disciplinary investigations in the circumstances where there were parallel criminal proceedings against the employee (in this case a prison officer). The EAT ruled that the employer's decision to postpone a disciplinary hearing whilst the police were still gathering evidence (in relation to allegations of orchestrating violence among prisoners and planting drugs on a specific prisoner) was 'entirely proper'. It took the view that the employer had wide discretion to do this.

Capability or performance dismissals

For a dismissal on grounds of capability or poor performance to be fair, employers need to demonstrate that the employee in question received adequate training, was informed of the problems with his or her performance and given an opportunity to improve. (Many large employers have capability procedures which are different from the usual disciplinary procedure.) In addition, it may be necessary to consider redeployment to another job. However, the ACAS *Code* states that where an employee's first incidence of unsatisfactory performance is 'sufficiently serious', for example, a serious breach of health and safety, it may be appropriate to move directly to a final written warning.

Medical capability

In situations of ill health, it is essential for employers to consult with employees, base their decisions as far as possible on medical evidence, consider alternative employment and, if appropriate, consider the duty to make reasonable adjustments (under the Equality Act 2010).

The importance of **consultation** in cases of medical incapability has been put this way: 'discussions and consultation will often bring to light facts and circumstances of which the employers were unaware, and which would throw new light on the problem . . . only one thing is certain and that is that if the employee is not consulted and given an opportunity to state his case, an injustice may be done' (Mr Justice Phillips in *East Lindsey District Council* v *Daubney* [1977] IRLR 181, EAT).

Medical evidence should be consulted and used by the employer to determine whether to dismiss or not. The employer should seek this from the employee's general practitioner or occupational health doctor (or, as appropriate, a specialist). In April 2010, the general practitioner's medical certificate was replaced with a new 'statement of fitness to work' (the so-called 'fit note'). The motivation behind this was to encourage employees absent for capability reasons to return to work in some capacity, even though they may be unable to undertake the full range of their work activities. Doctors therefore now must either declare that the employee is 'not fit for work' or that they 'may be fit for work taking account of the following advice'. In the latter situation, the form lists four possible modifications that would facilitate a return to work which doctors can tick (phased return, amended duties, altered hours and workplace adaptations), and also provides space for them to add relevant comments (IDS 2010).

Employers will be well advised to pay close attention to these new statements in dealing with capability issues. If they dismiss without taking account of advice provided in a fit note then it may be difficult to prove a fair dismissal. In contrast, if a doctor's statement notes that an employee in question is not fit for work then this could be used by an employer as evidence that they could not make any changes that would have allowed the employee return to work. Employers are however advised to act cautiously and obtain another opinion, as dismissal on the basis of a GP's diagnosis without a further examination by a specialist may be unfair (*Crampton* v *Dacorum Motors Ltd* [1975] IRLR 168, ET; IDS 2010).

The importance of making sure to consult medical evidence was highlighted in *City of Edinburgh Council* v *Dickson* [2010] EAT 0038/09. Here the employer in question dismissed an employee for accessing pornography on a school computer without investigating his claim that this behaviour was the result of a hypoglycaemic episode caused by diabetes. This case illustrates how medical evidence may also be relevant to cases of conduct, considered below, and more generally highlights how careful employers need to be to not jump to quick conclusions based on what appear to be straightforward circumstances or facts.

If the employee does not consent to the employer having access to medical evidence, the employer must act on the facts available. Important guidance on the situation where an employee's incapability was caused by her employer was provided in *McAdie* v *Royal Bank of Scotland* [2007] IRLR 895, CA (see Exhibit 8.6). With regard to alternative employment, the employer should explore the possibility of this, but is not obliged to create a job.

Retirement and capability

The abolition of the default retirement age is likely to make dismissal on grounds of capability or performance more important in future. Employers need to take care in this regard not to subject older workers to unnecessarily different performance or monitoring regimes, as that would be likely to constitute age discrimination (IDS 2011). However it may be possible for different treatment to be justified under the age discrimination legislation as a proportionate means of achieving a legitimate aim. For example, holding annual career planning meetings with employees in their sixties and above may enable an employer to take steps to retain the extensive knowledge and expertise that older workers possess in situations where they do want to retire (*ibid.*).

EXHIBIT 8.6

Ill-health dismissal

McAdie v Royal Bank of Scotland [2007] IRLR 895, CA

The complaint. In this case the employer dismissed a long-serving employee who had been off work for over a year on grounds of incapacity. Her incapacity had been caused by workplace bullying and the employer's subsequent mishandling of the grievance she had raised in that regard. Mrs McAdie brought a claim for unfair dismissal which an employment tribunal upheld on the basis that her illness had been caused by her employer's unreasonable behaviour, i.e. the tribunal determined that it was unfair for the employer to dismiss the employee for an illness it had caused. The employer appealed to the EAT.

EAT ruling. It allowed the appeal, ruling that the fact that an employee's incapacity was caused by their employer did not mean that it would never be possible to dismiss on grounds of incapability. If this were the case, employers would be obliged to retain employees indefinitely even if they were incapable of any work.

Instead, the proper approach to adopt was to decide whether it was reasonable to dismiss the employee in all the circumstances, which included a consideration of the employer's responsibility for the employee's incapability. The EAT noted that where an employer is responsible for an employee's incapacity it should normally be expected to 'go the extra mile' in finding alternative employment or putting up with a longer period of sickness absence than would otherwise be reasonable.

Court of Appeal judgment. Mrs McAdie subsequently appealed to the Court of Appeal. This was reported as in 'complete agreement' with the EAT. It stated that the key question in unfair dismissal cases is whether or not the employer acted reasonably in the circumstances. The employer's responsibility for an employee's incapacity is relevant, but it is only one factor to consider when determining whether or not a dismissal is fair.

Conduct dismissals

Similar to situations of poor performance, employees guilty of misconduct should generally be provided with an opportunity to improve their behaviour. An issue arising in cases of misconduct is that an employer may not have absolute proof that a particular employee was guilty of the misconduct in question. However, in the case of *British Home Stores Ltd v Burchell* [1978] IRLR 379, the EAT set out a three-stage test for employers to satisfy in order to fairly dismiss on grounds of misconduct in these circumstances. The employer needs to:

1 demonstrate it held a *genuine belief* that the employee in question was guilty of misconduct;

2 show it had *reasonable grounds for that belief*; and

3 demonstrate that it had *conducted as much of an investigation into the matter as was reasonable in the circumstances*.

This means that although employers are required to undertake a reasonable investigation, they are not required to have irrefutable proof or evidence as to an employee's guilt in order to fairly dismiss. Clearly, this **standard of proof** is substantially below that in criminal proceedings where proof of guilt has to be 'beyond reasonable doubt'.

In the process of carrying out a misconduct investigation, evidence from an informant can be used. The EAT has provided guidance on how this might be approached and suggests that steps be taken to preserve anonymity where required:

- There should be a written statement setting out the information from the informer, noting any circumstantial evidence and confirming why the evidence might not be fabricated.
- Investigations should take place.
- If the informant refuses to attend a disciplinary hearing, he or she should be interviewed by an appropriate manager.
- The written statement should be provided to the employee who is alleged to have committed the offence.
- Full notes should be taken of the proceedings (*Linfood Cash and Carry Ltd* v *Thomson and Another* [1989] IRLR 235).

Failure to follow a fair procedure and the '*Polkey* principle'

A question that has historically caused great interest and debate in the area of dismissal is whether a dismissal decision that is fair in substance but procedurally flawed, should be regarded as fair or unfair for the purposes of the legislation. For example, if an employee guilty of blatant stealing was dismissed without a formal disciplinary meeting or appeal would this be fair or unfair? Historically, the case of *British Labour Pump* v *Byrne* [1979] ICR 347 established that where it could be shown that a procedural irregularity made 'no difference' to the actual dismissal decision, the dismissal should be regarded as fair. However, this rule was overturned by a judgment of the House of Lords in the case of *Polkey* v *AE Dayton Services* [1987] IRLR 503, which determined that where an employer failed to follow a fair procedure the dismissal would be regarded as unfair even though on the merits of the case the dismissal might be seen to be warranted or fair unless the employer could, exceptionally, show that to comply with the proper procedure would have been futile and would not have affected the decision to dismiss. The judgment also provided that where a dismissal was unfair on purely procedural grounds, the tribunal in question should reduce the compensation payable, with the exception of the basic award, to reflect the fact that the dismissal decision was fair in substance.

◗ Statement of reasons for dismissal

Dismissed employees with one year's continuous service with an employer are entitled to request from their employer a written statement of the reasons for their dismissal. Employees working on a fixed-term contract which expires without being renewed are also entitled to such a statement. Women who are dismissed while pregnant or on maternity leave are entitled to receive such a statement from their employer without requesting it and do not need to have one year's service. Once requested the statement must be provided within 14 days. The statement must outline what the employer believed to be the reason or reasons for the dismissal.

An employee may complain to an employment tribunal if an employer unreasonably fails to provide the statement or if the reasons given are inadequate or untrue, and a tribunal may award the employee two weeks' pay as a remedy if it finds in the employee's favour (as at February 2011 the value of a week's pay for the application of this remedy was set at £400). Written statements provided by employers are admissible as evidence in unfair dismissal cases.

▶ The statutory right to be accompanied

The Employment Relations Act 1999 (s 10) created a right for all workers (not just employees) to be accompanied during formal disciplinary and grievance meetings by a fellow worker or an employed official of a trade union or an accredited workplace union representative. A primary intention behind the introduction of this new right was to provide workers and employees with some support in what are frequently stressful and possibly complex circumstances (Saundry *et al.* 2006).

The right applies in relation to formal disciplinary hearings including meetings that could result in the issuing of a formal warning or the taking of some other disciplinary action (e.g. suspension without pay, demotion or dismissal). The right does not apply to informal discussions, counselling sessions or investigatory meetings. However, the ACAS *Code of Practice* 2009 recommends as good practice that an employee is allowed to be accompanied at disciplinary investigations.

In relation to grievances, the right applies to meetings concerning an alleged breach by an employer of either a statutory or common law duty – for example where it is alleged that the employer has broken a contractual term (for instance, in relation to remuneration or job role) or infringed a statutory requirement, such as the duty not to discriminate on grounds of gender or race.

Notably, there is no requirement that if the employer recognises a trade union for the purposes of **collective bargaining**, then workers/employees have to avail themselves of the right to be represented by a union official.

The fellow worker or trade union representative has a right to address the hearing on the worker's behalf, put across the worker's case, sum up the worker's case and respond on his or her behalf to any views expressed at the hearing. They can also confer with the worker during the hearing but are not entitled to answer questions on their behalf.

If the right to be accompanied is infringed by an employer in some way, he or she is liable to pay compensation of up to two weeks' pay following a complaint to an employment tribunal by the employee or worker affected.

If an employee asks to be accompanied by a solicitor at a disciplinary or grievance meeting, this is a matter at the discretion of the employer. Such requests are most likely to arise in gross misconduct cases. An important consideration as to whether such requests are made or accepted can be whether the employee may be subject to criminal proceedings as a result of the misconduct. Relatedly, also of relevance is the possibility that a dismissal decision may ultimately lead to an individual being barred from a profession.

The latter issue was adjudicated on by the Supreme Court in the case of *R (on the application of G)* v *The Governors of School X* [2011] UKSC 30; [2011] All ER (D) 220 (Jun). This case involved a male teacher (G) who was dismissed by school governors for indecent conduct with a 15-year-old boy. G was denied legal representation at the disciplinary hearing. As a result of their decision the governors were obliged to refer G to the Independent Safeguarding Authority (ISA), which undertakes its own procedures to determine whether or not an individual should be put on a list of people banned from working in schools.

G sought a judicial review of the dismissal decision on the basis that the disciplinary hearing breached Article 6(1) of the European Convention on Human Rights, which states that an individual has a right to a fair hearing in the determination of his or her civil rights and obligations or any criminal charge against him or her.

G argued that by denying him legal representation when one of his civil rights (i.e. the right to work in teaching) was being determined, his employer's disciplinary procedure infringed the European Convention (which is legally binding in the UK). He therefore sought a re-hearing with legal representation.

His case ultimately came to the Supreme Court which decided, on a majority of four to one, that Article 6 of the ECHR did not apply to the disciplinary hearing in question because of the fact that the ISA proceedings were independent of the employer's decision and dealt with a different question (i.e. a decision on inclusion in the barred list). There was no reason to suppose that the ISA's decision would be unduly influenced by the employer's decision to dismiss. There was therefore no need for Article 6 to be engaged at the disciplinary hearing.

This case is therefore authority for the proposition that there is no right to legal representation at a disciplinary hearing where dismissal could lead to a process resulting in the barring of an individual from a profession, where the barring decision is sufficiently independent of the dismissal decision. The Supreme Court did however note that where a decision in one set of proceedings determines the outcome in subsequent proceedings that determine a person's civil rights, then, the right to a fair hearing and by implication legal representation, may be engaged at that first stage. In such situations, employers may therefore be required to allow legal representation.

Obtaining redress for unfair dismissal at an employment tribunal

There are several aspects to the process of obtaining redress:

- Does the complainant qualify?
- When must a complaint be made?
- What is the role of ACAS in these tribunal complaints?
- What is a compromise agreement?
- What issues concern an employment tribunal in making its decision?
- What remedies are available to successful complainants?
- Dismissal complaints and other grounds/causes of action.
- Relationship with wrongful dismissal claims.

We will look at each of these in turn (see also Chapter 1).

▶ Does the complainant qualify?

A complainant must be an 'employee' (i.e. have a contract of employment) (see Chapter 2) and have the required continuous service with an employer. The exception to these qualifying provisions is where the dismissal is for an automatically unfair reason. As noted above, at the time of writing the government had announced its intention to increase the qualifying period to claim unfair dismissal from one to two years from April 2012.

▶ When must a complaint be made?

A complaint about unfair dismissal must be made to the employment tribunal office within three months of the 'effective date of termination' (i.e. the date on which the dismissal took effect). This period can be extended by a tribunal when it considers that it was 'not reasonably practicable' for the complaint to be presented within that time (see **www.justice.gov.uk**).

▶ What is the role of ACAS in these tribunal complaints?

ACAS is under a statutory duty to offer conciliation of all unfair dismissal claims as well as other claims lodged before an employment tribunal with a view to promoting a settlement (Employment Tribunal Act 1996, s 18)(see also Exhibit 1.4). This involves ACAS being sent copies of applications to employment tribunals and an ACAS conciliation officer then communicating with both the employer and employee in question and attempting to reach an agreement between them to settle their case. This process is voluntary, the parties are under no obligation to agree to conciliation. The conciliation officer explains tribunal procedures and relevant legal principles but does not decide on the merits of the case; rather any agreement reached is at the discretion of the parties. However, if an agreement brokered by ACAS is reached on form COT 3, it will be legally binding.

Although conciliation is voluntary, a relatively high proportion of unfair dismissal claims are settled by means of ACAS conciliation: 41 per cent of unfair dismissal claims were settled in this way in 2010–11, while another 25 per cent were withdrawn before reaching the tribunal stage (Ministry of Justice/HM Courts and Tribunals Service 2011). These figures reflect the important role that ACAS plays in the resolution of disputes through conciliation and the provision of advice.

Since 2001 ACAS has also operated an arbitration scheme for the settlement of unfair dismissal disputes. In contrast to conciliation, this involves the parties agreeing in advance to be bound by the decision of an independent arbitrator whose decision is final. In submitting a claim to arbitration, an employee also agrees to give up the right to subsequently apply to an employment tribunal. The scheme is intended to provide an informal and speedy mechanism for the resolution of disputes, with arbitrators' decisions made on the basis of general principles of fairness and good conduct in employee relations as opposed to legal tests or rules. However, the scheme has had very limited take-up (ACAS Annual Reports).

The above figures outline how ACAS plays an important role in the resolution of unfair dismissal disputes. This may soon become more important, with a government consultation on measures to promote the resolution of employment disputes suggesting that in future it could be required that all claims be submitted to ACAS in the first instance, rather than the Tribunals Service (BIS 2011). ACAS would then have a short period of time to offer 'pre-claim conciliation', something that it has been doing on a voluntary basis across the country since 2009.

▶ What is a compromise agreement?

It is possible for the employer and the ex-employee to reach a compromise agreement (note that these are different to ACAS facilitated agreements on form COT3 mentioned above). This involves a settlement of the unfair dismissal claim and an agreement by the ex-employee not to proceed with the tribunal complaint. Normally, such agreements to preclude the exercise of statutory rights would be void (ERA 1996, s 203(1)). However, special provision is made for 'compromise agreements' provided they meet certain conditions (ERA 1996, s 203(3)–(4)). These conditions are:

● the agreement must be in writing;

● it must relate to the particular complaint;

● the ex-employee must have received independent legal advice on 'the terms and effect of the proposed agreement' and 'in particular, its effect on his ability to pursue his rights before an employment tribunal';

● the adviser can be a qualified lawyer, a trade union officer, employee or member who has been certified in writing by the union as competent and authorised to give advice; or an advice-centre worker who is certified and authorised to give advice;

● the adviser must have in force indemnity insurance;

● the agreement must identify the legal adviser; and

● 'the agreement must state that the conditions regulating compromise agreements under this Act are satisfied'.

In the 2010 Compromise Agreement Survey by XpertHR (Suff 2010: 2), the three most common situations for using compromise agreements were:

● where the cost of contesting an employment tribunal claim outweighs the cost of an agreement (59 per cent of employers responding);

● where there is a risk of damage to the organisation's reputation among customers (53 per cent);

● where dealing with senior members of staff who were leaving the organisation (52 per cent).

▶ What issues concern an employment tribunal in making its decision?

There are a number of issues that an employment tribunal will consider when reaching its decisions. These are examined earlier in this chapter and are merely summarised here:

● whether the complainant satisfies the qualifying conditions to claim unfair dismissal;

● whether there is a dismissal in law;

● whether the dismissal was for a fair or automatically unfair reason;

● whether or not the employer has behaved reasonably in all the circumstances;

● whether fair procedures were used;

● if the dismissal was unfair, what remedies are appropriate.

▶ What remedies are available to successful complainants?

There are three possible remedies available to employees who have been unfairly dismissed:

● reinstatement or re-engagement and

● compensation.

Reinstatement and re-engagement are the first remedies considered by tribunals if requested by the complainant. Reinstatement means that an employee gets his or her old job back, as if they had never been dismissed. Re-engagement means that the employee is taken back by the employer but in a different position. In both cases, employees' continuity of service and accrued rights are protected. In considering an order for reinstatement or re-engagement, tribunals are required to take into account whether the claimant wishes to be reinstated; whether it is practicable for the employer to comply with an order in this regard; and where the employee was partly at fault for the dismissal, whether it would be just to order reinstatement.

In practice these remedies are very rarely awarded, being ordered in only one per cent of unfair dismissal cases disposed of in 2009–10 (Ministry of Justice/The Tribunal Service 2010). An employment tribunal cannot force an employer to reinstate or re-engage an employee but where an order for reinstatement or re-engagement is not complied with, an employee is granted an 'additional award' of between 26 and 52 weeks' pay. (The amount of a 'week's pay' in this regard is normally determined annually; it was £400 as at February 2011) (see **www.bis.gov.uk** for the current rate.)

The remedy of compensation is the most common. This is made up of a basic award and an compensatory award. The former is a non-discretionary, standard award that is calculated on the basis of a formula relating to the number of years' continuous service of the employee, as follows:

- $1^{1}/_{2}$ weeks' pay for every year of employment over the age of 41 years;
- 1 week's pay for every year of service between the ages of 22 and 41 years;
- half a week's pay for every year of service completed before the age of 22.

The basic award is subject to a maximum amount, which at February 2011 was set at £12,000 (see **www.bis.gov.uk** for current rates).

The compensatory award is designed to compensate an employee for current and future loss of earnings. It is awarded at a level that is 'just and equitable' in the circumstances and also subject to a maximum limit (£68,000 as at February 2011). Notably, an employer's ability to pay an award is not a relevant consideration for tribunals in this regard (*Tao Herbs and Acupuncture Ltd* v *Jin* UKEAT/1477/09). Importantly, compensation is for financial loss only and its level is therefore not determined by the perceived reasonableness or otherwise of the employer's conduct. Importantly, employees have a duty to mitigate their loss, for example by looking for another job; if they fail to do so this can significantly reduce the compensation they are entitled to. Furthermore, compensation can be reduced by the tribunal because of the claimant's fault in contributing to his or her own dismissal. The reduction can be up to 100 per cent.

Following the Employment Act 2008, employment tribunals may adjust compensation awards if they feel that the ACAS *Code of Practice* has not been followed without good reason. Where the employer has unreasonably failed to comply with the Code the tribunal may increase any award to an employee by up to 25 per cent. Similarly, where the employee has unreasonably failed to comply with the Code the award they receive may be reduced by up to 25 per cent.

In situations of constructive dismissal a tribunal may reduce an employee's compensation where they have not attempted to resolve the problem internally by raising a grievance with their employer before applying to a tribunal. This would be consistent with the law as it stood up until April 2009, which required employees to have first raised a grievance with their employer before they would be entitled to claim constructive dismissal at a tribunal.

As outlined above, according to the '*Polkey* principle', the compensation payable may also be reduced where a dismissal is unfair on procedural grounds but where it was likely that if a proper procedure had been followed the employee would have been dismissed in any case. Any reduction here applies to the compensatory award only. Once tribunals have considered this, where relevant they then consider the possible significance of an employee's contributory conduct. Tribunals have the power to reduce the level of compensation payable to reflect contributory fault on the part of the employee (for example where an employee was guilty of theft and therefore effectively caused their own dismissal). Reductions in this regard may apply to both the basic and compensatory awards. These powers mean that compensation may in certain cases be reduced to zero.

The average compensation awarded by tribunals in unfair dismissal cases in 2010–11 was £8,924, with the median award being £4,591 (Ministry of Justice/The Tribunal Service).

▶ Dismissal complaints and other grounds/causes of action

Depending on the circumstances, employees who have been dismissed may be in a position to bring a claim additional to their complaint of unfair dismissal. For example, an employee who was dismissed on grounds of age or sexual orientation would be entitled to bring a claim for discrimination in addition to dismissal, as would a woman dismissed on grounds of pregnancy or maternity leave. An employee dismissed for claiming his or her entitlement to the national minimum wage may be able to bring a claim for unlawful deduction of wages under the Employment Rights Act 1996 in addition to one for dismissal (there would be no requirement for one year's service here, as this situation comes within the category of automatically unfair reasons for dismissal).

Bringing an additional claim may be advantageous from the point of view of the remedies that are awarded. In particular, while compensation paid as a remedy in unfair dismissal claims is subject to a maximum limit and does not take into account possible injury to feelings, there is no upper limit on the compensation that may be payable for unlawful discrimination and there may be an award for injury to feelings (see Chapter 5). However, it should be noted that tribunals are not permitted to award compensation for both discrimination and unfair dismissal in respect of the same act, i.e. compensation may only be awarded on one of these grounds.

As well as making it possible for tribunal applicants to make more than one claim, it is, of course, also the case that they may be able to bring a different claim instead of or as an alternative to one for unfair dismissal. This possibility is of particular importance to those employees who do not have the required one year's continuous service to claim unfair dismissal and also to casual workers who do not have employee status and therefore are unable to claim unfair dismissal at all.

▶ Relationship with wrongful dismissal claims

The nature of wrongful dismissal claims was explained earlier in the chapter. Remedies for this can, depending on the circumstances, be sought in either the courts or at an employment tribunal (see Table 8.2).

Table 8.2 **Redress for wrongful dismissal**

Claim	Time limit and qualifications	Comments
Damages of £25,000 or less for wages lost or breach of contract by the employer (not associated with an unfair dismissal claim) Damages may be awarded for the loss experienced; but *no* compensation for the wrongful dismissal itself Damages may be reduced because claimant has found new job; failed to mitigate his or her loss; or has received some payment from former employer	● 6 years; 5 years in Scotland ● No qualifying service necessary	Claims made in County Court in England and Wales, or in the Sheriff Court in Scotland If both wrongful and unfair dismissal claims are made (in separate proceedings) the tribunal or court may 'stay' one action – probably the wrongful dismissal claim – until the other has been determined. Because, in terms of money, there can be no double recovery
Damages over £25,000 for wages lost, or for breach of contract by the employer Damages (which are potentially unlimited) are for the loss experienced, but no compensation for the wrongful dismissal itself Damages may be reduced because claimant has found new job; failed to mitigate his or her loss; or has received some payment from former employer	● 6 years; 5 years in Scotland ● No qualifying service necessary	Claims made in High Court in England and Wales, or, in the Court of Session in Scotland Legal representation needed; and, if employee loses, employer's costs could be awarded against him or her
Damages of £25,000 or less for breach of contract by the employer – associated with an unfair dismissal claim (under Employment Rights Act 1996) Damages may be awarded for loss but *no* compensation for the wrongful dismissal itself. Additionally, limited compensation for unfair dismissal is possible only if claimant successful in the unfair dismissal claim	● Within 3 months of the dismissal ● Claimant must qualify to bring unfair dismissal claim at employment tribunal ● Claim must arise out of termination of employment	Possible for claims for wrongful dismissal to be made at employment tribunals since 1994 Legal representation *not* necessary for complainant. Employer's costs only awarded against employee in very limited circumstances

FRISHCO SUPERMARKET CASE STUDY

Scenario 8.1

The case of the bruised apple

Errol, a young man of 20, has been working at the store for two years as a General Assistant. One Saturday morning he was replenishing the fruit and vegetable shelves and he saw an apple had fallen on the floor and was bruised. Because he had had no breakfast that morning, he decided to eat it. **Sandra**, one the Team Leaders, notices him doing this and tells him that he is breaking the company's rules and he will be disciplined. He said it was the first time he had done such a thing and that he was 'starving'. In fact, he has a clean disciplinary record. He is told by **Sandra** to report to **Jez** the Deputy Manager on duty.

Question

What disciplinary action might be taken against Errol and by whom? If he was sacked, what might be his claim at an employment tribunal? In what circumstances could Frishco defend a dismissal?

Visit mylawchamber.co.uk/willey *to access sample HR documents to support this case study.*

FRISHCO SUPERMARKET CASE STUDY

Scenario 8.2

The case of discount card abuse

Staff with five years' service received a discount card for use in Frishco stores. **Pam**, a check-out assistant, had just received one. It was seen by the company as a generous benefit to reward loyalty. The card enabled staff to receive discounts of up to ten per cent on the retail price of goods – whether or not those goods were already discounted as sale goods or reduced for being close to their 'sell by' date. One of the principal rules of the discount card scheme was that goods to be bought were for personal use or consumption only. Multiple purchases would be regarded as an abuse of the scheme and the card would be withdrawn and the staff member would be subject to disciplinary action. The company had an electronic purchase review system which enabled them to monitor such transactions made on each card.

In mid-December, **Pam** was called to **Tony's** office one morning as she arrived for work. He told her that he had just received information from Head Office of concern about transactions that she had made during the past month. In total she had made some 20 transactions in four weeks. It appeared that she had bought a range of items from the four stores in the locality. Many were wine and spirits, tinned foodstuffs, chocolates and speciality biscuits. There were also purchases of Christmas decorations and crackers. These were in addition to the usual weekly grocery order that she made.

Tony said that there needed to be a disciplinary investigation with a view to taking disciplinary action against her. He told her that she would be suspended on full pay pending the outcome of the investigation; and that she was to surrender the discount card immediately.

Pam burst into tears and said she was sorry. She said she didn't understand that she had done wrong. She was only trying to help her son and his family because he had been just been made redundant and had three young children. She also had some family friends and neighbours who needed 'a little help'. **Tony** said that these points could be considered at the disciplinary investigation and hearing. He added that she was in 'serious trouble'.

Question

What advice would you give Frishco on the next step to be taken in relation to disciplinary action? What disciplinary action might be taken against Pam and by whom? If she is sacked, what might be her claim at an employment tribunal? In what circumstances could Frishco defend a dismissal?

Visit mylawchamber.co.uk/willey
to access sample HR documents to support this case study.

Grievances and disciplinary action

In this chapter various references have been made to the use of grievance procedures. Generally, grievances arise in the workplace in relation to terms of the contract of employment or in relation to the implementation of statutory employment rights and entitlements. However, there are two ways in which the grievance procedure can intertwine with disciplinary processes: in circumstances where an employee lodges a grievance during the process when disciplinary action is being considered against them; and in cases involving constructive dismissal. We will look at these in turn and also comment on general points of good practice relating to the lodging of grievances.

◗ Grievance raised in the course of disciplinary action

Good practice advice in this regard is provided in the ACAS *Code of Practice* 2009 (para 44):

> Where an employee raises a grievance during a disciplinary process the disciplinary process may be temporarily suspended in order to deal with the grievance. Where the grievance and disciplinary cases are related it may be appropriate to deal with both issues concurrently.

While grievances clearly need to be carefully considered and addressed, it is not the case that disciplinary hearings cannot proceed before related grievance procedures are completed (*Samuel Smith Old Brewery (Tadcaster)* v *Marshall and Another* UKEAT 0488/09).

◗ Constructive dismissal

As noted earlier, a claim alleging constructive dismissal is likely to have been preceded by a grievance about the unacceptable conduct of the employer. The grievance should have been raised through the formal workplace procedure. An employment tribunal will examine whether or not this internal step has been taken.

◗ General guidance about grievances

The ACAS *Code* 2009 (paras 31–43 (**www.acas.org.uk**)) sets out the following key guidance in relation to employee grievances:

- *Informing the employer.* 'This should be done in writing.'
- *Meeting.* The employer should hold this 'without unreasonable delay'.
- *Statutory right to be accompanied.* This should be granted where the complaint is about an employer 'not honouring the worker's contract or is in breach of legislation'.
- *Employer's decision.* This should be communicated 'without unreasonable delay' and 'where appropriate should set out what action the employer intends to take to resolve the grievance'.
- *Appeal.* This should be provided and heard promptly; and 'the appeal should be dealt with impartially and wherever possible by a manager who has not previously been involved in the case'.

Between 2004 and 2009, statutory dispute resolution procedures introduced by the Employment Act 2002 were in force. These made it mandatory for employers and employees to follow a specific three step procedure in formal disciplinary and grievance situations. This involved informing the employee or employer of the relevant issue in writing, holding a meeting to discuss it and allowing the employee or employer to appeal any decision made. Although these statutory procedures were repealed in 2009, case law relating to their operation is likely to have some continuing influence as a reference point for future tribunal rulings. Some of the important points to emerge from this are as follows:

- *Making a grievance*. The requirements regarding the raising of grievances were seen to be quite minimal. All an employee had to do was set out a grievance in writing, there was no need to expressly state that it constituted a formal 'grievance' or for comprehensive detail. Rather, the general nature or basis of the claim needed to be set out (*Mark Warner* v *Aspland* [2006] IRLR 87, EAT; *Canary Wharf Management Ltd* v *Edebi* [2006] IRLR 416, EAT).

- *Format*. A grievance could be contained in a letter of resignation (*Shergold* v *Fieldway Medical Centre* [2006] IRLR 76, EAT) and likewise a solicitor's letter (*Mark Warner* v *Aspland* [2006] IRLR 87, EAT).

Conclusion

There are various elements which employers need to take account of with regard to discipline and dismissal at work. However, for the most part the law in this area is relatively straightforward, with the adoption of a common sense approach generally enabling employers to satisfy the legal requirements. The categories of both fair and unfair reasons for dismissal are arguably both logical and encompassing, while the requirement for dismissal decisions to be reasonable is arguably also a suitable and appropriate provision. The ACAS *Code of Practice* and advisory handbook on discipline and grievance constitute very useful supplementary sources to the provisions in the Employment Rights Act 1996, providing helpful guidance for employers and employees alike. In addition, the repeal of the demanding and rather confusing three-step statutory dispute resolution procedures has simplified the law in this area.

There are, therefore, strong reasons to conclude that dismissal law is beneficial for both employers and employees alike. For employers, it outlines clear rules and guidelines to be followed; while from an employee perspective it ensures not only that employers must have a valid reason for dismissal but that the dismissal decision and process followed are fair and reasonable. The emphasis in the ACAS *Code of Practice* on the use of disciplinary processes as a means of facilitating improved performance rather than simply punishing deviant behaviour is beneficial for employees, while the provisions relating to automatic unfair reasons for dismissal and constructive dismissal provide them with particular protection.

It is also very evident that the existence of the unfair dismissal legislation has had a direct impact on employers' actions and behaviour in this area. The introduction of dismissal legislation in 1972 prompted many British employers to formalise their activities and approaches to discipline and dismissal. The extent to which this has occurred is demonstrated by the WERS 2004 survey, which found that 91 per cent of workplaces in Britain had a formal disciplinary/dismissal procedure, and 88 per cent a formal grievance procedure (Kersley *et al.* 2006: 215).

The legislation, therefore, has undoubtedly enhanced the legal protection of employees. However, it has also been heavily criticised by academics writing from an employment rights perspective and is seen to have a number of serious weaknesses (Earnshaw *et al.* 2000; Collins 1992, 2003; Collins *et al.* 2005; Anderman 2001). The fact that protection against unfair dismissal applies only to employees with specified continuous service is highlighted as a serious deficiency, while the minimal use of reinstatement and re-engagement as remedies also attracts great criticism.

In addition, a number of the provisions of the Employment Rights Act 1996 and the manner in which they have been interpreted and implemented by the courts have been highlighted as detrimental to the goal of providing employees with strong protection from being unfairly dismissed. In particular, academics note how the 'range of reasonable responses' test used to assess the reasonableness of a dismissal decision, arguably provides employers with too much leeway in making dismissal decisions (Collins 1992, 2003; Smith and Baker 2010). It is suggested that the fact that there is no one, fixed standard of reasonableness and that tribunals are not permitted to substitute their decision for that of the employer, means that the former are largely prevented from developing strong general standards or principles regarding the reasonableness of dismissal decisions.

The use by courts and tribunals of the 'some other substantial reason' provision provokes similar criticism – it is argued that this provision has been interpreted in such a way as to too easily enable employers to establish a fair reason for dismissal. Collins (2004) has undertaken a very detailed critique of the unfair dismissal legislation and outlines numerous suggestions for reform which address the weaknesses.

More broadly, there is clearly much room for improvement in employers' policy and practice regarding discipline and dismissal. There is a strong need for managers and employees to be informed and trained in the requirements of the legislation and, in particular, the application of rules and procedures relating to discipline and dismissal (Earnshaw *et al.* 1998, 2000).

Exercises

8.1   **Jason**. Jason, 22, has worked as a customer service representative at Easywheels, a large car rental company, for two years. He is a full-time, permanent employee. Working in a team of four, his job involves taking customer bookings over the phone and processing them via the company's computer system. His hours are 8.30 to 5. Over the last four months his performance has been less than satisfactory. He has been between 20 and 40 minutes late for work on a number of occasions during this time. This is due to the fact that having recently split from his girlfriend, he is now living with his parents and so has a longer commute to work than before. He received an informal (oral) warning and a formal (written) warning from his line manager after the third and fourth times he was late. He has just been late for work for a fifth time.

In addition to the lateness, in each of the last two weeks Jason has failed to stay for an allocated evening shift (from 5.30 to 7.30), which all employees are required to do one day a week, explaining that he was 'stressed' and needed to go home to rest.

Jason's line manager asks you, Easywheels' HR manager, how his case should be handled in light of the continuing lateness and recent unexplained absences. In particular, she wants to know whether the company may be able to dismiss Jason for poor performance. What advice would you give the manager?

8.2   **Sarah**. Sarah has worked for five years as Product Designer at a small manufacturer of high quality pottery products employing 50 people. Her job involves physically drawing out designs and making trial runs of new product orders by hand before they are manufactured as full commercial runs. One weekend, while rock climbing, Sarah falls and badly breaks her right arm. She is taken to hospital and has an operation on the arm. While this successfully reinforces her bone structures she is left with permanent tissue and muscle damage meaning that she is no longer able to draw designs or operate a kiln (used to make the pottery products). While distraught at what has happened, Sarah is determined to return to work in some capacity. On hearing of the accident and seeing a copy of the medical diagnosis, the managing director of Sarah's company invites her, in writing, to a meeting to discuss her situation. In the letter he outlines the problematic nature of her position given the ongoing requirements of the business. At the meeting the MD tells Sarah that he will have to appoint a replacement for her immediately due to the need to keep up with customer orders. In addition, although a vacancy will shortly be coming available in the marketing department, as Sarah does not have the necessary qualifications for this job, he explains that she is not eligible to apply. Sarah is subsequently informed of her dismissal in writing. She is given an opportunity to appeal but her appeal is rejected.

Sarah asks for your advice about her rights and any action she might take against her employer.

8.3   **Jo**. Jo, with six years' service, works as a trader at GNC, one of the larger stock-broking firms in the City. Very few female traders are employed by GNC and she is the only woman in her department. Like many companies in the City, GNC is a fast-paced working environment with a somewhat 'macho' working **culture**. Jo has recently been dismayed to see that following a change in line management in her department, the 'macho' culture has become more noticeable over the last year or so. The new department manager has created an informal rule whereby all team members are expected to participate in 'team building' sessions in a pub or wine bar at least two evenings a week. Having two small children, Jo informally objected to this to the manager, but was told that 'it is important for all members of the department to attend' these events. Jo has suffered significant stress as a result of having to attend, in particular, due to her not being able to go home to her family but also as a consequence of the heavy drinking that takes place. She discusses the issue with her line manager's direct superior. However, he too treats the complaint as nothing serious, noting that 'this sort of thing is happening all across the City'. Most recently, after the announcement of the company's annual results, all the brokers were required to attend a social function that lasted from 6pm to 2am where there was strong peer pressure to drink a large amount of alcohol in celebrating the company's success. As a result, Jo falls ill. Her doctor informs her that she is suffering from stress and will need to take three months off work.

Jo contacts a friend who studies employment law for advice about her situation, in particular, any relevant rights she has and also regarding the company's obligations towards her. What advice would the friend give her?

Feedback on these exercises is provided in the Appendix to this textbook.

References

Advisory, Conciliation and Arbitration Service. Annual Reports. London: ACAS (www.acas.org.uk).

Advisory, Conciliation and Arbitration Service (2004) *Code of Practice on Disciplinary and Grievance Procedures*. London: ACAS.

Advisory, Conciliation and Arbitration Service (2009) *Code of Practice on Disciplinary and Grievance Procedures*. London: ACAS.

ACAS (2011): *Discipline and Grievances at Work: The ACAS Guide*, London: ACAS.

Anderman, S. (1986) 'Unfair Dismissals and Redundancy', in Lewis, R. (ed.) *Labour Law in Britain*. Oxford: Blackwell.

Anderman, S. (2001) *The Law of Unfair Dismissal* (3rd edn). London: Butterworth.

Collins, H. (1992) *Justice in Dismissal: the Law on Termination of Employment*. Oxford: Clarendon.

Collins, H. (2003) *Employment Law*. Oxford: Oxford University Press.

Collins, H. (2004) *Nine Proposals for the Reform of the Law on Unfair Dismissal*. London: Institute of Employment Rights.

Collins, H., Ewing, K. and McColgan, A. (2005) *Labour Law: Text and Materials* (2nd edn). Oxford: Hart.

Department for Business, Innovation and Skills (2011) *Resolving Workplace Disputes: a Consultation*, London: Department for Business, Innovation and Skills.

Earnshaw, J., Goodman, J., Harrison, R. and Marchington, M. (1998) *Industrial Tribunals, Workplace Disciplinary Procedures and Employment Practice*. London: Department of Trade and Industry, URN 98/564, February 1998.

Earnshaw, J., Marchington, M. and Goodman, J. (2000) 'Unfair to Whom? Discipline and Dismissal in Small Establishments', *Industrial Relations Journal*, 31(1): 62–73.

Equal Opportunities Review (2011) 'Default Retirement Age To Go', No. 209, February.

IDS (2010) 'Encouraging the Not-quite Fit Back to Work', *IDS Employment Law Brief*, No. 904, July: 13–18.

IDS (2011) 'Abolition of the Statutory Retirement Regime', *IDS Employment Law Brief*, No. 922, April: 12–19.

Kersley, B., Alpin, C., Forth, J., Bryson, A., Bewley, H., Dix, G. and Oxenbridge, S. (2006) *Inside the Workplace: Findings from the 2004 Workplace Employment Relations Survey*. London: Routledge.

Knight, K. and Latreille, P. (2000) 'Discipline, Dismissals and Complaints to Employment Tribunals', *British Journal of Industrial Relations*, 38(4): 533–55.

Ministry of Justice/HM Courts and Tribunals Service (2011) *Annual Tribunal Statistics, 2010–11*, London: Ministry of Justice (www.justice.gov.uk/publications).

Ministry of Justice/The Tribunals Service (2010) *Employment Tribunal and EAT Statistics 2009–10 (GB)*, London: Ministry of Justice/The Tribunals Service (www.justice.gov.uk/publications).

Saundry, R. *et al.* (2006) *Employee Representation in Grievance and Disciplinary Matters – Making a Difference?* Employment Relations Research Series, No. 69. London: Department of Trade and Industry (www.bis.gov.uk).

Smith, I. and Baker, A. (2010) *Smith and Wood's Employment Law* (10th edn). Oxford: Oxford University Press.

Suff, R. (2010) *Compromise Agreements: a Mutual Benefit or Tribunal Avoidance Tactic?* IRS Employment Review, 18 October 2010 (www.xperthr.co.uk).

Useful websites

Advisory, Conciliation and Arbitration Service (ACAS) **www.acas.org.uk**

Business Link **www.businesslink.gov.uk**

Department for Business, Innovation and Skills **www.bis.gov.uk**

Direct.gov **www.direct.gov.uk/employment**

Visit **www.mylawchamber.co.uk/willey** to access study support resources including realistic HR documentation to accompany the case studies in the book, an online chapter on collective labour law, interactive multiple choice questions, annotated weblinks, a glossary, glossary flashcards, key case flashcards, a legal newsfeed and legal updates.

Chapter 9

Wages and equal pay

Structure of the chapter

- *Introduction*: the growth of the legal regulation of pay
- *The context*: economic, social welfare and social and political policy issues in relation to pay; 'fair' pay and status differences, gender pay gap, sex and race discrimination and minimum pay
- *Legal provisions*: definitions: wages and pay; common law of contract and pay; information about pay; methods of payment; overpayment; pay deduction; fines; disciplinary action; shortages and losses in retail employment; statutory national minimum wage; equal pay
- *Employment policies and practices*: contracts of employment and collective agreements; information and records
- *Exercises*

Introduction

The legal regulation of pay, like working time, is an issue that goes to the heart of the employment relationship and as such has generated considerable controversy. In the past 30 years, pay has been the subject of growing legal regulation by Parliament, notably the enactment of equal pay legislation (see later section of this chapter), a statutory framework on lawful and unlawful pay deduction, and the introduction of a statutory national minimum wage.

Prior to the 1970s, although law regulated aspects of pay, it did so primarily through the **common law** of contract – particularly through the implied **duty** on the employer to pay wages and not to make unauthorised deductions. These duties remain important but have been affected by the expanding body of **statute law**. This statute law has concerned itself both with the *transaction* (the paying and receiving of wages that are due) and with the *level of pay*. The latter is reflected in the legal framework governing equal pay (between men and women) and, since 1998, in that relating to the statutory national minimum wage.

Statute law also regulates the transaction through the provisions of the Employment Rights Act 1996 (s 1), outlining contractual information to be disclosed, and is relevant in assisting employees to calculate whether they have received their correct pay. This is supplemented by the requirement for employers to provide an itemised pay statement (s 8) which must contain information on the gross amount of salary; the amount of any variable or fixed deductions (s 9) and the purposes for which they are made. The itemised pay statement must also provide details of the amount of wages or salary payable, and where different parts are paid in different ways, the amount and method of payment or part-payment.

The context

The context within which the law on remuneration has been developed has been characterised by two broad sets of factors (Davies 2009):

1 The primacy, given by policy-makers, to the **economic determinants** of pay and the view that it should reflect the free play of market forces;

2 The view that pay levels should be influenced by **standards of social justice**. That individuals have a right to such things as a minimum wage, and that men and women, a right to equal pay, acknowledging there may be occasions when market forces either do not work or do not reflect concerns of equity and fairness.

Much legislation involves a blend of these economic and social justice issues. We will look at each in turn.

▶ Economic issues

Much of the concern of legislation is with 'pay' or 'wages'. (These terms are defined below in the section on the legal framework.) However, there are certain elements in the wider package of 'remuneration' or 'total reward' that a person might acquire from employment, including private health insurance, a company car, non-contributory pension scheme, and it is important in any individual case to be clear whether discussion is about 'pay' or broader issues of 'remuneration'.

▶ The importance of pay to employees

Economists have traditionally worked with a model of human behaviour embodied in the concept of 'economic man', that individuals are rational, utility maximisers and will seek out opportunities to earn as much as they can. On this basis pay is the prime determinant of why people work and why they work where they do. Even relaxing this strict instrumental view slightly it is clear that pay is important as an *extrinsic reward* for work done. It provides purchasing power for goods and services, helps a person maintain or improve their standard of living, and is frequently important as an indication of social status (Phelps Brown 1979). However, as psychologists, sociologists and indeed many economists acknowledge, people may also derive *intrinsic reward* from work such as recognition, power and status and self-esteem. Individuals will differ in the significance they attach to these rewards or sources of satisfaction but it reminds us that people's motivations about work and employment are often complex and interlinked, and that they may not be solely motivated by a desire to maximise their income.

▶ The importance of pay to employers

Pay is normally assumed to be important for employers in addressing three basic objectives. First, that of **recruitment**: here comparative salaries with competitor organisations are likely to influence an employer's ability to recruit staff. Organisations with an established reputation for paying salaries above those of their competitors may well secure the pick of available recruits in the labour market. Second, the issue of staff **retention**: pay may affect this through paying salaries above the market rate, lengthy salary scales where more experienced and competent employees receive higher rewards, and through loyalty bonuses and share options. Third, pay may be important for employers in influencing **motivation**, in that cash inducements may be used to change attitudes and/or improve or modify performance.

In terms of meeting some or all of these objectives, organisations have a choice of payments systems available to them (see Exhibit 9.1).

EXHIBIT 9.1

Payment systems

The payment systems available normally fit into one of three categories:

1 *Time-based pay*. Pay is usually related to hours, weeks or months of work. Such systems focus on grade rates. They tend to be found in more bureaucratic organisations where the pattern of work is relatively stable and easy to define.

2 *Output-based pay*. Pay is normally related to some measure of an employee's performance. It includes systems that link pay to some quantified measure such as the volume or value of output (such as piecework, profit-sharing), as well as those that are linked to more subjective assessments of performance through appraisal schemes (such as performance-related pay).

3 *Skill-based pay*. Under this system, pay is related to the skill, experience and competence possessed by an employee. This is most commonly used for technical and 'knowledge' workers. It is intended to raise the quality and **flexibility** of the workforce. It is appropriate when the pace of change is rapid so that new ideas, methods and technology are being introduced regularly.

Payments under these systems may be fixed (e.g. basic weekly wages) with rates only changeable by agreement. Alternatively, payments may vary according to the amount of time an employee attends work or the time of day attended. So, for example, longer attendance can result in overtime pay, and night and shift working in special premium rates. Much output-based pay can be variable and as well as those examples identified above; those in sales-related work, who are often paid by commission (the volume of sales), may have a very large proportion of their pay determined in this way.

▶ Public policy: free markets and regulation

Under a pure 'free market' system employers are free to set whatever pay level they choose and the payment system they feel most appropriate. Furthermore, they are free to decide whether or not to pay 'wages' for work done, make deductions where they feel these are appropriate under the employment relationship and which (if any) benefits to provide. In practice, although employers do have considerable freedom in these areas there are constraints in their operation that affect employers' decision-making.

The main ways in which the free market is modified concern questions of equity and fairness and a perception that left to its own devices, the free market may operate against the interests of some of the weakest and most vulnerable groups in the labour market (Rubery and Edwards 2003). Historically, these concerns have been voiced by trade unions through the collective bargaining process, but with the marked decline in bargaining coverage since the 1970s they are themes that have been increasingly asserted through legislation. Developments in the areas of equal pay, the national minimum wage, and constraints on employers' abilities to make lawful deductions from pay are illustrations of this shift and point to the recognition of social factors in the determination of pay that are dealt with below.

Contrasting positions on this issue of pay and the free market can be seen through a comparison of the policies of Conservative governments (1979–97), and those of the Labour governments (1997–2010). Much of the emphasis of labour market policy in the 1980s and 1990s was in removing what were seen as impediments to the efficient operation of a free market. Laws to curb the power and influence of trade unions and collective bargaining, and the abolition of Wages Councils (which established minimum pay levels in selected industries) were attempts to restore the primacy of economic factors in determining pay and other terms and conditions of employment (the specific details of this are contained in Exhibit 9.2). The gradual undermining of collective influence on pay throughout this period was part of a broader 'de-collectivisation' of pay regulation and employment relations and a simultaneous strengthening of individual performance factors in relation to pay (Charlwood 2007).

The de-collectivisation of pay regulation provides an important context for labour market interventions in the period since 1997. From a position in the mid-1970s where 80 per cent of workplaces in the UK and a similar percentage of employees had pay set by collective bargaining (Brown 2010), bargaining coverage had fallen to around 36 per cent of employees by the turn of the century (EIROnline 2002). The historical importance of joint regulation of terms and conditions of employment, whereby pay and other substantive terms became incorporated into contracts of employment is important both legally and practically. Its contraction, and the virtual disappearance of multi-employer bargaining from the private sector (Williams and Adam-Smith 2010) are linked to the decline of union presence and the decentralisation of employment relations, and have paved the way for a more explicit re-regulation of employment terms by management, particularly in the private sector (Grimshaw and Rubery 2010, Brown and Nash 2008). It is now the case that there is no collective bargaining in almost three-quarters of all workplaces (Williams and Adam-Smith 2010: 259) and because:

> Most workers fall outside the scope of joint regulation and collective solidarity amongst workers is low . . . many individual workers will be unlikely to address problems about pay or other workplace issues because of a weak bargaining position; the time and effort required; or a fear of damaging their reputation.
>
> (Pollert and Charlwood 2009, in Grimshaw and Rubery 2010: 354)

These concerns point to the potential for widening disparities in pay and for some groups of workers to be excluded from protection and to be at risk of exploitation

EXHIBIT 9.2

Government labour-market policy initiatives

Conservative (1979–1997)

- Abolition of the House of Commons Fair Wages resolution affecting public sector contracts.
- The abolition of Wages Councils (1993) – apart from that for agricultural workers.
- Gradual reduction in use of 'comparability' as a basis for pay determination in the public sector.
- Introduction of competitive tendering and market testing in the public sector.
- Use of legislation to erode the power and influence of trade unions, in particular, in relation to the 'closed shop' and industrial action.
- Attempts in the public sector to encourage greater flexibility and remove many groups from collective bargaining coverage.
- Support for the de-recognition of trade unions.
- Promotion of performance related pay in public and private sectors.

Labour (1997–2010)

- *Fair Deal at Work* White Paper: attempted balance of individual employment rights and promoting employers' business interests.
- Introduction of statutory national minimum wage.
- 'Relaxed' about high bonuses in financial services sector.
- Strong commitment to equal pay.
- Efficiency drives, 'contracterisation' and *some* public expenditure constraints had a variable impact on public sector pay.
- Statutory right of trade union recognition enacted.
- Restrictive legislation on industrial action remained in force.

Conservative–Liberal Democrat (from 2010)

- Commitment to national minimum wage (NMW) in principle.
- Abolition of Agricultural Wages Board and inclusion of these workers under NMW.
- Enactment of most of the equal pay provisions of the Equality Act 2010.
- Decision not to implement pay audit provisions.
- Two-year pay freeze from 2010 for public sector workers.
- Proposed a 'fair pay review' for public sector workers.
- Reforms of public sector pensions involving greater contributions, extended length of service and 'career average' rather than final salary pensions.

because of the absence of any effective representation or enforceable employment rights. They helped shape an emerging agenda of the Labour party in opposition and although, once in office, the Labour governments retained many of the free market approaches and initiatives of their Conservative predecessors, from 1997 to 2010, labour market interventions were focused; directed mainly at expanding and in some areas, establishing individual statutory rights. The main objective seemingly to establish a legal minimum floor of rights below which individuals would not be permitted to fall (Davies and Freedland 2007). In the area of pay, the single most important development was the establishment of a Low Pay Commission and resulting legislation – the National Minimum Wage Act (NMWA 1998).

▶ Social welfare factors

As we have seen, although there have been elements of consistency in government policy between Conservative and Labour governments, the period since 1997 marked a shift in policy concerns towards assisting the most vulnerable groups and individuals in the labour market. In addition to the NMW and other individual employment protection, there was a focus on the interlocking of pay and certain in-work social benefits. The late 1990s had witnessed increasing concern over the creation of a 'poverty trap' whereby an individual lost certain in-work benefits as pay increased. As a consequence employment could make little change to disposable income and in many instances discouraged individuals from working more hours. Furthermore it could serve to entrench not only 'in-work' poverty but also a 'dependency culture'.

One of the areas highlighted by the first report of the Low Pay Commission (1998: 31) was the relationship between pay levels and social security benefits. The Commission pointed out that from the mid-1970s those on median earnings and those highest earners had experienced a significantly greater increase in earnings than the lowest paid (see Atkinson 2003; Machin 2003 on rising inequality). The Commission concluded that:

> The widening distribution of earnings has led to a substantial degree of in-work poverty, particularly among families with young children and a consequential increase in earnings than the lowest-paid workers.   (Low Pay Commission 1998: 32)

The effects of this can be seen from the growth in Family Credit (and before this Family Income Supplement) from £200 million in 1987–88 to £2,000 million in 1996–97. In 1999, Family Credit was replaced by the Working Families Tax Credit and in 2003 two new schemes – the Working Tax Credit and the Child Tax Credit – replaced the Working Families Tax Credit. According to work undertaken by the New Policy Institute on its Poverty Site (**www.poverty.org.uk**) these changes have not achieved the success that was anticipated. The generous eligibility criteria introduced as a result of the changes in 2003 meant that the proportion of working-age households in receipt of tax credits stood at 17 per cent in April 2010. This equates to 3.2 million working, working-age households in receipt of tax credits over and above those just receiving the family element of tax credit. This is double the number in 2002 and three times that in 2000 (Parekh *et al.* 2010, **www.poverty.org.uk**).

▶ Social policy

The concerns surrounding the social-welfare poverty trap have been a major stimulus to establishing new legal standards in relation to pay. Social policy in respect of remuneration has a number of aspects. Some of these relate directly to government policy and others have evolved in managerial policy approaches. The issues involved are:

- fair pay;
- status differences in remuneration between manual and non-manual workers;

- pay levels and sex and race discrimination;
- minimum pay;
- new social objectives.

We will look at each in turn.

Fair pay

The concept of fairness in pay is controversial. Free market economists would argue that fairness is determined by market forces, and in the labour market this equates to the value an employer places on the knowledge and skills, the human capital of the individuals concerned. If the market dictates a cleaner is worth £6.00 an hour and a professional footballer £100,000 a week then this is fair. A counter view would point to the existence of monopsony power in parts of the labour market that mean that outcomes such as pay do not always reflect the free play of market forces (an example could be where local employers facing limited competition for less skilled staff take advantage of their market position and pay below the 'market rate'). It is argued further that these pressures are likely to impact particularly on the most vulnerable, so that protection in the form of minimum pay legislation may be necessary to ensure some element of fairness for these groups.

Additionally, fairness can mean a fair reward for the work undertaken, something that extends to comparative pay. This notion of 'felt fair' (Jacques 1967) resonates with the work of psychologists such as Adams (1965) associated with the concept of equity theory – that individuals not only equate their effort to outcomes, but also equate it to that of others, and where a discrepancy exists individuals will experience some distress and seek to redress this. In terms of comparative pay, the law has played a role. In 1891, the House of Commons adopted the Fair Wages Resolution whereby employers engaged on government contracts should pay at least the wage level generally recognised for the sector or locality concerned. The Resolution was revised in 1946, and ultimately repealed in 1983 as part of the then Conservative government's free-market economic policies. Although Labour governments after 1997 came under pressure to reintroduce such a measure, they chose not to revive it, presumably because they felt that the national minimum wage created a more wide-ranging basis for equal pay.

Notions of fairness frequently impinge upon organisational decisions about pay through the operation of job evaluation schemes. Such schemes mediate the impact of market forces and provide a broader defence of pay differentials, something that has acquired particular importance in the area of equal pay (see discussion below).

Status-based pay

The status divide has long been a feature of employment in Britain and refers to the distinction between manual (or 'blue collar') and non-manual (or 'white collar') workers. Historically, there was a clear distinction between these broad groups reflected in very different terms and conditions of employment. Manual workers generally worked longer hours, had fewer holidays, no provision for sick pay nor for pensions, and had less employment security. Frequently they were subject to one week's notice to terminate their **contracts** of employment, and pay was normally on a weekly basis, and in manu-facturing often fluctuated by virtue of being output-based. In some cases pay was even on a daily basis, depending on the availability of work, a phenomenon characteristic of industries such as port transport prior to de-casualisation in 1947 and some parts of construction. Inevitably hourly rates of pay for manual workers were frequently lower than the equivalent rates paid to 'white collar' staff.

Since the 1960s changes to these status distinctions have taken place although the extent of these has been the subject of debate (McGovern *et al.* 2007). In any event the impact of legal and political initiatives in encouraging change in this area has been limited. Moves towards **single status** and harmonisation of conditions of employment have been initiated mainly by employers for reasons related to the management of their organisations.

Pay and discrimination

In general, discussion of pay and discrimination has tended to focus on the provisions of the Equal Pay Act 1970 (now the Equality Act 2010, Part 5, Chapter 3) where direct comparisons are made in particular organisations between the pay of men and women. As we shall see, there are strong historical reasons for this and it remains an important and enduring issue but there is increasing recognition that other sources of discriminatory treatment operate in relation to pay, particularly those of race and ethnicity (Clark and Drinkwater 2007, Foster 2007, Heath and Cheung 2006, Platt 2007). There is now considerable evidence to suggest that certain minority groups (in some cases linked to migrant worker status) become trapped in low-paying work irrespective of gender and qualifications (Low Pay Commission 2008, 2009).

Despite this evidence, the law continues to require claims of unequal pay to be framed within the parameters of gender, rather than some other discrimination ground and this forms the basis of our discussion of the legal aspects of pay and discrimination later in this chapter. There, reference is made to discrimination in relation to general levels of pay, seen particularly in earnings distribution figures, giving rise to potential direct and indirect sex discrimination.

In this section we focus on the broader contexts surrounding discrimination and pay beginning with discussion of the pay gap between men and women. This is followed by a brief summary of the evidence for pay discrimination affecting other protected characteristics.

Equal pay and the gender pay gap

It is often difficult to appreciate that even as late as the 1960s the belief that men should be paid more than women for doing the same or similar work was widely held in the UK. Although some professions, such as teaching and the Civil Service, had established the principle and practice of equal pay for 'like work' in the 1950s, in many areas a combination of factors meant entrenched practices were slow to change. The catalyst for legal change came with a strike by female machinists working at the Ford Motor Company in Dagenham in 1967, supported by the then Secretary of State for Employment and Productivity, Barbara Castle. It was Barbara Castle who drafted what was to become the Equal Pay Act 1970, and in acknowledging the extent of change required in some areas, gave employers five years to comply with the act's requirements, which become fully effective on 1 January 1975.

Following the passing of the Act, progress on reducing the gender pay gap was immediate (see Table 9.1) and by the end of the decade the gap for those working full time had declined from 36 per cent in 1970 to around 28 per cent by 1980. However, from

Table 9.1 **Gender pay gap mean (median) hourly earnings in UK***

Year	Full-time pay gap	Part-time gap
1970	36.2%	48.5%
1976	26.5%	40.5%
1987	26.6%	43.7%
1993	23.5%	41.4%
1998	21.1% (17.4%)	41.9% (44.1%)
2002	20.1% (15.5%)	42.6% (44.5%)
2005	17.1% (13.0%)	37.6% (40.7%)
2007	16.9% (12.4%)	35.8% (39.4%)
2008	17.3% (12.6%)	36.9% (40.2%)
2009	16.4% (12.2%)	35.3% (39.7%)
2010	15.5% (10.2%)	34.5% (38.8%)

* *Source*: Perfect 2011, Pike 2011, Leaker 2008, Barnard 2008: figures pre-1998 relate to Britain, and to UK after this date; from 1998 figures in brackets median pay gap.

1975 and 1987 it changed little, before narrowing by almost a quarter in the ten years prior to the introduction of the national minimum wage. Despite this progress, the gender pay gap remains a third higher in the UK than the average for the EU as a whole.

Furthermore, as Table 9.1 demonstrates, in view of the over-representation of women in part-time work, an exclusive focus on the full-time gap can be misleading. When account is taken of this, the picture of a narrowing gap is more qualified. As Fredman has noted:

> The statistics on women's pay . . . show unequivocally that (three) decades of equal pay legislation has been unable to close the gap between the average remuneration of men and women. Indeed, in the twenty-two years from 1974 and 1996 the gap narrowed by a mere 5.9%.   (Fredman 1997: 225–226)

These concerns echoed those at a political level and the election of a Labour government in 1997 ushered in a number of public policy initiatives designed to examine and ultimately address the persistent pay gap between men and women (see Exhibit 9.3).

It is also the case that the picture of aggregate trends in the gender pay gap disguises important variations by occupations and between and within regions (Perfect 2011). The gap remains highest in south-east England and lowest in Northern Ireland but within the South-East wide disparities exist. In the City of London it has been estimated that women working full time earn on average 55 per cent less than their male colleagues (TUC 2008, *Guardian* 9 April 2009), with an Equality and Human Rights Commission survey of 50 companies revealing that men received around five times more in bonus payments than their female colleagues (BBC News 6 September 2009).

The reasons for the gender pay gap and its persistence are complex but some understanding of them is necessary in order to explore the role that law can play in addressing

EXHIBIT 9.3

The changed political agenda 1997–2010

The period of Labour governments from 1997–2010 demonstrated a significant shift in policy concern with equality and specifically equal pay. The following are the major initiatives that took place in this area over the period.

● Women and Equality Unit (established in 1997) replaced by Women and Work Commission (2004).

● Equalities Review (2007).

● Discrimination Law Review (2007).

● Establishment of Equality and Human Rights Commission (October 2007).

● Equality Acts (2006, 2010).

● Family friendly policies, anti-discrimination legislation (2002–06).

● Equality duties of public sector employers (from 5 April 2011 Public Sector Equality Duty (PSED) required to demonstrate equality across all strands).

and alleviating the gap. Conventional economic analyses have tended to emphasise the contribution made by differences in human capital (skills) as being a major source of earnings differences and attributing a large part of the gender pay gap to this (Hakim 2004). However, in research conducted on behalf of the Women and Work Commission, Olsen and Walby (2004) estimated that less than ten per cent of the gender pay gap was attributable to this. Rather, that over a third of the gap was the result of gender differences in working patterns (periods of part-time work and interruptions to careers), around a fifth the result of labour market rigidities including occupational segregation, and almost two-fifths the result of direct discrimination or career preferences.

Similarly Grimshaw and Rubery (2007) suggest three factors are critical in accounting for the gender pay gap.

● The *under-valuing of women's work*: that women's skills are often not recognised or valued in the way men's skills are, that women's work is concentrated in particular occupations and that work is more marginal for women than men, reflected in the over-representation of women in part-time work.

● The *gender segregation in employment*: that women are 'vastly over-represented in low paid, part-time, unskilled work' (Ashtiany 2007: 6), with women facing a significant part-time penalty (Manning and Petrolongo 2004, 2008) and men far more likely to work in larger firms often with more favourable terms and conditions of employment.

● An *employment penalty for mothers*: with the Equalities Review in its Final Report identifying 'becoming mothers as the single biggest cause of women's inequality in the labour market' (2007: 66). It links strongly to part-time working and significant problems in obtaining jobs (Berthoud and Belkesaune DWP 2007).

In so far as the law can have an impact on these, equal pay and minimum wage legislation has tended to focus upon the first issues – the circumstances where women tend to be paid less than men for the same performance in the same job and that the jobs they perform often attract lower wages than jobs undertaken by men. Sex discrimination law has had an impact on the second issue in helping to remove barriers to gender segregation and areas such as parental leave and paternity leave have tried to address work–life balance questions highlighted in the third.

Pay discrimination and other groups

Until recently, pay discrimination for groups other than women had been less well researched and documented. However, research conducted for the Low Pay Commission and the Equality and Human Rights Commission has shed considerable light on the issues faced by certain ethnic minorities, migrant workers and young workers (EHRC 2010, Metcalf 2009). The position on ethnic minorities is mixed. In general such workers are more likely to be working in low paying sectors (LPC 2008: 75) but there are marked differences between ethnic groups, with Pakistanis and Bangladeshis likely to be most affected (EHRC 2010 Ch.11, LPC 2008: 8). It is also probable that there is under-recording of work in sectors such as clothing and hosiery where homeworking is dominant and (as well as being concentrated among women) undertaken largely by those from particular minority groups (LPC 1998: 38) and who have emerged as a specific concern in terms of low pay (LPC 2009, 2010).

In her study of ethnic minorities and the labour market, Foster (2007) found widespread evidence of ethnic minority groups experiencing lower earnings than whites with the earnings disadvantage of ethnic minority men 'a pervasive feature of the British labour market'. Breaking this down by gender and ethnic group, Platt (2007) exposed particular pay disadvantages for some minority groups with Pakistani women experiencing the highest pay gap among women, and Bangladeshi men the highest gap among men. Indeed, as Heath and Cheung (2006) have argued:

> Even after controlling for factors such as age, education and other personal character-istics there were still significant net disadvantages for Black Africans, Black Caribbeans, Pakistanis, and Bangladeshis with respect to unemployment, earnings and occupa-tional attainment.   (quoted in LPC 2008: 77, EHRC 2010)

Recent Low Pay Commission reports have also highlighted the employment difficulties faced by many young workers in recessionary periods. As well as a 2010 report which estimated that a fifth of those described as economically active between the ages of 16 and 24 were out of work (**www.poverty.org.uk**), the LPC has shown that 'high propor-tions of young people are paid at the youth and adult minimum wage rates' (LPC 2009: xv) indicating the 'major impact (of the NMW) on the earnings of younger people' (LPC 2009: xv).

Minimum pay

Policies to set minimum pay levels in Britain have focused on three sets of statutory initiatives. The first, lasting from the early twentieth century until 1993, was the system of Wages Councils established to cover workers in particular industries and sectors. The second, and most recent, has been the development of a statutory minimum wage applicable to all workers. The third initiative, which is voluntary, is the advocacy of a 'living wage' – at a level significantly above the NMW.

Wages Councils

Established under legislation in 1909, trade boards, as they were originally known, were devised as a means of addressing gaps in the coverage provided by **free collective bargaining** and the difficulties of developing trade union organisation in particular sectors of the economy. These trade boards (the name was changed in 1945 to Wages Councils) comprised representatives of employers, trade unions and government and were charged with setting and implementing statutory minimum pay for specific sectors in the economy, the so-called 'sweated industries' with 'wages barely sufficient to sustain existence' (Select Committee on the Sweating System 5th Report 1890, in Collins *et al.* 2005: 388). At the outset it was always envisaged that Wages Councils would be a temporary measure, eventually replaced by full-blown collective bargaining. At their peak in 1953, there were 66 Wages Councils, covering some 3.5 million workers in sectors such as retail distribution, catering and hotels, clothing, laundries, road haulage and agriculture. At the time of abolition in 1993 there were 35 Wages Councils left in existence (26 in Britain, nine in Northern Ireland).

Following abolition one Council, the Agricultural Wages Board, remained. This was a reflection of the original concerns of the legislators in 1909 to protect workers in sectors where union organisation was weak and employers relatively powerful. It was also an acknowledgement that despite its history low pay remained a problem in the sector and the hoped-for transition to free collective bargaining had not materialised. However, in October 2011, the Conservative–Liberal Democrat government abolished the Board and included agricultural workers under the National Minimum Wage (**www.defra.gov.uk**).

In terms of their operation, Wages Councils made Wages Orders that were enforced through a Wages Inspectorate. In the 14 years prior to abolition, the annual average number of completed prosecutions via the Inspectorate was only seven but as the Low Pay Commission noted, these figures understated their role as 'Inspectorate policy was to achieve compliance through advice and persuasion rather than legal action' (LPC 1998: 207).

As the earlier discussion indicated, the political climate of the 1980s and 1990s was not favourable to institutions that were felt to be interfering with free market forces. Wages Councils were an obvious target, seen as 'outdated and anachronistic institutions which inhibited labour market flexibility' (Williams and Adam Smith 2010: 276). The Conservative government's antipathy towards them was summed up by Nigel Lawson (then Chancellor of the Exchequer) as 'forcing employers to pay wages they cannot afford'. As well as adding to firms' costs, the other implication was that Wages Council rates could impact on jobs. The government's response was to reduce the remit of Wages Councils in 1986, and in 1993, with the exception of the Agricultural Wages Boards, to abolish them completely. At the time of abolition they covered 2.6 million workers.

Towards a national minimum wage

Although the concept of a national minimum wage has been well-established in a number of countries, featuring particularly in the employment legislation of many European states, political commitment to the idea in Britain is more recent. Historically, both the Labour Party and trade union movement preferred a minimum wage system that was limited to those areas where **collective bargaining** could not be achieved, in a context of a wider policy commitment to encourage and extend collective bargaining. However, the abolition of the Wages Council system, US evidence that minimum wage legislation brought benefits with limited negative effects (Card and Kreuger 1995) and Labour's own deliberations on employment relations policies led to a reappraisal.

During the 1990s, the Labour Party in opposition accepted a policy commitment to a national minimum wage as part of a package of labour market reforms designed to assist the low paid. Initially, the Party had considered determining the minimum wage on the basis of a formula – half the median male earnings – but after 1996, it developed the approach that it adopted once in government. The essential elements of this were:

- the establishment of a low pay commission involving employers, unions and independent members;
- **consultation** with employers and employees;
- the responsibility of the commission to set the national minimum wage;
- consideration being given to economic circumstances in the setting of the rate.

In office, the Labour government established the Low Pay Commission, comprising employer, union and academic representatives. In making initial recommendations, the Commission undertook a comprehensive research and consultation programme including 'visits to over sixty cities, towns and villages throughout the UK, where we heard directly from small firms, rural businesses, local outlets of national companies, low-paid workers, the unemployed and some operating on the fringes of the formal economy' (LPC 1998: 1).

The Commission produces annual reports and is given terms of reference by the government which include making recommendations as to the rate of the NMW. In making these recommendations the Commission is instructed to have regard to the wider economic and social implications; the likely effect on the level of employment and inflation; the impact on the competitiveness of business, particularly the small firms sector; and the potential costs to industry and to the Exchequer. In general, government has tended to follow its recommendations as to appropriate minimum rates; and the bands to which these rates should apply (for example, the adult rate for those aged 22 and over, the youth development rate and the rate for 16–17-year-olds).

The national minimum wage reflects a mix of economic and social justice considerations in its development and in its practice. As noted above, 'some groups of workers are more likely to be low paid than others' (LPC 1998: 35), with women, young workers, lone parents, homeworkers, **part-time workers** and those with disabilities particularly vulnerable. Indeed, women in low paid jobs are frequently seen as one of the main beneficiaries of the NMW (Machin 2011; Machin *et al.* 2002; Bain 1999; Metcalf 1999b, 2007; EOR 2010: 198) with the NMW credited with having contributed to a narrowing of the gender pay gap since its introduction.

The national minimum wage also reflects a broader shift in thinking about the role of legislation in affecting employer behaviour, one which became influential in shaping the agenda of minimum statutory rights in the early period of the Labour government. What has been termed 'new institutional economics' is described in Exhibit 9.4.

New social objectives

Our discussion of the national minimum wage provides an illustration of how legislation that provides a means of protecting the groups most 'at risk' in the labour market and most likely to find themselves in low paid jobs, also has wider social objectives that link to concerns about equality, social inclusion and participation in the wider society. To the discussion about low pay we could add social policy concerns regarding the 'living wage', particularly in London (see Exhibit 9.5), and emerging debates surrounding

EXHIBIT 9.4

New institutional economics and employment regulation

New institutional economics argues that the introduction of a minimum wage (and other forms of employment regulation) could have a positive impact on productivity and efficiency through a combination of 'shock effects' and 'efficiency wages' (Deakin and Wilkinson 1994; Sachdev and Wilkinson 1998). The 'shock' theory suggests that faced with rising costs firms will be 'shocked' into using resources more efficiently, so that rather than increasing costs, firms may find that they end up being more competitive as a result of the minimum wage. Similarly, the 'efficiency wage' theory suggests it may make sense to pay workers above the 'market rate', because such workers may be more motivated, work harder and more productively and value their jobs more highly if paid an efficiency wage (Davies 2004: 140). Taken together these institutional economics perspectives provide a set of options to policy makers that support the use of legislation to close off or significantly deter firms from pursuing a low wage, low skill employment strategy. Although the empirical evidence in support of shock and efficiency wage effects is mixed (Card and Kreuger 1995; Machin *et al.* 2002), they offer an important theoretical justification for minimum wage legislation and employment regulation generally and provide a counterpoint to traditional economic accounts of the operation of markets and the role of legal regulation.

EXHIBIT 9.5

The 'living wage'

The campaign. The concept of the 'living wage' arose from a campaign started in 2001 by London Citizens, an alliance of community groups, trade unions, universities, schools and religious organisations (**www.citizensuk.org**). Over the past decade it has achieved some success in improving pay levels in private sector organisations in the capital. It has, also, gained bipartisan political support from both Ken Livingston and Boris Johnson as Mayors of London; from Ed Milliband; and David Cameron, who described it as 'an idea whose time has come'. Those involved in the London campaign are advising counterparts in Cardiff, Glasgow, Leeds, Norwich and Oxford.

The rate. In the summer of 2011, the London rate was £8.30 per hour; and the rate outside London was £7.20. This is significantly above the national minimum wage at the time of £5.93 (see Table 9.2 below). This rate is entirely voluntary and cannot be enforced.

Corporate experience. Barclays Bank, for example, has benefited from significantly higher levels of staff retention as well as lower absenteeism and service quality since introducing a living wage in 2007. The bank's rate stands at £8.17 per hour and covers 700 cleaning, catering and mailroom staff. Most of the 115 organisations paying the living wage do so through their contracted suppliers of services.

An evaluation. Duncan Brown, Director, HR Business Development at the Institute for Employment Studies makes the following important point about the way in which implementing the 'living wage' would also help close the equal pay gap: 'Pay is generally falling in low-paid sectors which tend to be dominated by female staff, while high-paying male jobs are going up and up. The national minimum wage did more to close the equal pay gap than legislation, so implementing a living wage would help even further.'

Summarised from 'A Wage To Live With' by Anat Arkin, *People Management*, 24 February 2011 (**www.peoplemanagement. co.uk/features**).

Table 9.2 **Levels of the national minimum wage**

Date	National rate for 21 years and above	Rate for 18–20 year-olds	Rate for 16–17-year-olds (from October 2004)
April 1999	£3.60	£3.00	
June 2000	£3.60	£3.20	
October 2000	£3.70	£3.20	
October 2001	£4.10	£3.50	
October 2002	£4.20	£3.60	
October 2003	£4.50	£3.80	
October 2004	£4.85	£4.10	£3.00
October 2005	£5.05	£4.25	£3.00
October 2006	£5.35	£4.45	£3.30
October 2007	£5.52	£4.60	£3.40
October 2008	£5.73	£4.77	£3.53
October 2009	£5.80	£4.83	£3.57
October 2010	£5.93	£4.92*	£3.64
October 2011	£6.08	£4.98	£3.68

Source: Low Pay Commission

* Note that from 1 October 2010 the age at which workers become entitled to the adult rate fell from 22 to 21

widening inequalities in pay and rewards. As a recent review of the impact of recession on the UK labour market has argued:

> The level of inequality in the UK labour market, along several dimensions, is the outstanding area of concern.   (Gregg and Wadsworth 2011: 5)

Of particular recent interest has been the argument advanced by the writers of the influential *Spirit Level* thesis (Wilkinson and Pickett 2009). This is that countries with relatively high levels of income inequality suffer from greater social problems, higher crime rates and poorer health problems (Williams and Adam-Smith 2010), and that whilst we may be materially, substantially better off than we were 30 years ago, evidence suggests we are not necessarily happier (Layard 2005).

Within the European Union, the emergence of agendas relating to work–life balance and social exclusion have become increasingly important. Differences in employment rates, between age groups and ethnic background – reflecting different levels of engagement with the labour market and paid employment – have become central to concerns with social exclusion. Moreover, despite legislation, some groups appear to be particularly vulnerable to potential exploitation – for example migrant workers working in the 'informal economy' where non-compliance with aspects of legislation appears to be greatest (Croucher and White 2007).

The legal framework

In this section we will consider a number of legal issues under four broad areas:

1 the legal definition of 'wages' and 'pay';

2 the legal regulation of the pay transaction, covering the common law of contract and pay, information about pay, methods of payment, overpayment, pay deduction (including during **industrial action**), the use of fines as disciplinary action and the issue of shortages and losses in retail employment;

3 the principle of social justice influencing pay levels, particularly in respect of the national minimum wage;

4 equal pay.

▶ Definitions

Wages

It is important to ensure familiarity with the definitions of 'wages' and 'pay' under the various and separate pieces of legislation. Under the statutory national minimum wage legislation, a 'wage' is defined narrowly as a 'single hourly rate [that] the Secretary of State may from time to time prescribe' (ERA 1996, s 27(2)(e)). However, the wage protection provisions governing unauthorised deductions under the Employment Rights Act (1996, s 13) define 'wages' more broadly as any sum payable to a worker in connection with their employment (s 27). The term includes:

- 'any fee, bonus, commission, holiday pay or other emolument referable to his employment, whether payable under his contract or otherwise';
- statutory sick pay;
- statutory maternity pay;
- statutory paternity pay;
- statutory adoption pay;
- a guarantee payment (under ERA 1996, s 28);
- any payment for time off (under ERA 1996, Part VI and TULRCA 1992, s 169);
- remuneration on suspension on medical grounds (ERA 1996, s 64) and on suspension on maternity grounds (ERA 1996, s 68);
- any sum payable under reinstatement or re-engagement order (ERA 1996, s 113);
- any sum payable in pursuance of an order for the continuation of a contract of employment (ERA 1996, s 130; TULRCA 1992, s 164);
- remuneration under a protective award (TULRCA 1992, s 189);
- non-contractual bonus (ERA 1996 s 27(3)).

The items excluded from this definition of wages are loans, an advance on wages, expenses, pension, allowance or gratuity in connection with retirement or loss of office, redundancy payment and 'any payment to the worker otherwise than in his capacity as a "worker"' (ERA 1996, s 27(2)(e)).

Pay

In contrast, 'pay' under the terms of the Equality Act 2010 (Part 5), has been moulded by decisions of the ECJ interpreting Article 141 of the amended Treaty of Rome (now Art 157 of the Treaty on the Functioning of the European Union). These have defined pay as 'the ordinary basic or minimum wage or salary and any other consideration, whether in cash or in kind, which the worker receives directly or indirectly in respect of his employment from his employer' (Article 141). As discussed below in the section on equal pay, the relevant law defines pay broadly, encompassing not only basic pay but also redundancy pay, occupational pensions, incremental pay systems, sick pay and paid leave.

▶ Regulating the 'wage–work bargain' under common law

At the core of the employment relationship and employment contract is 'the express legal promise to perform work in return for a promise to pay wages'. Like other contracts this provides '**consideration**' (something of value by which one party obtains the promise of the other party). The employee promises to work for the employer and this agreement is underpinned by the employer's commitment to pay wages. In the absence of consideration, there can be no legally enforceable contract. Furthermore, the promise to perform work in return for wages also provides the distinctive mutuality of obligation necessary for any contract of employment to exist (Collins *et al.* 2005: 75) (see Chapter 2).

Although wages are the most common, they are only one form of consideration. There can be a valid contract of employment even if no wages are set. The consideration may be entirely based on commission or the chance to earn tips from customers. Furthermore, the employee might be on a remuneration system which is entirely output based. In these instances, there can be an implied term of the contract of employment that the employer will provide the employee with a reasonable amount of work.

Under contract law, in situations where an employee performs work required by the employer but the employer fails to pay agreed wages, the employee can in principle bring a claim for the missing wages. Equally, if an employee fails to perform the specified work, the employer does not have to pay wages. Thus under contract law the legal principle of 'no work, no pay' applies, although in practice this is affected by particular disputes arising out of the course of employment (Collins *et al.* 2005: 76). The impact of industrial action on this principle is considered in Exhibit 9.6.

As we noted earlier in this chapter, it is normal to make a distinction between time-service contracts, predicated on time-based payment systems and those based on pay linked to skill or performance. Time-service contracts offer remuneration on condition that an employee is available to perform work at the time prescribed by the employer and with pay calculated according to the amount of time labour power is made available. Performance-based contracts tend to make payment conditional on satisfactory completion of particular tasks or the achievement of specified targets (Deakin and Morris 2009: 267, Collins *et al.* 2005: 77). In general, the systems apportion risks of defective or non-completed work in different ways, with employers tending to bear risks under time-service contracts, and employees under performance-based contracts. The general shift in the UK towards contracts that contain a performance-related element has been in part a reflection of employer desire to shift risks associated with contractual performance on to the employee (Collins *et al.* 2005).

The distinction between these contractual arrangements is important. Performance-based and piecework contracts normally require the employer to pay wages only when the tasks have been satisfactorily completed – 'the right to payment depends upon the relevant work being finished' (Deakin and Morris: 2009: 267) – and although disputes may arise as to what constitutes satisfactory completion, the issues of when payment takes place and on what basis are clear-cut. The position under time-service contracts is potentially more complex. Here, the employee promises to be available and willing to work according to the employer's instructions for the hours laid down in the contract. In the case of time workers: 'No work meant no pay; the consideration for work is wages and the consideration for wages is work' (*Browning v Crumlin Valley Collieries Ltd* [1926] 1 KB 522, 528, in Deakin and Morris 2009: 267).

If an employer can show that an employee has failed to work his or her prescribed hours, or failed to perform the required tasks, then the employer may withhold payment of wages. Where there has been a **breach of contract** by the employee then an employer may seek **damages** to compensate for losses that result from the contractual breach. Similarly, if an employee comes to work but not for all the hours laid down in the contract, the employer can refuse any or all of the work offered and avoid any payment or the employer could accept the work offered and pay on a *pro rata* basis (see Collins *et al*. 2005: 77–8).

Industrial action

These issues have assumed particular importance where employees engage in industrial action short of a strike. In *Miles v Wakefield Borough Council* [1987] AC 539, HL a government registrar of births, deaths and marriages was contracted to work 37 hours per week including three hours on Saturday mornings. He refused to work Saturday mornings and his employer deducted $\frac{3}{37}$ ths of his salary to reflect this. Miles challenged the decision. The case, which went to the House of Lords, held that the employer could deduct this proportion of his salary but added that another option for the employer would have been to not pay any salary to Miles on the grounds that partial performance of the contract was actually no performance. This judgment was saying, in effect, that individuals could not pick and choose which parts of the contract they wished to perform. This was essentially the judgment in *Wiluszynski v LB Tower Hamlets* [1989] IRLR 259, where a local government officer refused, as part of ongoing industrial action, to deal with queries arising from councillors, despite performing all other duties, and where the Council concerned refused to pay any of his salary (see Exhibit 9.6 and *BT plc v Ticehurst* [1992] IRLR 219, CA). The judgment underlines the view that the contract of employment can be seen to be enforceable in its entirety, and although employers could choose to opt for part payment for part performance, legally they are entitled to refuse payment altogether. However, whether many employers would opt to enforce such a legal entitlement is debatable given the wider repercussions that could result from such a decision in terms of the climate and conduct of future employment relations.

Contract law, therefore, places an implied duty on employers to pay wages and not to make unauthorised deductions, but there are exceptions to these principles. Industrial action is one such example (ERA 1996, s 14(5)); another is 'poor workmanship' (*Sagar v Ridehalgh & Son Ltd* [1931] Ch 310, CA). In the case of time-service contracts, the employer would appear to be in a relatively strong position to argue that an employee has broken the wage–work bargain in the case of unsatisfactory performance. The argument resting on the implied obligation placed on the employee to perform the contract 'in good faith'.

EXHIBIT 9.6

Pay and industrial action

The ERA 1996 (s 14(5)) provides for appropriate deductions from wages in the case of industrial action. The key issues are:

- whether there has been a breach (fundamental or not) by the employee of the employment contract;
- whether the employee took part in the industrial action;
- in non-strike action, the extent of the 'partial performance' of the contract;
- whether or not the employer accepts or rejects this 'partial performance' of the contract;
- the appropriate amount of deduction for no work and for 'partial performance'.

In strike action, the principle of 'no work, no pay' usually prevails. In action short of a strike, the position is more complex. The Court of Appeal has set out several important principles about contractual obligations (*Wiluszynski v LB Tower Hamlets* [1989] IRLR 259):

- Employees are 'not entitled to pick and choose' what work they perform under the contract of employment.
- An employee cannot 'refuse to comply with his contract and demand payment.'
- An employer 'having told (an employee) that he was not required to attend for work (as a result of an employee's partial performance) and that if he did so it would be on a purely voluntary basis . . . could not, when he in fact attended, give him directions to work and at the same time not pay him.'
- An employer 'could not be expected to take action physically to prevent . . . staff who were refusing to comply with their contracts from entering [his] premises.'

Consideration of the character and volume of work is also an important factor. In the *Wiluszynski* case, although the refusal of local government officers to answer phone calls from councillors constituted a relatively small amount of their work in terms of time, it was work 'of considerable importance'.

See also *BT plc v Ticehurst* [1992] IRLR 219 where two managers who had participated in a short strike and withdrawn goodwill were sent home without pay because they refused to sign an undertaking to work in accordance with their contracts of employment. The court held that managers' contracts contained an implied term requiring them to further their employer's interests. In cases where partial performance has been accepted by an employer the issue has often been the appropriate calculation of remuneration for the part performance.

See *Royle v Trafford Borough Council* [1984] IRLR 184, HC, where a teacher refused to accept another five pupils into a class of 31 but continued to perform his other duties. He was ruled to have 'part-performed' the contract and the employer was entitled to make a deduction of $\frac{5}{36}$ ths of his salary over the relevant period of his refusal. The deduction made representing 'the notional value of the services rendered'.

However, 'in general, the power to refuse to pay full wages in response to the implied term to perform the contract in good faith will usually be subject to statutory controls over unlawful deductions' (Collins *et al.* 2005: 83) and it is to this that we now turn.

▶ Statutory regulation of unauthorised deductions

The Employment Rights Act 1996, provides a right for the 'worker' (not just the employee) 'not to suffer unauthorised deductions' (ERA 1996, s 13). A deduction is defined in the following way:

> Where the total amount of wages paid on any occasion by an employer to a worker employed by him is less than the total amount of the wages properly paid by him to the worker on that occasion (after deductions), the amount of the deficiency shall be treated . . . as a deduction made by the employer from the worker's wage.
>
> (ERA 1996, s 13(3))

An employer may only be able to make deductions from an individual's wages if the deduction is authorised in one of three ways:

1 *Act of Parliament*. As, for example, deduction of income tax and National Insurance contributions.

2 *Contract of employment*. A deduction may be authorised by a relevant provision of the contract of employment. Examples include the deduction of pension contributions, the possibility of a fine under relevant disciplinary procedures and the deduction of payments to meet cash shortfalls and stock deficiencies in retail import (see ERA 1996, ss 17–22, and discussion below).

3 *Individual consent*. A deduction may be authorised by the worker through his or her consent in writing to the deduction taking place. Common examples include agreement for trade union contributions deducted from salary, and monthly repayment of loans for annual travel passes.

In practice the courts have required strict conformity with the ERA 1996 (s 13) (Collins *et al.* 2005: 84) demanding that deductions should be part of a worker's contract and that the worker should have been adequately notified of its content.

▌ Cash shortages and deficiencies in retail employment

There is a statutory provision in respect of lawful deductions which is restricted to those engaged in 'retail employment'. This 'means employment (whether or not on a regular basis) involving the carrying out by the worker of retail transactions directly with members of the public or with fellow workers or other individuals in their personal capacities' or the collection by the worker of amounts payable in connection with retail transactions (ERA 1996, s 17(2)). A 'retail transaction' refers 'to the sale or supply of goods or the supply of services (including financial services)' (s 17(3)).

The origin of these specific provisions for retail employment lie in concerns relating to the operation of ss 1–2 of the Truck Act 1896 raised by studies (e.g. Goreily 1983), and latterly by case law (*Bristow v City Petroleum Ltd* [1988] ICR 165, HL). These pointed to the extent to which some retail workers worked under contracts of employment that permitted an employer to deduct the value of stock that went missing during a worker's shift. The issue was brought into sharp focus by the situation of attendants at self-service petrol stations who were having pay deducted when motorists who had filled up their cars with petrol then drove off without paying. Goreily (1983) cites two examples both involving attendants at self-service petrol stations. The first concerned an individual left 16 pence in their wage packet after their employer had made deductions for alleged till shortages; the second, an employee who had been deducted £250 in wages over a six-month period because of 'unexplained till shortages'. The *Bristow* case brought the issue to a head and to a wider audience, but ironically was decided after the Truck Act 1896, which made such deductions possible, had already been repealed and replaced by the Wages Act 1986 (the provisions of which are now contained in ERA 1996, s 17(2) and (3)).

The Employment Rights Act 1996 permits authorised deductions for those in retail employment but lays down a range of specific requirements:

- The deduction must be for cash shortage or stock deficiency.
- The worker must be notified in writing of the total liability (ERA 1996, s 20(1)(a)).
- The demand for payment must be in writing (ERA 1996, s 20(2)).
- That the limit for deduction of pay is set at 10 per cent of gross wages due on any given day (ERA 1996, s 18(1)).
- That deductions of up to 10 per cent of pay can be made on successive pay days.
- That the 10 per cent rule does not apply to the final pay day when the employer can demand full reimbursement.
- The rule can be applied for up to 12 months following the shortage being established (ERA 1996, s 20(2)).
- There must be a provision in the contract permitting the deduction (ERA, s. 13).

▶ Overpayment

An employer is not prevented from making deductions in respect of overpayment of wages or of expenses (ERA, s 14) in practice, several issues arise:

- Does the employee dispute whether or not there has been overpayment? If so, a complaint can be made in the county court.
- Was the overpayment a consequence of an error in law? If so, it is generally recoverable. However, if the employee knew of the error and it would be inequitable to allow the money to be retained, then recovery is possible.
- Was the overpayment the result of a mistake by the employer? The general position is that the employer can recover the money provided that he or she can prove that the mistake was one of fact (see *Kleinwort Benson Ltd* v *Lincoln City Council* [1998] 4 ER 513). However, the Court of Appeal in *Avon County Council* v *Howlett* [1983] IRLR 171 outlined a number of issues that need to be considered. The *Avon* case involved an employee who was on leave of absence through illness, and paid at the full rate for the whole of his period of illness, although under the contract should have received only half his normal pay after six months. When the mistake was discovered the employers tried to recover the overpayment (£1,007) which the employee had already spent. The Court of Appeal in *Avon* held that an employer's ability to recover overpayments is subject to a number of conditions:
  - whether or not the employer led the employee to believe that he or she was entitled to the money that was overpaid;
  - whether the employee genuinely believed that they were entitled to the money and spent it;
  - whether the overpayment was not the fault of the employee.

In the *Avon* case, the employee claimed first of all that the employer had made a representation of fact leading them to believe the money was theirs; second, that they changed their position in good faith, in reliance on the representation; and third, that the overpayment was not caused by their own fault (Deakin and Morris 2009: 273). These conditions were held to be satisfied and the employee retained the entire amount by which he had been overpaid.

FRISHCO SUPERMARKET CASE STUDY

Scenario 9.1

Has Erica been 'short changed'?

Erica, one of the checkout staff, gave a month's notice because she was moving away from south west London. She worked mostly on a day shift between 9.30am and 5pm. On her last day she received her final monthly pay slip. This indicated that she had a deduction of £50. Her hourly rate was £6.50. She normally worked for 35 hours per week and received £910 gross each four-week month.

Erica queried the underpayment of wages with **Mick**, one of the deputy store managers. He said that the company could make deductions for stock deficiencies and cash shortages. **She** told him that no one had discussed the matter with her; and that it was the first time in three years with the company that there has been a deduction in her pay. She denied being told a couple of weeks previously of the cash shortage in the till that she was working on. She pointed out that often she was not the only member of

the checkout staff to be on tills. He said that there was nothing he could do. The deduction was correct. **Tony**, the store manager, was not at work that day so **Erica** left without raising the issue with him. She felt very disgruntled. One of her colleagues, at her leaving party, suggested that she get advice from Citizens Advice.

Question

What further information might Citizens Advice need? What advice might they give Erica about her rights and remedies?

mylawchamber

Visit mylawchamber.co.uk/willey
to access sample HR documents to support this case study.

The National Minimum Wage Act 1998; NMW Regulations 1999

The passing of the National Minimum Wage Act 1998 and the National Minimum Wage Regulations 1999 mark a significant development in the statutory regulation of contractual terms. As one commentator suggested at the time: 'It is arguable that the most radical and far-reaching reform of employment rights made by the 1997 Labour government will prove to be the introduction of the national minimum wage' (Simpson 1999a: 2).

However, Simpson went on to point out that discussions about a minimum wage tended to be dominated by social and economic concerns, as mentioned above, with 'issues of legal policy either . . . completely ignored or relegated to the status of technical, and by implication, minor details' (1999a: 3). The Low Pay Commission was one element in turning a manifesto commitment into a workable policy. The other was to develop legislation that provided a comprehensive framework with maximum compliance, but which avoided any serious negative consequences for employment and the economy. The government attempted to do this through the National Minimum Wage Act 1998 which provides for minimum basic hourly rates of pay, with more detailed aspects of the regulation of the minimum wage left to the National Minimum Wage Regulations 1999.

The extent to which the legislation adequately addresses the issue of low pay remains contentious (see Simpson 1999a, 1999b). Here we detail the main elements of the legislation and the implications for HR practitioners.

▶ Coverage

The Act covers the whole of the United Kingdom, including Northern Ireland and relates specifically to those who work ordinarily in the UK and who are over the school leaving age. Unlike the common law terms regulating the contract of employment and therefore employees, the National Minimum Wage Act 1998 applies to **workers**, regardless of where they live or work, the sector in which they are employed or the company in which they work. A worker is here defined as an individual who works under either a contract of employment or 'any other contract . . . whereby the individual undertakes to do or perform personally any work or services for another party to the contract whose status is not by virtue of the contract that of a client or customer of any profession or business undertaking carried on by the individual' (NMWA 1998, s 54).

Under this definition the Act explicitly *includes*:

- part-time workers, temporary workers and agency workers (s 34);
- homeworkers (s 35);
- Crown employees (s 36); and
- there is a reserve power (s 41) that enables the Secretary of State to propose additional regulations extending the Act to a specific category of workers.

And *excludes* those who are:

- the genuinely self-employed (independent contractors);
- office holders (such as police officers);
- company directors who are not also employees of the company;
- serving members of the armed forces;
- volunteers and voluntary workers with charitable organisations;
- offshore workers;
- schoolchildren;
- those on work experience who are not trainees under contracts of employment;
- prisoners in custody, including those on remand (s 45); and
- sharefishermen and women (s 43).

National minimum wage rates

The Act provides for a facility for different rates to be determined for different age groups and according to whether a worker is a trainee (to address the concerns raised by some that paying younger workers adult rates may harm their employment prospects) which have been followed by policy makers. Furthermore, age discrimination law (now Equality Act 2010, sch 9, paras 11–12) specifically permits the use of age bands in determining the national minimum wage. Increases in the NMW are not automatically linked to prices or earnings and as we noted earlier, the government considers uprating the rates periodically in light of advice from the Low Pay Commission and the economic circumstances at the time. Changes are brought into force by regulations laid before Parliament (see Table 9.2).

In addition, in March 2010 the then Labour government, accepted the recommendation of the Low Pay Commission for a minimum apprentice rate. The rate of £2.50 came into effect in October 2010 and rose to £2.60 in October 2011.

▶ The national minimum wage and employers

The National Minimum Wage Act places a clear obligation on employers to pay workers remuneration which is not less than the NMW in any pay reference period (see below). An employer is here defined in relation to an employee or worker (s 54(5)) as: 'The person by whom the employee or worker is (or where the employment has ceased, was) employed'. This definition is the same as that found in the ERA 1996, s 230(4).

The National Minimum Wage Act 1998 also covers the position of 'superior employers' (s 48), common in parts of the construction industry. These are defined as:

> Where (a) the immediate employer of a worker is himself in the employment of some other person and (b) the worker is employed on the premises of that other person, that other person shall be deemed for the purposes of the Act to be the employer of the worker jointly with the immediate employer. (NMWA, s 48)

In the case of a worker being employed by different employers on separate but parallel contracts, then each employer is responsible for ensuring compliance with the NMWA.

▶ Calculating hourly rates

Once the rate for the NMW has been established the key issue becomes how the rate is then applied to different contractual arrangements governing pay and working time (Deakin and Morris 2009: 261). The main mechanism for this is via the provisions contained in the National Minimum Wage Regulations 1999 (implemented on 1 April 1999). These prescribe how to calculate a worker's hourly rate of remuneration for the purposes of determining compliance with the NMW. For some workers the calculation is relatively straightforward. However, difficulties arise where a person is paid by output or works on irregular patterns. The NMWA and the NMW Regulations address these issues through three core legal concepts (Simpson 1999a). These are the pay reference period, the total remuneration and working time.

- *Pay reference period* (s 1(4)). This is the time period for which the worker must be paid at least the national minimum wage. This is calculated by dividing the *total remuneration* by the total number of hours worked. The reference period is normally one month; or where a person has been employed for less time than this, that period.

- *The total remuneration*. This covers all 'payments that count towards the wage or remuneration of the worker, for the purposes of satisfying the employer's obligation to observe the minimum rate' (NMWR 1999, regs 30–37 in Deakin and Morris 2009: 262). Regulation 8 defines pay as payments paid to the worker in his capacity as a worker before any deductions are made; an amount that does not include 'any benefit in kind provided to the worker, whether or not a monetary value is attached to the benefit [reg 9], save an amount that can be deducted for living accommodation'.

The starting point in calculating total remuneration is the gross wage or salary (i.e. pay before deductions of income tax and national insurance contributions). As the LPC stated in its first report:

> In whatever way workers' pay is defined or whatever hours they work, only their 'standard' pay shall count towards the National Minimum Wage. Here incentive payments, such as commission, tips and gratuities paid via the payroll and piece rate, should count. In contrast, allowances and premium payments which are provided for non-standard work or hours (e.g. overtime and shiftwork premia) as well as all benefits with the exception of accommodation, should not count towards compliance. A worker should be entitled to the National Minimum Wage for each hour of actual working time, averaged over the worker's normal pay reference period up to a maximum of one month.
>
> (LPC 1998: 51)

In essence, total remuneration is calculated by adding up:

- all payments made by the employer during the pay reference period;
- any payments made in the period following or later reference periods relating to the 'earlier pay reference period';
- any amount permitted to be taken into account for the provision of living accommodation (accommodation is the only benefit-in-kind that is permitted to be used to count towards the national minimum wage). As of October 2011 the maximum an employer can count towards the calculation of the NMW is £4.73 per day or £33.11 per week.

When all these are taken into account the law provides for various deductions (regs 31–7). These include money paid during absences from work; payments by the employer as tips and gratuities from customers but not paid through the payroll (but see below).

Note that tips paid by credit card or cheque had been deemed to be the property of the employer and when an employer 'passed them on to the worker through the payroll they discharged part of their obligation to pay the national minimum wage' (*Nerva v RL&G Ltd* [1996] IRLR 461, Deakin and Morris 2009: 262). In practice, tips in areas such as hotels and restaurants are often pooled and then shared out between staff. This process is known as the 'tronc' system. The person responsible for the sharing out of tips, the 'troncmaster, frequently uses his or her own bank account for this purpose. As a result these are not payments made by the employer to the worker, because ownership of the money has passed to the troncmaster, and therefore were considered payments that could not count towards the national minimum wage (*Annabel's (Berkley Square) Ltd and Others v Commissioners for Her Majesty's Revenue and Customs* [2009] EWCA Civ 361).

Some restaurant chains took advantage of this and paid staff an hourly rate below the NMW, using revenue from service charges to top up wages to the legal minimum (Williams and Adam-Smith 2010: 256). However, following pressure from unions such as Unite and some national newspapers who pursued a 'fair tips' campaign, the National Minimum Wage Regulations were amended in October 2009 so that tips, gratuities, service charges and cover charges could no longer be used to make up national minimum wage pay. In addition, the government introduced a voluntary Code of Best Practice on Service Charges, Tips, Gratuities and Cover Charges (2009) (**www.bis.gov.uk**).

EXHIBIT 9.7

The NMW and working time: hourly rates

Wright v *Scottbridge Construction Ltd* [2001] **IRLR 589, EAT**

A nightwatchman. Mr Wright worked between 5pm and 7am seven nights a week. He received wages of £210 per week. He was expected to respond if intruders set off an alarm. Otherwise, he was allowed to read or watch television or sleep when on the premises. Sleeping facilities were provided. He claimed entitlement to the NMW for each hour that he was on the premises. The EAT ruled that where a worker was required to be on the employer's premises to carry out his duties over a specific number of hours, then, *all* the hours were eligible for the NMW. It noted a distinction in the situation where the employer allowed a worker time off to sleep (reg 15(1)).

South Manchester Abbeyfield Society v *Hopkins and Others* **UKEAT/0079/1**

Housekeepers in sheltered accommodation. A different approach was taken in relation to the circumstances of this case. The deputy housekeeper and another housekeeper, who worked shifts for a salary during the day, were required to spend time overnight 'on call'. They were provided with private accommodation to use. For the deputy this was fully serviced and both were provided with food. Reversing the employment tribunal decision, the EAT ruled that not all the hours spent 'on call' could be taken into account. A claim could only be made for hours that they were awake to undertake work.

Comment. The issue of what is relevant 'working time' under the National Minimum Wage Act is, obviously, important but it is, of course, dependent on the individual's contractual arrangements and the facts and circumstances of each case.

British Nursing Association v *Inland Revenue (National Minimum Wage Compliance Team)* [2002] **IRLR 480**

Nurse 'bank' administrator. The Court of Appeal, upholding decisions of the Employment Tribunal and EAT, determined the eligibility for the NMW of nurses who spent the night at home, answering phone calls requesting 'bank' nurses and allocating nurses. They were ruled to be working for the full shift and entitled to be paid the NMW for each hour of the shift. The Court of Appeal saw no difference between a worker in an office waiting for phone calls and a nurse in this case. To suggest that there were different rules for homeworkers was 'misconceived'.

- *Working time*. Under the regulations there are four different categories of employment types identified: time-work, salaried hours work, output work and unmeasured work.
  - *Time-work* relates to the specific number of hours that a person works to perform the work provided by the employer. See Exhibit 9.7 for cases in respect of hours that can be calculated as time working. The general position being that under time-work, time is included when a worker is required to be at the workplace, available for work, whether or not work is provided (Simpson 1999b).
  - *Salaried work* is where a worker is paid an annual salary for specific annual hours and paid in equal instalments (Deakin and Morris 2009: 263).
  - *Output work* relates to work in which payment is linked to the number of items or products produced and therefore an individual's performance. It can be calculated either by counting the number of hours spent on undertaking the work; and until

recently by reaching a 'fair estimate' agreement of the hours to be worked (regs 24–26). However since 2004 a system of 'fair piece rates' has operated whereby an employer must pay either the minimum rate for each hour actually worked, or put in place the 'mean hourly rate' for a particular rate or task (Deakin and Morris 2009: 263–4).

- *Unmeasured work* can be dealt with by paying at least the NMW for each hour worked; or by the employer and worker coming to a 'daily average' agreement to decide the number of hours the worker is likely to spend on work.

▶ Collective agreements and contractual terms

The Act makes it clear that 'any provision in any agreement (whether a worker's contract or not) is void in so far as it purports (a) to exclude or limit the operation of any provision of the Act or (b) to preclude a person from bringing proceedings under this Act before an Employment Tribunal' (NMWA 998, s 49(1)). The exceptions to this are in relation to conciliated complaints (under the Employment Tribunals Act 1996, s 18) and in respect of compromise agreements (ETA 1996, s 18(1)(dd); NMWA 1998, ss 3–11).

▶ Enforcement of the national minimum wage: civil proceedings

Significantly, the Act is enforceable through both civil action and criminal proceedings. It creates individual rights for workers and administrative enforcement via officers of Her Majesty's Revenue and Customs (HMRC); with criminal sanctions underpinning the obligation to pay at the NMW rate, the administrative obligations (such as record keeping) and, the officers' powers to enforce them.

Before discussing the enforcement measures in detail it is important to stress that the level of compliance with the NMW appears to be high (Metcalf 2007, Grimshaw and Rubery 2010) although it is recognised that problems persist in some areas with certain groups of workers (for example migrant workers in the informal economy). This has been reflected, since July 2005, in a policy of 'targeted enforcement', focusing publicity and enforcement on key low paying sectors in turn to 'tackle the minority of bad employers' (quote from Gerry Sutcliffe in BERR: National Minimum Wage Annual Report 2005–06: 29; see Exhibit 9.8). One illustration of this has been the establishment by HMRC in January 2010 of a Dynamic Response Team to work on the most high profile and complex National Minimum Wage cases, often concerning situations where employers are using migrant labour to undercut competitors by paying below the minimum wage.

In the next section we focus on the civil enforcement process which has three principal aspects: record-keeping, underpayment and the role of inspectors.

Record-keeping

There has been considerable emphasis placed in the Act on the need for an employer to keep records. Any employer of a worker who qualifies for the NMW has a duty to keep records, the purpose of which is to show that the worker is being remunerated at a rate at least equal to the NMW. Failure by an employer in these circumstances to maintain adequate records is a criminal offence.

A worker has the right to require their employer to produce 'relevant records' for establishing whether or not the worker has been paid at least the NMW; and to inspect and copy those records (s 10). There are three important provisions in the exercise of this right.

EXHIBIT 9.8

National minimum wage enforcement and effectiveness: key statistics

- 61,000 queries relating to the NMW were dealt with by the Pay and Work Rights helpline in 2005–06; 52,000 in 2006–07; and 34,700 in 2008–09 (replaced in September 2009 by new helpline).

- Between 1 April 1999 and April 2010, the helpline dealt with over 630,000 enquiries and over 32,000 complaints.

- The majority of complaints are from adult workers between the ages of 22 and 59.

- The sectors attracting complaints tend to remain consistent over time with the hospitality sector at the forefront of complaints followed by market services, hairdressing, retail and production/construction. The position of apprentices in hairdressing has been a particular focus of the attention of inspectors.

- The highest incidence of complaints now comes from the London area (with a significant rise since 2003–04), and the North West of England.

- In April 2009 there were estimated to be 242,000 jobs paying below the NMW and in that year over 1,700 cases of non-compliance were identified.

- Over 4,300 employers were subject to investigation in 2009–10 but there has been a steady fall in investigations from 5,500 in 2003–04 and 4,900 in 2006–07.

- Around £4.5 million in wage arrears was identified by compliance teams in 2009 (down from over £5 million in 2001–02).

- Around a third of part-time employees are still paid below £7 an hour (2010), indeed 3.5 million workers between the ages of 22 and retirement were paid less than £7 an hour (of which three-fifths worked part time) and a further 1.1 million aged 18–21 were paid less than £7 an hour (see **www.poverty.org.uk**).

- The LPC Report (2010) stated that in 2009 some 750,000 workers were being paid the adult rate of NMW (2010: xi). This represents around 3.2 per cent of all jobs held by adults.

- Workers for whom arrears had been identified rose in 2005–06 to 25,314 (from 14,057 in 2004–05) but fell back to £23,247 in 2008–09. The average arrears per worker fell from £340 to £193 over this period.

- There remain around one million low paid workers who benefit directly from the minimum wage and, since April 2009, the HMRC assisted 14,000 workers in re-couping over £3.5 million of wage arrears.

Source: Department for Business Enterprise and Regulatory Reform (BERR) *National Minimum Wage Annual Report 2005–06*, LPC Reports 2009, 2010, 2011.

1   The worker must have reasonable grounds for believing that he or she is being paid less than the NMW.

2   The worker must give the employer a written 'production notice' requesting the production of any relevant records relating to a particular period. This notice should also indicate whether the worker wishes to be accompanied.

3   The employer can determine where the inspection takes place, having given the worker 'reasonable' notice of the place and time. Having received the 'production notice', the employer must produce the relevant records within 14 days, although a later time can be agreed during those 14 days between the employer and the worker in question.

The failure of an employer to produce 'relevant records' at a specified place and time or to allow inspection and copying of them by the worker entitles them to complain to an employment tribunal within three months of the production deadline (s 11). Such a case may be heard by a tribunal chairperson sitting alone.

In the event that it is established that an employer prevented access to the 'relevant records' then, two remedies are available and must be granted:

- a declaration;
- an award to the worker of 80 times the national minimum wage in force when the award is made. This would be £486.40 with a NMW of £6.08. This award cannot be varied.

Underpayment

The second aspect to enforcement relates to underpayment. A worker still in employment who has been underpaid has a right to claim the difference between what has been paid (if anything) and the prevailing NMW. The worker may complain to an employment tribunal (under ERA 1996, s 23(1)(a) alleging unauthorised deduction of wages). Alternatively, the worker may bring an action for breach of contract in the county court. A former worker can allege breach of contract at an employment tribunal in relation to the termination of his or her employment. Workers who successfully complain to an employment tribunal are entitled to recover the amount of underpayment but no interest. Those who go to the county court are entitled to interest also.

The normal **burden of proof** is reversed in cases concerning national minimum wage underpayment before both employment tribunals and the county court. The assumption is therefore that a person was paid below the NMW and qualifies for the NMW. In the event that the claim or status of the applicant is disputed, it is for the employer to show that the worker was paid the NMW or is not a worker covered by the protection of the Act.

The Employment Act 2008 (s 8) changed the method by which arrears of the NMW are calculated for monies owed to a worker who has been paid less than the NMW. Arrears are calculated by reference to the current rate of NMW when the current rate is higher than that in force at the time of the underpayment. This change came into force on 6 April 2009. A worker is therefore repaid any underpayment of NMW by their employer at a higher rate if NMW has increased since the time of underpayment.

'Name and shame' policy

In January 2011, following advice from the Low Pay Commission, the government introduced a 'name and shame' policy to expose employers who 'show a wilful disregard for the National Minimum Wage' (Department of Business, Innovation and Skills 2011). In the aftermath of an investigation into a breach of NMW rules, HMRC may issue a Notice of Underpayment, if appropriate, giving details of the arrears that must be paid to the affected employees and the penalty for non-compliance. If any or all of the Notice is ignored by the employer, further steps can be taken in the courts or employment tribunals. This further action establishes a debt that is enforceable in law and various ways of enforcing payment can by pursued through the courts.

The objective of the 'naming and shaming' scheme is to raise awareness of NMW enforcement and deter employers who would otherwise be tempted to flout NMW law (**www.payroll-help.com**). Under the policy HMRC will only refer cases to the

Department of Business, Innovation and Skills where a Notice of Underpayment has been issued to the employer requiring the payment of arrears of the NMW to one or more workers or former workers. In the event of an employer's appeal against a Notice of Underpayment being partially accepted, but the criteria (including the financial criteria) still being met, the employer may still be named.

The role of inspectors

The third element of the enforcement process is the role of inspectors (NMWA 1998 s 13). The enforcement body for the NMW, Her Majesty's Revenue and Customs (HMRC), have powers vested in them, covering the following:

- *The serving of an enforcement notice on an employer* (NMWA 1998, s 19). This requires both the payment of the NMW to the worker or the worker concerned and any arrears. Such a notice is a warning to the employer. It is likely to have been preceded by informal discussions. The employer can appeal to an employment tribunal within four weeks of receiving the notice. Such an appeal can be heard by a tribunal chairperson sitting alone. A tribunal may rescind or amend an enforcement notice. To succeed in a complaint, an employer needs to show that, for example, the workers concerned were genuinely self-employed, or that the workers had not been underpaid or that the amount of the alleged arrears was wrong.

- *Making a complaint to an employment tribunal* (NMWA, s 20). If an employer fails to comply with an enforcement notice, HMRC can take civil proceedings to recover the money. The enforcement officer may, on behalf of the workers concerned, also complain to a tribunal that the employer has made an unauthorised deduction. The officer must be satisfied that the employer has a case to answer. This will involve scrutiny of the evidence and an interview with the employer, remembering that the burden of proof is on the employer to show wages were properly paid. Note though that a complaint by an enforcement officer does not take away the rights of individual workers to complain about non-compliance with an enforcement notice.

- *Taking other civil proceedings* (NMWA, s 20). This would be an alternative route through the county court.

- *The serving of a penalty notice* (NMWA, s 21). Where an employer fails to comply with an enforcement notice then a penalty notice may be served setting out the nature of the non-compliance and indicating a fine that must be paid within four weeks of receiving the penalty notice, the fine increasing the longer the employer takes to comply. The amount of the fine is twice the hourly rate of the NMW (currently in force) for each worker who is underpaid on each day of non-compliance. A penalty notice is not enforceable while the appeal process on an enforcement notice is still 'in train'. Furthermore, a penalty notice can itself be appealed against to an employment tribunal and so cannot be enforced until an employer's appeal has been decided upon. Again, a tribunal may rescind or amend such a notice.

- *Access to records* (NMWA, s 14). The NMWA (s 10) provides for employees to have access to records. In order to be effective in ensuring compliance the Act (ss 13–14) also provides for *administrative inspection* whereby inspectors are provided with certain powers in respect of an employer's records. They can require production of these. They have a right to require additional information to be produced and can enter an employer's premises 'at all reasonable times' in order to exercise any of these powers. The Employment Act 2008 (s 10) provides for an extension of these powers to allow HMRC inspectors not only to obtain NMW information from employers but also to physically remove this from the employer's premises for the purpose of copying.

Exhibit 9.9 details some successful cases involving the intervention of inspectors.

EXHIBIT 9.9

Some successful cases

A bar worker complained that they were not being paid NMW – £36 arrears identified and repaid. During the course of the review it was found that the hotel was using student labour, mainly from Spain. They were paid a small training allowance making them far cheaper to employ than locals. Once NMW legislation came into play, *arrears identified as owing to overseas workers totalled £27,247* (BERR: *NMW Annual Report 2003–04*).

In the south-east of England, a compliance officer investigated a failure to pay the NMW to an 81-year-old worker who was employed as a car polisher. The company was unaware of its liability to pay pensioners the NMW. *It promptly paid arrears of £3,000* (BERR: *NMW Annual Report 2001–02*).

In Belfast, a case involved workers working for a housing association and the interpretation of the phrase being 'on call'. Following extensive work, an agreement was reached with the employer and payment of £47,248 was made, split between three employees (BERR: *NMW Annual Report 2003–04*).

Following an anonymous complaint to the helpline, a hairdressing company was visited. It was found that a young lady with special needs had been employed since July 1999. She worked 36 hours per week and had been paid a training wage of £78 per week. The company thought they were doing her a favour by employing her. *Arrears of pay of £1,700 were paid and she was placed on the NMW rate* (BERR: *NMW Annual Report 2003–04*).

In a large company repairing and selling cars, a worker complained that he was an apprentice and not being paid the NMW after the appropriate exemptions ran out. HMRC investigated the employer who was found not to be operating the apprenticeship rules correctly. The result was a total of 13 apprentices who were due arrears under the Act. The total arrears due and paid were £10,676 (BERR: *NMW Annual Report 2003–04*).

One investigation involved an employer using workers from central and Eastern Europe. Foreign workers can find it difficult to open bank accounts and get accommodation without references and the employer had deducted £50 from each of the workers' pay for a letter confirming that they worked for the employer. Most deductions from pay reduce the amount of pay that counts for NMW purposes and as a result of this practice around 40 workers were underpaid an average of £78 for arrears covering a period of two years (the total arrears identified by HMRC were just over £3k) (BIS: *NMW Annual Report 2009–10*).

Source: NMW Annual Report, BERR, Department for Business Innovation & Skills, contains public sector information licensed under the Open Government Licence v.1.0.

❯ Enforcement of the national minimum wage: criminal action

Under the NMWA (s 31) an employer commits a criminal offence who:

- 'Refuses or wilfully neglects to remunerate the worker for any pay reference period at a rate which is at least equal to the national minimum wage' (NMWA, s 31(1)).

- Fails to keep records in accordance with any regulations made under NMWA, s 9.

- 'Knowingly causes or allows to be made' in a record 'any entry which he knows to be false in a material particular' (NMWA, s 31(3)).

- 'Produces or furnishes or knowingly causes or allows to be produced, any records or information which he knows to be false in a material particular' (NMWA, s 31(4)).
- 'Intentionally delays or obstructs an officer' seeking to enforce the Act (NMWA, s 31(5)).
- 'Refuses or neglects to answer any question, furnish any information or produce any document when required to do so' (NMWA, s 31(6)).

An employer's defence in respect of the refusal or wilful neglect to pay the NMW or of keeping required records is 'to prove that he exercised all due diligence and took all reasonable precautions to secure that the provisions of this Act and of any relevant regulations made under it, were complied with by himself and by any person under his control' (NMWA, s 31(8)).

The prosecutor in these cases can be HMRC enforcement officers; and all offences are triable without a jury. They can therefore be heard in a magistrates' court or a court of summary jurisdiction in Northern Ireland. In Scotland, proceedings are initiated by the procurator fiscal. Conviction is determined against the criminal **standard of proof** – that the evidence shows beyond reasonable doubt that the offence was committed. The maximum fine is set at level 5 (currently £5000), and the general view of government experts is that action in this area is likely to be rare. The Employment Act 2008 provides for additional criminal proceedings. Serious criminal offences relating to the NMW can now be heard in the Crown Court.

▶ Detriments and dismissal and the NMW

Under the NMWA (s 23), workers have the right not to be subject to any **detriment** because of the NMW or any reason related to its enforcement. The circumstances attracting such protection are where:

- A worker asserts in good faith his or her right to the NMW, right of access to records and right to recover the difference between what (if anything) the worker has been paid and the NMW.
- As a result of employees asserting their rights, the employer was prosecuted for an offence under the NMWA 1998.
- The individual worker qualifies, or will or might qualify for the NMW or for a particular, higher rate of the NMW.

Complaints about detrimental treatment have to be made to an employment tribunal within three months of an alleged detriment being complained of. Moreover, employees have the right not to be unfairly dismissed if the reason or principal reason for their dismissal (including selection for redundancy) is related to their entitlement to the NMW or its enforcement (ERA 1996a, s 104A). The NMWA thereby provides a further protection for unfair dismissal to employees but as elsewhere, not to workers in general. Where an employer is defending a tribunal claim, they must show the reason for any act or omission that may have taken place.

If a tribunal finds that detrimental treatment has taken place, it must make a declaration and may award compensation. If the complainant was not an employee and the detriment was the termination of the employment relationship, the amount of compensation awarded must not exceed the amount that the worker would have received if he or she had been an employee who had been unfairly dismissed. However, in any other case the amount of compensation awarded is not limited; it is the amount that the tribunal considers just and equitable.

Equal pay and the law

▶ The Equal Pay Act 1970 and European law

Legal measures to address questions of unequal pay – and by implication the gender pay gap – have largely rested upon the provisions of the Equal Pay Act 1970 (now Chapter 3 of the Equality Act 2010), the EU Equal Treatment Directive 2006 (which consolidates previous Directives) and Article 141 of the EC Treaty (now Article 157 of the Treaty of the Functioning of the European Union). The latter requires member states to:

> Ensure that the principle of equal pay for male and female workers for equal work or work of equal value is applied.   (Deakin and Morris 2009: 607)

In the UK, equal pay legislation marked the beginning of what became a comprehensive patchwork of legislation regulating discriminatory practices in the employment field (see Chapter 5) which is now consolidated under the Equality Act 2010. Under the 'equality of terms' provisions (Equality Act, Chapter 3) a woman undertaking equal work with that of a man in the same employment is entitled to equality in pay and other terms and conditions. The law regulates gender discrimination on the grounds of pay and other benefits, covering the disparate treatment between men and women in employment, irrespective of length of service. It *does not* encompass pay inequality on other grounds (for example, ethnic origin or disability). The legislation is supplemented by a statutory code of practice on Equal Pay (2010), drafted by the Equality and Human Rights Commission and approved by Parliament (**www.equalityhumanrights.com**).

▶ What is pay?

Although it is primarily intended to address pay equality issues for women the Act is available to any man or woman who believes they have been discriminated against in pay or other benefits. The claimant does not have to prove discrimination, but has to show that they have been less favourably treated in some contractual terms than a suitable comparator (actual but not hypothetical) of the opposite sex. The comparator may be a predecessor in the job. The Act effectively operates through the insertion of an equality clause into contracts of employment (Equality Act, s 66). In practice, this clause addresses any provision relating to what are now 'equality terms' and covers all aspects of the contractual pay and benefits package, including:

- basic pay;
- non-discretionary bonuses;
- overtime rates and allowances;
- performance-related benefits;
- severance and redundancy pay;
- access to pension schemes;

- benefits under pension schemes;

- hours of work;

- company cars;

- sick pay;

- fringe benefits such as travel allowances.

Case law, in particular the findings of the European Court of Justice, has given a wide construction to the concept of what is meant by pay (see Exhibit 9.10). Indeed, Article 157 of the Treaty on the Functioning of the European Union 2009 (previously Article 141 of the EC Treaty) which asserts the broad principle in EU law that men and women should receive equal pay for equal work, states that 'pay means the ordinary basic or minimum wage or salary and any other consideration, whether in cash or in kind, which the worker receives, directly or indirectly, in respect of his employment from his employer'.

It is important to emphasise that the effect of the equality clause is to secure equality in pay *and other benefits* for men and women employed on:

- like work (s 65.1(a));

- work rated as equivalent (s 65.1(b));

- work of equal value (s 65.1(c)).

Examples of what may constitute pay in equal pay cases is given in Exhibit 9.10.

EXHIBIT 9.10

What is 'pay'? Examples from equal pay case law

- *Sick pay* (*Rinner-Kunn* v *FWW Special-Gebaudereinigang GmbH and Co* [1989] IRLR 493, ECJ).

- *Bonuses* and other one-off *ad hoc* payments.

- Payments for retrospective performance or future loyalty (*Lewen* v *Denda* [2000] IRLR 67, ECJ).

- *Paid leave* (*Arbeiterwohlfahrt der Stadt Berlin* v *Botel* [1992] IRLR 423, ECJ).

- *Occupational pensions* (*Bilka-Kaufhaus GmbH* v *Weber von Hartz* [1986] IRLR 317, ECJ; *Barber* v *Guardian Royal Exchange Assurance Group* [1990] IRLR 240, CA).

- *Contributions* to pension schemes (*Lewen* v *Denda* [2000] IRLR 67, ECJ).

- *Severance pay* (*Kowalska* v *Freie and Hansestadt Hamburg* [1992] C-33/89, ECJ).

- *Travel concessions* (*Garland* v *British Rail Engineering Ltd* [1982] IRLR 111, ECJ).

- *Statutory and non-statutory redundancy pay* (*R* v *Secretary of State for Employment* ex parte *Seymour-Smith and Perez* [1999] IRLR 253, ECJ; *Rutherford and Another* v *Secretary of State for Trade and Industry* [2006] IRLR 551, HL; *Hammersmith and Queen Charlotte's Special Health Authority* v *Cato* [1987] IRLR 483, EAT).

- *Statutory unfair dismissal compensation* (*Seymour-Smith and Perez*; and *R* v *Secretary of State for Employment* ex parte *Equal Opportunities Commission* [1994] IRLR 176, HL).

Who is the comparator?

The Equality Act 2010, like the previous Equal Pay Act, requires an actual comparator (s 79). So, a woman has to compare herself with a man 'in the same employment'. This is defined as employment by the same employer or an associated employer; under a contract of service, apprenticeship or contract personally to carry out work or labour; at the same establishment, or at establishments in Great Britain (including the one at which the complainant works) and 'at which common terms and conditions of employment are observed either generally or for employees of the relevant classes' (s 79(4)).

It follows that a woman can claim equal pay with a man working:

- For the same employer at the same workplace.

- For the same employer but at a different workplace where common terms and conditions apply, for example at another branch of a store.

- For an associated employer; for example, at her employer's parent company.

- European law also allows a comparison to be made between employees who do not work for the same employer, but who are 'in the same establishment or service', particularly where the differences in pay are attributable to a 'common source' and there is a single body responsible for and capable of remedying the pay inequality. For example, where pay differences arise from a sector-wide collective agreement or from legislation.

Potential difficulties

The Act creates a number of potential areas of difficulty. In addition to the definitions of 'like work', 'work rated as equivalent' and 'work of equal value' (see below) the Act imposes a number of restrictions on those wishing to claim less favourable treatment.

The requirement under the Act for an individual claimant and for that claimant to provide an *actual* rather than a *hypothetical* comparator (although Article 157 does provide for the latter in cases of indirect 'pay' discrimination), limits considerably the scope of the legislation (Fredman 2008, Mongahan 2007: 55). But as one of the major causes of the gender pay gap is women's concentration in predominantly female workplaces (McGolgan 2005: 435) the requirement that the comparator must be one in the same employment and where 'common terms and conditions . . . are observed' for the employees concerned (s 79.4) restricts this still further (Fredman 2008). As Fredman (2002) makes clear:

> One of the chief causes of low pay among women is that so many women work in segregated workplaces, either doing 'women's work' or in the lower grades of mixed professions. A woman working in a segregated workplace is unlikely to find a male comparator doing like work or work of equal value.   (Fredman 2002: 96)

One illustration of the these limitations can be seen in the contrast of two decisions in Exhibit 9.11.

Mindful of these concerns, the Equality Act (s 71) pemits a claim for the tort of direct sex discrimination to be brought where a term relates to pay but an equality clause has no effect (Hepple 2011: 99). That is, if there are 'no comparators in the employer's establishment doing the work the employee could now bring a claim for the tort of direct sex discrimination *which allows a comparison with a hypothetical comparator*' (*ibid.*: 99, italics added). Hepple uses the example of women engaged in work that has been contracted out to an undertaking paying them less than they were receiving from their previous employer. Here there is no breach of the equality clause because the women are 'not in the same employment' but the employer's actions could constitute a tort of direct sex discrimination.

EXHIBIT 9.11

Two judgments on equal pay

Ratcliffe and Others v *North Yorkshire County Council* [1995] **ICR 833, HL**

The case involved women working as 'dinner ladies' for a local authority. Under pressure to cut costs the authority put the provision of school dinners out to tender as part of a Compulsory Competitive Tendering exercise. To try and retain the contract the Council cut labour costs of the DSO (Direct Service Operator, running the school dinner service within the Council at the time) by 25 per cent, involving a cut in pay for those staff. However, other staff in the Council working for other DSOs had not had their pay cut. At the time the rates of pay had been negotiated through a collective agreement negotiated by the National Joint Council covering local government workers (and prior to claim the jobs performed by claimants had been 'rated as equivalent' in value to those of their comparators).

The women took their case to a tribunal arguing that others employed by the same employer and previously on 'common terms and conditions' were now being discriminated against on the grounds of sex. The employer argued that it had to cut pay in order to win the contract and provided a defence of 'market forces' as a material factor in the decision (EqPA, s 3). The women won their case but did so because they were still employed by the DSO, which, like their comparator's DSO (which predominantly employed men), was still part of the local authority.

What is clear from the *Ratcliffe* case is that women whose work had been contracted out would find it much more difficult to pursue such a claim (see *Lawrence* below). First, there would no longer be 'the same employer' and they would only be able to use men employed by the same contractor as their comparator. More fundamentally, the decision in *Ratcliffe* could have had the perverse effect of substantially disadvantaging many DSOs engaged in a CCT exercise against outside contractors who were seeking to retain that work in-house, particularly where (as is often the case) those DSOs employed large numbers of women in areas such as cleaning, caring, and catering.

Lawrence v *Regent Office Care* [2002] **IRLR 822, ECJ (paraphrased)**

This was a case also brought by women who had previously been employed by North Yorkshire Council, but were now employed by an outside contractor, Regent Office Care, as their jobs had been transferred to the private sector. All ended up with less favourable terms and conditions than they had 'enjoyed' with the Council. They argued that they should still be able to compare themselves with men employed by the Council whose jobs, prior to contracting-out, had been rated as equivalent to those of the complainants. Because they no longer worked for the 'same employer' they could not rely on the provisions of the Equal Pay Act, and sought to use the broader concept of 'employer' contained in Article 141 (which applies to 'work carried out in the same establishment or service, whether private or public'). However, the EAT decision held that the rights conferred by Article 141 were not wide enough to permit employees of one company to compare themselves with work undertaken by a comparator working for another company, even where at one point, those employees and their comparators had worked for the same employer. On appeal, the Court of Appeal referred the matter to the European Court of Justice. This ruled that where the differences in pay between men and women workers (performing like work or work of equal value) cannot be attributed to a single source, this does not fall under the Treaty Article 141 (now 157). No single body is responsible for the inequality and cannot implement equal treatment. See *Allonby* v *Accrington and Rossendale College and Others* (C-256/01) [2004] ECR I-873; [2004] IRLR 224.

Source: ICLR.

The decisions in the *Ratcliffe* and *Lawrence* cases are important in light of the significant role of contracting out of work in many organisations and the potential afforded by the Equality Act (s 71). To these should also be added the declining importance both of collective bargaining in the UK, and of individuals working under 'common terms and conditions'. They also raise the potential of employers creating separate independent employing organisations as a way of avoiding compliance with the law, something that arguably arose most clearly in the case of *Allonby v Accrington and Rossendale College and Others* (C-256/01) [2004] ECR I-873; [2004] IRLR 224 (see Exhibit 9.12).

EXHIBIT 9.12

The *Allonby* case

Allonby v Accrington and Rossendale College and Others (C256/01) ECR I-873; [2004] IRLR 224

The claimant was working as a part-time teacher for Accrington and Rossendale College and with a number of colleagues was dismissed and then offered a contract to carry out the same work on a self-employed basis through an outside agency. She was now working on terms and conditions that were 'less favourable' than those she had enjoyed when working directly for the college, and lodged a number of claims under the Equal Pay and Sex Discrimination Acts. Her equal pay claim relied on a male comparator still employed full time as a lecturer in the college.

The equal pay case suffered in similar ways to that brought in *Lawrence*. She was now employed by a separate employing organisation, so although Allonby worked alongside her male comparator, they were not working for the same employer, nor were they associated employees. Furthermore, their terms and conditions were not common and did not come from a single source. The case went to the ECJ, which found against Allonby.

Although Allonby was successful in other aspects of her claims, notably that her exclusion from the pension scheme constituted indirect sex discrimination, as Fredman (2004) has argued, the judgment in *Allonby* concerning equal pay raises important questions about the effectiveness of equal pay laws in the face of employers 'who deliberately fragment the supervisory and remunerative dimensions of the managerial function'.

The bases for equal pay claims

- 'like work';
- 'work rated as equivalent';
- 'work of equal value'.

'Like work'

A woman is to be regarded as employed on 'like work' (s 65(2)) with men in the same employment 'if, but only if, her work and theirs is of the same or a broadly similar nature and the difference (if any) between the things she does and the things they do are not of practical importance in relation to terms and conditions of employment (*Shields v E. Coomes (Holdings) Ltd* [1978] ICR 1159, CA). In comparing her work and theirs, 'regard shall be had to the frequency or otherwise with which any such differences occur in practice as well as to the nature and extent of the differences' (s 65(3)). Further clarification has been provided by the EAT decision in *Capper Pass Ltd v Lawton* [1977]

QB 852, EAT where the judgment indicated that 'like work' should involve a general consideration of similarities and differences and that this should mean no account is taken of 'trivial differences not likely in the real world to be reflected in terms and conditions of employment' (McColgan 2005: 427).

'Work rated as equivalent'

This relates to circumstances where a woman is employed on work rated as equivalent with that of a man in the same employment. This could mean that the jobs undertaken by a woman and her comparator are very different in nature but that her job and his job have been given an equal value, in terms of the demands made on them under various headings (e.g. effort, skill, discretion) by a job evaluation study (s 65(4)). Such a study must have covered the jobs done by all or any of the employees in an undertaking or group of undertakings. Although there is a range of job evaluation techniques available to organisations (e.g. ranking, points method), non-analytical methods that provide greater scope for subjective judgements have been considered invalid by the courts (*Bromley* v *H & J Quick Ltd* [1988] ICR 623, CA). Job evaluation needs to be 'analytical', 'thorough in analysis and capable of impartial application' (*Eaton Ltd* v *Nuttall* [1977] ICR 272, EAT). In effect, job demands must, as far as possible, be subject to objective assessment; broken down by category (skill, effort, training); analysed; and then evaluated. (Exhibit 9.13 details the variety of schemes in more depth.)

Perhaps surprisingly in view of the significance of the issue of equal pay there is no legal requirement for an employer to operate a job evaluation scheme and many, particularly smaller organisations, do not. A question arises as to what happens in cases where an individual is claiming unequal pay but no satisfactory basis for comparison exists. The third of the grounds for claiming pay discrimination is the mechanism the law provides to address such claims, that of 'work of equal value'.

EXHIBIT 9.13

Job evaluation: analytical and non-analytical

Job evaluation is a set of processes designed to establish pay structures within an organisation and is a systematic process designed to establish the relative worth of jobs within a single work organisation. What job evaluation attempts to do is to provide some internal equity, by organising jobs into a hierarchy based on an evaluation of those jobs in terms of their skill, levels of responsibility, experience required and contribution to the organisation. This raises important questions of:

1 how the jobs are evaluated, in terms of the criteria used;

2 the choice of relevant factors in evaluating jobs;

3 who is doing the evaluation;

4 the broader issue of objectivity of the process and its overall validity.

In general, four methods are normally used in job evaluation.

Non-analytical

(a) Ranking method – ranking of jobs based on a subjective evaluation of value.

(b) Job-grading method – jobs are classified and then placed in grades or hierarchy.

Analytical

(c) Factor-comparison – evaluates jobs on the basis of a range of factors; these factors are weighted and benchmark jobs created from the factors that are then assigned a monetary value.

(d) Points method – works in a similar way to (c) but uses points to assign to each factor. The points are added up and a hierarchy of jobs produced which then equate to pay. The most commonly used job evaluation method.

In effect, job evaluation assigns pay to the job and, in theory, provides a pay structure that is objective and defensible from the employer's perspective. In practice, no scheme is entirely free from subjective bias, but (c) and (d) are more robust than (a) and (b). It also should be remembered that despite the advantages of job evaluation, many organisations (particularly small, private-sector companies) do not operate such schemes.

A 2002 e-reward report of 236 organisations revealed that less than half operated a job evaluation scheme and of these, 68 per cent of public and voluntary sector organisations operated one, in contrast to less than 40 per cent of private-sector employers. However the Workplace Employment Relations Survey 2004, covering a broader sample of workplaces, found that only one in five operated such schemes, although this rose to two in five in the public sector, and where trade unions were recognised. Of the schemes that were in operation, 70 per cent of those in the public sector and just over half in the private sector were points-based schemes. While the e-reward report implied that just over a third of its sample of employers was operating a job evaluation scheme that could be defended on equal pay grounds (**www.e-reward.co.uk** 2003), WERS 2004 suggests that this may be true of only one in seven workplaces (Kersley *et al.* 2006).

'Work of equal value'

This amendment to the law on equal pay was enacted in 1983. A claimant who is not employed on 'like work' or 'work rated as equivalent' can claim equal pay with a comparator in the same employment provided their work is of 'equal value' to that of the person they have specified as their comparator with 'reference to factors such as effort, skill and decision-making' (s 65(6)). In the absence of an existing evaluation system covering both jobs, 'equal value' is assessed either by an *independent expert* appointed by the employment tribunal or by the tribunal itself. The assessment of jobs involves an examination and comparison of the jobs in question in isolation, using whatever factors the expert or tribunal consider to be most relevant in the jobs. If the jobs are assessed as being of equal value in this context then, assuming the man is being paid more than the woman, discrimination on the grounds of sex is defined as having taken place. An early and particularly significant equal value case was that of *Hayward* v *Cammell Laird Shipbuilders Ltd (No. 2)* [1988] AC 894 (Exhibit 9.14).

Since the decision in *Hayward* the equal value provision has provided opportunities for some groups to make a serious challenge to entrenched pay discrimination. The case of *British Coal Corporation* v *Smith and Others* [1996] ICR 515 HL is notable not just for its legal significance but also for the time it took to resolve – 11 years! Similarly, the case brought in 1990 by the trade union USDAW against Sainsbury's sought to secure equal value for check-out operators with their mainly male warehouse comparators. The case was settled out of court and resulted in the introduction of a job evaluation exercise that led to a 20 per cent increase in rates of pay to the check-out operators. A number of schemes followed in other major retail outlets. More recently, the job evaluation scheme in the NHS *Agenda for Change* has resulted in major changes to pay for many

EXHIBIT 9.14

Equal value

Hayward v *Cammell Laird Shipbuilders Ltd (No. 2)* [1988] AC 894

The *Hayward* case turned on the question of whether pay should be 'equal' in overall terms (taking into account benefits such as free meals, etc.) or at the level of each element of the pay package (McColgan 1997: 148). Hayward was a canteen worker who presented an equal pay claim naming a painter, a joiner and an insulation engineer as her comparators. Her employer argued that equal pay in 'overall terms' was what mattered and that although Hayward's basic pay and overtime rates were lower than her comparators, her sickness benefits and meal breaks were more favourable than theirs, and that taken as a whole 'her contractual terms were no less favourable to her than their's were to them' (McColgan 2005: 425). The case went to the employment tribunal, the EAT and ultimately to the House of Lords. The earlier decisions of the tribunal and EAT rejected her claim, reflecting a concern that a woman who succeeds in claiming equal value with a man might trigger claims by men in different jobs, 'thereby ratcheting up the whole payment structure' (Fredman 1997: 245). Indeed, the EAT argued that agreeing to the Hayward claim 'would necessarily involve leap-frogging, [and] would . . . result in widespread chaos in industry and inflict grave damage on commerce' (transcript of EAT judgment [1986] IRLR 287, 291).

However, the House of Lords unanimously decided that s 1(2) of the EqPA meant what it said. That is, in the words of Lord Goff, if 'one looks at the man's contract and at the woman's contract, and if one finds in the man's contract a term benefiting him that is not included in the woman's contract, *then that term is included in hers'* (italics added, quoted in McColgan 2005: 425). In other words, each contractual term must be treated separately, it is not sufficient to compare total pay and so 'the employer is not entitled to argue that inequality with regard to one term is outweighed by an advantage elsewhere in the terms and conditions of the complainant and his or her comparator' (Deakin and Morris 2009: 631). It follows that differences in rates of pay cannot be offset by differences in working hours or in fringe benefits.

staff as has the restructuring of pay schemes in local authorities following the conclusion of a single status agreement in 1997. The situation in local authorities has proved particularly contentious, forcing a major restructuring of pay that benefited large numbers of staff, but which also precipitated a spate of equal value claims that caused considerable financial embarrassment for a number of local authorities (see Exhibit 9.15).

Despite very considerable advances resulting from the equal value route (s 1(2)(c)), it has not been without its problems. Prior to changes in 1996, the procedure for dealing with claims on equal value grounds provided for potentially long delays in resolving such cases both before and once they had reached a tribunal (see *British Coal* case above) and it has not been unusual for equal value cases to take over five years to resolve. The expense of such a complaint is often a sufficient deterrent to individuals, particularly in the absence of unions willing to support them.

Some acknowledgement of the problems experienced by those trying to pursue equal value claims came with the Employment Tribunals (Constitution and Rules of Procedure) (Amendment) Regulations 2004, which provided for the appointment of tribunal panels with specialist equal value expertise. It has attempted to make processes more 'user friendly' and has imposed time limits at various stages (McColgan 2005: 432). In the annex to the regulations, it states that equal value claims using independent experts should take no longer than 37 weeks to determine; those not involving these, no more than 25 weeks.

EXHIBIT 9.15

Equal value in local authorities

In 1997 local authorities in England signed a Single Status Agreement that required them to review pay structures 'using a job evaluation process and then develop their own local pay grades fixed to points on a national pay spine' with a view to ensuring equality proofing of pay structures (*Equal Opportunities Review* (2006): 16). This was originally to have been achieved by 2000 but progress was slow and it was only following the 2004–06 pay deal that the National Joint Council agreed that all local authorities would enter into negotiations 'with a view to reaching agreement on new local pay structures by April 2006, and complete and implement local pay reviews by 31 March 2007' (*ibid.*: 16). However, by the end of 2006, despite the 2004 NJC agreement requiring all local authorities to have completed and implemented equal pay reviews (Local Government Employers 2004), around two-thirds of councils still had not implemented a new pay structure prior to the 31 March 2007 deadline.

Achieving agreements locally has proved difficult in many authorities and has generated a considerable amount of litigation. A survey by local authority employers in 2009 estimated that almost 30 per cent of councils in England and Wales faced tribunal cases over equal pay issues arising from the review of pay structures. UNISON has been particularly active in supporting claims, often multiple claims on behalf of members in equal pay cases; as have 'no-win, no-fee' lawyers. Where agreement and implementation has taken place, the costs of this re-alignment of pay structures has been considerable because of back pay and pay protection issues. Some local authorities have had to find as much as six years' back pay for women who have experienced pay discrimination (*Redcar and Cleveland Borough Council v Bainbridge* [2007] IRLR 984, CA; UNISON 2007; LGE 2008, *Barker & Others v Birmingham City Council* ET/1305819/2006). The Local Government Employers estimated that local authorities might require £5 billion to cover back-pay liability; and some authorities have found that the implementation of new pay structures has led to a substantial worsening of their employment relations. In Birmingham, the City Council issued redundancy notices to 40,000 staff in September 2007; and acknowledged that new pay structures could mean lower pay for up to 7,000 staff, a development that prompted a strike of refuse collectors in December 2010.

Birmingham City Council has been the focus of one of the largest equal pay cases ever brought. In seeking to apply the single status agreement, the Council concluded a revised pay grading structure only in 2008. The new structure prompted a strike by 3,000 Council staff with UNISON claiming that it left many women in traditionally female dominated roles, underpaid. A resulting legal case was brought against the Council, and heard at the Employment Tribunal in November 2009. The case, *Barker & Others v Birmingham City Council* [2010] ET/1305819/2006, involved 4,000 Council workers and the women who brought it were employed on some 49 different jobs, including cleaners and school crossing attendants. They complained that despite being on the same pay grades they had been excluded from bonuses available to other jobs predominantly undertaken by men. These bonuses were worth up to 160 per cent of the latter's basic pay and the women sought compensation backdated to 2000. One example given concerned refuse collectors, where staff could receive substantial bonuses leading to earnings four times higher than that of women on the same pay grade. The Council did not dispute the bonus issue but claimed that the bonuses were 'a genuine reward for productivity and vital to reducing absenteeism'. The women won their case at the tribunal which meant they would qualify for up to six years' back pay with a cost to the Council estimated to be in excess of £400 million. At the time of writing (May 2011) the Council are considering a second appeal against the decision. Similar high profile cases have also affected councils in Bury (2010) and Sunderland (2011).

Furthermore, the influence of 'no-win, no-fee' lawyers has severely constrained unions in their role in assisting the moves to single status and has made them reluctant to negotiate local agreements (see *Allen v GMB* [2008] IRLR 690, CA). According to the Local Government Employers, the overall impact of introducing equality-based pay structures could mean as much as a permanent 5 per cent increase in costs for local authorities (LGE 2006).

❭ Indirect pay discrimination

It should be noted that unequal pay can arise as a result of either direct or indirect discrimination. As we discussed in the context section, unlawful pay discrimination occurs largely because women and men tend to do different jobs or to have different work patterns. That is, it is the nature of women's work, which has traditionally been undervalued, and how that work is undertaken, frequently on a part-time basis rather than through a male pattern of full-time permanent employment, that is critical to the discussion of unequal pay and the gender pay gap. These are factors that the Equality Act still appears ill-equipped to tackle, and where claimants look to Article 157 to combat such deficiencies.

❭ Employers' defences

Where a woman compares herself with a man (Equality Act 2010, s 65), and is found to be discriminated against by being paid less for 'like work', 'work rated as equivalent' or 'work of equal value' it may still be possible for the employer (s 69) to show that any variation between the woman's contract and the man's contract is genuinely the result of a *material factor* which is not the difference of sex **and** which is a proportionate means of achieving a legitimate aim (s 69(1)(a),(b)). That is, the equality clause will not operate if there are good reasons – encouraging loyalty, and other sound business reasons – which are 'not the difference of sex' (s 69(1)(a)) why a comparator man was paid more than a woman. As the relevant minister argued at the time

> The material factor defence to an equal pay claim should be able to succeed where the employer shows that the factor on which he relies to explain the difference in pay is real and not a sham; that it is not directly discriminatory, and if the complainant brings forward evidence that is indirectly discriminatory, the employer can show that reliance on the factor is nevertheless *justified and proportionate*.
>
> (Baroness Royal cited in Hepple (2011), italics added)

To qualify as a material factor (s 69.6) that which is relied upon may be a 'material difference', otherwise known as 'difference of practical importance', and where the onus is upon the employer to show the material factor defence applies. In the early years of the Equal Pay Act the 'material difference' defence had been assumed to be narrowly confined to factors 'personal' to the workers concerned (Collins *et al.* 2005). In *Rainey v Greater Glasgow Health Board* [1987] 1 AC 224, HL, it was held that such personal factors related to 'much longer length of service . . . superior skill or qualifications . . . bigger output or productivity . . . or owing to downgrading, in a protected pay category ('red circling') or to other factors personal to the worker in doing his job' (see Deakin and Morris 2009: 624). Subsequent cases have continued to permit a market forces defence as well as the use of 'separate collective bargaining structures', and 'administrative reasons', all of which encompass 'extrinsic factors' beyond the 'personal' equation.

However, the ECJ in particular has sought to limit the breadth of such defences. For example, in the *Enderby* case, the EAT accepted that collective bargaining arrangements could be a defence to an equal value claim, but when the case went to the ECJ it was held that:

It is not sufficient for an employer, faced with an equal pay claim, to explain the difference by reference to some factor, such as market forces, different pay structures or collective agreements . . . He or she must go further and establish . . . that the factor is neutral as regards sex, or, to the extent that it serves to disadvantage either sex, that reliance upon it is nevertheless justified, consistent with European law.

(*Enderby* v *Frenchay Health Authority* [1993] IRLR 591, ECJ)

Cases of indirect discrimination in respect of equal pay have required further justification from employers. The House of Lords decision (*Rainey* v *Greater Glasgow Health Board* [1987] 1 AC 224) that in cases of indirect discrimination an employer must show 'objectively justified grounds' for the difference in pay has been further extended by the decision in *Allonby* that in cases of indirect discrimination it has not been necessary to identify an actual comparator, merely to show that 'a much higher percentage of women than men' would be 'disadvantaged by the practice at issue' (Monaghan 2007: 431). More recently, the ECJ decision in *Cadman* v *HSE* [2006] IRLR 969 indicated that where length of service is used to determine pay, and this has a disparate impact between men and women, the employer should be required to show (1) that the use of the criterion takes into account business needs, and (2) that its use is proportionate, so as not to minimise its disadvantageous impact on women.

In summary, a factor which is 'not the difference of sex' (s 1(3)) must be one which is neither directly discriminatory nor, in the absence of adequate justification, indirectly discriminatory. Significantly, the ECJ added in *Danfoss* that where an undertaking operates a pay system 'wholly lacking in transparency, it is for the employer to establish that the pay system is not discriminatory, if a female worker establishes, in relation to a relatively large number of employees, that the average pay of women is less than that of men'. This decision has had a major impact on litigation in the equal pay area and one that has potentially significant implications for a number of private sector employers where pay systems are often less transparent than in the public sector.

The defence used by *Birmingham City Council* in Exhibit 9.15 is interesting in this regard. The Council argued that the bonus for a large number of council workers could be justified, effectively using a business case 'material difference' defence of its actions based on the claim that the bonus ensured attendance, quality of performance, productivity and completion of work on time (EOR 201/2011). In its judgment, the ET argued that the reasons given to justify the bonus scheme were in fact a 'sham', tainted by sex, so that the aims behind the use of bonuses for the jobs in question were not legitimate and the issue of whether this was a proportionate response did not arise.

▶ Pay transparency

In relation to pay transparency it is significant that in framing the Equality Act the Labour government came under considerable pressure to use the Act to compel employers to undertake regular pay audits as a means of giving greater exposure to the gender pay issue. Despite this pressure the government opted for 'greater dialogue and transparency in relation to pay' (Hepple 2011: 106). However, the Act (s 78) enables a minister 'to develop regulations to require private and voluntary sector employers with at least 250 employees in Britain to publish information relating to differences in pay between male and female employees' (Hepple: 107) with any regulations becoming effective after April 2013. In December 2010, the Conservative–Liberal Democrat government announced that this would not be required, preferring to tackle the gender pay gap by voluntary rather than statutory means and checking annually what progress is being made (**www.equalities.gov.uk**).

▶ Employment tribunal claims

Such claims must be made by individuals although, very frequently, the unequal pay complained of covers the remuneration of sometimes quite sizeable workgroups. As part of the complaint process, a complainant may use a questionnaire provided for under the Equality Act 2010 (s 138). Furthermore, the employment tribunal will take into account the provisions of the Code of Practice on Equal Pay (2010).

▶ Remedies in equal pay cases

The general position in equal pay cases (Equality Act, ss 127–129) is that where a tribunal finds in favour of a claimant, it makes an order requiring that the employer observes the equality clause in the contract of employment. The immediate effect is that a woman's pay is equalised with that of her male comparator (or vice versa). Where unequal pay has persisted for some time, it is also usual for the tribunal to order that back pay or payments in arrears are made to compensate for the period in which the pay was unequal. The sums of money involved can be considerable, and a recent case where a woman successfully compared herself with her male successor (*Bodman v API* (2006) ET/2403504/05) received £25,000 in compensation.

Where multiple claims are pursued, the costs to the employer could potentially run into millions of pounds (see Exhibit 9.15). In the case of back pay and payment in arrears it is for the claimant to show how long they 'have unlawfully been paid at a lower rate than [their] comparator', and since 1996 these payments have included interest. Furthermore, following the ECJ decision in *Levez v TH Jennings (Harlow Pools) Ltd* [1999] IRLR 36, up to six years' payments in arrears may be claimed. In general, claims tend to be relatively straightforward when they concern pay, but compensation is more complex when claims concern other benefits such as holiday entitlements or staff discounts, and in such cases tribunals must make a judgment about the level of compensation deemed appropriate although few clear guidelines exist on this point.

FRISHCO SUPERMARKET CASE STUDY

Scenario 9.2

Unequal pay?

The warehouse staff, who are all male, work on a shift rota that covers the following hours: 6am–9pm on weekdays (including Saturdays); and 10am–6pm on Sundays. They can be required to work 12-hour shifts if needed. For this they receive a 'flexibility payment' of £40 per week whether or not they work such shifts. They are paid a standard rate of £7 per hour.

Maggie, a general assistant, who has just joined the company following redundancy from a local authority, heard about this payment from a colleague at lunchtime.

The ten general assistants ('shelf-stackers') work 7am–8pm on weekdays (including

Saturdays) and 10am–5pm on Sundays. Three of these general assistants – all women – work regular part-time hours to fit in with their child-care commitments. The remaining staff (4 women and 3 men) work on a shift system. All general assistants (including the part-timers), in their contracts of employment, are required to 'be available' for flexible hours 'if needed'. However, they do not receive any flexibility payment. They receive the current national minimum wage (£6.08 per hour in October 2011).

Maggie, who had been a union workplace representative in her job at the local authority and had now joined the General Retail Workers' Union (GRWU), phoned **Des**, the Regional official, and said that she thought there was an equal pay issue involved.

Question

Is Maggie correct? What advice might Des give her regarded the handling of this issue?

Visit mylawchamber.co.uk/willey **to access sample HR documents to support this case study.**

Employment policies and practices

From the perspective of HR practitioners and employers more generally, there are several practical issues that need to be considered in the application of the law in respect of wages and equal pay. These can be dealt with in terms of contracts of employment and collective agreements; special agreements; information and records.

▶ Contracts of employment and collective agreements

The starting point for complaints about employment rights is inevitably the contract of employment. This will encompass any terms of a collective agreement with a trade union that is **incorporated** into the contract. Clearly, an employer needs to appreciate the importance of honouring contractual terms, particularly in respect of pay. Below we summarise the potential **repudiatory breaches of the contract** of employment that can arise and could result in **constructive dismissal** claims. These are:

- not paying wages due to a person for work undertaken;
- making deductions from pay without authorisation;
- varying pay without the consent of the individual employee (or where appropriate, the union);
- arbitrarily deducting overpayment of wages without consulting the employee concerned.

In addition:

- infringements of the 'equality of terms' provisions of the Equality Act 2010;
- issues relating to non-payment or under-payment of the NMW.

These would also constitute a breach of contractual terms and result in a claim against an employer.

The contract of employment is therefore a source of entitlements to particular remuneration. Furthermore, it can be the source for authority for certain pay deductions (see the earlier discussion of the retail trade and disciplinary fines and Chapters 2 and 3).

▶ Special agreements

There may be certain monies that an employer wishes to recover from an employee than might not be subject to contractual terms. A special agreement may be made. This should be in writing and should cover all relevant requirements and expectations. It should be made in advance of the expenditure being incurred. Examples of such special agreements could be:

● Where there is an undertaking to return company property on termination of employment. If that is not done, a special agreement may provide for permission to deduct the replacement value from the employee's final pay.

● An agreement by the employee to repay expenditure on expensive training courses if the employee leaves an organisation within a specified period of time.

● An agreement to repay a loan (for example for travel) during employment and on termination of employment.

▶ Information and records

It should be remembered that there already exist well-established rights to the provision of information to employees. Such rights to information relate to:

● *Statement of Initial Employment Particulars* (ERA 1996, s 1). Employees are to be told the scale or rate of remuneration or the method of calculating it, and the intervals at which it is paid (weekly, monthly or otherwise). A linked information requirement concerns hours of work. Taking these together, it is possible for an employee to calculate their hourly rate of pay.

● *Written itemised pay statement and a statement of fixed deductions* (ERA 1996, ss 8–9): This must contain the following information:
  ○ the gross amount of wages and salary;
  ○ the amounts of any variable and fixed deductions from gross pay and the reasons for them;
  ○ the net amount of wages or salary payable; and
  ○ where different parts of the net amount are paid in different ways, the amount and method of payment of each part-payment.

New information requirements were introduced under the National Minimum Wage Act 1998. A critical part of its effectiveness in terms of enforcement is the availability of adequate records, and as we have noted earlier, failure to maintain these is a criminal offence (NMWA 1998, s 31).

Exercises

Read the following scenarios and decide whether or not the workers concerned are subject to any infringement of their statutory rights.

National minimum wage

9.1 A person is aged 17 years and works for six hours on a Saturday afternoon in a burger bar. His employer pays him £3.50 per hour.

Is he protected under the NMWA?

9.2 A person is aged 19 years and delivers a free newspaper for five hours a week at weekends. She is paid £4.80 per hour.

Is she protected under the NMWA?

9.3 A 30-year-old waiter has been supplied to the Gradgrind Hotel by an agency. He also works on a casual basis in the restaurant of a separate employer in between engagements at the hotel. His pay from the hotel is £5.50 per hour. Because he is a cousin of the owner, he is provided with free accommodation, although he has to pay for food and heating. His hours and additional remuneration for a four-week period of work for the hotel were as follows:

Week 1: 12 hours

Week 2: 6 hours

Week 3: 8 hours

Week 4: 14 hours

Is he being paid a rate compliant with the national minimum wage?

9.4 A cleaner has worked for one specific cleaning company for the past two years. She is 20 years old and has been paid £5.00 per hour. Just before her 21st birthday, her supervisor says that she is sacked, maintaining that they do not need her anymore.

Advise her on her legal rights and what action (if any) may be available to her.

9.5 A woman, aged 29 years, has just started work in a small 'open all hours' shop. It employs fewer than 20 staff – all of whom work on some form of part-time contract. She believes that she has been wrongly paid because her hourly wages over the past month average less than £6.00 per hour. She calculated that she should have received an hourly rate in line with the NMW. She has been given a handwritten piece of paper stating the hours she worked, her gross pay, the deductions made for tax and National Insurance and her net pay. She asks the owner of the shop if she can check his pay records to make sure that she has not been underpaid. He refuses.

Advise her on her legal position and what, if anything, she can request from her employer.

Pay deduction

9.6 A man had a loan agreement with his employer. It stipulated that when he left employment, payments would continue until the debt was paid off. His contract of employment was terminated and the employer did not pay his final wages of £273.50, saying it was to cover the outstanding loan payments.

Advise on the legal position in respect of pay deductions in this case.

9.7   A shiftworker worked under a contract, part of which incorporated terms of a collective agreement, and which provided for a shift allowance. During a temporary stoppage in production he was not required to work shifts and the allowance was not paid. He claimed that this was unlawful deduction.

Advise the shiftworker on his legal position.

9.8   A man has been overpaid by £250 in one month's pay cheque because of an administrative error. His normal gross pay is £1,200 per month. He had heard rumours that the union had negotiated a pay increase and so he decides to spend the money on a new tumble-drier. The company asks him to repay the overpayment immediately.

Advise the man on his legal rights in relation to repaying the overpayment.

9.9   A van driver was given a document with details of the vehicle insurance policy under which he would be liable for the excess for damage caused during personal use of the van. Private mileage was also limited. Further provisions covered charges for private phone calls made from the van. The amount of £305 was deducted from his final wages; £155 of this was for the cost of repairs for damage during private use, although he had agreed to repair the van himself; £150 was a provisional deduction for both private phone calls and excess private mileage. He claimed the deduction was unlawful.

Advise the van driver.

9.10   A woman works at a small café. As a result of a shortfall in the till, her boss deducted £18 from her weekly pay of £150. Her boyfriend tells her that her employer cannot do that.

Is her boyfriend correct? Advise the woman.

Feedback on these exercises is provided in the Appendix to this textbook.

References

Adams, J.S. (1965) 'Inequity in Social Exchange', *Advanced Experiments in Social Psychology*, Vol. 62: 335–43.

Ashtiany, D. (2007) 'Discrimination Law – Where Did it Come From and Where is it Going', *Industrial Law Society Conference*, May.

Atkinson, A.B. (2003) 'Income Inequality in OECD Countries: Data and Explanations', *CESifo Economic Studies*, Vol. 49(4).

Bain, G.S. (1999) 'The National Minimum Wage: Further Reflections', *Employee Relations*, Vol. 21(1).

Barnard, A. (2008) 'Modelling the Gender Pay Gap in the UK', *Economic and Labour Market Review*, Vol. 2(8), August, ONS.

Berthoud, R. and Blekesaune, M. (2007) *Persistent Employment Disadvantage*, Research Paper No. 416. London, Department of Work and Pensions.

Brown, W. (2010) 'Negotiation and Collective Bargaining' in Colling, T. and Terry, M. (eds), *Industrial Relations: Theory and Practice* (3rd edn). Chichester: Wiley.

Brown, W. and Nash, D. (2008) 'What has Happened to Collective Bargaining Under New Labour?', *Industrial Relations Journal*, 39: 2: 91–103.

Card, D. and Krueger, A. (1995) *Myth and Measurement: The New Economics of the Minimum Wage*. Princeton: Princeton University Press.

Charlwood, A. (2007) 'The De-collectivisation of Pay Setting in Britain 1990–98, Incidence, Determinants and Impact', *Industrial Relations Journal*, Vol. 38: 1.

Clark, K. and Drinkwater, S. (2007) *Ethnic Minorities in the Labour Market: Dynamics and Diversity*. York: Joseph Rowntree Foundation.

Collins, H., Ewing, K. and McColgan, A. (2005) *Labour Law: Text and Materials* (2nd edn). Oxford: Hart.

Croucher, R. and White, G. (2007) 'Enforcing a National Minimum Wage: The British Case', *Policy Studies*, 28(2).

Davies, A.C.L. (2004) *Perspectives on Labour Law*, Cambridge: Cambridge University Press.

Davies, A.C.L. (2009) *Perspectives on Labour Law* (2nd edn). Cambridge: Cambridge University Press.

Davies, P. and Freedland, M. (2007) *Towards a Flexible Labour Market: Labour Legislation and Regulation Since the 1990s*. Oxford: Oxford University Press.

Deakin, S. and Morris, G. (2009) *Labour Law* (5th edn). Oxford: Hart.

Deakin, S. and Wilkinson, F. (1994) 'Rights v Efficiency: the Economic Case for Transnational Labour Standards', *Industrial Law Journal*, Vol. 23: 289.

Department for Business Enterprise and Regulatory Reform, *National Minimum Wage Annual Reports 2001–02, 2003–04, 2005–06*.

Department for Business, Innovation and Skills (2011) *National Minimum Wage: Policy on HM Revenue and Customs Enforcement, Prosecutions and Naming Employers who Flout National Minimum Wage Law*. London, BIS.

EIROnline (2002) 'Collective Bargaining Coverage and Extension Procedures', *Eurofound*, 18 December.

Equality and Human Rights Commission (2009) *Financial Service Inquiry: Sex Discrimination and Gender Pay Gap Report of the Equality and Human Rights Commission*. London, ECHR.

Equality and Human Rights Commission (2010) *How Fair is Britain*? London, ECHR.

Equal Opportunities Review (2010) 'Bonusability and Equal Pay', *Equal Opportunities Review*, 201.

Equal Opportunities Review (2010) 'NMW Impacts on Women's Pay', *Equal Opportunities Review*, 198.

Foster, C. (2007) *Ethnic Minorities in the Labour Market*. York: Joseph Rowntree Foundation.

Fredman, S. (1997) *Women and the Law*. Oxford: Oxford University Press.

Fredman, S. (2002) *Discrimination Law*. Clarendon Press: Oxford.

Fredman, S. (2004) 'European Developments – Marginalising equal pay Laws'. *Industrial Law Journal*, Vol. 33: 3.

Fredman, S. (2008) 'Reforming Equal Pay Laws', *Industrial Law Journal*, Vol. 37: 3.

Goreily, T. (1983) 'Arbitrary Deductions from Pay and the Proposed Repeal of the Truck Acts', *Industrial Law Journal*, Vol. 12(4).

Gregg, P. and Wadsworth, J. (2011) 'Introduction' in *The Labour Market in Winter*. Oxford: Oxford University Press.

Grimshaw, D. and Rubery, J. (2007) *Undervaluing Women's Work*, Working Paper Series No. 53. Manchester: Equal Opportunities Commission.

Grimshaw, D. and Rubery, J. (2010) 'Pay and Working Time: Shifting Contours of the Employment Relationship', in Colling, T. and Terry, M. (eds) *Industrial Relations: Theory and Practice* (3rd edn). Chichester: Wiley.

Hakim, C. (2004) *Key Issues in Women's Work* (2nd edn). London: Glasshouse Press.

Heath, A. and Cheung, S. (2006) *Ethnic Penalties in the Labour Market: Employers and Discrimination*. London: DWP.

Hepple, B. (2011) *Equality: The New Legal Framework*. Hart: Oxford.

Jacques, E. (1967) *Equitable Payment*. Harmondsworth: Penguin.

Ketsley, B. et al (2006) 'Inside the Workplace'. *Findings of the 2004 Workplace Employment Relations Survey*. London: Routledge.

Layard, R. (2005) *Happiness*. London: Allen and Lane.

Leaker, D. (2008) 'The Gender Pay Gap in the UK', *Economic and Labour Market Review*, Vol. 2(4), April.

Local Government Employers (2006) *Unblocking the route to equal pay in local government*. London: LGE.

Local Government Employers (2008) *Equal Pay: Case Law and Developments*. London: LGE.

Low Pay Commission (1998) *First Report*. London: LPC.

Low Pay Commission (2007) *National Minimum Wage: Low Pay Commission Report*. London: LPC.

Low Pay Commission (2008) *National Minimum Wage: Low Pay Commission Report*. London: LPC.

Low Pay Commission (2009) *National Minimum Wage: Low Pay Commission Report*. London: LPC.

Low Pay Commission (2010) *National Minimum Wage: Low Pay Commission Report*. London: LPC.

Low Pay Commission (2011) *National Minimum Wage: Low Pay Commission Report*. London: LPC.

Machin, S. (2011) 'Changes in UK Wage Inequality over the Last Forty Years', in Gregg, P. and Wadsworth, J. (eds) *The Labour Market in Winter: The State of Working Britain*. Oxford: Oxford University Press.

Machin, S. (2003) 'Wage Inequality Since 1979', in Dickens *et al.* (eds) *The Labour Market under New Labour*. Basingstoke: Palgrave.

Machin, S., Disney, R. and Rahman, L. (2002) *Where the Minimum Wage Bites Hard: The Introduction of the UK National Minimum Wage to a Low Pay Sector*. London: CEP, LSE.

Manning, A. and Petrolongo, B. (2004) 'The Part-Time Pay Penalty', Report for *Women and Equality Unit*, London, DTI.

Manning, A. and Petrolongo, B. (2008) 'The Part-Time Pay Penalty for Women in Britain', *Economic Journal Features*, Vol. 118.

McColgan, A. (2005) *Discrimination Law*. Oxford: Hart.

McColgan, A. (1997) *Just Wages for Women*. Oxford: Oxford University Press.

McGovern, P., Hill, S., Mills, C. and White, M. (2007) *Market, Class and Employment*. Oxford: OUP.

Metcalf, D. (1999a) 'The Low Pay Commission and the National Minimum Wage', *Economic Journal*, Vol. 109.

Metcalf, D. (1999b) *The British National Minimum Wage*. London: CEP, LSE.

Metcalf, D. (2007) *Why Has the British National Minimum Wage Had Little or No Impact on Employment*, CEP Discussion Paper, No. 781. London: Centre for Economic Performance, LSE.

Metcalf, H. (2009) *Pay Gaps Across the Equality Strands: A Review*, Equality and Human Rights Commission, Research Report 14. Manchester: EHRC.

Metcalf, H. and Rolfe, H. (2009) *Employment and Earnings in the Finance Sector: A Gender Analysis*, Equality and Human Rights Commission, Research Report 17. Manchester: EHRC.

Monaghan, K. (2007) *Equality Law*. Oxford: OUP.

Olsen, W. (2010) *The Gender Pay Gap in the UK 1995–2007: Part 1 – Research Report*. London: Government Equalities Office.

Olsen, L. and Walby, S. (2004) *Modelling Gender Pay Gaps*. Manchester: Equal Opportunities Commission.

Parekh, A., MacInnes, T. and Kenway, P. (2010) *Monitoring Poverty and Social Exclusion*. York: Joseph Rowntree Foundation/New Policy Institute.

Perfect, D. (2011) *Gender Pay Gaps*, Equality and Human Rights Commission, Briefing Paper 2. Manchester: EHRC.

Phelps Brown, H. (1979) *The Inequality of Pay*. Oxford: Oxford University Press.

Pike, R. (2011) 'Patterns of Pay: Results of the Annual Survey of Hours and Earnings 1997 to 2010', *Economic and Labour Market Review* (March).

Platt, L. (2007) *Pay Gaps: The Position of Ethnic Minority Men and Women*. Manchester: Equal Opportunities Commission.

Pollert, A. and Charlwood, A. (2009) 'The Vulnerable Worker in Britain and Problems at Work', *Work, Employment and Society*, 23(2): 343–362.

Rubery, J. and Edwards, P. (2003) 'Low Pay and the National Minimum Wage', in Edwards, P. (ed.) *Industrial Relations: Theory and Practice* (2nd edn). Oxford: Blackwell.

Sachdev, S. and Wilkinson, F. (1998) *Low Pay, the Working of the Labour Market and the Role of a Minimum Wage*. London: Institute of Employment Rights.

Simpson, R. (1999a) 'A Milestone in the Legal Regulation of Pay: the National Minimum Wage Act 1998', *Industrial Law Journal*, Vol. 28(1).

Simpson, R. (1999b) 'Implementing the National Minimum Wage: the 1999 Regulations', *Industrial Law Journal*, Vol. 28: 171.

Trades Union Congress (2008) *Closing the Gender Pay Gap: An Update Report for TUC Women's Conference 2008*. London: Trades Union Congress (www.tuc.org.uk).

Wilkinson, R. and Pickett, K. (2009) *The Spirit Level*. London: Penguin.

Williams, S. and Adam-Smith, D. (2010) *Contemporary Employment Relations* (2nd edn). Oxford: Oxford University Press.

Other

BBC News (6 September 2009) 'Gender Pay Gap in City is Shocking'.

Guardian (9 April 2009) 'City's "Shocking Gender Pay Gap" Revealed in Equality Report'.

Useful websites

National Group on Homeworking **www.ngh.org.uk**

Poverty Site **www.poverty.org.uk**

Visit **www.mylawchamber.co.uk/willey** to access study support resources including realistic HR documentation to accompany the case studies in the book, an online chapter on collective labour law, interactive multiple choice questions, annotated weblinks, a glossary, glossary flashcards, key case flashcards, a legal newsfeed and legal updates.

Chapter 10

Regulation of working time

Learning objectives

This chapter considers the extent to which working time has been and continues to be regulated through both voluntary measures and legal regulation. Having read the chapter you should be able to:

- Understand the historic role of voluntary regulation of working time
- Understand the piecemeal growth of legal regulation of working time in Britain
- Understand the essential purposes and provisions of European law on working time regulation
- Advise your organisation on the implications of the Working Time Regulations 1998 and the relevant case law

Structure of the chapter

- *Introduction*: the scope of working time and its regulation
- *The context*: the role of voluntary regulation; the long hours culture; social policy objectives; economic considerations; individual choice and working hours and the impact of the Working Time Regulations 1998 and recent amendments to this
- *The legal framework*: the traditional, piecemeal approach to the regulation of working time; the 1998 Working Time Regulations – regulating the organisation and duration of working time
- *Employment policies and practices*: developing a strategic approach to implementation; a checklist of action to be taken; some problem scenarios
- *Exercises*

Introduction

Working time is a central component of the employment relationship and of employment contracts. As Arrowsmith and Sisson (2000: 287) have noted:

> Working time, along with pay, is the defining feature of the employment relationship . . . For employers, the arrangement of working time helps determine the way in which goods and services can be provided. For employees, these working time patterns shape the very experience of work . . . [it is] one of the most contested areas of workplace industrial relations.

It is also an area where the nature and locus of regulation has exhibited a marked change in the past 30 years. Traditionally, working time for many was the subject of collective bargaining, with collective agreements the principal mechanism for determining basic hours of work, shift work, and in some case overtime hours. As we have noted at various points in this book, the period since 1980 has witnessed a prolonged decline in collective bargaining as a method for determining and regulating terms and conditions of employment, particularly for those in the private sector. Where collective bargaining has disappeared or become less comprehensive it has largely been replaced by managerial regulation of basic terms and conditions.

For much of the 1980s and 1990s, managerial regulation of working time proceeded within a fairly benign legal framework. Decisions about hours of work continued to be influenced by collective agreements elsewhere and shaped by custom and practice but the law placed few constraints on employers. Where collective bargaining was absent, employers were largely free to determine the number of hours adults could work, the number and length of rest breaks and holiday entitlement.

The experience of many other countries within mainland Europe was very different. Legal regulation of aspects of working time was well-established in many EU Member States and in the early 1990s, pressure built up to establish a comprehensive legal framework to regulate working time across the European Union. This culminated in the passing of the directive on the organisation of working time (hereafter the Working Time Directive) in 1993. This has now been consolidated into the 2003 Directive. Britain implemented the original directive five years later through the Working Time Regulations 1998.

This chapter focuses on how and why the shift to a statutory framework for regulating working time has taken place, how such working time is regulated and the issues raised for HR professionals. Before doing so, it addresses the often complex issue of what is meant by working time. Normally, it includes the following:

- the **number of hours** worked by an individual worker in a specified time period (e.g. the basic or standard working week);

- the arrangement of **'non-work' time** (e.g. rest periods, rest days and holidays);

- the **scheduling** and availability of working time (e.g. night work, Sunday working and part-time working);

- the **flexibility** of working time (part time, **job share**, casual, etc.);

- the **quality of work** (e.g. the adaptation of work to the worker).

In this chapter we will consider all of these issues.

Working time is measured and arranged in various ways, and so it is important to outline the commonly used definitions. The standard terms that occur in working time arrangements, collective agreements and the law are outlined in Exhibit 10.1.

EXHIBIT 10.1

Defining standard terms

Basic working week. The number of hours per week that an employee is expected to work. It will usually be an express term of the contract of employment and should be stated in the written statement of employment particulars (ERA 1996, s 1). For full-time workers this is usually specified as a number of hours above 30 per week. Historically, there was no general statutory provision on the length of the basic working week, in contrast to the position in some other countries, for example France. Although since 1998 there has been a statutory *maximum* working week (from which it is possible for workers to opt out), the length of this continues to depend on either management decision or the provision of a collective agreement.

Overtime. The number of hours per week performed in excess of the employing organisation's basic working week. Paid overtime has long been a significant feature of working time in Britain, particularly in manufacturing. In law, there is no specific ceiling on overtime. However, the regulations on the average maximum working week of 48 hours clearly have an impact on overtime arrangements (WTR 1998, reg 4).

Shift work. The Working Time Directive (2003) defines shift work as 'any method of organising work in shifts whereby workers succeed each other at the same work stations according to a certain pattern, including a rotating pattern and which may be continuous or discontinuous, entailing the need for workers to work at different times over a given period of days or weeks' (Article 2(5)).

    The Health and Safety Executive estimate the number of shift workers in the UK at 3.6 million (which equates to around 14 per cent of the total working population (HSE 2006), of whom around 60 per cent are men). The Labour Force Survey (July–September 2008) records that 1.3 million people are shift workers who work regularly at night. Overwhelmingly, these are white and male (Norman 2011: 7).

Annualised hours schemes. Under these schemes, the total number of hours worked each year are added together and then scheduled to be worked according to variations in customer demand for a product or service. This may result in variations in the length of working days at different times of the year. Bell and Hart (2005: 3) estimated that for 2002, between 3 and 4 per cent of full-time employees in the UK were covered by these arrangements. In general, annualised hours schemes appear to be more common in the private sector and among women in areas such as local government. The lowest incidence of such schemes are found among managers and administrators.

Weekend working. This is normally regarded as any working on a Saturday and/or a Sunday. Weekend working has increased significantly in recent years with over half of men and over a third of women working at least one day at the weekend.

Part-time working. Normally defined as a situation where an employee works a number of hours less than the employing organisation's basic working week. This can include, therefore, those who work hours just short of the basic week as well as those who may work as little as two hours per week. In official statistics it is usually specified as working up to 30 hours per week. According to the Labour Force Survey (2008), over a quarter of the working population works part time, although part-time working remains concentrated among certain groups and sectors, with around 85 per cent of part-time work undertaken by women.

Job share. This is a situation which 'involves dividing a single full-time job between two people who share the responsibilities, pay and benefits' (**www.acas.org.uk**). In principle the job could be split between more than two employees, but in any event those employees work on *pro-rata* terms and conditions of employment. Job sharing developed in the mid-1980s and is evident in a minority of organisations. ACAS reported that its introduction 'was greatest in industries which employ mainly white-collar staff such as public administration and banking' (ACAS 1988: 21). Despite a recent British Chambers of Commerce report of SMEs indicating that almost 17 per cent of organisations *offered* job shares to their employees (British Chambers of Commerce 2007), Labour Force Surveys (**www.statistics.gov.uk**) have consistently shown that only around one per cent of employees are actually job sharers.

Flexible hours. Those working flexible hours may well find their hours varying from day to day, week to week or month to month. Although driven in many cases by employer demands for flexibility to match hours of work with fluctuations in demand, there has also been a long history of this being instigated by employees, at least in some sectors of employment. In the latter, the employee may decide their arrival and departure time around a 'core time', in others these may reflect both employer and employee concerns, as with term-time working.

Zero-hours contracts. These are a development of flexible working, instigated by employers and which attracted considerable attention from the mid-1980s. There are three possible broad categories of such contracts:

1 where an employee attends the employer's premises but is only regarded as 'working' when their services are required by a customer or client;

2 where the employee is 'on call' (by telephone or at home) at specified times, should the employer require their services;

3 where an employee is part of a 'bank' of potential workers and either the employer will contact the employee to see if the worker wants work or, alternatively, the employee might contact the employer to see if work is available.

Although these contracts attracted much adverse publicity in some quarters when they began to be used in areas like retail in the 1980s, it remains unclear how prevalent they remain. In the *Fairness at Work* White Paper (1998: para 3.14), the Labour government estimated that around 200,000 people were on such contracts in the late 1990s. The Workplace Employment Relations Survey (2004) estimated around 5 per cent of workplaces employed at least some workers on zero hours contracts. The Commission on Vulnerable Employment Report (2007) points to a slight decline in their use throughout the decade.

The context

▶ Introduction

Hours of work remain a core element in the employment relationship and in our working and non-working lives more generally. In general, the hours we spend at work have exhibited a long-term downward trend (see below). However, because of technological changes and the spatial re-configuration of work, the growth of 'hot-desking', teleworking, the virtual office, and the blurring of work and leisure activities in certain occupations there is often a considerable gap between formal contracted hours and those actually worked. Changes that often significantly understate the true scale of working time.

Arguably a more significant trend in the UK has been a shift to more heterogeneous and individualised patterns of working hours both in terms of the duration of working time and in the periods when work is performed (Anxo *et al.* 2004, in Blyton 2010: 306). This dispersion of working hours in the UK and in working-time arrangements as part of a standard working-week (Williams and Adam-Smith 2010: 289) has given rise to a differentiated experience of working time and access to work–life balance arrangements amongst the workforce (Blyton 2010). Long hours working persists but remains heavily concentrated among certain groups of workers – male workers and managers (Williams and Adam-Smith 2010: 287) – and at the other extreme:

> The UK has a high share of employees working only part-time hours and high share of part-time jobs offering only relatively short hours per week.
>
> (Grimshaw and Rubery 2010: 364)

Despite this diversity, it has been concern over the relatively long hours worked by certain groups in the UK that has been at the forefront of debates surrounding the growth of legal regulation of working time. Part of this concern reflects the fact that some features of long hours working and of flexible working, such as paid overtime and shift working, have been established characteristics of particular sectors for a considerable time, such as manufacturing and the extractive industries (e.g. mining). What has changed, particularly in the last 30 years, has been the growth in various forms of flexible working, specifically the expansion of temporal flexibility – part-time working, shift and weekend working, overtime (that is now frequently unpaid for many groups), flexible hours and annualised hours working. Indeed, research conducted in the late 1990s indicated that on average 56 per cent of workers worked variable hours – ranging from 70 per cent in oil and gas extraction to 42 per cent in textile manufacture (Casey *et al.* 1997).

▶ Voluntary regulation

The volume, arrangement and regulation of working time in any economy are shaped by a range of factors that evolve over time. A defining characteristic of what Deakin and Morris (2009) have termed the *traditional model* of regulating working time in Britain has been the historical predominance of voluntary regulation – that is through collective agreements negotiated between employers and trade unions either on an industry-wide or single employer basis. Often covering very large numbers of employees, these agreements not only set the standard working week in the industries they covered but also influenced the regulation of working time in other industries. Where these agreements were appropriate to working patterns in the sector, they would also cover shift working arrangements and premium rates of pay for such shift working and overtime working.

In view of the fact that in Britain collective agreements have been presumed not to be legally enforceable, such voluntary regulation has been enforceable through the **incorporation** of terms into the contracts of employment of individual employees (see Chapter 2). Non-compliance by an employer would therefore, constitute **breach of contract**.

Generally, this voluntary regulation of working time concerned the standard working week of manual workers in unionised industries and sectors. In practice, through concerted action, unions would often use a 'pace-setting' national deal to set a new maximum

Table 10.1 **Standard nationally negotiated working week in engineering**

1920s	48 hours
1947	44 hours
1960	42 hours
1965	40 hours
1979	39 hours

basic working week which would act as a basis for agreements in other industries. Historically, the engineering industry provided this lead through national agreements. By the 1970s this covered over three million workers; and it meant that pressure could then be placed on employers in other sectors to provide comparable treatment. Such action was often successful. Employers frequently did not require much persuasion when faced with the threat of possible action should they not comply and, more pragmatically, the loss of staff to competitors that could follow non-compliance. The major changes to working time negotiated for manual workers through collective agreements in engineering are detailed in Table 10.1. These reflect the general reduction taking place throughout much of British industry at these times.

The 1979 agreement reflected an unsuccessful attempt to achieve a 35 hour week in the engineering industry, a campaign that continued throughout the 1980s. This campaign failed to secure a national agreement, although some individual companies in the industry negotiated local agreements at or close to this. By the late 1980s, national bargaining in engineering was terminated by the Engineering Employers' Federation (the employers' side of the national bargaining forum). A trend repeated in many other industries, as national bargaining was eroded by the de-regulationist policies of the 1980s (Deakin and Morris 2009: 282). As a result, this co-ordinated voluntary approach to regulating hours of work and other aspects of the employment relationship ceased to be a feature of British employment relations.

National or sector level agreements had some success, directly and indirectly, in establishing the standard working week for the majority of workers in Britain for much of the last century. These agreements were also significant in establishing paid holidays, with a general four week entitlement becoming widespread in the early 1980s (Deakin and Morris 2009: 281). Furthermore, these national agreements were frequently supported by local agreements on other aspects of working time such as overtime levels and shift-working arrangements.

However, voluntary regulation was rarely comprehensive and some groups remained outside the provision of collective agreements. An example of this is the question of paid holiday entitlement. Until the implementation of the Working Time Regulations, Britain was the only country in the EU where workers had no legal rights to paid annual leave. Consequently, in the mid-1990s there were 2.5 million workers who received no paid annual leave (most were **part-time workers** of whom 1.4 million were women); 4.1 million received fewer than three weeks of paid holiday; and 5.9 million, fewer than four weeks (Labour Force Survey, Autumn 1995 (**www.statistics.gov.uk**)).

It should also be noted that sector-level agreements, while important for establishing basic working hours and weeks, were less successful as a mechanism for *regulating* working time. For example, the Donovan Commission (1968) revealed the extent of practices such as overtime working in parts of manufacturing industry, whilst more recent research has shown actual hours worked in manufacturing have frequently exceeded the basic working week of 37–39 hours. Indeed the wide variety of non-standard working arrangements observable in Britain today is largely the historical product of this loose voluntary regulatory system (Deakin and Morris 2009: 282).

In contrast, many other countries saw the establishment of basic working hours and weeks through legislation in the first half of the twentieth century (Deakin and Morris 2009). Although legal regulation was not absent from British employment relations, it was partial and limited to particular groups of workers seen as requiring some specific protection. These aspects of 'regulatory law' (Kahn-Freund 1983) can be traced to the Factories Acts of the mid-nineteenth century, providing for regulation of working hours for women, children and young persons; and in the twentieth century were reflected in protection for those working in retail, establishing the right for minimum meal breaks, Sunday working hours and weekly half-day holidays.

▶ A long hours culture?

The voluntary regulation of working time (and specifically the standard working week) established what would become fundamental terms of the individual contract of employment. Although this specified the hours to be worked in a week, it did not provide a limit on working hours, merely a threshold beyond which any additional work would be paid at a higher hourly rate. This was so in the manufacturing industry in particular. For many workers in this sector, where some overtime working was often a contractual requirement, it was not uncommon to work considerably in excess of standard contractual hours of 40 hours, so that a working week would often in practice extend to 48 hours and in some cases well beyond this. On average full-time employees worked between three and four hours' overtime per week (Hart 2004), a figure which in manufacturing (particularly in the 1970s and beyond) rose to between four and six hours per week.

Today, the picture is more complex. Long hours working remains, and continues to be heavily concentrated among certain groups of workers, particularly male workers and managers (Williams and Adam-Smith 2010: 287) but there is also a large proportion of employees working only part-time hours and a high share of part-time jobs offering only relatively short hours per week (Grimshaw and Rubery 2010: 364). As Blyton (2010) notes, these variations reflect differential opportunities available to individuals within organisations:

> Employees at higher levels in employment hierarchies are generally able to secure much greater discretion over their work time . . . [whereas] . . . it is the case that a disproportionate number of those experiencing greatest unpredictability of work time and least control over hours are women . . . A reflection of the experience of those at lowest levels in employment hierarchies rather than a reflection of gender inequality *per se*.
> (Blyton 2010: 302)

However, recent evidence suggests a slight reversal in the trend towards longer hours working (Grimshaw and Rubery 2010: 366). The proportion of men working more than 45 hours per week rose from 33 per cent in 1992, to 37 per cent in 1996 but has fallen steadily since, with slightly over a quarter working more than these hours in 2010 (Reed 2010, ONS data). The evidence for women, where long hours working has been less common, suggests around 9 per cent worked more than 45 hours in 2007, roughly the same proportion as in the early 1990s. The Work–Life Balance surveys also support this trend, suggesting a marked increase in the number who work no overtime at all (from a third of employees in 2003 to almost half in 2006, Grimshaw and Rubery 2010).

For those concerned about long hours working these are positive developments but the extent to which legislation has contributed to these changes is unclear, even though this was obviously a concern of those framing the legislation. Indeed, much of the debate and rationale for the statutory regulation of working time in the 1990s focused on the scale and consequences of long hours working in the UK. Despite the recent decline, official statistics estimate that around 4.8 million people still regularly work over 45 hours per week – 29 per cent of men employed and 9 per cent of women (Labour Force Survey 2008), with the TUC identifying around 3.3 million people regularly working in excess of 48 hours (TUC 2008). Estimates have also suggested almost one in six workers commonly work more than 60 hours per week (Bunting 2005). These statistics need to be seen in the context of a falling average standard working week for men and women (see Table 10.1). The fact that such working appears to be related to stress and mental ill health (White and Beswick 2003) is clearly a cause for concern and reflects the current focus on working time as a health and safety issue (see below and Chapter 12).

The evidence for long hours working in the UK suggests that it is undertaken predominantly by men – 85 per cent of those working long hours (TUC 2008) – particularly those in their 30s and 40s with dependants, and is far more common in the private sector and within this, in manufacturing. A survey for the then Department of Trade and Industry, reported the following factors most likely to be associated with long hours working (Kodz *et al.* 2003a, 2003b):

- Men were more likely to work long hours than women.
- Men with children were slightly more likely than men without children to work long hours.
- Women with children less likely than women without to work long hours.
- People between the ages of 30 and 49.
- Private sector workers and particularly those in manufacturing.
- Managers, professionals and operative and assembly workers – with over two-thirds of managers and professional workers neither paid overtime nor given time off in lieu.

In the context of the EU, average hours worked by full-time employees in the UK is around the average of that for the EU as a whole (42.1 hours in 2007, Federation of European Employers 2011) with only the Netherlands (at over 46 hours) significantly higher than this, but drawing such comparisons requires care. Focusing on full-time employees is important, particularly in light of the high incidence of part-time working in the UK, but given the fact that long hours working appears to be largely a male phenomenon, when the analysis shifts to this specific group, the average hours worked beyond the standard working week in the UK is roughly double that found in other EU countries (Reed 2010, CIPD 2003).

The reasons for this tendency to work long hours are complex. For employees, the freedom to work the hours they choose and to maximise earnings is clearly important, particularly when employees have dependency responsibilities; and to this can be added the relatively low basic hourly rates that have prevailed in Britain for manual work in the past, making overtime working an attractive proposition. However, there is considerable evidence that the main factor contributing to long hours working has been the demands of the job, not the opportunity for additional earnings (Grimshaw and Rubery 2010: 366). In 2006, over a fifth of workplaces reported having managerial staff working in excess of 48 hours, but fewer than 10 per cent reported non-managerial staff working in excess of 48 hours in the past 12 months (from 15 per cent in 2003) (Grimshaw and Rubery p. 367). This confirms the growing importance of long hours working for those groups of managers and professionals with 'unmeasured working time' both in private manufacturing, and increasingly, the service sector (see below).

For employers, overtime and shift working represent relatively easy and attractive (although not necessarily cost effective) forms of flexibility. The ability to extend or rearrange the hours of existing employees is often seen as preferable to hiring new staff to take on additional work that may only be required for a limited period of time. With the rise of service sector employment, where part-time working is far more established than in manufacturing and where overtime is frequently unpaid, working long hours appears to be linked to increasing workload (Kodz *et al.* 2003a, 2003b), organisational **cultures** where such working may be expected (cultures emphasising 'presenteeism' for example), and in some cases multiple job holding where the opportunities to increase earnings are available.

Research points to a number of factors associated with increasing workloads. These are:

- new organisational initiatives (e.g. de-layering, project-based working, and a greater emphasis on customer focus);
- staff shortages;
- IT and e-mail overload.

The overall impression from the available research findings is that many people work long hours for a combination of reasons which can be difficult to disentangle, especially in an organisation or part of an organisation where a long hours culture is well-established (Kodz *et al.* 2003a, 2003b). This said, much of the available evidence points to long hours working among those having what, under the Working Time Regulations 1998, is designated as 'unmeasured working time' (such as managers), and those who have 'opted-out' of the regulations.

▶ Social issues

There are two broad social policy issues which relate to long hours and the regulation of working time: the health, safety and welfare of employees (see Chapter 12); and the impact on family life and work–life balance (see Chapter 11). Both issues have been policy concerns for the EU and recent British governments.

The originating Working Time Directive 1993 (now consolidated into the 2003 Directive) was significant primarily because it was conceived of as a ***health and safety*** measure, augmenting those related directives adopted under the 1989 Social Action Programme. A key feature of the directive is the expectation that *'work should be adapted to the worker'* (Article 13). In the early 1990s the then Conservative government was firmly opposed to the legal regulation of working time and to its construction as a health and safety measure, and challenged the legality of the directive at the ECJ. The challenge failed but delays in implementing the directive meant that the UK Working Time Regulations 1998 had to wait for the election of a Labour government sympathetic both to the broad thrust of the legislation and to its construction as a health and safety issue. The directive and the regulations have four elements that make up a health and safety dimension: maximum working time; patterns of breaks and leave from working time; health assessments; and job design.

The research undertaken for the Health and Safety Executive (Kodz *et al.* 2003a, 2003b; White and Beswick 2003) indicates 'clear grounds for concern' about the adverse effect of long hours working and the frequency of health and safety incidents. Kodz *et al.* (2003a, 2003b) note that much of the evidence on the impact of long hours working comes from a small number of occupations (e.g. long-distance road haulage, the medical professions) which makes it difficult to draw more general conclusions. Furthermore, the research indicates associations rather than causal links between long hours working and mental health and cardio-vascular problems. The evidence also suggests a relationship between employee health and specific work patterns, notably working unsociable hours and shift patterns.

The issue of **work–life balance** is explored in more detail in Chapter 11. Here it is sufficient to note both the political impetus to change and the social consequences of long hours. The government, in its consultation document on what was then proposed legislation (DTI 1997), commented that the 'long hours' culture as well as giving rise to potential health issues for those working the hours had other negative effects on other groups. It noted that the culture had historically created barriers to work for women with caring responsibilities, and had prevented many men from taking an active role in their children's upbringing (DTI 1997: para 10). The consequences for family life were revealed in research which found that a quarter of all fathers were working over 50 hours per week, and that almost 10 per cent were working more than 60 hours per week (Ferri and Smith 1996).

▶ Economic considerations

Although the achievement of social objectives in the form of health and safety has been at the forefront of recent debates about working time, economic considerations have also shaped discussion about working time and the precise nature of statutory regulation. First, there are those who extend the concerns of psychologists, arguing that the long hours culture has an adverse economic effect on output and productivity. Second, there are those who see compliance with the legislation as costly – increasing unit labour costs and administration. An illustration of this is a British Chambers of Commerce report (Smith 2004) which estimated the cumulative cost of the Working Time Regulations at that time at £11.1 billion (Smith 2004). A third concern, influential in France's adoption of a 35-hour week, has been a wish to reduce unemployment (OECD 2004). The relative importance of these economic factors remains unclear but there is little doubt that the influence of economic considerations on policy makers has been considerable.

▶ The effects on work performance

From an economist's perspective the issue of work performance tends to focus on concerns about productivity and unit costs. Efficiency in the use of human resources is about how such resources are utilised, measured in terms of their output, and in terms of how much it costs to produce that output. In principle, working longer hours should produce more output (more customers served, more cars produced), but there are good reasons for believing that productivity need not increase and that beyond a certain point productivity (and indeed quality) may fall, and unit labour costs may rise. Although the research by Kodz *et al.* (2003a, 2003b) suggested that it was not possible to establish conclusively whether long hours working affected productivity, there is some evidence from France, in the wake of the Aubry Laws that introduced a 35-hour week, to suggest that shorter working hours may be associated with higher levels of productivity (Ashkenazy 2008; Hayden 2006; OECD 2004). That is, shorter working hours, particularly where pay is maintained, may encourage more intensive and efficient working practices as firms have more of an incentive to use their resources more efficiently and effectively. (After being in force for over ten years, this French law was repealed in 2008 as a result of employer campaigning in a sympathetic conservative political climate.)

❯ Costs of compliance

This is a particularly difficult area to assess given the long-standing nature of working practices and the extent of embeddedness and institutionalisation that often comes with this. In view of the concern of the legislation to 'adapt work to the worker' and for a more general 'humanisation of work', there was considerable potential for a clash between the legislation and business cultures and practices. The government's efforts to address this through the decision to include an 'opt-out' in the Working Time Regulations, helped to allay the fears of many in the business community concerned about the costs of compliance, but angered others who saw this as undermining the aims and intent of the legislation and at worse, amounting to non-compliance with the directive (Bercusson 2003).

Research conducted on behalf of the then DTI, six months after the implementation of the Working Time Regulations, indicated considerable concern among employers about the costs and bureaucratic burden associated with new record-keeping requirements (Neathey and Arrowsmith 2001). However, the follow-up study undertaken 12 months later (Neathey 2003) found that, once established, record-keeping systems were seen as less of a problem and, in some cases, to have positive operational benefits.

Other government-sponsored work in 2001 (BMRB Social Research 2004) focusing on workers' experiences of the regulations pointed to considerable gaps in both the operation of the regulations 'on the ground' and in workers' awareness of the law on working time. Although this suggests either a degree of ignorance or deliberate non-compliance with the legislation it also points to the potential for considerable transitional costs for both businesses and their staff as they adjust to the new arrangements.

Ultimately, as in any other area of law, the costs of compliance are closely linked to the enforcement mechanisms in place to monitor the operation of the law. In the case of working time, enforcement falls to the Health and Safety Executive in the case of issues relating to weekly working time and night-work limits; and to individuals on issues concerning rest periods, breaks and paid leave. However, in light of the resource constraints on the time of HSE inspectors, firms (particularly very small firms) may escape close scrutiny on practices for significant periods of time.

The next section details the legal framework governing working time, with particular emphasis on the *New Model* for regulating the duration and organisation of working time (Deakin and Morris 2009: 282). It then considers the implications of these developments for HR professionals.

The legal framework

The current legal framework on working time regulation is considered under two headings:

● A brief review of piecemeal legal requirements that have developed in recent years in both statutory and **case law**, covering specific occupations or categories of workers.

● A detailed review of the Working Time Regulations 1998, amendments to these and relevant case law.

Piecemeal legal regulation

The piecemeal legislation covers the following: those working in certain specific occupations; those protected by sex discrimination law and by disability discrimination law; and those alleging overwork as a breach of contract.

▶ Specific occupations

Working time is regulated for some specific occupations particularly in the transport sector, and includes drivers of public-service vehicles and certain commercial vehicles. Monitoring (where required) is undertaken through the use of the tachograph. Legislation was enacted in 1968 to protect the public against risks which arise in cases where the drivers of motor vehicles are suffering from fatigue. The working hours of those who work 'in and around shops' and betting shop workers have been affected by the choice as to whether to work on Sundays; and by protection from victimisation if the employer subjected them to a detriment in the exercise of this choice (Employment Rights Act 1996, Part IV).

▶ Sex discrimination law

The relevant working time provisions of sex discrimination law relate to the repeal of the restrictions on night work undertaken by women (Sex Discrimination Act 1986); and the extent to which full-time work can be a condition of employment. The second area has arisen in case law and relates to women returning to work after maternity leave and concerns indirect sex discrimination (under the former Sex Discrimination Act 1975 and now the Equality Act 2010), and the question as to whether or not an employer can 'justify' the requirements to work full time in the individual case (see Chapters 5 and 11).

▶ Disability discrimination

Disability discrimination law since 1995 (now a provision in the Equality Act 2010) has placed a **duty** on an employer to make reasonable adjustments to accommodate a disabled person (EA 2010, s 20). One possible adjustment is an alteration to a person's working hours. This could include allowing the disabled person to work flexible hours to enable additional breaks to overcome fatigue arising from the disability, or changing the disabled person's hours to fit with the availability of a carer.

▶ Breach of contract

Under **common law**, breaches of two implied terms in the contract of employment – the duty to take reasonable care of an employee and the duty of mutual trust and confidence – can be invoked in circumstances where an employee is alleging physical or mental injury as a result of long working hours (Chapter 2). The duty of care issue in respect of working hours was brought into sharp focus by the case of *Johnstone v Bloomsbury Health Authority* [1991] IRLR 118, concerning a Senior House Officer at University College Hospital. Under the express terms of his contract, he was required to work 40 hours per week and to be 'on call', at the employer's discretion, for up to a further 48 hours. He claimed that he had been asked repeatedly to work long hours, at times in excess of 100 hours per week, and that this had caused him both physical (sleep deprivation, physical sickness) and mental problems (stress, depression) and that this had put his patients at risk. He was successful in his claim with the Court of Appeal ruling that as a general principle, any additional hours requirement coming from the employer had to be exercised in ways that conformed with the overall duty of care. (For more on the issue of work-related stress see Chapter 12.)

The Working Time Regulations 1998

The key recent developments in the legal regulation of working time have come through the Working Time Regulations. These implement two directives:

- on the organisation of working time (now in the consolidated 2003 directive, repealing the original 1993 directive); and
- provisions of the Young Workers Directive 1994.

The regulations came into effect on 1 October 1998. They were amended in 1999 in respect of record-keeping and unmeasured working time; and in light of later amending directives covering specific occupational groups (non-mobile workers in various transport industries (2000), seafarers (2002), workers in civil aviation (2004), and mobile workers in road transport (2002) who were exempted from the original 1993 directive). The core rights provided by the regulations are detailed in Exhibit 10.2.

▶ Who is covered?

The Working Time Regulations apply to workers over the minimum school leaving age and as such, have wide-ranging coverage. Those covered include 'employees' who work under a contract of employment and those who work under other forms of contract to work personally. The only people excluded are the genuinely self-employed and there are some special provisions that apply to 'young workers' (those over 16 but under 18).

EXHIBIT 10.2

Working Time Regulations: core provisions for adults

- A limit of 48 hours' work per week.
- An ability to 'opt out' of this average working week.
- A basic entitlement of 28 days' paid annual leave each year (from 2009).
- Statutory rest periods – a minimum of 20 minutes' rest in any period of work of six hours or more.
- A minimum of 11 hours of rest in any one 24-hour period.
- A minimum of 24 hours of rest in any seven-day period.
- Specific regulations governing those on shift work.
- For night workers, a minimum of eight hours of work in any 24-hour period.
- Free health checks for night workers.
- Specific restrictions apply to the working time of those aged 16–18.

In cases where there is some ambiguity about employment status, as in other areas of law, the facts and circumstances will be considered by the court and tribunal. In the case of *Byrne Brothers (Formwork) Ltd* v *Baird and Others* EAT/542/01, labour only contractors were held to be workers for the purposes of the regulations. On the facts of the case, the workers concerned had a contract of personal service – they undertook personally to provide work but did not work as part of 'any profession or business undertaking' – and with limited powers to delegate work, were found not to be engaged in business on their own account, and that the necessary mutuality of obligations existed between them and others.

Although the breadth of coverage of the regulations is wide, certain groups were excluded from the original 1993 directive. Subsequently, the EU has adopted amending directives that cover workers as follows:

- *Road transport*. Since August 2003, *non-mobile workers* have been covered by the full provisions of the Working Time Directive. This amends the situation where the ECJ ruled, in October 2001, that all workers in road transport, including office workers, were excluded from the 1993 directive (*Bowden and Others* v *Tuffnells Parcels Express Ltd* ECJ C-133/00). Also, from August 2003, mobile workers have been entitled to paid annual leave, a 48-hour maximum working week and health checks for night workers. In addition, the Road Transport Directive sets out detailed working time for drivers covered by European drivers' legislation. This was implemented in 2005.

- *Rail transport*. In August 2003, the directive was extended in full to both mobile and non-mobile rail workers. It provides **derogations** from the entitlements to daily rest, rest breaks, weekly rest and the night work provisions for rail workers whose activities are intermittent, whose hours of work are spent on trains and whose activities are linked to rail transport timetables and ensuring the continuity and regularity of rail traffic.

- *Air transport*. In August 2003, the directive was extended in full to non-mobile workers, with mobile workers entitled to paid annual leave, a 48-hour maximum working week, health checks for night workers and adequate rest. A **Social Partners'** Aviation Directive, covering civil aviation, was also implemented from December 2003. This limits the annual working time of airborne personnel to 2,000 hours, covers some elements of standby time and restricts flying time to 900 hours. It also requires 'appropriate' health and safety protection for all mobile personnel and contains provisions for a monthly and yearly number of rest days.

- *Sea transport*. In August 2003, the directive was extended in full to non-mobile workers, and together with the Seafarers' Directive implemented in 2002 and based on Convention 180 of the International Labour Organisation has extended protection to those working at sea. The Seafarers' Directive provides for a maximum working week of 72 hours and 14 hours of rest in any 24-hour period, or a minimum weekly rest requirement of 77 hours and 10 hours in any 24-hour period. It also provides for four weeks' paid annual leave and health assessments for night workers.

- *Junior doctors*. This has arguably been the most controversial area of application of the regulations. In principle, full implementation of the 48-hour week can be phased in over a possible 12-year period for this group. However, though the Working Time Regulations apply in full to junior doctors, following the Horizontal Amending Directive (2000/EC/34) the implementation of the 48-hour working week was gradually phased in over a five-year period from 1 August 2004 until 1 August 2009. A limit of 58 hours applied between 1 August 2004 to 31 July 2007, one of 56 hours between 1 August 2007 and 31 July 2009, and 48 hours from 1 August 2009. Furthermore, specific rules have been introduced for calculating reference periods, based on a normal period of 26 weeks.

- *Other groups*. In addition to these amendments, there have been specific extensions of the 1993 Working Time Directive to workers engaged in inland waterway and lake transport, sea fishing and working offshore.

With these amendments and exclusions noted, the Working Time Regulations now apply to all workers, extend to Crown employees, House of Lords and House of Commons staff, the police, and members of the armed forces. However, they have been held not to apply to children below the minimum school leaving age (*Addison v Ashby* [2003] ICR 667).

▌ Definition of working time

The regulations, following the directive, identify only **two** time periods associated with the employment relationship: *working time* and *rest periods*. The directive defines working time as 'any period during which the worker is working, at the employer's disposal and carrying out his activity or duties, in accordance with national laws and/or practice' (Article 2.1). The regulations, transposing the directive, define working time as:

- any period during which a worker is working, at his employer's disposal and carrying out his activity or duties;

- any period during which he is receiving relevant training, such as under a combined work/training scheme or an in-plant work-experience scheme (also defined in reg 2.1);

- any additional period which is to be treated as working time for the purpose of these Regulations under a relevant agreement (also defined in reg 2.1).

For most working people this definition is clear-cut. However, there are uncertainties in respect of workers who are 'on call' or who are on 'zero hours contracts'. How much time is to be designated as 'working time'? To help resolve the issue of what is 'working time' and what is not, the regulations permit the negotiation of a 'relevant agreement' between the employer and an individual employee. Such an agreement might be derived from a collective agreement with an **independent trade union** or by a 'workforce agreement' (see below). A relevant agreement must be in writing and be legally binding.

In its guidance on working time the former Department of Trade and Industry included the following as working time (see **www.bis.gov.uk**):

● working lunches, such as business lunches;

● when a worker has to travel as part of his or her work – for example a 24-hour mobile repair worker or travelling salesperson;

● when a worker is undertaking training that is directly related to his or her job;

● time spent working abroad if the worker works for an employer who carries on business in Britain.

Case law has clarified a number of issues (see Exhibit 10.3) particularly in respect of those who are 'on duty' on the employer's premises – available for work and possibly sleeping – but not actually carrying out tasks. Furthermore, case law provides a framework within which it is possible to consider the situation of 'zero hours contract' workers.

▶ Rest breaks and rest periods

A 'rest period' is defined in the directive as 'any period which is not working time' (art 2(2)). The regulations add 'other than a rest break or leave to which the worker is entitled under these Regulations' (reg 2(1)) (see issues raised in Exhibit 10.3). When

---

EXHIBIT 10.3

Defining 'working time'

The first two cases, one Spanish and one German, concern rulings by the European Court of Justice about doctors who were 'on call'.

SIMAP v *Conselleria de Sanidid y Consumo de la Generalidad Valenciana* [2000] **IRLR 845**

ECJ rulings.

● '... [T]o exclude duty "on call" from working time if physical presence is required would seriously undermine' the objective of securing breaks for health and safety reasons.

● The ECJ held that 'on call' time is classified as 'working time' when a worker is physically required to be at their place of work. However, when a worker is away from the place of work when 'on call' and free to take part in other activities so that even if they were at the disposal of their employer (in that it had to be possible to contact them) doctors could manage their time with fewer constraints and pursue their own interests, such on call time should not be classified as 'working time'. In such circumstances, only time linked to the actual provision of primary care services can be regarded as *working time*.

Landeshauptstadt Kiel v Jaeger [2003] **IRLR 804, ECJ**

The ECJ held that 'on call' duty, performed by doctors (who were required to be physically present in the hospital and who were permitted to rest or sleep in rooms provided for them there during periods when their services were not required) constituted, in its entirety, working time under the Working Time Directive. Periods of inactivity during on call duty was not a 'rest period'. It reaffirmed and extended the principles set out in the *SIMAP* case.

The other cases are from British courts applying the principles of the European law.

MacCartney v Oversley House Management **EAT/0500/05**

The claimant, a residential manager in a home for people over 60, had contracted hours of 'four days per week of 24 hours on site cover' during which she had to be on or near the premises, 'on call', attending to the residents with whom she was in contact by mobile phone, answering emergency and non-emergency calls or doing administrative work in a small office in her flat in the home. The issue was whether duty 'on call' was working time.

EAT's finding.

- She was entitled to a 20-minute *rest break* each day.
- She was 'working' for the purposes of the Working Time Regulations during the whole time that she was 'on call'. Because she was required to remain at a place determined by her employer (with a view to performing services if necessary as resident manager in a residential care home) the entire period of 'on call' time constituted working time for the purposes of the regulations. She had not been granted the appropriate *11-hour daily rest periods*.

Comment. An employer in this situation could ask employees to sign an 'opt-out'. However, if an individual refuses to do so, the employer will essentially be required to hire additional wardens (IRS *Industrial Relations Law Bulletin* 781.11, March 2006).

Gallagher and Others v Alpha Catering Services Ltd [2004] **IRLR 102, CA**

The claimants' job was to deliver meals to aircraft. It was a job that varies according to flight timetables and levels of business from day to day and as a result their shifts contained periods of downtime between loading and unloading aircraft, during which time they were in radio contact with their employers in case they were needed. They could take meals but were not allowed to sleep during 'down time'. Alpha Catering Services claimed that 'down time' constituted a rest break, but that it was entitled not to provide any formal breaks as the regulations provide for them to be excluded due to the need for continuous service at peak times. The issue was the status of 'downtime' under the Working Time Regulations.

The Court of Appeal ruled that periods of 'down time' during which a worker is still at his or her employer's disposal do not count as rest periods under reg 12. A rest period is an uninterrupted period of at least 20 minutes in a work period of more than six hours that the worker can use as he or she pleases.

Comment. This case stresses that the directive (and the regulations which implement it in Britain) are intended to protect the health and safety of the worker. It should close off the temptation for an unscrupulous employer to call 'down time' or waiting periods 'rest breaks' (IRS *Industrial Relations Law Bulletin* 753.8, January 2005).

considering the situation of an individual worker, the following specific provisions, relating to working time and rests/breaks, need to be considered **all together**.

Daily rest

For adult workers the regulations provide for 'a minimum daily rest period of 11 consecutive hours per 24-hour period' (adding) 'during which he works for his employer' (reg 10(1)). A young worker (defined as under 18 but over school leaving age) is entitled to a rest period of not less than 12 consecutive hours in each 24-hour period 'during which he works for his employer' (reg 10(2)).

One case in this area concerning bus drivers (*First Hampshire & Dorset Ltd* v *Feist and Others* EAT 0510/06) ruled that reg 10(1) did not apply to a worker where his or her activities involved the need for continuity of service or production. The regulations allow a worker to claim 'compensatory rest' where he or she is required to work during a period that would otherwise be a rest period or rest break (reg 24). However, mobile workers are specifically covered by an amendment enacted in 2003 that entitles them to 'adequate rest' that is sufficiently long and continuous to ensure that 'as a result of fatigue or other irregular work patterns' they do not cause injury to themselves, to fellow workers or to others; and that the worker 'does not damage his health either in the short term or in the longer term' (reg 24A). In the circumstances, the EAT said that the bus drivers were entitled to 'adequate rest' but not also to 'compensatory rest'.

Rest breaks

Where the working day is longer than six hours, every worker is entitled to a rest break. This break for **adult workers** is 'an uninterrupted period of not less than twenty minutes and the worker is entitled to spend it away from his workstation if he has one' (reg 12(3)) (see *Huges* v *Corps of Commissioners Management Ltd* [2011] EWCAiv 1061, CA on compensatory rest). For *young workers*, where the 'daily working time is more than four and a half hours', the entitlement is to a rest break of a least 30 minutes, 'which shall be consecutive if possible and he is entitled to spend it away from his workstation if he has one' (reg 12(4)). The aggregation of working time is required where a young worker works for more than one employer (reg 12(5)). This does not occur under any other provisions.

Weekly rest

For each seven-day period, every **adult worker** is entitled to a minimum uninterrupted rest period of 24 hours plus the 11 hours' daily rest. This shall 'in principle include Sunday.' The implication is a 35-hour period of rest. However, 'if objective, technical or work organisation conditions so justify, a minimum rest period of 24 hours may be applied.' For *young workers* this reduction may be not less than 36 hours (reg 11).

▶ Shift work and night work

Shift work

This is work subject to minimum daily rest; maximum daily working hours; breaks during working hours; weekly rest periods; maximum weekly hours. Derogations are possible under the directive (Article 17(2) and (3)) in respect of daily rest and weekly rest. The regulations provide some flexibility in respect of shift working, subject to the provision of compensatory rest (reg 24).

Night work

An aim of the directive is to ensure that 'normal hours of work for night workers do not exceed an average of eight hours in any 24-hour period'. This is also provided for in the regulations (reg 6(1)). This is averaged over a 17-week reference period but can be extended by derogations (see below). 'Night time' is defined as a period of at least seven hours' duration between 11pm and 6am (or midnight and 5am if there is a relevant agreement). A 'night worker' is defined as 'a worker who, as a normal course, works at least three hours daily working time during night time' (reg 2(1)) (see Exhibit 10.4). It is also possible for a collective or workforce agreement to modify or exclude the application of the provisions of the eight-hour maximum and the reference period (reg 23).

Although young workers should not work at night (reg 6A), there are certain permitted exceptions (regs 27 and 27A). In these circumstances they may work where there is no adult available and where it is necessary to maintain continuity of service or production or respond to a surge in demand for a service or product. They must be adequately supervised for their own protection. Furthermore, they may work when exceptional and unforeseen circumstances arise.

Health and safety issues

The directive aims to ensure that 'night workers whose work involves special hazards or heavy physical or mental strain do not work more than eight hours in any period of 24 hours during which they perform night work' (Article 8, reg 6). This type of work can be defined in collective agreements and may be defined as such following a risk assessment made under the Management of Health and Safety at Work Regulations 1999. Adult night workers are also entitled to a health assessment (and a young worker to a health and capacities assessment) before being required to perform night work, and periodically thereafter (reg 7). If a registered medical professional advises that a night worker is suffering from health problems caused by or aggravated by working at night, he or she has a right to be transferred to suitable day work if possible (reg 7(6)).

EXHIBIT 10.4

Night work: case law

Case law in respect of night work is limited. However, in one early case defining 'night work', the Northern Ireland High Court ruled that under the directive (Article 2(4)), a worker is a 'night worker' if he or she works at least three hours during the designated hours of night *as a normal course* (*R v Attorney General for Northern Ireland* ex parte *Burns* [1999] IRLR 315, NIHC). The applicant in this case worked a rotating shift system at the relevant time under which she had to work night time hours one week in three.

The NIHC held that the words *normal course* entailed simply that night time working should be a regular feature of the applicant's employment. The court firmly rejected the argument that the definition of a night worker will only apply *to someone who does such work exclusively or predominantly*. The Working Time Regulations also use the phrase 'as a normal course' (reg 2(1)).

▶ Paid annual leave

The Working Time Directive and Regulations provided for the first time a right to paid holiday entitlement in British employment law. The directive provided for paid annual leave of at least four weeks (Article 7) and although Britain secured a transitional arrangement of three weeks (with effect from October 1998), the four-week statutory minimum entitlement came into in force in November 1999 (reg 13). Initially, the regulations provided for a 13-week **qualifying period** before entitlement to the paid leave came into effect but this was challenged at the European Court of Justice, which ruled it to be unlawful (*R* v *Secretary of State for Trade and Industry* ex parte *BECTU* [2001] IRLR 559, ECJ). A worker's entitlement now accrues from the first day of employment. The EU Charter of Fundamental Rights was also relied upon and asserts the unqualified right of every worker to annual paid leave (Article 8). From October 2001, the British government amended the Working Time Regulations to give effect to this judgment.

The entitlement is for a worker to accrue one-twelfth of the annual leave entitlement each month from the first day of employment. Any week in which a worker has a contractual relationship with an employer – for all or part of the week – will count. Part-time workers are entitled to *pro rata* treatment. (See detailed guidance on Department for Business website, **www.bis.gov.uk**)

Workers who work irregular hours are entitled to be away from work for the statutory minimum number of weeks. The number of hours for which they are entitled to receive payment might create problems. However, the law permits an averaging process with overtime hours not normally included as part of the calculations unless, contractually, a worker is bound to work some overtime hours.

It is important to note that the entitlement to paid annual leave does not prevent the employer, under the contract of employment, from specifying when that leave is to be taken. This has been confirmed by the EAT (*Sumsion* v *BBC* (*Scotland*) [2007] IRLR 678). In this case, a carpenter on a 24-week fixed-term contract was required to be available for work six days a week. The BBC said that where he was not required to work on Saturdays these days should be taken as annual leave. The EAT found that there was nothing restricting the employer nominating these days (when he might be required to work) as leave days. There was nothing special about weekends if it was a working day.

One controversial aspect of the initial paid annual leave entitlement in Britain was the provision which permitted an employer to include the eight statutory public holidays in the 20-day entitlement. Following campaigning, particularly by the Trades Union Congress, the law was amended (see Exhibit 10.5) and under the Working Time (Amendment) Regulations (2007), the statutory minimum leave entitlement is now 28 days for those working a five-day week.

The issue of paid annual leave has given rise to much of the case law under the Working Time Regulations. In Exhibit 10.6 some of the more significant cases in this area are identified and described. Of particular interest have been the recent cases of *Stringer* and *Pereda* relating to leave entitlement during periods of sickness, whether such leave can be carried forward into a new leave period and whether unpaid holiday

EXHIBIT 10.5

Increased holiday entitlement

- *Increase*: from 20 days (four weeks) to 28 days (5.6 weeks).
- *Phased introduction*: 24 weeks from 1 October 2007 then to 28 days (5.6 weeks) from 1 April 2009.
- Any time off for bank and public holidays can be included in the additional entitlement. So, a worker's holiday entitlement will not increase if he or she already received four weeks plus public holidays.
- *Pro rata* provision for part-timers as already established.
- Some or all of the holiday entitlement may be carried over to the following year with the agreement of the employer and the member of staff.
- Payment in lieu of the additional holiday *not* permitted from 1 April 2009 except on termination of employment.
- No qualifying period for the additional holiday.

EXHIBIT 10.6

Case law and paid annual leave

Robinson-Steele v *RD Retail Services Ltd and Other Cases* [2006] **IRLR 386, ECJ**

Issue. *The legality of 'rolled up holiday pay' under the Working Time Directive.*

The ECJ held that:

- It is unlawful for an employer to 'roll up' holiday pay so that, in effect, the minimum period of paid annual leave to which a worker is entitled is replaced by an allowance paid in instalments throughout the period of employment alongside the worker's normal pay. Holiday pay should be allocated to a period of leave and paid at the time the leave is taken.
- An employer will not act unlawfully if it offsets against a worker's entitlement to holiday pay for a specific period of leave *sums already paid* under a rolled-up holiday pay arrangement (provided that the rolled-up payments were made 'transparently and comprehensibly').

Comment. The British government has amended its guidance on the Working Time Regulations 1998 to state that employers with rolled-up holiday pay arrangements should renegotiate the relevant contracts as soon as possible so that payment for annual leave is made at the time that the leave is taken (IRS *Industrial Relations Law Bulletin* 783.14, April 2006).

Federatie Nederlandse Vakbeweging v *Staat der Nederlanden* [2006] **IRLR 561, ECJ**

Issue. This was whether it was compatible with the directive for an EU member state to have a national law that allows for the possibility that an employee who has not fully taken minimum annual leave in a year might receive financial compensation for that leave in a subsequent year.

The ECJ ruled that, while it was not contrary to the directive to carry leave over, there was the possibility that financial compensation could create an incentive for annual leave to remain untaken. This was incompatible with the directive's health and safety objectives (cf. decision in *Stringer* below where focus is upon those unable to take leave in a designated leave year as a result of sickness).

Commissioners of Inland Revenue v *Ainsworth and Others* [2005] **IRLR 465, CA;** *Stringer and Others* v *HM Revenue and Customs* **(C-520/06) [2009] IRLR 214**

Issue 1. *Entitlement to holiday pay by those on sick leave.*

The case concerned a number of current and former employees of HMRC. The Court of Appeal held that workers absent through long-term sick leave who have exhausted their entitlement to sick pay are not entitled to four weeks' holiday pay when they have done no work during the leave year as this would give them an unjustified windfall not intended by the Working Time Regulations 1998. The judgment was appealed to the House of Lords (now the Supreme Court) which referred it to the European Court of Justice.

In a landmark decision the ECJ took a different view on the operation of the Directive and held that workers on sick leave continue to accrue annual leave. Moreover, that if they are prevented from taking it during sick leave they must be able to take it after they return to work even if this means carrying over the leave until the following year. In a further judgment the ECJ held that any decision on whether workers can take annual leave during periods of sick leave was one for Member States to decide for themselves.

The significance of the case lies in the fact that the UK's Working Time Regulations required employees to use all holiday within a year or effectively lose it. The decision of the ECJ essentially challenged this, and the subsequent Supreme Court decision 'confirmed the ECJ ruling did override the Working Time Regulations' on this issue (*Personnel Today*, 10 June 2009).

In response to the ECJ decision the Supreme Court held that reg 13(9) of the WTR 1998, which states 'leave . . . may only be taken in the leave year in respect of which it is due' does not comply with the directive; and confirmed that staff accrue paid holiday for their entire period of sick leave, and must be allowed to take it once they return or be paid in lieu of it if their employment ends (*Personnel Today*, 10 June 2009) (see also German case *Schultz-Hoff* v *Deutsche Rentenvesicherung Bund (C-350/06)* [2009] IRLR 214; and *NHS Leeds* v *Larnet* EAT/0088/11).

The Conservative–Liberal Democrat government has stated that 'where someone has been on sick leave, we propose to allow employers to limit the ability to carry over annual leave to the four weeks of leave required under the WTD (i.e. excluding the additional 1.6 weeks required by the WTR and any further contractual leave' (HM Government 2011: 7).

Issue 2. *Claims to enforce the right to annual leave and holiday pay.*

The Supreme Court ruled further that claims for unpaid statutory holiday pay and accrued holiday pay on termination can be made as unlawful deductions from wages under the ERA 1996, not just the WTR. This could potentially allow employees to claim unpaid holiday pay on termination of their employment going back several years provided such claims are made within three months of the employers' most recent failure to pay holiday pay.

These judgments in what is now known as the *Stringer* case mean, in effect, that workers can accrue and take statutory leave during a period of sick leave; that as a result of sick leave, a worker who is unable to take annual leave in an annual year can carry this over – up to a maximum of 5.6 weeks (28 days) when they return to work. Moreover, where a worker is denied holiday pay he or she can bring a claim for unauthorised deduction from wages, and in the event that their employment is terminated before they have had the opportunity to take annual leave because of sickness they are entitled to payment in lieu at their normal rate (BIS 2010).

Pereda v *Madrid Movilidad SA* **(C-277/08) [2009] All ER (D) 88 (Sep)**

This case concerned an employee of a Spanish company who had arranged to have a period of holiday leave, but then suffered an injury which meant that he was unable to take the leave. The case focused upon the issue of whether he was entitled to an alternative period of leave equivalent to that he had been unable to take through incapacity, even if the leave year had already ended. The ECJ held that he could take leave in this way and that to deny an individual this was incompatible with the directive, irrespective of whether the leave year had ended (Wallington 2009).

British Airways plc v *Williams* [2010] **IRLR 541, SC**

This case involves pilots and cabin staff at British Airways and has potentially important implications for the civil aviation industry generally. Although not specifically concerned with the Working Time Regulations it does relate to the level of pay required under Article 7 of the Working Time Directive.

The case concerns reg 4 of the Civil Aviation (Working Time) Regulations 2004, which do not include express provisions explaining how holiday pay should be calculated, only a right to 'paid annual leave of at least four weeks' (Ford 2010). The level at which holiday pay is set is a particular issue in parts of civil aviation where the pay of staff is subject to a number of fixed and variable components and where as a consequence total pay can vary significantly. The view of BA is that holiday pay should be paid at the basic rate and not include any taxable supplements (such as flying allowances) staff would have received had they been working. In effect, that it should be set at a level that would not discourage staff from taking a holiday.

Drawing upon previous decisions of the ECJ, the view of the claimants is that as in *Stringer*, workers should receive their 'normal remuneration' during periods of annual leave (Ford 2010). The case was referred to the European Court of Justice by the Supreme Court. The ECJ ruled in September 2011 that the remuneration of a worker in respect of annual leave must, in principle, be determined in such a way as to correspond to the normal remuneration received by the worker. In particular, pay linked intrinsically to the tasks performed by a worker should be included. In this case, the airline pilots 'flying allowance' should be taken into account in calculating 'normal remuneration'. The ECJ, however, ruled that there were circumstances where remuneration may comprise several components – some of which may not be relevant for inclusion. Determination on this should be made by national courts (*British Airways plc v Williams and others*, (C-155/10)).

time can be claimed back on termination of employment. A separate issue concerns the level at which holiday pay should be set for those on variable pay and who normally benefit from additional taxable allowances (*British Airways* v *Williams* [2010] UKSC 16, see Exhibit 10.6).

The timing of annual leave has also been raised in *Russell* v *Transocean International Resources Ltd* [2010] CSIH 82. This case involved workers on offshore installations. Normally, they worked two weeks offshore. This was followed by a two-week onshore 'field break'. The employer refused a request for annual leave to be taken during the offshore period stating that leave should be taken during an onshore 'field break'. The Scottish Court of Session (the equivalent of the Court of Appeal in England and Wales), hearing an appeal from the EAT, ruled that there was no provision in the Working Time Directive 2003 that suggested that an employer may not arrange that annual leave is taken when the worker would not otherwise be working. (The Court drew a comparison with the example of school teachers being required to take leave at specific times when the school was closed to pupils; and with manufacturing plants which may be closed for a specific holiday period.)

Enhanced leave under the contract

The statutory entitlement is to a *minimum* period of annual leave. It is possible that the employer might have an enhanced annual leave entitlement of more than 28 days. These additional days will be a contractual entitlement. Any dispute about them will be about the contract and not about the statutory entitlement. Furthermore, financial compensation for not taking this enhanced annual leave would be permissible if agreed by the employer and the employee.

FRISHCO SUPERMARKET CASE STUDY

Scenario 10.1

Do 'bank' staff have holidays?

Marion has been a member of the 'bank' of general assistants used by Frischo for 12 months when the 'bank' started. It is designed to deal with resourcing problems. In the agreement these staff have a mobility clause requiring them to be available to cover vacancies in any stores within the south-west London region. As a consequence Marion has, in the past year, worked *on average* two days per week. At some periods – Christmas, Easter and during August – she has often worked four or five days a week in different stores. Her husband, who works as a porter at a local NHS hospital, has told her that she should be entitled to some paid holiday. Marion has worked more frequently at the store where **Tony** is the manager and decides to ask about whether she is entitled to any paid holiday. Tony says that it is 'the first he has heard about it' and that it is not in the 'bank

staff' agreement. He added that paid holiday was for permanent staff only.

Question

Does Marion have any entitlement to paid annual leave? What steps might she take in-company to deal with the issue? If an in-company grievance is not successful, does she have any right to complain to an employment tribunal?

Visit **mylawchamber.co.uk/willey**
to access sample HR documents to support this case study.

FRISHCO SUPERMARKET CASE STUDY

Scenario 10.2

Long-term sick absence

Indira, a part-time administrative assistant, has been absent from work for three months (early November to the end of January) following severe injuries sustained in a road traffic accident. She is entitled to 28 days' statutory annual leave on a *pro rata* basis. The holiday year in the company is from 1 January until 31 December. Before she went on sick leave, **Indira** had already booked ten days' holiday over the Christmas period. This was the remainder of her entitlement for that holiday year. When she returned to work at the end of January, she made some comment to **Debbie**, her supervisor, about having 38 days' leave this new holiday year. When Debbie queried this, **Indira** explained that she should be able to take the leave she had booked over Christmas. Debbie said that as far as she was

aware this holiday was 'lost'. It was last year's and she couldn't take it. However, she agreed to talk to Caroline, the company Human Resources Manager, about it.

Question

What advice should Caroline give about Indira's situation?

Visit **mylawchamber.co.uk/willey**
to access sample HR documents to support this case study.

❱ Maximum working week

The directive (Article 6) states that the average working time for each seven-day period (including overtime) should not exceed 48 hours. Weekly working time can be averaged over a four-month (17-week) period. Sick leave and 'periods of paid annual leave' 'shall not be included or shall be neutral in the calculation of the average' (Article 16).

Reference period

The Working Time Regulations specify a 48-hour maximum for a seven-day period over a 17-week reference period. There are provisions (in conformity with the directive) to extend the reference period to:

- 26 weeks in certain circumstances (reg 4(5)) (reg 21), for example in security and survelliance work; or
- up to 52 weeks through a collective or workforce agreement (reg 23).

In calculating a person's average working time, certain periods are in effect 'neutral', for example when a person is sick, on maternity or other family leave or on holiday. Exhibit 10.7

EXHIBIT 10.7

Averaging examples

1 A worker has a standard working week of 40 hours and does overtime of 12 hours a week for the first 10 weeks of the 17-week reference period. No leave is taken during the reference period.
The total hours worked is:
17 weeks of 40 hours and 10 weeks of 12 hours of overtime

$$(17 \times 40) + (10 \times 12) = 800$$

Therefore, this average (total hours divided by number of weeks) is:

$$800 \text{ divided by } 17 = 47.1 \text{ hours}$$

The average limit of 48 hours has been complied with.
Where leave is taken within a referencing period the situation is as follows:

2 In the example above, let us assume that the worker takes three days' leave in the reference period.
The total hours worked is:
16 weeks of 40 hours and 2 days of 8 hours and 10 weeks of 12 hours of overtime.

$$(16 \times 40) + (2 \times 8) + (10 \times 12) = 776$$

To this has to be added the time taken on leave, which is three days of eight hours that should be added (3×8) taken from the next reference period:

$$(3 \times 8) = 24$$

His or her average, therefore, (total hours divided by number of weeks) is:

$$\frac{776 + 24}{17} = 47.1 \text{ hours}$$

Again, the average limit of 48 hours has been complied with.

Source: BIS (2008) *Your Guide to the Working Time Regulations: Sections 1–4*, Example 1, Section 2.

provides an example of how average working hours are calculated under the regulations; the first example comes from government guidance (see **www.bis.gov.uk** on the making of these calculations).

A young worker should not work more than eight hours per day and 40 hours per week. There is no opt-out available. In certain circumstances they may work longer hours where there is no adult available and where it is necessary to maintain continuity of service or production; or respond to a surge in demand for a service or product. An employer 'shall take all reasonable steps, in keeping with the need to protect the health and safety of workers' to ensure that these limits are complied with (reg 5A).

▶ The individual 'opt-out'

One of the key concessions obtained by the British government in its implementation of the directive has been securing agreement that individual workers may opt to work in excess of 48 hours per week.

This particular derogation from the regulations requires the worker to sign a simple opt-out agreement. The right for the individual worker to invoke the opt-out must comply with the following conditions (reg 5):

- the agreement must be in writing;
- it can be for a specific or indefinite period;
- notice to terminate agreement shall not exceed three months;
- if there is no notice period, then the agreement is terminable by seven days' notice;
- the only record required is that workers have signed the opt out;
- individuals have the right not to suffer detriment and are protected against unfair dismissal for failing to sign an opt-out if requested by the employer (ERA 1996, ss 45A and 101A). 'Detriment' can include pressure, harassment, disciplinary threats, over-looking for promotion, failure to provide pay and benefits to which the worker is entitled. For an example of a discriminatory dismissal, see *Morris v Turista Travel Ltd* ET case 2501197/99 (Exhibit 10.8).

Although the UK was the first EU member state to have used this option, 15 other EU members now have provision in their national implementing legislation for some sort of opt-out (*Hansard* 9 May 2011). In general, other countries have tended to follow the UK in relation to specific sectors (Collins *et al.* 2005), and it remains the subject of considerable controversy. The derogation relating to individual workers is subject to the general principles of the protection of the safety and health of workers as set out in the directive (Article 22) and as such should not impose excessive working hours, sufficient to harm the health of the individual worker (*Hone v Six Continents Retail* [2006] IRLR 49 CA (Exhibit 10.8)). Furthermore, such agreements can be subject to scrutiny by the 'competent authorities'. In the UK this is the Health and Safety Executive. If there is no opt-out, then it is lawful for workers to refuse to exceed the 48-hour maximum as ruled in *Barber v RJB Mining (UK) Ltd* [1999] IRLR 308, HC (see Exhibit 10.8).

In view of the controversy surrounding it, the individual opt-out has been subject to a prolonged examination by the Council of Ministers. Available research evidence shows:

- Its use is widespread in the UK with an estimated 19 per cent of employees (3.8 million) having signed an opt-out. Its use is most common in the private sector (especially in manufacturing/construction) and in larger workplaces.

EXHIBIT 10.8

Case law relating to maximum working week

Morris v *Turista Travel Ltd* **ET/2501197/99**

The issue was a discriminatory dismissal. The worker was given a draft contract which stated:

> You agree that the limit imposed by Regulation 4(1) and (2) of the Working Time Regulations 1998 . . . should not apply to your average weekly working hours. This part of your contract of employment . . . would have the effect that you may work longer hours than 48 hours average maximum working hours provided under the regulations. The opt out agreement which is effective from . . . may be terminated by either party giving the other party three months' notice in writing.

He refused to sign the opt-out and was sacked for his refusal. It was ruled as an unfair dismissal (under ERA 1996, s 101A).

Barber v *RJB Mining (UK) Ltd* [1999] **IRLR 308, HC**

The issue was the enforcement of the central provision in the directive/regulations – the 48-hour maximum working week (reg 4(1)).

The workers concerned had worked more than the maximum average hours permitted in an initial reference period. They worked under protest but sought a declaration of their rights and an **injunction** restraining the employer from requiring them to work additional hours beyond the maximum. It was ruled that this regulation is 'a mandatory requirement which must apply to all contracts of employment' (Mr Justice Gage). It was noted that this 'will have the effect of making it clear that [the employees] are entitled, if they so choose, to refuse to continue working until the average working hours come within the specified time limit.'

It has been commented that the reasoning in this case can be applied to the maximum length of night work (reg 6).

Hone v *Six Continents Retail* [2006] **IRLR 49, CA**

An employee's refusal to opt out of the 48-hour week, in combination with his very long hours, was held to be relevant in deciding that his subsequent stress-related mental health problems were reasonably foreseeable.

- There is substantial evidence that the opt-out is sought by employers as a precautionary measure. Around 81 per cent of establishments that had an opt-out reported no sustained long hours working.

In one of the most detailed research studies into the operation of the individual opt-out, Barnard and her colleagues have argued that it has been the principal means by which the potential impact of the directive has been diluted.

> The opt-out provides employers with a low-cost mechanism to avoid the 48-hour limit, and the ease with which it can be deployed is one of the reasons for the limited use by employers of the collective derogations. They are complex to arrange, in particular for employers who, in the absence of a recognised trade union, only have available the route of a workforce agreement.   (Barnard *et al.* 2003: 252)

The deliberations surrounding the 'opt-out' continue and show no signs of resolution, at least for the time being (see Exhibit 10.9). Indeed, the growing take-up of opt-out

> ### EXHIBIT 10.9

The 'opt-out' provision

In June 2008, the EU Social Affairs Council voted to allow the continuation of the 'opt-out' provisions despite Members of the European Parliament voting in 2005 to end it. Among the key provisions of the agreement:

● those workers who have opted-out will be subject to a maximum working week of 60 hours (averaged over three months) unless the Social Partners agree otherwise;

● the individual 'opt-out' will not be allowed to be signed before the contract of employment commences and not during the first four weeks of the contract;

● an individual 'opt-out' cannot run for longer than a year without renewal;

● the 'opt-out' provisions will be subject to further examination four years after implementation.

In December 2008, however, the European Parliament voted again to end member states' ability to opt out of the maximum weekly working week of 48 hours. The decision was referred for consideration by the European Council of Ministers, but in April 2009 it was announced that the European Parliament and Council of Ministers failed to reach an agreement – the Council wishing to retain the option without any end date and Parliament, to phase out the opt-out clause.

As of May 2011 the position was that the social partners were being consulted over a general review of the Working Time Directive including calculation of on call time and compensatory rest periods, a process that will inevitably involve a consideration of the opt-out provisions (*Hansard*: proceeding of the European Committee 9 May 2011). In the event that no agreement between the social partners is forthcoming, which seems likely given their respective positions, the general view is that the Commission will introduce draft amending legislation to change the directive in late 2011. However as Edward Davey MP, Minister for Employment Relations, stated in Parliament the government's position on the issue is clear:

> We are committed in our coalition agreement to limit the application of the Working Time Directive in the United Kingdom. In that context, our key priority is to ensure the retention of the individual's right to opt out of the 48-hour working week (*Hansard* 9 May 2011).

This suggests, as the Labour MP Michael Connarty noted in the same debate, that:

> If the Commission brings forward proposals to amend the directive [the government] will engage positively and constructively to secure additional security, especially about on call time and compensatory rest periods (*Hansard* 9 May 2011).

provisions in other member states coupled with the approach of the Conservative–Liberal Democrat government in the UK suggest its continued use is likely to persist into the foreseeable future.

▶ Unmeasured working time

Specific derogations from the regulations are permitted 'when, on account of the particular characteristics of the activity concerned, the duration of the working time is not measured and/or predetermined or can be determined by the workers themselves'. This 'unmeasured working time' applies particularly to 'managing executives and other persons with autonomous decision-making powers', 'family workers', and 'workers officiating at religious ceremonies in churches and religious communities' (art 17(1)) (reg 20(1)). As we saw in the earlier *Context* section it is those with 'unmeasured working time' who most frequently work in excess of 48 hours per week (Blyton 2010, Grimshaw and Rubery 2010).

Since 6 April 2006, the Working Time (Amendment) Regulations 2006 have been in force in respect of unmeasured working time and voluntary overtime by such workers as managing executives or others with 'autonomous decision-taking powers'. These replace the arrangements that have been in place since 1999.

The effect of the 2006 change is that a wide range of employers whose workers may choose to do additional work are required to take all reasonable steps to ensure that the total duration of their working time does not exceed an average of 48 hours a week. For many employers this is simply a case of asking affected workers to agree in writing that the limit on working time will not apply to them. If the 'opt-out' (reg 4(1)) is duly signed, this will remove the problem.

> However, should a worker refuse to sign, the employer will need to take care to ensure that he or she is not victimised as a result. Particular care is required if the individual decides to assert his or her rights under the Regulations, declines to opt out and reduces the amount of additional work that he or she does. If doing less work leads to the worker being given unfavourable appraisals or performance ratings, this could amount to an unlawful detriment under s 45A of the Employment Rights Act 1996.
>
> (IRS, *Industrial Relations Law Bulletin*, 780.4, March 2006)

▶ Derogations

The previous section has described some of the major **derogations** from the Working Time Regulations. The term 'derogation' is, to some extent, a novelty in British employment relations. It means a specified 'waiver'. If a derogation exists, there is expected to be some equivalent compensation in return. Derogations, under the directive, are qualified by the need to have 'due regard for the general principles of the protection of the safety and health of workers' (Article 17(1)). The directive permits member states to make derogations in various broad areas (Article 17):

- those who have a degree of control over their own time (unmeasured working time);
- where the worker's activities are such that his or her place of work and place of residence are distant from one another or his or her different places of work are distant from one another;
- groups on whom rigid controls on working time may be inappropriate (e.g. security workers where a permanent presence on site is required);
- in the case of activities involving the need for continuity of service or production;
- where there is a foreseeable surge in activity (particularly in agriculture, tourism and postal services);
- certain shift workers;
- in cases of accident or imminent risk of accident.

Derogations may be achieved through:

- collective or workforce agreements;
- relevant agreements (by individuals);
- individual agreements to 'opt out' of the 48-hour maximum working week limit.

▶ Collective and workforce agreements

These, as indicated above, constitute a means of implementing a derogation – which enables the Working Time Regulations to be implemented more flexibly. There are two forms of agreement:

● collective agreements negotiated with recognised independent trade unions;

● workforce agreements, in non-union workplaces, which are negotiated with elected workforce representatives or with the workforce as a whole.

Collective agreements

We have already noted the historic regulatory role of collective agreements in British employment relations, with these agreements subject to a statutory legal framework (Trade Union and Labour Relations Consolidation Act 1992, ss 178–179). Furthermore, as we have noted at various points, the express or implied 'incorporation' of provisions of a collective agreement into the terms of individual contracts of employment is an accepted process under contract law (see Chapter 2).

Under the Working Time Regulations, a collective agreement may 'modify or exclude the application' of the following regulations for 'particular workers or groups of workers' (reg 23):

● The reference period of 17 weeks can be extended 'for objective or technical reasons or reasons concerning the organisation of work to a period not exceeding 52 weeks'. This effectively ensures possible compliance of annual hours contracts with the regulations (reg 23(b)).

● The length of night work (regs 6(1) and 23b).

● Night work involving 'special hazards or heavy physical or mental strain' (reg 6(7)).

● Daily rest (reg 10).

● Weekly rest (reg 11).

● Rest breaks (reg 12).

Any modifications or exclusions negotiated to rest periods and night work are subject to the principle of 'compensatory rest' or other 'appropriate protection' (reg 24).

The use of collective agreements to modify or in some cases exclude the operation of a directive is well established in European employment law. In the context of mainland Europe where **collective bargaining** remains a significant determinant of the terms and conditions of many workers this reflects an understandable wish to see the implementation of legislation remaining sensitive to the institutions and realities of employment relations.

In many EU countries collective agreements cover between 65 and 90 per cent of workers, reflecting the continuing importance of sectoral and industry-wide bargaining in much of Europe. As we have seen, the UK and the Irish Republic have in contrast witnessed a steady decline in collective bargaining coverage in recent years. In the UK, the numbers covered by collective agreements has fallen from around 72 per cent of the workforce in the late 1970s to below 40 per cent today, with the major decline taking place in the private sector. One important consequence of this change is that the facilities provided by Europe to aid implementation of legislation are potentially less able to give effect to such developments in the UK because of the decline in union organisation and with it collective bargaining. In the area of working time, an attempt to rectify this situation has been through the development of 'workforce agreements', which are discussed below.

Workforce agreements

These agreements are able, in non-union organisations, to achieve the same modifications and exclusions as collective agreements. However, a workforce agreement can only be made between an employer and a workforce (or part of a workforce) whose terms and conditions are *not* set by collective bargaining. To have the status of a 'workforce agreement' the following conditions and requirements must be satisfied:

- It must be in writing.
- It must specify the date of application to the workers concerned.
- Before signature, 'all those workers to whom it is to apply must be provided by the employer with copies of the text of the agreement and with guidance'.
- It must be signed by either a majority of the relevant workforce or the representatives (or a majority of the representatives) of the relevant workforce.
- It should have an expiry date no later than five years after the commencement date, when it can be renewed or replaced (Working Time Regulations, Sch 1).

It has not been clarified explicitly in law but it is presumed that the government wishes a workforce agreement to have an equivalent legal role to a collective agreement. That is, it is presumed not to be legally enforceable unless specified by the parties and capable of incorporation into individual contracts of employment.

▶ Enforcement

There are two routes to enforcement of the regulations.

Individual entitlements

In common with other employment rights, these are enforceable through a complaint to an employment tribunal by a 'worker' irrespective of length of service, within three months of the act complained of, although the tribunal has the discretion to extend this period if it considers that 'it was not reasonably practicable' for the case to be presented (reg 30). As is usual with employment tribunal complaints, ACAS has a statutory duty to conciliate and attempt to achieve a settlement (reg 33; and Employment Tribunals Act 1996, s 18(1)).

These complaints can relate to the following:

- daily rest for adult workers and young workers;
- weekly rest for adult workers and young workers;
- in-work rest breaks for adult workers and young workers;
- paid annual leave.

Where an employment tribunal finds a complaint well founded, it 'shall make a declaration to that effect' and may make an award of compensation to be paid by the employer to the worker. The amount of compensation shall be such as the tribunal considers 'just and equitable in all the circumstances' having regard to 'the employer's default in refusing to permit the worker to exercise his right' and 'any loss sustained by the worker which is attributable to the matters complained of' (reg 30).

Limits

These (weekly working-time and night-work limits and health assessments for night workers) are enforced by the appropriate health and safety authorities (the Health and Safety Executive or local authority environmental health officers) (reg 28). The HSE is responsible for enforcing the working time limits where they apply in factories, building sites, mines, farms, fairgrounds, quarries, chemical plants, nuclear installations, schools and hospitals. Local authority environmental health officers have responsibility in the areas of retailing, offices, hotels and catering, sports, leisure and consumer services.

The powers of the inspectors provided in the Health and Safety at Work Act etc. 1974, apply to the enforcement of the Working Time Regulations 1998. A person guilty of an offence (HASWA 1974, s 33(1)) shall be liable to prosecution and on conviction in a magistrates' court, to a fine. If the conviction is on indictment, the fine is unlimited.

The number of working time cases can fluctuate significantly, depending on whether there are individual complaints or what are effectively groups of individual complaints. The number of claims made under the Working Time Regulations to the Employment Tribunal Service for the period since 2002–03 are detailed in Table 10.2.

Table 10.2 **Claims brought to tribunals under the Working Time Regulations**

Year	Number of employment tribunal claims
2010/11	68,400 (first three quarter statistics)
2009/10	95,200*
2008/09	23,976
2007/08	55,712
2006/07	21,167
2005/06	35,474
2004/05	3,223
2003/04	16,869
2002/03	6,436

* Accounted for a quarter of all ET claims but this includes multiple airline cases re-submitted every three months

Source: **www.justice.gov.uk**

Are the Working Time Regulations working?

Research into the impact and effectiveness of the regulations suggests they have fallen some way short of their aims, with their impact in particular being limited and uneven. Case study research (Neathey and Arrowsmith 2001; Neathey 2003; Barnard *et al.* 2003) has suggested a slow adjustment to the legislation and some significant costs in implementing the regulations. In general, the available evidence can be summarised as follows:

❱ Impact of the regulations

In an early attempt to study the impact of the regulations, Neathey and Arrowsmith (2001) surveyed 20 organisations; of these half indicated that the regulations had a 'marginal' or 'no impact' on their organisation of working time. This was confirmed in a follow-up study (Neathey 2003) and by separate research conducted by Barnard and her colleagues (2003), which concluded that the implementation of the directive had not led to widespread changes in the way working time was organised:

> In particular it has not been a catalyst for organisational reforms aimed at using a reduction in the length of the working week to bring about productivity improvements . . . [adding that] . . . employers and employees . . . remain wedded to a long-hours culture.
>
> (Barnard et al. 2003: 251–2)

According to Neathey and Arrowsmith (2001), where there was an impact of the regulations, it included a review of working practices which could involve taking a more strategic approach to the organisation of working time. However, this was evidenced in only a small number of the organisations in their original study.

❱ Areas of uncertainty

In the DTI-sponsored research (Neathey and Arrowsmith 2001), all but one of the case study organisations faced some difficulties interpreting provisions of the regulations. These included:

- *Defining Working Time*. In particular, this concerned travelling time and on call time (see earlier section).
- *Dealing with unmeasured working time*. There were differences of opinion about whether the amendment (Working Time Regulations 1999) had clarified this area. A complaint by the trade union AMICUS (now UNITE) alleging that the 1993 directive had not been fully implemented, was particularly concerned about the lack of obligation on employers to keep records of time worked voluntarily above normal working time, particularly for this group of workers.
- *Casual workers*. This was a particular problem for 'as and when' casuals in relation to their continuity of service and entitlements to paid annual leave.
- *Staff with more than one job*. The guide produced by the then DTI (2000: 26) suggested finding out this information from individuals and considering, if appropriate, an opt-out to disapply the 48-hour maximum.

Neathey and Arrowsmith (2001) also found significant misrepresentation by employers, particularly in relation to the 48-hour week and the definition of workplace agreements.

❱ The 48-hour maximum working week

The survey data in this area can appear conflicting. There are several issues involved:

- whether or not the employer has introduced the facility of the individual 'opt-out' (to be operated as and when required);
- the proportion of the employer's workforce covered by individual 'opt-outs';

- the actual use of the 'opt-out' to exceed the 48-hour maximum; and
- the use of the alternative mechanism – varying the reference period through a collective or workplace agreement.

The evidence presented earlier in this chapter points to 'long hours working' remaining a feature of working life for many in the UK, indicating the extent to which such practices are embedded in the culture of many organisations and accepted by those who work in them (TUC 2008; Hart 2004). The TUC (2002 (**www.tuc.org.uk**)) quotes one survey which reported that 47 per cent of companies had used 'opt-outs' for *some* of their workers, a figure that rose to 71 per cent in the case of companies employing between 500 and 5,000 employees. In 15 of the 20 companies surveyed by Neathey and Arrowsmith (2001), the proportion of the workforce regularly exceeding the limit was small. The principal method used was to encourage workers to sign forms opting out of the 48-hour limit. A third of employers had signed a collective or workforce agreement to vary the reference period and a similar proportion had changed working practices to reduce the hours worked by individual workers. These included revised shift arrangements and increases in staffing.

◗ Holidays

This area seems to have presented the fewest problems of adjustment for many organisations. In the Neathey and Arrowsmith research, only two of the 20 organisations had leave entitlement of less than four weeks. The only significant change concerned the provision of leave for casual workers, where for four of the organisations the cost implications of the definition of 'holiday pay' were important.

◗ Night work

The main implication of the regulations for most of the organisations with night workers concerned the health assessment requirements (Neathey and Arrowsmith 2001). However, once implemented these assessments did not lead to workers being moved away from night work.

A research survey (Norman 2011) observing 50 night workers over a period of time in 2009–10 reported a range of consequences for such workers:

> A growing body of medical evidence shows that working night shifts increases the likelihood of developing a range of health problems including cancers, gastro-intestinal conditions, cardio-vascular disease and problems in pregnancy . . . We observed that many night workers had poor diets . . . Tiredness and fatigue are the inevitable consequences of working at night and result in lowering cognitive performance and one's ability to concentrate. Night workers are more likely to cause or suffer from an accident at work (*ibid.*: 4).

◗ Collective and workforce agreements

In their study, Neathey and Arrowsmith found that five organisations with recognised unions had used the flexibilities provided through collective agreements, and three non-union establishments had used workforce agreements. In the latter, the involvement of employee representatives had taken the form of **consultation** rather than negotiation. Rather surprisingly, there has been little survey evidence or case study research in the past five years attempting a longer-term assessment of the regulations. In the meantime we await the findings of the Workplace Employment Relations Survey 2011 to allow us to shed more light on the impact and effectiveness of the regulations over more than a decade of their operation.

Employment policies and practices

▶ A strategic approach to implementation

In light of the traditional way of determining working time (through collective bargaining or unilateral employer decision), the regulations potentially have a disproportionate impact on British employee relations compared with these relations in other EU member states. Employers might be tempted to respond to the regulations in a piecemeal way. However, given their wide-ranging implications, there are good reasons for adopting a more strategic approach. There are a number of broad considerations for employers, which encompass corporate strategy, operational practice, the use of internal and/or external professional resources of advice and information, employee relations policy, and the contribution of personnel administration. These involve the following:

Identifying which members of their workforce are covered by the various provisions

This involves paying attention to specific grades of staff who might be covered by derogations, whether or not any are 'young workers', and those who work on particular working-time patterns (shift working and night work).

Using as appropriate, professional resources to diagnose workers' suitability for night work and shift work

This refers in particular to the issue of health and safety assessments, and the role of occupational health services within an organisation.

Identifying the impact of the regulations upon existing contractual terms and (where relevant) collective agreements

This involves considering whether or not the legislation limits any existing contractual terms (for example on working hours) or whether it requires the introduction of new contractual rights (paid holiday entitlement) to comply with the law.

Considering the ways in which, for operational reasons, the organisation might wish to utilise the opportunities available within the regulations through derogations

As we have seen there are three main ways to introduce flexibilities provided by the regulations: 'collective agreements', 'workforce agreements', and an 'individual voluntary agreement'. Furthermore, the 'opt-out' from the 48-hour week can be applied by all employers with the agreement of individual employees (reg 5).

As we have discussed earlier, for employers that recognise trade unions, the regulations provide for a collective agreement to modify or exclude the application of various of the regulations for 'particular workers or groups of workers'. The areas covered are the reference period for averaging working time (reg 4), the length of night work (reg 6(1)), night work involving special hazards of physical or mental strain (reg 6(7)), daily rest (reg 10), weekly rest (reg 11) and rest breaks (reg 12).

In the case of non-union workforces, workforce agreements are able to achieve these same modifications and exclusions. The agreements can only be made between an employer and a workforce (or part of a workforce) whose terms and conditions are **not** set by collective bargaining. The regulations stipulate requirements that must be satisfied in setting up representative machinery; these have been outlined in the earlier section on workforce agreements.

Deciding whether, procedurally, to use workforce or collective agreements, or agreements with individual workers to comply with the requirements

Individual employers need to weigh up the balances of advantages for their own organisations to determine which of the mechanisms to use.

Deciding on the likely use of individual voluntary agreements to disapply the 48-hour maximum working week

Individual employers need to consider the operational advantages of such agreements, to be aware of possible allegations of unlawful pressure to force employees to sign such agreements and to consider the operational implications that might arise if such an agreement is not secured or if it is not brought to an end by the employee.

Deciding on whether the staff (full time, part time, temporary, etc.) currently employed (as well as new staff) are already receiving the minimum annual paid leave entitlement

The regulations provide for a *minimum* period of paid leave. Employers may consider whether to enhance paid leave under the contract of employment.

Deciding on appropriate record systems

The records required cover the maximum working week, night work patterns, and the assessment of night workers. The guidance on this by the Department for Business Enterprise and Regulatory Reform states that in terms of the **maximum working week**, it is for the employer to determine the records to be kept, although the basis for such records may already be in existence.

In respect of **night working and health assessments**, it is for the employer to decide on the records to be kept. The employer needs to be able to 'show who is a night worker, when they had an assessment and the result of the assessment' (DTI 2000: para 4.5).

▶ Exploring the impact on organisations of the Working Time Regulations

In the final section we provide a suggested checklist that might help human resource practitioners consider, in a structured way, the impact of the regulations on their organisation. Finally, the scenarios in the Exercises will help in understanding further the practical application of the regulations.

A checklist for action

The following identifies the main questions and issues for HR practitioners to consider in securing compliance with the Working Time Regulations.

- What is the profile of the workforce in terms of:
  - Employment status (i.e. full time, part time, temporary, etc.)?
  - Working patterns (shift and night working, annual hours arrangements)?
  - Age (adult and young workers)?

- Do existing arrangements comply with the standards set in the regulations?

- Where an independent trade union is recognised for the staff in question, would it be more constructive to undergo this diagnosis jointly?

- Is any use to be made of 'individual voluntary agreements' to disapply the 48-hour working week average?

- Is there any working time which cannot be 'measured, predetermined or fixed by the employer'? Is it, therefore, appropriate to invoke the derogation?

- If trade unions are not recognised for particular groups of staff, what use might be made of 'workforce agreements' to achieve some flexibility in the implementation of the regulations?

- Is more detailed advice necessary on specific matters from, for example, the Department for Business and Regulatory Reform; the Advisory, Conciliation and Arbitration Service; the Health and Safety Executive; or any relevant employers' association?

- If necessary, does the organisation have its own (or access to) specialist health and safety/occupational services to assist in the preparation of health and safety assessments?

- What administrative arrangements need to be made to create (and maintain for two years) the necessary records; and can these records be integrated into existing computerised personnel records? Employers will need to hold records on the following to enable the competent authorities to monitor compliance (reg 8). These cover:
  - a worker's average working time, including overtime (reg 4.1);
  - the details of individual voluntary agreements to disapply the 48-hour working week maximum (reg 5);
  - the operation of night work (reg 6);
  - health and safety assessments (reg 7).

- What are the likely implementation costs for the organisation – in respect of changed terms and conditions of employment, record keeping, and the provision/funding of health and safety assessments?

Exercises: Some scenarios

10.1   A small non-unionised print shop employing around 19 people occasionally has to deal with rush orders requiring 70-hour weeks.

How can the employer deal with the 48-hour maximum average working week?

10.2   A call centre has traditionally defined '**work**' as the period when the worker is dealing with a customer on the telephone. Sometimes staff have attended their place of work for eight hours but only received six hours' pay.

Can this now be challenged at an employment tribunal? How should working time be defined?

10.3   Maggie, a waitress, has been employed by a catering company on an 'as required' basis for some 15 months. Generally, this means that she works four or five evenings a week. A friend told her that she should be entitled to some paid holiday. When she spoke to her manager, she said she was entitled to nothing.

What is her situation?

10.4   A freezer engineer is based at home. He is 'on call' (through a mobile phone) to a supermarket chain in a specific region. He is only paid by the supermarket for specific tasks he carries out, as and when required.

Is he a worker as defined by the regulations and therefore protected by them?

10.5   A worker in a medium-sized company tells her employer that she wants to terminate (in eight days' time) **an individual voluntary agreement** to disapply the 48-hour maximum working week limit. It has been in force for several months and no notice period is indicated for the termination of this agreement. The employer has indicated to her that it is not convenient to terminate the agreement and asks her for her reasons. She refuses to say and insists on ending the agreement. The employer does not say he will sack her immediately but implies that he might be looking for staff to replace her who will agree to disapply the limit.

Advise the worker on her legal rights under the regulations and the courses of action open to her.

10.6   A large, non-unionised international hotel employs on **night work**, a night manager and a night team of eight staff in its front office between the hours of 11pm and 8am. Each member of staff works an average of 45 hours per week (over five days). The night team comprises the assistant night manager, a cashier, two receptionists and four porters.

The length of the shift is important. There needs to be a short overlap between the new day shift and the night shift to deal with any outstanding problems. In the morning, the concierge department shift does not begin until 8am. This means that all the luggage of the guests arriving or departing in the morning before 8am is dealt with by the night staff. Furthermore, daytime staff start their shift at 7am. The one hour overlap between the two shifts is used for hand-over.

Are these arrangements still permissible under the Working Time Regulations?

10.7   A shift worker visited his GP about periods of giddiness which he started to experience. These arose from sleepless nights or days (depending on his shifts). The GP's medical report stated that the varying shift pattern was probably the cause of the disrupted sleep patterns. The report was sent to the employer with the worker's permission when he requested to be placed on normal daytime work. The company refused his request on the ground that it needed to operate a night shift with a full complement of staff and because it could not change at short notice. It stated that it would take six months to rearrange the shift patterns to accommodate his request.

What protections and rights does he have in law?

Feedback on these exercises is provided in the Appendix to this textbook.

References

Advisory, Conciliation and Arbitration Service (1988) 'Labour Flexibility in Britain', Occasional Paper 41. London: ACAS.

Anxo, D. *et al.* (2004) 'Implications for Working Time Policies', in Messenger, J., *Working Time and Workers' Preferences in Industrialized Countries. Finding the Balance*. London: Routledge.

Arrowsmith, J. and Sisson, K. (2000) 'Managing Working Time', in Bach, S. and Sisson, K. (eds), *Personnel Management: A Comprehensive Guide to Theory and Practice*. Oxford: Blackwells.

Ashkenazy, P. (2008) 'A Primer on the 35-hour Week in France 1997–2007', IZA Discussion Paper No. 3402.

Barnard, C., Deakin, S. and Hobbs, R. (2003) 'Opting Out of the 48-hour Week: Employer Necessity or Individual Choice? An Empirical Study of the Operation of Article 18(1)(b) of the Working Time Directive in the UK', *Industrial Law Journal*, Vol. 32, No. 4.

Bell, D. and Hart, R. (2005) *Annualised Hours Contracts*. London: ESRC (www.esrc.ac.uk).

Bercusson, B. (2003) 'Crunch Time for Working Time', *Thompson's Labour and European Law Review*, No. 83.

Blyton, P. (2010) 'Working Time, Work–Life Balance and Inequality', in Blyton, P., Heery, E. and Turnbull, P. (eds), *Reassessing the Employment Relationship*. Basingstoke: Palgrave Macmillan.

BMRB Social Research (2004) *A Survey of Workers' Experiences of the Working Time Regulations*, Employment Relations Research Series, No. 31. London: Department of Trade and Industry (www.bis.gov.uk).

British Chambers of Commerce (2007) *Work and Life: How Business is Striking the Right Balance*. London: BCC.

Bunting, M. (2005) *Willing Slaves: How the Overwork Culture is Ruling our Lives*. London: Harper Perennial.

Casey, B. *et al.* (1997) *Employers' Use of Flexible Labour*. London: PSI.

Chartered Institute of Personnel and Development (2003) *Living to Work*. London: Chartered Institute of Personnel and Development.

Collins, H., Ewing, K. and McColgan, A. (2005) *Labour Law: Text and Materials*. Oxford: Hart.

Commission on Vulnerable Employment (COVE) (2007) *Hard Work, Hidden Lives: The Full Report of the Commission on Vulnerable Employment*. London: TUC.

Deakin, S. and Morris, G. (2009) *Labour Law* (5th edn). Oxford: Hart.

Department of Trade and Industry (1997) *Measures to Implement Provisions of the EC Directive on the Organisation of Working: A Consultation Document*. London: Department of Trade and Industry (www.bis.gov.uk).

Department of Trade and Industry (2000) *Your Guide to the Working Time Regulations*. London: DTI.

Donovan Commission (1968) The Royal Commission on Trade Unions and Employers' Organisations (1965–68), Cmnd 3623. London: HMSO.

Federation of European Employers (2011) *Untangling the Myths of Working Time: How Long is the European Working Week*. London: Federation of European Employers.

Ferri, E. and Smith, K. (1996) *Parenting in the 1990s*. London: Joseph Rowntree Foundation and Family Policy Studies Centre.

Ford, M. (2010) *Working Time and the Right to Paid Annual Leave: The Implications of Stringer, Pereda and Williams*. London: Old Square Chambers.

Grimshaw, D. and Rubery, J. (2010) 'Pay and Working Time: Shifting Contours', in Colling, T. and Terry, M. (eds), *Industrial Relations: Theory and Practice*. London: Wiley.

Hart, R. (2004) *The Economics of Overtime Working*. Cambridge: Cambridge University Press.

Hayden, A. (2006) 'France's 35-hour Week: Attack on Business? Win-win reform? Or betrayal of Disadvantaged Workers', *Politics and Society*, Vol. 34: 2.

Health and Safety Executive (2006) *A New Guide on Managing Shift Work*. London: HSE (www.hse.gov.uk).

HM Government (2011) Consultation on Modern Workplaces. London: Department for Business, Innovation and Skills (www.bis.gov.uk).

Kahn-Freund, O. (1983) *Labour and the Law*. Oxford: Oxford University Press.

Kodz, J., Davis, S., Lain, D., Strebler, M., Rick, J., Bates, P., Cummings, J., Meager, N. and Anxo, D. (2003a) *Working Long Hours: A Review of the Evidence, Volume 1 – The Main Report*, Employment Relations Research Series, No. 16. London: Department of Trade and Industry (www.bis.gov.uk).

Kodz, J., Davis, S., Lain, D., Strebler, M., Rick, J., Bates, P., Cummings, J., Meager, N. and Anxo, D. (2003b) *Working Long Hours: Volume 2 – Case Studies and Appendices*, Employment Relations Research Series, No. 16. London: Department of Trade and Industry (www.bis.gov.uk).

Labour Force Survey (2008) (www.statistics.gov.uk).

Neathey, F. (2003) *Implementation of the Working Time Regulations: Follow-up Study*, Employment Relations Research Series, No. 19. London: Department of Trade and Industry.

Neathey, F. and Arrowsmith, J. (2001) *Implementation of the Working Time Regulations*, Employment Relations Research Series, No. 11. London: Department of Trade and Industry.

Norman, W. (2011) *Rough Nights: the Growing Dangers of Working at Nights*, London: The Young Foundation.

Organisation for Economic Co-operation and Development (2004) *Observer*, Discussion Paper No. 244, September. Geneva: OECD.

Personnel Today (10 June 2009) 'Workers Can Accrue Holiday Pay While on Sick Leave, the House of Lords has Ruled', *Personnel Today*.

Reed, J. (2010) *Flexible with the Truth: Exploring the Relationship between Labour Market Flexibility and Labour Market Performance*. London: Trades Union Congress.

Smith, D. (2004) 'Strangled', *Sunday Times*, 7 March.

Trades Union Congress (2008) *Return of the Long Hours Culture*. London: Trades Union Congress (www.tuc.org.uk).

Wallington, P. (2009) *The Working Time Regulations: Holiday Pay*. London: KBW.

White, J. and Beswick, D. (2003) *Working Long Hours*. Sheffield: Health and Safety Executive.

Williams, S. and Adam-Smith, D. (2010) *Contemporary Employment Relations* (2nd edn). Oxford: Oxford University Press.

Useful websites

Advisory, Conciliation and Arbitration Service **www.acas.org.uk**

Department for Business, Innovation and Skills **www.bis.gov.uk**

Equality and Human Rights Commission **www.equalityhumanrights.com**

UK Statistics Authority **www.statistics.gov.uk**

Trades Union Congress **www.tuc.org.uk**

Visit **www.mylawchamber.co.uk/willey** to access study support resources including realistic HR documentation to accompany the case studies in the book, an online chapter on collective labour law, interactive multiple choice questions, annotated weblinks, a glossary, glossary flashcards, key case flashcards, a legal newsfeed and legal updates.

Chapter 11

Family leave and work–life balance

Learning objectives

Having read this chapter you should be able to:

- Explain the reasons for the recent growth in interest in 'work–life balance' and appreciate the different approaches taken to defining this concept
- Summarise the primary pieces of legislation that apply in the area of family and dependency rights and outline their scope and main provisions
- Evaluate the grounds of action and remedies available to British workers in relation to the exercise of family and dependency rights

Structure of the chapter

- *Introduction*: a brief overview of the economic and social factors underpinning the recent growth of interest in work–life balance, and of attempts to define the concept
- *Legislation*: its scope and the relationship between legislative and contractual rights; rights and responsibilities in the areas of pregnancy and maternity, paternity, adoption, dependency and parental leave and the right to request flexible working; protection against dismissal or detriment for exercising family rights; the role of equality law in this area; enforcement procedures and remedies available for breach of the family rights outlined
- *Exercises*

Introduction

Work–life balance has arguably been the most high profile HR or employment related issue over recent years. It is one that HR practitioners are increasingly having to deal with, particularly in the context of the relatively **tight labour market** in recent years. Although the concept of 'work–life balance' is broad and rather nebulous, there has been notable recent legal intervention in this area with regard to rights to family leave. The goal of this chapter is to chart developments in this area and outline key rights and responsibilities of employers and **employees** alike.

❯ Factors underpinning the growing interest in work–life balance

Workforce interest in striking a balance between home and work is not necessarily a new phenomenon. Indeed, it may be argued that employers and their workforces have always been in conflict over where the latter should expend their time and energy, and that both have had to show flexibility at times (Clutterbuck 2003). However, the drivers and underlying social dynamics of employment have changed dramatically in the last quarter of a century, and this has resulted in the notion of 'work–life balance' (WLB) gaining increased prominence in the contemporary employment vernacular.

Early industrialisation and the introduction of mass machinery created two distinct spheres of life – home and work (Felstead *et al.* 2005). These two spheres remained relatively distinct throughout much of the twentieth century, but the progressive development of information and communications technology (ICT) over the last two decades, whilst maximising work efficiency, has extended the time and space of employment (e.g. via the use of e-mail and 'BlackBerrys'). The resulting 'work intensification' has been compounded by increased global competition and the shift in many western economies from production to service-oriented industries, which increasingly operate on the basis of instant availability to customers (Suff 2002).

At the same time, major demographic and social shifts including an increasing number of women entering the workforce, declining birth rates and a rapidly ageing population, have changed the profile, attitudes and needs of the workforce (MacInnes 2002). More employees than ever have caring responsibilities, whilst simultaneously being subjected to longer working hours (TUC 2005). The result is described by Hoschild (1997) as a 'time-bind' and by Madeline Bunting (2004) as a 'crisis of human sustainability' that threatens the very fabric of family life and indeed the health and stability of society at large.

The tight nature of the UK labour market until recently and the difficulty experienced by many organisations in recruiting and retaining staff has also been a significant recent 'push' factor, which has prompted the development and implementation of policies by employers on work–life balance and family friendly working (e.g. see CIPD 2007).

Legal and political developments have been important too. As with so many areas of employment regulation, the UK's membership of the European Union has had significant implications for the area of family rights and work–life balance. The Pregnant Workers Directive 1992 obliged the member states of the European Union to provide for a minimum 14-week maternity leave period, while also setting down standards for the protection of the health and safety of pregnant women. The Parental Leave Directive 1996 created a right to parental leave. In addition, the European Union's treaty articles and directives on gender equality have also been highly influential in this area.

Alongside these political/legal influences from Europe, UK government activity has become increasingly important. The Labour governments 1997–2010 introduced a range of measures aimed at increasing the number of women in the labour market and helping employees better balance work commitments and family life. The Conservative–Liberal coalition elected in May 2010 has outlined its strong commitment to the same objectives, with significant new legislation likely to be introduced in due course (HM Government 2011).

◗ Defining 'work–life balance'

This is a highly elastic concept that largely escapes precise definition. While previously it was seen to be centrally focused on the provision of assistance to workers with family and caring responsibilities, the contemporary notion of work–life balance represents a progression to practices that are intended to benefit all employees (Kodz *et al.* 2002). It is also now recognised that employee needs in relation to work–life balance change throughout life (Suff 2002), while the term 'balance' has acquired a dual meaning, referring both to the relationship between home and work and to the wider objective of meeting both employee and employer needs (Dex and Scheibl 1998). The notion of 'work–life balance', therefore, has evolved and become more inclusive (Suff 2002).

While conceptualisation of 'work–life balance' has therefore developed and expanded over time, this makes it difficult to identify precisely how this notion translates into policies and practices at workplace level. Indeed, work–life balance seems to be endowed with 'infinite elasticity' in the corporate context (IRS 2002: 6). Researchers have attempted to overcome this problem by grouping work–life balance practices into manageable categories, however these vary widely. For example, Dex and Smith (2002) categorise practices relating to 'hours of work' and 'location of work' separately, whereas IRS (2002) merges them into one group entitled 'flexible working (time and place)'. The definition of work–life balance in the Workplace Employee Relations Survey (WERS) series has focused on non-standard patterns of work and childcare assistance (Cully *et al.* 1999; Kersley *et al.* 2006). By contrast, Suff (2002) expands the definition to include previously unacknowledged practices such as 'employee development' and 'flexible careers'. Friedman and Greenhaus (2000) do the same, in defining Employee Assistance Programmes as a work–life balance practice.

It is therefore evident that a variety of approaches are taken to specifying what work–life balance means in practice. While some favour a narrow focus on perhaps the more obvious practices relating to the organisation of work, others are broader, encompassing a wider range of policies and practices. Although the validity of the latter approaches is recognised, the focus of this chapter is on more traditional practices relating to leave for family reasons and the organisation of work. This is because these are the areas regarding which legal regulations currently exist.

Legislation

▶ European law

As mentioned above, as in other areas European Union law has been very important in establishing minimum rules and standards in relation to pregnancy, maternity and other family rights. The Pregnant Workers Directive 1992 provides pregnant workers with a right to time off for ante-natal care, requires employers across Europe to take specific steps to protect the health and safety of pregnant women, and obliges them to provide a minimum of a 14-week, paid maternity leave period. The Parental Leave Directive 1996 provided rights to both parental and dependency leave. This has since been superseded by Directive 2010/18/EU, which introduces a number of changes to the original parental leave directive and must be implemented by 8 March 2012. The Equal Treatment Directive 2006 (which amends and consolidates previous equal treatment directives), prohibits less favourable treatment on grounds of pregnancy or maternity and provides women with the right to return to work after maternity leave.

▶ British law

The following acts and regulations give effect to this European legislation in a UK context as well as the additional rights and responsibilities created independently by the UK government. They contain the various rules and provisions that apply in the area of family and dependency rights and responsibilities:

- *Employment Rights Act 1996*: core provisions on maternity, adoption and dependency leave; also on right to time off for ante-natal care, flexible working and the right not to suffer detriment or dismissal on family grounds. This act has been added to and amended on various occasions.
- *Maternity and Parental Leave Regulations 1999* (as amended in 2002, 2006 and 2008): additional rules and provisions on maternity and parental leave.
- *Paternity and Adoption Leave Regulations 2002* (as amended 2006 and 2008): additional rules and provisions on paternity and adoption leave.
- *Additional Paternity Leave Regulations 2010 and Additional Statutory Paternity Pay (General) Regulations 2010*: implement the right to additional paternity leave and additional statutory paternity pay consequent to birth or adoption.
- *Flexible Working (Eligibility, Complaints and Remedies) Regulations 2002* (as amended 2009) *and Flexible Working (Procedural Requirements) Regulations 2002*: two sets of regulations containing additional rules and provisions on flexible working.
- *Management of Health and Safety at Work Regulations 1999*: cover health and safety of pregnant women.
- *Equality Act 2010*: specific provisions on the protected characteristic of 'pregnancy and maternity'; broader provisions on direct and indirect sex discrimination also relevant

It should be noted that at the time of writing the UK government was considering further radical changes in this area, which are discussed in relevant sections below (HM Government 2011). This is likely to lead to new legislation amending or replacing a number of the above acts or regulations.

▶ Relationship with contract of employment

The rights and entitlements provided by legislation in the area of family leave constitute basic, minimum standards which can be supplemented by more generous contractual provisions. The more advantageous composite rights resulting from the combination of statutory and contractual provisions are enforceable via the enforcement procedures specified for the former (i.e. within the context of a claim to an employment tribunal).

▶ Scope of statutory protection

This varies according to the employment status of individuals, as outlined in Table 11.1 below. Effectively, there are differences in respect to whether a worker is an 'employee' (i.e. with a **contract** of employment) or a 'worker on some other contract to work personally' (see Chapter 2).

As outlined in the table, the majority of rights and entitlements in relation to pregnancy/ maternity and family leave apply to those with 'employee' status only. Only 'employees'

Table 11.1 **Family and dependency rights by employment status**

Right or entitlement	Application
Ante-natal care	Employees only
Maternity leave	Employees only
Maternity pay	Employees only but definition used can encompass agency workers
Paternity leave	Employees only
Parental leave	Employees only
Adoption leave and pay	Employees only
Right to request flexible working	Employees only
Dependency leave	Employees only
Health and safety protection	All workers, i.e. employees, self-employed and casual workers
Protection from sex discrimination	Broad application: covers agency workers and self-employed may also be covered

are able to avail of entitlements to maternity, paternity, parental and adoption leave and the right to request flexible working. (This may change with regard to parental and dependency leave as a result of the Parental Leave Directive 2010.) However in relation to maternity pay, the definition of 'employee' adopted is relatively broad (the key issue is whether the organisation is liable to pay National Insurance contributions in relation to the worker in question) and hence agency workers may be entitled to this. Alternatively, they may be entitled to 'maternity allowance' (the Department of Work and Pensions provides detailed information on the rules governing statutory maternity pay – see **www.dwp.gov.uk/advisers/techguides**). Aside from this, at present the principal rights and entitlements of casual/atypical workers who lack employee status are in relation to health and safety and protection against discrimination.

The Management of Health and Safety at Work Regulations 1999 impose obligations on employers with regard to 'persons working' in their undertaking who may be pregnant or of childbearing age. The regulations therefore cover workers who do not have employee status.

In addition, the Equality Act 2010 (s 83(2)) applies to a broad notion of 'employment' including contracts to 'personally execute any work', which means that self-employed workers may be protected provided that they personally undertake the work in question themselves. The Equality Act (s 41) also expressly covers 'contract workers', a category that includes temporary agency workers (see Chapter 5).

Note that in addition to requiring a particular employment status, the above legislation (Table 11.1) imposes additional qualifying conditions relating to length of service as well as other considerations. These additional conditions will be outlined in the various sections below, but, for example, to be entitled to request flexible working, employees must have 26 weeks' continuous service with their employer and also be the parent of a child aged 17 or under or 18 or under if the child is disabled; or partner to such a parent; or carer of an adult.

Health and safety protection

The Management of Health and Safety at Work Regulations 1999 (regs 16–18A) oblige employers to protect the health and safety of pregnant women (see Chapter 12). Employers are required to carry out a risk assessment where there are women of childbearing age in the workplace and the work is of a kind which could involve risk to the health and safety of a new or expectant mother or to that of her baby. Where this is the case, employers should inform their employees of the need to provide written notification of pregnancy as soon as possible.

In addition to this general duty, employers are obliged to undertake a more specific risk assessment when they have been notified in writing that a worker is pregnant, has given birth within the previous six months, or is breastfeeding. Sick notes stating that an employee or worker was suffering from a pregnancy-related illness could amount to written notification, triggering the employer's duty to carry out an individual risk assessment (*Day* v *T Pickles Farms Ltd* [1999] IRLR 217, EAT).

The case of *O'Neill* v *Buckinghamshire County Council* [2010] IRLR 384, EAT has clarified the nature of an employer's obligations in this area. (It was adopting the approach previously set out by the Court of Appeal in *Madrassy* v *Nomura International plc* [2007] IRLR 246, CA.) Here the EAT explained that the obligation to carry out a risk assessment is triggered only in certain circumstances, namely where:

- the employee notifies the employer in writing that she is pregnant;
- the work could involve the risk of harm or danger to the expectant mother or her baby; and
- the risk arises from the processes or working conditions or physical or biological agents specified in the Pregnant Workers Directive.

In this case the employee in question was a school teacher, and the EAT found that the alleged stress inherent in teaching did not constitute a 'working condition' that would trigger a risk assessment. While *O'Neill* confirms that there is no general duty for employers to carry out an individual risk assessment for all pregnant employees, it is good practice to do so. It is argued that this avoids uncertainty over whether or not the duty applies and may enable measures that could make the pregnant employee more comfortable at work to be identified (the Health and Safety Executive provides useful guidance in this area – **www.hse.gov.uk/mothers**).

Where the obligation to carry out a risk assessment arises in respect of a pregnant worker, the courts have previously established that a failure to do so constitutes sex discrimination (*Hardman* v *Mallon t/a Orchard Lodge Nursing Home* [2002] IRLR 516 EAT). Such cases are now likely to come within the dedicated provisions concerning pregnancy or maternity discrimination or the broader provisions on direct discrimination contained in the Equality Act 2010 (see further below).

The case of *Stevenson* v *J M Skinner & Co* [2008] EAT/0584/07/DA provided guidance about conducting risk assessments. The EAT noted that there is no definition of 'risk assessment' in the legislation and that there is no requirement for an assessment to be in writing. The regulations state that a risk assessment must be 'suitable and sufficient' (reg 3). In addition, an employer is not obliged to physically give a risk assessment to an employee; rather they must record the findings of the assessment and provide information about those findings, which may be done orally. According to the EAT, 'a meeting with the employee where assessments are made and at which agreement is reached on the relevant risks, discharges the obligation on the employer'.

Employers must keep risk assessments under review due to the fact that the potential risks may vary at different stages of a pregnancy. In addition, risk assessments should be reviewed in the event of any change to an employee's work that could raise a previously unidentified risk.

Where a risk to the health of a pregnant woman is identified, employers must take steps to eliminate or reduce the risk. This may involve an alteration to the woman's hours or working conditions. If this is not possible she should be offered suitable alternative work. This must be suitable and appropriate for the employee to do in the circumstances and on terms and conditions not substantially less favourable than her normal terms and conditions (Employment Rights Act 1996 (s 67). If this is also not possible then the pregnant women should be suspended from work on full pay for as long as is necessary to protect the health and safety of both the employee and her child.

In *British Airways (European Operations at Gatwick) Ltd* v *Moore and Botterill* [2000] IRLR 296, EAT, the employer transferred cabin crew to ground duties during their pregnancy for health and safety reasons. The employees' flying allowance was discontinued as a result of the transfer. The EAT found that this temporary alternative employment was not suitable as because no flying allowance was payable, the alternative jobs were on terms and conditions substantially less favourable than those applicable to their normal jobs. It should, however, be noted that subsequent decisions of the European Court of Justice cast doubt on this decision, and appear to suggest that employers are not obliged to continue paying pregnant women pay components that are dependent on performance by the worker of specific functions (this is discussed further below).

Breastfeeding

Section 25(4) of the Workplace (Health, Safety and Welfare) Regulations 1992 requires employers to provide suitable facilities for workers who are pregnant or breastfeeding to rest. The HSE outlines that it is good practice to provide a safe and healthy environment for nursing mothers to express and store milk or to enable infants to be breastfed at or near the workplace. Employers could, for example, consider providing a private room, secure and clean refrigerators, facilities for sterilising and storing bottles, and paid time off to express milk or breastfeed.

Time off for ante-natal care

The Employment Rights Act 1996 (s 55) sets out this right for pregnant employees. It is a right not to be unreasonably refused time off to attend ante-natal care (for example an appointment with a midwife or doctor or hospital appointment) and, in addition, the right to be paid for this period of absence. The pregnant woman is required to seek permission before she takes this leave and if the employer requests, must provide evidence of an appointment (note that this duty does not apply to the first such appointment). The right is to time off within working hours, so an employer is not permitted to rearrange the woman's working hours or insist that she make up the hours lost another time. The employer can only refuse such a request if it is reasonable to do so. The government is considering also giving fathers or the mother's partner rights to attend such ante-natal appointments (HM Government 2011).

Maternity leave

From 1 April 2007, all pregnant employees have been entitled to take up to 52 weeks of maternity leave, regardless of their length of service with their employer. This entitlement is in two periods: 26 weeks of 'ordinary' maternity leave (OML) followed by 26 weeks of 'additional' maternity leave (AML) (ERA 1996, ss 71–73).

A woman can choose when to start her maternity leave. This can be any date from the beginning of the 11th week before the week the baby is due. However, there is a period of 'compulsory maternity leave' which is the two-week period following birth (this is four weeks for factory workers). An employer is criminally **liable** for non-compliance with this provision and may be fined (ERA 1996, s 72(5)). In order to be able to take up her right to maternity leave a woman must inform the employer of:

- the fact that she is pregnant;
- the expected week of childbirth;
- the date on which ordinary maternity leave is due to start.

This information must be provided 15 weeks before the expected week of childbirth and employers are entitled to request a medical certificate stating the date of the expected week of childbirth (EWC). Once an employer has been informed of the pregnancy, he or she is obliged to notify the woman of the date on which she will return to work within 28 days.

Maternity pay

Pregnant employees with 26 weeks' continuous service by the 15th week before the expected week of childbirth are entitled to Statutory Maternity Pay (SMP) during the period of ordinary maternity leave. Since 1 April 2007 the maternity pay period now lasts for 39 weeks. SMP is set at two levels. 'Higher rate' SMP is 90 per cent of a woman's average weekly earnings and is paid for the first six weeks. The amount a woman is due to be paid during this period is generally obtained by calculating her average earnings during the eight-week period up to and including the 15th week before the expected week of childbirth. Higher rate SMP is followed by 'lower rate' SMP, the level of which is reviewed annually (for current rates see **www.direct.gov.uk/en/MoneyTaxAnd Benefits/index.htm**) and was set at £128.73 a week as at May 2011. SMP is paid by the employer who then receives a rebate for the amount from the government.

The case of *Alabaster* v *Woolwich Building Society* [2004] IRLR 486, ECJ established that a woman on maternity leave is entitled to benefit from a pay rise awarded between the start of the reference period used to calculate average earnings for higher rate SMP, and the end of maternity leave. This position has been formalised by the Equality Act 2010 (s 74). Where this situation applies an employer is obliged to recalculate the level of maternity pay to include the pay rise and pay her the difference between the two amounts. Women who are not entitled to SMP but meet certain qualifying conditions based on their employment and earnings record may claim up to 39 weeks' Maternity Allowance from a Job Centre Plus office.

Contract of employment during maternity leave

The contract of employment continues to exist during both ordinary and additional maternity leave. Previously, all the contractual terms with the exception of those regarding remuneration, continued to apply during OML. During AML only a much smaller range of essential contractual terms applied. For example, while a woman on OML was legally entitled to continue benefiting from contractual terms relating to use of a company car or gym membership, a woman on AML was not, with only essential contractual terms such as those relating to duty of care or disciplinary procedures operational during AML. (Of course, a fuller range of terms could also be in force during AML if a woman's contract of employment expressly provided for this.)

However, decisions of the European Court of Justice (*Lewen v Denda* [2000] ICR 648; and *Land Brandenburg v Sass* [2005] IRLR 147) and a judicial review of the revised Sex Discrimination Act brought by the Equal Opportunities Commission in early 2007, challenged the legislation in this area. It was consequently amended by the Sex Discrimination Act (Amendment) Regulations 2008, to eliminate any legal distinction between the rights and treatment of women on OML and AML, and consequently in the types of claim they can bring in relation to these periods. This change affects employers who have previously provided non-pay benefits to women on OML but not on AML (e.g. contractual leave above the statutory minimum, company cars, gym membership or mobile phones).

The change in the law also has implications for the treatment of maternity leave in calculating length of service for the purposes of both statutory and contractual rights. While both the OML and AML periods have historically counted as periods of employment for the purposes of calculating service with reference to statutory rights (e.g. protection against unfair dismissal), only the OML period has counted as such in the calculation of service for the purposes of contractual rights (e.g. pension entitlements). However, the amendment to the law in this area now means that the AML period must now also be included in calculating length of service for the purposes of both statutory and contractual rights.

The Equality Act 2010 (s 74) stipulates that when a woman goes on maternity leave a 'maternity equality clause' is automatically read into her contract, which has a number of consequences. First, as outlined above, any pay increase awarded after the reference period but before the end of maternity leave which the woman would have received had she not been on leave, must be taken into account in calculating her maternity pay. In addition, when a woman returns to work and starts receiving her normal salary again, her employer must give her any pay increase she would have received had she not been on maternity leave. Second, the employer must pay any contractual bonus payment awarded or that would have been awarded during the maternity leave period. However, in calculating the bonus payable, the actual time during which a woman is on maternity leave will not be included, except for the compulsory maternity leave period. Any pay rise or bonus must be paid when they would usually be due.

Bonus payments during maternity leave

The question of the entitlement of a woman on maternity leave to receive bonuses is rather complex. If a bonus is part of her contract then she is not entitled to it during maternity leave, as she is not entitled to contractual pay during this period. However if a bonus to be paid either wholly or partly relates to a period when she was working then the bonus or a relevant *pro rata* amount should be paid; not to do so would constitute sex discrimination (*Lewen v Denda* [2000] ICR 648, ECJ).

In general terms, discretionary bonuses do not need to be paid to women on maternity leave. However there are two exceptions to this:

- a bonus must be paid relating to any period during which a woman is on compulsory maternity leave; and

- a discretionary bonus must be paid to the extent that it relates to a period when the woman was not on maternity leave (*Lewen v Denda* [2000] ICR 648, ECJ) (Equality Act 2010, Sch 9, para 17).

The position regarding *voluntary bonuses for future loyalty* is somewhat unclear, although the case of *Gus Home Shopping Ltd v Green and McLaughlin* [2001] IRLR 75, EAT, is authority for the proposition that not to pay such bonuses to women on maternity leave may be discriminatory.

Allowances

Another relevant issue concerns the entitlements of women who are redeployed or on medical suspension during pregnancy (but before maternity leave begins), in order to protect their health and safety. In *Gassmayr v Bundesminister fur Wissenschaft und Forschung* [2008] ECJ C-194/08, an employer refused to pay on-call payments to a doctor who was on medical suspension because of risk to her pregnancy. The employer's view was that because she couldn't work she could not be on-call. Ms Gassmayr contended that this contravened the Pregnant Workers Directive 1992. The ECJ ruled that Article 11 of this directive does not preclude withholding allowances in these circumstances – i.e. which depend on the performance of a specific task – provided the woman's income does not fall below the national sick pay levels. However, employers cannot withhold allowances that do not depend on performance.

Similarly, in *Parviainen v Finnair Oyj* (C-471/08), the ECJ ruled that an air hostess transferred to ground work during her pregnancy was not entitled to retain a number of supplementary allowances paid to flight crew. The principle established was that while a pregnant woman transferred to another position remained entitled to the pay components or allowances relating to her professional status (for example her seniority, length of service and professional qualifications), there is no requirement to maintain those 'dependent on the performance by the worker of specific functions in particular circumstances'. This decision appears to be contrary to current UK law, where the Employment Rights Act (s 67) states that women transferred to an alternative job on grounds of pregnancy must be transferred on terms 'not substantially less favourable' than they enjoyed before. For example, in *British Airways (European Operations at Gatwick) Ltd v Moore* [2000] IRLR 296, the EAT held that BA was in breach of s 67 by not providing pregnant cabin crew employed on alternative ground-based work the allowances to which they were entitled when they were working normally (*Equal Opportunities Review*, August 2000).

Pension schemes during maternity leave

The Equality Act introduced a 'maternity equality rule' into all occupational pension schemes (s 75). The effect of this is that employees on maternity leave continue to be members of their pension scheme, with this period also counting for the calculation of benefits. However the accrual of pension rights takes place during paid maternity leave only. During the latter employees make their standard pension contribution, based on the maternity pay received during the period. In contrast, the employer must continue to pay any earmarked contributions based on the pay the woman would have received had she been working normally.

'Keeping in touch days' and contact during maternity leave

From April 2007 it has been possible for employees to do up to ten days work during maternity leave without breaking that period. These are known as 'keeping in touch days' and in addition to some pieces of work they are also envisaged to encompass training sessions or appraisals. These keeping in touch days can be paid, at a rate agreed between the employer and employee. There is no right for an employer to insist that an employee works such a day; nor for an employee to insist on working. This is seen to be a significant change as previously if a woman undertook paid work during maternity leave she would lose her entitlement to maternity pay for the week in question and her leave period would automatically come to an end.

Another change introduced by the Work and Families Act 2006 is that employers are now allowed to have 'reasonable contact' with employees during the maternity leave period. This is envisaged to enable an employer to provide an update regarding developments at the workplace and also allow communication regarding arrangements for the return to work.

Returning to work after maternity leave

The Employment Rights Act (ss 71 and 73) provides women with the right to return to work after ordinary and additional maternity leave. If a woman wishes to return early from maternity leave she must inform her employer eight weeks in advance.

A woman returning to work after OML has the right to return to the same job on the same terms and conditions as before, as if she had not been absent. Those returning after AML also have a right to return to the same job on the same terms and conditions as before. However if it is 'not reasonably practicable' for the woman to return to the same job, she is entitled to a similar job that is 'suitable' and 'appropriate for her to do in the circumstances'; and 'on terms and conditions not less favourable than those which would have applied if she had not been absent' (Maternity and Parental Leave etc. Regulations 1999, regs 18 and 18A). To date, there has been only one decision of the Employment Appeals Tribunal to consider the meaning of the 'same job', in the case of *Blundell* v *St Andrew's Catholic Primary School* [2007] EAT 0329/06/RN (see Exhibit 11.1).

Redundancy situations

Where there is a redundancy situation, women on OML or AML are entitled to be offered a 'suitable alternative vacancy' where one exists (this may be at an associated employer) (Maternity and Parental Leave etc. Regulations 1999, reg 10). The new job must be such that the work is suitable and appropriate for her to do in the circumstances and, in addition, with provisions as to capacity, place and other terms and conditions that 'are not substantially less favourable' than if she had continued to be employed under the previous contract. The implication here is that employers are essentially required to discriminate in favour of women on maternity leave in redundancy situations (See Chapter 3).

What is the 'same job'?

Blundell v *St Andrew's Catholic Primary School* [2007] **EAT 0329/06/RN**

Facts. This case involved a female primary school teacher who before her maternity leave was teaching the 'reception' class. However, after returning from leave, she was assigned to teach a year two class and she claimed that this was not a return to the same job.

EAT judgment. It held that she *had* in fact been returned to the same job. It set out how the relevant provisions in the Maternity and Parental Leave Regulations 1999 (reg 2) require three different factors to be taken into consideration:

- 'the nature of the work she is employed to do in accordance with the contract of employment'; and
- the 'capacity'; and
- the 'place' of the old and new jobs being undertaken.

In the case in question, the EAT outlined that Ms Blundell had been employed as a teacher in the school, not specifically as a teacher of the reception class. The nature of the work was therefore the same. The place of work (i.e. the school) was also the same, as was the capacity (i.e. of teacher). The employer had not therefore breached the legislation. An important observation made was that where the precise job a woman was doing before she went on maternity leave was variable, the key question to consider is whether the nature of the job she is given on her return was 'outside the boundary of what was permissible'; whether the new job was 'outside the normal range of variability which she could reasonably have expected'. In *Blundell* this was not the case.

Paternity leave

The right to paternity leave was first introduced in 2003 following the adoption of the Paternity and Adoption Leave Regulations 2002. Up until 2011 this consisted of a right to take two weeks' leave at the time of birth or adoption, provided certain qualifying conditions were met. However the Work and Families Act 2006 incorporated the power for government to create a right to up to six months 'additional paternity leave' on top of the basic two week entitlement (henceforth categorised as 'ordinary paternity leave'). This was implemented by the Additional Paternity Leave Regulations 2010, which came into force in April 2011 for fathers of children whose expected week of birth is on or after 3 April 2011. Matching for adoption has the same date. The two rights are discussed in turn below.

Ordinary Paternity Leave (OPL)

Employees with 26 weeks' continuous service by the end of the 15th week before the EWC are eligible for ordinary paternity leave. The employee must be the father of the child or either married to or the partner of the child's mother (the partner may be same sex). Where the employee is not the child's father they should have the main responsibility for the upbringing of the child (apart from any responsibility of the mother). Both ordinary and additional paternity leave can be taken with regard to a child's placement for adoption.

To gain entitlement, employees must also satisfy a number of notification requirements. They must provide written notification to their employer outlining when the baby is due, when the OPL is to start and whether one week or two week's leave are requested. This information must be provided at least fifteen weeks before the week in which the baby is due.

The amount of OPL an employee is entitled to does not increase in the case of multiple births. OPL must be taken as one week or two weeks together. It is not possible to take days here and there or one week now and another later on. The leave must also be taken within the eight weeks following birth. The leave is paid, with Ordinary Statutory Paternity Pay (OSPP) paid at the same rate as lower rate SMP (£128.73 as at April 2011). Workers who are not eligible for OPL may still be able to claim OSPP.

Employees taking ordinary paternity leave have rights to return to work similar to those relating to the taking of ordinary maternity leave.

Additional Paternity Leave (APL)

The eligibility requirements for APL outlined in the Additional Paternity Leave Regulations 2010 are the same as those for ordinary paternity leave. The regulations outline the right to up to 26 weeks extra leave (the minimum amount of leave that can be taken is two weeks). APL must be taken as one block in multiples of complete weeks.

APL can only be taken once the mother has returned to work and from week 20 after the birth of the child, and it must also be taken within 12 months of the birth. There are a number of written notification requirements that fathers/partners have to comply with. They must provide their employer with a 'leave notice', 'employee declaration' and 'mother declaration' at least eight weeks in advance of the leave being taken. The leave notice must specify the expected week and date of birth and the dates on which the APL is to start and end. The employee declaration must outline that the purpose of the leave is to care for the child and that the applicant is either the child's father or the mother's partner. The mother's declaration must outline the mother's name, address and National Insurance number and the date she intends to return to work. In addition it must confirm that the applicant is the child's father or mother's partner, and also that that he or she is the only one exercising the entitlement to APL in respect of the child. An employer may request a copy of the child's birth certificate and the name and address of the mother's employer. Once an employer has been notified of a leave request they are obliged to confirm the relevant dates in writing within 28 days.

Fathers on APL can receive the balance of the mother's statutory maternity pay if there is an entitlement, in the form of Additional Statutory Paternity Pay (ASPP). If the mother is not entitled to SMP or Maternity Allowance, the APL can be taken but it is unpaid.

The contract of employment during paternity leave and the return to work

The contract of employment remains in force during both OPL and APL and the father is entitled to continue to receive contractual benefits, except for those concerning pay. The provisions here are similar to those that apply during maternity leave. Similar provisions also apply regarding contact with the employer and 'keeping in touch days'.

The right to return to work after both ordinary and additional paternity leave are the same as those that apply in relation to ordinary maternity leave. Where the employee returns to work after having taken two or more consecutive periods of statutory leave including a period of parental leave of over four weeks, then the rights to return are similar to those relating to additional maternity leave.

Employees are protected against detriment or dismissal related to paternity leave (e.g. for taking or applying for paternity leave). Also similar to the position regarding maternity leave, where a redundancy situation arises employees on additional (but not ordinary) paternity leave are entitled to be offered a 'suitable alternative vacancy' on terms and conditions not substantially less favourable than those in their previous role.

Parental leave

The Maternity and Parental Leave etc. Regulations 1999 (regs 13 and 14) provide that employees, with one year's continuous service who have or expect to have 'parental responsibility' for a child under the age of five, have a right to parental leave for the purposes of 'caring for' that child. Adoptive parents are also entitled to take parental leave. This statutory leave is unpaid. However, the employer may agree to payment under the employee's contract of employment.

The intention of the government was to enable employers to provide contractual entitlements to parental leave, but where this does not take place the statutory 'default' scheme applies. The details of the latter are as follows:

- Employees are entitled to take 13 weeks of unpaid parental leave up to the fifth birthday of each child they have for the purposes of caring for that child. The entitlement in relation to disabled children is 18 weeks up until the 18th birthday.

- Leave must be taken in minimum periods of one week (this rule does not apply in relation to disabled children). A maximum of four weeks leave can be taken in relation to an individual child in a particular year.

- Employees must give their employer 21 days' notice of leave and its duration.

- The employer may postpone leave for up to six months (although not at the time of birth and adoption) where their business would be 'unduly disrupted'.

- Written notice of postponement outlining the reasons for the same and providing a date when the postponed leave may be taken must be given to the employee within seven days of receiving their request.

- The contract of employment continues during parental leave, although only a narrow range of provisions apply during this period including those concerning the duties of implied trust and confidence and good faith, and notice and disciplinary procedures.

- At the end of parental leave employees have the right to return to the same job. However if the length of leave is greater than four weeks or parental leave is combined with additional maternity leave, then if it is not reasonably practicable for the employee to return to the same job, there is an entitlement to return to another job that is suitable and appropriate.

Two developments are likely to lead to changes in the parental leave provisions over the next few years.

Developing European law

First, a revised European Directive on Parental Leave was agreed in 2010 (Directive 2010/18/EU), which must be implemented in the UK by 2012. Like the original passed in 1996, this directive provides rights to parental leave to take care of a child up to the age of eight (it is notable that the UK legislation applies to children up to the age of five only). The revised directive increased the minimum period of parental leave entitlement from three to four months. It states that at least one of these months should be provided on a non-transferable basis (i.e. it would not be possible to transfer this period of leave between parents). The intention here is to promote greater sharing of parental responsibilities. The directive also encourages employers to maintain contact with employees during parental leave and requires EU member states to ensure that workers returning from parental leave may request changes to their working hours and/or patterns for a set period of time.

British government policy

Alongside and in addition to this revised directive, another likely driver of future change in this area is the policy of the Conservative–Liberal Democrat government. In May 2011 it set out ideas for major reform of family rights (HM Government 2011). Included were proposals to increase parental leave entitlements in line with the revised directive. A significant pillar of the intended reform is a plan to reduce the maternity leave period to 18 weeks, scrap the right to additional paternity leave and instead reclassify the current remaining 34 weeks of maternity leave as a more generic category of parental leave (HM Government 2011). Within this 34 weeks, four weeks would be allocated exclusively for both the mother and father to take, with the remaining weeks to be shared and possibly taken concurrently and on a flexible basis. This leave would be paid in line with the current regulations regarding maternity and paternity leave. In addition, the new category of parental leave would be supplemented by the current entitlement of 13 weeks' unpaid leave up to the child's fifth birthday. It remains to be seen how exactly these ideas would be implemented in practice.

Adoption leave

The Paternity and Adoption Leave Regulations 2002 (reg 15) provide that an employee who is the adoptive parent of a child newly placed for adoption may take adoption leave. To qualify an employee must have 26 weeks of continuous service by the week in which he or she is notified of being matched with a child for adoption. As with maternity leave, adoption leave is divided into two periods: 26 weeks' 'ordinary' adoption leave and 26 weeks' 'additional' leave. Only one adoptive parent is entitled to take adoption leave, although the other may be eligible to take paternity leave if they meet the relevant criteria (see below). Statutory Adoption Pay is also provided, which is the same as lower rate statutory maternity pay. The rules as to terms and conditions during leave and the right to return to work that apply in relation to maternity leave also apply with regard to adoption leave.

The adoptive parent's partner can take both ordinary and additional paternity leave provided they meet the eligibility requirements and comply with the notification procedures for these. The rules and procedures for adoptive parents wishing to take paternity leave are essentially the same as those for other parents.

Dependency leave

A right to 'dependency leave' was introduced in 1999 (ERA 1996, s 57A). This is a right for employees to take a 'reasonable amount' of time off, to 'take action which is necessary' to deal with unexpected events concerning a dependant. Key aspects are as follows:

- There is no **qualifying period** for the right.
- The circumstances or activities regarding which the right to leave applies are as follows:
  - Provision of assistance to a dependant who falls ill, gives birth, or is injured or assaulted.
  - When arrangements need to be made for the care of a dependant who is ill or injured.
  - When a dependant dies.
  - Where there is unexpected disruption to arrangements for the care of a dependant.
  - To deal with an unexpected incident involving a child of the employee at school or other educational establishment.
- 'Dependant' is defined as a person's spouse or civil partner, child, parent or someone living with the employee other than a tenant or lodger. The legislation also provides that persons other than these (e.g. an elderly neighbour) who reasonably relies on the employee for assistance come within the definition of a dependant.

To validly take up this right, employees are obliged to inform their employer about the reason for their absence as soon as reasonably practicable and how long the absence is likely to last. The employer is obliged not to unreasonably refuse a request. There has been relatively little **case law** regarding these provisions but the case of *Qua v John Ford Morrison Solicitors* [2003] IRLR 184, EAT established the nature of the right (see Exhibit 11.2).

A later case, *RBS v Harrison* EAT/0093/08, has provided guidance on the interpretation of the regulations. In this case, Mrs Harrison, who worked as a part-time insurance claims advisor, learned that her child minder would not be available to look after her children in two weeks' time. She tried to find a replacement but was unable

---

EXHIBIT 11.2

The case of *Qua* v *John Ford Morrison Solicitors*

Qua v *John Ford Morrison Solicitors* [2003] **IRLR 184, EAT**

Facts. In this case a legal secretary working for a firm of solicitors was dismissed after taking 17 days off in a nine-month period in order to care for her sick son, who had a long-term illness.

Judgments. The tribunal and subsequently the Employment Appeals Tribunal found that her dismissal had not been automatically unfair and that the employer was not in breach of the dependency leave provisions. They outlined that the dependency leave rights enable an employee to take time off to arrange for the care of a dependant, but that they do not allow an employee to take time off to provide the care him or herself 'beyond the reasonable amount necessary to enable them to deal with the immediate crisis'. The statutory right applies to unforeseen and unexpected events as opposed to foreseeable or ongoing events. Leave to provide longer-term care would come under the heading of parental leave.

The EAT stated that in determining what is a reasonable amount of time off work, an employer should always take account of the individual circumstances of the employee. It noted that in the vast majority of cases it may be that no more than a few hours or, at most, one or possibly two days, would be regarded as reasonable to deal with the particular problem which has arisen.

Importantly, the EAT also noted that in its view the disruption caused to the employer's business by the employee's time off is not relevant to the question of whether a reasonable amount of time was taken.

to do so and therefore subsequently informed her line manager and asked if she could have the day in question off. She was told that she could not and that any absence would be unauthorised. Mrs Harrison went ahead and took the day off and as a result was given a verbal warning. She claimed at an employment tribunal that this was a detriment relating to the right to dependency leave.

Both the employment tribunal and Employment Appeal Tribunal ruled that she had been subject to a detriment. The key issue on appeal was whether it had been necessary for Mrs Harrison to take the day off to deal with the unexpected disruption of her childcare. The EAT noted that in deciding whether an employee is entitled to take time off, tribunals may take into account the amount of time passing between the employee becoming aware of the relevant disruption and the actual disruption itself. This element of time was seen to be primarily relevant to the consideration of whether it was necessary for the employee to take the time off. The EAT outlined that while the regulations are not confined to dealing with sudden emergencies, the more time an employee has before the disruption in question the greater the likelihood that a tribunal will find that it was not necessary to take the time off. In short, the reasoning was that the more time the employee has the better able they will be to explore alternative arrangements, for example taking parental leave. It is up to tribunals to decide on the basis of all the relevant facts in each case whether the employee's action was necessary in the circumstances.

Right to request flexible working

This was introduced in 2003 (Employment Rights Act 1996, Part VIIIA; and the Flexible Working Regulations 2002). Employers are obliged to consider applications for flexible working from employees who have 26 weeks' continuous service and children under the age of 17 (or 18 if disabled). The purpose is to enable an employee to 'care for' his or her child. In addition to mothers, fathers, guardians, foster and adoptive parents, partners of the same sex are entitled to apply if they have or expect to have responsibility for the upbringing of the child.

The right originally applied to parents of children under six, being extended to parents of older children in 2009. Another important change was that from April 2007, carers of adults were also made eligible. This category encompasses those caring for a spouse, partner, 'near relative' or another adult who is not within one of these categories but lives in the same house as the employee. The term 'near relative' covers parents, grandparents, adult children, siblings, uncles and aunts. In-laws, family members via adoptive relationships, step-relatives and half-blood relatives are also covered.

An employee can make an application to change terms and conditions relating to:

- hours of work;
- times required to work;
- place of work (specifically the choice is between working at home or at the employer's premises) (ERA 1996, s 80F).

Practices which come within these three categories include a change from full-time to part-time work; job-sharing; 'flexi-time'; compressed, annualised and staggered hours; term-time, home and shift working. Importantly, the legislation does not provide an automatic right to flexible working but rather a right *to apply* for this and a duty on the employer *to consider* the application.

A specific decision-making process is set out which must be followed. The employee must make the flexible working request in writing, outlining the proposed change, the effect it is likely to have on the employer and how this might be dealt with. The employer must then either agree or hold a meeting within 28 days to discuss the request and inform the employee of the decision in writing within 14 days. The employer must also provide an opportunity for the employee to appeal a decision where a request has been rejected and inform the employee of the appeal decision (14 day deadlines again apply to each of these steps, although these periods can be extended by agreement). The employee has a statutory right to be accompanied at these meetings by a fellow worker or a workplace or full-time union official (Employment Relations Act 1999, s 10).

An employer may only refuse a request on eight 'business grounds' which are exhaustively outlined in the legislation (s 80G):

- burden of additional cost;
- detrimental impact on ability to meet customer demand;
- detrimental impact on performance of the business;
- detrimental impact on quality;
- inability to reorganise work among existing staff;
- inability to recruit additional staff;
- insufficiency of work during periods employee proposes to work;
- if the change is incompatible with planned structural changes.

Where an application is rejected, the written notice provided to the employee must specify the ground or grounds for refusal from this list and explain why they apply in the circumstances. Importantly, from an employee's perspective, any contract variation resulting from a flexible working request will be permanent unless otherwise agreed at the outset. In addition, employees may make only one variation application per year.

An employee is not permitted to apply to an employment tribunal claiming breach of the flexible working legislation until they have appealed their employer's decision regarding their application and received the outcome of the same. A tribunal can award a remedy where the stipulated procedure was not followed; the decision to reject was based on incorrect facts; or the ground for refusal was not one of those permitted. In terms of remedies, tribunals can make a declaration, ordering an employer to reconsider an application and/or award compensation. Tribunals have no power to order a request to be granted and in addition, they are not permitted to examine the reasonableness of a decision to reject a request, with their role largely limited to monitoring that the correct procedure was followed. This gave rise to concerns on the part of analysts and commentators that the right would, in effect, be very weak.

The case of *Commotion v Rutty* [2006] IRLR 171, EAT provided welcome clarification on this matter. Mrs Rutty, a warehouse assistant, applied for part-time working when she became responsible for the care of her grandchild. Her employer rejected the request on the grounds that it would have a detrimental effect on company performance and ability to meet customer demand. She took a case to an employment tribunal which decided that there was no evidence that there would be a detrimental impact on performance of the business if her request had been granted. It therefore awarded her a remedy under the legislation. Her employer appealed the decision to the Employment Appeals Tribunal, challenging the tribunal's power to examine the substance of the employer's decision in this way.

The EAT held that it was necessary for tribunals to enquire into the details of the cases before it in order to establish whether the decision to reject a flexible working request was based on incorrect facts. It therefore decided that the tribunal was right to examine the evidence on which the company's decision was made and, in light of this, to find against it. This case suggests that while tribunals may in general have limited powers to examine the reasonableness of employers' decisions to refuse flexible working requests, they are nevertheless to consider the substantive basis of these decisions to a significant degree.

A notable feature of the flexible working legislation is the possibility for disputes to be resolved under a dedicated **arbitration** scheme operated by ACAS, rather than by an employment tribunal. The intention here is to provide a more speedy and less legalistic mechanism for dispute resolution. Claimants are free to choose whether to submit their claim to arbitration or to apply to a tribunal.

Like parental leave, this area may change significantly in the coming years. At the time of writing the government was considering making the right to request flexible working available to all employees and, in addition, introducing a number of changes to the manner in which it is exercised with a view to making the right more user friendly (HM Government 2011).

Protection from detriment and dismissal

Employees have a right not to be dismissed (ERA 1996, s. 99) or subjected to detriment short of dismissal (ERA ss 47C, 47E) for exercising their entitlements to the various forms of family leave and flexible working, or for other reasons related to these rights, pregnancy or maternity. Where the reason or principal reason for dismissing an employee is related to pregnancy, the taking of maternity leave or another of the rights in this area, the dismissal will be automatically unfair. Importantly, this protection applies regardless of length of service. An employee dismissed during pregnancy or maternity leave is entitled to a written statement of the reasons for dismissal (see Chapter 8). Examples of detriment short of dismissal would include a failure to promote or provide training on the grounds of a woman's pregnancy or a man's application for parental leave.

An interesting recent case regarding pregnancy-related dismissal was considered by the European Court of Justice (*Mayr* v *Bäckerei und Konditorei Gerhard Flöckner OHG* [2008] Case C-506/06, ECJ) (see Exhibit 11.3).

▶ Family rights and sex discrimination

No comparator

Although the need for a male comparator in discrimination law has historically been a substantial obstacle, the European Court of Justice ruled in the early 1990s that the EU Equal Treatment Directive 1976 encompassed protection against adverse treatment on the grounds of pregnancy and maternity. The latter was held to be a form of direct sex discrimination (*Dekker* v *Stichting Vormingscentrum Voor Jonge Volwassen Plus*

EXHIBIT 11.3

When is a woman pregnant?

Mayr v *Bäckerei und Konditorei Gerhard Flöckner OHG* [2008] (Case C-506/06), ECJ

Facts. This case concerned an Austrian waitress, Ms Mayr, who, having been undergoing in vitro fertilisation treatment (IVF treatment), was dismissed from her job. When dismissed, M's ova had been removed from her body and fertilised by her partner's sperm, but had not yet been transferred to her uterus. She brought a claim under the Austrian law on maternity protection, which prohibits dismissal during pregnancy. She argued that as her ova had been fertilised, she should be classed as pregnant for the purposes of the legislation.

Judgment. The case was referred to the European Court of Justice which ruled that, for the purposes of the EU's Pregnant Workers Directive, which prohibits dismissal of women on grounds of pregnancy, in cases of IVF the earliest a pregnancy could be said to begin is the date of implantation. The directive, therefore, was not applicable to her situation. This case is binding on UK courts. It means that in future it will be automatically unfair to dismiss a woman on the ground that she has undergone IVF treatment involving ova implantation, but not to dismiss a woman who has merely undergone fertilisation treatment.

Comment. This decision may seem quite harsh. However, this is alleviated by the fact that the ECJ also ruled that although a woman in Ms Mayr's position could not benefit from the law on pregnancy dismissal, she could claim sex discrimination in breach of the Equal Treatment Directive (see further below).

[1991] IRLR 27). In the *Dekker* case, a female candidate for a training instructor's position who, although regarded as the most suitable candidate, was not appointed because she was pregnant. The ECJ held that the fact that she had not been employed for a reason connected with pregnancy was contrary to the Equal Treatment Directive. Essentially, European judges have therefore supported the common sense view that adverse or less favourable treatment on grounds of pregnancy or maternity is sex discrimination and that no male comparator is necessary. This position was formalised by the revised Equal Treatment Directive 2002, subsequently consolidated into the Equal Treatment Directive 2006. British law was amended to this effect by means of the insertion of a new provision into the former Sex Discrimination Act 1975.

Equality Act 2010

This act (see Chapter 5) has brought together the various elements of UK discrimination law into one piece of legislation. This protects against discrimination because of pregnancy or maternity. Pregnancy and maternity are a 'protected characteristic' (s 4). Unfavourable treatment of a woman because of pregnancy or illness suffered as a result of pregnancy during the 'protected period' constitutes unlawful discrimination (s 18). Importantly no comparator is required. In addition, the employer's motive is irrelevant. Unfavourable treatment on grounds of pregnancy or maternity automatically constitutes discrimination.

Where a pregnant woman has the right to OML and AML, the 'protected period' runs from the beginning of the pregnancy to the end of the additional maternity leave period or, if earlier, to when she returns to work. If the woman is not entitled to maternity leave, the protected period runs until two weeks after the pregnancy. Unfavourable treatment against a woman because she is on compulsory maternity leave or exercising or seeking to exercise the right to ordinary or additional maternity leave is also prohibited (s 18). An example of such discrimination would be where an employer treats a woman unfavourably due to the fact that she has been off sick during her pregnancy with a pregnancy-related illness.

Other examples of the type of actions targeted by the provisions on unfavourable treatment include a decision not to recruit, promote or train, or dismissal on grounds of pregnancy; not giving a woman on maternity leave an opportunity to undergo a performance appraisal (and thereby benefit from a pay rise) or not informing her of a vacancy in her area. In addition, failure to undertake a risk assessment or a decision not to recruit a pregnant woman on health and safety grounds may also constitute discrimination, providing that the woman can demonstrate she suffered a detriment.

For example, in the case of *Mannell v Clinton Cards plc* ET/2304416/04, the employer failed to carry out a specific risk assessment in relation to Ms Mannell, a manager at one of its stores. Ms Mannell felt compelled to resign due to the fact that long hours and high levels of stress in the job were impacting negatively on her pregnancy. The tribunal found that the employer's failure to carry out the risk assessment led to Ms Mannell suffering a detriment (i.e. having to resign her job) and decided that the employer, therefore, was guilty of discrimination.

Unfavourable treatment because of pregnancy or maternity outside the protected period is covered by the Equality Act's wider provisions on sex discrimination, namely on direct sex discrimination (s 13) and on indirect discrimination (s 19). Whereas the requirement of section 18 is to simply demonstrate '*unfavourable*' treatment, under section 13 it is necessary to show '*less favourable treatment*', i.e. a comparator – whether real or hypothetical – is required (see Chapter 5). For example, to invoke a capability procedure against a woman who was off sick due to a pregnancy-related illness after the end of the maternity leave period, would not necessarily constitute discrimination. It would only be so if the woman could demonstrate less favourable treatment compared to a man who had been off sick for a similar period (s 13).

Discrimination against women undergoing IVF treatment

As indicated earlier, the case of *Mayr v Bäckerei und Konditorei Gerhard Flöckner OHG* [2008] (Case C-506/06, ECJ) (see Exhibit 11.3) has extended the protection offered by the law in this area to cover women at an advanced stage of IVF treatment. Although as outlined above, in that case the European Court of Justice decided that for the purposes of protection against dismissal under the Pregnant Workers Directive 1992, a woman having IVF treatment needs to have undergone implantation of ova, it also decided that for the purposes of the Equal Treatment Directive, it was sufficient for a woman to have undergone fertilisation treatment. The court ruled that it was appropriate to draw an analogy between women at such an advanced stage of IVF treatment and pregnant women. Less favourable treatment of such a woman because of that fact, would therefore constitute sex discrimination under the Equality Act (s 13). British employers should take note of this decision, given the increasing number of female employees having IVF treatment.

Discrimination because of association and perception

Another European Court of Justice decision, *Coleman v Attridge Law* [2008] (C-303/06), ECJ, has had important consequences for those with caring responsibilities. Ms Coleman, who had a disabled son, brought a case to an employment tribunal claiming that she had been subject to less favourable treatment than parents of non-disabled children on ground of her association with her disabled son. The Employment Tribunal referred her case to the European Court of Justice to establish whether such 'disability discrimination by association' was unlawful. The ECJ ruled that it was, that the Equal Treatment in Employment Framework Directive 2000 prohibits discrimination by association on grounds of disability, age, sexual orientation, religion or belief, etc. This decision was of great significance because it meant that employees with caring responsibilities, for example for disabled children or elderly parents, could be protected from being discriminated against on that basis.

The Equality Act 2010 (see Chapter 5) includes provisions outlawing discrimination because of association. Protection against associative discrimination covers age, disability, gender reassignment, race, religion or belief, sex and sexual orientation. While pregnancy or maternity are not directly covered, a worker treated less favourably because of association with a pregnant woman or a woman who has recently given birth, *may* have a claim for direct sex discrimination. This issue was considered in *Kulikaoskas v Shellfish and Another* [2011] ICR 48. The Scottish EAT held that an employee who claimed that he was dismissed because of his partner's pregnancy could not bring a claim for associative discrimination under the former Sex Discrimination Act. Case law is likely to establish whether the Equality Act provisions on associative sex discrimination are to be interpreted in a similar manner.

Similar to association, there is no express protection against less favourable treatment on grounds of perception of pregnancy or maternity in the Equality Act 2010; however, here again a worker may be protected under the sex discrimination provisions.

FRISHCO SUPERMARKET: CASE STUDY

Scenario 11.1

Time off for care

Jack, one of the checkout staff, has worked for the company for five years. He is a good worker with a clean disciplinary record. He is 48 years old, divorced and lives with his father who has multiple sclerosis. His father's health has deteriorated progressively in the past three years. He is now only able to walk with great difficulty and has a wheelchair for trips out. He needs personal care to help him bathe and go to the toilet. **Jack** is his primary carer. There are workers who come daily from a social care agency to help provide assistance.

During the past month the service from the agency has deteriorated with staff attending late and **Jack** having to undertake tasks to assist his father. Consequently, **Jack** has been late for work on three occasions – by up to 30 minutes. He has explained the situation to **Jez**, a deputy store manager. He was, generally, unsympathetic and told Jack to sort the situation out otherwise he would be disciplined. He denied that 'dependency leave' was relevant to **Jack**'s case.

The situation with the social care agency became worse. **Jack** not only attended work late ➡

more regularly but had to take extended lunch hours to make sure that his father was fed. **Jez** decided that 'enough was enough' and that **Jack** should attend a disciplinary hearing for a formal warning. Jack attended the hearing. He was unrepresented and given a formal written warning. He did not appeal. A month later the situation had not improved and he was given a final written warning and warned that, if there was no improvement, he would be sacked.

Maggie, a general assistant, saw **Jack** looking very distressed one lunchtime and he explained his situation to her. He said he was afraid he would lose his job. She is a union member and said that she thought he had some rights and that the company could not treat him that way. She offered have a word with her union official.

Question

What might Maggie find out about the law covering Jack's situation? What action might he take against the company for the way he has been treated?

Visit mylawchamber.co.uk/willey *to access sample HR documents to support this case study.*

Indirect sex discrimination

The concept of indirect sex discrimination is also relevant in the area of pregnancy, maternity and family rights. For example, an employer's policy of refusing requests for part-time working may adversely affect women attempting to balance work with family commitments – e.g. women returning from maternity leave. Such a policy would be an example of a 'provision, criterion or practice' which puts women at a 'particular disadvantage'. These are two of the conditions that are required to establish a case of indirect discrimination (see Chapter 5). Unless the employer can show that such a rule or policy is a 'proportionate means of achieving a legitimate aim', a detriment or disadvantage suffered as a consequence will be classed as unjustified indirect discrimination.

A notable trend here is the reliance by tribunal applicants on the law on indirect discrimination in cases relating to flexible working requests. Case law shows that even though an employer may satisfy the requirements of the flexible working legislation, a decision to reject a request for flexible working may still be held to be indirectly discriminatory.

An example is the case of *Webster* v *Princes Soft Drinks* ET/1803942/04, which involved a request by a senior accountant to transfer to part-time work following her return from maternity leave. The tribunal in this case found that although the employer had complied with the requirements of the flexible working regulations, they had indirectly discriminated against Ms Webster. The employer had highlighted the large number of staff to be managed as a reason for refusing the request, yet Ms Webster had only three people reporting directly to her. The employer also argued that a job-share arrangement would be inefficient and that a full-time position was necessary in order to respond promptly to requests from head office for financial information. The tribunal was not persuaded by these arguments and concluded that no convincing reasons had been provided for the insistence on full-time work. The company had therefore indirectly discriminated against Ms Webster.

The high profile case, *British Airways plc* v *Starmer* [2005] IRLR 862 is also relevant in this context (see Exhibit 11.4).

EXHIBIT 11.4

Reducing a pilot's hours of work

British Airways plc v *Starmer* [2005] **IRLR 862, EAT**

Facts. The employer refused a request from a female pilot to go to a 50 per cent fractional contract in order to be able to look after her new baby, and instead only permitted her to move to a 75 per cent contract.

Judgments. A tribunal and subsequently the Employment Appeal Tribunal held that the decision to only permit part-time working at 75 per cent of a full-time contract was a 'provision, criterion or practice' for the purposes of the Sex Discrimination Act. The EAT held that the tribunal had been correct in finding that British Airways had not provided sufficient justification for this decision and that there had therefore been indirect discrimination against Mrs Starmer. Resource constraints including the burden of additional costs and inability to reorganise work had been put forward by the employer, with the tribunal finding that the reasons outlined were not sufficient to justify the discriminatory effect of the decision made. In addition, a general policy of BA that inexperienced pilots should not be permitted to work below 75 per cent of a full-time contract was rejected. The EAT ruled that the circumstances of individual workers needed to be considered.

Discrimination cases by men

Although the bulk of decisions in this area relate to discrimination against women, in certain situations men may also be able to successfully bring a discrimination claim. While men are not usually in a position to claim indirect discrimination due to the fact that they are in general less likely than women to have family or caring commitments, a man may have a case for direct discrimination if a request to work flexibly is refused. For example, in *Walkingshaw* v *The John Martin Group* ETS/401126/00, a man requested a transfer to a two and a half day week in order to enable him to care for his baby son. His request was rejected but he succeeded in a claim for direct discrimination, as the tribunal found that his employer had always accommodated requests by women for flexible working. Mr Walkingshaw could also have compared himself with how a hypothetical female comparator in the same post would have been treated.

It is noteworthy that where a man is claiming direct sex discrimination, the legislation states that no account is to be taken of the special treatment afforded to a woman in connection with pregnancy or childbirth (Equality Act 2010, s 13(6)(b)). However in a recent case (*Eversheds Legal Services* v *de Belin* [2011] IRLR 448, EAT), the EAT held that the more favourable treatment of a woman in this way was subject to a test of proportionality (i.e. that the more favourable treatment needed to be proportionate); and if this was not the case then a finding of direct sex discrimination in favour of a man was possible. In that case, a solicitor, Mr de Belin, was made redundant in part due to the fact that a female colleague on maternity leave was awarded a maximum score on a certain aspect of a redundancy scoring exercise without reference to her actual performance. The EAT held that this was not a proportionate action on the part of the employer, and as a consequence came to a finding of direct sex discrimination (see Chapter 3). This case goes against established principle and it therefore remains to be seen whether the courts will in future apply require proportionality in the more favourable treatment of women in connection with pregnancy or childbirth (*Equal Opportunities Review*, May 2011).

Harassment

The Equality Act 2010 (s 26) prohibits harassment related to specified 'protected characteristics' – excluding pregnancy and maternity. However, harassment because of pregnancy or maternity would constitute harassment related to sex and is therefore unlawful. In the case of *Nixon* v *Ross Coates Solicitors and another* UKEAT/0108/10, the EAT held that gossip about an employee's pregnancy was harassment under the Sex Discrimination Act. This case would be likely to be decided in the same way under the new legislation.

Enforcement and remedies

The issue of enforcement of family rights is rather complex. For some of the rights outlined in this chapter specific enforcement provisions and remedies apply, while the enforcement of others is via general provisions. It is also possible that employees can bring more than one claim, for example a claim for discrimination in addition to one for detriment or dismissal. Table 11.2 outlines the grounds on which employees may bring a case and the remedies available. This is based on various provisions of the Employment Rights Act 1996 and the Equality Act 2010.

A notable element of the legislation in this area is that a dismissal for a pregnancy, maternity or other family-related reason is automatically unfair and the employee will be entitled to claim unfair dismissal regardless of their length of service (the usual service qualification does not apply – see Chapter 8). In addition to a dismissal of an employee by an employer for one of these reasons, a woman or man subjected to detriment on grounds of pregnancy, maternity or other family rights may be entitled to resign and claim unfair **constructive dismissal**. This is where an employer's actions or conduct causes a fundamental or **repudiatory breach of contract** (see Chapter 8). Examples of this could be where a woman is not promoted on grounds of pregnancy or where an employer fails to undertake a health assessment in relation to a pregnant woman (e.g. *Mannell* v *Clinton Cards*). An employer's failure to inform a woman on maternity leave of vacancies arising in her department may also constitute grounds for constructive dismissal where the woman in question had a legitimate expectation that she would be so informed (*Visa International Service Association* v *Paul* [2004] IRLR 42, EAT).

As is evident from Table 11.2, the primary remedy available for breach of family rights is compensation. The legislation does not permit tribunals to order an employer to allow leave to be taken. At best tribunals are empowered to order an employer to reconsider a request, but this only applies to flexible working. Compensation awarded is generally that which is 'just and equitable' in the particular situation. In the case of breach of the flexible working regulations, the level of compensation a tribunal can order is capped at eight weeks' pay, with the level of a week's pay for this purpose set by legislation. At February 2011 a 'week's pay' was defined as £400, so this would mean a maximum compensation award of £3,200. In discrimination cases, compensation levels are uncapped and may include compensation for injury to feelings.

Employees seeking to bring a claim on one or more of the above grounds must apply to an employment tribunal within three months of the act in question. However, following the ACAS *Code of Practice on Disciplinary and Grievance Procedures* (2009), before doing so they should first try to resolve the situation with their employer. Specifically, they should submit a written grievance about the issue in question, attend any meeting

Table 11.2 **Grounds of action and remedies relating to family rights**

Claim	Summary	Possible remedies
Leave		
● Unreasonable refusal of time off for ante-natal care or failure to pay for time off work ● Unreasonable refusal of time off for dependency leave ● Refusal or unreasonable postponement of parental leave request	Specific enforcement provisions relating to ante-natal care, dependency and parental leave	Declaration Compensation
Flexible working provisions		
● Failure to follow stipulated procedure for flexible working application ● Decision based on incorrect facts ● Grounds for refusal not one of those permitted	Specific provisions relating to flexible working applications	Declaration Compensation (up to a maximum of eight weeks' pay – £3,200 as at February 2011) Order to reconsider flexible working request
Detriment for family and domestic reasons	Covers detriment in form of any act or failure to act by employer in relation to exercise by employee of rights regarding pregnancy, maternity leave, adoption leave, paternity leave, parental leave, dependency leave and flexible working	Declaration Compensation
Unfair dismissal	Dismissal for a family/dependency leave or flexible working related reason automatically unfair regardless of length of service	Re-engagement Reinstatement Compensation
Pregnancy/maternity discrimination and sex discrimination	Unfavourable treatment on grounds of pregnancy/maternity is discrimination; less favourable treatment is also direct sex discrimination; indirect sex discrimination, discrimination on grounds of association/perception and harassment also relevant	Declaration Recommendation Compensation (potentially unlimited and including compensation for injury to feelings in addition to financial loss)

that is arranged and also appeal any decision if allowed to do so. If they do not take these steps any compensation subsequently awarded by a tribunal could be reduced by up to 25 per cent. Under the Employment Relations Act 1999, they would have a statutory right to be accompanied at such grievance or appeal meetings by a fellow worker or trade union official (see Chapter 8).

Employment policy and practice

There is a great deal of information available on the take-up and implementation of the various rights, entitlements and obligations outlined above. The government has sponsored comprehensive surveys on work–life balance and flexible working at regular intervals, while the Workplace Employee Relations Survey series (which is sponsored by the Department for Business, Innovation and Skills and ACAS, among other organisations) provides representative data on a range of relevant practices. Evidence is also available from a number of other sources such as reports of the former Equal Opportunities Commission and dedicated 'think tanks' or organisations such as Working Families. This section summarises some of the principal findings from these sources. It outlines trends and highlights what are perceived to be both positive aspects or 'success stories' and weaknesses or failures regarding the practice of family leave, flexible working and 'work–life balance' in the UK.

▶ Maternity leave

A government-sponsored survey of new parents in 2005 (Smeaton and Marsh 2006) provided information on trends in maternity leave, which was comparable with a similar survey conducted in 2002. Some of the key findings were as follows:

- Nearly half of mothers took six months' maternity leave in 2005 (compared with 9 per cent in 2002), while 14 per cent took 52 weeks (5 per cent in 2002).

- Eighty per cent of mothers returned to work after maternity leave and of these, 80 per cent returned to the same employer (59 per cent in 2002).

- The majority of returning mothers made a change to their employment pattern, with three-quarters returning on a part-time basis.

- Overall, the return to work was found to be easier for women in 2005 than 2002, due to greater employer flexibility and support.

Additional information on trends in maternity leave is available from the Third Work–Life Balance Employer's Survey carried out in 2007 (Hayward *et al.* 2007). This found that 53 per cent of the workplaces surveyed in 2007 allowed all mothers 12 months of maternity leave despite the fact that the survey was conducted at a time when they were not obliged to do so. Fifteen per cent of workplaces, covering 41 per cent of employees, paid maternity pay at a rate higher than the statutory minimum. The finding that many employers exceed statutory requirements with regard to maternity leave entitlements has also been confirmed by smaller scale surveys (Foster 2008). Another significant finding from the Third Work–Life Balance Employer's Survey was that 83 per cent of women going back to work from maternity leave returned to the same or a very similar job (Hayward *et al.* 2007). Relatedly, the proportion of mothers who changed employer upon returning to work after maternity leave fell from 41 per cent in 2002 to 14 per cent in 2007 (BIS 2010: 15).

These figures demonstrate that British employers have become more generous in the provision of maternity rights over the last number of years. The authors of these studies, although recognising the influence of a range of different factors, highlight the changes in the legislation on maternity leave and pay and flexible working as being important influences behind these trends. The survey evidence also shows how employers have in general adapted well to the changes introduced (for example 'keeping in touch days'). Nevertheless it is noted how smaller employers find it difficult to comply with the various legislative requirements and provisions, in particular the requirement to hold a job open for a woman on maternity leave (Foster 2008; BIS 2010).

While these surveys and reports emphasise the extent of positive employer engagement with pregnancy and maternity at work, more recent evidence highlights how the downturn in the UK economy from 2009 has created a more difficult environment. There has been much anecdotal and some more formal evidence (e.g. Working Families 2011) that the rights of pregnant women and those on maternity leave are being increasingly disregarded, for example by employers failing to consult with women on maternity leave in redundancy situations or failing to offer them suitable alternative vacancies as required by law.

▶ Paternity leave

A 2005 survey (Smeaton and Marsh 2006) found that 93 per cent of fathers with employee status whose partners had given birth took time off work around the time of birth. The numbers of days off taken by fathers at this time had risen since 2002, with the proportion taking more than two weeks' leave increasing from 22 per cent to 36 per cent. Like those with regard to maternity leave, this trend was seen to be connected with the introduction of the statutory right to paternity leave in 2003. Seventy-one per cent of fathers made a change to their working arrangement following birth, for example 36 per cent worked more regular hours, while 27 per cent changed working hours to fit with their partner's job. The fathers surveyed also reported a substantial increase in the availability of flexible working patterns (e.g. part-time working or flexi-time) between 2002 and 2005.

Findings from the Workplace Employee Relations Survey (WERS) series similarly demonstrate an increase in paternity leave provision over time: while in 1998, 48 per cent of British workplaces provided paid paternity (or other discretionary) leave at the time of childbirth, by 2004, 92 per cent of workplaces were doing so (Whitehouse *et al.* 2007: 20). The new legislation on additional paternity leave implemented in 2011 might be expected to stimulate increased employer provision of paternity leave rights and entitlements.

▶ Parental leave

The provision by employers of parental leave has increased notably since the introduction of legislation on this in 1999. In 1998, 38 per cent of workplaces in Britain allowed employees to take parental leave, but by 2004 this had increased to 73 per cent (*ibid.*). However it is evident that the actual *take-up* of parental leave remains very low. A survey conducted in 2007 found only 14 per cent of employers to have had at least one employee who had taken parental leave in the previous 12 months (Hayward *et al.* 2007: 7). A survey conducted the previous year found that only one per cent of all employees and 6 per cent of employees who were parents of dependent children (up to the age of 18), had taken such leave (Hooker *et al.* 2007: 122).

▶ Dependency leave

The survey evidence demonstrates that British employers are willing to give employees leave at short notice to deal with emergencies: 99 per cent of employers state that they almost always or sometimes grant time off for employees to care for a family member or to deal with a household emergency (Hayward *et al.* 2007: 17). For their part, 71 per cent of British employees surveyed in 2007 thought that their employer would 'almost always' give them time off at short notice to care for a dependant. Thirty-eight per cent reported that they had experienced an emergency at short notice during the working week. Of these, 90 per cent said they had taken time off to deal with such an emergency. This proportion was equivalent to 34 per cent of all employees surveyed. Over half (52 per cent) of the employees who had taken time off to deal with an emergency had taken fully paid leave (Hooker *et al.* 2007: 114, 229–30).

▶ Awareness and use of the right to request flexible working

The Third Work–Life Balance Employee survey (conducted in 2006) contained a number of questions about the right to request flexible working (Hooker *et al.* 2007). Over half of all employees (56 per cent) said that they were aware of this right. This compared with 41 per cent in 2003, immediately before the right came into force. A higher proportion of parents with children under six (i.e. those legally entitled to the right to request at that time) were aware of the right than were other employees (65 per cent compared with 53 per cent). Over the two years preceding the survey, 17 per cent of employees had made a request to their employer to change their working pattern (the 2003 survey produced an identical result). Twenty-two per cent of women had made such a request, compared with 14 per cent of men. In 60 per cent of cases requests were fully agreed to, while in 18 per cent they were partially agreed to. Seventeen per cent of requests were rejected, with the remaining five per cent still to be decided at the time of the survey.

Interestingly, women were more likely to be successful than men in making a request – 66 per cent of female workers had their request fully agreed to compared with 53 per cent of men. Part-timers were also more likely than full-timers to have their request agreed to (74 per cent compared with 57 per cent).

A survey conducted in 2008 identified low levels of awareness about eligibility to the right to request flexible working (Elsmore 2009). Just 19 per cent of eligible parents knew that parents in their situation were entitled to request flexible working, while only one in ten eligible carers were aware they had the right.

▶ Flexible working practices

The report on the Third Work–Life Balance Employee Survey (Hooker *et al.* 2007) contained figures on the availability and take-up of flexible working practices in 2006 and also tables comparing the 2006 figures with those from the previous two work–life balance employee surveys conducted in 2000 and 2003.

Some of the information provided on trends in *availability* of flexible working practices over this period is reproduced in Table 11.3. The availability of part-time working, flexi-time, term-time working, a compressed working week and annualised hours, all increased quite noticeably between 2000 and 2006. In contrast, there was stability in the availability of reduced hours and job sharing. It is notable that working reduced hours, flexi-time or job sharing was possible for around half of employees in Britain in 2006, while term-time working and a compressed working week were available to over a third. Homeworking and annualised hours were relatively uncommon, with only around a quarter of employees reporting that they were available to them.

A survey of employers undertaken in 2007 also provided data on availability of flexible working (Hayward *et al.* 2007). This survey asked employers whether any employees at their workplace had used any of six forms of flexible working (part-time, job sharing, flexi-time, compressed working week, reduced hours for limited period, or working from home) in the previous 12 months. At least one of the six types of flexible working arrangement was available for employees to use in 95 per cent of workplaces surveyed, and had been used by an employee in the last 12 months in 85 per cent. Eighty four per cent of workplaces had two or more flexible working arrangements available, while only four per cent had no flexible working arrangements available.

Apart from the availability of flexible working practices, various studies and reports also provide figures on the actual *take-up* of these practices. Trends in the proportion of employees reporting take-up of flexible working practices between 2000 and 2006 are presented in Table 11.4. Although the authors of a report on these figures advise that they be treated with caution, the table appears to demonstrate that while the availability of flexible working practices may be relatively high, their take-up in practice tends to be rather lower, with a high degree of stability in this over time.

Although over half of the employees surveyed in 2006 stated that they were currently working flexibly or that they had done so in the previous 12 months, at most 27 per cent reported adopting the individual practices specified. While over a quarter of employees were working part time or flexi time, only around one in ten were working reduced hours, a compressed week, term-time working, annualised hours or home working. Only six per cent of employees were job sharing.

The results from a survey of British employees conducted in 2008 are outlined in Table 11.5 (Elsmore 2009). This table again shows a high proportion of respondents reporting that they work flexibly (69 per cent), but also rather lower proportions adopting individual flexible working practices. Nearly a third worked on a flexi-time basis and over a quarter part time, with other forms of flexible working affecting at most a fifth.

There is evidence that the difficult business environment in recent years has prompted firms to increase their adoption of flexible working practices, with the latter seen to be enable employers to reduce costs as well as save jobs and retain skilled employees. In this regard, 45 per cent of respondents to the Confederation of British Industry's 2009 *Employment Trends Survey* had increased their use of flexible working, with an additional 13 per cent intending to do so (CBI 2009). While this is a positive development in that it reflects increased openness to and adoption of flexible working practices, some negative

Table 11.3 **Trends in *availability* of flexible working arrangements 2000–06, percentage of employees reporting availability of practices**

	2000	*2003*	*2006*
Part-time working	49	67	69
Reduced hours for a limited period	56	62	54
Flexi-time	32	48	53
Job share	46	41	47
Term-time working	22	32	37
Compressed working week	25	30	35
Annualised hours	17	20	24
Regular home working	n/a	20	23
One or more arrangements available	–	85	90
No arrangement available/don't know	–	15	10

Source: adapted from Hooker *et al.* (2007: 61). The Third Work-Life Balance Employee Survey: Main Findings. HMSO.

Table 11.4 **Trends in *take-up* of flexible working arrangements 2000–06, percentage of employees reporting use of practices**

	2000	*2003*	*2006*
Part-time working	24	28	27
Reduced hours for a limited period	n/a	13	12
Flexi-time	24	26	27
Job share	4	6	6
Term-time working	14	15	13
Compressed working week	6	11	9
Annualised hours	2	6	8
Regular home working	n/a	11	10
Not worked flexibly in last 12 months	–	49	44
Currently working flexibly or has done so in the last 12 months	–	51	56

Source: adapted from Hooker *et al.* (2007: 62)

Table 11.5 **Flexible Working Practices 2008, percentage of employees reporting use of practices**

Work practice	*Parents – child under 6*	*Parents – older children*	*Carers*	*All employees*
Works flexibly	71	78	78	69
Part-time working	33	32	45	29
Term time only working	14	23	24	16
Job-sharing	7	8	17	8
Flexi-time	30	33	33	32
Compressed hours	17	14	17	16
Annualised hours	19	16	17	20
Work form home	17	22	13	15
Other	28	26	28	23
Number of respondents	216	264	180	1288

Source: Elsmore (2009), Caring and Flexible Working, *Research Summary*, Department for Work and Pensions. HMSO.

trends in this regard have also been in evidence. Other research has highlighted how in many cases managers have used business pressures as a reason *to refuse* flexible work practices, with this particularly affecting women returning to work from maternity leave (Working Families 2011).

▶ Degrees of success with flexible working and 'work–life balance'

The above evidence demonstrates that family leave and flexible working policies and practices are becoming more common in the British labour market. It is clear that the introduction and strengthening of the various pieces of legislation have partly under-pinned this, prompting employers to reassess and amend their policies and practices. It is also evident that business considerations and general labour market pressures have been important push factors. Therefore, there is a substantial amount of positive evidence or 'good news' regarding flexible working and work–life balance in the UK. On the other hand, it is also clear that there continue to be many obstacles to the implementation of family friendly/flexible working policies and practices. This section explores the question of 'degrees of success' in this area in some detail.

Senior managers

In a report entitled *Hours to Suit: Working Flexibly at Senior and Managerial Levels*, Working Families 2007 presents the findings from semi-structured interviews conducted with 23 senior managers working reduced hours or flexibly, the large majority of whom were located in the private sector. Eight worked at City-based organisations and the majority had direct responsibility for managing a team of people. Eighteen of the 23 worked reduced hours, with eight job sharing and the other ten working patterns such as a two-, three- or four-day week.

A key objective of the report was to address and challenge directly the common pre-sumption that flexible working is not possible or feasible in senior, managerial positions, by drawing on examples of senior managers who are successfully working in this way.

The report is based on detailed case studies of each of the individual managers. Overall, they demonstrate how these managers were able to have successful careers while working on a flexible basis. The use of flexible/reduced hours was found to lead to advantages or improvements for the employing organisations in the areas of recruitment and retention. In addition, these practices improved the motivation, enthusiasm, effectiveness and loyalty of the managers in question. There was a strong view that flexible working was compatible with the roles and responsibilities of senior managers. The development of information and communication technologies greatly facilitated the flexible working patterns adopted (e.g. homeworking).

Despite these positive findings, there is a lot of other research which reports that family life and working flexibly are often not compatible with senior management positions. The continuing dominance of long hours working and traditional work patterns in such positions was one of the key obstacles identified by the Women and Work Commission report (2006) as impeding the progress of women into higher level organisational positions. While noting the significant recent improvements in employer support for and adoption of flexible working practices, the more recent report of the Family Friendly Working Hours Taskforce set up by the government highlighted similar concerns (DWP 2010). A study of women working in senior positions in the financial sector outlines the difficulties they experience in combining motherhood with career progression (Odgers Berndtson/Muika Leadership 2011).

Employee performance

A report based on a two-year research project undertaken by Cranfield School of Manage-ment examines the impact of flexible working patterns on employee performance

(Working Families 2008). The research for this report involved surveys, semi-structured interviews and focus groups at seven leading British companies. The majority of flexible workers and co-workers and managers of the same were of the view that flexible working had either a positive or neutral impact on the quantity and quality of work undertaken. The majority of employees reported that flexible working had a positive effect in reducing and managing stress levels, although for some individuals flexible working was itself a source of stress. Flexible workers had higher levels of organisational commitment than those not working flexibly; and in some cases they had a higher level of job satisfaction.

While the findings were therefore generally positive, some negative findings emerged from the report in addition to the observation about stress levels mentioned above. There was a general belief among respondents that adopting flexible working practices could harm their careers. In addition, the availability of flexible working was seen to be very much dependent on the culture of the organisation and views of line managers, with some of the latter not being supportive of it. In addition, the feasibility of flexible working was found to be contingent on the nature of work that individuals were doing – while some jobs were well suited to it others by their very nature were not (e.g. senior management roles).

Motherhood

Case study research by Gatrell (2007) provides sobering evidence about employers' policies and practice in relation to pregnancy and motherhood. Gatrell (2007) conducted interviews with 20 working mothers, seven of whom were working full time and the remaining 13 reduced hours. The interviews highlighted how many organisations were effectively alien environments for pregnant women, with managers, colleagues and clients all being ill at ease with pregnant women, thereby creating very uncomfortable working environments for them.

While each of the women's organisations had policies promising equal opportunities to 'fractional' employees (i.e. those working reduced hours), the working mothers found that in practice fractional working was only available to those who were prepared to accept demotion or limited career opportunities. For example, Eleanor, a senior education manager in a public-sector organisation, was refused reduced hours on grounds of her seniority; she was told that if she wanted to work reduced hours she would have to accept a demotion. Another woman, Sarah-Jane, was obliged to give up her status as a hospital consultant when she returned to work on 80 per cent time.

Gatrell (2007: 472–3) concludes that the experience of the mothers she researched indicates that 'fractional working is not as conducive to "work life balance" as may be assumed, because it is accompanied by heavy penalties in terms of limited career prospects and blocked promotion'. She argues that 'business case' arguments in favour of flexible working for professional women are insufficient to counter employers' discriminatory behaviour regarding fractional working. Rather, what is first required is an open discussion of the various 'taboos' that exist in organisations with regard to motherhood and paid work and a change in fundamental attitudes towards the same.

The extent to which many British employers continue to be uncomfortable dealing with pregnancy and maternity was graphically illustrated by a report of the former Equal Opportunities Commission (EOC 2005). This presented the results of a 2005 survey of

1,000 pregnant or previously pregnant women which showed that 45 per cent of the women surveyed had experienced dismissal or disadvantageous treatment on grounds of pregnancy, which the authors calculated as being equivalent to 200,000 women per year across the labour market as a whole. Seven per cent of such women had been dismissed, made redundant or treated so badly they were forced to leave work (equivalent to 30,000 in total). Young, low income, ethnic minority women and those with short job tenure were particularly negatively affected, while discrimination was especially prominent in firms employing fewer than ten people. As outlined above, the difficult business environment in recent years is seen to have led to an increase in maltreatment of pregnant women by employers (Working Families 2011).

Critical perspectives on the legislation

While the fact that it has substantially strengthened employee rights and had positive effects on employer policy and practice is recognised, the legislation on family rights and 'work–life balance' has attracted some strong criticism. For example, some authors (e.g. Smith and Thomas 2003: 421) have highlighted the fact that the maternity leave provisions do not provide women with the right to return to work on *different* terms and conditions, for example on a part-time basis. Requests for the latter would need to be made under the flexible working provisions, yet these have also been the subject of much criticism. In particular, it is noted that they do not give employees a right to flexible working but only a right *to apply* to work flexibly (Anderson 2003). In addition, it is argued that the legislation provides employers with a wide scope to justify refusal of an employee's application (i.e. the eight 'business grounds'). Further, it is suggested that the role and involvement of employment tribunals in this area is very weak. Their remit is seen to be largely procedural, with the fact that they are not permitted to examine the reasonableness or otherwise of an employer's decision highlighted (*ibid.*).

The legislation on parental leave has also been criticised along a number of dimensions, such as that the leave is unpaid, that employers can postpone the taking of it, and that the right to such leave is only provided to parents of children up to the age of five whereas the Parental Leave Directive envisaged application to children up to age eight (McColgan 2000). It must be noted, however, that the current government intends to strengthen entitlements in this area (HM Government 2011).

Conclusion

It is evident from the above evidence and discussion that there is a need for balance and some healthy scepticism when evaluating the extent to which progress has been made in promoting family rights, work–life balance and flexible working in the UK labour market. While a range of legislative provisions have been introduced and subsequently enhanced and there is evidence of increasing adoption by employers of family leave and flexible working policies, the legislation also has a number of apparent weaknesses and there continue to be many problematic aspects regarding employers' policies and practices in these areas.

Exercises

11.1 **Pauline and Kate** work for a public relations (PR) agency employing 30 people, Pauline as an administrator and Kate as an account manager in the 'politics' section of the business (which offers PR advice to government departments and political parties). Both have recently completed a period of maternity leave, Pauline having taken OML and Kate AML, and, therefore, are planning to return to work.

In Pauline's case, when she reports for work at the end of her leave she is informed by her manager that she cannot have her old job back, as the company wishes to keep on her temporary replacement, Elaine, who the manager says is more efficient. In addition, she is told that there is no other job she can do.

Similarly, Kate is not allowed to return to her old job. Her manager insists that Rob, who she trained up to cover for her during her maternity leave, keeps the job for the reason that 'this is better from the point of view of the customers'. Kate, therefore, is assigned to the position of account manager in the agency's other main department, 'corporate' (which advises private sector companies on how to improve their profiles in the press and media). Although at the same salary grade and location as her previous job, Kate wonders whether the company is allowed to do this.

Pauline and Kate ask you for advice as to any rights and remedies they may be entitled to arising from their employer's actions.

11.2 **Sarah and Lucy** work full time for a food manufacturer that supplies ready-meals to the larger British retail chains. Sarah, who has been with the company for three years, works as a senior quality control manager, a position which involves overall responsibility for the quality and safety of products manufactured in the factory. She has a child aged four and has applied in writing to the HR manager to transfer to part-time work. Lucy has one year's service as a marketing manager, with responsibility for developing and overseeing marketing campaigns. She has recently returned from maternity leave and has also applied in writing to transfer to part-time work.

The HR manager holds meetings with both women to discuss their requests. Following this Sarah and Lucy's line managers (the operations and marketing directors respectively) are asked to provide a report on the likely operational and business consequences of a transfer by them to part-time working. The operations director provides a detailed report which outlines that the importance and responsibility of the role requires there to be a senior quality control manager on site on a full-time basis. In addition, it notes that creating a job share arrangement would also not be feasible due to the difficultly in recruiting someone to work part time in such a senior, specialist position. In contrast, Lucy's manager provides only a very brief note stating that 'this position is not suitable for part-time work'. Both requests to work part time are therefore rejected.

What entitlements or rights do Lucy and Sarah have in relation to their requests and what causes of action or remedies might their employer's refusal give rise to?

11.3 **Tom** has worked as a team leader for FirstCall Direct, an insurance company employing 3,000 people, for two years. His partner has recently given birth to twins. She has now returned to work and the twins have started at nursery. Tom wants to be able to take and collect the twins from the nursery and therefore makes an application for his hours to be reduced so that he can work from 10–4 instead of 9–5.30. Although similar requests by female teamleaders have been accepted, his line manager rejects his request, explaining that 'we can't have all our teamleaders working flexi-time, there need to be enough teamleaders in place to supervise the staff'. He appeals this decision but his manager rejects his appeal, stating that he should 'just get on with doing the job you're employed to do'.

Tom asks for your advice regarding his position. What advice would you give regarding any rights or remedies he may be entitled to arising from his employer's actions?

11.4 **Paula** has worked as a tax solicitor at a large law firm for the last three years. Due to her extensive expertise in the tax field and recent success in winning a number of high-profile cases, she has been told by the managing director that she would make an 'ideal candidate' to become a partner at the firm, and that she should apply for the position in the next round of internal vacancies. Paula duly does so and is subsequently called for interview. The interview goes extremely well with strong indications that she will get the position. However, towards the end of the interview Paula informs the panel that as she is three months pregnant she will soon have to go on maternity leave. The chair of the interview panel expresses his shock at this, noting that he was under the impression that Paula was a 'career woman', and that it would be difficult for the company to arrange cover during her maternity leave. Paula subsequently receives a letter informing her that she has not been successful in her application due to the 'outstanding calibre' of other applicants.

Advise Paula on any claim she may have against her employers.

Feedback on these exercises is provided in the Appendix to this textbook.

References

Anderson, L. (2003) 'Sound Bite Legislation: the Employment Act 2002', *Industrial Law Journal*, March, Vol. 32(1): 37–42.

BIS (2010) *Work and Families Act 2006 Evaluation Report*, BIS Employment Relations, London: Department for Business, Innovation and Skills.

Bunting, M. (2004) *Willing Slaves – How the Overwork Culture is Ruling our Lives*. London: HarperCollins.

Confederation of British Industry (2009) *Employment Trends 2009: Work Patterns in the Recession*. London: Confederation of British Industry.

Chartered Institute of Personnel and Development (2007) *Work–life Balance Factsheet* (April 2007). London: Chartered Institute of Personnel and Development (available from www.cipd.org.uk).

Clutterbuck, D. (2003) *Managing Work–Life Balance: A Guide for HR in Achieving Organisational and Individual Change*. London: CIPD.

Cully, M., Woodland, S., O'Reilly, A. and Dix, G. (1999) *Britain at Work: as Depicted by the 1998 Workplace Employee Relations Survey*. London: Routledge.

Dex, S. and Scheibl, F. (1998) 'Should We Have More Family-Friendly Policies?', *European Management Journal*, 16(5): 586–99.

Dex, S. and Smith, C. (2002) *The Nature and Pattern of Family-Friendly Employment Policies in Britain*. London: for the Joseph Rowntree Foundation by the Policy Press.

DWP (2010) *Flexible Working: Working for Families, Working for Business*, A report by the Family Friendly Working Hours Taskforce. London: Department for Work and Pensions.

Elsmore, K. (2009) 'Caring and Flexible Working', *Research Summary*. London: Department for Work and Pensions.

Equal Opportunities Commission (2005) *Greater Expectations: EOC's Investigation into Pregnancy Discrimination*. London: EOC.

Felstead, A., Jewson, N. and Walters, S. (2005) *Changing Places of Work*. New York: Palgrave Macmillan.

Foster, C. (2008) 'Maternity, Paternity and Parental Rights Policies – an EOR Survey', *Equal Opportunities Review*, No. 178, 1 July 2008.

Friedman, S. and Greenhaus, J. (2000) *Work and Family – Allies or Enemies? What Happens when Business Professionals Confront Life Choices*. New York: Oxford University Press.

Gatrell, C. (2007) 'A Fractional Commitment? Part-time Work and the Maternal Body', *International Journal of Human Resource Management*, 18(3): 462–75.

Hayward, B., Fong, B. and Thornton, A. (2007) *The Third Work–Life Balance Employer Survey: Main Findings*, Employment Relations Research Series, No. 86. London: Department for Business, Enterprise and Regulatory Reform.

Hooker, H., Neathey, F., Casebourne, J. and Munro, M. (2007) *The Third Work–Life Balance Employee Survey: Main Findings*, Employment Relations Research Series, No. 58. London: Department of Trade and Industry.

HM Government (2011) *Consultation on Modern Workplaces*. London: Department for Business, Innovation and Skills (**www.bis.gov.uk**).

Hoschild, A. (1997) *Time Bind*. New York: Metropolitan Books.

Industrial Relations Services (2002) 'Hanging in the Balance', *IRS Employment Review*, 766: 6–11.

Kersley, B., Alpin, C., Forth, J., Bryson, A., Bewley, H., Dix, G. and Oxenbridge, S. (2006) *Inside the Workplace: Findings from the 2004 Workplace Employment Relations Survey*. London: Routledge.

Kodz, J., Harper, H. and Dench, S. (2002) *Work–Life Balance: Beyond the Rhetoric*, Report 384. Brighton: Institute for Employment Studies.

MacInnes, J. (2002) 'Work–Life Balance and the Demand for Reduction in Working Hours: Evidence from the British Social Attitudes Survey 2002', *British Journal of Industrial Relations*, 43(2): 273–95.

McColgan, A. (2000) 'Family Friendly Frolics? The Maternity and Parental Leave, etc. Regulations 1999', *Industrial Law Journal*, 29(2): 125–44.

Odgers Berndtson/Muika Leadership (2011): *Past Perspectives; Future change. A Study into the Experiences of Senior Women in Financial Services*. London: Odgers Berndtson/Muika Leadership.

Smeaton, D. and Marsh, A. (2006) *Maternity and Paternity Rights and Benefits: Survey of Parents 2005*, Employment Relations Research Series, No. 86. London: Department of Trade and Industry.

Smith, I.T. and Thomas, G. (2003) *Smith and Wood's Industrial Law* (8th edn). London: Lexis Nexis.

Suff, P. (2002) *Work–Life Balance*, Management Review No. 24. London: IRS.

Trades Union Congress (2005) *Future of Work: TUC Economics Department Briefing*. London: Trades Union Congress (available at **www.tuc.org.uk/work_life/tuc.11016.fo.cfm**).

Whitehouse, G., Haynes, M., MacDonald, F. and Arts, D. (2007) *Reassessing the 'Family-Friendly Workplace': Trends and Influences in Britain, 1998–2004*, Employment Relations Research Series, No. 76. London: Department for Business, Enterprise and Regulatory Reform.

Women and Work Commission (2006) *Shaping a Fairer Future*. London: Women and Work Commission, London: Department of Trade and Industry.

Working Families (2007) *Hours to Suit: Working Flexibly at Senior and Managerial Levels*. London: Working Families.

Working Families (2008) *Flexible Working and Performance: Summary of Research*. London: Working Families and Cranfield University School of Management.

Working Families (2011) *Report on Working Families Helpline 2010*. London: Working Families.

Useful websites

Department for Business, Innovation and Skills **www.bis.gov.uk**

Department for Work and Pensions **www.dwp.gov.uk**

Direct.gov **www.direct.gov.uk/employment**

Business Link **www.businesslink.gov.uk**

Health and Safety Executive **www.hse.gov.uk/mothers**

Chartered Institute of Personnel and Development **www.cipd.co.uk**

Trades Union Congress **www.tuc.org.uk**

Visit **www.mylawchamber.co.uk/willey** to access study support resources including realistic HR documentation to accompany the case studies in the book, an online chapter on collective labour law, interactive multiple choice questions, annotated weblinks, a glossary, glossary flashcards, key case flashcards, a legal newsfeed and legal updates.

Chapter 12

Health, safety and welfare at work

Introduction

Health, safety and welfare are woven into operational management and the employment relationship in various important ways. Among key factors managers need to consider are:

- *The management of health and safety*. This involves dealing with a wide range of health and safety implications of the following: the nature of the technology used and related ergonomic considerations; the nature of the products and materials used; work organisation; the scheduling of working time; appropriate staffing levels; the nature of reward systems; and the relevance of training and development for staff.

● **Information**. Information necessary to consider the nature and extent of risk at work is likely to be drawn, as appropriate, from various academic disciplines: physics, chemistry, biology, engineering, medicine, etc. Furthermore, financial considerations are also important: in respect of injuries and accidents and also the implementation of health and safety standards. This, in turn, requires knowledge of relevant details of the legal framework affecting work in the organisation. So, health and safety management is an integrative area involving the interlocking of many specialisms.

● **Employee relations context**. It is also important to remember that health and safety standards and good practice are implemented in an employee relations context. Standards and practice can control and influence how employees behave, how they are paid, staffing levels, their welfare and the conditions under which they work. So, the management of health and safety needs to be linked to both strategic and day-to-day decision-making processes within organisations, as well as to specialist functions (finance, HRM and safety) and also to employee relations processes.

The concepts

'Health', 'safety' and 'welfare', are frequently used in ways which gloss over the differences between them. The terms are not defined in the Health and Safety at Work etc. Act 1974 nor in the European Framework Directive 1989.

❱ Health

The International Labour Organisation defines 'health' in relation to work as 'not merely the absence of disease or infirmity; it also includes the physical and mental elements affecting health which are directly related to safety and hygiene at work' (Convention 155 concerning Occupational Safety and Health and the Working Environment). So, for example, workplace stress, exposure to toxic fumes and substances are likely to create hazards and harm to a person's health. The person might sustain some illness or medical condition from which he or she might recover.

The prohibition of smoking in certain public places and in the workplace is regarded as a public health matter. It was prohibited in various public and work places in Scotland (by the Scottish government) in 2006 and in England and Wales and in Northern Ireland in 2007 (by Parliament and the Welsh Assembly as appropriate). There are limited exemptions to the bans. Employers and managers who control premises need to display non-smoking notices and take reasonable steps to ensure that staff, customers and visitors do not smoke in the premises. The Health and Safety Executive is **not** responsible for enforcement but supports local authorities in their responsibilities. Fines for breaches of the legislation may be imposed (see **www.hse.gov.uk**). The relevant legislation is: Health Act 2006; Prohibition of Smoking in Certain Premises (Scotland) Regulations 2006; Smoke-free Premises, etc. (Wales) Regulations 2007.

❱ Safety

This concerns protection from risk of injury, disease or death. It focuses on preventative steps that can be taken and possible protections to deal with hazards (e.g. working practices, scheduling of working time, training, staffing levels, protective clothing and the physical guarding of machinery). There are substantial links with the concept of 'health' and, unsurprisingly, the two terms are invariably linked.

▶ Welfare

This is a term rarely used in discussions. Yet it is explicitly part of the general duties placed on an employer (Health and Safety at Work etc. Act 1974, s 2(1)). The World Health Organisation speaks of 'a state of complete physical, mental and social well-being that does not consist only in the absence of illness or infirmity'. It interlocks with the other concepts. By adopting protective and preventative measures, it is anticipated that employees' welfare will be taken into account. Generally, it concerns minimising stress at work; helping employees reconcile the competing demands on their time (e.g. work and care for children or a disabled relative); evidence of concern for employees who are suffering personal problems (e.g. bereavement, financial or domestic difficulties); and support for employees who may have drug and alcohol problems.

Legal framework

▶ An initial broad overview

Both civil and criminal law are involved in the regulation of health and safety at work (see Exhibit 12.1).

Civil law

Civil law encompasses:

- **liability** of employer for breach of the contractual duty to take reasonable care;
- liability of employer for the **tort** of **negligence**;
- liability of employee for contributory negligence;
- **dismissal** of employee for breach of safety rules;
- **constructive dismissal** for employer's fundamental breach of the contract of employment.

Criminal law

Criminal law involves the prosecution of an employer (usually by the Health and Safety Executive) for breaches of health and safety standards. If successful, this might result in a fine or, in exceptional cases, imprisonment. In addition, there is the possibility of prosecution by the Crown Prosecution Service for corporate homicide or manslaughter.

So, in varying ways, civil and criminal law cover employees as well as employers and individual managers. They also cover contractors and suppliers. They draw on the **common law** of contract and tort, **statute law** and regulations approved by Parliament and, in part, provisions deriving from European directives. One way of illustrating this potential diversity of law involved in health and safety is to take a simple, yet serious, workplace accident and consider the legal consequences that might result (see Exhibit 12.2).

The range of legal action briefly outlined here is now discussed in more detail under the following headings: the common law, statute law, rights of employees, and consultation and representation.

EXHIBIT 12.1

Health and safety at work: summary of principal legal action and liabilities

Which legal issues?	Who is liable?	Who can take action – for what?	Where?	Employer's possible defence/arguments
Civil Common law of contract: breach of contractual duty of care; possible repudiatory breach	Employer	Employee, for constructive dismissal. Compensation and possible reinstatement/re-engagement	Employment tribunal	No fundamental breach. No breach at all
Civil Common law of tort: negligence	Employer	Employee for personal injury – whether physical or psychiatric. Claim for damages	County Court or High Court	Contributory negligence. The injury was not 'foreseeable'. The employee consented to work in hazardous workplace
Civil Breach of safety rules by employee	Employee and employer	Employer can take disciplinary action up to dismissal. Employee may claim unfair dismissal	Employment tribunal	Employee had been trained and instructed to comply with rules
Criminal Breach of safety rules by employer; breach of duties under Health and Safety at Work etc. Act 1974	Employer Managers and directors Employee Contractors Suppliers	Health and Safety Executive for breach of Health and Safety at Work etc. Act 1974.* Fine or imprisonment	Magistrates' Court or Crown Court	Providing a safe workplace 'so far as is reasonably practicable'
Criminal Gross breach of the duty of care (i.e. gross negligence) because of management and organisation of work	Employer	Director of Public Prosecutions (in England, Wales and Northern Ireland) and Procurator Fiscal (in Scotland) under Corporate Manslaughter and Corporate Homicide Act 2007. Fine	Crown Court	No gross breach. Contributory negligence

* See Enforcement Policy Statement (**www.hse.gov.uk**)

> ### EXHIBIT 12.2

The unguarded machine

The incident: a machine operator loses a finger on an unguarded machine.

1 ***Tort of negligence***. Under civil law, the employer appears to have neglected to meet the common law duty to take reasonable care of the employee. It is, therefore, possible for the employee to sue the employer (for damages) for this *negligence* in the county court. However, in his defence, the employer might be able to say that the employee contributed to the injury by deliberately removing the guard – in breach of workplace rules. The court would need to decide, then, on the facts, whether or not there was *contributory negligence*. If this is established, any damages awarded could be reduced by up to 100 per cent – depending on the extent it was decided that the employee contributed to an injury.

2 ***Disciplinary action***. The employer might feel that, if the employee broke workplace rules, then there should be disciplinary action. The disciplinary procedure would need to be followed fully (in accordance with the ACAS *Code on Disciplinary and Grievance Procedures* 2009). The outcome could include *a warning or even dismissal*. If the employee was dismissed, depending on the circumstances, he or she might claim unfair dismissal at an employment tribunal. The employee's success would depend on the facts and circumstances of the case (see Chapter 8).

3 ***Constructive dismissal***. Under civil law, an additional course of action is possible. The employee's injury might be entirely the fault of the employer. Furthermore, it might be the latest in a series of injuries that the employee has sustained in this employer's employment. Clearly, the employer is failing to comply with the implied contractual duty to take reasonable care of the employee. In these circumstances, the employee could view the employer's behaviour as a *fundamental breach of the contract of employment*. An employee can accept the employer's repudiation of the contract and resign. If he or she is an 'employee' and has sufficient length of service, a claim for unfair constructive dismissal at an employment tribunal can be made (see Chapter 8).

4 ***Prosecution***. Criminal law might also be used involving the prosecution of the employer, *not* by the employee, but by the Health and Safety Executive. This prosecution would be brought under the Health and Safety at Work etc. Act 1974 in either the magistrates' court or the Crown Court (depending on the seriousness of the accident). Given that physical injury was sustained in an accident, criminal proceedings are probable. Evidence in such criminal proceedings would be the employer's failure to provide a safe system of work (including the way health and safety was managed) under the HASAWA 1974, and under regulations relating to the guarding of machinery that were not complied with. For a conviction, the court would need to be satisfied 'beyond reasonable doubt' of the employer's guilt (the criminal standard of proof). The most likely outcome, then, would be a fine. In very serious cases, imprisonment is possible. A successful prosecution could help an individual's subsequent claim for compensation for the injury and also for proving a repudiatory breach of the contract of employment.

Common law

There are two aspects of the common law relevant to health and safety at work: the tort (i.e. a civil wrong) of negligence, and the implied contractual duty of care owed by an employer to an employee.

▶ Tort of negligence

An employer is under a duty to take reasonable care of the health and safety of each individual employee at work. Effectively, this comprises the provision of a safe place of work, safe plant and equipment, and competent and safe fellow employees. What is regarded as 'reasonable' will depend on such matters as the scale of the risk; whether risk of harm is, from the facts available to the employer, reasonably foreseeable; the seriousness of the consequences for the employee if the risk was not dealt with and the employee was injured; and the cost and practicality of preventing the risk.

An employer will, then, breach this duty if he fails to prevent reasonably foreseeable risks. A breach of this duty (i.e. the employer's neglect) usually provides the basis of personal injury claims. In this context both physical and/or mental health issues are relevant. So, if an employee suffers from a recognised psychiatric illness or condition and it can be proved on the balance of probabilities (the relevant **standard of proof** in civil matters) that the illness was caused by the respondent employer's breach of duty, then that employer is liable. One illustration of some of the issues relating to employer negligence and personal injury claims is seen in the *Walker* case (Exhibit 12.3).

EXHIBIT 12.3

The *Walker* case

Walker v *Northumberland County Council* [1995] **IRLR 35, HC**

This early case relating to work-related stress involved a social services officer who alleged a failure by his employer to deal with excessive workload. Mr Walker said that his employer failed in a number of respects. First, the county council had not responded to his requests to restructure the department to provide more field officers to deal with increasing case work (particularly in respect of child abuse cases). Secondly, after he had suffered a nervous breakdown and subsequently returned to work, promises of assistance from a seconded member of staff and weekly visits by his boss were not delivered upon. Thirdly, during his four-month absence, a substantial volume of paperwork had built up. Fourthly, the number of pending childcare cases continued to grow at a considerable rate. Ultimately, within a few months, he had a second nervous breakdown and was dismissed by the council on grounds of permanent ill health. He claimed damages against the council for breach of its common law duty of care in failing to take reasonable steps to avoid exposing him to a workload that endangered his health.

He was successful at the High Court (and the matter was *not* taken on appeal to the Court of Appeal). The duty of care owed to Mr Walker was ruled as encompassing the prevention of foreseeable psychiatric illness. An out-of-court settlement of £175,000 was agreed in 1996. (More detail on the current law on work-related stress is considered later in this chapter.)

Negligence claims are usually made in respect of one employer where there is strict liability. The personal injury arises from the negligence of that employer. However, it is important to note that, in certain cases, harm to health, arising from negligence, may not easily be attributed to one employer. The House of Lords ruled on this issue in the circumstances of workers suffering from mesothelioma. They had contracted this condition in the course of their employment with a number of employers as a result of exposure to asbestos dust. In 2002, the House of Lords made a **landmark judgment** in respect of tortious liability. It ruled on a test case (*Fairchild* v *Glenhaven Funeral Services Ltd and Others* [2002] IRLR 533) and several related cases which concerned liability for mesothelioma. Previously, the Court of Appeal had held that where a claimant suffered or might suffer mesothelioma as a result of exposure in the course of employment with more than one employer to asbestos dust, then he or she could *not* recover damages from any of the employers. This was because it could not be established, on the balance of probabilities, when the claimant inhaled the fibre which led to the development of mesothelioma. However, the House of Lords overturned this ruling. The defendant employers should be regarded as jointly and severally liable for the wrong.

Repudiatory breach of contract

A second aspect of common law relevant to health and safety issues concerns the implied contractual term: the employer's duty of care to the individual employee. Failure to meet this duty may be a repudiatory breach of the contract. If the employee accepts the breach, he or she can resign and claim unfair constructive dismissal at an employment tribunal. Alternatively, he or she might remain in employment but seek remedies in either the High Court or the county court. These remedies may include a declaration of contractual rights, damages, and an **injunction** which could prevent an anticipatory breach of contract.

Liability and vicarious liability

The issue of liability for breach of health and safety law covers both common law, and the duties under statute law (which are outlined in more detail below in Exhibit 12.7).

Common law

As we have seen, an employer is liable under this for breaches of duty (i.e. the tort of negligence) which are 'in the course of employment'. The issue of **vicarious liability** can also arise. This can occur, for example, where an employee injures a fellow worker or a customer or a contractor. The injured person may sue the employer for the injury because the employer is vicariously liable for the 'acts and omissions' of his or her employees. In practical terms, it is advantageous to the injured person because of the significantly better financial and insurance position of the employing organisation. It also acknowledges the employer's ultimate responsibility for the organisation of the work in question and for the deployment and training of staff.

A point of uncertainty that can arise in such cases is the meaning of 'in the course of employment'. Among the issues under health and safety law are:

● whether or not the employee is carrying out tasks wrongly;
● whether the work was performed by the employee negligently;
● whether the acts are outside working hours;
● whether the employee was travelling to or from work;
● whether the employee behaved violently (e.g. towards a customer or fellow worker).

Clearly, courts will need to consider the facts and circumstances of each case to establish liability.

An employer's defences

In such common law claims an employer might have defences available. The two principal ones that may be possible: '*volenti not fit injuria*' and contributory negligence.

Volenti non fit injuria

Translated from Latin, this means 'no wrong is done to one who consents'. For this defence to be effective in health and safety matters, the employer would need to establish that the employee not only knew of the risk and continued working but also consented freely to work. This might be difficult for the employer to prove because the employee might have been ordered to work or, alternatively, the employee needed to work in such a way to carry out his duties. The view of academic lawyers is that *volenti* 'rarely succeeds' in industrial injury and employment cases (Smith and Thomas 2000: 734).

As to liability for breaches of statutory duty, 'the position is even clearer, for it has been held that *volenti* does not apply at all to an action for breach of a statutory duty laid upon the employer by the relevant legislation' (Smith and Thomas 2000: 735). The authors added: 'the principal reason being that it would be contrary to public policy to allow an employee by agreement or consent to "contract out" of his statutory protection.'

Contributory negligence

Contributory negligence can arise when an employee disobeys a safety instruction given by the employer or is reckless and, consequently, sustains an injury. It applies to all cases involving breaches of both statutory duties as well as common law actions. (Statutory duties are set out below.)

Statute law

The following section outlines:

- the primary legislation: the Health and Safety at Work etc. Act 1974;
- secondary legislation: principally, the Management of Health and Safety at Work Regulations 1999 with references to some other key regulations;
- Corporate Manslaughter and Corporate Homicide Act 2007;
- Fatal Accidents Act 1976.

▶ Health and Safety at Work etc. Act 1974

Origin

Following the recommendations of the Robens report (Robens 1972), a broad political consensus resulted in the enactment of the Health and Safety at Work etc. Act 1974. This had a number of purposes – both explicit and implicit:

- to extend the coverage of health and safety protection to a wider range of working people;
- to rationalise existing health and safety law;
- to impose general duties upon all employers;
- to permit some flexibility in implementation by qualifying the duties with the phrase 'as far as is reasonably practicable';
- to encourage self-regulation by employers and workforce representatives;
- to ensure that relevant information is available to employers and employees;

- to provide clear enforcement procedures and specific enforcement agencies (the Health and Safety Executive and, as appropriate, local authorities);
- to establish a tripartite body, the Health and Safety Commission, comprising employers, unions and certain independent people, to review and advise the Secretary of State on health and safety policy. (The HSC was abolished in 2008, and a reconstituted Health and Safety Executive is the principal body for overseeing and the legislation.)

Who is covered?

It covers all employers and every aspect of work. It brought into legal protection some seven million additional working people. The Act applies to the Crown (s 48). It covers an employer's responsibilities to contractors and to the general public. Domestic servants in a private household are exempt (s 51).

What is the nature of the Act?

It is described as enabling legislation. To promote health and safety standards in the workplace, regulations can be laid before Parliament, under the authority of the Act. The Act sets general duties. Regulations, made under the Act, are more precise, setting detailed prescriptions. Examples of these regulations are the Control of Noise at Work Regulations 2005; Health and Safety (Display Screen Equipment) Regulations 1992; the Management of Health and Safety Regulations 1999. Regulations can cover procedures to be adopted in the management of health and safety as well as standards of safety practice in the workplace. Furthermore, there are regulations prescribing arrangements for safety consultation and representation.

What are the general duties?

These are placed on employers, employees, self-employed persons and on designers, manufacturers, importers and suppliers.

Employers' duties to employees

The Act states that 'it shall be the duty of every employer to ensure, so far as is reasonably practicable, the health, safety and welfare at work of all his employees' (HASAWA 1974, s 2(1)). Several comments can be made about this basic duty.

- First, it is qualified by the phrase 'as far as is reasonably practicable'. Invariably, a balance is to be struck between risk reduction/minimisation and the cost, time and trouble involved.

- Secondly, it is important to remember that this all-encompassing duty relates to welfare, as well as health and safety and should result in appropriate employer policies.

- Thirdly, this duty is extended to other particular matters. These cover:
  - the provision and maintenance of plant and systems of work that are, so far as is reasonably practicable, safe and without risks to health;
  - arrangements for ensuring, so far as is reasonably practicable, safety and absence of risks to health in connection with the use, handling, storage and transport of articles and substances;
  - provision of information, instruction, training and supervision as is necessary to ensure, so far as is reasonably practicable, the health and safety at work of employees;

- any place of work under the employer's control, the maintenance of it in a condition that is safe and without risks to health and the provision and maintenance of means of access to and egress from it that are safe and without such risks – all so far as is reasonably practicable;
- provision and maintenance of a working environment for employees that is, so far as is reasonably practicable, safe, without risks to health, and adequate as regards facilities and arrangements for their welfare at work (HASAWA 1974, s 2(2)).

An employer, in complying with health and safety duties, may not impose any levy on an employee (s 9).

Employers' duties to non-employees

Employer's duties towards employees are, also, extended to cover responsibilities to non-employees. 'It shall be the duty of every employer to conduct his undertaking in such a way as to ensure, so far as is reasonably practicable, that persons not in his employment who may be affected thereby are not thereby exposed to risks to their health or safety' (s 3(1)). A parallel duty is imposed upon self-employed persons towards non-employees (s 3(2)). Furthermore, there are general duties placed upon 'persons concerned with premises to persons other than their employees' (s 4).

In interpreting this duty (s 3), the Court of Appeal (*R v Board of Trustees of the Science Museum* [1993] 3 All ER 853) adopted a **purposive** approach and emphasised the 'risk' of harm as opposed to evidence that actual harm had been sustained. (This approach differs from the common law approach which requires evidence of actual harm for **damages** to be awarded.)

Employers' duty to promote self-regulation

The general duties on employers, outlined above, are supplemented by further ones, designed to promote self-regulation.

- First, '. . . it shall be the duty of every employer to prepare and as often as may be appropriate revise a written statement of his *general policy* with respect of the health and safety at work of his employees and the organisation and arrangements for the time being in force for carrying out that policy, and to bring the statement and any revision of it to the notice of all his employees' (s 2(3)). (Those employing fewer than five employees are exempt from this requirement.) (See Exhibit 12.11 below.)

- Secondly, there are provisions on *safety representatives* and on the establishment of a *safety committee* (s 2(4)–(7)). They are created within the context of the following general duty on an employer 'to consult any such representatives with a view to the making and maintenance of arrangements which will enable him and his employees to co-operate effectively in promoting and developing measures to ensure the health and safety at work of employees and in checking the effectiveness of such measures' (s 2(6)). The roles and functions are discussed in more detail below.

- Thirdly, as seen later, there are supplementary duties arising from the Management of Health and Safety at Work Regulations 1999, particularly in respect of risk assessment, health surveillance of employees, and the protection of pregnant and young workers.

Duties of employees and others

The general duties on employees do not absolve an employer from its primary responsibility for health and safety at work. The Act states that 'it shall be the duty of every employee while at work (a) to take reasonable care for the health and safety of himself and other persons who may be affected by his acts or omissions at work; and (b) as regards any duty or requirement imposed on his employer or any other person by or under any of the relevant statutory provisions, to co-operate with him so far as is necessary to enable that duty or requirement to be performed or complied with' (HASAWA 1974, s 7).

These duties are supplemented by those in the Management of Health and Safety at Work Regulations 1999 (reg 14). An employee must 'use any machinery, equipment, dangerous substance, transport equipment, means of production or safety device provided to him by the employer in accordance both with any training . . . and instructions . . .' (reg 14). Additionally, an employee must inform the employer of situations which he or she reasonably believes 'represented a serious and immediate danger to health and safety', or of shortcomings in the employer's arrangements for health and safety protection.

An ancillary duty affects a wide range of people (including employees): 'No person shall intentionally or recklessly interfere with or misuse anything provided in the interests of health, safety, or welfare in pursuance of any of the relevant statutory provisions' (s 8).

Finally, in respect of general duties, designers, manufacturers, importers and suppliers of 'any article for use at work' must, as far as is reasonably practicable, ensure that the article is designed and constructed so as to be safe when properly used; must carry out testing and examination; must ensure that information is available about the article, its testing and its use; must carry out research to minimise any risks; and must ensure safe installation (s 6).

▶ What is the role of regulations?

The HASAWA 1974 was constructed as enabling legislation to be supplemented by specific regulations (s 15). Regulations that have been prepared and approved by Parliament over the past 40 years fall into two broad categories:

- *Hazards*. These set standards for dealing with specific hazards at work (e.g. noise, manual handling operations, eye protection).
- *Procedures*. These set procedural requirements for all employers (e.g. relating to the management of health and safety and information disclosure, and to the role and functions of safety representatives).

The range of regulations is considerable (see **www.hse.gov.uk**). Their relevance to particular employers, obviously, varies. Some can be industry-specific. Others are more widespread in their application because the incidence of certain workplace hazards (e.g. the use of visual display units) extends across many industries and sectors. Regulations relating to procedures are, also, generally of broad application. The most fundamentally important of these is the Management of Health and Safety at Work Regulations 1999. Its provisions are considered next. Other key regulations are briefly outlined in Exhibit 12.4.

▶ The Management of Health and Safety at Work Regulations 1999

These implement requirements of the European Health and Safety Directive 1989. They apply to all employers in respect of their own employees and 'persons not in his employment arising out of or in connection with the conduct by him of his undertaking' (reg 3). (See in Exhibit 12.7 reference to the issue of liability in *R* v *Associated Octel Ltd* [1994] IRLR 540.) They set out ways in which risk and health and safety can be managed systematically. There are several key provisions.

EXHIBIT 12.4

Some other key regulations

Control of Noise at Work Regulations 2005. These cover workers and the self-employed in all industry sectors. They set duties on employers to prevent damage to or loss of workers' hearing; or causing the suffering of tinnitus. There are parallel duties for designers, manufacturers, importers and suppliers. Daily personal noise exposure levels for workers are specified and must be assessed. Employers must reduce unacceptable noise exposure levels as far as is reasonably practicable.

Health and Safety (Display Screen Equipment) Regulations 1992. These cover the users of such equipment and are considered in detail in the final section of this chapter dealing with employment policies and practices. (See Exhibit 12.12)

Manual Handling Operations Regulations 1992. As far as reasonably practicable, employers are to avoid manual handling operations (e.g. lifting, pushing, pulling, carrying or moving) and consider whether such operations are necessary or could be achieved in a different way, or be automated or mechanised. A suitable assessment of the operations should be carried in consultation with employees. Risk should be reduced to the lowest level practicable. Attention should be paid to workers who have been pregnant and those with health problems. Weight limits are specified.

Workplace (Health, Safety and Welfare) Regulations 1992. These cover a wide range of workplaces (but excluding extractive industries, construction sites and outdoors agricultural and forestry workplaces). There are provisions on e.g. workplace temperatures, rest facilities, lighting, ventilation, cleanliness, space, and workstations.

Provision and Use of Work Equipment Regulations 1992. They cover all workers, including those working off-shore and the self-employed. Employers' duty is to ensure the suitability of work equipment for its purpose (by design, construction or adaptation). They must take account of likely risks (e.g. a wet or flammable atmosphere). Work equipment must be effectively maintained. All persons who use or supervise the use of work equipment must have received adequate information and health and safety training.

Personal Protective Equipment at Work Regulations 1992. They cover workers and the self-employed. Employers must provide suitable, properly maintained personal protective equipment for workers who may be exposed to health and safety risks.

Control of Substances Hazardous to Health Regulations (COSHH) 2002. These cover, among other matters, employers' duties, prohibitions relating to certain substances, risk assessment, the prevention and control of exposure to substances hazardous to health, and monitoring exposure and health surveillance.

Reporting of Injuries, Diseases and Dangerous Occurrences Regulations (RIDDOR) 1995. They specify notification procedures (to the Health and Safety Executive or the local authority, as appropriate) for injuries, dangerous occurrences, work-related diseases (such as arsenic or lead poisoning) and for deaths of employees; and stipulate records to be kept by employers.

Risk assessments

General

The first step must be to make 'suitable and sufficient assessment' of risks in the work-place (reg 3). The assessment must look at the way work is actually done (which may sometimes be different from the way the employer expects it to be done). It must enable the employer to identify and prioritise significant risks and decide on appropriate action. Appropriate action can involve a number of considerations:

- whether the risk can be eliminated completely – for example, by not using a specific substance or by redesigning the way in which work is carried out;

- whether the hazard can be tackled at source – for example, isolating noisy machinery in an acoustic booth rather than providing ear protection;

- whether work should be adapted to the individual worker and not the other way – so avoiding monotonous work and work at a predetermined rate;

- making sure that all workers (including part-timers, temporary staff and trainees) are informed in 'comprehensible' form (reg 10) of safety standards and expectations about how work is to be carried out.

'Avoidance of risk' does not require the elimination of all possible risk to the employee but merely the reduction of risk to the lowest acceptable level (*New Southern Railway Ltd* v *Quinn* [2006] IRLR 266).

Pregnant and breast-feeding workers

Particular attention must be paid to the risks to which this group are exposed (regs 16, 16A and 17). These can include physical hazards (such as noise, vibration, radiation, physical effort, etc.), and biological and chemical hazards. The employer should undertake:

- An assessment of the risks and a consideration of any protective measures that would avoid it.

- If the risk cannot be avoided, then the employer should consider altering the woman's working conditions or hours of work.

- If such alteration is unreasonable or would not avoid the risk and there is no suitable work available, then the last resort is suspension on full pay for as long as necessary to protect the health and safety of both the employee and her child.

In *O'Neill* v *Buckinghamshire County Council* [2009] UKEAT/0020/09, the Employment Appeal Tribunal confirmed that employers had no general obligation to undertake a risk assessment for every pregnant worker. Failure to do so is not automatically sex discrimination. The duty to provide a risk assessment is triggered only:

- when the employee has notified the employer in writing that she is pregnant;

- when the work involves risk of harm or danger to the expectant mother or her baby; and

- when the risk arises from working arrangements or from legally specified physical, biological or chemical agents in the workplace.

This approach had previously been set out by the Court of Appeal in *Madarassy v Nomura International plc* [2007] IRLR 246, CA (See also Chapter 11).

Young people

An employer must assess particular risks for young people, taking into account their inexperience, lack of awareness of potential risks and immaturity. Where the risks cannot be adequately controlled, young people should not be employed for that work (e.g. where the work is beyond their physical or psychological capacity, or work which involves exposure to harmful agents or radiation; or presents a risk to health from extreme cold or heat, noise or vibration). If children under the minimum school-leaving age are employed, then parents must be given details of the risk assessment and control measures (reg 19).

Health and safety arrangements

These follow from risk assessment and require effective planning, organisation, control of health and safety, review; and should also include health surveillance arrangements (reg 5).

Health surveillance

Where appropriate, the regulations require the employer to provide 'such health surveillance as is appropriate' of their workforce (reg 6). Central to this is monitoring. This can be carried out on various levels. For example, supervisors could be trained to check people's hands if they work with a substance which can cause skin rashes; whereas occupational health staff could undertake specific medical tests and examinations.

Competent persons

One or more such persons shall be appointed by an employer 'to assist him in undertaking the measures he needs to take to comply with the requirements and prohibitions imposed upon him by or under the relevant statutory provisions' (reg 7). Such a person

---

Activity 12.1

Assessing risks

In small groups, discuss the working conditions of any number of the following and decide on the risks that you think that staff might encounter; and on the steps that the employer might and should take to deal with them:

- call-centre worker;
- bus driver;
- nurse in a hospital's accident and emergency department;
- social worker;
- school teacher;
- traffic warden;
- solicitor;
- prison officer;
- pharmacist in a retail chemist shop.

For guidance on risk assessment, see *Five Steps to Risk Assessment*, available from **www.hse.gov.uk**.

must have sufficient training and experience or knowledge and other qualities to enable the function to be carried out. The person appointed must have:

- a good understanding of the principles of risk assessment and prevention;
- a knowledge of the employer's business and the work carried out by employees;
- awareness of the limitations of their own ability and when other expertise may be required.

Serious or imminent danger

Employers must plan in advance for foreseeable emergencies such as fire, a bomb scare, the release of toxic fumes, etc. Arrangements may involve a full evacuation of the work premises. In such an event, there should be sufficient trained, designated people to supervise the evacuation. Staff who are required to enter a hazardous area (e.g. to close down a process) should be specially trained (reg 8).

◗ The machinery for enforcing health and safety standards

Two levels are provided for in the legislation:

- *Workplace*: safety representatives and safety committees in combination with the relevant employer.
- *Public authority level*: the Health and Safety Executive, which manages Health and Safety Inspectors (HSIs). Local authority inspectors regulate lower risk workplaces – e.g. shops, offices, pubs and cinemas. The principal focus in this chapter is on the HSE.

Workplace level consultation and representation

Workforce representation, through the establishment of safety representatives and safety committees, was seen, from the origin of the Health and Safety at Work Act 1974, as central to a 'self-regulation' model for implementing effective health and safety standards. The Trades Union Congress has undertaken biennial surveys of union safety representatives to record their experiences in the role (see TUC (2010)).

Between the mid-1970s and 1996, Britain had a flawed system of representation. The 1977 Safety Representatives and Safety Committees Regulations were restricted to union safety representatives where trade unions were recognised by an employer. As unionisation diminished during the 1980s and 1990s, employees in the rapidly expanding non-union sector were without any legally enforceable rights of representation. This did not comply with the 1989 European Directive on Safety and Health. Article 11 outlined the responsibilities of 'workers' representatives' – with no distinction between unionised and non-unionised organisations. So, in 1996, the Health and Safety (Consultation with Employees) Regulations were approved by Parliament. These complement the 1977 regulations. Together they create a general framework of representation rights. There are several issues in this legal framework that we will consider:

- safety representation;
- the functions of safety representatives;
- information disclosure;
- protections against detriments;
- remedies and redress for detriments and dismissal.

Safety representation

Under the *1977 regulations*, a **recognised independent trade union** may appoint safety representatives from among the employees 'in all cases where one or more employees are employed by an employer by whom it is recognised' (reg 3.1). The person 'so far as is reasonably practicable' shall 'either have been employed by his employer throughout the preceding two years or have had at least two years' experience in similar employment' (reg 3.4). The *1996 regulations* merely describe 'representatives of employee safety'. Such a person will have been elected from a group of employees 'to represent that group [for] the purposes of . . . consultation' (reg 4.1b).

A safety committee should be established by an employer 'having the function of keeping under review the measures taken to ensure the health and safety at work of his employees and such other functions as may be prescribed' (HASAWA, s 2(7)). Under the *1977 regulations*, two union-recognised safety representatives are needed to request a committee (reg 9). The *1996 regulations* have no parallel provision. Under these regulations, consultation can be directly with the workforce, with one representative or with more than one (reg 4). The creation of a safety committee is subject to management discretion.

The functions of safety representatives

1977 regulations: in unionised workforces, the functions are:

- to represent employees in consultation with the employer (reg 4);
- to investigate potential hazards and dangerous occurrences at the workplace and examine the causes of accidents at the workplace;
- to investigate health and safety complaints made by any employee he or she represents;
- to make representations to the employer on general matters arising out of investigations;
- to make representations to the employer on general matters affecting the health, safety or welfare of the employees at the workplace;
- to carry out inspections in a number of circumstances: where there has been no inspection for the past three months; where there has been 'a substantial change in the conditions of work'; where there has been 'a notifiable accident or dangerous occurrence in a workplace or a notifiable disease has been contracted'; where the employer has 'any document relevant to the workplace and to the employees' (regs 5, 6 and 7);
- to represent the employees in consultation at the workplace with Health and Safety Inspectors and any other enforcing authority;
- to attend meetings of safety committees in connection with any of these functions.

1996 regulations: in non-union workforces, the functions are:

- to make representations to the employer on potential hazards and dangerous occurrences at the workplace which affect, or could affect, employees (reg 6);
- to make representations to the employer on general matters affecting the health and safety at work of the employees and, in particular, on such matters consulted about with the employer (see reg 3 below);
- to represent the employees in consultation at the workplace with inspectors.

These functions are exercised in the context of 'the duty of the employer to consult' provisions (reg 3). The employer 'shall consult in good time' (with either the workforce directly or with representatives) particularly regarding:

- the introduction of any measure at the workplace which may substantially affect the health and safety of those employees;

- arrangements for nominating 'competent persons' (MHSW Regulations, reg 7);

- any health and safety information he or she is required to provide to those employees by or under the relevant statutory provisions;

- the planning and organisation of any health and safety training he or she is required to provide to those employees by or under the relevant statutory provisions;

- the health and safety consequences for employees of the introduction (including planning) of new technologies into the workplace.

The *1996 regulations* are silent about inspections – though they could be implied from some of the above provisions.

Disclosure of information

Obviously, consultation and representation can only be effective if information is adequate. The *1977 regulations* (reg 7) for union safety representatives specify:

- ***Inspection***. 'Safety representatives shall for the performance of their functions ... if they have given the employer reasonable notice, be entitled to inspect and take copies of any document relevant to the workplace or the employees the safety representatives represent which the employer is required to keep ... except a document consisting of or relating to any health record of an identifiable individual.'

- ***Information***. An employer shall make available to safety representatives the information, within the employer's knowledge, necessary to enable him or her to fulfil his or her functions except information which 'would be against the interests of national security'; the disclosure of which would infringe some statutory provision; information which relates to an individual (unless he or she has consented to disclosure); or information which would, if disclosed, cause 'substantial injury to the employer's undertaking'; or 'any information obtained by the employer for the purpose of bringing, prosecuting or defending any legal proceedings'.

The *1996 regulations* provide a general duty to provide information (reg 5) to either employees directly or with their representatives 'as is necessary to enable them to participate fully and effectively in the consultation' and for representatives 'in the carrying out of their functions under these Regulations'. The exceptions set out in the 1977 regulations (reg 7.2) are restated.

This information disclosure is in the context of the general duty on the employer 'to provide such information . . . as is necessary to ensure, as far as is reasonably practicable, the health and safety at work of his employees' (HASAWA, s 2(2)(c)).

Protection against 'detriments' and unfair dismissal

Certain protections are enacted to help ensure the credibility of workforce safety representatives and their independence from undue employer influence. These are outlined below in relation to the general protections for employees and for specific postholders.

There are statutory protections 'from suffering detriments in employment' (Employment Rights Act 1996, s 44); and parallel protection against unfair dismissal (s 100).

'Detriment' is construed as putting a person at a disadvantage. It includes disciplinary warnings and dismissal, temporary transfers to other work and suspensions from work, refusals to grant a pay rise or allocate overtime to an employee, and overlooking an employee for promotion. In this context it is stated that 'an employee has the right not to be subjected to any detriment by any act, or any deliberate failure to act, by his employer done on the ground that' he or she exercised certain statutory rights (ERA 1996, s 44(1)) (see also Chapter 8).

There are five circumstances covered by protection:

1 *'Competent persons'* (appointed under MHSW Regulations 1999): who 'having been designated by the employer to carry out activities in connection with preventing or reducing risks to health and safety at work,' this employee 'carried out (or proposed to carry out) any such activities' (ERA 1996, s 44(1)(a)).

2 *Safety representatives or safety committee members*: where an employee performed or proposed to perform the functions of this role.

3 *Election of safety representatives*: where an employee took part or proposed to take part in consultation with the employer or in an election of safety representatives (Health and Safety (Consultation with Employees) Regulations 1996).

4 *Informing the employer of hazards*: where 'being an employee at a place where (i) there was no such representative or safety committee, or (ii) there was such a representative or safety committee but it was not reasonably practicable for the employee to raise the matter by those means, he brought to his employer's attention, by reasonable means, circumstances connected with his work which he reasonably believed were harmful or potentially harmful to health or safety' (ERA 1996, s 44(1)(c)).

It is expected that the employee would raise his or her complaint through the organisation's grievance procedure. This would be regarded as 'reasonable means' – whereas a direct complaint, in the first instance, to a director or an external body, like the HSE, would not be. Furthermore, the employee must show 'reasonable belief'. In an unfair dismissal case, the EAT provided the following guidance (*Kerr v Nathan's Wastesavers Ltd* EAT/91/95). An employee must show:
- belief that, in fact, the circumstances were harmful, or potentially harmful, to health and safety;
- that he or she had in mind reasonable grounds to sustain that belief;
- that those grounds were based on all the relevant circumstances of the case.

5 *Serious and imminent risk*: this relates to leaving the workplace where there is such a risk – which may be a one-off incident or an on-going situation. Protection against detriment relates to 'circumstances of danger which the employee reasonably believed to be serious and imminent and which he could not reasonably have been expected to avert, he left (or proposed to leave) or (while the danger persisted) refused to return to his place of work or any dangerous part of his place of work' (s 44(1)(d)). Such protection also concerns 'circumstances of danger which the employee reasonably believed to be serious and imminent' where 'he took (or proposed to take) appropriate steps to protect himself or other persons from the danger' (s 44(1)(e)).

The issue of 'reasonable belief', arises. One aspect of this is the extent to which 'objective' evidence is required for the employee to sustain his or her 'subjective' belief that there is a 'serious and imminent danger'. It appears that there is no absolute

---

EXHIBIT 12.5

The van driver

Rawlings v *Barraclough t/a Independent Delivery Services Ltd* 2.5.95, COIT, 15595/95

A van driver refused to drive what he said was a defective vehicle and was dismissed. His employer had assured him that the vehicle was in a safe condition. Although he had obtained no expert evidence, it was provided before the tribunal where it was stated that the vehicle would have failed its MOT test and would have been ruled as unroadworthy. The tribunal commented that the assurance about the vehicle's safety given by the company was 'so informal and so undetailed that [he] was still entitled to hold his belief notwithstanding the fact that others had driven the van in the meantime'. The dismissal was ruled to be unfair.

---

obligation upon the employee to acquire such evidence – but, clearly, it can help (see Exhibit 12.5).

The question of whether the steps which the employee 'took or proposed to take were appropriate is to be judged by reference to all the circumstances including, in particular, his knowledge and the facilities and advice available to him at the time' (ERA 1996, s 44(2)). Furthermore, if an employer can show that what the employee did was 'so negligent' that 'a reasonable employer' would have taken action against such an employee, then 'an employee is not to be regarded as having been subjected to a detriment' (ERA 1996, s 44(3)). To this extent, an employer has a defence.

Remedies and redress for detriments and dismissal

● *Complaints to an employment tribunal.* An employee who believes that he or she has suffered such a detriment may complain to an employment tribunal. There are no qualifying conditions. The right covers all 'employees' irrespective of age, hours of work or length of service. A complaint must be lodged within three months of the unfair dismissal or the detrimental treatment. A tribunal has discretion to extend this three-month period. Where a detrimental act continues over a period, the date of the act is the last day of that period.

● *Detriments short of dismissal.* If an employee successfully complains of this detrimental treatment, the employment tribunal must make a declaration to that effect and may award (unlimited) compensation which it regards as 'just and equitable' in all the circumstances. This will involve consideration of any loss sustained by the employee and any injury to feelings. The employee must mitigate his or her loss. Compensation might be reduced because the employee's behaviour contributed to the circumstances.

● *Dismissal.* If the detrimental treatment is dismissal and the claim successful, then an ex-employee may be awarded compensation or an order for re-engagement or reinstatement can be made. Basic and compensatory awards are calculated in the normal way.

● *Dismissal of safety representatives.* If the person is dismissed for undertaking his or her duties as a safety representative, member of a safety committee or as a 'designated employee', then additional remedies are available. The first is interim relief (ERA 1996, s 128). A claim for this must be made to the employment tribunal within seven days immediately following the effective date of termination. If it appears to the tribunal that the employee is 'likely' (ERA 1996, s 129(1)) to establish that the reason for the dismissal is one prohibited under s 100, and the employer is willing, then it may order the reinstatement or re-engagement of the employee pending the final determination of the case at a hearing or settlement (e.g. through ACAS **conciliation**). Re-engagement means re-employment on terms that are 'not less favourable' than those that would have applied had the employee not been dismissed (ERA 1996, s 129(3)(b)). The employee may 'reasonably' refuse re-engagement (ERA 1996, s 128(8)(a)).

If no agreement is reached on reinstatement or re-engagement, the tribunal must make an order for the continuation of the contract of employment from the date of termination until the date of determination or settlement of the complaint. Unreasonable refusal of re-engagement by an employee will result in the tribunal making no order to continue the contract of employment (ERA 1996, s 129(8)(b)). An order to continue the contract of employment is 'an order that the contract of employment continue in force . . . for the purposes of pay and any other benefit derived from employment, seniority, pension rights and other similar matters' and for the purposes of determining the employee's continuity of employment (ERA 1996, s 130(1)).

Health and Safety Executive and inspectors

❱ What are the roles of the HSE?

In terms of the day-to-day management of health and safety at work, the statutory roles of health and safety inspectors are significant (HASAWA 1974, s 20). These are:

Entering premises

- at any reasonable time (or in a situation which in his opinion is or may be dangerous, at any time) to enter any premises which he believes it is necessary for him to enter;
- to take with him a constable if he has reasonable cause to apprehend any serious obstruction in the execution of his duty;
- to take with him any person duly authorised by his [the inspector's] enforcing authority; and any equipment or materials required.

Investigation

- to make such examination and investigation as may in any circumstances be necessary;
- as regards any premises which he has power to enter, to direct that those premises or any part of them, or anything therein, shall be left undisturbed for as long as is reasonably necessary for the purpose of any examination or investigation;
- to take such measurements and photographs and make such recordings as necessary;
- to take samples of any articles or substances found in any premises which he has power to enter, and of the atmosphere in or in the vicinity of any such premises.

Action on substances or equipment

- if an article or substance appears to him to have caused or to be likely to cause danger to health and safety, to have it to dismantled or subjected to any process or test; or, if necessary, destroyed;

- in the case of any such article or substance, to take possession of it and detain it for so long as is necessary for all or any of the following purposes, namely
  - to examine it;
  - to ensure that it is not tampered with before his examination of it is completed;
  - to ensure that it is available for use as evidence in any proceedings for an offence.

Obtaining information

- to require any person (whom he has reasonable cause to believe to be able to give any information relevant to any examination or investigation) to answer (in the absence of persons other than a person nominated by him to be present and any persons whom the inspector may allow to be present) such questions as the inspector thinks fit to ask and to sign a declaration of the truth of his answers;

- to require the production of, inspect, and take copies of, or of any entry in, any books or documents.

Requiring assistance

- to require any person to afford him such facilities and assistance with respect to any matters or things within that person's control or in relation to which that person has responsibilities as are necessary to enable the inspector to exercise any of the powers conferred on him by this section (HASAWA 1974, s 20(2)).

▶ What are the powers of the HSE?

- *Improvement notice* (HASAWA 1974, s 21). This may be issued by an Inspector and requires a person (usually an employer) to remedy a contravention of statutory provisions within a specified time period (normally 21 days). Appeal is possible to an employment tribunal within 21 days and this suspends the notice (HASAWA 1974, s 24). During 2009–10, the HSE issued 5,811 of these notices (see **www.hse.gov.uk/statistics**).

- *Prohibition notice* (HASAWA 1974, s 22). This is issued to prevent a person from carrying on activities where there is or may be a 'risk of serious personal injury'. Such a notice can have immediate effect. Again, appeal is possible to an employment tribunal. However, appeal does not rescind the notice. This can only be done after a tribunal hearing (HASAWA 1974, s 24). During 2009–10, the HSE issued 47 deferred prohibition notices and 3,876 immediate prohibition notices (see **www.hse.gov.uk/statistics**).

- *Prosecutions*. Criminal proceedings may be initiated in the courts for offences under the relevant statutory provisions. An Inspector is authorised (HASAWA, s 39) to prosecute in magistrates' courts in England and Wales. In all other proceedings, the consent of the Director of Public Prosecutions is required. Contrary to the usual rules in criminal proceedings, it is for the defendant to prove what was reasonably practicable. Specific provision on the onus of proof is set out in the Act (HASAWA 1974, s 40). During 2009–10, the HSE initiated 1,026 prosecutions which resulted in 735 convictions. The average fine was £15,817 (see **www.hse.gov.uk/statistics**). (See Exhibit 12.6 and Exhibit 12.7.)

EXHIBIT 12.6

Prosecutions

R v Porter [2008] **EWCA Crim 1271, CA**

An appeal in 2008 against conviction illustrates some of the issues involved in the incidence of risk and an organisation's duty (HASAWA 1974, s 3) to non-employees. The Court of Appeal quashed a headteacher's conviction for accidental injuries sustained by a three-year-old pupil on school property.

R v Norwest Holst Construction Ltd and Costain Ltd [2009] **Croydon Crown Court**

The prosecution of the companies was dismissed because the court found 'no case to answer'. It was stated by the judge that the victim who was killed had 'gone off on a frolic of his own' and the companies could not have foreseen the risk. They had taken all reasonably practicable steps to avert risk.

EXHIBIT 12.7

Health and Safety at Work Act: liability for infringements

An employer is liable for complying with the general duties 'as far as is reasonably practicable' and for compliance with relevant statutory provisions (HASAWA 1974, ss 2–4).

Directors and managers. It is possible for these to be personally liable for offences. 'Where an offence under any of the relevant statutory provisions committed by a body corporate is proved to have been committed with the consent or connivance of, or to have been attributable to any neglect on the part of, any director, manager, secretary or other similar officer of the body corporate or a person who is purporting to act in any such capacity, he as well as the body corporate shall be guilty of that offence and shall be liable to be proceeded against and punished accordingly' (HASAWA 1974, s 37(1)).

Non-employees employed by independent contractors. The issue of liability in circumstances where an organisation employs contractors was clarified by the Court of Appeal (*R v Associated Octel Ltd* [1994] IRLR 540). Interpreting the duty under HASAWA 1974, s 3(1), it established the liability of an employer for injuries caused to non-employees who were employed by independent contractors – whether or not the employer had actual control over how the work was carried out. Liability is subject to the defence of 'as far as is reasonably practicable'.

In this case a contractor's employee was badly burned in a flash fire that resulted from an explosion. This occurred when a lamp (which was not a safety lamp) broke and ignited acetone vapour within the tank he was cleaning. The court found that the cleaning and maintenance of the chlorine tank did form part of Octel's 'undertaking' and that it was reasonably practicable for Octel to give the contractor instructions on carrying out the work and on the safety measures to be adopted. Each case, of course, would be considered on its own facts.

An employee. He or she is liable for failing to take reasonable care of his or her health and safety and that of other people, and for failing to co-operate with the employer in the implementation of health and safety standards (HASAWA 1974, s 7). In practice, it is unlikely that an employee would have criminal proceeding taken against him or her unless the safety breach was so serious and, perhaps, involved recklessness or deliberate misuse of equipment, etc. (HASAWA 1974, s 8). Usually, a breach of safety rules by an employee would be dealt with through the internal disciplinary procedure.

Safety representatives. They are not legally liable for carrying out their function or for not carrying out their function. In the Safety Representatives and Safety Committees Regulations 1977 (reg 4.1) it is made clear that 'no function given to a safety representative by this paragraph shall be construed as imposing any duty on him'. In guidance to the regulations, the HSE states that 'a safety representative by accepting, agreeing with or not objecting to a course of action taken by the employer to deal with a health or safety hazard, does not take upon himself any legal responsibility for that course of action'. Furthermore, it is stated that the former Health and Safety Commission directed that the HSE 'shall not institute criminal proceedings against any safety representative for any act or omission by him in respect of the performance of functions assigned to him by the Regulations . . .' (Guidance Note 11).

Corporate Manslaughter and Corporate Homicide Act 2007

This legislation was implemented in April 2008. It fills a significant gap in health and safety protection for working people. Historically, corporate manslaughter cases rarely came before the courts. Criminal liability of employers for unlawful killing has been very difficult to establish. Prosecutors have had to prove beyond reasonable doubt – the criminal standard of proof – that the individuals responsible for the death were 'the directing mind and will' and had the necessary 'guilty mind' (*mens rea*). These individuals had to be personally liable. The first successful prosecution did not occur until 1994, involving OLL Ltd which ran an activity centre. Four young people, on a canoeing trip organised by the company, drowned in Lyme Bay, Dorset. The conviction of OLL Ltd was possible because it was a small organisation. It was clear that its managing director was the embodiment of the company. He was gaoled for three years for the manslaughter. Other cases involving the death of working people were much more problematic (see Exhibit 12.8).

As a consequence of public concern about the limitations of the law and political campaigning, the Corporate Manslaughter and Corporate Homicide Act 2007 was eventually enacted. This does not hinge on personal liability but on the liability of the organisation. This legislation is applicable across the UK. It is not retrospective. So, it will only apply to fatalities caused by gross management failings that occur after the Act came into force on 6 April 2008. The new offence, under the CMCHA 2007, is 'intended to complement, not replace, other forms of accountability such as prosecutions under health and safety legislation and is specifically linked to existing health and safety requirements' (Ministry of Justice guidance, 2007, **www.justice.gov.uk**). In the Ministry's view, the Act will be 'reserved for the very worst cases of corporate mismanagement leading to death'.

▶ Key provisions of the 2007 Act

- *Organisations covered*. All companies and other corporate bodies operating in the UK, in the private, public and third sectors. So it includes, for example, private companies operating in the UK whether foreign-owned or not, local authorities, NHS trusts, police services, Crown bodies and incorporated charities and voluntary organisations. Subcontractors may be liable where they owe a duty of care to the victim. The jurisdiction relates to harm resulting in death within the UK; in the UK's territorial waters; on a British ship, aircraft or hovercraft; on an oil rig or other offshore installation already covered by UK criminal law.

- *The offence*. An organisation commits the new offence if the way in which its activities are managed or organised causes a death and this amounts to a gross breach of a duty of

EXHIBIT 12.8

The case of Simon Jones

Simon Jones, 24, a student on casual work, started a labouring job for Euromin, a Dutch-owned firm, at Shoreham Docks on 24 April 1998. It was provided through a Brighton employment agency, Personnel Selection. His job involved unloading cobblestones from a ship. He was given no training and was provided with no safety equipment. He worked in the hold of the ship hooking bags of cobbles onto chains. The chains had been welded into the crane's open grab. Within two hours of starting work, he was dead. His head was crushed and partially severed by a two-tonne crane grab, which had been brought too low over the hold and accidentally closed on his head.

The question of prosecution for manslaughter against the general manager was considered by the Crown Prosecution Service (CPS). It took the view that there was 'no realistic prospect of a conviction'. However, in March 2000, the High Court ordered the CPS to reconsider. This was the first successful judicial review of a decision not to prosecute for manslaughter over a workplace death. In November 2001, the prosecution of Euromin and of the general manager opened at the Old Bailey.

It was alleged that the system of work was not safe. The principal defects were that:

- welding the hook attached to the grab was dangerous and done for speed and economy;
- instructions in the cab that no one should be in the grab's area when it is operating were ignored;
- the 'hatchman' responsible for communication between the crane operator and the hold was not experienced and was a Polish speaker with little knowledge of English.

On a majority verdict, the jury cleared the general manager of manslaughter. The company was found guilty of two breaches of safety regulations and fined £50,000 and ordered to pay £20,000 costs.

(www.simonjones.org.uk.)

care owed to the deceased (i.e. gross negligence). Juries will consider how the fatal activity was managed or organised throughout the organisation, including any systems and processes for managing safety and how these were operated in practice. A substantial part of the failure within the organisation must have been at a senior level (i.e. those who make significant decisions about organisational policy and procedure). It should be noted that directors, senior managers or other individuals cannot be prosecuted under this Act. It is the organisation that faces criminal proceedings. Nevertheless, failures by senior managers to manage health and safety adequately will leave organisations vulnerable to corporate manslaughter/homicide charges. It is important to note that existing law (HASWA 1974) allowing individuals to be prosecuted still remains in force.

- *Duty of care*. The Act does not create new duties. These are already owed in the civil law of negligence. A gross breach of the duty of care arises where the organisation's conduct falls far below what could have been reasonably expected. A judge will decide whether or not a duty of care is owed.

- *Exemptions*. The offence does not apply to deaths that are connected with the management of particular activities (e.g. military combat operations; police operations dealing with terrorism and violent disorder). The legislation also lists partial exemptions.

- *Decision to prosecute*. Investigations into workplace deaths will be carried out by the police, in partnership with the Health and Safety Executive, or local authority or other regulatory authorities (e.g. the Office of Rail Regulation). In England and Wales and in Northern Ireland, the consent of the relevant Director of Public Prosecutions is needed before corporate manslaughter proceedings can be initiated in the courts by the Crown Prosecution Service. In Scotland, all decisions to prosecute are taken by the Procurator Fiscal. It is also important to note that other health and safety charges may be brought at the same time as a prosecution under the CMCHA 2007 (see Exhibit 12.9).

It is not necessary for the management failure to have been the *sole* cause of death. The prosecution, however, needs to show that 'but for' the management failure, including the substantial element attributable to senior management, the death would not have occurred. Whilst the injury and the death may, usually, occur at the same time, it is recognised that death may occur sometime after the injury. This will not preclude a prosecution. Neither does a person's death abroad – if the injury was sustained in the UK.

◗ Penalties

An organisation guilty of the offence is liable for *an unlimited fine*. The court may impose *a publicity order*, requiring the organisation to publicise details of its conviction and fine. Courts may also require an organisation, through *a remedial order*, to take steps to address the failures behind the death (see Exhibit 12.9).

EXHIBIT 12.9

First corporate manslaughter prosecution

The prosecution was brought by the Crown Prosecution Service before a jury at Winchester Crown Court. Cotswold Geotechnical Holdings (CGH) in 2008 was a company of eight employees. It was charged in relation to the death, on 5 September 2008, of 27-year-old Alexander Wright, a junior geologist employed by the company. He was taking soil samples from inside a 3.5 metre-deep pit that had been excavated as part of a site survey when the sides collapsed and crushed him. He died of traumatic asphyxiation. The Gloucestershire Police worked with the Health and Safety Executive to investigate the case.

Peter Eaton, the director in overall control of the company, was charged with:

● gross-negligence manslaughter under common law;

● an offence contrary to the Health and Safety at Work Act 1974, s 37 regarding neglect on his part as director of the company.

In October 2010, Eaton was found to be too ill to stand trial and the judge ruled that charges against him be dropped.

The company was charged with:

● corporate manslaughter;

● failing to discharge a duty contrary to Health and Safety at Work Act 1974, s 33.

The trial concluded in February 2011 when the company was unanimously convicted of corporate manslaughter. The company was fined £385,000 on 17 February 2011. (This was below the starting point for fines of £500,000 in the sentencing guidelines published by the Sentencing Council.) Because the company was in financial difficulties it was allowed by the Court to pay £38,500 each year for a ten-year period. On appeal (May 2011) the Lord Chief Justice upheld the fine.

See Sentencing Council *Definitive Guideline: Corporate Manslaughter and Health and Safety Offences Causing Death* (2010) (**www.sentencingcouncil.judiciary.gov.uk/guidelines**).

The Fatal Accidents Act 1976

Although not considered part of the normal range of health and safety legislation, a House of Lords ruling on employer liability has created an important legal precedent (see Exhibit 12.10).

EXHIBIT 12.10

Employer's liability for suicide

Corr (Administratrix of Estate of Thomas Corr (Deceased)) v *IBC Vehicles Ltd* [2008] **UKHL 13**

Facts. Mr Corr worked as maintenance engineer on presses producing car panels. In 1996 while he was mending a fault, an automated arm moved unexpectedly striking his head and severing his right ear. He underwent reconstructive surgery and thereafter lived with some disfigurement as well as severe headaches, persistent unsteadiness and sleeping difficulties. He also developed post-traumatic stress disorder – suffering flashbacks and nightmares. He was diagnosed with depressive illness that required hospital treatment. In 2002, during a particularly severe depressive episode, his feeling of hopelessness worsened to such an extent that he jumped to his death from a multi-storey car park. Prior to the accident he had been happily married with an equable temperament and no psychiatric problems.

Claims. Mr Corr's widow brought proceedings against the employer on behalf of her husband's estate (which was awarded by the High Court). She also brought a claim for damages under the Fatal Accidents Act 1976, which enables the executor or administrator of a person whose death was caused by a wrongful act to claim damages on behalf of the deceased's dependants. The High Court, on the second claim, took the view that although the employer had breached its duty to protect her husband from personal injury (including psychiatric injury) his suicide was not a 'reasonably foreseeable' consequence of the accident. The matter went on appeal to the Court of Appeal (which found in Mrs Corr's favour) and, then, on further appeal (by the employer) to the House of Lords.

House of Lords judgment. Lord Bingham's judgment, which reflected the majority legal opinion:

- *Duty of care*: Mr Corr's employer owed him a duty to take reasonable care to avoid causing him personal injury (physical or psychological).
- It was common ground that the employer had breached that duty, causing injury of both kinds.
- Although Mr Corr was not insane (under the legal definition), he was not fully responsible for committing suicide.
- He would not have acted as he had but for the injury that he had suffered at work.
- So, the act could not be said to fall outside the scope of the employer's duty of care.
- **Foreseeability.** A person who commits a tort, who reasonably foresees the damage occurring, need not, to become liable, foresee the precise form of that damage.
- Suicide is not outside the bounds of what is reasonably foreseeable for those with severe depression.
- *Causation*. Mr Corr's decision to take his life was not a voluntary, informed decision taken by him as an adult of sound mind. It was the response of a man suffering from a severe depressive illness, caused by his employer's negligence, which impaired his ability to make reasoned judgements.
- *Contributory negligence*. Mr Corr had no causal responsibility for his death. This was assessed at zero per cent. (This was not a unanimous view.)

Employment policies and practices

> The promotion of safety and health at work is first and foremost a matter of efficient management. But it is not a management prerogative. In this context more than most, real progress is impossible without the full co-operation and commitment of all employees. How can this be encouraged? We believe that work people must be able to participate fully in the making and monitoring of arrangements for safety and health in their place of work.
>
> (Robens 1972: 18)

The Chartered Institute of Personnel and Development (1996) has elaborated the business case in these terms: 'effective management of the health and welfare of people at work: contributes to performance improvement and increases competitive advantage; reduces unacceptable losses associated with ill-health and injuries; and lowers absenteeism, improves morale and reduces litigation costs'.

A structured approach to health and safety management involves consideration of procedures and institutions; and also how an employer might tackle particular health and safety issues. The discussion below considers some general issues relating to safety management and looks at how some of the key risks and hazards at work might be handled.

Managing health and safety:

- the creation of a safety culture;
- the formulation and implementation of safety policies;
- the contribution of an occupational health service;
- the availability of an employee assistance programme.

Handling particular workplace risks:

- use of display screen equipment;
- work-related stress.

❯ Managing health and safety

Creating a safety culture

A 'safety culture' within an organisation needs to demonstrate a high degree of safety consciousness throughout the organisation. Safety should be perceived as a dimension of most, if not all, activities. Safety standards should be integrated into work operations, job design, working-time scheduling and reward systems. Appropriate training should be given to managers and employees. There should be regular and genuine consultation – backed by information disclosure. Standards should be enforced through inspections and monitoring.

So, in certain industries, such as nuclear power, coal mining, chemicals, some sectors of engineering, air transport and the railways, health and safety is regarded as a central management issue – not just operationally but also in the employee relations system. Two factors encourage this: the nature of the hazards that exist and the serious consequences that might follow from an accident, and, in many instances, the presence of strong workplace trade unionism. Policies are developed which are concerned with not merely minimising risks but also setting and implementing standards on an integrated manner – i.e. linked to work organisation, payment systems and staffing levels, etc.

However, in industry at large, several factors already mentioned limit the achievement of such a culture: management and workforce perceptions about the seriousness of risks within their workplace; the balance between risk minimisation or elimination on the one hand, and the associated economic costs on the other; the conflicts of interests and expectations between employees and their employer; and the contribution of the workforce consultation to the achievement of safety standards.

A safety policy

Employers (except those with fewer than five employees) are under a statutory duty (HASAWA 1974, s 2(3)) to prepare and update a written safety policy. This should outline the organisation and arrangements in force for implementing health and safety standards (see Exhibit 12.11). Employees should be informed about the policy. Guidance on the details has been issued by the Health and Safety Executive. In prosecutions for breaches of health and safety regulations, an employer's adoption (or not) of a safety policy can be used in evidence.

Occupational health service

An occupational health service (OHS) resourced by an employer is likely to have access to a wide range of occupational health practitioners including physicians, hygienists, psychologists, ergonomic experts and occupational health nurses. These may be employees or used on a consultancy basis. Such a service will help an employer comply with duties under health and safety law. It may, indeed, extend beyond legal obligations to pioneer standards of good practice. Obviously, an OHS is more likely to be provided by larger organisations. It is, however, possible for smaller ones to subscribe to a group service, covering a number of employers. It is estimated that about half of employees are covered by an OHS.

An OHS will have four broad, related functions concerning both the physical and psychological health:

1 *Prevention* will cover pre-employment assessment of an individual's suitability for particular tasks by means of a pre-employment questionnaire and/or a medical examination (subject to the Equality Act 2010, s 60, see Chapter 5). Also, it will be achieved by regular surveillance of particular risks and hazards associated with the workplace. This would involve periodic reviews of materials, processes and procedures; periodic health reviews of staff, and monitoring the effectiveness of personal protection measures. Finally, the OHS would be responsible for the training and supervision of first aiders.

2 *Treatment* would cover medical treatment by OHS staff of minor illnesses and accidents.

3 *Monitoring* would encompass the monitoring and support of sick employees and pregnant workers; the recording of accidents, sickness and absence; compliance with the organisation's notification duties under the Reporting of Injuries, Diseases and Dangerous Occurences Regulations 1995; and monitoring of work-related stress.

4 *Health promotion* could include the provision of counselling and treatment (e.g. in relation to stress, harassment, drug and alcohol abuse), guidance on redesigning the work environment, general feedback to improve work practices, referral to specialists for treatment and professional advice, and the promotion of health education programmes.

EXHIBIT 12.11

Recommended provisions of a safety policy

- *Statement* of the organisation's commitment to good health and safety practice, phrased in terms which emphasise not merely management efficiency, but also the human resource management objectives of valuing staff. It might also draw attention to commitments to reduce accidents, injuries and work-related sick absence, and to promote employee welfare. It could be linked to the organisation's overall mission statement (if one exists).

- Explanation of *possible risks* and *preventative measures* (including for dealing with emergencies).

- *Outline of procedures* for implementing, monitoring and reviewing health and safety standards. This can cover consultation with safety representatives; and also periodic formal in-company inspections and 'spot-checks'.

- Commitment to the provision and funding of *appropriate training*, and an indication of how statutory obligations will be complied with.

- Commitment to *dissemination of relevant information* to employees and other interested people (i.e. contractors, customers, the public).

- Commitment to maintain *adequate recording* of risk assessments, accidents, injuries and dangerous occurrences.

- *Statement of ultimate responsibility* of chief executive and board of directors (or equivalent people) for compliance with legal standards.

- *Statement of the responsibilities of managers and supervisors* for implementation and monitoring of safety standards.

- Outline of roles of *specialist and advisory functions* (e.g. safety officers, occupational health staff, medical advisers and nurses).

- Indication of those who are designated as '*competent persons*', and of their role and function in implementing safety policy.

- Statement of functions of *trade union* or *employee safety representatives*.

- Outline of the *consultation arrangements* with trade union or employee safety representatives.

- Procedure for employees to raise *health and safety grievances* and issues.

- Statement of the *rights and responsibilities of individual employees*.

Employee assistance programmes and counselling

These programmes are an important aspect of the promotion of employee welfare. Given the legal duties placed upon an employer, counselling and assistance is essential. An EAP may be resourced by professionally qualified specialists employed by the company (as well as specially trained employees). It may also rely on the use of appropriately qualified external consultants. Some companies have such programmes, others use *ad hoc* counselling.

The role of EAPs has expanded over the years. Many work-related and non-work factors can, and do, have an impact on an employee's attendance at work and his or her performance. These factors cover, for example, personal traumas like death in the immediate family; divorce; the diagnosis of a serious, possibly incurable, illness; harassment at work or within the family; or having to deal with a traumatic situation in the course of employment. Consequently, the employee's behaviour may show evidence of, for example, post-traumatic stress, other symptoms caused by stress and/or a too heavy reliance on alcohol, or drug abuse.

◗ Handling particular workplace risks

Use of display screen equipment

The Health and Safety (Display Screen Equipment) Regulations 1992 implement the European Display Screen Equipment Directive. They cover most types of display screen equipment. Excepted pieces of equipment are, for example, screens in drivers' cabs and on other means of transport, portable systems not in prolonged use, cash registers, calculators or other equipment with a small data display. The European Court of Justice ruled that the term 'graphic display screen' in the directive must be interpreted to include screens that display film recordings in analogue or digital form. So the employer of a film cutter had to plan into her daily work breaks and changes in activity (*Dietrich v Westdeutscher Rundfunk* (2000) case C-11/99) (see Exhibit 12.12 and *Exercises*).

EXHIBIT 12.12

Provisions of the Display Screen Equipment Regulations 1992

The whole workstation is covered:

- the display screen equipment and software, including keyboards and other inputting devices;
- optional accessories added to the DSE;
- equipment: disk drive, phone, modem, printer, document holder, work chart, desk or other equipment;
- the immediate work environment around the DSE.

Minimum requirements applicable to workstation use must be satisfied:

- *display screen*: well-defined characters of adequate size, stable image, easily adjustable brightness and contrast, easily tilting and swivelling screen, no reflective glare;
- *keyboard*: tiltable and separate from the screen, sufficient space in front of keyboard, matt surface, easy-to-use, adequately contrasted symbols on keys;
- *work surface*: sufficiently large and low-reflecting surface, allows a flexible arrangement of equipment, adequate space;
- *work chair*: stable, allows user easy movement and comfortable position, adjustable height (seat), adjustable height and tilt (seat back), footrests available on request;
- *space*: designed to allow operator to change positions;
- *lighting*: satisfactory lighting conditions, appropriate contrast between screen and background, prevention of glare through positioning of artificial lighting;
- *reflections*: positioning must prevent sources of light, such as windows, from causing distracting reflections on the screen;
- *noise*: must not distract attention or disturb speech;
- *heat*: must not produce excess heat causing discomfort;
- *radiation*: reduced to negligible levels in respect of user's safety, except for the visible part of the electromagnetic spectrum;

- *humidity*: establishment and maintenance of an adequate level;
- *software and systems*: software must be suitable for the task, easy to use and adaptable to the level of user's knowledge, no quantive or qualitative checking facility may be used without user's knowledge, principles of software ergomonics must be applied.

Users. The regulations only apply to 'users' of display screen equipment – a person who 'habitually uses display screen equipment as a significant part of normal work'. Considerations in deciding whether a person is a user are: whether DSE work is an essential part of a job; how long a person spends on the machine, etc.

Under the Display Screen Equipment Regulations, there are four health and safety protection issues:

1 **Daily work routine**. This could be achieved by periodic breaks or job rotation (i.e. carrying out tasks that do not involve the similar use of hands and arms). The HSE suggests that breaks should be taken before onset of fatigue and before productivity starts to fall. Breaks should be part of working time. Short and frequent breaks are better than occasional longer breaks. Where possible, 'users' should have discretion and individual control over how they do their jobs and when they take breaks.

2 **Risk assessment**. This should be systematic and comprehensive. The likely risks: postural problems mainly caused by workstation design; visual problems such as sore eyes, headaches caused by glare, poor lighting; and stress and fatigue caused by workstation design, workload intensity. These risks can result in work-related upper-limb disorders (repetitive strain injury). Any risk must be reduced as quickly as possible. This could be fairly simple – repositioning or renewing equipment or providing the worker with some control over the tasks. The risk assessment should be reviewed where there is a significant change to the workstation, in the workforce or its capabilities or where new risks are established. As far as teleworkers are concerned, risks must be assessed regardless of whether the workstation is provided partly or wholly by the employer.

3 **Eyesight**. Users entitled to a full eye and eyesight test by qualified optician or medical practitioner. The employer's liability for the cost of 'corrective appliances', usually spectacles, only applies to 'special' appliances required for DSE use or to special modifications to the user's normal spectacles.

4 **Information and training**. Users must be provided with adequate health and safety training in the use of the workstation – tailored to the work the user does. Information must relate to all aspects of the workstation, daily work routine, and eyesight requirements.

▶ Work-related stress

This has been regarded, by many observers and working people, as both a consequence of working conditions (e.g. noise, dust, extremes of temperature); and a by-product of various managerial policies and practices:

- business process re-engineering, 'market testing' and competitive tendering;
- delayering, downsizing and fears of job insecurity;
- work intensification to increase labour productivity (see *Dickens* case – Exhibit 12.15);
- greater surveillance and monitoring of staff;
- the expansion of the flexible labour market;
- failure to tackle workplace bullying and harassment (see Chapter 7);
- tensions in the reconciliation of work and non-work (particularly family) life.

It continues to be identified as an important feature of working life. The British Academy reported (Chandola 2010) a marked increase of between 4 and 6 per cent in work 'stressors' (such as workload, conflict, job security and organisational change) between spring 2009 and spring 2010. It stated that since 1992, annual increases had been between 0.5 and one per cent. The Trades Union Congress (2010) in its eighth biennial survey of safety representatives recorded that 62 per cent of representatives identified stress as a 'top five concern'. Twenty-seven per cent of representatives said it was the 'most important' hazard in their workplace. It was more prevalent in the public and the private sector; and in larger workplaces.

The Health and Safety Executive (2010), using data from the Labour Force Survey, estimated that 415,000 people in the UK (2008–09), who worked in the year, believed that they were suffering from 'stress, depression or anxiety caused or made worse by their current or past work'. An estimated 11.4 million working days (full-day equivalent) were lost through self-reported stress, depression or anxiety caused or made worse by work. Significantly higher than average prevalence rates were in the following industries: 'public administration and defence', 'health and social work' and 'education'. They occurred in the following occupation groups: professionals in health, social welfare and teaching; 'corporate managers' and 'business and public service associate professionals'.

The concept of stress

'Stress' is, however, a general term that can be misused. It is suggested in the scientific literature that a person can experience anxiety in two possible ways: through physical hazards at work (e.g. the danger of fire or explosion, the threat of violence, the danger of injury from equipment), or from psycho-social hazards. This latter set of hazards has been described by the International Labour Organisation as involving the interaction of job content, work organisation and management, together with environmental and organisational conditions together with an employee's competences. The psycho-social stressors have been categorised as shown in Exhibit 12.13.

'Stress' is not a medical condition. It is a *cause* of physical and/or mental ill-health. So, as a result of work-related stress, a person may exhibit various reactions:

- *adverse health conditions*: increased heart rate, heart disease, high blood pressure, thyroid disorders, ulcers, panic attacks, depression, headaches, blurred vision, aching neck and shoulders;
- *behavioural consequences*: irritability, anxiety, insomnia, poor concentration, reliance on the consumption of alcohol, tobacco and other drugs.

A person's response to the different types of pressure will, of course, vary. So widespread has been the public concern and discussion about stress that action on various levels has begun to be taken. Since 1995, the Health and Safety Executive has published guidance. In this, it clearly asserted the duty of employers:

> Ill health resulting from stress caused at work has to be treated the same as ill health due to other physical causes present in the workplace. This means that employers do have a legal duty to take reasonable care to ensure that health is not placed at risk through excessive and sustained levels of stress arising from the way people deal with each other at their work or from the day-to-day demands placed on their workforce. Employers should bear stress in mind when assessing possible health hazards in their workplaces, keeping an eye out for developing problems and being prepared to act if harm to health seems likely. In other words, stress should be treated like any other health hazard.   (**www.hse.gov.uk/stress**)

EXHIBIT 12.13

Psycho-social stressors

The context of work

- *Organisation function and culture*: poor task environment and lack of definition of objectives; poor problem-solving environment; poor development environment; poor communications; non-supportive culture.

- *Role in organisation*: role ambiguity; role conflict; high responsibility.

- *Career development*: career uncertainty; career stagnation; poor status or status incongruity; poor pay; job security and redundancy; low social value to the work.

- *Interpersonal relationships at work*: social or physical isolation; poor relationships with superiors; interpersonal conflict and violence; lack of social support.

- *Home/work interface*: conflicting demands of work and home; low social or practical support at home; dual career problems.

The content of work

- *Task design*: ill-defined work; high uncertainty in work; lack of variety or short workcycles; fragmented or meaningless work; underutilisation of skill; continual exposure to client/customer groups.

- *Workload/work-pace* (quantitative and qualitative): lack of control over pacing; work overload or underload; high levels of pacing or time pressure.

- *Work schedule*: shiftworking; inflexible work schedule; unpredictable work hours; long or unsocial hours.

- *Decision latitude/control*: low participation in decision-making; lack of control over work; little decision-making in work.

Source: Cox (1993).

Stress and the law

An employer's legal liability for work-related stress is considered under three headings:

- personal injury/negligence claims for damages in the county court or the High Court;

- constructive dismissal claims at an employment tribunal;

- disability discrimination claims at an employment tribunal.

The issues relating to the last two are considered elsewhere in this textbook (see Chapters 8 and 5 respectively). Recent case law in the Court of Appeal relating to personal injury claims has provided some detailed and valuable guidance which is considered here.

❱ Personal injury claims

In these claims the following legal issues are relevant:

- The claim involves the tort of negligence – i.e. the employer's neglect to take reasonable care of the employee. The tort is not committed until an injury is actually suffered.

- It must be shown that the personal injury suffered was 'reasonably foreseeable' and that the circumstances at work were a material cause of the injury. Such a claim will also involve consideration of the Court of Appeal's guidance (see Exhibit 12.14).

EXHIBIT 12.14

Stress cases: Court of Appeal guidance on 'foreseeability'

Source: *Sutherland v Hatton* [2002] **IRLR 263**

It is important to remember that all cases should be judged on their own facts and circumstances.

- ***Employer liability***. The ordinary principles of employer liability apply. There are no special control mechanisms applying to claims for psychiatric or physical illness or injury arising from stress of doing the work the employee is required to do.
- ***The threshold question***. Whether this kind of harm to this particular employee was reasonably foreseeable. This has two components: (i) an injury to health as distinct from occupational stress which (ii) is attributable to stress at work (as distinct from other factors).
- ***Answering the threshold question***: The relevant factors include:
  - *The nature and extent of the work done by the employee*. Is the workload much more than is normal for the particular job? Is the work particularly intellectually or emotionally demanding for this employee? Are demands being made of this employee unreasonable when compared with the demands made of others in the same or comparable jobs? Or are there signs that others doing this job are suffering harmful levels of stress? Is there an abnormal level of sickness or absenteeism in the same job or the same department?
  - *Signs from the employee of impending harm to health*. Does he or she have a particular problem or vulnerability? Has he or she already suffered from illness attributable to stress at work? Have there recently been frequent or prolonged absences which are uncharacteristic of him or her? Is there reason to think that these are attributable to stress at work, for example, because of complaints or warnings from him or her or others?
- ***Foreseeability***. This depends upon what the employer knows or ought reasonably to know about the individual employee. Because of the nature of mental disorder, it is harder to foresee than physical injury. But it may be easier to foresee in a known individual than in the population at large. An employer is usually entitled to assume that the employee can withstand the normal pressures of the job, unless he or she knows of some particular problem or vulnerability.
- ***The test***. This is the same whatever the employment; there are no occupations which should be regarded as intrinsically dangerous to mental health.
- ***Taking at face value***. The employer is generally entitled to take at face value what he or she is told by his or her employee unless he or she has good reason to think to the contrary. He or she does not generally have to make searching enquiries of the employee or seek permission to make further enquiries of his or her medical advisers.
- ***Triggering the duty to take steps***. The indications of impending harm to health arising from stress at work must be plain enough for any reasonable employer to realise that he or she should do something about it.
- ***Breach of duty***. The employer is only in breach of the duty if he or she has 'failed to take the steps which are *reasonable* in the circumstances', bearing in mind (i) the magnitude of the risk of harm occurring; (ii) the gravity of the harm which may occur; (iii) the costs and practicality of preventing it; and (iv) the justifications for running the risk.
- ***What is reasonable?*** In deciding this, the following are relevant: the size and scope of the employer's operation and the demands it faces. These include the interests of other employees and the need to treat them fairly, for example, in the redistribution of duties.
- ***Reasonable expectation***. An employer can only reasonably be expected to take steps which are likely to do some good. The court is likely to need expert evidence on this.
- ***Confidential advice service***. An employer which offers this, with referral to appropriate counselling or treatment services, is unlikely to be found in breach of duty.

- *Dismissal or demotion*. If the only reasonable and effective step would have been to dismiss or demote the employee, the employer will not be in breach of duty in allowing a willing employee to continue in the job.

- *Identification of steps*. In all cases, therefore, it is necessary to identify the steps which the employer both could and should have taken before finding him or her in breach of his or her duty of care.

- *Material contribution*. The claimant must show that the breach of duty has caused or materially contributed to the harm suffered. It is not enough to show that occupational stress has caused the harm.

- *More than one cause*. Where the harm suffered has more than one cause, the employer should only pay for that proportion of the harm suffered which is attributable to his or her wrongdoing, unless the harm is truly indivisible. It is for the claimant to raise the question of apportionment.

- *The assessment of damages*. This will take account of any pre-existing disorder or vulnerability and of the chance that the claimant would have succumbed to a stress-related disorder in any event.

EXHIBIT 12.15

Applying the Court of Appeal guidance

Two cases illustrate the way in which the courts subsequently dealt with **personal injury claims** arising from work-related stress:

Bonser v RJB Mining (UK) Ltd [2004] **IRLR 164, CA**

Facts. Christine Bonser was employed by RJB Coal Mining as its technical support and training manager from 1995. (She had in fact worked in the coal industry for 20 years.) She was said to be conscientious, extremely hardworking and skilled. However, unknown to her employer, she was also emotionally vulnerable, having suffered a five-month period of depression (during her previous employment). She also had severe pre-menstrual stress which had required hormone therapy. Furthermore, her husband had given up work because of his emotional vulnerability which had put additional pressure on her. In the summer of 1996, Ms Bonser's line manager and his boss agreed to introduce a scheme to promote greater efficiency. All requests for project work and meetings were to be channelled through the line manager to ensure that the support resource (of which Ms Bonser formed a part) was being properly controlled and allocated. However, efficiency was not achieved. Teams suffered uneven workloads at a time when management were also paying close attention to the achievement of deadlines and were objectively assessing performance.

This change forced Ms Bonser to pack into an already long working week additional and often unexpected work. In August 1996, she had booked a much-needed holiday. But she was told shortly before she was due to go on leave that she would have to complete a project that would take an estimated 40 hours of extra work. She broke down in tears and told her line manager that she was exhausted and felt that her holiday was under threat. Eventually, in February 1997, following continuing pressure at work, she suffered a psychiatric breakdown and was unable to continue working in April 1997. She was dismissed in May 1998.

Judgments. In the High Court, the judge found that the demands placed on employees were excessive and that it should have been apparent that some and Ms Bonser, in particular, would not be able to cope. He also had regard to the incident in August 1996, when she broke down in tears. She was awarded damages of over £38,000. The matter was appealed to the Court of Appeal.

The issue, arising from the Court's ruling in the *Sutherland v Hatton* case, is the 'test' of whether a person claiming damages for psychiatric injury shows not merely a risk of stress from overwork but also a 'reasonably foreseeable risk' of psychiatric breakdown. The specific issues in the Court's guidance are:

- An employer is normally entitled to assume that employees are up to the normal pressures of the job.
- There is a distinction between signs of stress and signs of impending harm to health. Stress may, but not usually, lead to damage to health.

On the facts of the Bonser case, a single incident where the employee had broken down in tears showed that she may have been vulnerable to stress from overwork; but it was not sufficient to foretell the psychiatric breakdown she subsequently suffered some months later. The Court of Appeal overturned the High Court award of damages, saying that she did not meet the requirements of the test. It reached its decision with 'considerable misgivings', noting that the High Court judge had formed a very adverse view of the senior manager involved, whose conduct was 'justly condemned as cavalier'. However, in the light of the *Hatton* 'test', it found it could reach no other decision.

Dickens v *O2plc* [2009] IRLR 58, CA

Facts. Susan Dickens, an accountant, had worked for O2 since 1991. She had been conscientious, hard-working and reliable. From March 2001 she was demonstrating symptoms caused by stress. She had irritable bowel syndrome and was undertaking counselling arranged by her doctor. In August 2001, she was transferred to another job but did not received the expected training and support. In March 2002, exhausted, she asked to be moved to a less stressful job. She made various representations to managers. Eventually, she asked for six months off work. A referral was made to occupational health but nothing was done. In June 2002, she was 'signed off' work by her doctor as unfit because of anxiety and depression. She remained on sick leave until she was dismissed in November 2003.

Judgments. The county court found O2 liable for the psychiatric injury which was negligently caused by excessive stress in the course of employment. It awarded £109,754 which took account of the fact that about 50 per cent of Ms Dickens' illness was contributed to by 'non-tortious' factors – i.e. not related to the employer's negligence.

The Court of Appeal ruled that O2 could reasonably foresee Ms Dickens' ill health. It was insufficient to merely suggest that she should seek counselling. The employer's failure to address her problems had materially contributed to her illness. The Court stated that once she had told the manager about her condition some responsibility passed to the employer.

The Court upheld a county court decision to award damages for psychiatric injury due to excessive work-related stress.

- The claimant must show that the stress caused a recognised disorder or recognised psychiatric illness. This raises the possibility of association with disability discrimination if the person can show that he or she is disabled within the meaning of that Equality Act 2010.
- Consideration will be given as to whether or not there was a breach of the Health and Safety at Work etc. Act 1974 and any appropriate regulations.
- Consideration will be given as to whether the employer exercised the duty to be proactive and take initiatives in dealing with these matters (*Barber* v *Somerset County Council* [2004] IRLR 475).
- If the court finds the employer negligent, it will set damages to be paid to the claimant.
- If there was a breach by the employer of the implied contractual term of mutual trust and confidence and of the duty to take reasonable care, there may be a constructive dismissal claim if the employee resigned alleging a repudiatory breach of contract.

Conclusion

The issue of health and safety has, in recent years, had a 'bad press'. Tabloid newspapers have publicised stories (some untrue) of various restrictions and prohibitions. Underlying this negative attitude among some members of the public and some politicians are a number of factors: concerns by organisations about litigation for personal injury; some instances of obsessive and ill-informed decisions and restrictions; some over-zealous assessments of risk.

Lord Young (2010) was commissioned by Prime Minister David Cameron to investigate 'the rise of the compensation culture', 'the current low standing that health and safety legislation now enjoys', and to suggest solutions. In his report, he made proposals for (among others) dealing with compensation claims, professionalising health and safety consultants and simplifying risk assessment procedures for 'low hazard workplaces' such as offices, classrooms and shops. However, he is positive in his assessment of the Health and Safety at Work Act etc. 1974. He described the Act as a 'rational, proportionate approach' which has provided 'an effective framework for business and individuals for almost 40 years'.

Indeed, the Health and Safety Executive was able to report that Britain (between April 2009 and March 2010) had the lowest rate of fatal occupational injuries in Europe at 152 and down from 179 the previous year. It also had one of the lowest levels of work-related ill health (**www.hse.gov.uk/statistics**). Nevertheless, several issues remain important: work-related stress (as considered above); and whether corporate manslaughter legislation will be effective in dealing with gross negligence by organisations. Furthermore, the issue of exposure to violence in certain occupations continues to be a concern.

Inevitably, the adequacy of resources to deal with the enforcement of standards must also be a concern. The funding of the Health and Safety Executive has been cut by 35 per cent. The TUC (2010) has reported from its survey that 49 per cent of workplaces have never been visited by a Health and Safety Inspector. (The figure for companies employing fewer than 50 people is 16 per cent.) A consequence of the public expenditure cutbacks on enforcement agencies (the HSE and local authorities) is that more emphasis needs to be placed on the role of workplace safety representation and on the issue of worker involvement. This would be consistent with the strategy of the Health and Safety Executive in which worker involvement is a key theme (HSE 2009). It is clear that much work needs to be undertaken to stimulate this – particularly in non-union organisations. A survey carried out by the Royal Society for the Prevention of Accidents found that in its experience 'there are few representatives of employee safety elected in non-unionised workplaces' – despite the 1996 Regulations (Fidderman and McDonnell: ROSPA 2010: 5). Furthermore, it found that although companies reported different barriers to worker involvement in health and safety, 'the most commonly cited were lack of resources, knowledge, time and imperative'. Other barriers mentioned by a significant number of those surveyed were 'fear of managers; lack of respect shown by managers; transient workforces; remote and peripatetic workers; and cultural attitudes within the workplace, local community and wider society' (*ibid.*: 13).

Exercises

12.1 **The VDU operators: a safety grievance**. This case study encourages you to draw upon material in the regulations that have been outlined earlier – particularly the Management of Health and Safety at Work Regulations 1999 and the Health and Safety (Display Screen Equipment) Regulations 1992. Also, you will need to consider the 1977 and 1996 regulations on safety representation and consultation. The primary issue to be considered is how compliance by the employer can be ensured and how standards can be monitored, bearing in mind the employer's duty to ensure the health, safety and welfare of employees 'so far as reasonably practicable'.

The facts. Helen McDonald is one of eight VDU operators who work in the Central Administrative Services Department at the head office of a food processing company in Leeds. She has worked for six months in the department's open-plan office. She spends between 75 and 95 per cent of her working time at a VDU.

She has complained, on four occasions, to her supervisor about headaches arising from her work. The supervisor has been generally unsympathetic. Helen has just returned from two days' self-certified sick absence because of a severe migraine attack.

At lunchtime on her first day back she is chatting to Wendy who is the safety committee representative at the head office. Helen tells her that she is very unhappy about the working conditions for the VDU operators. She mentions her headaches and the pains that some other staff get. She feels that management should do something about it.

A two-stage task:

1 In syndicates, carry out a diagnostic exercise by listing the issues that you think arise under the following categories:
   ● operational issues for the company;
   ● job design;
   ● health and safety requirements;
   ● employment relations.

2 Students are allocated to one of two syndicate groups: 'an employer group' and 'an employee group'. Consider the following questions:
   ● *What are your objectives in resolving the grievance in terms of health and safety standards and in terms of employment relations?*
   ● *What would be your preferred outcome for resolving the grievance?*
   ● *What constraints might exist to limit your achievement of this preferred outcome?*

12.2 **Matt: workplace violence**. Matt works as a nurse in the accident and emergency department of a hospital. Late one Saturday evening, whilst he is attending a patient, he is headbutted by another patient who complains drunkenly that he has been 'waiting for hours' to be seen by a doctor. Matt has to go off duty for medical attention and, subsequently, he has a three-day sick leave.

His union representative complains to the management of the hospital trust that insufficient attention has been paid to the safety of A&E staff. He cites several incidents in the past 12 months of both verbal and physical abuse.

Consider the employer's liability for both Matt and other staff in the A&E department; and outline the steps that you think the hospital trust might reasonably take.

12.3 **Maggie: drinking at work**. Maggie has worked as a broker in a City of London financial institution. The work was very pressurised. Like many of the staff, she relaxed after work with colleagues at a pub near the office. Sometimes she went home on the train fairly drunk. Gradually, the situation became worse. On a couple of occasions she had come into work – once after lunch and once early in the morning – under the influence of alcohol. She was given an informal warning by her manager on the first occasion and a formal warning for the second incident.

Over the following weeks, there was no improvement. One afternoon, she was found slumped at her desk in a drunken state. After a disciplinary hearing, she was given a final written warning and was required to undertake counselling for alcohol abuse, under the supervision of Occupational Health.

Shortly after this incident, she was off work because of sickness. It transpired that she had a liver problem. She was signed off work by her general practitioner for six months. Her health did not improve significantly and she was eventually on sick leave for over 12 months. Her manager consulted the HR department with a view to dismissing her.

What advice would the HR director give the manager about the law and on the approach that the company should adopt?

Feedback on these exercises is provided in the Appendix to this textbook.

Further reading

Broughton, A. *et al.* (2009) *Managing Stress and Sickness Absence: Progress of the Sector Implementation Plan Phase 2*. Health and Safety Executive Research Report RR694: Institute for Employment Studies (**www.employment-studies.co.uk**).

Donaldson-Feilder, E. *et al.* (2009) *Preventing Stress: Promoting Positive Management Behaviour*. Investors in People, Health and Safety Executive and Chartered Institute of Personnel and Development (**www.cipd.co.uk**).

European Foundation for the Improvement of Living and Working Conditions (2010) *Health and Safety at Work in SMEs: Strategies for Employee Information and Consultation* (**http://www.eurofound.europa.eu/docs/ewco/tn0911028s/tn0911028s.pdf**).

European Foundation for the Improvement of Living and Working Conditions (2010) *Physical and Psychological Violence at the Workplace* (**http://www.eurofound.europa. eu/pubdocs/2010/54/en/1/EF1054EN.pdf**).

European Foundation for the Improvement of Living and Working Conditions (2010) *Work-related Stress* (**http://www.eurofound.europa.eu/docs/ewco/tn1004059s/ tn1004059s.pdf**).

Health and Safety Executive (2010) *Statistics on Occupational Fatalities and Injuries* (April 2009–March 2010) (**www.hse.gov.uk**).

Health Work Wellbeing (Leeds Metropolitan University) (2010) *Work-related Stress: What the Law Says* (with the CIPD, HSE and ACAS) (**www.stressguidance.org**).

Tyers, C. *et al.* (2009) *Organisational Responses to the HSE Management Standards for Work-related Stress: Progress of the Sector Implementation Plan Phase 1.* Health and Safety Executive Research Report RR693: Institute for Employment Studies (**www.employment-studies.co.uk**).

References

Advisory, Conciliation and Arbitration Service (2009) *Code of Practice on Disciplinary and Grievance Procedures.* London: ACAS.

Chandola, T. (2010) *Stress at Work.* London: British Academy Policy Centre (www.britac.ac.uk).

Chartered Institute of Personnel and Development (1996) *Occupational Health and Organisational Effectiveness*, Key Facts, September. London: CIPD.

Cox, T. (1993) *Stress Research and Stress Management: Putting Theory to Work*, Contract Research Report 61. London: Health and Safety Executive.

Fidderman, H. and McDonnell, K. (2010) *Worker Involvement in Health and Safety: What Works?* Royal Society for the Prevention of Accidents and the Health and Safety Executive. London.

Health and Safety Executive (2009) *Be Part of the Solution* (www.hse.gov.uk/strategy/index.htm).

Health and Safety Executive (2010) *Self-reported Work-related Illness and Workplace Injuries in 2008–09: Results from the Labour Force Survey* (www.hse.gov.uk/statistics).

Robens, Lord (1972) *Report of the Committee of Inquiry on Safety and Health at Work.* London: HMSO.

Sentencing Council (2010) *Definitive Guidelines: Corporate Manslaughter and Health and Safety Offences Causing Death* (www.sentencingcouncil.judiciary.gov.uk/guidelines).

Smith, I. and Thomas, G. (2000) *Smith and Wood's Industrial Law.* London: Butterworth.

Trades Union Congress (2010) *Eighth Biennial TUC Safety Representatives' Survey* (www.tuc.org.uk/extras/safetyrepssurvey2010.pdf).

Lord Young (2010) *Common Sense Common Safety.* London: HM Government Cabinet Office (lordyoungreview@dwp.gsi.gov.uk).

Other legal materials

International Labour Organisation: Convention 155 concerning Occupational Safety and Health and the Working Environment.

Useful website

Health and Safety Executive **www.hse.gov.uk**

Visit **www.mylawchamber.co.uk/willey** to access study support resources including realistic HR documentation to accompany the case studies in the book, an online chapter on collective labour law, interactive multiple choice questions, annotated weblinks, a glossary, glossary flashcards, key case flashcards, a legal newsfeed and legal updates.

Chapter 13

Conclusion

Introduction

At the time of writing, in late 2011, some 18 months after the inconclusive 2010 general election, it is clear that employment law and equality law is, in relation to some essential provisions, in a period of flux.

Some of the economic and social themes impacting on legislation over the past 20 years remain important – particularly at a time when the government's deficit reduction strategy is a principal driver of change. This strategy – together with some policy aspirations and objectives under the umbrella and rather nebulous term 'fairness' – are significant in moulding both legal standards and processes for dealing with employment matters.

Any evaluation of these actual or proposed legislative changes requires some consideration of certain basics. Two particular questions – important in the past and still relevant today – need to be considered:

- What are legal standards for in relation to employment?
- In whose interests are they enacted, implemented and amended?

What are legal standards for in relation to employment?

Essentially, legal standards are designed to achieve two fundamental purposes:

- To address the inherent imbalance of power in the employment relationship between employers and working people.
- To assert, as public policy, certain principles and standards both in terms of employers' treatment of their employees; and in the procedural processes used to deal with workplace disputes and other issues.

The balance of economic power

It is worth recalling the point made earlier (Chapter 2) that the two parties in the employment relationship – the employer and the employee – are often spoken of as if they are of equal status. However, the economic reality of employment shows that, in practice, there is, usually, no equality. In discussing the employment contract, Wedderburn (1986) described the situation this way: 'The individual employer is from the outset an aggregate of resources, already a collective power in social terms . . . In reality, save in exceptional circumstances, the individual worker brings no equality of bargaining power to the labour market and to this transaction central to his life whereby the employer buys his labour.'

The instrument used to regulate this relationship – the contract of employment – is a flawed instrument and needs statute law to rectify both the inherent imbalance of interest reflected in it and also its discriminatory character (see Chapter 2). Sir Otto Kahn-Freund 1983: 18) described it as 'a command under the guise of an agreement' – with the employer as the commander.

This remains very much the situation today. Despite the expansion of employment and equality law over the past 40 years, employers still have considerable discretion to determine key elements of the employment relationship: the terms and conditions under which employment is offered; decisions about whether employment is to be terminated; whether indirect discriminatory treatment can be 'objectively justified'; whether health and safety standards have been established 'so far as is reasonably practicable'. Having said that, it is accepted that there are constraints on an employer's conduct of the employment relationship and that legal measures have become stronger in some respects. But, it is argued, that they needed to.

Historically, employers have been subject to measures to modify their treatment of working people. Essentially, there have been two ways in which this arose:

- through collective bargaining with trade unions and the creation of voluntary standards about pay and other conditions of employment; and

- through legislation and the common law of contract.

The use of collective bargaining as an instrument of regulation of the employment relationship developed, in particular, in the period between 1919 and 1979. This was at a time when the body of law regulating employment was sparse. British employment relations was described by Sir Otto Kahn Freund (1983) as characterised by the 'abstention of the law'. The employment relations system was, generally, described by employers, trade unionists and academic commentators as 'voluntarist'.

It was, of course, never the situation that the 'voluntary system' delivered comprehensive high standards. Many working people were excluded because the density of trade union membership only ever exceeded half the workforce in the late 1970s. There was still evidence, in many surveys, of arbitrary treatment by employers – breaching contracts of employment, wrongfully dismissing people. There was also clear evidence, within the voluntary system and outside, of in-built discrimination. Collective agreements until 1970 provided for separate 'women's rates of pay'. Manual workers had inferior terms and conditions to white-collar workers – despite the fact that their work was often more hazardous, strenuous and insecure. So, the 'voluntary system' does not characterise a golden age. But as a means for curbing some of the more exploitative excesses of some employers, it achieved some positive outcomes. In some large organisations it produced an orderly system of employment relations that satisfied both employers and working people most of the time.

The contribution of trade unions to the regulation of terms and conditions of employment began to diminish from the 1980s as a result of two principal factors: the restructuring of the British economy resulting in a considerable contraction of the membership base of unions; and severe legislative controls on union action – particularly in respect of the pressure that they could exert against employers in disputes (through the use of various forms of industrial action) (see **web chapter** on *Collective employment law*).

In 1988, the Trades Union Congress complained to the International Labour Organisation about various aspects of British law on industrial action and trade unions. A Committee of Experts reported that 'our labour law has fallen below acceptable standards on no less than six quite different grounds' in relation to the ILO Convention 87 on Freedom of Association. Aside from specific concerns, the Committee commented on 'the general complexity of the legislation itself' (Ewing 1989: 21).

The Labour government (1997–2010) did not alter in any fundamental way the structure of industrial action law. It did, however, enact legislation in respect of representation – on recognition for collective bargaining; and on the individual's statutory right to be represented in grievances and disciplinary hearings. Overall, however, the increase in trade union recognition and membership has been slight. There has been no restoration (particularly in the private sector) of unions, through collective bargaining, as the primary source of voluntary workplace 'rules'.

One consequence of the decline in trade union membership and of recognition was the isolation of individual workers or workgroups from some forms of collective advice and support and, in particular, sources of representation. This trend coincided with the tendency for workplaces, particularly in the private sector, to be, for obvious economic reasons, smaller and fragmented. Any concept of 'collective power' became unrealistic in these circumstances.

Alongside these developments, from the early 1970s, statutory regulation of employment began to develop. This alternative method of regulating the employment relationship began – at least theoretically – to gain significance. The rationale for such regulation was explicitly to impose specific public policy standards into the employment relationship. A major consequence for employers, in particular, was the '**juridification**' of employment relations and human resource management.

The rationale for a framework of legal regulation is still there in an economy buffeted by considerable turbulence; in a society where there are evident concerns about equality and social justice; and in businesses where the impact of technological change and competitors' behaviour in global markets can be substantial. This context inevitably results in the matter discussed below about whose interests should be reflected in this legal framework. Should there be a balance of interests? Should one set of interests trump another?

Standards of public policy

The second fundamental purpose of legal standards is to assert and promote particular standards of public policy. There are two aspects to this: ethical standards; and the minimum standard approach.

▶ Ethical standards

These derive from various legal sources. They are invariably part of wider sets of standards concerning the treatment of groups of people in civil society as a whole (e.g. women, people of different nationalities and ethnic origin). Most derive from international conventions – many of which were adopted after the experience of World War Two and of Nazism and Fascism:

- The United Nations' Universal Declaration of Human Rights (1946).

- The Council of Europe's European Convention on Human Rights and Fundamental Freedoms (1950) – the main provisions of which are incorporated in the Human Rights Act 1998.

- The International Labour Organisation (a United Nations agency) has promulgated various conventions related to fair treatment in employment. The most recent was the Convention on Domestic Workers 2011, which the British government did not sign.

- The European Union's treaties and directives – in particular those promoting with equal treatment. Under the European Communities Act 1972 the treaties are subscribed to by Britain; and directives must be transposed into British law.

These ethical standards, in varying ways, mould provisions of UK law. This is either because under treaty obligations we are required to comply, as in the case of our obligations to the European Union or, on occasion, it is the result of domestic campaigning. So, for example, it is worth recalling that Britain was, within the European Union, in the forefront in adopting race equality legislation.

Nowadays, in terms of the regulation of the employment relationship, ethical standards are central to, for example, the main piece of equality legislation, the Equality Act 2010. Ethical standards also infuse the treatment of employees in, for example, dismissals.

▶ Minimum standards

Standards of treatment in employment can, in fact, be enacted as *absolute* standards or as *minimum* standards. Examples of the former exist particularly in health and safety legislation. However, the tendency of most governments in the past 50 years has been to create minimum standards. The rationale is to provide a floor of rights (or, as far as remuneration is concerned, and in the language of the Council of Europe, a 'decency' threshold) below which individuals will not fall. At the same time, employers are provided with flexibility to offer enhanced conditions above the minima. This approach is reflected in statutory provisions on, for example, contractual information, redundancy pay, maternity leave, notice to terminate employment, the minimum wage and paid annual leave. Effectively, as suggested in Chapter 2, it can be argued that we have moved decisively towards a minimum contract of employment.

A consequence of standards being promoted in public policy has been that HR professionals and other managers need to be highly sensitive to legal standards. Employers, as we have seen, still have some discretion but this is narrowing. In most organisations, decisions relating to employment relations are now more likely to be reached by reference to these legal standards. Even where trade union recognition has been conceded by an employer, the standards set in collective agreements must reflect legal standards where they exist. It can be argued, of course, that this 'juridification' (Lewis 1986: 29–30) of human resource management is more likely to be found in larger organisations which have professional support and the advice of human resource practitioners. Certainly, evidence suggests that some managers, particularly in smaller organisations, are either ignorant of the legal standards or deliberately flout them. Clearly, if a minimum standards culture is promoted by government, then steps to provide advice and guidance must be continually under review to aim at ensuring compliance.

In whose interests are legal standards enacted, implemented and amended?

The preceding discussion has drawn attention to the original purposes of much legal regulation affecting employment. It was – in circumstances of an imbalance of economic power – to protect vulnerable workers, to address arbitrary treatment by employers, and to eradicate exploitation and discrimination. Inevitably, legislative measures setting legal standards would conflict with two fundamental concerns of employers: the 'right to manage'; and their economic interests.

▶ The right to manage

Essentially, this (see Chapter 1) is a matter of concern because an employer has to be accountable for its decision-making. The employer can be judged (literally) in external forums for actions that it takes – whether, for example, on redundancies and other dismissals; or on whether treatment is discriminatory.

▶ Employer economic interests

This second area of concern continues to be an important – if not dominant – part of political debates and representations to legislators. The tension here is between, on the one hand, social justice for working people and, on the other hand, employers' concerns about such issues as unit labour costs and cost-effectiveness generally; and about competitiveness, profits and profitability.

Governments have responded to these concerns, to some extent, by claiming sensitivity to avoiding too much bureaucracy and unnecessary 'burdens on business'. As a consequence, specific legislation does include opportunities for flexible responses to meet the operational and employment relations circumstances of businesses. Examples of this include the derogations in the Working Time Regulations 1998 and the 'opt out' from the maximum working week; the facility to 'justify objectively' certain forms of discrimination; the ability to provide enhancements above the minimum standards; the ability to defend certain treatment as 'reasonable' in the circumstances. Cost considerations can be factors in some of these situations.

▶ Survey evidence

Various surveys have reported employers' concerns about employment law. A survey of 500 micro businesses (i.e. employing fewer than ten employees) found that 'employment law does have a negative effect on business growth and that the concern about employment law is less about paperwork but probably more about cost, complexity and the perceived cost of "getting it wrong"' (The Better Regulation Executive, 2010: 16). Particular issues of concern were fear of unfair dismissal claims and the operation of maternity and paternity leave rights.

An often-cited complaint of employers is the administrative burden of employment regulation. The Labour government commissioned research on this. In a survey of over 1,000 business owners, directors and HR managers, it was found that the five most frequently undertaken 'information obligations' were 'providing a written statement of employment particulars (79 per cent); maintaining records of working time (71 per cent);

making changes to written statements of employment particulars (56 per cent); maintaining records of national minimum wage (50 per cent); approving a request for flexible working (43 per cent)' (Lambourne *et al.* 2008: 5). The researchers concluded from other responses that '74 per cent of respondents found preparing/providing information for the obligation easy'. However, their knowledge of employment law was a little problematic: 45 per cent were 'confident' in their knowledge. 'One of the biggest challenges businesses faced was keeping up to date' (*ibid.*: 9).

Other research evidence suggests that, for small organisations, although employment legislation was of 'rising in importance as a constraint' (Dickens *et al.* 2005: 25) it has been noted that 'administration workload' created by legislation was a particular concern (Blackburn and Hart 2002).

Nevertheless, surveys undertaken, for example, for the Chartered Institute for Personnel and Development (see **www.cipd.co.uk**), show that some employers do see the standards of employment law and discrimination law as important underpinning for standards of good human resource management practice. This in turn is argued as contributing to business success.

Employers, of course, are not uniform in terms of size or the approaches and policies they adopt towards employment relations. There are marked differences in respect of knowledge of the law and espousal of good employment practice. The literature of employment relations provides various categorisations of management style (e.g. Fox 1966; Purcell and Sisson 1983). In summary, there are probably three broad theoretical 'types' of organisation which can be considered in an assessment of likely compliance with the law:

- *'Sophisticated' organisations* which have a strategic perspective and develop policies which generally reflect professional standards of human resource management and comply with employment law. Faced with a complainant's success at employment tribunal, these employers may well revise corporate policy to try to ensure no repetition of any breaches of good practice. They have a concern about 'reputation'. There is likely to be clear evidence of 'juridification' in such organisations.

- *'Pragmatic' or 'opportunistic' organisations* which react to situations as they arise and, generally, will only comply with good employment practice if there is a legislative 'stick' used against them. They may adopt a 'light touch' to compliance. In some instances they 'chance it', in that they are aware of legal standards but hope to avoid complying in the hope that an employment tribunal complaint will not be made.

- *'Exploitative' organisations* which are ignorant of the law or deliberately flout it.

It is difficult to quantify the numbers of organisations in these categories. However, an interesting snapshot is provided in the data provided in surveys of employment tribunal claims. There is a marked tilt towards smaller organisations as respondent employers: 27 per cent of cases were from organisations that employed fewer than 25 people; and 9 per cent from those employing 25–49 people. Overwhelmingly, these were likely to be in the private sector given that 72 per cent of claims came from that sector (Peters 2010: xix).

As far as successful outcomes at employment tribunal are concerned, it is reported that 'as in 2003, claimants who brought a claim against a small organisation (with less than 25 employees) were a little more likely than those who brought cases against larger employers to be successful at a full tribunal' (Peters 2010: 80 and Table 9.6).

There is an issue about the conduct of work relationship in small organisations. Admittedly, the character of these relationships can be and is different in nature to those in larger organisations. Whether proposed exemptions from new legislation (as suggested by the Conservative–Liberal Democrat government) is the way forward is arguable. It may reduce some administrative costs but, in terms of the promotion of employees' interests, there is little or no justification for it.

An inevitable question, then, is whether there is substance in the views of employers generally that employment regulation is a 'burden' administratively and an inhibitor to economic growth. Interestingly, the Chartered Institute of Personnel and Development has examined this in a report, *Work Horizons: The Economic Rights and Wrongs of Employment Regulation* (2011). It draws attention to research by the Organisation of Economic Co-operation and Development (2006) and comments that 'the UK labour market is already one of the least regulated and most flexible in the developed world'; according to OECD rankings 'only in the United Sates and Canada is employment regulation less strict than in the UK' (2011: 2 and 5). It adds that 'job creation potential is strong, structural unemployment is low and there is little convincing evidence that employment regulation accounts for the long-standing productivity gap between the UK and major competitor economies' (*ibid.*).

The current state of employment and equality law

Any evaluation about the current state of employment and equality law must, therefore, consider the two broad questions posed at the beginning of this chapter.

- What are legal standards for in relation to employment?
- In whose interests are they enacted, implemented and amended?

Bearing these in mind, the key issues to be considered here are:

- The ideological objectives and principles underpinning the legislative policies of the Conservative–Liberal Democrat government.
- Equality law.
- The promotion of labour market flexibility.
- Dispute resolution reform.

▶ Conservative–Liberal Democrat government ideological objectives and principles

The government has no *explicit* strategy for the reform of employment and equality law. It has not published a coherent policy statement reflecting its social and economic objectives unlike some predecessor governments – for example, *Fair Deal at Work* (1968) published by the Conservative Party and influencing its policy in government between 1970–74; and *Fairness at Work* (1998) of the Labour government elected in 1997. It has, however, identified some key objectives in *The Coalition: Our Programme for Government* (**http://webarchive.nationalarchives.gov.uk**) (see Exhibit 13.1). These provide a standard against which to assess the subsequent delivery of policy initiatives and legislative amendments.

EXHIBIT 13.1

The Coalition: Our Programme for Government

- The Government believes that there are many barriers to social mobility and equal opportunities in Britain today with too many children held back because of their social background and too many people of all ages held back because of their gender, race, religion or sexuality. We need concerted government action to tear down these barriers and help to build a fairer society.

- We will promote equal pay and take a range of measures to end discrimination in the workplace.

- We will undertake a fair pay review in the public sector to implement our proposed '20 times' pay multiple.

- We will look to promote gender equality on the boards of listed companies.

- We support the National Minimum Wage because of the protection it gives to low-income workers and the incentives to work it provides.

Subsequently, the measures proposed and implemented have been dealt with in a piecemeal way. However, overarching principles underpinning legislative changes have been discerned from political statements, consultation documents and from the adoption of policy reports commissioned and published by the government.

Consequently, two overarching political/ideological objectives can be discerned: a commitment to pursue a deficit reduction strategy; and the gradual reduction of state activity in the provision of services. These are linked and obviously have a clear economic imperative attaching them. Below we will consider the ways in which these economic objectives strongly influence policy measures on employment relations and equality law. Before doing that, further comment needs to be made about four related issues: the economic imperatives; the 'Red Tape Challenge'; 'gold-plating' and the general approach to regulation from the European Union.

- **Economic imperatives.** In March 2011 the government published *Plan for Growth* (**www.hm-treasury.gov.uk**). The emphasis was to remove barriers to growth particularly for smaller businesses. One such proposal was to exempt, from April 2011 for three years, 'start-ups' and employers of fewer than ten employees from compliance with *new* laws. However, family-friendly laws are exempt from this (**www.equalities.gov.uk**). In addition, there were proposals to curtail or review certain provisions of equality law in the interests of business. Although this approach has found favour with various employers' organisations, the CIPD Chief Economic Adviser has taken a different view: 'A balanced assessment shows that underlying problems of structural unemployment and productivity shortfalls in the UK economy cannot be attributed to any negative impact of employment regulation, but are due instead to relatively low rates of capital investment, long-standing deficiencies in the supply and quality of work related skills, poor management of available skills in the workplace and work disincentives stemming from the operation of the welfare benefit system. Further de-regulation of an already relatively de-regulated labour market will do nothing to help solve these structural problems and might well exacerbate them' (**www.cipd.co.uk/pressoffice**, 23 May 2011).

- **'Red Tape Challenge'**. A particular concern has been this campaign to remove 'red tape' for businesses in order to eradicate what is perceived as 'bureaucracy' (**www.bis.gov.uk**). The 'Challenge' runs until April 2013. Members of the public, businesses and other organisations are invited to comment on particular regulations (there are 21,000 in total). After 2013, the relevant government department has three months to justify the regulations' continued existence. Measures include a 'one in one out' rule (where no new regulation is brought in without other regulations being cut); the insertion of 'sunset clauses' into regulations to ensure that they are reviewed regularly and, if ineffective, rescinded. Employment and equality regulations are included as one of the six key areas.

  The problem with this approach is the emotive language used. One employment lawyer has commented that 'red tape is not necessarily a bad thing' (Darren Newman, *Employers' Law*, May 2011). It is accepted that some legislation may be out of date or cumbersome to administer. But governments should not lose sight of the fact that legislation can have certain fundamental purposes of enacting protections and entitlements for working people and are designed to hold employers, in particular, to account. Newman comments further that 'instead of a proper structured debate around key employment law areas, we are being asked to comment on a random assortment of minor regulations, some of which merely amend some technical aspect of primary legislation and others that are obsolete. It is very difficult to see the point of an exercise that invites comment about obscure regulations with little relevance to anyone, while completely ignoring those areas of law to which employers do have to pay close attention.'

- **'Gold-plating'**. This phrase – used widely in various statements and speeches – is very much part of political rhetoric to create an impression of disproportionate treatment. Eradicating it would result in the 'bare minimum' that is necessary rather than the establishment and maintenance of standards of good employment practice. In the context of promoting business interests, this new principle was adopted in respect of European legislation. The 'copy out' approach to the transposition of EU directives into UK law is to be adopted in future. This means that our domestic legislation will not provide enhancements over and above the provisions in the directive.

  An example of this approach is found in the terms of reference of the Löfstedt Review into health and safety legislation (see below). The review is asked to consider whether health and safety law has 'unnecessarily enhanced the requirements of an EU directive.'

- **General approach to EU law**. The government is reviewing ways in which EU legislation is made. The Department for Business, Innovation and Skills stated that it 'will be talking with business organisations about the European Commission's plan for future legislation, working closely with other European countries to make sure that regulations work well on the ground and improving how evidence is used by the European Parliament and Council' (News release, 15 Dec 2010, **www.bis.gov.uk**).

Against the background of these economic and ideological approaches we will review the state of three sets of employment law: equality law; labour market flexibility; and dispute resolution.

Equality law

The approach to equality law, given the Conservative–Liberal Democrat *Programme for Government*, has been mixed. The Equality Act 2010 (which received the Royal Assent in the 'wash-up' just prior to the dissolution of Parliament before the 2010 general election) has been broadly implemented with effect from October 2010. Initially, it was seen as having multi-party support in terms of its essential framework and statutory objectives. Indeed, the rescinding of the default retirement age (DRA) has been widely commended – apart, interestingly, from some employer's organisations who regarded retirement as a crude and arbitrary way of getting rid of staff and as an alternative to effective performance management of older workers.

However, as indicated in Chapters 4, 5 and 7, there have been a number of statutory provisions which have not been implemented or subject to possible repeal. This, inevitably, raises questions about the continuing degree of multi-party support. Having said that, the fundamental structure of the legislation remains intact.

- **Socio-economic duty** (EA 2010, s 1). It was decided not to proceed with this. The previous Labour government envisaged this as a duty which would require public authorities to focus on strategic decisions and consider 'how they can better target their policies and resources to help those who are most disadvantaged'. It made it clear that this duty was 'not about creating a new equalities strand or protected characteristic'. Nor was it 'creating new justiciable rights for individuals' (*The Equality Bill: Duty to Reduced Socio-economic Inequality – a Guide*, January 2010, **www.equalities.gov.uk**). As an instrument for public authorities to scrutinise their strategies and evaluate the consequence of their policies, the duty might have assisted in the achievement of the improved social mobility and equal opportunities in the Conservative-Liberal Democrat *Programme for Government* (see Exhibit 13.1).

- **Gender pay reporting**. The Conservative–Liberal Democrat government announced in December 2010 that it did not require employers with more than 250 staff to report their gender pay gap from 2013 (Equality Act 2010, s 78). They may do this on a voluntary basis. However, in its consultation paper, *Modern Workplaces* (HM Government 2011: 8), it states that 'there is still a significant gender pay gap and continuing evidence of non-compliance with the law'. It added that 'the gender pay gap has multiple and complex causes and the Government is committed to working with business to address these, in particular through improving flexibility at work, encouraging greater transparency and ensuring effective enforcement of equal pay law'.

  The proposal here is **not** to activate the gender pay gap reporting provision. It is to establish a scheme contingent on a complaint having been made successfully at an employment tribunal. 'We propose to require employment tribunals which have found an employer to have discriminated in contractual or non-contractual pay matters to make that employer conduct a pay audit unless the tribunal is satisfied it would not be productive to do so' (see also Chapter 9).

- **Combined discrimination: dual characterstics**. It has been decided not to implement this provision in the Equality Act 2010 (s 14). Non-implementation was, curiously, announced in HM Treasury's 2011 Budget document, *Plan for Growth*; it is not clear what economic benefit is to be achieved for employers. The statutory provision was intended to create a more effective basis for a complaint. However, it still remains the situation that parallel and separate claims in relation to two 'protected characteristics' may be made.

● **Third party harassment**. The Budget paper *Plan for Growth* announced that this provision in the Equality Act (s 40) is being reviewed as being 'unworkable'. This is questionable. Certainly, employment lawyers have argued that other legal steps might be taken by complainants to deal with such harassment (see Chapter 7).

As a concluding point in respect of equality law, the interplay between measures under the deficit reduction strategy and their discriminatory impact and consequences for equal treatment – particularly in relation to gender equality – has caused some considerable tensions. This issue was considered as part of the context to equality law in Chapter 4.

The promotion of labour market flexibility

The 'flexible workforce' remains a significant feature of the British labour market. It has been central to government policy for the past 30 years – irrespective of party. Whilst there has been an economic imperative to promote labour flexibility, there has also been a tension between the business interest in greater flexible working and the public policy commitment to employment protection and social justice for various groups of atypical and flexible workers.

There are two aspects to this issue: generalised employment protection for specific categories of flexible workers (e.g., part-time workers); and opportunities for particular workers to request flexible working arrangements (e.g. depending on family responsibilities).

▶ Specific categories of workers

Over the past 15 years the European Union has promulgated measures to provide employment protections and rights for three categories of 'atypical' workers: part-time workers, fixed-term workers, and temporary agency workers (see Chapter 2). The first two EU directives (implementing social partners' agreements) were transposed into British law as the Part-time Workers Regulations 2000 and the Fixed-term Employees Regulations 2002. The Labour government restricted the scope of the second to 'employees' rather than 'workers' – clearly, narrowing the protection.

The Temporary Agency Workers Directive – the final part of the triumvirate of legislation – was adopted in October 2008. Its purpose is to provide agency workers with equal treatment in their basic employment conditions in comparison with those of staff employed in the client company. In May 2008, the Labour government brokered a deal between the Confederation of British Industry (CBI) and the Trades Union Congress (TUC) which granted agency workers equal treatment after 12 weeks of employment in the client organisation. This social partners' agreement formed the basis of the Agency Workers' Regulations 2010 to implement the directive. On arrival in office the Conservative–Liberal Democrat government reviewed these new Regulations and their proposed implementation date in October 2011. Having considered the legal complexity of delay, it was decided to proceed with them.

Although there is some framework of protection for these specific categories of workers, there are exclusions from the laws and there remain two significant groups of working people who are liable to exploitation: casual workers; and certain temporary agency workers – specifically, migrant workers recruited by gangmasters. This is despite the enactment of the Gangmasters' (Licensing) Act 2004 (see Chapter 2).

▶ Requesting flexible working

The continuing feminisation of the labour market, the persistence of traditional caring responsibilities being undertaken by women, flexibility of working time and the 'long hours culture' continue to be factors in discussions about policies designed to accommodate work and non-work life. Indeed, there has been welcome progress in the political arena with family and dependency issues being acknowledged by both major political parties, during the past decade, as important policy matters.

The range of leave entitlements and the facility to request flexible working are helpful as is equality law (see Chapters 5 and 11). Judicial decision-making and judicial creativity have shown some signs of pushing the boundaries of discrimination law as evidenced in the *Coleman* case (see Exhibit 5.12). Politically, this is an aspect of 'flexibility' which will continue to remain important to governments, irrespective of political party.

The Conservative–Liberal Democrat government has published a consultation paper, *Modern Workplaces*, outlining some proposals to promote developments in this area (HM Government, 2011). The consultation is about 'plans for a culture of flexible, family-friendly employment practices'. Three of the policy areas identified are:

- A system of flexible parental leave.
- A right for all employees to request flexible working.
- Changes to the Working Time Regulations 1998 affecting the interaction of annual leave with sick leave and family-friendly leave.

The consultation paper, in its preamble, indicates that these measures are not just business-driven but may take account of the balance of employer economic interests and the social concerns of working people. So, 'encouraging flexible working generally will give all employees the opportunity to contribute more widely to society, whether as carers, disabled people, volunteers or simply as citizens. It will also help employers to recruit, motivate and retain their workforces and so build successful businesses as well as increasing productivity.'

These aspirations are commendable. However, the issue of compliance with existing statutory rights by organisations is still problematic – particularly in respect of pregnant workers who remain vulnerable to dismissal and other detrimental treatment. More fundamentally, the culture of organisations needs to be examined to ensure coherent policies in this area – possibly with enhancements. Furthermore, employer willingness to acknowledge that parenting is a male as well as female social responsibility is limited. Flexibility and leave arrangements for fathers needs to be facilitated.

Dispute resolution reform

This is a continuing concern for employers and governments. However, it is also a concern for working people who wish to ensure effective resolution of workplace problems and some proper redress for wrongs done to them. The enactment in 2004 by the Labour government of the statutory dispute resolution procedures for grievances and dismissals proved a failure and they were rescinded. The emphasis returned to workplace resolution using voluntary measures like mediation and conciliation; and encouragement to follow the standards of good procedural practice is the route now being adopted. The ACAS *Code of Practice on Disciplinary and Grievance Procedures* 2009 provides firm recommendations on practice. A respondent employer's compliance with this Code continues to be used in evidence at an employment tribunal hearing. In addition, good employment practice suggests that employers, in their internal procedures, might consider the processes of mediation (strongly advocated by, among other bodies, ACAS and the Chartered Institute of Personnel and Development) and also the ACAS services of conciliation. Overall, it is to be hoped that workplace resolution develops more effectively in the immediate future – partly to limit complaints being made to an employment tribunal, but also to provide more immediate redress for complainants and to help improve the quality of employment relations.

The proposals of the Conservative–Liberal Democrat government in respect of dispute resolution contain a blend of helpful administrative reforms of legal processes used by complainants together with a contentious further restriction on the opportunity of employees to complain about and seek redress for workplace wrongs (see Exhibit 13.2).

Aspects of these proposed dispute resolution measures are commented on below.

▶ Mediation and conciliation

ACAS, understandably, welcomes the proposals on these – but with justification. The Chair of ACAS said that 'pre-claim conciliation is a highly effective way of resolving disputes before they reach an employment tribunal and offers substantial savings for employers, employees and the taxpayer. It is quicker, cheaper and less stressful.' Research (Peters *et al.* 2010) has shown that employers could typically spend five days on an employment tribunal claim and seven and a half days if the complainant went to a hearing. It could spend five days if the claim was settled by ACAS. The average cost to an employer for a pre-claim conciliation case is £475 compared to £5,690 for an employment tribunal claim. (This does not, of course, include any settlement figure or compensation awarded.)

▶ The employment tribunal process

This has been criticised by academic researchers. As early as 1985, tribunals were described as 'quasi courts' (see Chapter 1). Employment relations practitioners have also commented on the need for reform. The Confederation of British Industry (2011) describes it as 'remote, slow, legalistic and costly.' Brendan Barber, General Secretary of the Trade Union Congress, has stated that 'everyone wants to see a quicker and more efficient tribunal system' but adds that 'taking away people's rights and pricing vulnerable workers out of the system is the worst possible way to achieve this' (TUC press release, 19 April 2011). The CIPD (2011: 12) supports measures to 'reduce the cost of the employment tribunal system.'

▶ Unfair dismissal qualifying period

Daniel Barnett, an employment lawyer, has described this proposal as 'moderately good news for business but bad news for employees' (**bulletins@emplaw.services.co.uk**, 1 November

EXHIBIT 13.2

Dispute resolution reform proposals

The measures aim to:

- Achieve more early resolution of workplace disputes so that parties can resolve their own problems in a way that is fair and equitable for both sides without having to go to an employment tribunal;
- Ensure that, where parties do need to come to an employment tribunal, the process is as swift, user friendly and effective as possible;
- Help businesses feel more confident about hiring people.
- **Mediation and conciliation**. A new requirement is proposed that all claims should be submitted to ACAS in the first instance rather than to the Tribunal Service. Pre-claim conciliation would not be mandatory but ACAS could give advice and a claim could only proceed if it had been lodged with ACAS for a month.
- **Tackling weaker cases**. These cases are described as imposing an unjustifiable burden on businesses and it is proposed that employment tribunals have powers to strike them out in a greater range of circumstances. In relation to these cases, it is proposed that employment judges should be able to require claimants to pay a deposit of £1,000 (currently £500); and that maximum costs would rise from £10,000 to £20,000.
- **Reasonable settlements**. Stronger encouragement for these to be made at various stages in the employment tribunal process. The claim form (ET1) to include a statement of loss.
- **Simplification of employment tribunal process**. It is proposed that witness statements could be 'taken as read' unless directed by the employment judge.
- **Fee for bringing an employment tribunal claim**. An intention is stated of introducing a fee.
- **Payment of expenses**. It is proposed to withdraw these in tribunal hearings 'encouraging parties to settle earlier and to think more carefully about the number of witnesses they call, so potentially reducing length of hearings'.
- **Qualifying period for unfair dismissal claims**. It is proposed to extend this from 12 months to two years. Other employment rights that are available on 'day one' would be unaffected. This would result in between 3,700–4,700 fewer tribunal claims.
- **Financial penalties for employers**. Consideration is being given to penalising employers which have breached an individual's rights rather than just compensating claimants. The cap on the penalty would be £5,000 and payable to the Exchequer and not to the claimant. This is to 'send a clear message to an employer, and employers more generally, that they must ensure that they comply with their employment law obligations'.

Source: *Resolving Workplace Disputes: Public Consultation* (2011) (**www.bis.gov.uk**).

At the Conservative Party Conference (2011) the Chancellor of the Exchequer announced the two-year qualifying service (from April 2012) and the introduction of fees (from April 2013). Both measures are subject to Parliamentary approval..

2010). 'In theory, employers would have an extra year to dismiss unreasonably – but they could still face allegations of discrimination (or unfair dismissal claims where no qualifying period is required, i.e. whistleblowing and certain health and safety, maternity and trade union-related dismissals. Since such claims tend to be more expensive to defend than "ordinary" unfair dismissal claims, it is unclear whether employers will find this proposal an entirely favourable change.'

Barnett added that there might be a sex discrimination aspect to the proposed policy. 'In June 1999, the House of Lords held by a 3:2 majority in *R v Secretary of State for Employment ex parte Seymour Smith* that the (then) two year qualifying period for unfair dismissal was potentially discriminatory against women, as women were statistically less likely than men to accrue two years' employment. However, they also held that the Secretary of State for Employment could justify the social policy behind the two-year threshold, namely opportunities in the labour market, which mean the two year qualifying period was permitted to stand.' He commented that 'it is likely a similar result would occur today if the increase to two years was challenged'. (The Labour government reduced the qualifying period to 12 months in 1999 – resisting representation from trade unions to bring it down to six months.)

The Trades Union Congress in its response to the consultation paper, among other matters, drew attention to the discriminatory effect of the increased qualifying period for young people, ethnic minority employees and female part-time workers. Quoting official statistics (Labour Force Survey, Autumn 2010, **www.statistics.gov.uk**) it reports that the following have less than two years' service:

- 59.2 per cent of employees aged 24 years and under;
- 30.1 per cent of ethnic minority employees (compared with 24.3 per cent of white employees);
- 32.4 per cent of part-time employees (compared with 22 per cent of full-time employees); and
- 500,000 female part-time workers will lose out directly as a result of the extended qualifying period.

The CIPD (2011: 12) has commented that the measure to increase the qualifying period is 'questionable'.

▶ Fees etc.

The Trades Union Congress states that the introduction of these will have 'disproportionate impact on low paid workers'. It refers to the Survey of Employment Tribunal Applications 2008 (Peters *et al.* 2010) which records that 70 per cent of tribunal claimants have average or below average earnings; and 35 per cent earn less than £15,000 p.a.

The Confederation of British Industry, the employer's organisation, supports fees, saying that it would help ensure that only 'reasonable claims' are made (**www.cbi.org.uk**).

Although not formally part of the BIS's consultation on dispute resolution, the issue of legal aid generally has been also subject to consultation (**www.justice.gov.uk**). Legal aid has been available for advice at employment tribunal and for representation in Employment Appeal Tribunal hearings and employment-related claims in the civil courts. The Ministry of Justice has proposed to remove legal aid from employment disputes (except for legal advice on discrimination claims prior to employment tribunal hearings).

The Ministry, summarising responses to its proposals, said that: 'many argued that employment cases were not solely money claims, but also involved important employment rights . . . They argued that claims often raised complex and difficult issues for litigants; the employer was often represented and there was an inequality of arms . . .' (2011, para 73).

The subsequent comments reflect an interesting attitude: 'We do not consider that applicants in these [employment] cases are likely to be particularly vulnerable. We consider that, given the need to prioritise resources, employment matters are of a lower importance than cases involving life, liberty or homelessness . . . [and so they] do not represent as high a priority for funding.'

Health and safety regulation

Health and safety has had a bad press – particularly in some tabloid newspapers. In his 2010 report commissioned by Prime Minister David Cameron, Lord Young is balanced in his comments on the principal statute, the Health and Safety at Work Act etc. 1974. He describes it as an 'effective framework'.

A more fundamental and substantial review of health and safety legislation was commissioned from Professor Ragnar Löfstedt (May 2011). It was stated that 'the review is part of a package of changes to Britain's health and safety system to support the Government's growth agenda and cut red tape.' How fundamental the potential reform of health and safety legislation will be is uncertain at the time of writing. The Terms of Reference have a wide scope (**www.dwp.gov.uk**):

> The review will consider the opportunity for combining, simplifying or reducing the approximately 200 statutory instruments that are owned by the Health and Safety Executive, by learning lessons from health and safety regimes in other countries, and considering the extent to which regulations:
>
> - have impacted on positive health and safety outcomes and businesses;
> - have led to unreasonable outcomes, or inappropriate litigation and compensation; and
> - have unnecessarily enhanced the requirements of an EU directive.

Enforcement of individual rights

This issue involves a number of perennial problems – only a few of which are being tackled.

▶ Access to statutory rights

This access can be restricted in two, often interlocking, ways:

1 by employment status: e.g. only 'employees' are able to claim unfair dismissal;
2 by length of service with an employer: e.g. 12 months' continuous service for unfair dismissal complaints; 26 weeks for the right to request flexible working.

In recent years, the qualifications relating to the number of hours worked, age limits over 65 years, and the size of the employer's workforce have been removed. Nevertheless, although three key employment rights are available to the wide category of 'workers' irrespective of length of service (under Working Time Regulations 1998, National Minimum Wage Act 1998, and in respect of wage deduction), the restrictions on unfair dismissal claims and those for statutory redundancy pay exclude vulnerable groups from important remedies. The proposal of the Conservative–Liberal Democrat government to introduce a two-year qualifying period for unfair dismissal claims is a further significant restriction. It affects not just employees who are directly dismissed by their employer but individuals who resign because of the unacceptable conduct of their employer and claim constructive dismissal.

▶ Managing individual complaints

Much survey evidence of the employment tribunal process (DTI 2002; Haywood *et al.* 2004; Aston *et al.* 2006; Armstrong and Coats 2007; Hammersley *et al.* 2007; Latreille 2007; Peters 2010) shows that it can be stressful, consume a great deal of time and may be costly to the individual in terms of the resources needed. There is also evidence of potential complainants not lodging a complaint because of these factors. The financial assistance that could be available is to be removed under legal aid reforms (**www.justice. gov.uk**). Advice may be available from the Citizens Advice Bureaux. Some 'no win no fee' lawyers may be willing to take cases. Otherwise, unless a person is a member of trade union or has their own resources, there can be disparate treatment in the way in which their complaint can be dealt with – particularly in comparison with the resources available to most employers. Using the language of the European Convention on Human Rights 1950, there is no 'equality of arms'.

This individual complaint process and the imbalance of resources is of particular significance in many discrimination cases. There can be complexities in both the law and in the evidence in such cases where patterns of discrimination or harassment are alleged.

Conclusion

It is dangerous to predict future developments and directions in employment law. Indeed, the field is littered with many unanticipated consequences. Those trends that are certain are the continued 'Europeanisation' of employment and discrimination law; further intricate legal arguments about the eligibility of 'workers' for employment protection in the flexible labour market; debates about the extension of effective rights for parents and carers; the continued 'juridification' of HRM and employment relations; and ever-present concerns about the extent to which working people have effective access to complaints procedures and remedies.

Whatever government is in office, there have been inevitable fundamental issues to be resolved relating to the regulation of the employment relationship. Two questions, in particular, are of concern for practitioners:

- Can a balance of interest be achieved between working people and employers?
- What is the economic justification for changes to employment and equality law?

These are questions to be debated. It is sufficient, at this stage, to end with a comment from the Chartered Institute of Personnel and Development (2011: 12):

> The CIPD agrees with the Government that regulation should be a last resort but where considered necessary be implemented in as light-touch a way as possible, be simple to understand and involve a minimum of red tape. We also agree that existing regulations should be subject to review and think the Government is right to push the EU Commission in the direction of better regulation and away from what at times seems to be an ideological predilection for more regulation.

However, while agreeing with much of the Government's regulatory reform agenda, the CIPD cautions against the possibility that the current better regulation agenda might start to drift towards a deregulation agenda.

On this basis the CIPD believe the prime focus of regulatory reform should be on streamlining the red tape that accompanies regulation rather than on watering down the substance of existing employee rights and entitlements. Moreover, proposals for deregulation should be subject to equally robust analysis as those for new regulation and not be driven by ideological assertion or in response to policy lobbying by influential vested interests.

References

Armstrong, K. and Coats, D. (2007) *The Costs and Benefits of Employment Tribunal Cases for Employers and Claimants*, Employment Relations Research Series No. 83. London: Department for Business Enterprise and Regulatory Reform (www.bis.gov.uk).

Aston, J. *et al.* (2006) *The Experience of Claimants in Race Discrimination Employment Tribunal Cases*, Employment Relations Research Series, No. 55. London: Department of Trade and Industry (www.bis.gov.uk).

The Better Regulation Executive (2010) *Lightening the Load: the Regulatory Impact on UK's Small Businesses* (www.bis.gov.uk).

Blackburn, R. and Hart, M. (2002) *Small Firms' Awareness and Knowledge of Individual Employment Rights*, Employment Relations Research Series, No. 14. London: Department of Trade and Industry (www.bis.gov.uk).

Chartered Institute of Personnel and Development (2011) *Work Horizons: the Economic Rights and Wrongs of Employment Regulation*. London: CIPD (www.cipd.co.uk).

Confederation of British Industry (2011) *Settling the Matter: Building a More Efficient and Effective Tribunal System* (www.cbi.org.uk).

Department of Trade and Industry (2002) *Findings from the 1998 Survey of Employment Tribunal Applications*, Employment Relations Research Series, No. 13. London: Department of Trade and Industry (www.bis.gov.uk).

Dickens, L. *et al.* (2005) *Review of Research into the Impact of Employment Relations Legislation*, Employment Relations Research Series, No. 45. London: Department of Trade and Industry (www.bis.gov.uk).

Ewing, K. (1989) *Britain and the ILO*, London: Institute of Employment Rights.

Fox, A. (1966) *Industrial Sociology and Industrial Relations*, Research Paper 3, Royal Commission on Trade Unions and Employers' Associations, Cmnd 3623. London: HMSO.

Hammersley, G. *et al.* (2007) *The Influence of Legal Representation at Employment Tribunals on Case Outcome*, Employment Relations Research Series, No. 84. London: Department for Business Enterprise and Regulatory Reform (www.bis.gov.uk).

Haywood, B. *et al.* (2004) *Findings from the Survey of Employment Tribunal Applications 2003*, Employment Relations Research Series, No. 33. London: Department of Trade and Industry (www.bis.gov.uk).

HM Government (2011) *Consultation on Modern Workplaces*. London: Department for Business, Innovation and Skills (www.bis.gov.uk).

Kahn-Freud, O. (1983) *Kahn-Freud's Labour and the Law* (P. Davies and M. Freedland, eds) London: Stevens.

Lambourne, E. *et al.* (2008) *Employment Law Admin Burdens Survey* 2008 (www.orc.co.uk).

Latreille, P. (2007) *The Settlement of Employment Tribunal Cases: Evidence from SETA 2003*, Employment Relations Research Series, No. 61. London: Department for Business Enterprise and Regulatory Reform (www.bis.gov.uk).

Lewis, R. (1986) 'The Role of the Law in Employment Relations', in Lewis, R. (ed.) *Labour Law in Britain*. Oxford: Blackwell.

Ministry of Justice (2011) *Reform of Legal Aid in England and Wales: the Government Response* (www.justice.gov.uk).

Peters, M. *et al.* (2010) *Findings from the Survey of Employment Tribunal Applications 2008*, Employment Relations Research Series, No. 107. London: Department for Business, Innovation and Skills (www.bis.gov.uk).

Purcell, J. and Sisson, K. (1983) 'Strategies and Practices in the Management of Industrial Relations', in Bain, G. (ed.) *Industrial Relations in Britain*. Oxford: Blackwell.

Wedderburn, Lord (1986) *The Worker and the Law*. Harmondsworth: Penguin Books.

Lord Young (2010) *Common Sense, Common Safety*. London: HM Government Cabinet Office.

Useful websites

Advisory, Conciliation and Arbitration Service **www.acas.org.uk**

Chartered Institute of Personnel and Development **www.cipd.co.uk**

Confederation of British Industry **www.cbi.org.uk**

Department for Business, Innovation and Skills **www.bis.gov.uk**

Department for Work and Pensions **www.dwp.gov.uk**

Equalities Office **www.equalities.gov.uk**

HM Treasury **www.hm-treasury.gov.uk**

Trades Union Congress **www.tuc.org.uk**

Appendix: Feedback on exercises

In considering these exercises, it is important to remember the necessity to comply, as appropriate, with the ACAS *Code of Practice on Disciplinary and Grievance Procedures* (2009). Failure to follow the recommendations can be used in evidence at an employment tribunal (see Exhibits 8.1 and 8.2 in Chapter 8).

Chapter 3: Managing change in the employment relationship

▶ Contract variation

3.1.1 *Samantha*. The issue is whether or not Samantha has a mobility clause in her contract of employment. If there is one, it could be implied through custom and practice (although this would be relatively rare); or it could be an express term. This means that it would be in writing in the offer letter or in the contractual information she was given when she started employment. If there was such a mobility clause and the employer implemented it in a reasonable way then she should comply with it. A distance of four miles might well be regarded as reasonable and it may well be an arrangement that she has complied with on previous occasions.

A related issue that could arise, even if the mobility clause is part of the contract, is the issue of indirect sex discrimination. For example, if Samantha has caring responsibilities, she might argue that the clause puts her at a 'disadvantage'. The employer would need to justify the clause objectively (see Chapter 5). Taken overall, it would be sensible and good practice for the employer to consult with Samantha about what was required and to consider any problems that she might have.

If there is no mobility clause, then the employer should consult with Samantha about varying the place of work under her contract of employment. The issues of sex discrimination and reasonable distance could be considered. If Samantha does not agree the variation, then the employer may terminate her contract of employment for 'some other substantial reason' (in this case 'business need') and offer a new one incorporating the changed place of work. She has the choice of accepting or refusing this new contract. She may, if she has one year's continuous service, claim unfair dismissal at an employment tribunal. However, if the employer has a good reason ('business need' can be such a reason); and has handled the matter in a procedurally correct way and in accordance with the ACAS *Code of Practice on Disciplinary and Grievance Procedures*, then the dismissal is likely to be fair.

3.1.2 *Locksmith Engineering*. The issue is the nature of the pay increase under the contract of employment. If it is *discretionary*, then the employer may be able to refuse to award the increase. If it is *contractual*, then it would be a breach of contract not to make the payment and individual employees could sue for non-payment of wages due (Employment Rights Act 1996, Part II). It would, in fact, be a repudiatory breach of contract because pay is an essential term of the contract. So, it could result in resignation and claims of constructive dismissal. An employer could avoid the consequences of breach of contract by terminating with due notice the existing contracts of employment, consulting with staff and offering a new contract without any term relating to an automatic annual pay increase.

3.1.3 *Beryl*. The issue is whether Beryl can be instructed to carry out the tasks involved in the new and complex computerised system. An implied term in her contract of employment is the duty to obey the lawful and reasonable instructions of her employer. There is nothing unlawful in what the employer is requiring her to do. Whether it is reasonable is dependent on the answers to a number of questions. The principal ones are:

- Do the tasks that she is being required to undertake fall within her job description?
- Do they substantially change the work that she is normally required to do?
- Is she to be provided with training and support in order to undertake the new tasks?
- Has the employer consulted with her about the proposed changes? (see the *Cresswell* case)

If she persists in refusing to attend the training, then the employer might take disciplinary action. Alternatively, he might terminate her contract of employment for 'some other substantial reason' (on the grounds of 'business need') and offer her a new contract on condition that she participates in the training programme.

3.1.4 *Jamila*. The issue is whether she can be instructed to carry out the requirement of the employer. The task falls within the job description and the implied contractual duty of a retail assistant to promote her employer's business (see issues in Exercise 3 above). She is unlikely to be able to claim constructive dismissal because there is no evidence of a repudiation of her contract of employment by her employer.

▶ Managing redundancies

3.2.1 Assuming the redundancies are genuine and there is a decline in the need for particular grades of staff, the employer will have to determine which print operators are to be made redundant (i.e. against which criteria); and to consult with them individually about the redundancy. Once the consultation process is completed, notice of the termination of their employment should be given to them. It should be due notice – i.e. what they are entitled to under their contracts of employment.

3.2.2 As in the previous case, assuming the redundancies are genuine and the business circumstances require a reduction in the number of employees, the employer should select staff according to specific objective criteria. Selection according to employment status is potentially discriminatory. It could be discriminatory on the grounds of sex if more women are on temporary contracts than men. It could also be potentially discriminatory under the Fixed-term Employees (Prevention of Less Favourable Treatment) Regulations 2002 – in terms of comparative treatment with permanent employees. Furthermore, it could also be that some workers on temporary contracts could have considerable service – up to four years before they become permanent. This might exceed the length of service of staff on permanent contracts if LIFO ('last in first out') was to be used as a criterion.

The approach to be adopted in terms of good practice (and possibly avoidance of claims under discrimination law) is to set out objective criteria for the selection of staff – whether they are permanent or temporary. Such criteria could include performance standards, disciplinary issues, absence record, etc.

3.2.3 *Trisha*. There are two principal issues here: the fact that Trisha's job is being made redundant under the reorganisation; and the question of whether her new post is suitable alternative employment. On this latter issue, she might argue that there has been a diminution of her status – in terms of direct responsibility to a course leader and in terms of autonomy. Having said that, the tasks remain generally the same and she could reasonably be expected to undertake the work required. The employer should provide a 'trial period'. If at the end of that she is dissatisfied with the post, then the employment may be terminated. There may be another factor involved in the case. This is the potential for indirect sex discrimination. The 'provision, criterion or practice' which the employer needs to justify objectively is the requirement to work occasionally until 7pm. If she has dependency responsibilities, she may be disadvantaged by this provision. The employer, however, may be successful in defending it because of the operational needs of the college.

▶ Managing transfers

3.3.1 The key issue here is whether or not the new employer (the 'transferee') is able to vary contracts of employment of the staff transferred. Essentially, the contracts of employees of the transferor are protected throughout the transfer situation. This period is not defined. It is unlawful to vary contracts if the variation is connected with the transfer. However, the law was amended in 2006, when it became permissible for a transferee to vary contracts for an economic, technical or organisational reason entailing a change in the workforce.

In this case, it is difficult to see the justification for the common pay structure being established. It could be argued that this is for reasons of harmonisation and is connected with the transfer. The deployment of staff might be an 'organisational' reason 'entailing changes in the workforce' if it is necessary to merge two separate workforces. If such changes are to be proposed, they must be discussed and, if they are contractual, agreed with the staff.

3.3.2 There are two aspects to this transfer. First of all, the contracts of the staff transferred: these must be preserved through the transfer. If they incorporate terms of collective agreements, they will continue and 'live on' in the future – whether the transferee is union-free or not. Secondly, there is the issue of transferee's attitude to trade union recognition. The transferee can derecognise the union after the transfer. This will not, however, affect the issue of incorporated terms deriving from collective agreements.

3.3.3 The transferee is liable for this employment tribunal claim. They should have been notified of it by the transferor as part of the 'employee liability information'. If the transferor failed to tell the transferee of a grievance or complaint that was known to it, then the transferee can take legal proceedings against the transferor.

The transferee must respond to the employment tribunal complaint.

3.3.4 The Transfer of Undertakings (Protection of Employment) Regulations 2006 protect 'employees'. The self-employed workers would be excluded from protection during the transfer. They would have no rights under the Regulations. They may have certain rights under their contracts with the transferor and that organisation should ensure that they are complied with. The seasonal contract staff could be 'employees'. By considering their employment status and, in particular, the issue of mutuality of obligation, it might be possible to determine their entitlements under the Regulations.

Chapter 5: Equality law and the workplace

5.1 Taking the *Ladele* case by itself, there are several points that can be made. Clearly, any harassment and bullying against people who object to civil partnerships is not acceptable and is contrary to discrimination law. The central issue is whether it is indirectly discriminatory to require a member of staff to comply with specific key requirements of the job. The responsibilities of a registrar are to perform important public duties. The employer should make clear the nature of those responsibilities. Given the diverse nature of British society, the probability is that a registrar of civil marriage and partnership ceremonies is likely to encounter people with whose views he or she does not necessarily agree. The employer could inquire of the employee if there were any circumstances in which he or she would feel uncomfortable. In that situation it might be possible, operationally, to arrange the allocation of work to avoid such a conflict of values. Whether the employer could require a registrar to perform ceremonies they disapproved of and could justify it in accordance with the equality law is highly questionable. Also, failure to perform the required duties by the member of staff may be grounds for dismissal. The issue here which could arise is whether that would be direct discrimination on grounds of religious belief.

5.2 This is an actual case from 2003. The tribunal found that the failure to invite Mrs Hill to the event and the subsequent comments were direct sex discrimination and that, because of the employer's unacceptable behaviour forcing her to resign, she was constructively dismissed because of the repudiation of her contract. The failure to invite her to an event designed to reward hard work was 'a refusal to afford her access to a benefit' and she was subjected to a detriment. The employer's failure to recognise the upset caused by effectively making a joke of it and then trying to dismiss her concerns enhanced the upset. She was awarded £3,000 for injury to feelings, and £22,219 for loss of earnings and interest.

5.3 The reliance by some managers on 'commitment' might be a genuine attempt to appoint someone who will work to a high standard in the organisation. The problem with the term is that it can be used in a coded way to sift out people who may want some flexibility in employment arrangements and who may not be at ease with a 'long hours culture'. Such a view could well be indirectly discriminatory on the grounds of sex; it may also be discriminatory under disability law which requires the employer to consider some reasonable adjustment. If it appears to be potentially indirect sex discrimination, the manager must be prepared to justify objectively the provision, criterion or practice as a genuine business need. If adjustments are needed under disability legislation, then these must be reasonable and it they cannot be made, reasons should be given.

5.4 The size of the business is not relevant. She is likely to be a disabled person within the meaning of the Act and is protected as an applicant for employment. She clearly is suitable for the post but the withdrawal of the verbal offer is discriminatory. The employer should formally reinstate the offer and consult with her about any reasonable adjustments that she might need. It may be that careful management of her workload might help. If the offer is not reinstated, then she may make a claim at employment tribunal for direct discrimination on the grounds of disability.

5.5 Lou is protected under the Equality Act 2010 from the time of the diagnosis of multiple sclerosis even if the symptoms are not manifest. He has suffered a detriment because he was not considered as suitable for short-listing. This was not for any reason relating to his capability but to do with assumptions about his long-term health. He should be offered an interview and should be considered for the promotion. If he is refused the post, it must be for objective reasons. Otherwise he would be able to complain of direct discrimination. If he is offered the post, it may be that the nature of it is such that reasonable adjustments could be made more easily to accommodate him in the long term. As evidence of good practice, the employer would also need to consult with him on any adjustments – which might be small-scale initially.

5.6 The culture of this organisation is probably profit-driven and generally unsympathetic to good employment practice and to the requirements of discrimination law. The difficulty will be with the Chief Executive who no doubt is very influential in determining policy. One approach would be to identify the risks of the action he wishes to take and suggest ways of meeting his objectives lawfully. Age discrimination law is central. An advertisement which conveys the intention to discriminate is unlawful. A person specification setting out age group may be unlawful unless it can be objectively justified as a genuine business need. More critically for such a senior post, the person specification should be identifying experience and qualifications. If flexible working is being ruled out, then the rationale for this needs to be considered. Is it necessary for the business? If a structured, legally compliant approach is not adopted then the business may incur costs in terms of management time and possible compensation should there be an employment tribunal complaint. Much will depend on how the Chief Executive is likely to respond to the 'stick'.

5.7 This is a case of indirect discrimination on racial grounds. The specification of GCSE qualifications sets a standard of proficiency that the employer is looking for in applicants. However, it may be possible that such proficiency is evident in a range of other qualifications. The employer would need to objectively justify the indirect discrimination. It is unlikely that he would be able to demonstrate a genuine business need specifically for GCSE qualifications.

5.8 The issue here is whether or not there is a genuine occupational qualification on racial grounds. It is very much a borderline case. Clearly, there is to be liaison with the Chinese community. However, the nature of the job is fund-raising and administrative. It does not involve promoting culture identity or welfare directly but rather facilitating the work of other people through funding. One key issue might be the extent to which the postholder has to be proficient in a Chinese language to improve liaison. In this case, there may be a case for clarifying this in the person specification. Even then, a Chinese speaker may not have to be of Chinese ethnic origin.

5.9 This relates to the issue of occupational requirement because of religion or belief. There are two possible aspects to this. First, a requirement which is usually appropriate is that for a person who is promoting a particular faith or system of belief. This does not arise in this case. Secondly, the preservation or promotion of an 'ethos' in religious organisations. This appears to be the reason behind this specific OR. Given the nature of the work he would be required to perform, it is difficult to see how such an OR can be defended. If he suspected that he was being discriminated against because of his religion, then he might be able to claim direct discrimination on grounds of religion or belief at employment tribunal. He is protected as an applicant for employment and may make a complaint at an employment tribunal.

Chapter 7: Harassment and bullying at work

7.1 This scenario outlines some deeply-embedded cultural issues. To tackle these, a multi-level approach is necessary. The initial step must be the development of a strategy involving commitment from senior management to a detailed plan. The plan should consider several issues – ways of effectively gaining commitment from managers, the training necessary to achieve the proposed strategic outcomes, effective procedures for dealing with individual complaints, monitoring processes.

In evaluating the steps necessary for dealing with this cultural problem, draw on your own experience from any organisation in which you have worked. Think about the practicalities of implementing change and how any consequential further problems might be tackled. It might also be worth considering the relevant section of Chapter 6 concerning strategic approaches to eradicating discrimination.

7.2 *Indira*. The harassment that Indira experiences is, in part, 'personal' (in that it is directed to her) and also as a part of a general harassing culture within the organisation. Under the Equality Act 2010 an issue that has to be considered is whether the harassment is 'because of the sex of the recipient' or 'unwanted conduct of a sexual nature'. The e-mail message is likely to be the latter. The comments in the lift seem as if they are the former.

Indira clearly finds both sets of behaviour upsetting. In the terms of the legislation they are 'unwanted'. She has rightly mentioned her concern to her supervisor who, wrongly, has suggested 'laughing off' the matter. Tom, as an observer could complain about the harassment of Indira.

Angela in the HR department must, because of the employer's liability for discrimination and harassment, take the issue seriously as a formal grievance. First she should investigate what has happened. There may be some difficulty in establishing the facts of the unwitnessed incident in the lift. Nevertheless, if she forms a 'reasonable belief' that Jez behaved in the way that Indira claims (and this is probable given his reputation and his knowledge that she had complained about the e-mail message), then, Angela can accept, on the balance of probabilities, that Indira's version of events is true.

The issue for the employer, then, is whether to initiate disciplinary action against Jez. A view needs to be taken by the employer of the seriousness of Jez's conduct – is it gross misconduct or relatively minor? If he is guilty of misconduct, the appropriate penalty needs to be considered. If he is guilty of gross misconduct, then, the employer's starting point for a penalty could be dismissal. Depending on the circumstances (his record, length of service and any remorse he might show) then he could be given a warning – first formal or a final warning.

This response by the employer could be evidence of them taking 'such steps as were reasonably practicable' to deal with Indira's individual complaint. There are, of course, other more deep-seated problems about the culture of the organisation. The approaches suggested in the answer to Exercise 7.1 are worth considering.

If nothing effective is done to deal with Indira's complaint, then, she might be able to argue a breach of the implied contractual term of 'mutual trust and confidence'. There would be a repudiation of the contract and she could resign and complain to an employment tribunal of constructive dismissal – providing she has twelve months' continuous service. Alternatively, she might complain of harassment under the provisions in the Equality Act 2010. She would not need to resign in order to make such a complaint. Furthermore, any compensation awarded would be uncapped.

7.3 *Ronke*. The critical issue in this case is whether or not the remark of Joan Philips about 'you people' constitutes harassment on racial grounds or whether it refers to people like Ronke who have been long-serving members of staff. If it is the latter Joan's behaviour is more likely to be 'bullying' rather than harassment as outlawed under discrimination law. It may be difficult to prove that it is racial harassment unless there is some additional evidence of similar attitudes and behaviour. If it is accepted as bullying, then, it is still serious enough for senior management to deal with. Of particular concern is the power relationship between the two women; and in addition the need in a relatively small office environment for good working relationships to exist. So, in the circumstances, Ronke might be advised to raise the issue with Joan's boss as a grievance. She might indicate that she is prepared to participate in formal mediation. This is could be a constructive way of helping resolve issues and achieving a satisfactory outcome for both parties. If the issue is not resolved, then, Ronke might resign and claim constructive dismissal at an employment tribunal.

7.4 *Issac and Harry*. Issac's behaviour is offensive and unwanted. He is entitled to have his religious beliefs about homosexuality. However, he does not have complete freedom of expression. Harry has made clear his objection to Isaac's comments. He has also mentioned the situation to his manager. The manager, as a 'reasonable step', should have discussed the matter with Isaac and Harry separately; and then, if appropriate, to try and mediate between the two of them. His failure to do this, probably, resulted in the continuing escalation of the inter-personal difficulties.

There are three principal sets of issues to be dealt with:

- *The fight*: This is gross misconduct. Establishing the facts of what happened and whether or not there was any provocation is critically important. Clearly, Harry had struck the first blow. However, in all the circumstances (including possible provocation), it may not be regarded by the employer as serious enough to dismiss him for gross misconduct.

- *Harry's grievance*: This should be dealt with prior to any disciplinary hearing. The facts that are established are material to the background of any disciplinary issues – i.e. management's failure to deal with Harry's earlier complaint about Isaac's persistent and escalating offensive behaviour.

- *Isaac's behaviour*: This also needs to be tackled. There is evidence of a breach of disciplinary rules by his harassing behaviour. Some disciplinary warning might be appropriate.

If Harry were to be dismissed, then, he may have grounds to claim unfair dismissal at an employment tribunal. The employer could probably succeed in such a case if it proved that it was reasonable in all the circumstances – including the seriousness with which they viewed fighting – to dismiss Harry for gross misconduct. Perhaps a more certain complaint might be a claim by Harry under equality law (the Equality Act 2010) that he had been harassed by association with his son's sexuality. He would claim that the employer was vicariously liable for this harassment.

Chapter 8: Discipline and dismissal

8.1 **Jason**. The HR manager should firstly explain to Jason's line manager that Jason is protected against unfair dismissal under the Employment Rights Act 1996 as he is an employee with more than one year's continuous service. The company therefore needs to be very careful in how they handle his case.

For a dismissal to be fair under the ERA it needs to firstly come under one of the potentially fair reasons for dismissal. That this is the case in this scenario is very obvious – Jason's lateness and absence from work clearly relate to the 'conduct' ground. In addition to establishing a potentially fair reason for dismissal, employers are obliged to demonstrate that the actual decision to dismiss was reasonable in the circumstances.

In establishing whether a dismissal was reasonable or not, employment tribunals will refer to the principles and procedural guidance outlined in the ACAS *Code of Practice on Disciplinary and Grievance Procedures*. The ACAS code outlines that before action is taken in response to a breach of disciplinary rules, organisations should inform the employee of the issue in question, undertake a comprehensive investigation, give the employee the opportunity to put their case forward, and also allow them to appeal any decision made. Jason would have a right to be accompanied at any formal disciplinary meeting.

Easywheels may have taken such procedural steps before issuing Jason with a written warning. The company may therefore be justified in giving him a final written warning outlining that if he is late again he could be dismissed. This would arguably be within the 'range of reasonable responses' an employer might implement in such circumstances. Jason's recent absences from work could also be classed as misconduct, which could potentially support the issuing of a final written warning.

However the circumstances of the case would perhaps suggest that the employer should look more closely into Jason's situation before issuing a final written warning and subsequently dismissing. Specifically, Jason's claim that his recent absences have been a result of stress should be carefully examined. The ACAS guide on discipline and grievance at work recommends that employers should check whether there are any special circumstances such as personal issues that may be affecting performance, in advance of disciplinary meetings. It would be good practice therefore for Easywheels to speak to Jason about this and possibly offer some form of counselling or other assistance if he is indeed found to be suffering from stress or depression, if they have not already done so. In addition, if not already considered an adjustment of working arrangements – for example a later starting time and/or temporary exemption from having to work in the evening – should also be discussed. Dismissing Jason without considering such issues and taking these additional steps could potentially be seen by a tribunal to be unfair.

If these additional steps were not undertaken and Jason was indeed found to have been unfairly dismissed, a tribunal could order him to be reinstated or reengaged or alternatively award compensation.

8.2 Sarah. As an employee (we can assume this from the facts of the case) with more than one year's continuous service, Sarah is protected against unfair dismissal under the ERA 1996. Sarah could therefore apply to an employment tribunal claiming that her dismissal was unfair. Her employer would have to demonstrate that she was dismissed for a fair reason and that the decision to dismiss was reasonable in the circumstances. The most obvious fair reason for dismissal here is capability, i.e. that Sarah is no longer physically capable of doing her job. In relation to the reasonableness of the decision, the company's status as a small business would be expressly taken into account by a tribunal. In particular, the small size of the company may mean that it does not have the financial resources to continue employing Sarah for a long period of time or to make potentially costly adjustments to her role (e.g. by modifying existing equipment); while there may also be limited opportunities to provide her with alternative work. The company's need to supply customer orders would also be seen to be of paramount importance.

By writing to her about the situation, holding a meeting to discuss it and providing for an appeal, Sarah's managing director has followed key procedural steps outlined in the ACAS code of practice. However it is well established that in capability cases tribunals generally require employers to take particular, additional procedural steps in order for dismissals to be fair. Employers should consult closely with the employee, consider carefully the medical evidence on the employee's condition and also whether it is possible to provide him or her with alternative employment or make an adjustment to the job so that they can continue working. In this case it is clear that the employer has examined the relevant medical evidence, consulted with Sarah and to a limited extent considered the issue of alternative employment. However a tribunal could decide that the employer has given insufficient consideration to whether Sarah could take up the marketing vacancy. In addition, the managing director has not considered whether the making of adjustments to her role or the equipment used might enable Sarah to continue in her current position. This would suggest that the dismissal on grounds of capability might be found to be unfair, in which case Sarah could be reinstated, reengaged or awarded compensation.

There is a second main aspect of this case, namely the possibility of a claim for disability discrimination, which Sarah could consider including in her application to a tribunal. Under the Equality Act 2010, employers are obliged to make 'reasonable adjustments' for disabled employees to enable them to work or continue working effectively. To be classed as disabled under the EA 2010, Sarah must have a 'physical or mental impairment' which has a substantial and long-term adverse effect on her ability to carry out 'normal day-to-day activities'. She does have a physical impairment that is long-term and which has a substantial adverse effect on her ability to carry out normal day-to-day activities (the effect on 'manual dexterity' is arguably key here).

The duty to make reasonable adjustments may include adjustment to equipment being used or the exact nature of the job undertaken. A tribunal would therefore closely consider, for example, whether if some piece of equipment were introduced Sarah could continue her design work. In addition, *Archibald v Fife Council 2004* established that the duty to make reasonable adjustments may, depending on the circumstances, require companies to consider transferring employees who have become disabled into positions which they do not necessarily have the qualifications or experience for (see Chapter 5). It is therefore likely that a tribunal would hold that the employer in this case is in breach of the EA 2010 due to the fact that it has not properly addressed the duty to make reasonable adjustments. No consideration has been given to possible adjustments to her existing job that would enable Sarah remain in employment, while the possibility of her transferring to do the job coming up in the marketing department has arguably not been considered sufficiently. A tribunal could also therefore make a declaration and recommendation and award compensation for disability discrimination.

8.3 Jo. As Jo has six years' service she is protected against unfair dismissal. The circumstances of her case suggest a possible claim for unfair constructive dismissal. Such a claim arises where, by reason of their conduct, an employer is responsible for a fundamental or 'repudiatory' breach of the contract of employment that entitles the employee to resign and treat the contract as having come to an end. By not taking Jo's complaint and concerns seriously it is arguable that the employer has failed in its duty to take reasonable care of her and is therefore guilty of a fundamental breach of contract, which could entitle her to resign and claim constructive dismissal.

However following the ACAS code of practice on discipline and grievance, before resigning and making an application to a tribunal, Jo should try to resolve her situation with her employer. She should submit a written grievance about the company's policies and treatment of her, attend any meeting that is arranged and also appeal any decision if allowed to do so. If she does not take these steps any compensation subsequently awarded to her by a tribunal could be reduced by 25 per cent. If GNC did not respond satisfactorily to her grievance and she did take a case to a tribunal, it would be likely that she would be found to have been unfairly dismissed and therefore awarded compensation. (It would perhaps be unlikely that she would want to be either reinstated or reengaged.)

Although there is no clear evidence of direct sex discrimination or sexual harassment, the facts also raise the possibility of a claim for indirect sex discrimination under the Equality Act 2010. This may arise where an employer applies a provision, criterion or practice equally to male and female workers which puts a woman 'at a particular disadvantage' compared with men, and which cannot be shown to be a 'proportionate means of achieving a legitimate aim'. In this case, due to childcare commitments the requirement for all team members to attend evening social events twice a week is likely to put women at a particular disadvantage compared to men (and has put Jo at a disadvantage), and it would therefore be up to GNC to justify it. It would be very difficult for GNC to demonstrate that the social outings were justifiable and it may also therefore be liable for indirect sex discrimination. Remedies for this would be a declaration, recommendation and/or compensation (potentially unlimited and for injury to feelings in addition to financial loss).

Chapter 9: Wages and equal pay

▶ National Minimum Wage

9.1 He is a 'worker' protected under the National Minimum Wage Act 1998. He is entitled to receive the rate applicable to 16–17-year-olds (set at £3.68 per hour in

October 2011 and usually varied upwards each year). Advice can be given by Her Majesty's Revenue and Customs helpline. He has been underpaid and can complain to an employment tribunal for underpayment of his wages. He would be expected to lodge a grievance with his employer initially. The employer must not subject the employee to detrimental treatment nor dismiss them if the reason of principal reason is enforcing rights under the Act.

9.2 She is a 'worker' protected under the National Minimum Wage Act 1998. She is entitled to receive the rate applicable to 18–20-year-olds (set at £4.98 per hour in October 2011 and usually varied upwards each year). Advice can be given by Her Majesty's Revenue and Customs helpline. She has been underpaid and can complain to an employment tribunal for underpayment of her wages. She would be expected to lodge a grievance with her employer initially. The employer must not subject the employee to detrimental treatment not dismiss them if the reason of principal reason is enforcing rights under the Act.

9.3 He is a 'worker' protected under the National Minimum Wage Act 1998. The pay reference period is four weeks. His relevant pay comprises basic pay (paid at £5.00 per hour – **below** the national minimum wage set at £6.08 per hour in October 2011). He is, however, being provided with free accommodation. In terms of remuneration, this has a notional value under the Act. In October 2011, it was £4.73 per day; £33.11 per week.

9.4 She has been paid at just above the appropriate rate for 18–20-year-old (set at £4.98 per hour in October 2011; but usually varied upwards each year). The key issue is the real reason for her dismissal. Is it her performance or conduct or redundancy; or is it that she is becoming eligible for the higher rate of the national minimum wage (set at £6.08 per hour in October 2011)? She would be able to claim unfair dismissal if the reason or principal reason was that she was being deliberately prevented from asserting her right to be paid the full rate.

9.5 She is entitled to see her pay records. She is also entitled to receive an appropriate itemised pay statement if she is an employee. She can report the employer to Her Majesty's Revenue and Customs. It can take action against the employer – even in the criminal courts if there is a deliberate refusal to pay the national minimum wage.

◗ Pay deduction

9.6 It is an unlawful deduction to withhold money in respect of a loan. An employee must agree to it. A complaint, irrespective of length of service can be made by a 'worker' to an employment tribunal.

9.7 It would depend on the terms of the collective agreement as it was 'incorporated' into the contract of employment. If the agreement says that the shift allowance should be paid, then, the employer is deducting it unlawfully. A complaint, irrespective of length of service can be made by a 'worker' to an employment tribunal.

9.8 In law, he is required to pay the money back to his employer. In requiring repayment, the employer should, according to case law, be reasonable. It was not a large sum of money, so, it is feasible that he might have thought that the money was legitimately his. Since he has already spent the money, the employer should consider an agreement that he pays it by instalments over, perhaps, six months. Any agreement should take account of his normal outgoings. The employer cannot deduct the money from his pay packet without consultation and his agreement.

9.9 The deduction of £155 seems to breach an agreement that the employee made to repair the van himself. The other deductions were provisional and, so, based on little firm evidence. The employer may have good reason for wanting to withhold or deduct some money. But this should be done with the employee's agreement.

9.10 Her boyfriend is right! The maximum permissible deduction in retail employment (which a café is) is ten per cent of a week's gross wages (i.e. £15) – unless it is the final week of employment.

Chapter 10: Regulation of working time

10.1 Presumably, only a proportion of the total workforce is likely to be required to work in excess of the maximum. These would be the 'relevant workforce'. Two possible routes are available to the employer under the Working Time Regulations 1998. First, the employer could ask each employee to make individual agreements to disapply the maximum 48-hour working week. From the employer's point of view this might not provide continuing operational certainty because employees can give notice to terminate such agreements.

The second way would be to negotiate a 'workforce agreement'. This can be done in non-union workplaces. It would enable the averaging period of 17 weeks to be extended to 52 weeks. This would apply only to relevant members of the workforce. It would need to be signed by a majority, if not all, and would become a new condition of employment.

10.2 Under the Working Time Regulations 1998, 'working time' is defined as 'any period in relation to a worker during which he is working, at his employer's disposal and carrying out his activities or duties'. In this case, it is arguable that for the 8-hour shift the worker is at the employer's 'disposal' – dealing with in-coming calls; waiting for calls; and, depending on operational circumstances, available to cover colleagues at short notice; and to take over any other duties that the employer might allocate. The worker is unlikely to have any freedom of action in that 8-hour period. He or she will not be permitted to leave the workplace without permission.

The interpretation of the directive's provision on 'working time' by the European Court of Justice in the *SIMAP* [2000] and *Jaeger* [2003] cases suggests strongly that these call-centre workers are entitled to regard the entire 8-hour shift as working time (aside from any rest breaks).

10.3 Maggie is what is usually called a 'casual worker'. Despite this employment status she has protection and entitlements under the Working Time Regulations 1998. These regulations cover the wide category of 'workers'. She is entitled to paid annual leave. The statutory minimum under the regulations is 28 days. Because Maggie is not a full-time worker but only works occasional hours she is entitled to *pro rata* paid annual leave, depending on how much work she has done (in comparison to a full-time worker). The

European Court of Justice has ruled that the entitlement to paid annual leave means that the worker must have the time off work. The leave entitlement cannot be 'bought out' by means of an additional payment to wages (see the case of *Robinson-Steele* [2006]).

10.4 There are a number of factors in this case. The starting point is whether or not he is working solely for the supermarket chain. Assuming that he is, although he is working on an 'as and when required' basis, he is a protected worker under the Working Time Regulations 1998.

However, it could be that although he has an ongoing commitment to the supermarket chain, he is also able, provided he gives the supermarket priority, to undertake other work (e.g. repairing and installing domestic fridges and freezers). So, some of his work is self-employment which he can 'pick and choose' to do. He is still a protected worker in relation to the work he does for the supermarket.

A final possibility is that if contacted to undertake work for the supermarket he is not personally required to undertake it and he can contract out the work to another engineer known to him. In this case, he is likely to be self-employed in relation to the work he does for the supermarket and not covered by the Working Time Regulations which explicitly exclude self-employed workers.

10.5 The worker is entitled to terminate the agreement; and in the absence of an agreed notice period, to do this with at least seven days' notice. It was short-sighted of the employer not to provide for a notice period in the written agreement which can be for any period up to (but no longer than) three months. The worker does not have to provide reasons for wanting to end the agreement. The implied threat of dismissal by the employer is unlawful. She was exercising her right – irrespective of the operational difficulties that might be caused to the employer. She has a right not to suffer any detriment, including dismissal, for asserting her right (Working Time Regulations, regs 29 and 30). Any detrimental action by the employer could result in a complaint to an employment tribunal.

10.6 Several issues arise in this case:

● The definition of night time.

● Whether particular staff are 'night workers'.

● The length of night work.

In this exercise, staff are normally working nine hours in a 24-hour period. Operationally, there are good reasons for this. However, in terms of their strict entitlements, it is not acceptable. If the hotel did not wish to change its shift-work arrangements, it could use the derogation provision and, as a non-union company, negotiate a workforce agreement.

10.7 The employer's duty under the Working Time Regulations 1998 is to have regard to the health and safety of night workers (reg 7). There should be a health assessment and further assessments at regular intervals. There needs to be consideration of whether patterns of working hours breach the regulations. As far as the circumstances of his ill-health are concerned, there is advice taken from a registered medical practitioner; and the employee has made a request to the employer. The employer is also under a duty to take reasonable care of the employee. Knowing about the ill-health, the employer may make himself liable for a personal injury claim if he does not respond to the request in a positive way. The employer may also be liable for a repudiation of the contract of employment (by breaching mutual trust and confidence) if he rejects or ignores the request out of hand. A constructive way might be to consult with the employee, consider the medical report in detail and any prognosis in it, and review whether suitable alternative employment is possible. If it is not possible, the employer may consider possible dismissal on the grounds of medical incapacity.

Chapter 11: Family leave and work–life balance

11.1 Pauline and Kate. Under the Employment Rights Act 1996 and the Maternity and Parental Leave Regulations 1999, after her period of OML, Pauline is entitled to return to the same job that she held previously on the same terms and conditions as before, as if she had not been absent. Not permitting an employee to return to work after maternity leave constitutes a dismissal. Further, any dismissal on grounds of pregnancy or maternity is automatically unfair regardless of an employee's length of service. Pauline could therefore claim unfair dismissal at an employment tribunal. (She would need to appeal her employer's decision under the organisation's disciplinary procedure.) Possible remedies for this would be reinstatement, re-engagement or compensation.

Because she has suffered unfavourable treatment/detriment because of her pregnancy and maternity leave, Pauline would also be entitled to bring a case for discrimination because of the 'protected characteristic' of 'pregnancy and maternity' under the Equality Act 2010. Under this Act there is no upper limit on the compensation that might be awarded and an award for injury to feelings may also be covered (see Chapter 5).

After her period of AML, Kate is also entitled to return to the same job that she held previously on the same terms and conditions as before, as if she had not been absent. However, if it is not reasonably practicable for her to return to the same job, her employer can offer her a similar job which is 'suitable and appropriate' and no less favourable in terms of capacity, place and other terms and conditions.

In this instance, the employer may be justified in arguing that it was not reasonably practicable for Kate to return to her old job on the basis of the need for continuity in dealing with customers and in view of the small size of the company. In terms of the alternative job Kate has been offered, given that it is broadly similar in terms of content and also at the same seniority and pay levels and location as her previous job, a tribunal might arguably decide that the employer's actions met the conditions specified in the legislation and that the employer therefore did not infringe Kate's employment rights on her return.

11.2 Sarah and Lucy. This case is clearly related to the right to request flexible working contained in the Employment Rights Act 1996. Under this Act, employers are obliged to consider applications for flexible working from employees with children under 17 years (or 18 years if the child is disabled); or if the employee is a carer of a dependent adult. The employee must have 26 weeks' continuous service with the employer.

Both Lucy and Sarah meet the service requirement and therefore qualify for the right to apply for flexible working. Importantly, they do not have an automatic right to flexible working but rather only a right to apply for this. They have followed the correct procedure set out in the Act by applying in writing to the HR manager.

An employer may only refuse a request for flexible working on 'business grounds' which include such factors as detrimental impact on quality, or inability to recruit additional staff. Although tribunals are not permitted to consider the reasonableness or merits of an employer's decision, they will ensure that companies have genuinely considered the issue and provided arguments or evidence under the list of relevant grounds in the Act (see, for example, the case of *Mehaffy v Dunnes Stores* ET/1308/76/08).

In this exercise, a tribunal would arguably be likely to hold that the company has met its obligations in relation to Sarah's request in that substantial, genuine, business-related reasons for the refusal have been outlined. In contrast, it is questionable whether it has provided sufficient evidence in relation to Lucy's request. Lucy therefore needs to follow the procedure stipulated for the resolution of requests in this area: namely to appeal the decision to her employer. If her appeal is rejected, she may bring a claim to an employment tribunal. If the complaint is found in her favour, a tribunal could order the company to reconsider her request and/or award Lucy compensation.

There is an additional aspect to this case: the possibility that the employer's refusal to the requests to transfer to part-time working may constitute indirect discrimination under the Equality Act 2010. To claim indirect discrimination, Sarah and Lucy would need to establish that their employer was applying a 'provision, criterion or practice' that put women 'at a particular disadvantage' compared with men and which cannot be shown to be a 'proportionate means of achieving a legitimate aim'. In this case, due to childcare commitments, the requirement to work full time puts women at a particular disadvantage compared to men; and it will be up to the employer to show that this requirement is a proportional means of achieving a legitimate (a business) aim. In this regard, it is arguably again the case that the employer satisfies the necessary requirements in relation to Sarah. (However, see *Webster v Princes Soft Drinks* [2005] (*Equal Opportunities Review* 145) where refusing a job share to a senior manager was held to be discriminatory).

It is doubtful if this is so in relation to Lucy. If Lucy is successful in a claim for indirect sex discrimination, an employment tribunal could make a declaration, recommendation and award compensation, and an award for injury to feelings.

11.3 Tom. This case is also related to the right to request flexible working (Employment Rights Act 1996). Tom meets the qualification requirements because he has more than 26 weeks' continuous service with his employer; and his children are under the age of six years.

The reason for the employer's refusal of the request – that it is not possible for all team leaders to be on flexitime and there need to be a sufficient number of team leaders in place to supervise staff – is potentially valid. It could come under one of the headings required in the Act such as detrimental impact on quality or performance of the business. However, an employment tribunal would require evidence from the company that granting Tom's request would have a detrimental impact, particularly in view of the fact that other requests have been accepted.

The fact that requests by female colleagues have been accepted could mean that the company might be found to be guilty of direct sex discrimination against Tom under the Equality Act 2010. (Such direct sex discrimination against a male employee who had requested flexible working was found in *Walkingshaw v the John Martin Group* ETS/401126/00. Requests from women in the organisation had been accepted. This case was determined under the previous Sex Discrimination Act 1975.)

To succeed in a sex discrimination claim, Tom needs to establish facts from which an 'inference' of discrimination can be drawn. It is then up to his employer to provide evidence that their actions were not in fact discriminatory in nature. Tom could argue that 'but for' his sex (i.e. the fact that he is a man), his request would have been accepted. His line manager's statement that he should just 'get on with' his job could also be highlighted as possibly discriminatory in nature, particularly if similar requests by female employees did not obtain the same reaction. His employer would then need to prove that no discrimination had in fact taken place.

An employment tribunal could order the company to reconsider Tom's flexible working request if it is found that it has not been genuinely considered and/or award him compensation. If he successfully claimed direct sex discrimination the possible remedies are a declaration, recommendation, compensation and an award for injury to feelings.

11.4 Paula. Under the Employment Rights Act 1996 and the Maternity and Parental Leave Regulations 1999, Paula is protected against a detriment or dismissal on grounds that she is pregnant or will take maternity leave. These rights apply regardless of length of service. The facts of the case strongly indicate that despite being well qualified, Paula has not been promoted to the partner position because she is pregnant and will go on maternity leave. She has therefore clearly suffered a detriment and would be entitled to a declaration and compensation for this at an employment tribunal. In addition, the nature of her treatment may entitle her to resign and claim constructive dismissal on the grounds that her employer has broken its duty of mutual trust and confidence. For this she would receive compensation. However, before applying to a tribunal (either for detrimental treatment or dismissal) she would need to use the company's grievance procedure.

It is also likely that Paula would be able to make a discrimination claim because she is pregnant. 'Unfavourable treatment' because of the 'protected characteristic' of pregnancy and maternity is unlawful under the Equality Act 2010 (see Chapter 5). Possible remedies would be unlimited compensation for discrimination and an award for injury to feelings.

Chapter 12: Health, safety and welfare

12.1 The VDU operators: safety grievance

1 The issues that might arise:

- *Operational issues:*
    - the need to get work done;
    - the availability of substitute staff for job rotation.
- *Job design*
    - the amount of time spent on the VDU;
    - the feasibility of job rotation.
- *Health and safety requirements*
    - the work environment in the office (lighting, heating, ventilation, etc.);
    - the layout of the workstation;
    - compliance of the equipment with approved technical standards;
    - personal issues (e.g. the incidence of headaches and other physical pains).
- *Employee relations*
    - the duty to consult;
    - the implications of establishing a consultation arrangement in a non-union organisation;

- provision of training for representatives;
- time off for representatives;
- the relationship of the supervisor with the staff.

2 The differences and areas of possible consensus that might arise are:

Objectives:

- *Employer*
  - get work done;
  - improve quality of working relations;
  - minimise cost of any action.
- *Employees*
  - resolve grievance;
  - improve working environment;
  - ensure compliance with the regulations;
  - establish some regular consultation on health and safety issues.

Preferred outcomes:

- *Employer*
  - discussion with Helen individually to try and resolve her grievance;
  - some form of non-union consultation (as and when necessary) – possibly through team briefings.
- *Employees*
  - resolution of Helen's grievance;
  - more breaks from VDU work; and some job rotation;
  - consultative committee to meet monthly, supported by a Head Office representative;
  - possibly a claim for union recognition.

Constraints:

- cost of any action;
- commitment of management to follow through such action;
- extent to which staff are committed to achieve their objectives.

12.2 Matt: workplace violence

The employer is liable under the contract to take reasonable care of Matt. It also has a statutory duty under the Health and Safety at Work etc. Act 1974 to ensure the health, safety and welfare of staff and to provide a safe system of work. The employer needs to take steps which will demonstrate that it does take reasonable care of its staff; and will also demonstrate to the Health and Safety Executive that it is not criminally liable for failing to meet its statutory duties.

Among the steps the hospital could take are the following:

- The formulation, in agreement with the unions, of a policy on violence. This could provide a coherent basis for the following proposed action.

- A risk assessment of the probability of violence in the workplaces – in relation to the physical environment and also to particular times of day.

- Consideration of the suitability of various physical alterations to the working environment.

- Consideration of whether any protective equipment is necessary.

- Training for staff in conflict minimisation.
- Provision of additional and immediate support staff who could be 'on call' to assist in dealing with a serious incident.
- Provision of counselling for staff who are victims of violence.
- Preparedness to support the prosecution of the perpetrators of violence.

12.3 Maggie: drinking at work

Initially, there is clearly consideration of a disciplinary approach. Certainly, drunkenness at work is invariably regarded as gross misconduct and may lead to dismissal. However, it becomes apparent that there are welfare issues in this case. As a consequence, the employer rightly considers adopting a 'twin track' approach with a disciplinary dimension and a requirement to undertake counselling. In this way the employer is demonstrating that reasonable care is being taken of Maggie whilst at the same time reinforcing workplace standards of conduct.

The state of Maggie's health deteriorates and dismissal is considered. To defend a dismissal, the employer would need to show that there was a fair reason for the dismissal and that it was reasonable in the circumstances to dismiss the person for that reason. The fair reason would be 'medical incapability'. However, she has become a disabled person within the meaning of the Equality Act 2010 (see Chapter 5). So, the issue to be considered is whether the employer is able to make reasonable adjustments for her continued employment. If the employer is unable to make such adjustments, then termination of her employment is possible. The employer may be able to show that it behaved reasonably in all the circumstances by the provision of counselling and employee assistance when the alcohol problem first arose.

Note: (q.v.) after a word means that it is defined in this Glossary.

Act of Parliament: see **statute law** below.

Arbitration: Dispute resolution process where the arbitrator (usually a single person but may be a panel) is invited by the parties in dispute to resolve the dispute by making an award (i.e. a decision). The arbitrator is an independent person and may be appointed under the auspices of ACAS. There are two possible types of arbitration: *collective* (relating to disputes between an employer and trade unions), and *individual* (relating to an employer and an employee who has made a complaint or grievance). An example of the latter is the scheme operated by ACAS for resolving unfair dismissal and flexible working claims as an alternative to an employment tribunal claim.

Breach of contract: Circumstances in which one party to a contract does not comply with the terms of the contract (q.v.). Many breaches are minor and may be resolved by an employee lodging grievance with the employer or, alternatively, by an employer taking disciplinary action against an employee. Some breaches are serious (e.g. non-payment of wages due; or allowing persistent bullying to continue). These would be fundamental (i.e. repudiatory) breaches – the equivalent of tearing up the contract. The employee may accept the repudiation and resign and possibly claim constructive dismissal (q.v.).

Burden of proof: Sometimes this is referred to as the 'onus of proof'. It is the responsibility of a party to tribunal or court proceedings to prove an allegation by reference to certain facts and circumstances that are presented in evidence.

Case law: Law set out in judicial decisions. This can help clarify and interpret the law – particularly statute law (q.v.) – and create precedents (q.v.).

Civil law: This is a mixture of statute law (q.v.) and common law (q.v.). It concerns disputes between private individuals (including organisations). In these cases someone is sued. There are two branches of civil law: the law of contract (q.v.) and the law of tort (q.v.). The bulk of employment and discrimination law is civil and so is subsumed under the law of contract or tort. The standard of proof (q.v.) under this branch of law is 'the balance of probabilities'.

Codes of practice: There are both voluntary and statutory codes. Voluntary codes have no legal significance but they can be important in setting standards of good employment practice. Statutory codes do have legal importance. They are used by courts and tribunals in considering the extent to which an employer is liable for a breach of particular statutory employment rights. They are particularly important in respect of discrimination law and dismissal (see Chapters 5, 6 and 8).

Collective bargaining: A process where an employer and a recognised trade union (q.v.) negotiate about differences of interest. These are likely to be about terms and conditions of employment (e.g. pay and working time). They may also be about the extent of workplace consultation (q.v.) and about the scope of collective bargaining itself. The successful outcome of negotiations is a collective agreement.

Common law: Part of English law based on rules developed by judges over many centuries.

Conciliation: Dispute resolution process where the conciliator (usually an officer from ACAS) aims to facilitate a settlement between the two parties in dispute. The settlement is one that the parties agree to themselves. It is not imposed by the conciliator. There are two possible types of conciliation: *collective* (relating to disputes between an employer and trade unions); *individual* (usually arising in relation to complaints made by working people to an employment tribunal). In relation to individual conciliation, ACAS has a statutory duty to promote a settlement where there is an employment tribunal claim.

Consensual variation: The situation where an employee and an employer agree to a change to the terms of a contract of employment (see Chapter 3).

Consideration: Something of value (usually wages) with which the employer buys the agreement of the employee to be ready willing and able to work under a contract of employment (see Chapter 2).

Constructive dismissal: An enforced resignation that is equivalent to dismissal from employment. It arises as a result of the employer's unacceptable behaviour showing that he or she does not intend to be bound by the contract's essential terms and so there is a repudiatory breach of contract (q.v.).

Consultation: A process where an employer and workforce representatives (and occasionally, the whole workforce itself) discuss employment relations-related issues. Theoretically, there are two types of consultation: pseudo consultation and genuine consultation. The former is where the employer is effectively giving information but is not influenced by the views of employees. The second is where there is a full dialogue and the employer responds to employees' opinions and may make changes to any proposed action. There are various statutory duties to consult (e.g. collective redundancies, transfers of undertakings, health and safety). In redundancies the individual employee is expected to be consulted.

Contract: A legally binding agreement, normally between two parties. With a contract of employment, it arises as a result of an offer of terms of employment and the acceptance by the employee of those terms. There must be consideration (q.v.) and an intention of the parties to create legal relations. The contract cannot agree to do something illegal. If it did, it would be void. Because it is an agreement, it is a basic principle that it can only be varied by consent.

Contributory negligence: see **negligence** below.

Criminal law: This is mainly in statutes (q.v.) and concerns wrongs against society (e.g. theft, actual bodily harm, public order). To convict a defendant the prosecution, usually the Crown Prosecution Service, has to prove the case beyond reasonable doubt – the highest standard of proof (q.v.). Around 98 per cent of criminal cases are heard in the magistrates' courts. More serious matters are dealt with before a judge and jury at the Crown Court. Punishments can involve, for example, a fine, a community order or imprisonment. In the employment sphere, it is possible for prosecutions to be brought, for example, by the Health and Safety Executive (see Chapter 12); and by HM Revenue and Customs for infringements of the National Minimum Wage Act 1998 (see Chapter 9).

Culture: Organisational culture refers to the range of values, traditional practices and standards that apply. The culture of an organisation can be an important factor in facilitating or obstructing the effective implementation of, for example, discrimination law or health and safety standards.

Custom and practice: This may be a term of a contract of employment if it is well-known, reasonable and it is certain that the individual knows the effect of the custom on himself or herself.

Damages: Sum of money awarded by a court as compensation for a tort (q.v.) or breach of contract (q.v.).

Derogation: A waiver from the provisions of a statute that is permitted under that legislation (e.g. the Working Time Regulations 1998).

Detriment: Action by an employer which causes disadvantage, harm or damage to an employee (e.g. by victimisation or harassment, overlooking in promotion, depriving of benefits). It is a factor in discrimination law and in the statutory protection provided for employee representatives and workplace trade union officials.

'Direct effect': A doctrine developed by the European Court of Justice for the implementation of European law by member states. An article of the Treaty of Rome will have direct effect if it is clear and unambiguous, unconditional and needs no further action to come into force apart from legislative action by the member state (e.g. Article 157 on equal pay). It applies both horizontally (i.e. conferring rights on individuals against each other) and vertically (i.e. conferring rights that can be enforced against the state and emanations of the state (q.v.)). The provisions of directives (q.v.), on the other hand, only have vertical direct effect where they are clear, unambiguous and require no further action to be implemented.

Directives: The principal means by which European employment law is made. A directive is binding on member states and must, within a given timescale, be transposed fully into the law of each member state. Failure to do this can result in infraction proceedings (q.v.). In Britain, directives are enacted either through statute law (q.v.) or through regulations (q.v.).

Dismissal: The termination of an employee's employment – with or without notice. The law requires that a fair reason is given for the dismissal; that the disciplinary process leading to dismissal conforms with standards of fairness and natural justice (q.v.); and that the decision to dismiss is reasonable in all the circumstances. An employee may allege at an employment tribunal that the dismissal is *unfair* (against various statutory criteria and case law); or that the dismissal is *wrongful* (e.g. it has not been terminated in accordance with the terms of the contract).

Duty: Legal obligation on either an employer or an employee to carry out some action or to stop some particular act. Some duties are set out in statute law (q.v.) – e.g. the duty to consult about collective redundancies. Some are implied under the common law (q.v.) into the contract of employment – e.g. the duty to pay wages; or the duty on the employee to obey lawful and reasonable instructions.

Economic activity rate: This is used in labour market analysis to provide an indication of the percentage of people in a particular group (for example, women or disabled people) who are either in employment or, if unemployed, are actively seeking work.

Emanation of the state: A description of organisations that carry out public/state functions. They may not necessarily be part of central or local government. Examples would include the National Health Service or some privatised utilities (gas, water and electricity). This status is particularly relevant in relation to the application, or 'direct effect' (q.v.), of European Union law (see Chapter 1).

Employee: Defined in law as someone who works under a contract of employment. Case law has developed tests to establish employee status. Courts will look for the existence of mutuality of obligation (see Chapter 2).

ETO: An abbreviation for 'economic, technical and organisational'. It relates to the reasons that employers might give, under the Transfer of Undertakings (Protection of Employment) Regulations 2006, for either dismissing employees or for varying contracts of employment (see Chapters 3 and 8).

Ex parte: (Latin) This expression, which means 'on behalf of', is used in the heading of some law reports with the name of a particular individual making an application to the court in question.

Flexibility: A term used in relation to a large number of management employment practices. The concept of the *flexible firm* was used in the 1980s to suggest a theoretical model which encompassed all forms of flexibility. *Numerical flexibility* describes the extent to which and ways in which an employer can vary the size of the workforce (e.g. through the use of casual and part-time workers). *Functional flexibility* concerns flexibility of task and arises when job demarcations are removed. *Temporal flexibility* is working-time flexibility. *Geographic flexibility* concerns the location of work and workers' mobility.

Foreseeability: The ability to foresee particular consequences arising from an event or set of circumstances. It has been used, for example, in relation to whether or not stress at work can result in some foreseeable or predictable harm to physical or mental health (see Chapter 12).

Framework agreement: These are reached, usually under European law, between the 'social partners' (q.v.). Such agreements usually set out particular objectives and general principles which can be embodied in directives of the European Union. Examples include those on Part-time Work 1997; Fixed-term Work 1999.

Francovich **claims:** The possibility of such claims arose from an Italian case in the European Court of Justice (*Francovich and Bonifaci v Republic of Italy* [1992] IRLR 84). The ECJ ruled that a citizen, not just an employee, can sue their government if it has failed to implement an EU directive. The individual would need to show that he or she has sustained loss and that there was a clear link between the government's failure and the damage suffered. In Britain, a claim can be made in the High Court.

Free collective bargaining: Bargaining whereby an employer and trade unions can negotiate terms of the agreement without any constraint imposed by legislation or government policy. Historically, the most significant interference with free collective bargaining has been the statutory imposition through incomes policies of the percentage increase in pay that can be awarded. Legislation does mould the terms of collective bargaining by requiring compliance for example, with standards set in discrimination law (see Chapter 5).

Immunities: An immunity is a protection, provided under law, against prosecution or claims for damages for some action which otherwise would be unlawful. Specifically, in employment relations, there are two sets of immunities applicable to trade unions: those which allow them to exist and engage in collective bargaining with employers; and those which enable them lawfully to undertake specified industrial action. These trade union immunities are enacted in statute law (q.v.) (See website chapter).

Incorporation: Process whereby the terms of collective agreements are included, as appropriate, into individual contracts of employment. So, for example, the appropriate rates of pay (under a payment system); or the relevant standard working week will be applied to the individual. Through this process of incorporation the terms of the collective agreement relating to a particular individual become legally enforceable (see Chapters 2 and 3).

'Independent' trade union: A trade union which is not under the control or dominance of a particular employer through the provision of funds or facilities or not liable to employer interference in the running of its affairs. Legislation provides particular standards and a certificate of independence is conferred by the Certification Officer (Trade Union and Labour Relations Act 1992, ss 5 and 6). An 'independent' union has statutory rights in respect of, e.g. consultation in business transfers; and in collective redundancies.

Industrial action: Sanctions imposed by working people (usually organised by trade unions) against an employer. It arises because of a trade dispute (q.v.). Broadly, there are two categories of industrial action: a strike whereby work stops completely; and 'industrial action short of a strike' (e.g. working to rule, boycotting various tasks, overtime bans, etc.).

Infraction proceedings: Proceedings initiated in the European Court of Justice by the European Commission against an EU member state for not implementing particular European law – either in part or in its entirety.

Injunction: A court order requiring a person (including an employer or a trade union) to stop a certain course of action. Usually, a temporary or interlocutory injunction is granted initially, pending a full hearing of the claim before the court. A person who breaches an injunction is guilty of contempt of court and may be subject to a fine or imprisonment. (An **interdict** in Scotland.)

Job share: Circumstances where a full-time job is split between, usually, two employees who then receive *pro rata* (q.v.) conditions of employment.

'Juridification': The extent to which decisions by employers in relation to terms and conditions of employment and the treatment of individual workers is made by reference to legal standards. The extent of employer discretion continues to narrow with the promotion of widespread minimum standards; the concept of less favourable treatment; and the conferring of entitlements on working people.

Landmark case: Usually refers to a significant case which is the first interpretation by one of the higher courts of particular legislation. It is likely to be a precedent (q.v.).

Leading case: Any ruling by the higher courts which provide an authoritative interpretation of law and legal principles.

Liability: This arises in circumstances when wrongs have been committed. Examples include breach of contract, breach of discrimination law or of health and safety law. It concerns the issue of who is answerable in law for the wrong. Usually under employment law it is the employer. The employer may also be 'vicariously liable' for the behaviour (acts and omissions) in the course of employment of his workforce or of a contractor. A defence for the employer, depending on the legislation involved, may be that he or she took reasonable steps to prevent the wrong being committed. In employment, most issues of liability are civil. However, it is possible for an employer to be criminally liable if specified in particular legislation (e.g. relating to health and safety; national minimum wage) – in which case the employer would be prosecuted in the criminal courts by the relevant agency.

LIFO: It stands for 'last in first out'. A traditional selection method used in redundancies. Generally, it recognises the job rights of longer serving employees by making those with relatively short service the first to be made redundant. It is not recommended as good practice and may be discriminatory under both sex and age discrimination law.

Living wage: This is a concept promoted by various campaigning groups which argue that the National Minimum Wage is set at too low a level. It promotes wage levels (within London and outside London) above the NMW; and encourages companies voluntarily to implement these higher rates.

Mens rea: (Latin) This means the 'guilty mind'. It is the state of mind that prosecutors have to prove that a defendant had at the time of committing a crime in order to secure a conviction. Common examples of *mens rea* are **intention** to do something; ***recklessness*** about the consequences of particular action; and ***negligence***. This can have particular relevance in the law on health and safety at work (see Chapter 12).

Natural justice: These rules, developed under common law (q.v.), are applicable in courts and tribunals. Under dismissal legislation, they influence the way in which disciplinary proceedings should be conducted. There are two principal rules: a person should have an opportunity to state his or her case and to answer the other side's case; and no one should be a judge in his or her own cause.

Negligence: Carelessness or neglect. The most common examples in employment arise in the area of health and safety where it is claimed an employer neglected to take reasonable care of the employee. An employer sued by an employee in a negligence claim may himself or herself claim that the employee was also negligent (e.g. for failing to wear protective equipment). If this contributory negligence is proved, it could result in the employee's damages (q.v.) being reduced, depending on the circumstances, by up to 100 per cent (See Chapter 12).

'Non-standard' employment relationships: Employment relationships other than the full-time, permanent employment relationship. They involve flexible (q.v.) arrangements under which work is carried out – either in relation to working time, duration or place of work (e.g. whether it is on the employer's premises or at home). Such work is also described as 'atypical' work (see Chapter 2).

Part-time worker: Someone who works less than the normal working week set in a particular organisation. No specific hours are stipulated under law.

Precedent: A judgment or ruling of a court that is used as an authority for reaching a decision in subsequent cases. In English law, decisions of the Supreme Court (and formerly the House of Lords) are binding on the Court of Appeal and all lower courts. Likewise, decisions of the Court of Appeal and, below that, the High Court are binding on lower courts. Decisions of lower courts (and of employment tribunals) do not create any binding precedent.

Prima facie: (Latin) It means 'from a first impression' or 'on the face of things'. Under discrimination law, a *prima facie* case made by a complainant whereby he or she presents an outline case of the facts known to him or her which are said to point to discriminatory treatment (see Chapter 5).

Procedural issues: In employment relations, these concern the operation of procedures used to structure the relationship between an employer and his or her workforce and, if relevant, recognised trade unions (q.v.). The procedures can concern grievances, discipline and dismissal, harassment, redundancies, consultation, health and safety matters, arrangements for negotiating terms and conditions, collective dispute resolution procedures.

Pro rata **principle:** (Latin) In employment it refers to proportionality in the treatment of individuals under terms of the contract of employment. In particular, it relates to the comparative treatment of full-time employees and part-time employees. So, for example, if a part-timer works for half of a full-time employee's standard working week, then the part-timer would be entitled to half the relevant holiday entitlement; and proportional treatment in relation to most other terms and conditions of employment.

Purposive interpretation: An approach adopted by the European Court of Justice for the interpretation of EU legislation. The judiciary consider the purposes of the legislation as set out by the legislators and this can mould their ruling on specific matters. As an approach it contrasts with the 'literal' approach (focusing on the precise meaning of words in the statute) adopted by the judiciary in Britain.

Qualified majority voting (QMV): It is used to approve certain EU legislation. It is a weighted voting system that requires more than a simple majority (i.e. over 50 per cent) to approve a measure. It has been used to approve health and safety directives and the Working Time Directive (which was ruled by the European Court of Justice to be health and safety law).

Qualifying period: The period of continuous employment with an employer that an employee (q.v.) or worker (q.v.) must have in order to claim certain statutory rights.

Recognition of a trade union: This describes the situation in which an employer agrees voluntarily (or is required in law) to negotiate with one or more trade unions about specific terms and conditions of employment (See website chapter).

Regulations: see **statutory instruments** below.

Remedy: This is any method available at law for enforcing rights or for obtaining redress for their infringement. It can include an injunction (q.v.); damages (q.v.); or a declaration.

Repudiatory breach of contract: see **breach of contract** above.

Right to manage: Not a legal right. It is essentially management rhetoric to claim economic rights over the recruitment, deployment and remuneration of employees. It is freedom to manage – sometimes referred to as 'managerial prerogatives'. Common law (q.v.) and, in particular, statute law (q.v.) have limited this freedom by imposing standards of conduct, duties and minimum terms and conditions of employment.

Single status: Common treatment and terms and conditions of employment for employees whether they are manual workers or non-manual workers.

Social partners: Representative bodies of European trade unions and public and private sector employers: ETUC (European Trade Union Confederation); CEEP (European Centre for Enterprises with Public Participation); BUSINESSEUROPE (formerly UNICE) representing private sector employers; UEAPME (representing small and medium-sized enterprises). Within the process of EU law-making, these bodies are consulted regularly on new European Commission proposals for social policy and employment legislation. They may negotiate framework agreements (q.v.) which can then form the basis of directives (q.v.) (e.g. that relating to Parental Leave 1996).

Socialisation: The process through which an individual's attitudes, values and standards of behaviour are inculcated and developed particularly within the family, within education, in religious organisations, in the workplace and within society at large.

'Standard' employment relationship: The most common form of employment relationship, characterised by being full-time and 'permanent' – i.e. the employee is on an 'open-ended' contract.

Standards of proof: There are two: beyond reasonable doubt; and the balance of probabilities. The first is used in criminal (q.v.) cases to establish conviction. The second arises in civil (q.v.) proceedings and is generally construed as follows: that it is more probable than not that something said to have happened did happen. This standard is used in employment tribunal cases.

Statute law: Law made by Parliament in the form of Acts of Parliament. It usually reflects the political policies of the government of the day; and also measures proposed by backbench MPs if approved by Parliament. It is interpreted by judges and new statute law can overturn judge-made law. Alongside statutory instruments (q.v.), it is a principal means for transposing EU directives into domestic law.

Statutory instruments: They are delegated legislation and are presented as regulations to Parliament and come into force subject to its approval. Regulations are made under the authority of a particular Act of Parliament. For example, the Working Time Regulations 1998 were made under the European Communities Act, s 2. Other examples include those made under the Health and Safety at Work etc. Act 1974. Alongside statute law (q.v.), regulations are a principal means of transposing EU directives into domestic law.

'Subsidiarity': This concept relates to the political question of which is the most appropriate level for legal regulation and decision-making within the European Union. Proponents of 'subsidiarity' support the greatest possible devolution of regulation and decision-making to the level of the member states.

Substantive issues: In employment relations, this refers to the terms and conditions of employment under which an employee is employed.

Summary dismissal: Dismissal (q.v.) without notice.

Superior courts: Primarily, these are the Supreme Court and the Court of Appeal because their decisions create precedents (q.v.) on the interpretation of the law. (In the instance of employment cases not appealed to the level, the Employment Appeal Tribunal, is a source of precedent.)

Terms: These are the provisions of a contract of employment. They may be express (e.g. pay and hours) or implied from common law (q.v.) (e.g. the duty to take reasonable care).

Tight labour market: Economic circumstances where there are various forms of labour and skill shortage and it is difficult for employers to recruit particular staff.

Tort: A civil (q.v.) wrong other than a breach of contract (q.v.). In employment relations, examples include claims of personal injury (whether physical or psychological) through negligence. Claims are usually initiated in the High Court. Trade unions can commit 'economic' torts when they take industrial action against an employer because the industrial action damages the employer's business. The enactment of immunities (q.v.) provides some protection from trade unions being sued.

Trade dispute: A dispute between a workforce (usually unionised) and an employer about various terms and conditions of employment and employment-related procedural issues (See website chapter).

Transferee: The employing organisation that receives a workgroup/workforce from a transferor (q.v.) in a business transfer.

Transferor: The employing organisation that transfers to a transferee (q.v.) a work group/ workforce in a business transfer.

Vicarious liability: see **liability** above.

Victimisation: A form of detriment (q.v.). It involves singling out a person for unfair and usually unlawful treatment. Particular forms of victimisation to prevent claims being made to employment tribunals are specifically prohibited under the discrimination law.

'Voluntarism': The situation where the state leaves employers and employees (probably through the medium of trade unions) relatively free to determine the nature of the employment relationship and terms and conditions of employment. Legislation plays a minimal role in regulating employment relations (see website chapter).

Unilateral variation: The circumstances where an employer imposes, without agreement with individual employees, changed terms and conditions of employment. It contrasts with consensual variation (q.v.) (see Chapter 3).

White Paper: A document published by government in which it sets out proposals for legislative action. Usually, they are open to limited consultation by interest groups.

Worker: A person who has an employment relationship with an organisation. It covers employees (q.v.) and others required to work personally. It does not cover the self-employed (see Chapter 2).

Index

Note: entries in **bold** refer to Glossary